AMERICA'S #1 CAMPUS-BASED TESTPREP.

ACT* • PLAN* • EXPLORE*
Victory

Student Text
Volume 2

ACT • PLAN • EXPLORE • SAT • PSAT • GRE • GMAT • LSAT • MCAT • TOEFL • GED • PRAXIS • PSAE • WorkKeys • Stanford • ITBS • State Tests
CollegePrep™ • Learning Styles • Guidance Services • Professional Development • Motivation & Admissions Workshops • Data Services • Formative Assessment

*ACT, PLAN, and EXPLORE are registered trademarks of ACT, Inc., which does not endorse this product.

About Cambridge Educational Services:

Cambridge Educational Services was founded in order to help all students, regardless of income, meet standards and perform to the best of their abilities on standardized tests and in the classroom. Our mission is to provide assessment services and program materials that make quality school improvement programs possible for a wide range of student ability levels. Our goal is to help students achieve test scores that reflect their true potential and ability. Our programs help thousands of students each year reach their goals, such as becoming National Merit Scholars, gaining admission to the colleges of their choice, and earning valuable scholarships. Cambridge publishes a variety of school improvement and preparation titles and products including student texts, teacher's guides, skills review manuals, software, and assessment services.

Cambridge Publishing, Inc., Chicago National Headquarters, Des Plaines, IL 60018

© 1994, 1995, 1996, 1997, 2000, 2003, 2004, 2005, 2009 by Cambridge Publishing, Inc.
All rights reserved. First edition 1994
Ninth edition 2009

Printed in the United States of America
12 11 10 09   1 2 3 4 5

ISBN-13: 978-1-58894-083-4

Portions reprinted from ACT
© 2005 by Thomas H. Martinson
All rights reserved

TABLE OF CONTENTS

Course Overview

HOW TO USE THIS BOOK

Cambridge ACT • PLAN • EXPLORE Victory Student Text, Volume 2, 9th Edition is organized into four parts:

1) items resembling the real ACT, PLAN, and EXPLORE that your instructor will use to teach tested concepts and applicable strategies (Test Mechanics, Concepts, and Strategies);
2) four full-length ACT practice tests (Practice Test Reinforcement);
3) a diagnostic post-assessment and information to help you make sense of the results (Post-Assessment);
4) recommendations for continuing your study after the course, as well as for preparing your college applications (Personal Action Plan).

The following introduction will briefly explain how to use each part of this volume.

SOLVING PROBLEMS THAT LOOK LIKE THOSE FOUND ON THE TEST

Test Mechanics, Concepts, and Strategies make up the heart of this course and, in particular, the *Cambridge ACT • PLAN • EXPLORE Victory Student Text, Volume 2, 9th Edition*. This part of volume 2 contains items that look like those found on the real ACT, PLAN, and EXPLORE. When compared with items on the real tests, the items in this part of the book have similar content, represent the same difficulty levels, and can be solved by using the same problem-solving skills and alternative test-taking strategies.

There are five chapters in Test Mechanics, Concepts, and Strategies, each chapter representing a core component of the ACT, PLAN, and EXPLORE:

- English

- Mathematics

- Reading

- Science

- Writing

Each of the above chapters begins with a course concept outline, which acts as a syllabus, listing the concepts that are tested for each item-type. The items in each chapter are organized to correspond with the respective outline. For each concept in the outline, there is a group of items. The group contains a greater number of items if the item-type appears with great frequency on the real test, and it contains a lesser number of items if the item-type appears with less frequency. Although the concepts are not grouped in this way on the real ACT, PLAN, or EXPLORE, we organize the lessons in this manner so that the concepts are emphasized and reinforced. After you learn the concepts, you will be able to practice applying this conceptual knowledge on the practice tests.

TAKING PRACTICE TESTS

In the Practice Test Reinforcement portion of volume 2, there are four full-length ACT practice tests. In these tests, the items not only mimic the real test in content and difficulty level, but they are also arranged in an order and with a frequency that simulates the real ACT, PLAN, and EXPLORE.

Your instructor will ask you to complete either some or all of these items in class, or he or she will assign them as homework. If you are taking these four tests at home, you should take two *without* time restrictions and then take two *with* time restrictions. Taking the test without time restrictions will help you get a sense of how long it would take for you to comfortably and accurately solve an item. Applying the time pressure then forces you to pace yourself as you would on the real test. If you complete all four of the practice tests, any test anxiety you may have will be greatly reduced.

TAKING A POST-ASSESSMENT AND MAKING SENSE OF YOUR RESULTS

In order to know how far you've come since the pre-assessment, you have to take a second official, retired ACT, PLAN, or EXPLORE. You will take this post-assessment under actual testing conditions. You will then receive a second student summary report to help you determine final areas for review. The *Winning Strategies* section entitled *How to Use the Post-Assessment Report* shows you how to identify particular areas of study, as well as exact items in your textbook, upon which to focus as you continue to prepare for the real test.

CREATING AN ACTION PLAN

The last part of volume 2 provides a short guide to help you design a personal action plan for the days or weeks between the end of the course and the real test. At this stage of the course, you will put into action what you learned in earlier *Winning Strategies* sections to make the most of your remaining study time and review the following additional *Winning Strategies* sections that will help you beyond the course:

- The *Planning for Further Study* section includes advice on how to make the most of an effective and concrete action plan, addressing such issues as maximizing your remaining course time and prioritizing material to be reviewed before taking the actual test. Empty calendars are offered to get your action plans started.

- The *Application Preparation* section teaches you how to highlight your unique qualities to maximize your chances of admission into your first-choice school.

- The *Six Ways to Jumpstart Your College Admissions Essays* section gives examples of actual college admissions essay questions/responses and shows you how to ace the essay.

Test Mechanics, Concepts, and Strategies

Highlights:

Learn everything you need to know about the five tested core subjects: English, Mathematics, Reading, Science, and Writing.

Identify the test mechanics information you need to know to make a positive impact on your test score.

Review the most commonly-tested concepts on the ACT, the PLAN, and the EXPLORE.

Discover the powerful alternative test-taking strategies that will give you an edge when taking the ACT, the PLAN, and the EXPLORE.

Snapshot of Test Mechanics, Concepts, and Strategies:

This part of the student text contains many items that look like those found on the ACT, the PLAN, and the EXPLORE. When compared with items on the real test, these items have the same content, represent similar difficulty levels, and are solved by using the same concepts and alternative test-taking strategies. You will go over these items with your instructor in class.

English

CAMBRIDGE TESTPREP™

ENGLISH

COURSE CONCEPT OUTLINE: WHAT YOU ABSOLUTELY MUST KNOW

I. Test Mechanics (p. 9)

II. Lesson (p. 15)

A. Preliminaries

1. What Is Tested
2. Directions
3. Item Profiles
4. Notational Information
   a. Underlined Words or Phrases
   b. Boxed Numbers
   c. Bracketed Numbers
   d. Boxed Information

B. Item-Types

1. Grammar and Usage
2. Sentence Structure
3. Punctuation
4. Strategy
5. Organization
6. Style

C. Usage and Mechanics Review

1. Grammar and Usage
   a. Subject-Verb Agreement (Item #1, p. 15)
      i. Material Inserted Between Subject and Verb (Items #2–7, p. 15)
      ii. Inverted Sentence Structure (Items #8–9, p. 15)
      iii. Compound Subjects (Items #10–12, p. 16)
   b. Pronoun Usage
      i. Pronouns Must Have Antecedents (Items #13–14, p. 16)
      ii. Antecedents Must Be Clear (Item #15, p. 16)
      iii. Pronoun-Antecedent Agreement (Items #16–19, p. 16)
      iv. Pronouns Must Be in Proper Case (Items #20–21, p. 16)
   c. Adjectives versus Adverbs
      i. Adjectives Modify Nouns; Adverbs Modify Verbs (Items #22–23, p. 17)
      ii. Linking Verbs (Items #24–25, p. 17)
      iii. Watch for Adjectives Posing as Adverbs (Items #26–28, p. 17)
   d. Double Negatives (Items #29–30, p. 17)
   e. Nouns and Noun Clauses (Items #31–33, p. 17)
   f. Faulty or Illogical Comparisons (Items #34–38, p. 18)
   g. Verb Tense
      i. Principal Parts of Verbs (Items #39–41, p. 18)

TEST MECHANICS

BASICS

It would not be too far wrong to say that the English Test is a test of your understanding of the rules of grammar, and that announcement should be enough to strike dread into the hearts of most students: "You mean like '*i* before *e* except after *c*'?" No, that's a rule of spelling, not grammar, and the English Test does not test spelling. Actually, the English Test doesn't really test your knowledge of the formal rules of grammar either, though it does test your ability to write using those rules.

You might be asked to correct an error.

Example:

The recently created wildlife refuge, which includes nearly 30 small ponds for migrating geese and ducks, <u>were</u> made possible by substantial gifts by an anonymous donor to the Wildlife Protection Fund.

A. NO CHANGE
B. was
C. have been
D. being

The correct answer is (B) because the sentence should read "refuge...was," not "refuge...were." But you would not be asked to state the grammatical rule that explains the error or how to correct it: *a verb must agree in both number and person with its subject.*

The items used by the English Test fall into one of two categories: Usage and Mechanics and Rhetorical Skills. The Usage and Mechanics category (UM) includes all of the items that you would normally associate with a writing test, such as choosing proper verb tense and pronoun usage, while the Rhetorical Skills category (RH) includes items that ask about the development of a selection, such as crafting topic sentences and selecting effective transitions. You'll see specific examples of both types in the "Anatomy" section that follows.

ANATOMY

DIRECTIONS: In the passages below, certain parts of the sentences have been underlined and numbered. In the right-hand column, you will find different ways of writing each underlined part; the original version is indicated by the "NO CHANGE" option. There are also items that ask about a section of the passage or the passage as a whole. These items do not refer to an underlined portion of the passage; they are identified by a number or numbers in a box.

For each item, choose the alternative that you consider to be the best. Select the answer choice that best expresses the intended idea, is most acceptable in standard written English, or is most consistent with the overall tone and style of the passage. Read the passage through once before you begin to answer the accompanying items. Finding the answers to certain items may depend on looking at material that appears several sentences beyond the item. So, be sure that you have read far enough ahead before you select your answer choice.

PASSAGE I

Although you might not think it, the Antarctic waters are rich in nutrients. The lack of <u>ice, combined</u>
                                                             1
with shallow coastal waters, provides the top layers of the ocean with added sunlight, so polynyas (large open areas of waters surrounded by sea ice) offer ideal conditions for phytoplankton blooms. Because the ice around polynyas is thin in the early spring when the long days begin, they are the first areas to get strong sunlight. The open waters retain more heat, further thinning ice cover and leading to early, intense, and

The directions for the English Test are fairly long, and it would take you a while to read them during the test. You'd be wasting valuable time that could be used to answer questions. By the time you get to the test, you'll know what to do in the English Test, so skip the directions altogether.

short-lived plankton blooms. These blooms feed krill,
<u>a tiny, shrimp-like animal</u>, which in turn are eaten by
₃

Adelie Penguins, seabirds, seals, whales, and other
animals.

    <u>Because</u> relatively small in area, coastal polynyas
₄

play an important role. In eastern Antarctica, more than
90 percent of all Adelie Penguin colonies live next to
coastal polynyas. Polynya productivity explains, to a
great extent, the increase and decrease in penguin
population.

1. A. NO CHANGE
   B. ice combined
   C. ice combined,
   D. ice—combined

2. The writer is considering deleting the information in parentheses in Sentence 2. If the writer removed this material, the essay would primarily lose:

   F. a transition from the first paragraph to the second paragraph.
   G. further examples of the animals that depend upon krill for food.
   H. a definition of a term that might be unfamiliar to the reader.
   J. additional information about the climate of Antarctica.

3. A. NO CHANGE
   B. tiny, shrimp-like animals
   C. a tiny animal like a shrimp
   D. an animal like a tiny shrimp

4. F. NO CHANGE
   G. Although
   H. Therefore
   J. Furthermore

The first item tests punctuation. When you insert an aside or clarifying remark, you need to set off that material from the main part of the sentence, usually with commas—one at the start and one at the end of the material. The original sentence is correctly punctuated. So, (A) is the correct answer.

Why does the writer include the parenthetical material? To define a key term that might otherwise be unfamiliar to the reader. So, (H) is the correct answer.

The original sentence lacks parallelism. In the main part of the sentence, the writer is talking about krill in the plural: "krill...which in turn are eaten." But in the appositive phrase, the writer uses the singular "animal." "Animal" is not parallel to "krill," which is used here as a plural noun. So, (B) is the correct answer.

In the fourth item, "because" is a word used to introduce an explanation, so the reader expects the information in the independent clause to be the outcome of the information provided in the dependent ("because") clause. The writer, instead, intends to contrast the two ideas in the sentence: even though polynyas are small in area, they are very important to Adelie Penguins. So, (G) is the correct answer.

PACING

The English Test consists of five passages, each approximately 300 words in length and with 15 corresponding questions, for a total of 75 questions. The time limit is 45 minutes. So, a fairly simple and easy-to-follow plan is to allocate 9 minutes to each of the five passages:

First Passage		
Task	*Allotted Time*	*Remaining Time*
Read Passage	1.5 minutes	43.5 minutes
Answer Questions	7.5* minutes	36 minutes

Second Passage		
Task	*Allotted Time*	*Remaining Time*
Read Passage	1.5 minutes	34.5 minutes
Answer Questions	7.5* minutes	27 minutes

Third Passage		
Task	*Allotted Time*	*Remaining Time*
Read Passage	1.5 minutes	25.5 minutes
Answer Questions	7.5* minutes	18 minutes

Fourth Passage		
Task	*Allotted Time*	*Remaining Time*
Read Passage	1.5 minutes	16.5 minutes
Answer Questions	7.5* minutes	9 minutes

Fifth Passage		
Task	*Allotted Time*	*Remaining Time*
Read Passage	1.5 minutes	7.5 minutes
Answer Questions	7.5* minutes	0 minutes

*Approximately 30 seconds per question

This schedule describes what would happen in a perfect world; but, of course, the ACT is not a perfect world. Some questions are going to take longer than others, particularly those that ask about the overall development of the passage. This means that you'll need to spend less time on the simple grammar questions, building up a time reserve for those more difficult items that are coming. And the more difficult questions are usually placed at the end of a passage because that's where it makes sense to ask, "What is the main idea?" and "How could the passage be improved?" The schedule actually gives you a feedback loop that lets you know whether you need to skip some questions. For example, if you are nearing the "36 minutes left in the section" mark and still have two or three questions to do on the first passage, then skip any Rhetorical Skills items and go straight away to the next passage. The Rhetorical Skills items take longer, and there will be some simple grammar items waiting to be cherry-picked in the next passage.

GAME PLAN

1. DON'T READ THE DIRECTIONS

By the time you get to the test, you'll know what to do when you see the English Test just by the way it looks. Let the appearance of the questions on the page be all the direction you need, and then get started immediately.

2. DO THE PASSAGES IN ORDER

Unlike the Reading Test with passages that fall into categories such as Humanities and Natural Sciences, the passages on the English Test are not really about any particular subject-area. Of course, the passages do have a topic and some questions do ask Reading-type questions, but the English questions basically test usage, not reading comprehension. In Reading, there is an advantage to predetermining an order for the passages; in English, however, you should just do them in the order presented.

3. START EACH SET OF QUESTIONS BY READING THE PASSAGE

You really need to read the passage before you start answering questions because some questions will not make sense without the proper context. Since the passages are about 300 words in length, you can finish a read-through in a little more than a minute. Read primarily for overall development so that you'll understand the logic in the author's presentation, and don't worry overly much about details. Later, you can study the specific parts of the passage in which the various questions appear.

4. READ ANY QUESTIONS WITH UNDERLINED PARTS, LOOKING FOR ERRORS

When a question asks about rewriting an underlined part, begin by reading the sentence, looking for an error. If you can spot an error, then you're more than halfway home. Later in the English Lesson, you'll cover the important principles of writing and grammar that are tested, and there is a list of these principles provided in the English Course Concept Outline (p. 5). You can treat this outline as a checklist of important things to look for in English items.

5. WORK BACKWARDS FROM THE ANSWER CHOICES

If you are having difficulty locating the right answer, use the answer choices to help you. Compare each answer choice with the original, and explain to yourself what the important difference is between the two of them. This can help you see an error that you may have overlooked. Additionally, you can compare choices to each other, asking yourself, in what way is this choice better or worse than the other one? Again, this technique can help you uncover a hidden error and make the right choice.

6.   DON'T LOOK FOR SPELLING OR CAPITALIZATION ERRORS

These topics are not tested, so don't waste your time looking for errors of this sort. Even if you think you've found a spelling mistake (and you're almost certain to be wrong anyway), there is nothing you can do with the information. The correct response is correct because it "follows the requirements of standard written English."

7.   MAKE EDUCATED GUESSES

You should be able to eliminate some answer choices on most questions because they introduce new errors that are not found in the original. Or, a choice may fail to correct an error that you know to be in the underlined part of the sentence. You should always guess, even if you are unable to eliminate any answer choices, because there is no penalty for guessing on the ACT. However, your chances improve if you are able to eliminate even one answer choice.

8.   DON'T BE AFRAID TO PICK "NO CHANGE"

Choose (A), "NO CHANGE," if you think that the original is correct as written. Many students automatically refuse to pick "NO CHANGE" because they figure that there must be something wrong with the original—even if they are unable to say what. But this reasoning is faulty. "NO CHANGE," when it is an option, is statistically as likely to be correct as is one of the other three choices.

LESSON

The items in this section accompany the English Lesson. They demonstrate the English skills and concepts that are tested by the ACT, the PLAN, and the EXPLORE. You will work through the items with your instructor in class. Answers are on page 591.

DIRECTIONS: Items #1–114 consist of two types of items: (1) When four separate parts of a sentence are underlined, identify the underlined part that contains an error. Some of these sentences may not contain any errors; in such a case, choose "No change." No sentence contains more than one error, and no sentence contains an error that is not underlined. (2) When a single part of a sentence is underlined or the entire sentence is underlined, identify the re-phrasing that best expresses the meaning of the underlined material. (A) is always NO CHANGE, which indicates that the underlined material is correct as written.

1. The professor <u>were traveling</u> in Europe <u>when</u> she
               A   B

   <u>received</u> notice of <u>her</u> promotion. <u>No change</u>
     C   D   E

2. The professor <u>voted Teacher of the Year</u> by the
                      F

   students <u>were traveling</u> in Europe <u>when</u> she
           G   H

   received notice of <u>her</u> promotion. <u>No change</u>
                 J   K

3. Most teachers, unless <u>they have</u> an appointment
                      A

   to a prestigious university, <u>earns</u> relatively
                          B

   <u>less as</u> a teacher <u>than they might</u> in business.
     C   D

   <u>No change</u>
       E

4. Many nutritionists now <u>believe</u> <u>that</u> a balanced
                       F   G

   diet and not large doses of vitamins <u>are</u> the <u>best</u>
                             H   J

   guarantee of health. <u>No change</u>
                      K

5. Television comedies <u>in which</u> <u>there is</u> at least
                    A   B

   one <u>really detestable</u> character <u>captures</u> the
         C   D

   interest of viewers. <u>No change</u>
                    E

6. The opposition to smoking in public places <u>are</u>
   <u>prompting many state legislatures to consider</u>
   banning smoking in such locations.

   (F) NO CHANGE
   (G) is prompting many state legislatures to consider
   (H) are prompting many state legislatures considering
   (J) is prompting many state legislatures considering
   (K) is prompting many state legislatures' consider

7. Diplomats sent to an unstable region or a genuinely hostile territory usually <u>is assigned an aide or chauffeur who function</u> also as a bodyguard.

   (A) NO CHANGE
   (B) are assigned an aide or chauffeur who function
   (C) are assigned an aide or chauffeur who functions
   (D) is assigned an aide or chauffeur that function
   (E) are assigned an aide or chauffeur which functions

8. <u>Though</u> this is the wealthiest country in the
     F

   world, within a <u>few</u> blocks of the White House
                G

   <u>there is</u> scores of homeless people <u>who live</u> on
     H   J

   the streets. <u>No change</u>
               K

9. <u>Just</u> a few miles from the factories and
   A

   skyscrapers <u>stand</u> a medieval castle <u>which looks</u>
   B   C

   <u>exactly as</u> it did in the 12th century. <u>No change</u>
   D   E

10. John, his wife, and the rest of his family <u>plans</u>
    F

    <u>to attend</u> the award dinner <u>to be given</u> by the
    G   H

    company for the employees with the <u>most</u>
    J

    seniority. <u>No change</u>
    K

11. Either the governor or one of his close aides

    <u>prefer</u> <u>not to have</u> the Senator <u>seated at</u> the head
    A   B   C

    table where he <u>would be</u> conspicuous. <u>No change</u>
    D   E

12. <u>Surrounded by</u> layers of excelsior, none of the
    F

    crystal goblets <u>were broken</u> <u>when</u> the workers
    G   H

    <u>dropped</u> the crate. <u>No change</u>
    J   K

13. During her rise to fame, she betrayed many of her
    friends, <u>and because of it</u>, very few people trust
    her.

    (A) NO CHANGE
    (B) and in spite of it
    (C) and because of her friends
    (D) and even though
    (E) and because of her behavior

14. In New York City, <u>they</u> are brusque and even
    F

    rude <u>but</u> quick <u>to come to</u> one another's
    G   H

    assistance <u>in a time of</u> crisis. <u>No change</u>
    J   K

15. Ten years ago, the United States <u>imported</u> ten
    A

    times <u>as much</u> French wine as Italian wine, but
    B

    today Americans <u>are drinking</u> more of <u>it</u>.
    C   D

    <u>No change</u>
    E

16. Although a police officer <u>used to be</u> a symbol of
    F

    authority, today <u>they receive</u> <u>little</u> respect
    G   H

    <u>from most</u> people. <u>No change</u>
    J   K

17. The Abbot <u>was</u> an effective administrator
    A

    <u>who attempted to</u> assign each monk a task
    B

    <u>particularly suited</u> to <u>their</u> talents and training.
    C   D

    <u>No change</u>
    E

18. After three years of college education, a person

    <u>should be allowed to</u> apply to graduate school,
    F

    <u>because</u> by that time <u>you are</u> ready <u>to choose</u> a
    G   H   J

    profession. <u>No change</u>
    K

19. <u>If one wishes</u> <u>to apply for</u> a scholarship, <u>you</u>
    A   B   C

    must submit a <u>completed</u> application by March 1.
    D

    <u>No change</u>
    E

20. The judges <u>were</u> unable to make a final decision
    F

    on a single winner, so <u>they</u> divided the first prize
    G

    <u>between</u> John and <u>he</u>. <u>No change</u>
    H   J   K

21. Although Peter <u>had been looking</u> <u>forward to</u> the
         A   B

    debate for weeks, a sore throat <u>prevented him</u>
                                        C

    taking <u>part</u>. <u>No change</u>
           D   E

22. The company's mission statement took into consideration the <u>significant changes</u> that were made in the field of technology.

    (F) NO CHANGE
    (G) significantly changes
    (H) significant changed
    (J) significantly changed
    (K) significantly to change

23. When asked about the chance that the defenders might concentrate their forces at the beachhead, the general responded <u>tart that he was fully</u> aware of all the possibilities.

    (A) NO CHANGE
    (B) tartly that he was full
    (C) tart that he was full
    (D) tart that he fully was
    (E) tartly that he was fully

24. When the door burst open, Kevin <u>looked up angry</u> from his desk.

    (F) NO CHANGE
    (G) was looking up angry
    (H) looked up angrily
    (J) looks up angrily
    (K) looked angry up

25. The director explained that the scene required Edmund <u>to look distraughtly</u> on hearing the news of his sister's death.

    (A) NO CHANGE
    (B) looking distraughtly
    (C) to have looked distraughtly
    (D) to have looked distraught
    (E) to look distraught

26. Some psychologists maintain that a child <u>who</u>
                                                F

    <u>has seen</u> violence on television <u>is</u> more likely to
    G   H

    react <u>violent</u> in situations of stress. <u>No change</u>
          J   K

27. The <u>recent created</u> commission <u>has done</u> nothing
        A   B

    to address the problem <u>except to approve</u> the
                            C

    color of <u>its</u> stationary. <u>No change</u>
             D   E

28. The track meet begins at 10:00 am, so the team needs to depart from the school <u>at a reasonable early hour</u>.

    (F) NO CHANGE
    (G) at a reasonably early hour
    (H) during a reasonable early hour
    (J) while a reasonably early hour
    (K) at a reasonably hour that is early

29. <u>Not hardly</u> a sound <u>could be heard</u> in the
        A   B

    auditorium <u>when</u> the speaker <u>approached</u> the dais
               C   D

    to announce the result of the contest. <u>No change</u>
                                             E

30. Although she <u>had been hired</u> by the magazine
                 F

    <u>to write</u> book reviews, <u>she knew</u> <u>scarcely nothing</u>
    G   H   J

    about current fiction. <u>No change</u>
                            K

31. The reason Harriet <u>fired</u> her secretary is <u>because</u> he
                       A   B

    <u>was</u> <u>frequently</u> late and spent too much time on
    C   D

    personal phone calls. <u>No change</u>
                           E

32. <u>The reason the manager changed catchers was</u> <u>because</u> he hoped that the opposing side would put in a left-handed pitcher.

   (F) NO CHANGE
   (G) The reason that catchers were changed by the manager was because
   (H) The reason the manager changed catchers which
   (J) The manager changed catchers because
   (K) The manager changed catchers, the reason being

33. I read in a magazine <u>where</u> scientists <u>believe</u> that
                A   B

  <u>they</u> <u>have discovered</u> a new subatomic particle.
   C   D

  <u>No change</u>
    E

34. The company <u>offers</u> a plastic key card
              F

  so that employees <u>can carry</u> it in <u>their</u> <u>wallet</u>.
                G   H   J

  <u>No change</u>
    K

35. The great pianist Vladimir Horowitz <u>plays</u> the
                          A

  music <u>of</u> the Romantic Era <u>better than</u> <u>any pianist</u>
      B   C   D

  in history. <u>No change</u>
          E

36. <u>Like Neil Simon, many of Tennessee Williams'</u> <u>plays</u> reflect a culture familiar to the playwright.

   (F) NO CHANGE
   (G) Many of Tennessee Williams' plays, like Neil Simon's
   (H) Many of Tennessee Williams' plays, like Neil Simon
   (J) Many of Neil Simon and Tennessee Williams' plays
   (K) As with the plays of Neil Simon, many of Tennessee Williams' plays

37. Educators <u>are</u> now expressing <u>their</u> concern that
          A   B
American school children <u>prefer</u> watching
                 C
television <u>to books</u>. <u>No change</u>
       D   E

38. The novels of Nathaniel Hawthorne <u>contain</u>
                              F

  characters who <u>are</u> every bit <u>as</u> sinister and
           G   H

  frightening <u>as the master</u> of cinematic suspense,
            J

  Alfred Hitchcock. <u>No change</u>
               K

39. After the broken glass and other debris were cleaned up, we realized that the thief <u>had took</u> not only the necklace but a valuable ring as well.

   (A) NO CHANGE
   (B) had taken
   (C) was took
   (D) was taken
   (E) were took

40. Everyone was very surprised <u>when Sylvia brought</u> her grandfather to music class and asked him to perform several Spanish songs on the guitar.

   (F) NO CHANGE
   (G) because Sylvia bringing
   (H) while Sylvia brought
   (J) that Sylvia brang
   (K) for Sylvia to bring

41. The sheriff called off the search for the escaped convict because he doubted that <u>the convict can successfully cross the river because the current was so swift</u>.

    (A) NO CHANGE
    (B) the convict successfully crossed the river because the current was so swift
    (C) the convict successfully crossed the river being that the current was so swift
    (D) the convict would have been successful in crossing the river, the current being so swift
    (E) a successful attempt to cross the river was made by the convict because the current was so swift

42. Elaine is the favorite to win the final event because she <u>had always run</u> well at the 100-meter distance.

    (F) NO CHANGE
    (G) has always run
    (H) have always run
    (J) always ran
    (K) will always run

43. My computer crashed several times before I <u>finally figured out that I had loaded</u> a corrupted copy of the program.

    (A) NO CHANGE
    (B) had finally figured out that I loaded
    (C) had finally figured out that I had loaded
    (D) finally had figured out that I loaded
    (E) figured out finally that I would load

44. At the current rate of consumption, we <u>have exhausted</u> our supply of firewood before the weather turns warm.

    (F) NO CHANGE
    (G) had exhausted
    (H) exhausted
    (J) will exhaust
    (K) will have exhausted

45. The will is going to be read at 3:00 pm, so the lawyer has asked that all family members <u>are present</u> in the office at that time.

    (A) NO CHANGE
    (B) are presently
    (C) are going to be present
    (D) be present
    (E) being present

46. A dangerous situation could arise if the override switch were left open and the water <u>drops</u> below 50% of capacity.

    (F) NO CHANGE
    (G) dropped
    (H) allowed to drop
    (J) allowed dropping
    (K) allows to drop

47. The teacher began <u>to discuss</u> the homework
                          A
    assignment <u>when</u> he <u>will be</u> interrupted <u>by</u> the
                     B   C   D
    sound of the fire alarm. <u>No change</u>
                                    E

48. The conductor <u>announced</u> that the concert would
                      F
    resume <u>as soon as</u> the soloist <u>replaces</u> the broken
                G   H
    string on <u>her</u> violin. <u>No change</u>
                 J   K

49. <u>Many</u> patients begin <u>to show</u> symptoms again
     A   B
    after <u>they</u> <u>stopped</u> taking the drug. <u>No change</u>
           C   D   E

50. The winter was so severe <u>that</u> <u>several</u> of Hillary's
                                 F   G
    prize rose bushes <u>had sustained</u> <u>serious</u> damage
                          H   J
    from the frost. <u>No change</u>
                          K

51. <u>In contrast of</u> the prevailing opinion, the
    A

    editorial <u>lays</u> the blame <u>for</u> the strike on the
    B   C

    workers and <u>their</u> representatives.   <u>No change</u>
    D   E

52. Although ballet and modern dance are both

    <u>concerned in</u> movement in space to musical
    F

    accompaniment, the training for ballet <u>is more</u>
    G   H

    rigorous <u>than that</u> for modern dance. <u>No change</u>
    J   K

53. By midnight the guests still <u>had not been served</u>
    A

    anything <u>to eat</u>, so <u>they</u> were <u>ravishing</u>. <u>No change</u>
    B   C   D   E

54. The <u>raise</u> in the number of accidents <u>attributable</u>
    F   G

    to drunk drivers <u>has prompted</u> a call for <u>stiffer</u>
    H   J

    penalties for driving while intoxicated. <u>No</u>
    K

    <u>change</u>

55. The idea of trying <u>completing</u> the term paper <u>by</u>
    A   B

    Friday <u>caused</u> Ken <u>to cancel</u> his plans for the
    C   D

    weekend. <u>No change</u>
    E

56. Psychologists <u>think</u> that many people eat
    F

    <u>satisfying</u> <u>a need</u> for affection that is not
    G   H

    otherwise <u>fulfilled</u>. <u>No change</u>
    J   K

57. The armor plating on the new tank protects more
    vulnerable <u>areas than the armor on the old tank, it</u>
    <u>costs</u> about three times as much to manufacture
    and install.

    (A) NO CHANGE
    (B) areas than the armor on the old tank, because
        it costs
    (C) areas than the armor on the old tank, and it
        costs
    (D) areas than the armor on the old tank which
        costs
    (E) areas than the armor on the old tank, it costs

58. <u>The filibuster continued late into the night some</u>
    Senators slept sitting upright in the chairs while
    others slumped over their desks.

    (F) NO CHANGE
    (G) As the filibuster continued late into the night,
        some
    (H) Because of the filibuster continuing late into
        the night, some
    (J) The filibuster continued late into the night
        with
    (K) The filibuster, which continued late into the
        night, some

59. The weather forecast predicted heavy <u>rain, the</u>
    baseball game was postponed until the following
    day.

    (A) NO CHANGE
    (B) rain while the
    (C) rain, so the
    (D) rain the
    (E) rain or the

60. The devastation caused by the flood was <u>so</u>
    <u>complete, it</u> was impossible to tell that the pile of
    debris had once been a house.

    (F) NO CHANGE
    (G) so complete, and it
    (H) so complete that it
    (J) so completely, it
    (K) so that it

61. The audience, dazzled by the sequined costumes and brilliant lights and applauded wildly.

    (A) NO CHANGE
    (B) The audience, dazzled by the sequined costumes and brilliant lights, applauded wildly.
    (C) The audience was dazzled by the sequined costumes and brilliant lights applauding wildly.
    (D) The audience, applauding wildly and dazzled by the sequined costumes and brilliant lights.
    (E) Dazzled by the sequined costumes and brilliant lights, the applauding audience.

62. Most of the delegates, who were from smaller villages and rural areas and so opposed any plans to improve conditions in the large cities.

    (F) NO CHANGE
    (G) Most of the delegates from smaller villages and rural areas and so opposed any plans to improve conditions in the large cities.
    (H) The delegates, most of whom were from smaller villages and rural areas and so opposed any plans to improve conditions in the large cities.
    (J) The delegates who opposed any plans to improve conditions in the large cities and were from smaller villages and rural areas.
    (K) Most of the delegates, who were from smaller villages and rural areas, opposed any plans to improve conditions in the large cities.

63. Carlos telephoned to say that weather had delayed his plane, but he will not be able to attend the meeting.

    (A) NO CHANGE
    (B) plane, so he will
    (C) plane, but he was
    (D) plane when he will
    (E) plane because he could

64. By the fifth inning, Cindy was showing signs of fatigue and walked three consecutive batters, so the coach refused to take her out of the game.

    (F) NO CHANGE
    (G) batters, when
    (H) batters, moreover
    (J) batters during
    (K) batters, but

65. Because the wetlands were protected by federal law, the owners were not able to build the shopping center that they had planned.

    (A) NO CHANGE
    (B) In fact
    (C) However
    (D) Moreover
    (E) So that

66. Victoria was nominated to the office of club president, or it is doubtful that she would serve even if elected.

    (F) NO CHANGE
    (G) president so
    (H) president, though
    (J) president, in that
    (K) president, even

67. The driving snow made the roadway slippery and reduced visibility to no more than a few feet, and fortunately there were no accidents despite the heavy volume of traffic.

    (A) NO CHANGE
    (B) but fortunately there were no
    (C) and fortunately there were some
    (D) while fortunately there were no
    (E) so fortunately there were no

68. The land surrounding Las Vegas is characterized by parched red dunes and flats with dry ravines, but it is almost entirely lacking in vegetation.

    (F) NO CHANGE
    (G) and they are
    (H) and it is
    (J) but they are
    (K) but are

69. Kari was just about to mail in her deposit for her second-choice school <u>and that was when the letter arrived notifying her</u> of her acceptance at her first choice.

(A) NO CHANGE
(B) and then the letter that arrived notified her
(C) when she received notification by letter
(D) and then they told her
(E) when she learned

70. <u>Although the American relay team did not qualify for the finals, the</u> anchor runner dropped the baton shortly after the hand-off.

(F) NO CHANGE
(G) When the American relay team did not qualify for the finals, the
(H) The American relay team did not qualify for the finals, and the
(J) The American relay team did not qualify for the finals because the
(K) Not qualifying for the finals, the American relay team's

71. To abandon <u>their</u> homes, leave behind their
          A

families, and <u>traveling</u> across the ocean <u>required</u>
          B   C

great courage on the part of the immigrants

<u>who moved</u> to America. <u>No change</u>
   D   E

72. The review <u>praised</u> the wit, charm, and
          F

<u>interpreting</u> of the recitalist <u>but never once</u>
   G   H

<u>mentioned</u> her voice. <u>No change</u>
   J   K

73. To acknowledge that <u>one has</u> something to learn
              A B

<u>is taking</u> the first step on the road to true
C D

wisdom. <u>No change</u>
        E

74. The students are <u>critical of</u> the dean because he <u>is</u>
             F   G

either <u>unfamiliar or</u> doesn't care about the urgent
       H

<u>need for</u> new student housing on campus.
J

<u>No change</u>
K

75. Baseball <u>has and</u> probably always will be the
       A

sport <u>that</u> <u>symbolizes</u> for people <u>in</u> other
     B   C   D

countries the American way of life. <u>No change</u>
                                   E

76. <u>Letters were received by the editor of the newspaper that complained of its editorial policy.</u>

(F) NO CHANGE
(G) Letters were received by the editor of the newspaper having complained of its editorial policy.
(H) The editor of the newspaper received letters complaining of the newspaper's editorial policy.
(J) Letters were received by the editor in which there were complaints to the editor of the newspaper about its editorial policy.
(K) Letters were received by the editor complaining of the newspaper's editorial policy by the editor.

77. Riding in a coach and wearing the crown jewels, <u>the crowd cheered the royal couple.</u>

(A) NO CHANGE
(B) cheering for the royal couple was done by the crowd
(C) the royal couple was cheered by the crowd
(D) the royal couple's cheering was done by the crowd
(E) the royal couple, who was being cheered by crowd

78. <u>Wrapped in several thicknesses of newspaper, packed carefully in a strong cardboard carton, and bound securely with tape, the worker made sure that the fragile figurines would not be broken.</u>

(F) NO CHANGE
(G) Wrapped in several thicknesses of newspaper, packed carefully in a strong cardboard carton, and then binding the carton securely with tape, the worker made sure that the fragile figurines would not be broken.
(H) The figurines, having been securely wrapped in several thicknesses of newspaper, packed carefully in a strong cardboard carton which was then securely bound with tape, the worker made sure would not be broken.
(J) The worker, wrapping the figurines in several thicknesses of newspaper, packing them carefully in a strong cardboard carton, and securely binding the carton with tape, made sure that they would not be broken.
(K) To make sure that the figurines would not be broken, the worker wrapped them in several thicknesses of newspaper, packed them carefully in a strong cardboard carton, and securely bound the carton with tape.

79. Mary Lou was awarded the gold medal because she <u>scored</u> <u>more points than any child participating</u> in the field day.

(A) NO CHANGE
(B) more points than any other child participating
(C) most points than any child participating
(D) more points than any child who had participated
(E) more points as any child participating

80. <u>Appearing</u> in his first American tour, the British singer's album rose to the top of the charts.

(F) NO CHANGE
(G) While appearing
(H) While he was appearing
(J) When appearing
(K) Upon appearing

81. I think that Dore's illustrations of Dante's *Divine Comedy* <u>are excellent; but my favorite drawing is</u> "Don Quixote in His Library."

(A) NO CHANGE
(B) are excellent, but my favorite drawing is "Don Quixote in His Library."
(C) are excellent and my favorite drawing is "Don Quixote in His Library."
(D) are excellent in that my favorite drawing is "Don Quixote in His Library."
(E) are excellent even though "Don Quixote in His Library" is my favorite drawing.

82. <u>Practically</u> all nitrates are crystalline and <u>readily</u>
　　F　　　　　　　　　　　　　　　　　　G

<u>soluble, and</u> they are characterized by marked
　　H

decrepitation <u>when</u> heated on charcoals by a
　　　　　　　J

blowpipe. <u>No change</u>
　　　　　　K

83. The door <u>was</u> <u>ajar,</u> and the house <u>had been</u>
　　　　　A　　B　　　　　　　　　　C

<u>ransacked.</u> <u>No change</u>
　D　　　　　E

84. Since many diseases and insects cause serious

damage to <u>crops,</u> special national legislation has
　　　　　F

been passed to provide for the quarantine of

imported <u>plants;</u> and under provisions of various
　　　　　G

<u>acts,</u> inspectors are placed at ports of entry to
　H

prevent smugglers from bringing in plants

<u>that might be</u> dangerous. <u>No change</u>
　J　　　　　　　　　　K

85. <u>A full train crew consists of a motorman, a</u>
    <u>brakeman, a conductor, and two ticket takers.</u>

    (A) NO CHANGE
    (B) A full train crew consists of a motorman, a
        brakeman, a conductor and two ticket takers.
    (C) A full train crew consists of a motorman,
        brakeman, conductor, and two ticket takers.
    (D) A full train crew consists of, a motorman, a
        brakeman, a conductor, and two ticket takers.
    (E) A full train crew consists of a motorman
        brakeman a conductor and two ticket takers.

86. The procedure requires that you open the outer

    cover <u>plate,</u> remove the <u>thermostat,</u> replace the
          F   G

    broken <u>switch, and then</u> replace the thermostat.
           H   J
    <u>No change</u>
       K

87. <u>After</u> Peter finished painting the bird <u>feeder</u> he
    A   B

    <u>and</u> Jack <u>hung it</u> from a limb of the oak tree.
    C   D

    <u>No change</u>
       E

88. <u>When</u> Pat explained to his mother that ten was
    F

    the highest mark <u>given</u> on the entrance <u>test</u> she
                     G   H

    <u>breathed</u> a sigh of relief. <u>No change</u>
    J   K

89. <u>Tim hopes to score well on the exam because he</u>
    <u>plans to go to an Ivy League school.</u>

    (A) NO CHANGE
    (B) Tim hopes to score well on the exam and he
        plans to go to an Ivy League school.
    (C) Tim hopes to score well on the exam,
        because he plans to go to an Ivy League
        school.
    (D) Tim hopes to score well on the exam, and he
        plans to go to an Ivy League school.
    (E) Tim hopes to score well on the exam he
        plans to go to an Ivy League school.

90. <u>In this impoverished region with its arid soil a</u>
    <u>typical diet may contain only 800 calories per</u>
    <u>day.</u>

    (F) NO CHANGE
    (G) In this impoverished region with its arid soil;
        a typical diet may contain only 800 calories
        per day.
    (H) In this impoverished region, with its arid soil,
        a typical diet may contain only 800 calories
        per day.
    (J) In this impoverished region with its arid soil,
        a typical diet may contain only 800 calories
        per day.
    (K) In this impoverished region with its arid soil:
        a typical diet may contain only 800 calories
        per day.

91. <u>Begun</u> in 1981 and completed in <u>1985</u> the bridge
    A   B

    <u>provided</u> the first link <u>between</u> the island and the
    C   D

    mainland. <u>No change</u>
               E

92. <u>To slow the bleeding Van tied a tourniquet</u>
    <u>around the lower portion of the leg.</u>

    (F) NO CHANGE
    (G) To slow the bleeding—Van tied a tourniquet
        around the lower portion of the leg.
    (H) To slow the bleeding, Van tied a tourniquet
        around the lower portion of the leg.
    (J) To slow the bleeding, Van tied a tourniquet,
        around the lower portion of the leg.
    (K) Van tied a tourniquet, to slow the bleeding,
        around the lower portion of the leg.

93. <u>Niagara Falls, which</u> forms part of the border
    A   B

    between the United States and <u>Canada,</u> was the
                                  C

    site of a saw mill <u>built by the French in 1725.</u>
                       D

    <u>No change</u>
       E

94. Secretary of State <u>Acheson, however,</u> made a
                         F   G

    <u>reasoned</u> defense <u>of</u> the treaty. <u>No change</u>
     H   J   K

95. Until the end of the 18th <u>century,</u> the only
                            A

    musicians in <u>Norway,</u> were simple
                 B

    unsophisticated peasants <u>who</u> traveled <u>about.</u>
                        C   D

    <u>No change</u>
     E

96. Prizes <u>will be</u> awarded in each <u>event,</u> and the
        F   G

    <u>participant, who compiles the greatest overall total,</u>
                           H

    <u>will receive</u> a special prize. <u>No change</u>
     J   K

97. Since learning of the dangers of <u>caffeine, neither</u>
                              A   B

    my wife <u>nor</u> I have consumed any <u>beverage,</u>
             C   D

    containing caffeine. <u>No change</u>
                    E

98. After months of separation, Gauguin finally joined Van Gogh <u>in Arles in October of 1888, Gauguin left a few weeks later</u>.

    (F) NO CHANGE
    (G) in Arles; Gauguin, however, leaving a few weeks later
    (H) in Arles, while Gauguin left a few weeks later
    (J) in Arles, it was three weeks later when Gauguin was gone
    (K) in Arles, in October of 1888, but left a few weeks later

99. <u>By the middle of June,</u> the foliage on the trees
     A

    and the underbrush <u>was</u> lush and green and so
                        B

    thick <u>that</u> it was impossible to see <u>very far, into</u>
         C   D

    the woods. <u>No change</u>
                 E

100. Students who plan to graduate with joint majors <u>must, declare</u> their intention and identify the two areas of study by the end of their junior years.

    (F) NO CHANGE
    (G) must declare
    (H) must, declaring
    (J) must declaring
    (K) must declared

101. <u>He grew up on a farm in Nebraska; he is now the captain of a Navy ship.</u>

    (A) NO CHANGE
    (B) He grew up on a farm in Nebraska, he is now the captain of a Navy ship.
    (C) He grew up on a farm in Nebraska he is now the captain of a Navy ship.
    (D) He grew up on a farm; in Nebraska he is now the captain of a Navy ship.
    (E) He grew up on a farm in Nebraska but he is now the captain of a Navy ship.

102. <u>The Smithtown players cheered the referee's decision; the Stonybrook players booed it.</u>

    (F) NO CHANGE
    (G) The Smithtown players cheered the referee's decision the Stonybrook players booed it.
    (H) The Smithtown players cheered the referee's decision, the Stonybrook players booed it.
    (J) The Smithtown players cheered the referee's decision: the Stonybrook players booed it.
    (K) The Smithtown players cheered the referee's decision, but the Stonybrook players booed it.

103. <u>When</u> John entered the <u>room;</u> <u>everyone</u> stood <u>up</u>.
　　　A　　　　　　　　　B　　　C　　　　　D

No change
　E

104. Clem <u>announced</u> <u>that</u> the prize <u>would be</u> donated
　　　　　　　F　　　　G　　　　　　　　H

to Harbus <u>House;</u> a well-known charity.
　　　　　　　J

No change
　K

105. The nineteenth-century composers Wagner and
Mahler did more than just write <u>music, they</u>
<u>conducted</u> their own works.

(A) NO CHANGE
(B) music, in that they conducted
(C) music; they conducted
(D) music, with their conducting of
(E) music; as conductors, they did

106. The <u>seemingly</u> tranquil lane has been the scene of
　　　　　　F

many crimes <u>including:</u> two <u>assaults,</u> three
　　　　　　　　G　　　　　H

<u>robberies,</u> and one murder.　<u>No change</u>
　　　J　　　　　　　　　　　　　　　K

107. In addition to test <u>scores, college</u> admissions
　　　　　　　　　　　　A

officers take into consideration many other

factors such <u>as: grades,</u> extracurricular <u>activities,</u>
　　　　　　　　B　　C　　　　　　　　　　D

<u>and</u> letters of recommendation.　<u>No change</u>
　D　　　　　　　　　　　　　　　　　　E

108. <u>Peter notified Elaine. The guidance counselor,</u>
<u>that he had been accepted.</u>

(F) NO CHANGE
(G) Peter notified Elaine the guidance counselor,
that he had been accepted.
(H) Peter notified Elaine, the guidance counselor
that he had been accepted.
(J) Peter notified Elaine, the guidance counselor,
that he had been accepted.
(K) Peter notified Elaine that the guidance
counselor had been accepted.

109. <u>Peanuts—blanched or lightly roasted, add an</u>
<u>interesting texture and taste to garden salads.</u>

(A) NO CHANGE
(B) Peanuts—blanched or lightly roasted—add
an interesting texture and taste to garden
salads.
(C) Peanuts: blanched or lightly roasted, add an
interesting texture and taste to garden salads.
(D) Peanuts, blanched or lightly roasted—add an
interesting texture and taste to garden salads.
(E) Peanuts blanched or lightly roasted; add an
interesting texture and taste to garden salads.

110. The rug gets its striking colors from the weaver's
skilled use of <u>dyes—both natural and synthetic to</u>
create shades in subtle variations.

(F) NO CHANGE
(G) dyes—both natural and synthetic, to create
(H) dyes, both natural and synthetic—to create
(J) dyes—both natural and synthetic—to create
(K) dyes—both natural and—synthetic to create

111. <u>The first chapter of *The Scarlet Letter* is "The</u>
<u>Custom House."</u>

(A) NO CHANGE
(B) The first chapter of *The Scarlet Letter* is
"The Custom House".
(C) The first chapter of *The Scarlet Letter* is The
Custom House.
(D) The first chapter of *The Scarlet Letter* is *The
Custom House.*
(E) The first chapter of "*The Scarlet Letter*" is
"The Custom House."

112. According to legend, <u>King Arthurs court</u> consisted of twenty-four knights, each of whom was chosen by Arthur for a special talent or virtue.

    (F) NO CHANGE
    (G) King Arthurs' court
    (H) King Arthur's court
    (J) King's Arthur court
    (K) Kings' Arthur court

113. In the turmoil of our <u>modern times,</u> it is important to try to keep in mind the fundamental moral values that structure our society.

    (A) NO CHANGE
    (B) modern times'
    (C) modern time's
    (D) modern-like times'
    (E) modern and time

114. While he addresses the barbell, <u>a weightlifters face</u> has an expression of deep concentration which immediately gives way to one of complete exertion during the lift and to total exhaustion as the bar is allowed to fall to the ground.

    (F) NO CHANGE
    (G) the weightlifters face
    (H) the weightlifters faces
    (J) the weightlifters' face
    (K) a weightlifter's face

DIRECTIONS: Punctuate the following paragraph.

115. On Monday Mark received a letter of acceptance from State College He immediately called his mother herself a graduate of State College to tell her about his acceptance When he told her he had also been awarded a scholarship she was very excited After hanging up Mark's mother decided to throw a surprise party for Mark She telephoned his brother his sister and several of his friends Because the party was supposed to be a surprise she made them all promise not to say anything to Mark Mark however had a similar idea a party for his mother to celebrate his acceptance at her alma mater He telephoned his brother his sister and several of his parents' friends to invite them to a party at his house on Saturday night and he made them all promise to say nothing to his mother On Saturday night both Mark and his mother were surprised

DIRECTIONS: The following passages are early drafts of essays. Some parts of the passages need to be rewritten. Read each passage and answer the items that follow. Some items are about particular sentences or parts of sentences and ask you to improve sentence structure and word choice. Other items refer to parts of the passage or the entire passage and ask you to consider organization and development. In making your decisions, follow the conventions of standard written English.

Items 116–120 are based on the following essay, which is a response to an assignment to write about an issue that is facing America and what might be done to resolve it.

[1] *In my mind, one of the most pressing issues facing America today is healthcare.* [2] *One aspect of the problem is lack of access to a doctor.* [3] *Many people just cannot afford to pay for a visit to a doctor.* [4] *They avoid going to the doctor until they are really sick.* [5] *If they were treated in the first place, they wouldn't get so sick.* [6] *This practice not only causes human suffering but is wasteful.* [7] *Health insurance for surgery is also an issue.* [8] *Many people do not get adequate health insurance with their jobs and cannot afford to pay for it.* [9] *The inability to pay for health insurance also creates an unfair distribution of healthcare in America.*

[10] *An even more important aspect of the healthcare problem in America is the choices that people make for themselves.* [11] *Take smoking for example.* [12] *Scientific evidence proves that smoking causes lung cancer and other diseases.* [13] *Yet, many people continue to smoke, and young people continue to start smoking.* [14] *There are other health problems such as being overweight and using drugs that may also come from private choices.*

[15] *Some government assistance is needed for those who cannot afford medical care or health insurance.* [16] *The most important thing is for people to be concerned with their own health.* [17] *If we take care of ourselves by eating better, exercising more, and avoiding destructive choices, we will all live longer, healthier, and happier lives.*

116. The author considers inserting the following factual statement between sentences 13 and 14:

Nicotine, which is found in tobacco, is one of the most addictive chemicals known to science.

Would this statement add to the development of the paragraph?

(A) Yes, because the paragraph identifies smoking as a serious problem.
(B) Yes, because the sentence explains why young people start to smoke.
(C) No, because scientific evidence is irrelevant to the author's point.
(D) No, because the addictive mechanism behind smoking is not relevant.
(E) No, because essays should emphasize positive points, not negative ones.

117. Which of the following revisions to sentence 15 best clarifies the author's position?

(F) NO CHANGE
(G) Some government assistance is needed for those who cannot afford medical care or health insurance and people need to be concerned with their own health.
(H) The most important thing is for people to be concerned with their own health and for them to ask for government assistance.
(J) Even though some government assistance is needed for those who cannot afford medical care or health insurance, the most important thing is for people to be concerned with their own health.
(K) OMIT sentence 15

118. In context, which of the following best describes the main purpose of the essay?

(A) To expose faulty reasoning
(B) To evaluate a theory set forth earlier
(C) To provide specific illustrations
(D) To propose a solution to a problem
(E) To persuade the reader to change an opinion

119. In writing this passage, the author was most probably addressing

   (F) a convention of surgeons
   (G) a group of concerned citizens
   (H) a meeting of insurance executives
   (J) a conference of tobacco executives
   (K) an assembly of noted scientists

120. What should be done to sentence 7 to strengthen the organization of the essay?

   (A) NO CHANGE
   (B) Begin a new paragraph
   (C) Switch sentence 6 with sentence 7
   (D) Switch sentence 7 with sentence 8
   (E) OMIT sentence 7

<u>Item 121</u> is based on the following essay, which is a response to an assignment to write about a chore for which you have a responsibility and why you like or dislike doing the chore.

Each year, my family plants a vegetable garden. Both my parents work, and with this it is the job of the children to tend the garden.

Work starts several weeks before the growing season actually begins. We put little pots of soil containing seeds that must sprout before they are planted outdoors on the sun porch. Then, my father prepares the ground with a rototiller. The danger of frost is past, it is time to plant.

For the first few weeks, we water the seed beds regularly and pull weeds by hand. Once the plants are established, the leaves of the good plants block the sunlight so weeds can't grow. However, there are other jobs such as staking tomatoes and tending to running vines.

Then the blossoms appear and are pollinated by bees and other insects. As small vegetables appear, the blossoms drop off. They continue to grow and later in the summer begin to ripen. Up to this point, tending the garden has been a chore, but now it becomes a pleasure. Each afternoon, we pick the ripe ones and wash them so that they are ready for cooking. I suppose that I feel proud that I have helped to feed my family. I have to admit that I enjoy the taste of the freshly picked vegetables.

121. Which of the following best describes the overall organization of the passage?

   (F) Chronological development
   (G) Explanation of two sides of an issue
   (H) Generalization of a statement with illustrations
   (J) Posing a question and then answering it
   (K) Citing an authority and then drawing a conclusion

Items 122–127 are based on the following essay, which is a response to an assignment to write about a significant activity or experience from the summer vacation.

On my vacation to Alaska, I took a trip to Porcupine. In 1905, Porcupine was a thriving town of 2,000 people, retail stores, and a post office. Hardly any of the town remains today, but there is still gold there, and our guide showed us how to pan for gold. It's easy to learn how, and anyone can do it. [1]

The technique of panning depends on the weight of gold. It's about 20 times heavier than water, so the gold stays at the bottom of a stream and gets caught in the sand in slow flowing water around bends and along the edge of the stream. It can also get stuck in small crevices of rock and even wedged into pieces of wood.

You need to find where the gold is. There's no sense in panning for gold in a stream where there isn't any, so go to a stream where people have found gold before. Then concentrate on those areas that are most likely to trap the little bits of gold.

Keep moving the pan until about half the original material has been carried away. Lift the pan out of the water, tilt it toward the side with the riffles (the small ridges), and swirl until the water is gone. Repeat this process until nearly all the material is gone.

To start panning, put a few handfuls of material into your gold pan. Then submerge the pan in the water of the stream. Hold the pan under the surface and move it in a circular motion so that the lighter material sloshes over the edge. You have to be careful not to be too aggressive or you'll send your gold downstream along with the silt and other debris.

Use a small stream of water suction pipette (or even a spray bottle with a concentrated setting on the nozzle) to sort the gold from the remaining debris. Pick up the flecks with a tweezers or your fingers and place them in a small glass container such as a test tube or a medicine bottle.

Panning takes practice, patience, and luck, but even a little bit of gold is a big thrill. You're probably not going to find a lot of gold.

122. Which of the following sentences inserted at [1] would best introduce the remaining paragraphs of the essay?

(A) Gold is one of the most valuable substances on earth.
(B) Just follow these simple instructions.
(C) I try to do a lot of different things on my vacations.
(D) Did you even know that there was a gold rush in Alaska?
(E) Porcupine, the town, was named for the small quilled animal.

123. Which of the following sequence of paragraphs is most logical?

(F) NO CHANGE
(G) 6, 4, 5
(H) 4, 6, 5
(J) 5, 4, 6
(K) 5, 6, 4

124. What is the most appropriate location for the final sentence in paragraph 2?

(A) NO CHANGE
(B) As the first sentence of paragraph 2
(C) In paragraph 2, following the sentence ending "…weight of gold."
(D) As the first sentence of paragraph 3
(E) As the last sentence of paragraph 4

125. Is the parenthetical note following the word "riffles" in paragraph 4 appropriate?

(F) Yes, because it clarifies a technical term for the reader.
(G) Yes, because it presents an idea that is essential to the passage.
(H) No, because it distracts the reader from the directions for panning.
(J) No, because the author does not cite a source for the definition.
(K) No, because technical jargon is out of place in this essay.

126. What would be the most effective place for the following sentence: "Panning takes practice, patience, and luck, but even a little bit of gold is a big thrill"?

    (A) WHERE IT IS NOW
    (B) At the end of the passage
    (C) At the beginning of paragraph 2
    (D) At the beginning of paragraph 6
    (E) At the beginning of the essay

127. Suppose the author had been assigned to write a brief essay on an interesting travel destination. Assuming that all of the following statements are true, would this essay successfully fulfill the assignment?

    (F) Yes, because many gold-seekers came to Porcupine during the 19th century.
    (G) Yes, because panning for gold would be a fun activity on a trip.
    (H) No, because very little remains today of the town of Porcupine.
    (J) No, because most people have never before heard of Porcupine.
    (K) No, because many people prefer silver jewelry to gold jewelry.

128. Angela is hoping to save enough for a trip to Europe, during which <u>the small village where her grandparents were born will be visited</u>.

    (A) NO CHANGE
    (B) the small village where her grandparents had been born will be visited
    (C) she will visit the small village where her grandparents were born
    (D) there will be a visit to the small village where her grandparents were born
    (E) a visit to the small village where her grandparents were born will be included

129. <u>Finally and at long last</u> the old dog opened his eyes and noticed the intruder.

    (F) NO CHANGE
    (G) Finally
    (H) So finally
    (J) Yet at long last
    (K) Finally and long lastingly

130. The speaker declared that <u>alternative ways of utilizing</u> waterfront land ought to be explored.

    (A) NO CHANGE
    (B) alternatives of use for
    (C) alternative utilizations of
    (D) alternative ways of utilization of
    (E) alternate uses of

131. <u>Since only</u> the ruling party <u>is allowed to</u> vote, <u>its</u>
    F   G   H

    members are able to maintain the <u>existing</u> status
             J

    quo. <u>No change</u>
      K

132. Each year, the geese <u>make</u> their <u>annual</u> <u>migration</u>
          A   B   C

    from Northern Canada to <u>their winter habitats</u> in
            D

    the United States. <u>No change</u>
          E

133. <u>Although</u> the committee met for over two weeks
     F

    and issued a 50-page report, <u>its findings</u> were
             G

    <u>of little</u> <u>importance or</u> consequence. <u>No change</u>
     H   J   K

134. <u>Along with an end to featherbedding and no-show jobs</u>, the new head of the Transit Authority has eliminated many other inefficient employment practices.

    (A) NO CHANGE
    (B) In addition to eliminating featherbedding and no-show jobs
    (C) Not only did he end featherbedding and no-shows jobs,
    (D) Besides featherbedding and no-show jobs coming to an end
    (E) Together with the ending of featherbedding and no-show jobs

–31–

135. <u>Being that</u> the hour <u>was</u> late, we <u>agreed</u> to adjourn
   F   G   H

 the meeting and <u>reconvene</u> at nine o'clock the
        J

 following morning. <u>No change</u>
        K

DIRECTIONS: In the selections below, certain parts of the sentences have been underlined and numbered. In the right-hand column, you will find different ways of writing each underlined part. Choose the one that best expresses the idea and uses standard written English. If you think the original version is the best, choose "NO CHANGE." The answer to many questions depends upon material that follows the underlined part. So, be sure that you have read far enough ahead before you select your answer choice.

Appalachia's European Settlers

The first Europeans who adopted Appalachia as

home, followed the trails pounded out by those
136

earliest mountain engineers: the buffalo, elk, deer, and
137

other wild game. (Later, they found the great traces
138

forged by the Indian tribes on their trading and
138

fighting forays.) Gradually, these first Europeans
138

hewed out passages that become part of America's
139

history, and portions of which may still be discovered

along today's interstates and back roads. Their very

names connect us to the past in the region: The Great
140

Warrior's Trail, Boone's Trace (which became the

Wilderness Road), and the Cumberland Gap.

136. (A) NO CHANGE
(B) home followed
(C) home: followed
(D) home; followed

137. (F) NO CHANGE
(G) engineers, the
(H) engineers the
(J) engineers. The

138. (A) NO CHANGE
(B) Great traces forged by the Indian tribes, however, were later found on their trading and fighting forays.
(C) (Finding later, great traces forged by the Indian tribes, on their trading and fighting forays.)
(D) Later, they found the great traces forged by the Indian tribes on their trading and fighting forays.

139. (F) NO CHANGE
(G) will become a part of
(H) became part of
(J) became part

140. (A) NO CHANGE
(B) connecting us to
(C) connected us to
(D) connect us

Geographic isolation greatly influenced the
₁₄₁
region's culture. From the beginning, numerous ethnic

groups contributed to Appalachian settlement. During

the late 1600s and into the next century, Germans

from the Rhineland settled in the Great Appalachian

Valley. Building fat barns and tight houses on the
₁₄₂
fertile fields of Pennsylvania, Maryland, Virginia, and

North Carolina. They were the "Pennsylvania Dutch."

The German settlers made important
₁₄₃
contributions. One of the important contributions
₁₄₃
made by German settlers to frontier life was the

Pennsylvania rifle—also called the Kentucky rifle and

the Long rifle. A weapon born of necessity and

economy, its extended barrel assured greater accuracy
₁₄₄
and precision than could be achieved with the old
₁₄₄
muskets, and its smaller bore required less powder

and lead for each shot (precious commodities). Such
₁₄₅
rifles were highly prized possessions, and their

manufacture was one of the central industries of

pioneer Appalachia.

141. (F) NO CHANGE
(G) Geographically isolated
(H) Isolated geographically
(J) Isolated geography

142. (A) NO CHANGE
(B) Valley, building
(C) Valley: building
(D) Valley,

143. For the sake of the logic and coherence of this paragraph, the underlined sentence should be:
(F) left as it is now.
(G) placed in parentheses.
(H) placed in quotation marks.
(J) omitted.

144. (A) NO CHANGE
(B) accuracy as well as precision
(C) accuracy plus precision
(D) accuracy

145. The most appropriate placement of the underlined phrase in this sentence would be:
(F) where it is now.
(G) after the word "powder."
(H) after the word "lead."
(J) after the word "each."

CHALLENGE ITEMS

The passages and items in this section reflect both the format and difficulty range of passages and items on the real English Test, though difficult material is emphasized. Answers are on page 591.

DIRECTIONS: In the passages below, certain parts of the sentences have been underlined and numbered. In the right-hand column, you will find different ways of writing each underlined part; the original version is indicated by the "NO CHANGE" option. There are also items that ask about a section of the passage or the passage as a whole. These items do not refer to an underlined portion of the passage; they are identified by a number or numbers in a box.

For each item, choose the alternative that you consider to be the best. Select the answer choice that best expresses the intended idea, is most acceptable in standard written English, or is most consistent with the overall tone and style of the passage. Read the passage through once before you begin to answer the accompanying items. Finding the answers to certain items may depend on looking at material that appears several sentences beyond the item. So, be sure that you have read far enough ahead before you select your answer choice.

PASSAGE I

Significance of Symbolism in Medieval Art

Art of the Middle Ages is first and foremost a

sacred script, the symbols and meanings of which are
1

well settled. A circular halo placed vertically behind
1

the head of a figure signifies sainthood, meanwhile
2

the halo impressed with a cross signifies divinity.

A tower with a window indicates a village, and
3

should an angel be watching from the battlements,

that city is thereby identified as Jerusalem.

Mathematics is also an important element of

this iconography. "The Divine Wisdom," wrote Saint

1. (A) NO CHANGE
   (B) is well settled
   (C) are settled well
   (D) would be settled

2. (F) NO CHANGE
   (G) sainthood, because
   (H) sainthood because
   (J) sainthood, while

3. (A) NO CHANGE
   (B) (Do NOT begin a new paragraph) A tower
   (C) Towers
   (D) Having a tower

Augustine, "reveals itself everywhere in <u>numbers." A</u>
4
<u>doctrine</u> derived from the <u>Neoplatonists who</u> revived
4   5
the teachings of Pythagoras. And numbers require
symmetry. At Chartres, a stained-glass window shows
the four prophets Isaac, Ezekiel, Daniel, and Jeremiah
carrying on their shoulders the four evangelists
Matthew, Mark, Luke, and John.

<u>Every painting</u> is also an allegory, showing us
6
one thing and inviting us to see another. <u>In this</u>
7
<u>respect, the artist was</u> asked to imitate God, who had
7
hidden a profound <u>meaning behind</u> the literal and
8
who wished nature to be a moral lesson to man. In a
painting of the final judgment, the foolish virgins can
be seen <u>by us</u> at the left hand of Jesus and the wise on
9
the right, and we understand that this symbolizes
those who are lost and <u>those that have been saved</u>.
10

<u>Within such a system,</u> even the most mediocre
11
talent was elevated by the genius of centuries, <u>and</u> the
12
first artist of the Renaissance broke with the tradition
at great risk. Even when they are great, medieval

4. (F) NO CHANGE
(G) numbers," which
(H) numbers." This doctrine was
(J) numbers" which

5. (A) NO CHANGE
(B) Neoplatonists that
(C) Neoplatonist's that
(D) Neoplatonist's who

6. (F) NO CHANGE
(G) (Do NOT begin a new paragraph) Every painting
(H) However, every painting
(J) (Do NOT begin a new paragraph) However, every painting

7. (A) NO CHANGE
(B) Furthermore, the artist was
(C) The artist, however, was
(D) Generally, artists are

8. (F) NO CHANGE
(G) meaning which was behind
(H) meaning being behind
(J) meaning behind and in back of

9. (A) NO CHANGE
(B) by all of us
(C) by each of us
(D) OMIT the underlined portion.

10. (F) NO CHANGE
(G) those who have been saved
(H) those who are saved
(J) the saved

11. (A) NO CHANGE
(B) (Do NOT begin a new paragraph) Within such a system,
(C) (Do NOT begin a new paragraph) Inside of such a system,
(D) (Do NOT begin a new paragraph) To be inside such a system,

12. (F) NO CHANGE
(G) with
(H) however
(J) since

artists are no more than the equals of the old masters who passively followed the sacred rules. When they are not outstanding, they <u>scarcely</u> avoid banality and insignificance in their religious works.

13. (A) NO CHANGE
(B) always
(C) ever
(D) OMIT the underlined portion.

> Items 14–16 ask about the preceding passage as a whole.

14. The author most likely wrote this essay for which of the following?

(F) A scholarly art journal
(G) A book tracing the history of mathematics
(H) A history of the Catholic Church
(J) A book surveying the history of Western art

15. The author relies on which of the following to develop the passage?

(A) Examples
(B) Extensive quotations from other authorities
(C) Statistics
(D) Personal experience

16. The author probably quotes Saint Augustine in order to:

(F) ridicule his position.
(G) emphasize the importance of numbers and symmetry.
(H) prove the importance of Church teaching.
(J) illustrate Augustine's knowledge of art.

PASSAGE II

Pursuit of the Bottomless Pit

A persistent and universal symbol in the

mythology of virtually every <u>culture, is</u> that of a
₁₇

bottomless pit or an engulfing whirlpool. It was the

maw of the <u>abyss: and those</u> venturing too close were
₁₈

dragged inward toward chaos by an irresistible force.

Socrates <u>(a Greek philosopher who committed</u>
₁₉

<u>suicide)</u> talked of a chasm that pierced the world
₁₉

straight through from side to side. Ulysses <u>also</u>
₂₀

<u>encountering it,</u> as did a mythical Cherokee who
₂₀

escaped, but not before he was drawn down to the

narrowest circle of the maelstrom where he could peer

into the netherworld of the dead. <u>Many primitive</u>
₂₁

<u>cultures bury their dead with tools in the belief that</u>
₂₁

<u>the tools will be useful to them in the afterlife.</u>
₂₁

<u>On the other hand, the search</u> for a solution to
₂₂

one of <u>astronomys'</u> most persistent and perplexing
₂₃

riddles, black holes, could be viewed <u>by one</u> as a
₂₄

17. (A) NO CHANGE
(B) culture is
(C) culture are
(D) cultures are

18. (F) NO CHANGE
(G) abyss, and those
(H) abyss meanwhile those
(J) abyss due to the fact that

19. (A) NO CHANGE
(B) (a philosopher from Greece who committed suicide)
(C) (a Greek philosopher who had committed suicide)
(D) OMIT the underlined portion.

20. (F) NO CHANGE
(G) also encountered it,
(H) also encountered them,
(J) encountered them also,

21. For the sake of the logic and coherence of this paragraph, the underlined sentence should be:
(A) left as it is now.
(B) placed before the word "Ulysses."
(C) placed at the end of the passage.
(D) omitted.

22. (F) NO CHANGE
(G) The search
(H) (Do NOT begin a new paragraph) The search
(J) Also, the search

23. (A) NO CHANGE
(B) astronomy's
(C) astronomy
(D) astronomys

24. (F) NO CHANGE
(G) by one astronomer
(H) by those
(J) OMIT the underlined portion

continuation of the search for the whirlpool that is
25

the maw of the abyss, a depth our telescopes cannot

reach and from which nothing will have returned.
26

What is incredible to contemplate, and what sets us
27

apart from the ancients, is that we think we have a fair

idea not only as to how they are formed, but also how
28

large they are and so forth. A combination of theory

and observation have led to the growing suspicion
29

among astrophysicists that the nucleus of virtually

every galaxy harbors a massive black hole.

25. (A) NO CHANGE
    (B) continuing the search of
    (C) continuation to the search for
    (D) continuation for the search for

26. (F) NO CHANGE
    (G) will return
    (H) returns
    (J) returning

27. (A) NO CHANGE
    (B) setting us
    (C) and that sets us
    (D) and we are set

28. (F) NO CHANGE
    (G) about
    (H) not about
    (J) OMIT the underlined portion.

29. (A) NO CHANGE
    (B) has led to
    (C) has led
    (D) led

PASSAGE III

Tradition Preservation During Meiji Restoration

Instead of casting aside traditional values during the Meiji Restoration of 1888, those who strove to dismantle feudalism and to modernize the country chose to preserve three traditions as the foundations <u>on</u> <u>which they could build a modern Japan upon</u>.
30

The <u>older</u> tradition and basis of the entire
31

Japanese value system was <u>respect for and even</u> <u>worshipping</u> the Emperor. During the early centuries
32

of Japanese history, the Shinto cult, in which <u>the</u> <u>Imperial family traced its ancestry to the Sun Goddess</u>,
33

became the people's sustaining faith. <u>Being later</u> <u>subordinated</u> to imported Buddhism and Confucianism,
34

Shintoism was perpetuated in Ise and Izumo, the great shrines of the Imperial family, until the Meiji modernizers established it as a quasi state religion to unify the people and restore the Emperor as the symbol of national unity and the object of loyalty <u>to</u> <u>the Japanese</u>.
35

30. (F) NO CHANGE
    (G) on which they could be building a modern Japan upon
    (H) upon which they could build a modern Japan
    (J) upon which they someday could probably build a modern Japan

31. (A) NO CHANGE
    (B) oldest
    (C) old
    (D) OMIT the underlined portion.

32. (F) NO CHANGE
    (G) respecting and even worshipping
    (H) respect for and even worship of
    (J) respect and even worship

33. (A) NO CHANGE
    (B) the Imperial family got its ancestry traced back to the Sun Goddess
    (C) the Imperial family's ancestry was traced back to the Sun Goddess
    (D) the Sun Goddess was considered to be the ancestor of the Imperial family

34. (F) NO CHANGE
    (G) Later subordinated
    (H) Later subordinated,
    (J) Subordinated later,

35. (A) NO CHANGE
    (B) the Japanese had
    (C) by the Japanese
    (D) for the Japanese

Another tradition that was enduring was the
36

hierarchical system of social relations based on

feudalism. Confucianism prescribed a pattern by ethical
37

conduct between groups of people within a fixed

hierarchy. Four of the five Confucian relationships

(those between ruler and subject, husband and wife,

father and son, and elder brother and younger brother) 38

were vertical since they required loyalty and obedience
39   40

from the inferior toward the superior and benevolence
41

and protection from the superior to the inferior.
41

Only the fifth relationship, that between friend and
42

friend—was horizontal. A third tradition was respect
43

36. (F) NO CHANGE
(G) Another tradition
(H) (Do NOT begin a new paragraph) Another
tradition
(J) The other tradition

37. (A) NO CHANGE
(B) patterns by
(C) a pattern for
(D) patterns with

38. Is the author's use of parentheses appropriate?
(F) Yes, because the examples are irrelevant to
the passage.
(G) Yes, because although the information is
relevant, the material is not part of the main
development of the passage.
(H) No, because the examples are relevant to the
meaning of the sentence.
(J) No, because the material is essential to the
reader's understanding of the passage.

39. (A) NO CHANGE
(B) was
(C) are
(D) could be

40. (F) NO CHANGE
(G) vertical, they
(H) vertical, since it
(J) vertical, being they

41. (A) NO CHANGE
(B) and also benevolence and protection from the
superior to the inferior
(C) with the benevolence and protection being
from the superior to the inferior
(D) and from the superior to the inferior, the
benevolence and protection

42. (F) NO CHANGE
(G) relationship that
(H) relationship—that
(J) relationship

43. (A) NO CHANGE
(B) Furthermore, a
(C) (Begin a new paragraph) A
(D) (Begin a new paragraph) Also a

for learning, another basic <u>idea of Confucius</u>. In
44

traditional Japan, study was the absolute duty of man.

It was a religious <u>mandate as well</u> as a social duty and
45

was a means of promoting a harmonious and stable

society. <u>The individual's behavior</u> was strictly
46

prescribed by law and custom. Only the Samurai had

the right to retaliate with force if they were displeased.

<u>But his</u> primary duty was to the lord.
47

44. (F) NO CHANGE
    (G) Confucius idea
    (H) idea of Confucianism
    (J) Confucianism idea

45. (A) NO CHANGE
    (B) mandate as well as being
    (C) mandate as well,
    (D) mandate,

46. (F) NO CHANGE
    (G) An individual behavior
    (H) Behavior by individual's
    (J) The individuals behavior

47. (A) NO CHANGE
    (B) But their
    (C) Being that their
    (D) Because their

> Item 48 asks about the preceding passage
> as a whole.

48. The best description of the development of this
    essay would be:

    (F) argument and rebuttal.
    (G) a personal narrative.
    (H) a three-part exposition.
    (J) question and answer.

TIMED-PRACTICE QUIZZES

This section contains three English ACT quizzes. Complete each quiz under timed conditions. Answers are on page 591.

DIRECTIONS: In the selections below, certain parts of the sentences have been underlined and numbered. In the right-hand column, you will find different ways of writing each underlined part; the original version is indicated by the "NO CHANGE" option. There are also items that ask about a section of the passage or the passage as a whole. These items do not refer to an underlined portion of the passage; they are identified by a number or numbers in a box.

For each item, choose the alternative that you consider to be the best. Select the answer choice that best expresses the intended idea, is most acceptable in standard written English, or is most consistent with the overall tone and style of the passage. Read the passage through once before you begin to answer the accompanying items. Finding the answers to certain items may depend on looking at material that appears several sentences beyond the item. So, be sure that you have read far enough ahead before you select your answer choice.

A. QUIZ I (32 items; 20 minutes)

PASSAGE I

Shakespeare's Mirror of Life

No writer can please many readers and please

them for a long time <u>excepting by</u> the accurate
₁

representation of human nature. Shakespeare,

<u>however</u>, is above all writers, the poet of human
₂

nature, the writer who holds up to his readers a

<u>faithful and true</u> mirror of manners and life.
₃

    Shakespeare's characters are not modified by

the customs of particular places unknown to the rest

of the world, by peculiarities of study or professions

known <u>to just a few, or</u> by the latest fashions or
₄

popular opinions.

1. (A) NO CHANGE
   (B) except by
   (C) except for
   (D) excepting

2. (F) NO CHANGE
   (G) moreover
   (H) therefore
   (J) furthermore

3. (A) NO CHANGE
   (B) faithful
   (C) faithfully true
   (D) true and real

4. (F) NO CHANGE
   (G) about by only a few, and
   (H) to just a few, but
   (J) to only a few, since

Shakespeare's characters are <u>each</u> genuine
₅

representations of common humanity. Hamlet and

Othello <u>act and speak</u> according to the general
₆

passions and principles that affect all of us. In the

writings of other poets, <u>whoever they may be,</u> a
₇

character is too often an individual; in <u>that of</u>
₈

<u>Shakespeare,</u> it is commonly a species. Other
₈

dramatists can gain attention only by using

exaggerated characters. Shakespeare <u>has no heroes;</u>
₉

<u>his</u> scenes <u>only</u> are occupied by persons who act and
₉   ₁₀

speak as the reader thinks he or she <u>would of spoken</u>
₁₁

or acted on the same occasion. This, therefore, is the

praise of <u>Shakespeare that</u> his drama is the mirror of
₁₂

life. ⬜₁₃

5. (A) NO CHANGE
   (B) every
   (C) all
   (D) each one a

6. (F) NO CHANGE
   (G) acting and speaking
   (H) acted and spoke
   (J) acted and spoken

7. (A) NO CHANGE
   (B) whoever they may be
   (C) whomever they may be,
   (D) OMIT the underlined portion.

8. (F) NO CHANGE
   (G) the one of Shakespeare,
   (H) those of Shakespeare's,
   (J) those of Shakespeare,

9. (A) NO CHANGE
   (B) has no heroes: his
   (C) has no heroes his
   (D) has no heroes, his

10. The most appropriate placement of the underlined phrase in this sentence would be:

    (F) where it is now.
    (G) after the word "act."
    (H) before the word "act."
    (J) after the word "occupied."

11. (A) NO CHANGE
    (B) would have speaked
    (C) would have spoken
    (D) would speak

12. (F) NO CHANGE
    (G) Shakespeare,
    (H) Shakespeare. That
    (J) Shakespeare: that

13. Is the final sentence an appropriate ending?

    (A) Yes, because it makes a final point about Shakespeare that was not previously mentioned and will leave the reader with something to think about.
    (B) Yes, because it is a summary of what was said in the introductory paragraph and will give the reader a sense of closure.
    (C) No, because it is irrelevant to the essay and will leave the reader confused.
    (D) No, because it is so repetitious that it will make the reader impatient.

Items 14–17 ask about the preceding passage as a whole.

14. What assumption is the essay's author making?

(F) Everyone believes Shakespeare is a good writer.

(G) No one has ever heard of Shakespeare.

(H) An accurate representation of human nature is important for great art.

(J) We could not understand Shakespeare's characters in the twentieth century.

15. Where might you find this essay published?

(A) In a book of literary criticism

(B) In a journal for Renaissance scholars

(C) In a Shakespeare biography

(D) In a sociology textbook

16. Which of the following is NOT a strategy the author uses to make his/her point?

(F) Comparison

(G) Argument

(H) Examples

(J) Personal anecdote

17. Which of the following would most strengthen the author's argument that Shakespeare is the poet of human nature?

(A) A discussion of Shakespeare's poetry

(B) An analysis of the characters Hamlet and Othello

(C) Biographical background on Shakespeare

(D) A description of Shakespeare's Globe Theater

PASSAGE II

Diary of a Black Hole

[1]

In the course of billions of years, millions of stars may <u>sometimes occasionally</u> be concentrated into a region, or regions, only a few light years across,

18.

<u>and in these crowded conditions colliding</u> with one another. Some of these collisions <u>would occur</u> at high speeds, in which case the stars are partially or completely torn apart. Other collisions are gentle <u>bumps, but the stars coalesce</u>. The bigger the star

<u>becomes, the more likely</u> it is to be hit again and the faster it grows until it reaches instability, collapses on itself, <u>and forms a black hole</u>.

[2]

When most of the stars and gas in the core of a galaxy <u>has been</u> swallowed up by the black hole, the nucleus of the galaxy settles down <u>to a relative</u> quiet existence. This is probably the state of the nucleus of our own galaxy, but every hundred million years or

18. (F) NO CHANGE
(G) sometimes, occasionally
(H) occasionally
(J) off and on

19. (A) NO CHANGE
(B) colliding
(C) and in these crowded conditions, they collide
(D) which causes them to collide

20. (F) NO CHANGE
(G) will occur
(H) to occur
(J) occur

21. (A) NO CHANGE
(B) bumps, since the stars
(C) bumps, and the stars coalesce
(D) bumps, with the stars coalescing

22. (F) NO CHANGE
(G) becomes the more
(H) becomes the more,
(J) becomes; the more

23. (A) NO CHANGE
(B) and a black hole is formed
(C) and when this happens a black hole is formed
(D) and thus a black hole is formed at this very moment

24. (F) NO CHANGE
(G) have been
(H) will have been
(J) would have been

25. (A) NO CHANGE
(B) to a relatively
(C) for a relative and
(D) relatively

so it may flare upto a brightness 100 times its present
____
26

level when a globular cluster or especially large gas

cloud of enormous size spirals into the nucleus.
____
27

[3]

Once formed, a central "seed" black hole grows

mainly through the accretion of gas accumulated in

the nucleus; gas obtained from disrupted stars, from
____
28

supernova explosions, or from stars torn apart by the

gravitational field of the black hole. Perhaps an entire

galaxy can collide with another galaxy, and the result
____
29

would be the transfer of large amounts of gas from one
____
29

galaxy to each other.
____
30

26. (F) NO CHANGE
    (G) up
    (H) up to
    (J) OMIT the underlined portion.

27. (A) NO CHANGE
    (B) of great enormity
    (C) which is huge
    (D) OMIT the underlined portion.

28. (F) NO CHANGE
    (G) nucleus and gas
    (H) nucleus. Gas
    (J) nucleus gas

29. (A) NO CHANGE
    (B) galaxy to result in
    (C) galaxy. Such a collision could result in
    (D) galaxy with the results that

30. (F) NO CHANGE
    (G) to the other
    (H) an other
    (J) and another

Items 31 and 32 ask about the preceding passage
as a whole.

31. Which of the following represents the most logical
    sequence for the paragraphs?

    (A) 1, 2, 3
    (B) 1, 3, 2
    (C) 2, 3, 1
    (D) 3, 1, 2

32. The author's intended audience is most likely:

    (F) astronomers.
    (G) young children.
    (H) high school students.
    (J) physicists.

B. QUIZ II (29 items; 20 minutes)

PASSAGE I

The Influence of the Southwest on Artists

Georgia O'Keeffe, <u>who's</u> death <u>at age ninety-</u>
¹   ²

<u>eight</u> closed one of the most fertile chapters of
²

American <u>creativity and flourished</u> as a maverick in
³

her life and work. <u>Since other</u> painters spent a season
⁴

or two in the country trying to come to terms with the

scenes and settings of the Southwest—O'Keeffe stayed

a lifetime. When the canvases of other <u>artists, working</u>
⁵

<u>in the region</u> faded from view and <u>then were neglected</u>
⁵   ⁶

<u>in the chronicle of American visual history</u>, her
⁶

stylized images made an <u>indelible and permanent</u>
⁷

impression on countless eyes.

Between 1900 and 1945, the region now called

New Mexico both fascinated <u>and also it perplexed</u> two
⁸

1. (A) NO CHANGE
    (B) which
    (C) that
    (D) whose

2. (F) NO CHANGE
    (G) at the old age of ninety-eight
    (H) at the age of ninety-eight years
    (J) when she was ninety-eight years old

3. (A) NO CHANGE
    (B) creativity, and flourished
    (C) creativity—flourished
    (D) creativity, flourished

4. (F) NO CHANGE
    (G) Because other
    (H) In that other
    (J) Other

5. (A) NO CHANGE
    (B) artists working in the region,
    (C) artists working in the region
    (D) artists, who worked in the region

6. (F) NO CHANGE
    (G) got neglected then in the chronicle of
        American visual history
    (H) were also then neglected in the American
        visual history chronicle
    (J) then they were also totally neglected in the
        chronicle of American visual history

7. (A) NO CHANGE
    (B) indelible
    (C) indelible—and permanent—
    (D) indelible but permanent

8. (F) NO CHANGE
    (G) and perplexed
    (H) while perplexing
    (J) but perplexed

generations of American artists. Despite successes,
9

many of those artists wearied of the industrial world

of the east. The vast expanse of the West offered a
10

promise for inspiration. For these artists, life and art,
10

so separate in New York and Paris, seemed

inextricably bounded in Southwestern cultures.
11

Painters of every persuasion were convinced that
12

sampling this mysterious phenomenon will strengthen
13

and enrich their own work. Most were touched by

what D.H. Lawrence called the "spirit of the place."

Besides the scenic beauty bathed in clear golden light.
14

The rich traditions of New Mexico's Indian and
14

Hispanic people who were living there became
15

frequent subjects of the artists who traveled to Taos

and Santa Fe.

9. (A) NO CHANGE
   (B) Despite successes
   (C) In spite of their successes
   (D) Ensuring successes,

10. (F) NO CHANGE
    (G) America's West, with its vast expanse, offered an inspiring promise.
    (H) America's vast expanse of the West offered a promise for inspiration.
    (J) Offering a promise of inspiration to the artists was the vast expanse of the American West.

11. (A) NO CHANGE
    (B) inextricably bound
    (C) inextricable bounding
    (D) inextricably bounding

12. (F) NO CHANGE
    (G) could be convinced
    (H) will be convinced
    (J) are convincing

13. (A) NO CHANGE
    (B) would strengthen
    (C) strengthens
    (D) strengthening

14. (F) NO CHANGE
    (G) light, the
    (H) light the
    (J) light: the

15. (A) NO CHANGE
    (B) who lived there
    (C) living there
    (D) OMIT the underlined portion.

> Items 16 and 17 ask about the preceding passage as a whole.

16. Is the author's quote of D. H. Lawrence in the last paragraph appropriate?

    (F) Yes, because the author is talking about how this spirit inspired artists, and the quote strengthens his argument.
    (G) No, because the author has already made his point about the spirit, and the quote is redundant.
    (H) No, because the author does not make it clear that Lawrence is an authority on the subject.
    (J) Yes, because it is always a good idea to end an article with a quotation.

17. How might the author have developed the essay so that it was more interesting?

    (A) The author could have told an anecdote about D. H. Lawrence.
    (B) The author could have eliminated all mention of Georgia O'Keeffe.
    (C) The author could have discussed the settling of New Mexico.
    (D) The author could have been more specific about the other artists who went to the Southwest.

PASSAGE II

Chippewa Chief Demands Timber Payment

Early in November 1850, the work of a logging detail from Fort Gaines in the Minnesota Territory was interrupted by a party of Chippewa warriors who demanded payment for the timber. The loggers
[18]
refused, so the Indians, acting at the direction of Chief
[18]   [19]
Hole-in-the-Day confiscated the government's oxen.
[19]
The loggers had established their camp on Chippewa

lands without his authorizing it. Therefore, in a move
[20]   [21]
designed to force reimbursements for the timber,

Hole-in-the-Day was ordering his braves to seize the
[22]
oxen.

Captain John Todd, the commanding officer at Fort Gaines, demanded that the cattle had to
[23]
be returned to them. The chief's reply was firm,
[23]

and at the same time, it was friendly. In his message
[24]
to Captain Todd, Hole-in-the-Day explained that he

had delayed to seize the cattle until he could meet
[25]
Todd in council and had sent a messenger to the officer requesting a conference at Crow Wing.

18. (F) NO CHANGE
(G) The loggers refused—
(H) The loggers refused:
(J) The loggers refused so

19. (A) NO CHANGE
(B) that acted at the direction of Chief Hole-in-the-Day,
(C) acting at the direction of Chief Hole-in-the-Day,
(D) (acting at the direction of Chief Hole-in-the-Day),

20. (F) NO CHANGE
(G) without his authorization
(H) without their authorizing it
(J) without his authorization of it

21. (A) NO CHANGE
(B) Henceforth
(C) Since
(D) On the contrary

22. (F) NO CHANGE
(G) gave orders that
(H) orders
(J) ordered

23. (A) NO CHANGE
(B) the return of the cattle
(C) the cattle's returning
(D) that they return the cattle

24. (F) NO CHANGE
(G) but, at the same time, it was friendly
(H) yet friendly
(J) at the same time—friendly

25. (A) NO CHANGE
(B) delayed to have seized
(C) delayed to seized
(D) delayed seizing

When Todd did not come, he <u>acted, additionally</u> he
                                    26
later decided that since the army had not paid for

timber cut the previous winter, he intended to keep

the oxen until the tribe <u>was reimbursed by</u> all the
                              27
timber taken for the fort. Hole-in-the-Day concluded

by saying, "Do not think hard of me, but I do as

others would—the timber is mine." 28

26. (F) NO CHANGE
    (G) acted but additionally
    (H) acted. Additionally,
    (J) acted additionally,

27. (A) NO CHANGE
    (B) reimbursed for
    (C) reimbursed
    (D) was reimbursed for

28. Is the author's use of the quote in the final
    paragraph appropriate?
    (F) Yes, because it neatly summarizes the main
        point of the essay.
    (G) No, because the chief's thoughts were irrele
        vant to the events.
    (H) Yes, but the author should have included a
        quotation from Captain Todd.
    (J) No, because quotations have no place in
        expository writing.

    Item 29 asks about the preceding passage
    as a whole.

29. Which of the following best describes the overall
    character of the essay?
    (A) Description of a scene
    (B) Narration of events
    (C) Comparison of two theories
    (D) Argument for a change

C. QUIZ III (31 items; 20 minutes)

PASSAGE I

The Con Game is No Game

Most people have a certain crime <u>that one</u>
<u>believes</u> should be ranked as the worst of all crimes.

For some, <u>its'</u> murder; for others, it may be selling

drugs to children. I believe, <u>moreover,</u> that the worst

of all crimes may be the confidence scheme.

The confidence scheme may seem an <u>odd</u>

choice for the worst crime since con games are

usually <u>nonviolent. Although,</u> it is a crime that ranks

in heartlessness. Con artists are the most devious,

the most harmful, and the most disruptive members of

society because <u>they break</u> down the most important

bonds of the social <u>order, honesty and trust</u>.

The con games themselves are <u>simplistic</u>
<u>almost infantile</u>. They work <u>on account of a con artist</u>

<u>can</u> win complete confidence, talk fast enough to

1. (A) NO CHANGE
   (B) that they believe
   (C) which one believes
   (D) that you believe

2. (F) NO CHANGE
   (G) they are
   (H) it's
   (J) its

3. (A) NO CHANGE
   (B) however
   (C) further
   (D) therefore

4. (F) NO CHANGE
   (G) obvious
   (H) irrelevant
   (J) apt

5. (A) NO CHANGE
   (B) nonviolent, though
   (C) nonviolent, but
   (D) nonviolent, and

6. (F) NO CHANGE
   (G) it breaks
   (H) of its breaking
   (J) of them breaking

7. (A) NO CHANGE
   (B) order, honesty, and trust
   (C) order: honesty and trust
   (D) order: honesty, and trust

8. (F) NO CHANGE
   (G) simplistic; almost infantile
   (H) simplistic, almost infantile
   (J) simplistic, yet almost infantile

9. (A) NO CHANGE
   (B) on account of a con artist's ability to
   (C) owing to a con artist's ability to
   (D) because a con artist can

keep the victim slightly confused, <u>and dangling</u>
₁₀

enough temptation to suppress any suspicion or

skepticism. The primary targets of these criminals

<u>will be</u> the elderly and <u>women. (And they prefer to</u>
₁₁ ₁₂

<u>work in large crowds.)</u>
₁₂

10. (F) NO CHANGE
    (G) and dangles
    (H) and has dangled
    (J) and dangle

11. (A) NO CHANGE
    (B) to be
    (C) are
    (D) is

12. (F) NO CHANGE
    (G) women, and the con artists prefer to work in
        large crowds.
    (H) women, preferring, of course, to work in large
        crowds.
    (J) women (who prefer to work in large crowds).

Items 13–15 ask about the preceding passage
as a whole.

---

13. Which of the following is most probably the
    author's opinion rather than a fact?
    (A) Con artists are the most disruptive members of
        society.
    (B) Most con games are nonviolent.
    (C) Most of the targets are the elderly and women.
    (D) Most con games are simple.

14. What would be the most logical continuation of
    the essay?
    (F) A description of some confidence games
    (G) An account of the elderly as crime victims in
        society
    (H) An account of the author's experience with
        con artists
    (J) An explanation of crowd psychology

15. What would strengthen the author's contention
    that con games rank first in heartlessness?
    (A) Statistics to show the number of people who
        were taken in by the con artist
    (B) A discussion of the way the police handle the
        problem
    (C) An example that shows how the con artist
        breaks down honesty and trust
    (D) An example to illustrate that con games are
        nonviolent and simple

PASSAGE II

Elizabeth I's Intellect Ruled Supreme

Elizabeth I had a sensuous and indulgent

nature that she inherited from her mother, Anne

Boleyn (who was beheaded by Henry VIII).
16

Splendor and pleasure is the very air she breathed.
17

She loved gaiety, laughter, and wit. Her vanity

remained even, to old age. The vanity of a coquette.
18

The statesmen who she outwitted believed,
19

almost to the end, that Elizabeth I was little more

than a frivolous woman who was very vain. But the
20

Elizabeth whom they saw was far from being all of
21

Elizabeth. The willfulness of Henry and the triviality

of Anne played over the surface of a nature so hard
22

like steel—a purely intellectual temperament. Her
22

vanity and caprice carried no weight whatsoever in
23

state affairs. The coquette of the presence chamber

had became the coolest and hardest of politicians at
24

the council board.

16. (F) NO CHANGE
(G) (having been beheaded by Henry VIII)
(H) beheaded by Henry VIII
(J) OMIT the underlined portion.

17. (A) NO CHANGE
(B) is,
(C) were
(D) were,

18. (F) NO CHANGE
(G) remains, even to old age, the
(H) remains, even to old age the
(J) remained, even to old age, the

19. (A) NO CHANGE
(B) that she outwitted
(C) whom she outwitted
(D) who she was outwitting

20. (F) NO CHANGE
(G) and she was also very vain
(H) known for her great vanity
(J) OMIT the underlined portion.

21. (A) NO CHANGE
(B) to be
(C) having been
(D) OMIT the underlined portion.

22. (F) NO CHANGE
(G) as hard as
(H) so hard as
(J) as hard like

23. (A) NO CHANGE
(B) no matter what
(C) whatever, at all
(D) whatever, despite everything

24. (F) NO CHANGE
(G) became
(H) used to become
(J) becomes

It was this part that gave her marked <u>superiority</u> [25] <u>over</u> [25] the statesmen of her time. No <u>more nobler a group</u> [26] of ministers ever gathered round the council board than those of Elizabeth, but she was the instrument of none. She listened and she weighed, but her policy, as a whole, was her own. It was the policy of good sense, <u>not genius, she</u> [27] endeavored to keep her throne, to keep

England out of war, <u>and she wanted</u> [28] to restore civil and religious order.

25. (A) NO CHANGE
(B) superiority in regard to
(C) superiority about
(D) superior quality to

26. (F) NO CHANGE
(G) nobler a group,
(H) nobler a group
(J) more nobler of a group,

27. (A) NO CHANGE
(B) not genius she
(C) not genius. She
(D) —not genius, she

28. (F) NO CHANGE
(G) wanting
(H) and wanting
(J) and

Items 29–31 ask about the preceding passage as a whole.

---

29. What might logically have preceded this essay?
(A) Some biographical background on Elizabeth I
(B) A discussion of the wives of Henry VIII
(C) A discussion of the politics of Tudor England
(D) A discussion of the policies of Elizabeth's ministers

30. This essay is most probably taken from a:
(F) scholarly work on Renaissance England.
(G) biography of Elizabeth I.
(H) diary kept by one of Elizabeth's ministers.
(J) political science textbook.

31. Which of the following would most strengthen the essay?
(A) Knowing who the ministers were and what their policies were
(B) Examples of Elizabeth's dual nature
(C) A discussion of Henry VIII's policies
(D) A discussion of the role of the woman in Tudor England

CAMBRIDGE TESTPREP™

ENGLISH

STRATEGY SUMMARY SHEET

GENERAL STRATEGIES:

1. After you have memorized the directions, they can be safely ignored; therefore, do not waste valuable test time by re-reading instructions.

2. Read the entire selection for comprehension of the overall meaning. Look for possible errors. Mentally note how to correct possible errors.

3. Study the answer choices, looking for one that matches your anticipated answer.

4. Compare the answer choices. What makes them different from one another?

5. Do not choose answer choices that introduce new errors or change the meaning of the selection.

6. Use the Checklist for Possible Writing Errors, presented below, when searching for errors.

STRATEGIES FOR USAGE AND MECHANICS CONTENT AREA:

1. Check for grammatical errors.

   a. Look for obvious subject-verb agreement problems. The test-writers may try to obscure agreement by inserting material between the subject and the verb, inverting the sentence structure so that the verb precedes the subject, or introducing compound subjects.

   b. Check for proper pronoun usage. Remember that all pronouns must have antecedents. The pronoun must clearly refer to the antecedent and must agree in case, number, and person.

   c. Be alert to the proper usage of adjectives and adverbs. Note that adjectives modify nouns, while adverbs modify verbs. Also, adjectives, not adverbs, follow linking verbs. Lastly, watch out for adjectives posing as adverbs. Sometimes, adjectives can be transformed into adverbs by adding "ly," so it is important to identify whether the modifier is an adjective or an adverb.

   d. Watch for double negatives. Even though double negatives are sometimes used colloquially, they are not grammatically correct.

   e. Check for proper noun clause introductions. A noun clause is a group of words that functions as the subject of a sentence and must be introduced with "that." Note that "because" and "why" should not be used to introduce noun clauses.

   f. Watch for illogical comparisons. Comparisons can only be made between similar objects. Be alert to the use of the comparative form of an adjective (for comparing two objects) and the superlative form of an adjective (for comparing three or more objects). Remember that some adjectives and adverbs express the highest degree of quality; therefore, they cannot be improved upon.

g. Check for improper verb and mood shifts. The same verb tense and mood should be used within a sentence or paragraph unless there is a valid reason for a change. Also, be alert to the improper usage of verb tenses in general. Make sure that the verb tense within a sentence or a paragraph is logical.

h. Make sure that the choice of verb tense in a sentence reflects the sequence and the duration of the events described.

i. Check for diction errors such as wrong prepositions, improper word choice, and gerund-infinitive switching.

2. Check for sentence structure errors.

a. Check to see if the sentence is a run-on.

b. Be aware of comma splice errors in sentences.

c. Check to see if the sentence is a fragment.

d. Make sure the sentence contains logical coordinating conjunctions.

e. Watch for faulty parallelism in a sentence. Note that whenever elements of a sentence perform similar or equal functions, they should have the same form.

f. Be alert for sentence structures in which a thought that is interrupted by intervening material is completed later in the sentence. Check that the interrupted thought is correctly completed. A simple way to check for this type of error is to read the sentence without the intervening material—the sentence should make sense, be grammatically correct, and represent a complete thought.

g. Look for misplaced modifiers. Modifiers should be placed as close as possible to what they modify. Errors in placement of modifiers create ambiguous and illogical constructions.

h. Be alert to misplacements or omissions of certain elements of a sentence. These errors lead to unintended meanings. Make sure the intended meaning of the sentence follows from its logical structure.

3. Check for punctuation errors.

a. Check to see if the comma is used correctly in the sentence. The following list summarizes the most important uses and misuses of commas.

i. Use a comma before coordinating conjunctions.

ii. Use commas for clarity.

iii. Use commas to separate coordinate adjectives, words in a series, and nouns in direct address.

iv. Use commas to separate quotations and introductory phrases.

v. Use pairs of commas to set off appositive, parenthetical, and non-restrictive elements.

vi. A comma should not be used to separate a subject from its verb.

vii. Commas should not be used to set off restrictive or necessary clauses or phrases.

viii. A comma should not be used in place of a conjunction.

b. Check for correct semicolon usage. The following list summarizes the appropriate uses of semicolons.

    i.   Use a semicolon to separate two complete ideas.

    ii.   Use a semicolon to separate a series of phrases with commas and a series of numbers.

    iii.   Use a semicolon to separate independent clauses.

    iv.   Do not use semicolons to separate dependent clauses.

c.   Check for correct colon usage. The following list summarizes the rules for colon usage.

    i.   A colon should be placed after the salutation in a business letter.

    ii.   Use a colon to separate hours from minutes.

    iii.   Colons are used to precede lists of three of more items or long quotations.

    iv.   A colon should be used to introduce a question.

    v.   Do not use colons to introduce or to call attention to elaboration or explanation if that is already signaled by expressions such as "like," "for example," or "such as."

d.   Check for correct end-stop punctuation. Make sure that any material that includes a period is a complete sentence.

e.   Check for correct usage of dashes. The following are the rules for situations requiring the use of a dash.

    i.   Use a dash for emphasis or to set off an explanatory group of words.

    ii.   Use a dash before a word or group of words that indicates a summation or reversal of what preceded it.

    iii.   Use a dash to mark a sudden break in thought that leaves a sentence unfinished.

f.   Check the selection for quotation errors. Quotation marks are used to enclose the actual words of a speaker or writer, to emphasize words used in a special or unusual sense, and to set off titles of short themes or parts of a larger work. Quotation marks are not used for indirect quotations or to justify a poor choice of words.

g.   Check for correct apostrophe usage. Apostrophes are most commonly used to show possession. They are also used when a noun is used to modify another noun or a gerund.

h.   Check to see if a punctuation mark is needed to clarify the selection.

STRATEGIES FOR RHETORICAL SKILLS CONTENT AREA:

1. Check to see if the strategy used by the writer is appropriate.

a.   Make sure that all supporting material is appropriate to the selection.

b.   Be alert to opening, transitional, and concluding sentences. Check to see if they are effective or if they need improvement.

c.   Read the selection for the main ideas and identify the main purpose of the entire passage.

d.   Look for diction, purpose, and tone clues that identify the writer's audience.

2. Check for organization errors.

   a. Check the sentence-level structure. Sentences should appear in a logical and appropriate order within the paragraph.

   b. Check the paragraph-level structure. Paragraphs should be divided logically and unified around a central theme.

   c. Check the passage-level structure. Passages should follow an identifiable pattern of development, with paragraphs appearing in a logical order.

3. Check for stylistic problems.

   a. Make sure that the sentences are concise and to the point.

      i. Look for awkward sentences or weak passive verbs.

      ii. Look for needlessly wordy sentences.

   b. Check for ambiguous sentences. Such sentences run two or more ideas together and require further clarification to separate and connect the disparate ideas.

   c. Check for idiomatic usage.

ADDITIONAL STRATEGIES FROM IN-CLASS DISCUSSION: _____

_____

_____

_____

_____

_____

_____

_____

_____

_____

_____

_____

_____

Mathematics

CAMBRIDGE TESTPREP™

MATHEMATICS

COURSE CONCEPT OUTLINE: WHAT YOU ABSOLUTELY MUST KNOW

I. Test Mechanics (p. 69)

II. Lesson (p. 77)

A. Preliminaries

B. Item-Types

1. Arithmetic (Item #1, p. 77)
2. Algebra (Items #2–6, p. 77)
3. Coordinate Geometry (Item #7, p. 78)
4. Geometry (Items #8–10, p. 78)
5. Trigonometry (Item #11, p. 79)
6. Statistics and Probability (Item #12, p. 79)

C. General Strategies

1. A Note about Figures (Items #13–16, p. 79)
2. Important Facts about the Answer Choices
   a. Answer Choices Are Arranged in Order
   b. Wrong Choices Correspond to Conceptual Errors (Item #17, p. 80)
3. "Signal" Words Require Special Attention (Items #18–21, p. 80)
4. Answer the Question Being Asked (Items #22–30, p. 80)
5. "Cannot Be Determined…" (Item #31, p. 81)
6. Additional Helpful Hints

D. Arithmetic Review and Strategies

1. Simple Manipulations—Just Do It! (Items #32–33, p. 82)
2. Complicated Manipulations—Look for Shortcuts
   a. Simplifying (Item #34, p. 82)
   b. Factoring (Items #35–36, p. 82)
   c. Approximation (Items #37–39, p. 82)
   d. The "Flying-X" Method (Item #40, p. 82)
   e. Decimal-Fraction Equivalents (Items #41–42, p. 83)
3. Solving Complicated Arithmetic Application Items (Items #43–44, p. 83)
4. Common Arithmetic Items
   a. Properties of Numbers (Items #45–53, p. 83)
   b. Sets: Union, Intersection, and Elements (Items #54–58, p. 84)
   c. Absolute Value (Items #59–61, p. 85)
   d. Complex Numbers (Items #62–63, p. 85)
   e. Percents (Items #64–70, p. 85)
   f. Ratios (Items #71–72, p. 86)
   g. Proportions and Direct-Inverse Variation (Items #73–79, p. 87)
5. Arithmetic Strategy: "Test-the-Test" (Items #80–85, p. 88)

TEST MECHANICS

BASICS

The ACT Mathematics Test, according to the test-writers, presupposes a knowledge of pre-algebra and algebra, intermediate algebra and coordinate geometry, and geometry and trigonometry. And the ACT Mathematics items are pretty much the same kind of questions you'd see on a regular test—except that they are multiple-choice questions.

In reality, however, you do not have to know all of those topics to do pretty well on the test. Intermediate algebra, coordinate geometry, and trigonometry combined account for less than 40% of the test. Here is the breakdown of questions by topic on the ACT Mathematics Test:

60 questions; 60 minutes

Content	Approximate Number	Approximate Percent
Pre-Algebra	14	23%
Elementary Algebra	10	17%
Intermediate Algebra	9	15%
Coordinate Geometry	9	15%
Plane Geometry	14	23%
Trigonometry	4	7%

This means that you could blow off all of the trigonometry and the hardest half of the coordinate geometry and intermediate algebra, miss another 9 questions, and still get a 24 on the math. And 24 is a pretty good score. For a very respectable score of 21 or so (well above the average of everyone in the country who's thinking about college), you need a raw score of about 33, which you can get if you blow off all the trigonometry, intermediate algebra, and coordinate geometry and keep your wrong answers down to 5.

This is not a recommended strategy. You want to make sure that you answer any questions you know how to answer. But these little "thought experiments" show that you can do quite well on the math even if you're not exactly a math whiz.

ANATOMY

DIRECTIONS: Solve each item and choose the correct answer choice. Then, fill in the corresponding oval on the bubble sheet.

Allocate time wisely. Try to solve as many items as possible, returning to skipped items if time permits.

Calculator use is permitted on this test; however, some items are best solved without the use of a calculator.

Note: Unless otherwise stated, assume all of the following.

1. Illustrative figures are NOT necessarily drawn to scale.
2. The word "average" indicates arithmetic mean.
3. The word "line" indicates a straight line.
4. Geometric figures lie in a plane.

1. Paulo bicycled $6\frac{1}{3}$ miles on Wednesday and $8\frac{2}{5}$ miles on Thursday. How many miles did he bicycle during those two days?

   A. $14\frac{2}{15}$
   B. $14\frac{1}{4}$
   C. $14\frac{3}{8}$
   D. $14\frac{11}{15}$
   E. $14\frac{13}{15}$

You really do not need the directions at all. Problem-solving is your standard-issue Mathematics item.

You can use a calculator, and there will be further discussion of this in class.

Also, figures are not necessarily drawn to scale, but the issue is much more complicated than that. The figures are, in fact, almost always to scale, but, again, there will be extended discussion of the issue in class.

This item is an easy one. It's solved just by addition: $6\frac{1}{3}+8\frac{2}{5}=\frac{19}{3}+\frac{42}{5}=\frac{95}{15}+\frac{126}{15}=\frac{221}{15}=14\frac{11}{15}$. *So, (D) is the correct answer choice.*

2. The average weight of five packages in a shipment is 8.7 pounds. The weights of four of the packages are 6.3 pounds, 7.5 pounds, 8.9 pounds, and 9.6 pounds. What is the weight of the fifth package?

   F. 8.5
   G. 8.8
   H. 9.4
   J. 11.2
   K. 12.3

This item is a bit more difficult. First, set up an equation: $\frac{6.3 + 7.5 + 8.9 + 9.6 + x}{5} = 8.7$. *Then, solve for the missing weight:*

$$(6.3 + 7.5 + 8.9 + 9.6) + x = (8.7)(5)$$
$$x = 43.5 - 32.3 = 11.2$$

So, (J) is the correct answer choice.

3. If $3x + 4 = 7x - 2$, $x = ?$

   A. $-\frac{1}{4}$
   B. $\frac{1}{2}$
   C. $\frac{3}{5}$
   D. $\frac{2}{3}$
   E. $1\frac{1}{2}$

For this item, you need to solve for x:

$$3x + 4 = 7x - 2$$
$$3x - 7x = -2 - 4$$
$$-4x = -6$$
$$4x = 6$$
$$x = \frac{6}{4} = \frac{3}{2} = 1\frac{1}{2}$$

So, (E) is the correct answer choice.

4. The ratio of the radii of two circles is 3:4. What is the ratio of their areas?

   F. 7:1
   G. 3:4
   H. 9:16
   J. $3:4\pi$
   K. $9:16\pi$

With this item, since the ratio of the radii of the two circles is 3:4, the ratio of their areas is $\frac{\pi(3)^2}{\pi(4)^2} = \frac{9\pi}{16\pi} = \frac{9}{16} = 9:16$, *so the answer is (H).*

There are three other features of the "Anatomy" of Mathematics items to note:

- *Answer choices are arranged in order.* For most Mathematics items, answer choices are arranged from largest to smallest or vice versa. However, there are some exceptions. Choices that consist entirely of variables do not follow the rule, and items that ask "which of the following is the biggest?" obviously do not follow the rule. This feature makes it easier to find your choice in the list, and it sets up an important test-taking strategy called the "Pick C." Method, which you'll learn about later in the Mathematics Lesson.

- *Answer choices are well-defined.* The choices are not created so that you have to do "donkey math." You are not likely to find a problem with answer choices like:

    A. $183.27
    B. $183.28
    C. $183.29
    D. $183.30
    E. $183.31

    You might find answers like this on an ordinary math test but not on the ACT. Instead, the choices usually correspond to errors in thinking—not errors in arithmetic. This feature is important because it is the basis for a couple of time-saving strategies that you'll learn shortly.

- *Items are arranged on a ladder of difficulty.* Of course, you can't tell this from the four examples provided here, but the ladder is an important feature of the math test. Given that the problems become more difficult as you proceed, you're obviously going to have to make some important decisions about speed and skipping items. You'll get more advice on this in the lesson.

PACING

Mathematics items are arranged on a ladder of difficulty, so you'll need a pacing plan that helps you move more quickly through the easier items at the beginning of the test and allows you to build up a time reserve for the harder items that are toward the end. The following table summarizes the timing for this approach:

60 questions; 60 minutes

Item Numbers	Time to Spend Per Item	Remaining Time
1–10	36 seconds	54 minutes
11–20	42 seconds	47 minutes
21–30	54 seconds	38 minutes
31–40	66 seconds	27 minutes
41–50	72 seconds	15 minutes
51–60	90 seconds	0 minutes

This table is a schedule for the best of all possible math worlds. It's intended to be a guideline, not a rule. Try to stay on schedule, but be prepared to adjust your timing according to how many items it is realistic to expect that you'll be able to do. Trying to stay on a schedule during the test will help you to avoid the two biggest time-sucks ever created for a timed test.

First, staying on schedule will ensure that you are not plodding through the easy items earlier in the test. At the beginning, with a 60-minute time limit, it will seem to you like you've got all the time in the world. But you don't. From the moment the flag drops, you're behind schedule and playing catch-up. So, keep that sense of urgency about you.

Second, the schedule will serve as a constant reminder that you cannot afford to spend too much time on any one problem. If you make a mistake and spend 3 minutes on item #22, you'll find that you're falling badly behind schedule. Leave that problem, hoping you'll have time at the end of the test to come back and finish it. But spending 3 minutes to get +1 when 3 minutes could get you +5 is a score-killer.

GAME PLAN

1. FOR STARTERS

As you get started, take a few seconds to preview the Mathematics Test. It's 99.99% certain that you're going to find everything in place and just as you expected. But a quick overview will guarantee against any unanticipated changes. Do NOT, however, read the directions. Remind yourself of your pacing plan and then get to work.

2. ANSWER THE QUESTION THAT IS BEING ASKED

a. READ THE QUESTION CAREFULLY

Some problems are fairly simple, but others are more complex, particularly practical word problems and more difficult geometry problems. The more complex the question, the easier it is to misread and set off down the wrong track. If the question is very long, then underline the key part of the question.

Example:

If Mark traveled 20 miles in 3 hours and Lester traveled twice as far
in half the time, what was Lester's average speed?

b. PAY ATTENTION TO UNITS

Some questions require you to convert units (e.g., feet to inches or hours to minutes). The question stem will tell you what units to use, and if the test-writer senses any possible confusion, the units for the answer choices will be emphasized—underlined or in bold face or capitalized. When you see a word emphasized with any of those signals, circle it and put a star beside it. It is very important.

Example:

A certain copy machine produces 13 copies every 10 seconds.
If the machine operates without interruption, how many copies
will it produce in an hour? ✳

c. PAY ATTENTION TO THOUGHT-REVERSERS

A thought-reverser is any word, such as "not," "except," or "but," that turns a question inside out. As shown, below, make sure that you mark the thought-reverser so that it is staring you in the face as you work the problem.

Example:

How many integers in the set of integers from 1 to 144,
inclusive, are NOT a square of an integer?

3. USE THE ANSWER CHOICES

In the Mathematics Lesson, you will learn some very powerful test-taking strategies that use the answers. For now, there are two procedural points to consider.

a. ELIMINATE ANSWER CHOICES THAT CANNOT BE CORRECT

Sometimes, the array of answers will include choices that, taken at face value, seem to be plausible, but when examined more carefully, must be incorrect.

Example:

In the figure above, a circle with center O and a radius of 2 is inscribed in a square. What is the area of the shaded portion of the figure?

A. $2 - \pi$
B. $4 - 2\pi$
C. $16 - 2\pi$
D. $16 - 4\pi$
E. $16 - 6\pi$

Since the radius of the circle is 2, the side of the square is 4. Then, the shaded area is just the square, which is $4 \cdot 4 = 16$, less the circle, which is $\pi(2)^2 = 4\pi$. So, $16 - 4\pi$, (D), is the correct answer choice. Take a closer look at (A) and (B). Since π is approximately 3.14, both (A) and (B) are negative. Area, however, cannot be a negative number, so (A) and (B) must be wrong; and you can eliminate them without doing any other work. If this were all you were able to accomplish, you would still want to guess because you would be making an educated guess—1 out of 3 answer choices. (Note: Even if you are unable to eliminate answer choices, you still must guess, even if randomly, since the ACT does not penalize for wrong answers.)

b. USE THE ANSWER CHOICES TO CHECK YOUR MATH

While the ACT does not test "donkey math," some items do require a calculation or two. One of the fundamental rules of math in school is "check your work." On the ACT, however, this is a real time-suck. Let's say that you do a calculation (with or without your calculator) and the result is $23.10. If one of the choices is $23.10, pick it, mark your answer sheet, and move on to the next item. Do NOT check your arithmetic. The possibility that you did the arithmetic, made a mistake, and still got a number like 23.10 is just too remote to consider. On the other hand, if you do not find a choice that matches your calculation, then you'd better check both your set-up of the problem and your arithmetic to find the error. In this way, the answer choices function as a feedback loop on the accuracy of your manipulations.

4. DON'T GO CALCULATOR CRAZY

Just because you are allowed to use a calculator on the test does not mean that you should try to solve every problem with your calculator. In fact, for most problems, the calculator is the less efficient method of arriving at a solution. Assume, for example, that you have to do the following arithmetic to get your answer:

$$\left(\tfrac{2}{3}\right)\left(\tfrac{7}{4}\right)\left(\tfrac{1}{6}\right) =$$

Since using a calculator would require that you enter decimal equivalents for these fractions, it's going to be easier to do the arithmetic with a pencil than with a calculator:

$$\left(\tfrac{2}{3}\right)\left(\tfrac{7}{4}\right)\left(\tfrac{1}{6}\right) = \frac{2 \cdot 7 \cdot 1}{3 \cdot 4 \cdot 6} = \frac{14}{72} = \frac{7}{36}$$

By all means, use the calculator since it will be a definite advantage, but don't automatically assume that every problem requires its use.

LESSON

The items in this section accompany the Mathematics Lesson. They demonstrate the Mathematics skills and concepts that are tested by the ACT, the PLAN, and the EXPLORE. You will work through the items with your instructor in class. You may use any available space in the section for scratch work. Answers are on page 593.

DIRECTIONS: Solve each item and choose the correct answer choice. Then, fill in the corresponding oval on the bubble sheet.

Allocate time wisely. Try to solve as many items as possible, returning to skipped items if time permits.

Calculator use is permitted on this test; however, some items are best solved without the use of a calculator.

Note: Unless otherwise stated, assume all of the following.

1. Illustrative figures are NOT necessarily drawn to scale.
2. The word *average* indicates arithmetic mean.
3. The word *line* indicates a straight line.
4. Geometric figures lie in a plane.

1. If the price of fertilizer has been decreased from 3 pounds for \$2 to 5 pounds for \$2, how many more pounds of fertilizer can be purchased for \$10 than could have been purchased before?

   (A) 2
   (B) 8
   (C) 10
   (D) 12
   (E) 15

2. Five students formed a political club to support a candidate for local office. They project that club membership will double every three weeks. Which of the following can be used to find the number of members that the club projects to have after twelve weeks?

   (F) $5(2^{\frac{2}{3}})$
   (G) $5(2^{\frac{3}{2}})$
   (H) $5(2^{\frac{12}{3}})$
   (J) $5(2^{\frac{3}{12}})$
   (K) $5+5(2^4)$

3. If $\frac{2x-5}{3} = -4x$, then $x = ?$

   (A) -1
   (B) $-\frac{5}{14}$
   (C) 0
   (D) $\frac{5}{14}$
   (E) 1

4. A vending machine dispenses k cups of coffee, each at a cost of c cents, every day. During a period d days long, what is the amount of money in dollars taken in by the vending machine from the sale of coffee?

   (F) $\frac{100kc}{d}$
   (G) kcd
   (H) $\frac{dk}{c}$
   (J) $\frac{kcd}{100}$
   (K) $\frac{kc}{100d}$

5. If $f(x) = 2x-3$ and $g(x) = x^2-2$, then $f(g(2)) = ?$

   (A) -1
   (B) 0
   (C) 1
   (D) 4
   (E) 7

6. If $|x+3| = 5$, then $x = ?$

    (F) -8 or 2
    (G) -2 or 8
    (H) -8
    (J) -2
    (K) 2 or 8

7. In the figure above, line m has a slope of 1. What is the y-intercept of the line?

    (A) -5
    (B) -3
    (C) 0
    (D) 3
    (E) 7

8. If a circle has a radius of 1, what is its area?

    (F) $\frac{\pi}{2}$
    (G) π
    (H) 2π
    (J) 4π
    (K) π^2

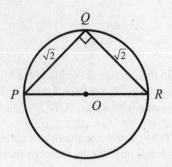

9. In the figure above, ΔPQR is inscribed in a circle with center O. What is the area of the circle?

    (A) $\frac{\pi}{2}$
    (B) $\frac{\pi}{\sqrt{2}}$
    (C) π
    (D) $\pi\sqrt{2}$
    (E) 2π

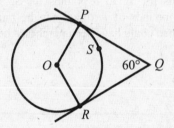

10. In the figure above, $\overline{QP}$ is tangent to circle O at point P, and $\overline{QR}$ is tangent to circle O at point R. What is the degree measure of the minor arc PSR?

    (F) 30
    (G) 60
    (H) 90
    (J) 120
    (K) 180

11. In the figure below, sin(A) = ?

(A) $\frac{3}{4}$

(B) $\frac{3}{5}$

(C) $\frac{4}{5}$

(D) $\frac{5}{3}$

(E) $\frac{5}{4}$

12. What is the average of 8.5, 7.8, and 7.7?

(F) 8.3

(G) 8.2

(H) 8.1

(J) 8.0

(K) 7.9

13. In the figure above, x = ?

(A) 15

(B) 30

(C) 45

(D) 60

(E) 120

Note: Figure not drawn to scale.

14. In the figure above, what is the length of $\overline{AB} + \overline{CD}$?

(F) 5

(G) 10

(H) 15

(J) 20

(K) 40

Items #15–16 refer to the following figure.

Note: Figure not drawn to scale.

15. Which of the following must be true?

I. $\overline{PS} < \overline{SR}$

II. $z = 90$

III. $x > y$

(A) I only

(B) I and II only

(C) I and III only

(D) I, II, and III

(E) Neither I, II, nor III

16. Which of the following must be true?

I. $\overline{PR} > \overline{PS}$

II. $z > x$

III. $x + y = z$

(F) I only

(G) I and II only

(H) I and III only

(J) I, II, and III

(K) Neither I, II, nor III

17. In a certain year, the number of girls who graduated from City High School was twice the number of boys. If $\frac{3}{4}$ of the girls and $\frac{5}{6}$ of the boys went to college immediately after graduation, what fraction of the graduates that year went to college immediately after graduation?

    (A) $\frac{5}{36}$

    (B) $\frac{16}{27}$

    (C) $\frac{7}{9}$

    (D) $\frac{29}{36}$

    (E) $\frac{31}{36}$

18. A jar contains black and white marbles. If there are ten marbles in the jar, then which of the following could NOT be the ratio of black to white marbles?

    (F) 9:1
    (G) 7:3
    (H) 1:1
    (J) 1:4
    (K) 1:10

19. If n is a negative number, which of the following is the least in value?

    (A) $-n$
    (B) $n-n$
    (C) $n+n$
    (D) n^2
    (E) n^4

20. If a machine produces 240 thingamabobs per hour, how many <u>minutes</u> are needed for the machine to produce 30 thingamabobs?

    (F) 6
    (G) 7.5
    (H) 8
    (J) 12
    (K) 12.5

21. Of the 120 people in a room, $\frac{3}{5}$ are women. If $\frac{2}{3}$ of the people are married, what is the maximum number of women in the room who could be <u>unmarried</u>?

    (A) 80
    (B) 72
    (C) 48
    (D) 40
    (E) 32

22. Three friends are playing a game in which each person simultaneously displays one of three hand signs: a clenched fist, an open palm, or two extended fingers. How many unique combinations of the signs are possible?

    (F) 3
    (G) 9
    (H) 10
    (J) 12
    (K) 27

23. If $\frac{1}{3}$ of the number of girls in a school equals $\frac{1}{5}$ of the total number of students, what is the ratio of girls to boys in the school?

    (A) 5:3
    (B) 3:2
    (C) 2:5
    (D) 1:3
    (E) 1:5

24. Peter walked from point P to point Q and back again, a total distance of 2 miles. If he averaged 4 miles per hour on the trip from P to Q and 5 miles per hour on the return trip, what was his average walking speed in miles per hour for the entire trip?

    (F) $2\frac{2}{9}$
    (G) 4
    (H) $4\frac{4}{9}$
    (J) $4\frac{1}{2}$
    (K) 5

25. After a 20-percent decrease in price, the cost of an item is D dollars. What was the price of the item before the decrease?

    (A) 0.75D
    (B) 0.80D
    (C) 1.20D
    (D) 1.25D
    (E) 1.5D

26. On a certain trip, a motorist drove 10 miles at 30 miles per hour, 10 miles at 40 miles per hour, and 10 miles at 50 miles per hour. What portion of her total driving time was spent driving 50 miles per hour?

    (F) $1\frac{13}{51}$
    (G) $\frac{5}{7}$
    (H) $\frac{5}{12}$
    (J) $\frac{1}{3}$
    (K) $\frac{12}{47}$

27. What is the <u>maximum</u> number of non-overlapping sections that can be created when a circle is crossed by three straight lines?

    (A) 3
    (B) 4
    (C) 5
    (D) 6
    (E) 7

28. At Glenridge High School, 20 percent of the students are seniors. If all of the seniors attended the school play, and 60 percent of all the students attended the play, what percent of the <u>non-seniors</u> attended the play?

    (F) 20%
    (G) 40%
    (H) 50%
    (J) 60%
    (K) 100%

Water Usage in Cubic Feet

29. The water meter at a factory displays the reading above. What is the <u>minimum</u> number of cubic feet of water that the factory must use before four of the five digits on the meter are again the same?

    (A) 10,000
    (B) 1,000
    (C) 999
    (D) 666
    (E) 9

30. A telephone call from City X to City Y costs $1.00 for the first three minutes and $0.25 for each additional minute thereafter. What is the <u>maximum</u> length of time, in minutes, that a caller could talk for $3.00?

    (F) 8
    (G) 10
    (H) 11
    (J) 12
    (K) 13

31. In the figure below, $m + n + o + p + q + r = ?$

    (A) 360
    (B) 540
    (C) 720
    (D) 900
    (E) Cannot be determined from the given information

32. $\frac{8}{9} - \frac{7}{8} = ?$

(F) $\frac{1}{72}$

(G) $\frac{1}{8}$

(H) $\frac{1}{7}$

(J) $\frac{15}{72}$

(K) $\frac{15}{7}$

33. $\sqrt{1 - \left(\frac{2}{9} + \frac{1}{36} + \frac{1}{18}\right)} = ?$

(A) $\frac{1}{5}$

(B) $\sqrt{\frac{2}{3}}$

(C) $\frac{5}{6}$

(D) 1

(E) $\sqrt{3}$

34. $\frac{1}{2} \cdot \frac{2}{3} \cdot \frac{3}{4} \cdot \frac{4}{5} \cdot \frac{5}{6} \cdot \frac{6}{7} \cdot \frac{7}{8} = ?$

(F) $\frac{1}{56}$

(G) $\frac{1}{8}$

(H) $\frac{28}{37}$

(J) $\frac{41}{43}$

(K) $\frac{55}{56}$

35. $86(37) - 37(85) = ?$

(A) 0

(B) 1

(C) 37

(D) 85

(E) 86

36. Which of the following is a prime factorization of 120?

(F) (2)(2)(15)

(G) (2)(3)(4)(5)

(H) (2)(2)(3)(10)

(J) (2)(2)(2)(3)(5)

(K) (2)(2)(3)(3)(5)

37. $-4.01(3.2) + 0.2(0.4) = ?$

(A) −12.752

(B) −4.536

(C) 0.432

(D) 1.251

(E) 12.783

38. $\frac{0.2521 \cdot 8.012}{1.014}$ is approximately equal to:

(F) 0.25

(G) 0.5

(H) 1.0

(J) 1.5

(K) 2.0

39. Which of the following fractions is the largest?

(A) $\frac{111}{221}$

(B) $\frac{75}{151}$

(C) $\frac{333}{998}$

(D) $\frac{113}{225}$

(E) $\frac{101}{301}$

40. If $z = \frac{x+y}{x}$, $1 - z = ?$

(F) $\frac{1 - x + y}{x}$

(G) $\frac{x + y - 1}{x}$

(H) $\frac{1 - x - y}{x}$

(J) $-\frac{y}{x}$

(K) $1 - x - y$

41. $0.125 \cdot 0.125 \cdot 64 = ?$

    (A) 0.625
    (B) 0.125
    (C) 0.5
    (D) 1
    (E) 8

42. $\frac{0.111 \cdot 0.666}{0.166 \cdot 0.125}$ is approximately equal to which of the following?

    (F) 6.8
    (G) 4.3
    (H) 3.6
    (J) 1.6
    (K) 0.9

43. If the senior class has 360 students, of whom $\frac{5}{12}$ are women, and the junior class has 350 students, of whom $\frac{4}{7}$ are women, how many more women are there in the junior class than in the senior class?

    (A) $(360 - 350)(\frac{4}{7} - \frac{5}{12})$
    (B) $\frac{(360 - 350)(\frac{4}{7} - \frac{5}{12})}{2}$
    (C) $(\frac{4}{7} \cdot \frac{5}{12})(360 - 350)$
    (D) $(\frac{4}{7} \cdot 350) - (\frac{5}{12} \cdot 360)$
    (E) $(\frac{5}{12} \cdot 360) - (\frac{4}{7} \cdot 350)$

44. If the price of candy increases from 5 pounds for $7 to 3 pounds for $7, how much less candy (in pounds) can be purchased for $3.50 at the new price than at the old price?

    (F) $\frac{2}{7}$
    (G) 1
    (H) $1\frac{17}{35}$
    (J) 2
    (K) $3\frac{34}{35}$

45. If n is any integer, which of the following is always an odd integer?

    (A) $n - 1$
    (B) $n + 1$
    (C) $n + 2$
    (D) $2n + 1$
    (E) $2n + 2$

46. Which of the following expressions represents the product of two consecutive integers?

    (F) $2n + 1$
    (G) $2n + n$
    (H) $2n^2$
    (J) $n^2 + 1$
    (K) $n^2 + n$

47. If n is any integer, which of the following expressions <u>must</u> be even?

    I. $2n$
    II. $2n + n$
    III. $2n \cdot n$

    (A) I only
    (B) II only
    (C) III only
    (D) I and II only
    (E) I and III only

48. If n is the first number in a series of three consecutive even numbers, which of the following expressions represents the sum of the three numbers?

(F) $n+2$
(G) $n+4$
(H) $n+6$
(J) $3n+6$
(K) $6(3n)$

49. If n is an odd number, which of the following expressions represents the third odd number following n?

(A) $n+3$
(B) $n+4$
(C) $n+6$
(D) $3n+3$
(E) $4n+4$

50. If n is any odd integer, which of the following expressions must also be odd?

    I. $n+n$
    II. $n+n+n$
    III. $n \cdot n \cdot n$

(F) I only
(G) II only
(H) III only
(J) II and III only
(K) I, II, and III

51. If n is a negative number, which of the following expressions must be positive?

    I. $2n$
    II. n^2
    III. n^5

(A) I only
(B) II only
(C) III only
(D) I and II only
(E) II and III only

52. If $0 < x < 1$, which of the following expressions is the largest?

(F) x
(G) $2x$
(H) x^2
(J) x^3
(K) $x+1$

53. If $-1 < x < 0$, which of the following expressions is the largest?

(A) -1
(B) x
(C) $2x$
(D) x^3
(E) $x-1$

54. If set $S = \{2, 3, 4\}$ and set P is the set of all products of different elements in set S, then set $P = ?$

(F) $\{6, 8, 12\}$
(G) $\{6, 8, 18\}$
(H) $\{6, 8, 12, 24\}$
(J) $\{6, 8, 12, 18, 24\}$
(K) $\{6, 8, 12, 18, 24, 36\}$

55. If set X is the set of all integers between 1 and 24, inclusive, that are evenly divisible by 3, and set Y is the set of all integers between 1 and 24, inclusive, that are evenly divisible by 4, what is the set of all elements in both sets X and Y?

(A) $\{12\}$
(B) $\{3, 4\}$
(C) $\{12, 24\}$
(D) $\{4, 12, 24\}$
(E) $\{3, 4, 12, 24\}$

56. If x is an element of set X, in which set X is the set of integers evenly divisible by 3 such that $6 < x < 11$, and y is an element of set Y, where set Y is the set of integers evenly divisible by 4 such that $7 < y < 12$, what is the intersection of sets X and Y?

(F) $\{\}$
(G) $\{8\}$
(H) $\{9\}$
(J) $\{12\}$
(K) $\{8, 12\}$

57. If set S is the set of all positive odd integers and set T is the set of all positive even integers, then the union of sets S and T (the set of all elements that are in either set or both sets) is the set of:

(A) positive integers.
(B) integers.
(C) even integers.
(D) odd integers.
(E) real numbers.

58. In a certain school, each of the 72 music students must participate in the marching band, the orchestra, or both. If only music students participate, 48 students total participate in the marching band, and 54 students total participate in the orchestra, how many students participate in both programs?

(F) 6
(G) 18
(H) 24
(J) 30
(K) 36

59. $|-2| + 3 - |-4| = ?$

(A) -5
(B) -4
(C) -1
(D) 1
(E) 9

60. $|5| - |-5| + |-3| = ?$

(F) -8
(G) -3
(H) 3
(J) 8
(K) 13

61. $|-3| \cdot |-4| \cdot -5 = ?$

(A) -60
(B) -30
(C) -7
(D) 20
(E) 60

62. $(3 + i)(4 - 3i) = ?$

(F) $12 + 3i^2$
(G) $12 - 3i^2$
(H) $9 - 5i^2$
(J) $9 - 5i$
(K) $15 - 5i$

63. $\frac{1}{2 - i} = ?$

(A) -2
(B) -1
(C) $\frac{2 + i}{5}$
(D) $\frac{2 - i}{5}$
(E) $\frac{2 + i}{3}$

64. A jar contains 24 white marbles and 48 black marbles. What percent of the marbles in the jar are black?

(F) 10%
(G) 25%
(H) $33\frac{1}{3}\%$
(J) 60%
(K) $66\frac{2}{3}\%$

65. A group of 3 friends shared the cost of a tape recorder. If Andy, Barbara, and Donna each paid $12, $30, and $18, respectively, then Donna paid what percent of the cost of the tape recorder?

(A) 10%
(B) 30%
(C) $33\frac{1}{3}$%
(D) 50%
(E) $66\frac{2}{3}$%

66. Twenty students attended Professor Rodriguez's class on Monday and 25 students attended on Tuesday. The number of students who attended on Tuesday was what percent of the number of students who attended on Monday?

(F) 5%
(G) 20%
(H) 25%
(J) 80%
(K) 125%

67. If the population of a town was 20,000 in 1997 and 16,000 in 2007, what was the percentage decline in the town's population?

(A) 50%
(B) 25%
(C) 20%
(D) 10%
(E) 5%

Items #68–70 refer to the following table.

Capitol City Fires	
Year	Number of Fires
2002	100
2003	125
2004	140
2005	150
2006	135

68. The number of fires in 2002 was what percentage of the number of fires in 2003?

(F) 25%
(G) $66\frac{2}{3}$%
(H) 80%
(J) 100%
(K) 125%

69. The number of fires in 2006 was what percentage of the number of fires in 2005?

(A) 90%
(B) 82%
(C) 50%
(D) 25%
(E) 10%

70. What was the percent decrease in the number of fires from 2005 to 2006?

(F) 10%
(G) 25%
(H) 50%
(J) 82%
(K) 90%

71. A groom must divide 12 quarts of oats between two horses. If Dobbin is to receive twice as much as Pegasus, how many quarts of oats should the groom give to Dobbin?

(A) 4
(B) 6
(C) 8
(D) 9
(E) 10

72. If the ratio of John's allowance to Lucy's allowance is $3:2$, and the ratio of Lucy's allowance to Bob's allowance is $3:4$, what is the ratio of John's allowance to Bob's allowance?

   (F) $1:6$
   (G) $2:5$
   (H) $1:2$
   (J) $3:4$
   (K) $9:8$

73. If 4.5 pounds of chocolate cost $10, how many pounds of chocolate can be purchased for $12?

   (A) $4\frac{3}{4}$
   (B) $5\frac{2}{5}$
   (C) $5\frac{1}{2}$
   (D) $5\frac{3}{4}$
   (E) 6

74. At Star Lake Middle School, 45 percent of the students bought a yearbook. If 540 students bought yearbooks, how many students did <u>not</u> buy a yearbook?

   (F) 243
   (G) 540
   (H) 575
   (J) 660
   (K) 957

75. In the equation $y = kx$, k is the constant of variation. If y is equal to 6 when $x = 2.4$, what is the constant of variation?

   (A) 0.4
   (B) 2.5
   (C) 3.4
   (D) 3.6
   (E) 14.4

76. A train traveling at a constant speed, k, takes 90 minutes to go from point P to point Q, a distance of 45 miles. What is the value of k, in miles per hour?

   (F) 20
   (G) 30
   (H) 45
   (J) 60
   (K) 75

77. The cost of picture framing depends on the outer perimeter of the frame. If a 15" x 15" picture frame costs $35 more than a 10" x 10" picture frame, what is the cost of framing, in dollars per inch?

   (A) $3.50
   (B) $2.75
   (C) $2.25
   (D) $1.75
   (E) $1.50

78. Walking at a constant speed of 4 miles per hour, it took Jill exactly 1 hour to walk home from school. If she walked at a constant speed of 5 miles per hour, how many <u>minutes</u> did the trip take?

   (F) 48
   (G) 54
   (H) 56
   (J) 72
   (K) 112

79. Ms. Peters drove from her home to the park at an average speed of 30 miles per hour and returned home along the same route at an average speed of 40 miles per hour. If her driving time from home to the park was 20 minutes, how many minutes did it take Ms. Peters to drive from the park to her home?

   (A) 7.5
   (B) 12
   (C) 15
   (D) 24
   (E) 30

80. Which of the following is the larger of two numbers the product of which is 600 and the sum of which is five times the difference between the two?

    (F) 10
    (G) 15
    (H) 20
    (J) 30
    (K) 50

81. If $\frac{1}{3}$ of a number is 3 more than $\frac{1}{4}$ of the number, then what is the number?

    (A) 18
    (B) 24
    (C) 30
    (D) 36
    (E) 48

82. If $\frac{3}{5}$ of a number is 4 more than $\frac{1}{2}$ of the number, then what is the number?

    (F) 20
    (G) 28
    (H) 35
    (J) 40
    (K) 56

83. If both 16 and 9 are divided by n, the remainder is 2. What is n?

    (A) 3
    (B) 4
    (C) 5
    (D) 6
    (E) 7

84. The sum of the digits of a three-digit number is 16. If the tens digit of the number is 3 times the units digit, and the units digit is $\frac{1}{4}$ of the hundreds digit, then what is the number?

    (F) 446
    (G) 561
    (H) 682
    (J) 862
    (K) 914

85. If the sum of five consecutive integers is 40, what is the smallest of the five integers?

    (A) 4
    (B) 5
    (C) 6
    (D) 7
    (E) 8

86. If $a^3 + b = 3 + a^3$, then $b = ?$

    (F) 3^3
    (G) $3\sqrt{3}$
    (H) 3
    (J) $\sqrt[3]{3}$
    (K) $-\sqrt{3}$

87. Which of the following expressions is equivalent to $4a + 3b - (-2a - 3b)$?

    (A) $2a$
    (B) $12ab$
    (C) $2a + 6b$
    (D) $6a + 6b$
    (E) $8a + 9b$

88. If $x = 2$, what is the value of $x^2 + 2x - 2$?

    (F) -2
    (G) 0
    (H) 2
    (J) 4
    (K) 6

89. If $x = 2$, then $\frac{1}{x^2} + \frac{1}{x} - \frac{x}{2} = ?$

    (A) $-\frac{3}{4}$
    (B) $-\frac{1}{4}$
    (C) 0
    (D) $\frac{1}{4}$
    (E) $\frac{1}{2}$

90. If $\frac{1}{3}x = 10$, then $\frac{1}{6}x = ?$

   (F) $\frac{1}{15}$
   (G) $\frac{2}{3}$
   (H) 2
   (J) 5
   (K) 30

91. If $p = 1$, $q = 2$, and $r = 3$, then $\frac{(q \cdot r)(r-q)}{(q-p)(p \cdot q)} = ?$

   (A) -3
   (B) -1
   (C) 0
   (D) 3
   (E) 6

92. $\frac{9(x^2 y^3)^6}{(3x^6 y^9)^2} = ?$

   (F) 1
   (G) 3
   (H) $x^2 y^3$
   (J) $3x^2 y^3$
   (K) $x^{12} y^{12}$

93. $2(4^{-\frac{1}{2}}) - 2^0 + 2^{\frac{3}{2}} + 2^{-2} = ?$

   (A) $-2\sqrt{2} - \frac{1}{4}$
   (B) $2\sqrt{2} - \frac{1}{4}$
   (C) $2\sqrt{2}$
   (D) $2\sqrt{2} + \frac{1}{4}$
   (E) $2\sqrt{2} + \frac{5}{4}$

94. Which of the following expressions is equivalent to $\frac{x^2 - y^2}{x + y}$?

   (F) $x^2 - y^2$
   (G) $x^2 + y^2$
   (H) $x^2 + y$
   (J) $x + y^2$
   (K) $x - y$

95. Which of the following expressions is equivalent to $\frac{x^2 - x - 6}{x + 2}$?

   (A) $x^2 - \frac{x}{2} - 3$
   (B) $x^2 - 2$
   (C) $x - 2$
   (D) $x - 3$
   (E) x

96. Which of the following is the factorization of $6x^2 + 4x - 2$?

   (F) $(6x + 1)(x - 3)$
   (G) $(6x + 3)(x - 1)$
   (H) $(3x - 1)(2x - 2)$
   (J) $(2x + 2)(3x - 1)$
   (K) $(2x + 4)(3x - 2)$

97. In a certain game, a player picks an integer between 1 and 10, adds 3 to it, multiplies the sum by 2, and subtracts 5. If x is the number picked by a player, which of the following correctly expresses the final result of the game?

   (A) $x + (3)(2) - 5$
   (B) $3x + 2 - 5$
   (C) $2(x + 3 - 5)$
   (D) $2(x + 3) - 5$
   (E) $(2)(3)(x) - 5$

98. At 9:00 a.m., when the heat is turned on, the temperature of a room is 55°F. If the room temperature increases by n°F each hour, which of the following can be used to determine the number of hours needed to bring the temperature of the room to 70°F?

   (F) $(55 + 70)(n)$
   (G) $(55 - 70)(n)$
   (H) $\frac{(70 - 55)}{n}$
   (J) $\frac{n}{(70 - 55)}$
   (K) $\frac{n}{(55 + 70)}$

99. In a geometric sequence of positive numbers, the fourth term is 125 and the sixth term is 3,125. What is the second term of the sequence?

    (A) 1
    (B) 5
    (C) 10
    (D) 25
    (E) 50

100. City University projects that a planned expansion will increase the number of enrolled students every year for the next five years by 50 percent. If 400 students enroll in the first year of the plan, how many students are expected to enroll in the fifth year of the plan?

    (F) 200
    (G) 600
    (H) 675
    (J) 1,350
    (K) 2,025

101. Jimmy's uncle deposited $1,000 into a college fund account and promised that at the start of each year, he would deposit an amount equal to 10% of the account balance. If no other deposits or withdrawals were made and no additional interest accrued, what was the account balance after three additional annual deposits were made by Jimmy's uncle?

    (A) $1,030
    (B) $1,300
    (C) $1,331
    (D) $1,500
    (E) $1,830

102. A tank with a capacity of 2,400 liters is filled with water. If a valve is opened that drains 25 percent of the contents of the tank every minute, what is the volume of water (in liters) that remains in the tank after 3 minutes?

    (F) 1,800
    (G) 1,350
    (H) 1,012.5
    (J) 600
    (K) 325.75

103. If $(2+3)(1+x) = 25$, then $x = ?$

    (A) $\frac{1}{5}$
    (B) $\frac{1}{4}$
    (C) 1
    (D) 4
    (E) 5

104. If $2x + 3 > 9$, which of the following can be the value of x?

    (F) −4
    (G) −3
    (H) 0
    (J) 3
    (K) 4

105. If $\frac{12}{x+1} - 1 = 2$, and $x \neq -1$, then $x = ?$

    (A) 1
    (B) 2
    (C) 3
    (D) 11
    (E) 12

106. If $\frac{x}{x+2} = \frac{3}{4}$, and $x \neq -2$, then $x = ?$

    (F) 6
    (G) 4
    (H) 3
    (J) 2
    (K) 1

107. If $\frac{x}{x-2} - \frac{x+2}{2(x-2)} = 8$, and $x \neq 2$, which of the following is the complete solution set for x?

   (A) {}
   (B) {−2}
   (C) {2}
   (D) {4}
   (E) {8}

108. If $\frac{3}{x-2} > \frac{1}{6}$, which of the following defines the possible values for x?

   (F) $x < 20$
   (G) $x > 0$
   (H) $x > 2$
   (J) $0 < x < 20$
   (K) $2 < x < 20$

109. If $\sqrt{2x+1} - 1 = 4$, then $x = ?$

   (A) −5
   (B) −1
   (C) 1
   (D) 12
   (E) 24

110. Which of the following is the complete solution set for $\sqrt{3x-2} - 3 = -4$?

   (F) {}
   (G) {−1}
   (H) {1}
   (J) {−1, 1}
   (K) {1, 2}

111. If $\sqrt{2x-5} = 2\sqrt{5-2x}$, then $x = ?$

   (A) 1
   (B) 2
   (C) $\frac{5}{2}$
   (D) 10
   (E) 15

112. Which of the following is the complete solution set for $\sqrt{x^2+9} = 5$?

   (F) {−4, 4}
   (G) {−4}
   (H) {0}
   (J) {4}
   (K) {}

113. If $4^{x+2} = 64$, then $x = ?$

   (A) 1
   (B) 2
   (C) 3
   (D) 4
   (E) 5

114. If $8^x = 2^{x+3}$, then $x = ?$

   (F) 0
   (G) 1
   (H) $\frac{2}{3}$
   (J) 3
   (K) $\frac{3}{2}$

115. If $3^{2x} = \frac{1}{81}$, then $x = ?$

   (A) −2
   (B) $-\frac{3}{2}$
   (C) $-\frac{2}{3}$
   (D) $\frac{2}{3}$
   (E) $\frac{3}{2}$

116. If $5^3 = (\sqrt{5})^{-2x}$, then $5^x = ?$

    (F) $\frac{1}{125}$

    (G) $\frac{1}{25}$

    (H) $\frac{1}{5}$

    (J) 5

    (K) 25

117. Which of the following is the complete solution set for $\left|\frac{2x+1}{3}\right| = 5$?

    (A) $\{-8, -7\}$

    (B) $\{-8, 7\}$

    (C) $\{-7, 8\}$

    (D) $\{7\}$

    (E) $\{8\}$

118. Which of the following is the complete solution set for $|x + 6| = 3x$?

    (F) $\{-3, \frac{3}{2}\}$

    (G) $\{-\frac{3}{2}, 3\}$

    (H) $\{\frac{3}{2}, 3\}$

    (J) $\{3\}$

    (K) $\{\}$

119. Which of the following is the complete solution set for $|2x - 1| > 3$?

    (A) All real numbers

    (B) The null set

    (C) All real numbers less than −1 or greater than 2

    (D) All real numbers less than −2 or greater than 1

    (E) All real numbers less than −3

120. If $|3x - 6| > 9$, then which of the following must be true?

    (F) $-3 < x < 2$

    (G) $-2 < x < 3$

    (H) $x < -3$ or $x > 2$

    (J) $x < -1$ or $x > 5$

    (K) $x < -1$ or $x > 9$

121. Which of the following identifies exactly those values of x that satisfy $|-2x + 4| < 4$?

    (A) $x > -4$

    (B) $x < 4$

    (C) $x > 0$

    (D) $0 < x < 4$

    (E) $-4 < x < 0$

122. If $f(x) = x^2 + x$, what is the value of $f(-2)$?

    (F) −8

    (G) −2

    (H) 2

    (J) 8

    (K) 12

123. Given: $y = f(x) = \left(\frac{6x^2 - 2^{-x}}{|x|}\right)^{-\frac{1}{2}}$ for all integers. If $x = -1$, what is the value of y?

    (A) 2

    (B) $\frac{1}{2}$

    (C) $\frac{1}{4}$

    (D) $-\frac{1}{2}$

    (E) −2

124. If $f(x) = x + 3$ and $g(x) = 2x - 5$, what is the value of $f(g(2))$?

    (F) −2

    (G) 0

    (H) 2

    (J) 4

    (K) 10

125. If $f(x) = 3x + 2$ and $g(x) = x^2 + x$, what is the value of $g(f(-2))$?

    (A) 15

    (B) 12

    (C) 6

    (D) 3

    (E) −2

126. If $f(x) = 2x^2 + x$ and $g(x) = f(f(x))$, what is the value of $g(1)$?

    (F) 3
    (G) 18
    (H) 21
    (J) 39
    (K) 55

127. If $f(x) = 3x + 4$ and $g(x) = 2x - 1$, for what value of x does $f(x) = g(x)$?

    (A) −5
    (B) −2
    (C) 0
    (D) 3
    (E) 7

128. If $\boxed{x} = x^2 - x$ for all integers, then $\boxed{-2} = ?$

    (F) −6
    (G) −2
    (H) 0
    (J) 4
    (K) 6

129. If $\boxed{x} = x^2 - x$ for all integers, then $\boxed{\boxed{3}} = ?$

    (A) 27
    (B) 30
    (C) 58
    (D) 72
    (E) 121

130. If $f(x) = 3x - 2$ and $-5 < x < 5$, which of the following defines the range of $f(x)$?

    (F) $-17 < f(x) < 13$
    (G) $-13 < f(x) < 17$
    (H) $-5 < f(x) < 12$
    (J) $0 < f(x) < 17$
    (K) $3 < f(x) < 13$

131. If $f(x) = \frac{x+2}{x-1}$, for which of the following values of x is $f(x)$ undefined?

    (A) −2
    (B) −1
    (C) $\frac{1}{2}$
    (D) 1
    (E) 2

132. If $f(x) = \frac{2-2x}{x}$, which of the following defines the range of $f(x)$?

    (F) All real numbers
    (G) All real numbers except −2
    (H) All real numbers except 0
    (J) All real numbers except 2
    (K) All real numbers greater than 2

133. If $|4x - 8| < 12$, which of the following defines the possible values of x?

    (A) $-8 < x < -4$
    (B) $-4 < x < 8$
    (C) $-1 < x < 5$
    (D) $1 < x < 5$
    (E) $4 < x < 8$

134. The cost of making a call using a phone-card is $0.15 for dialing and $0.04 per minute of connection time. Which of the following equations could be used to find the cost, y, of a call x minutes long?

    (F) $y = x(0.04 + 0.15)$
    (G) $y = 0.04x + 0.15$
    (H) $y = 0.04 + 0.15x$
    (J) $y = 0.15 - 0.04x$
    (K) $y = 0.04 - 0.15x$

135. If $x + y = 3$, then $2x + 2y =$

    (A) $-\frac{2}{3}$
    (B) $\frac{1}{2}$
    (C) $\frac{2}{3}$
    (D) 6
    (E) Cannot be determined from the given information

136. If $2x + y = 8$ and $x - y = 1$, then $x = ?$

    (F) -2
    (G) -1
    (H) 0
    (J) 1
    (K) 3

137. If $7x = 2$ and $3y - 7x = 10$, then $y = ?$

    (A) 2
    (B) 3
    (C) 4
    (D) 5
    (E) 6

138. If $2x + y = 8$ and $x - y = 1$, then $x + y = ?$

    (F) -1
    (G) 1
    (H) 2
    (J) 3
    (K) 5

139. If $4x + 5y = 12$ and $3x + 4y = 5$, then $7(x + y) = ?$

    (A) 7
    (B) 14
    (C) 49
    (D) 77
    (E) 91

x	-2	-1	0	1	2
y	$\frac{10}{3}$	$\frac{8}{3}$	2	$\frac{4}{3}$	$\frac{2}{3}$

140. Which of the following equations correctly describes the relationship between the values x and y in the table above?

    (F) $3x + 2y = 6$
    (G) $3x - 2y = 3$
    (H) $3x + 3y = -6$
    (J) $6x + 4y = 7$
    (K) $2x + 3y = 6$

141. Which of the following is the solution set for $2x^2 - 2x = 12$?

    (A) $\{-3, -2\}$
    (B) $\{-2, 3\}$
    (C) $\{\frac{2}{3}, 3\}$
    (D) $\{\frac{3}{2}, 2\}$
    (E) $\{2, 3\}$

142. If $x^2 - 3x = 4$, then which of the following shows all possible values of x?

    (F) $\{4, 1\}$
    (G) $\{4, -1\}$
    (H) $\{-4, 1\}$
    (J) $\{-4, -1\}$
    (K) $\{-4, 1, 4\}$

143. If $x^2 - y^2 = 0$ and $x + y = 1$, then $x - y = ?$

    (A) -1
    (B) 0
    (C) 1
    (D) 2
    (E) 4

144. Which of the following is the solution set for $3x^2 + 3x = 6$?

    (F) $\{1, -2\}$
    (G) $\{1, 2\}$
    (H) $\{\frac{1}{2}, 1\}$
    (J) $\{\frac{1}{2}, \frac{1}{3}\}$
    (K) $\{-1, -2\}$

145. Which of the following is the solution set for $2x^2 - 3x = 2$?

    (A) $\{\frac{1}{2}, 2\}$
    (B) $\{-\frac{1}{2}, 2\}$
    (C) $\{-\frac{1}{2}, -2\}$
    (D) $\{2, -2\}$
    (E) $\{2, 4\}$

146. Diana spent $\frac{1}{2}$ of her weekly allowance on a new book and another $3 on lunch. If she still had $\frac{1}{6}$ of her original allowance left, how much is Diana's allowance?

    (F) $24
    (G) $18
    (H) $15
    (J) $12
    (K) $9

147. In a certain game, a player had five successful turns in a row, and after each one, the number of points added to his total score was double what was added the preceding turn. If the player scored a total of 465 points, how many points did he score on the first play?

    (A) 15
    (B) 31
    (C) 93
    (D) 155
    (E) 270

148. At a certain firm, d gallons of fuel are needed per day for each truck. At this rate, g gallons of fuel will supply t trucks for how many days?

    (F) $\frac{dt}{g}$
    (G) $\frac{gt}{d}$
    (H) dgt
    (J) $\frac{t}{dg}$
    (K) $\frac{g}{dt}$

149. Y years ago, Paul was twice as old as Bob. If Bob is now 18 years old, how old is Paul today in terms of Y?

    (A) $36+Y$
    (B) $18+Y$
    (C) $18-Y$
    (D) $36-Y$
    (E) $36-2Y$

150. After filling the car's fuel tank, a driver drove from point P to point Q and then to point R. She used $\frac{2}{5}$ of the fuel driving from P to Q. If she used another 7 gallons to drive from Q to R and still had $\frac{1}{4}$ of a tank left, how many gallons does the tank hold?

    (F) 12
    (G) 18
    (H) 20
    (J) 21
    (K) 35

151. If pencils cost x cents each, how many pencils can be purchased for y dollars?

    (A) $\frac{100}{xy}$
    (B) $\frac{xy}{100}$
    (C) $\frac{100y}{x}$
    (D) $\frac{y}{100x}$
    (E) $100xy$

152. A merchant increased the original price of an item by 10 percent. If she then reduces the new price by 10 percent, the final price, in terms of the original price, is equal to which of the following?

    (F) a decrease of 11 percent
    (G) a decrease of 1 percent
    (H) no net change
    (J) an increase of 1 percent
    (K) an increase of 11 percent

153. Harold is twice as old as Jack, who is three years older than Dan. If Harold's age is five times Dan's age, how old (in years) is Jack?

    (A) 2
    (B) 4
    (C) 5
    (D) 8
    (E) 10

154. A tank with capacity T gallons is empty. If water flows into the tank from pipe X at the rate of X gallons per minute, and water is pumped out by pipe Y at the rate of Y gallons per minute, and X is greater than Y, in how many <u>minutes</u> will the tank be filled?

(F) $\frac{T}{Y-X}$

(G) $\frac{T}{X-Y}$

(H) $\frac{T-X}{Y}$

(J) $\frac{X-Y}{60T}$

(K) $\frac{60T}{XY}$

155. Machine X produces w widgets in five minutes. Machine X and machine Y, working at the same time, produce w widgets in two minutes. How long will it take machine Y working alone to produce w widgets?

(A) 2 minutes, 30 seconds
(B) 2 minutes, 40 seconds
(C) 3 minutes, 20 seconds
(D) 3 minutes, 30 seconds
(E) 3 minutes, 40 seconds

156. If a train travels m miles in h hours and 45 minutes, what is its average speed in miles per hour?

(F) $\frac{m}{h+\frac{3}{4}}$

(G) $\frac{m}{1\frac{3}{4}h}$

(H) $m(h+\frac{3}{4})$

(J) $\frac{m+45}{h}$

(K) $\frac{h}{m+45}$

157. On a playground, there are x seesaws. If 50 children are all riding on seesaws, two to a seesaw, and five seesaws are <u>not</u> in use, what is the value of x?

(A) 15
(B) 20
(C) 25
(D) 30
(E) 35

158. In the figure below, what is the length of $\overline{PQ}$?

(F) $\sqrt{2}$
(G) $\sqrt{3}$
(H) 3
(J) 4
(K) 5

159. In the figure above, the line segment joining points (3,3) and (7,3) forms one side of a square. Which of the following CANNOT be the coordinates of another vertex of the square?

(A) (3,−1)
(B) (3,7)
(C) (7,−3)
(D) (7,−1)
(E) (7,7)

160. Which of the following is a graph of the line that passes through the points (−5,3), (−1,1), and (3,−1)?

(F)

(J)

(G)

(K)

(H)

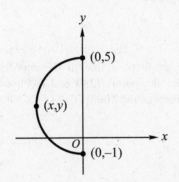

161. In the figure above, what are the coordinates, (x,y), of the point on the semicircle that is farthest from the y-axis?

(A) (−4,−4)
(B) (−3,−3)
(C) (−2,−3)
(D) (−3,2)
(E) (3,2)

162. In the figure above, the area of $\triangle ABC$ is 8. What is the value of k?

(F) 2
(G) $2\sqrt{2}$
(H) 4
(J) $4\sqrt{2}$
(K) 8

163. In the figure below, what is the slope of the line?

(A) −3
(B) −2
(C) −1
(D) 1
(E) 2

164. In the figure above, which two sides of polygon *PQRST* have the same slope?

(F) $\overline{PQ}$ and $\overline{QR}$

(G) $\overline{PQ}$ and $\overline{RS}$

(H) $\overline{PQ}$ and $\overline{ST}$

(J) $\overline{QR}$ and $\overline{RS}$

(K) $\overline{RS}$ and $\overline{ST}$

165. Line *l* is the graph of the equation $y = \frac{3x}{2} + 2$. The graph of which of the following equations is perpendicular to line *l* at (0,2)?

(A) $y = \frac{3x}{2} - 2$

(B) $y = \frac{2x}{3} - 2$

(C) $y = -\frac{2x}{3} + 2$

(D) $y = -\frac{3x}{2} + 3$

(E) $y = -3x + 4$

166. If set $A = \{(-2,3); (-1,1); (-4,-5)\}$, and set $B = \{(3,4); (4,3); (2,-1)\}$, how many lines can be drawn with a positive slope that include exactly one point from set *A* and one point from set *B*?

(F) 2

(G) 3

(H) 4

(J) 5

(K) 6

167. A line includes the points (2,3) and (3,6). What is the equation of the line?

(A) $y = 2x - 3$

(B) $y = 3x - 3$

(C) $y = \frac{3x - 3}{2}$

(D) $y = 3x + 3$

(E) $y = x - 3$

168. Which of the following is the equation for the line with slope of 2 that includes point (0,2)?

(F) $y = x - 1$

(G) $y = 2x - 1$

(H) $y = 2x - 2$

(J) $y = 2x + 2$

(K) $y = x + 1$

169. Which of the following is the equation for the line that includes points $(-1,1)$ and $(7,5)$?

(A) $y = \frac{x}{2} + 2$

(B) $y = \frac{x}{2} + \frac{3}{2}$

(C) $y = \frac{x}{2} + \frac{2}{3}$

(D) $y = 2x + \frac{3}{2}$

(E) $y = 2x + 2$

170. If the graph of a line in the coordinate plane includes the points (2,4) and (8,7), what is the *y*-intercept of the line?

(F) 6

(G) 4

(H) 3

(J) −1

(K) −3

171. If the slope and *y*-intercept of a line are −2 and 3, respectively, then the line passes through which of the following points?

(A) (−5,−10)

(B) (−5,10)

(C) (−2,3)

(D) (3,4)

(E) (4,−5)

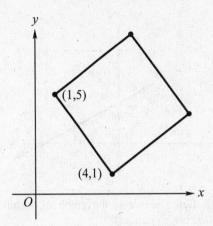

172. What is the distance between the points $(-3,-2)$ and $(3,3)$?

(F) $\sqrt{3}$
(G) $2\sqrt{3}$
(H) 5
(J) $\sqrt{29}$
(K) $\sqrt{61}$

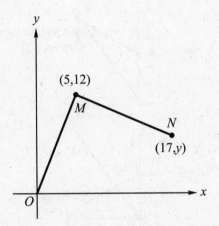

173. In the coordinate plane above, $\overline{MO} \cong \overline{MN}$ and $\overline{MO} \perp \overline{MN}$. What is the value of y?

(A) 5
(B) 7
(C) 12
(D) 13
(E) 17

174. In the figure above, what is the area of the square region?

(F) 4
(G) 8
(H) $8\sqrt{2}$
(J) 16
(K) 25

175. In the coordinate plane, what is the midpoint of the line segment with endpoints $(-3,-5)$ and $(5,7)$?

(A) (1,1)
(B) (1,6)
(C) $(3,\frac{7}{2})$
(D) (4,6)
(E) (8,12)

176. The figure above is the graph of which of the following equations?

(F) $x + 2y = 6$

(G) $2x + y = 6$

(H) $x + \frac{y}{2} = 6$

(J) $\frac{x}{2} + y = 2$

(K) $x - 3y = 2$

177. A school rented the ballroom of a hotel for a dance. The cost of the rental is $1,500 plus $5.00 per person who attends. Each person who attends will pay an admission charge of $12.50. If x represents the number of people who attend, which of the graphs can be used to determine how many people must attend for the admission charges to cover exactly the cost of renting the ballroom?

(A)

(B)

(C)

(D)

(E)

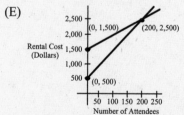

178. Which of the following is the graph of the inequality $y \geq 2x$?

(F)

(J)

(G)

(K)

(H)

179. Which of the following is the graph of the equation $(x-1)^2 + y^2 = 4$?

(A) (0,2), (−2,0), (2,0), (0,−2)

(D) (1,2), (−1,0), (3,0), (1,−2)

(B) (0,1), (−2,−1), (2,−1), (0,−3)

(E) (0,3), (−2,1), (2,1), (0,−1)

(C) (1,3), (−1,1), (3,1), (1,−1)

180. Which of the following is the graph of the equation $\frac{x^2}{9} + \frac{y^2}{16} = 1$?

(F)

(J)

181. The figure above shows the graph of a function $g(x)$. How many times does the graph cross the x-axis?

(A) 1
(B) 2
(C) 3
(D) 4
(E) 5

(G)

(K)

(H)

182. The figure above shows the graph of $f(x)$ in the coordinate plane. For the portion of the graph shown, for how many values of x is $f(x) = 3$?

(F) 0
(G) 1
(H) 2
(J) 3
(K) 4

183. The figure above represents the graph of $y = f(x)$ in the coordinate plane. Which of the following is the graph of $y' = f(x-1)$?

(A)

(D)

(B)

(C)

(E)

184. If the triangle in the figure above is reflected across the y-axis and then reflected across the x-axis, which of the following graphs shows the resulting position of the triangle?

(F)

(J)

(G)

(K)

(H)

185. In the figure above, $x = ?$

    (A) 45
    (B) 60
    (C) 75
    (D) 90
    (E) 120

186. In the figure above, $x = ?$

    (F) 45
    (G) 60
    (H) 90
    (J) 105
    (K) 120

187. In the figure above, l_1 is parallel to l_2. Which of the following <u>must</u> be true?

    (A) $w = a$
    (B) $y + b = 180$
    (C) $w = a$ and $y + b = 180$
    (D) $y + b = 180$ and $x + d = 180$
    (E) $w = a$, $y + b = 180$, and $x + d = 180$

188. In the figure above, $x = ?$

    (F) 30
    (G) 45
    (H) 60
    (J) 75
    (K) 90

189. In the figure above, what is the sum of the indicated angles?

    (A) 540
    (B) 720
    (C) 900
    (D) 1,080
    (E) 1,260

190. In the figure above, what is the length of $\overline{AB}$?

    (F) 2
    (G) $2\sqrt{3}$
    (H) 4
    (J) $4\sqrt{2}$
    (K) 8

191. In the figure above, what is the length of $\overline{PQ}$?

(A) 1
(B) $\sqrt{2}$
(C) $2\sqrt{2}$
(D) 4
(E) 5

192. In a right isosceles triangle, the hypotenuse is equal to which of the following?

(F) Half the length of either of the other sides
(G) The length of either of the other sides multiplied by $\sqrt{2}$
(H) Twice the length of either of the other sides
(J) The sum of the lengths of the other two sides
(K) The sum of the lengths of the other two sides multiplied by $\sqrt{2}$

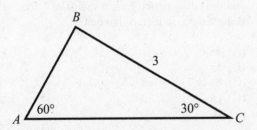

193. In the triangle above, what is the length of $\overline{AC}$?

(A) 2
(B) $\sqrt{3}$
(C) $2\sqrt{3}$
(D) $3\sqrt{3}$
(E) 6

194. In the figure above, the perimeter of $\triangle PQR =$?

(F) $12 + \sqrt{3}$
(G) $12 + 2\sqrt{3}$
(H) $12 + 4\sqrt{3}$
(J) 28
(K) 56

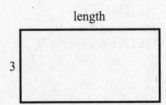

195. In the figure above, what is the area of $\triangle MNO$?

(A) $\frac{1}{2}$
(B) $\frac{\sqrt{2}}{2}$
(C) 1
(D) $\sqrt{2}$
(E) 2

196. If the area of the rectangle above is 18, what is the perimeter?

(F) 9
(G) 12
(H) 18
(J) 24
(K) 30

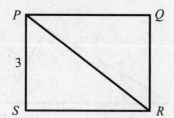

197. In the figure above, $PQRS$ is a rectangle. If $\overline{PR} = 5$ centimeters, what is the area, in square centimeters, of the rectangle?

(A) 2
(B) 3
(C) 4
(D) 8
(E) 12

198. If the width of a rectangle is increased by 10% and the length of the rectangle is increased by 20%, by what percent does the area of the rectangle <u>increase</u>?

(F) 2%
(G) 10%
(H) 15%
(J) 32%
(K) 36%

199. If the area of a circle is equal to 9π, which of the following is (are) true?

    I. The radius is 3.
    II. The diameter is 6.
    III. The circumference is 6π.

(A) I only
(B) II only
(C) III only
(D) I and II only
(E) I, II, and III

200. In the figure above, O is the center of the circle, and $\overline{PQ}$ is tangent to the circle at P. If the radius of circle O has a length of 6, what is the area of the shaded portion of the figure?

(F) π
(G) 3π
(H) 6π
(J) 9π
(K) 12π

Note: Figure not drawn to scale.

201. The figure above shows two pulleys connected by a belt. If the centers of the pulleys are 8 feet apart and the pulleys each have a radius of 1 foot, what is the length, in feet, of the belt?

(A) 4π
(B) 8π
(C) $8 + \pi$
(D) $16 + \pi$
(E) $16 + 2\pi$

202. In the figure above, a circle is inscribed in an equilateral triangle. If the radius of the circle is 1, what is the perimeter of the triangle?

(F) $\sqrt{3}$
(G) $2\sqrt{3}$
(H) $3\sqrt{3}$
(J) 6
(K) $6\sqrt{3}$

203. The figure above shows two circles of diameter 2 that are tangent to each other at point P. The line segments form a rectangle and are tangent to the circles at the points shown. What is the area of the shaded portion of the figure?

(A) $8-2\pi$
(B) $8-\pi$
(C) $4-2\pi$
(D) $4-\pi$
(E) 2π

204. If a circle of radius 1 foot is inscribed in a square, what is the area, in square feet, of the square?

(F) $\frac{\sqrt{2}}{2}$
(G) 1
(H) $\sqrt{2}$
(J) 2
(K) 4

205. An isosceles right triangle is inscribed in a semicircle with a radius of 1 inch. What is the area, in square inches, of the triangle?

(A) $\frac{\sqrt{2}}{3}$
(B) $\frac{1}{2}$
(C) 1
(D) $\sqrt{2}$
(E) $2\sqrt{2}$

206. In the figure above, $BCDE$ is a square with an area of 4. What is the perimeter of $\triangle ABE$?

(F) 3
(G) 4
(H) 6
(J) 8
(K) 12

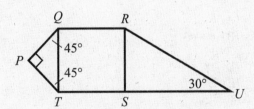

207. In the figure above, if $QRST$ is a square and the length of $\overline{PQ}$ is $\sqrt{2}$, what is the length of $\overline{RU}$?

(A) $\sqrt{2}$
(B) $2\sqrt{2}$
(C) $\sqrt{6}$
(D) 4
(E) $4\sqrt{3}$

208. In the figure above, *PQRS* is a square, and $\overline{PS}$ is the diameter of a semicircle. If the length of $\overline{PQ}$ is 2, what is the area of the shaded portion of the diagram?

(F) $4 - 2\pi$
(G) $4 - \pi$
(H) $4 - \frac{\pi}{2}$
(J) $8 - \pi$
(K) $8 - \frac{\pi}{2}$

210. In the figure above, $x = ?$

(F) 30
(G) 65
(H) 120
(J) 150
(K) 170

211. The perimeter of the triangle shown above is:

(A) $3\sqrt{2}$
(B) 6
(C) 7.5
(D) 9
(E) 15

209. If the lengths of the sides, in inches, are as marked on the figure above, what is the area, in square inches, of the quadrilateral?

(A) 6
(B) $6 + \sqrt{3}$
(C) 12
(D) 18
(E) 24

212. In the figure below, $x = ?$

(F) 120
(G) 150
(H) 180
(J) 210
(K) 240

213. In the figure above, x = ?

(A) 30
(B) 45
(C) 60
(D) 75
(E) 90

214. In the figure above, what is the length of $\overline{AC}$?

(F) $30\sqrt{2}$
(G) 50
(H) 75
(J) $60\sqrt{2}$
(K) 100

215. In the figure above, what is the area of square ABCD?

(A) 2
(B) $2\sqrt{2}$
(C) 4
(D) $4\sqrt{2}$
(E) 8

216. In the triangle above, the measure of ∠BAC is 30° and the length of $\overline{AB}$ is 2. Which of the following best approximates the length of $\overline{AC}$?

(F) 0.8
(G) 1.0
(H) 1.7
(J) 1.9
(K) 2.3

217. For the figure below, $\sin(\theta) = \frac{12}{13}$. Which of the following is INCORRECT?

(A) $\cos(\theta) = \frac{5}{13}$

(B) $\tan(\theta) = \frac{12}{5}$

(C) $\cot(\theta) = \frac{5}{12}$

(D) $\sec(\theta) = \frac{13}{5}$

(E) $\csc(\theta) = \frac{12}{13}$

218. In the right triangle below, the length of $\overline{AB}$ is 5 centimeters and $\angle A$ measures 30°. What is the length, in centimeters, of $\overline{BC}$? [$\sin(30°) = 0.5$]

(F) 4

(G) $3\frac{1}{2}$

(H) $2\frac{3}{4}$

(J) $2\frac{1}{2}$

(K) 2

219. If $\sin(60°)$ is equal to $\frac{\sqrt{3}}{2}$, what is the value of $\sin^2(30°) + \cos^2(30°)$?

(A) $\frac{\sqrt{3}+1}{2}$

(B) $\sqrt{5}$

(C) $\frac{\sqrt{5}}{2}$

(D) $\frac{3}{4}$

(E) 1

220. Which of the following is equivalent to $\frac{\sin(A)}{\cos(A)}$?

(F) $\tan(A)$

(G) $\cot(A)$

(H) $\sec(A)$

(J) $\csc(A)$

(K) $\frac{1}{\tan(A)}$

221. In the figure above, $\triangle PQR$ and $\triangle QRS$ are isosceles right triangles. If $\overline{QP} = 3$, what is the length of $\overline{QS}$? [$\sin(45°) = \frac{\sqrt{2}}{2}$]

(A) $\sqrt{2}$

(B) $2\sqrt{2}$

(C) 4

(D) 6

(E) 8

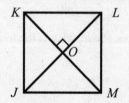

222. If the area of the square $JKLM$ in the figure above is 4, what is the sum of the lengths of the diagonals $\overline{JL}$ and $\overline{KM}$? [$\sin(45°) = \frac{\sqrt{2}}{2}$]

(F) $\frac{\sqrt{2}}{2}$

(G) $2 + \frac{\sqrt{2}}{2}$

(H) $4\sqrt{2}$

(J) $4 + 4\sqrt{2}$

(K) $8\sqrt{2}$

223. In the figure above, O is the center of the circle with radius 10. What is the area of $\triangle AOB$?
$[\sin(30°) = \frac{1}{2}; \sin(60°) = \frac{\sqrt{3}}{2}]$

(A) $10\sqrt{3}$
(B) 10
(C) 25
(D) $25\sqrt{3}$
(E) 50

224. If the average of 35, 38, 41, 43, and x is 37, what is x?

(F) 28
(G) 30
(H) 31
(J) 34
(K) 36

225. The average weight of 6 packages is 50 pounds per package. Another package is added, making the average weight of the 7 packages 52 pounds per package. What is the weight, in pounds, of the additional package?

(A) 2
(B) 7
(C) 52
(D) 62
(E) 64

226. The average of 10 test scores is 80. If the high and low scores are dropped, the average is 81. What is the average of the high and low scores?

(F) 76
(G) 78
(H) 80
(J) 81
(K) 82

227. In Latin 101, the final exam grade is weighted two times as heavily as the mid-term grade. If Leo received a score of 84 on his final exam and 90 on his mid-term, what was his course average?

(A) 88
(B) 87.5
(C) 86.5
(D) 86
(E) 85

228. In a group of children, three children are 10 years old and two children are 5 years old. What is the average age, in years, of the children in the group?

(F) 6
(G) 6.5
(H) 7
(J) 7.5
(K) 8

229. The number of employment applications received by All-Star Staffing each month during 2002 was as follows: 8, 3, 5, 3, 4, 3, 1, 0, 3, 4, 0, and 7. What is the median number of applications received in 2002?

(A) 3
(B) 4
(C) 5
(D) 6
(E) 7

230. William's monthly electric bills for last year were as follows: $40, 38, 36, 38, 34, 34, 30, 32, 34, 37, 39, and 40. What is the mode of the bills?

(F) $33
(G) $34
(H) $35
(J) $36
(K) $37

231. If set $A = \{1, 2, 3, 4, 5, 6\}$ and set $B = \{1, 2, 3, 4, 5, 6\}$, what is the probability that the sum of one number from set A and one number from set B will total 7?

    (A) $\frac{1}{12}$

    (B) $\frac{5}{36}$

    (C) $\frac{1}{6}$

    (D) $\frac{1}{5}$

    (E) $\frac{1}{3}$

234. The figure above shows a dartboard consisting of two concentric circles with center O. The radius of the larger circle is equal to the diameter of the smaller circle. What is the probability that a randomly thrown dart striking the board will score a 3?

    (F) $\frac{1}{16}$

    (G) $\frac{1}{8}$

    (H) $\frac{1}{4}$

    (J) $\frac{1}{2}$

    (K) $\frac{3}{4}$

232. If a book is selected at random from the collection shown above, which of the following has the greatest probability of being selected?

    (F) A book by Mary Smith
    (G) A textbook
    (H) A mystery
    (J) A book written by either Carol Kim or Victor Brown
    (K) A biography

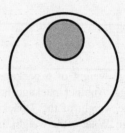

Note: Figure not drawn to scale.

233. If a jar contains r red marbles, b blue marbles, and g green marbles, which of the following expresses the probability that a marble drawn at random will NOT be red?

    (A) $\frac{-r}{r + b + g}$

    (B) $\frac{r}{r + b + g}$

    (C) $\frac{b + g - r}{b + g + r}$

    (D) $\frac{r}{b + g}$

    (E) $\frac{b + g}{b + g + r}$

235. An underwater salvage team is searching the ocean floor for a lost signal device using a large circular search pattern and a smaller circular search pattern with a radius equal to one-third that of the larger pattern. If the device is known to be inside the boundary of the larger search area, what is the probability that it is NOT located in the shaded portion of the figure?

    (A) $\frac{1}{9}$

    (B) $\frac{1}{6}$

    (C) $\frac{1}{3}$

    (D) $\frac{1}{2}$

    (E) $\frac{8}{9}$

Gross Receipts of Store X

Number of Corporation X Employees

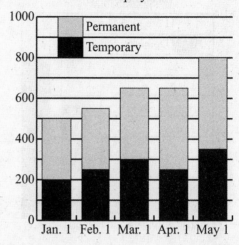

236. During the week shown in the graph above, what was the greatest increase in sales from one day to the next?

(F) $50
(G) $100
(H) $150
(J) $200
(K) $250

238. Based on the data presented above, what was the difference, if any, between the number of permanent workers employed by corporation X on March 1st and the number of permanent workers employed by corporation X on April 1st?

(F) 0
(G) 50
(H) 100
(J) 150
(K) 200

237. If the graph above represents expenditures by corporation X in two different years, what was the approximate ratio of expenditures in 2006 to those in 2007?

(A) $\frac{1}{5}$

(B) $\frac{2}{5}$

(C) $\frac{1}{2}$

(D) $\frac{2}{3}$

(E) 2

Company *T* Domestic Sales
(in millions of dollars)

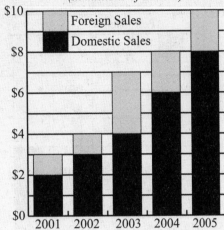

Number of Packages Shipped Monthly
by PostExpress

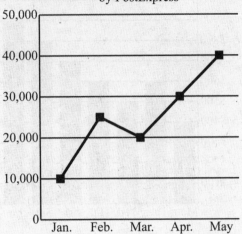

239. Based on the data presented above, what was the difference in the value of foreign sales by company *T* between 2003 and 2005?

(A) $1,000,000
(B) $2,000,000
(C) $3,000,000
(D) $5,000,000
(E) $6,000,000

240. Based on the data presented above, what was the approximate total number of packages shipped by PostExpress for the months January, February, and March, inclusive?

(F) 40,000
(G) 55,000
(H) 60,000
(J) 70,000
(K) 85,000

GOVERNMENT EXPENDITURES

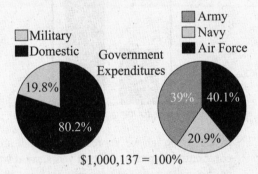

$1,000,137 = 100%

241. Based on the data presented above, approximately how much money was spent on the Air Force?

(A) $39,704
(B) $79,409
(C) $96,123
(D) $198,027
(E) $401,054

PetProducts 2002 Foreign Sales
(Total = $2,000,000)

242. Based on the data presented above, what was the dollar value of foreign sales to Europe by PetProducts in 2002?

(F) $200,000
(G) $400,000
(H) $1,200,000
(J) $1,600,000
(K) $2,000,000

T-Shirt Prices			
	Blue	*Red*	*White*
Small	$5.00	$6.00	$7.00
Large	$5.75	$6.50	$7.25
Extra Large	$6.50	$7.25	$8.00

243. Based on the data presented above, what is the total cost of 5 large blue t-shirts, 8 small red t-shirts, and 4 extra large white t-shirts?

(A) $56.00
(B) $88.25
(C) $105.50
(D) $108.75
(E) $135.00

244. The above scatterplot shows the video-game playing habits of 20 students. The graph most strongly supports the conclusion that the number of hours per week spent playing video-games:

(F) is constant from age 10 to age 18.
(G) increases as age increases from 10 to 18.
(H) decreases as age increases from 10 to 18.
(J) is constant for ages 10 through 14 and then decreases.
(K) is constant for ages 10 through 14 and then increases.

CHALLENGE ITEMS

The items in this section reflect both the format and difficulty range of items on the real Mathematics Test, though difficult items are emphasized. You may use any available space in the section for scratch work. Answers are on page 593.

DIRECTIONS: Solve each item and choose the correct answer choice. Then, fill in the corresponding oval on the bubble sheet.

Allocate time wisely. Try to solve as many items as possible, returning to skipped items if time permits.

Calculator use is permitted on this test; however, some items are best solved without the use of a calculator.

Note: Unless otherwise stated, assume all of the following.

1. Illustrative figures are NOT necessarily drawn to scale.
2. The word *average* indicates arithmetic mean.
3. The word *line* indicates a straight line.
4. Geometric figures lie in a plane.

1. Nine playing cards from the same deck are placed as shown in the figure above to form a large rectangle of area 180 sq. in. How many inches are there in the perimeter of this large rectangle?

    (A) 29
    (B) 58
    (C) 64
    (D) 116
    (E) 210

2. If each of the dimensions of a rectangle is increased by 100%, by what percent is the area increased?

    (F) 100%
    (G) 200%
    (H) 300%
    (J) 400%
    (K) 500%

3. What is 10% of $\frac{1}{3}x$ if $\frac{2}{3}x$ is 10% of 60?

    (A) 0.1
    (B) 0.2
    (C) 0.3
    (D) 0.4
    (E) 0.5

4. In the figure above, M and N are midpoints of sides $\overline{PR}$ and $\overline{PQ}$, respectively, of $\triangle PQR$. What is the ratio of the area of $\triangle MNS$ to that of $\triangle PQR$?

    (F) 2 : 5
    (G) 2 : 9
    (H) 1 : 4
    (J) 1 : 8
    (K) 1 : 12

5. A cube has an edge that is 4 inches long. If the edge is increased by 25%, by what percent is the volume increased?

    (A) 25%
    (B) 48%
    (C) 73%
    (D) 95%
    (E) 122%

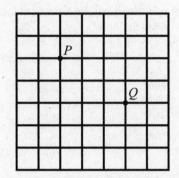

6. In the graph above, the axes and the origin are not shown. If point *P* has coordinates (3,7), what are the coordinates of point *Q*, assuming each box is one square unit?

(F) (5,6)
(G) (1,10)
(H) (6,9)
(J) (6,5)
(K) (5,10)

7. The average of 8 numbers is 6; the average of 6 other numbers is 8. What is the average of all 14 numbers?

(A) 6
(B) $6\frac{6}{7}$
(C) 7
(D) $7\frac{2}{7}$
(E) $8\frac{1}{7}$

8. The front wheels of a wagon are 7 feet in circumference and the back wheels are 9 feet in circumference. When the front wheels have made 10 more revolutions than the back wheels, what distance, in feet, has the wagon gone?

(F) 126
(G) 180
(H) 189
(J) 315
(K) 630

9. Doreen can wash her car in 15 minutes, while her younger brother Dave takes twice as long to do the same job. If they work together, how many minutes will the job take them?

(A) 5
(B) $7\frac{1}{2}$
(C) 10
(D) $22\frac{1}{2}$
(E) 30

10. In the figure above, the sides of the large square are each 14 inches long. Joining the midpoints of each opposite side forms 4 smaller squares. What is the value of *y*, in inches?

(F) 5
(G) 6
(H) $6\frac{5}{8}$
(J) $6\frac{2}{3}$
(K) 6.8

Note: Figure not drawn to scale.

11. In the figure above, $PQRS$ is a parallelogram, and $\overline{ST} = \overline{TV} = \overline{VR}$. If $\angle PTS = 90°$, what is the ratio of the area of $\triangle SPT$ to the area of the parallelogram?

(A) $\frac{1}{6}$

(B) $\frac{1}{5}$

(C) $\frac{2}{7}$

(D) $2\frac{1}{3}$

(E) Cannot be determined from the given information

12. If $p > q$ and $r < 0$, which of the following is (are) true?

I. $pr < qr$

II. $p + r > q + r$

III. $p - r < q - r$

(F) I only

(G) II only

(H) I and III only

(J) I and II only

(K) I, II, and III

13. A pound of water is evaporated from 6 pounds of seawater that is 4% salt. What is the percentage of salt in the remaining solution?

(A) 3.6%

(B) 4%

(C) 4.8%

(D) 5.2%

(E) 6%

14. John is now three times Pat's age. Four years from now, John will be x years old. In terms of x, how old is Pat now?

(F) $\frac{x+4}{3}$

(G) $3x$

(H) $x + 4$

(J) $x - 4$

(K) $\frac{x-4}{3}$

15. In the figure above, what percent of the area of rectangle $PQRS$ is shaded?

(A) 20

(B) 25

(C) 30

(D) $33\frac{1}{3}$

(E) 35

16. A cylindrical container has a diameter of 14 inches and a height of 6 inches. Since one gallon equals 231 cubic inches, what is the approximate capacity, in gallons, of the tank?

(F) $\frac{2}{3}$

(G) $1\frac{1}{7}$

(H) $2\frac{2}{7}$

(J) $2\frac{2}{3}$

(K) 4

17. A train running between two towns arrives at its destination 10 minutes late when it goes 40 miles per hour and 16 minutes late when it goes 30 miles per hour. What is the distance, in miles, between the two towns?

(A) $8\frac{6}{7}$

(B) 12

(C) 192

(D) 560

(E) 720

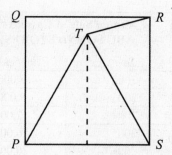

18. In the figure above, *PQRS* is a square and *PTS* is an equilateral triangle. What is the degree measure of ∠*TRS*?

(F) 60
(G) 75
(H) 80
(J) 90
(K) Cannot be determined from the given information

19. In the figure above, $\overline{PQ}$ is parallel to $\overline{RS}$, $y = 60°$, and $z = 130°$. What is the degree measure of ∠*x*?

(A) 90
(B) 100
(C) 110
(D) 120
(E) 130

20. Paul can paint a fence in 2 hours and Fred can paint the same fence in 3 hours. If Paul and Fred work together, how many hours will it take them to paint the fence?

(F) 5
(G) $2\frac{1}{2}$
(H) $1\frac{1}{5}$
(J) 1
(K) $\frac{5}{6}$

21. A motorist drives 60 miles to her destination at an average speed of 40 miles per hour and makes the return trip at an average speed of 30 miles per hour. What is her average speed, in miles per hour, for the entire trip?

(A) 17
(B) $34\frac{2}{7}$
(C) 35
(D) $43\frac{1}{3}$
(E) 70

22. An ice cream truck drives down Willy Street 4 times a week. The truck carries 5 different flavors of ice cream bars, each of which comes in 2 different designs. If the truck runs Monday through Thursday, and Monday was the first day of the month, by what day of the month could Zachary, buying 1 ice cream bar each time the truck drives down the street, purchase all of the different varieties of ice cream bars?

(F) 11th
(G) 16th
(H) 21st
(J) 24th
(K) 30th

23. If $N! = N(N-1)(N-2)\ldots[N-(N-1)]$, what does $\frac{N!}{(N-2)!}$ equal?

(A) $N^2 - N$
(B) $N^5 + N^3 - N^2 + \frac{N}{N^2}$
(C) $N + 1$
(D) 1
(E) 6

24. In the figure above, ABC is an equilateral triangle with a perpendicular line drawn from point A to point D. If the triangle is "folded over" on the perpendicular line so that points B and C meet, the perimeter of the new triangle is approximately what percent of the perimeter of the triangle before the fold?

(F) 100%
(G) 78%
(H) 50%
(J) 32%
(K) Cannot be determined from the given information

Note: Figure not drawn to scale.

25. In the figure above, $\overline{AB}$ is three times longer than $\overline{BC}$, and $\overline{CD}$ is two times longer than $\overline{BC}$. If $\overline{BC}$ is removed from the line and the other two segments are joined to form one line, what is the ratio of the original length of $\overline{AD}$ to the new length of $\overline{AD}$?

(A) $3:2$
(B) $6:5$
(C) $5:4$
(D) $7:6$
(E) $11:10$

26. If $(x+1)(x-2)$ is positive, then:

(F) $x < -1$ or $x > 2$.
(G) $x > -1$ or $x < 2$.
(H) $-1 < x < 2$.
(J) $-2 < x < 1$.
(K) $x = -1$ or $x = 2$.

Annual Sale of Cassettes ABC SOUND STORES	
Year	Number Sold
2002	7,000
2003	9,000
2004	12,000
2005	16,000
2006	20,000
2007	24,000

27. In the above table, which yearly period had the smallest percent increase in sales?

(A) 2002–2003
(B) 2003–2004
(C) 2004–2005
(D) 2005–2006
(E) 2006–2007

28. If s, t, and u are different positive integers and $\frac{s}{t}$ and $\frac{t}{u}$ are positive integers, which of the following CANNOT be a positive integer?

(F) $\frac{s}{u}$
(G) $s \cdot t$
(H) $\frac{u}{s}$
(J) $(s+t)u$
(K) $(s-u)t$

Note: Figure not drawn to scale.

29. In the figure above, $\overline{AD} = \overline{DC}$. What is the value of $\overline{AD} + \overline{DC}$?

(A) $18\sqrt{2}$
(B) 18
(C) $10\sqrt{2}$
(D) 10
(E) $6\sqrt{2}$

30. For the figure below, which of the following statements is true?

(F) $\sin(\theta) = \frac{b}{c}$

(G) $\tan(\sigma) = \frac{a}{b}$

(H) $\cos(\theta) = \frac{c}{a}$

(J) $\sin(\theta) = \cos(\sigma)$

(K) $\cot(\sigma) = \tan(\sigma)$

31. In the figure below, if $\arcsin(s) = 2[\arcsin(d)]$, then $x = ?$

(A) 15

(B) 30

(C) 45

(D) 60

(E) 75

32. In the figure below, if $\overline{AC}$ is the diameter of the circle, B is a point on the circle, and $\sin(\theta) = \frac{1}{2}$, then $\sin(\phi) = ?$

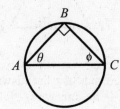

(F) $\frac{\sqrt{2}}{3}$

(G) $\frac{\sqrt{3}}{3}$

(H) $\frac{\sqrt{3}}{2}$

(J) $\frac{2\sqrt{2}}{3}$

(K) $\frac{2\sqrt{3}}{2}$

33. The figure below is a possible graph of which of the following equations?

(A) $y = 2[\sin(x)]$

(B) $y = \sin(x) + 2$

(C) $y = \csc(x) + 1$

(D) $y = \csc(x) - 1$

(E) $y = \sec(x) + 1$

34. If θ is an acute angle and $\cos(\theta) = \frac{b}{c}$, $b > 0$ and $c > 0$ and $b \neq c$, then $\sin(\theta)$ is equal to which of the following?

(F) $\dfrac{b}{\sqrt{b^2 - c^2}}$

(G) $\dfrac{c}{\sqrt{b^2 - b^2}}$

(H) $\dfrac{\sqrt{b^2 - c^2}}{b}$

(J) $\dfrac{\sqrt{b^2 - c^2}}{c}$

(K) $\dfrac{\sqrt{c^2 - b^2}}{c}$

TIMED-PRACTICE QUIZZES

This section contains three Mathematics quizzes. Complete each quiz under timed conditions. You may use any available space in the section for scratch work. Answers are on page 593.

DIRECTIONS: Solve each item and choose the correct answer choice. Then, fill in the corresponding oval on the bubble sheet.

Allocate time wisely. Try to solve as many items as possible, returning to skipped items if time permits.

Calculator use is permitted on this test; however, some items are best solved without the use of a calculator.

Note: Unless otherwise stated, assume all of the following.

1. Illustrative figures are NOT necessarily drawn to scale.
2. The word *average* indicates arithmetic mean.
3. The word *line* indicates a straight line.
4. Geometric figures lie in a plane.

A. QUIZ I (16 items; 20 minutes)

1. In the triangle above, $x =$?

    (A) 24
    (B) 20
    (C) 16
    (D) 12
    (E) 10

2. A normal dozen contains 12 items, and a baker's dozen contains 13 items. If x is the number of items that could be measured either in a whole number of normal dozens or in a whole number of baker's dozens, what is the <u>minimum</u> value of x?

    (F) 1
    (G) 12
    (H) 13
    (J) 25
    (K) 156

3. In the figure above, what is the degree measure of the <u>smaller</u> of the two angles formed by the hour and minute hands of the clock?

    (A) 45
    (B) 60
    (C) 90
    (D) 120
    (E) 240

4. Starting from points that are 200 kilometers apart, two trains travel toward each other along two parallel tracks. If one train travels at 70 kilometers per hour and the other travels at 80 kilometers per hour, how much time, in hours, will elapse before the trains pass each other?

    (F) $\frac{3}{4}$
    (G) 1
    (H) $\frac{4}{3}$
    (J) $\frac{3}{2}$
    (K) 2

5. A student begins heating a certain substance with a temperature of 50°C over a Bunsen burner. If the temperature of the substance will rise 20°C for every 24 minutes it remains over the burner, what will be the temperature, in degrees Celsius, of the substance after 18 minutes?

(A) 52
(B) 56
(C) 60
(D) 65
(E) 72

6. If the ratio of men to women in a meeting is 8 to 7, what fractional part of the people at the meeting is women?

(F) $\frac{1}{56}$
(G) $\frac{1}{15}$
(H) $\frac{1}{7}$
(J) $\frac{7}{15}$
(K) $\frac{8}{7}$

7. The object of a popular board game is to use clues to identify a suspect and the weapon used to commit a crime. If there are 3 suspects and 6 weapons, how many different solutions to the game are possible?

(A) 2
(B) 3
(C) 9
(D) 12
(E) 18

8. The average weight of three boxes is $25\frac{1}{3}$ pounds. If each box weighs at least 24 pounds, what is the greatest possible weight, in pounds, of any one of the boxes?

(F) 25
(G) 26
(H) 27
(J) 28
(K) 29

9. If n subtracted from $\frac{13}{2}$ is equal to n divided by $\frac{2}{13}$, what is the value of n?

(A) $\frac{2}{3}$
(B) $\frac{13}{15}$
(C) 1
(D) $\frac{13}{11}$
(E) 26

10. In the figure above, what is the area of the quadrilateral?

(F) 18
(G) 15
(H) 12
(J) 9
(K) 8

11. In the figure above, what is the length of $\overline{BC}$? [$\sin(30°) = \frac{1}{2}$]

(A) 2
(B) 3
(C) $3\sqrt{3}$
(D) 6
(E) $6\sqrt{3}$

12. After being dropped from a height of h meters, a ball bounces 3 meters high on the third bounce and $\frac{4}{3}$ meters high on the fifth bounce. What is the value, in meters, of h?

(F) $\frac{27}{8}$

(G) $\frac{9}{2}$

(H) $\frac{27}{4}$

(J) $\frac{81}{8}$

(K) $\frac{27}{2}$

13. Set $A = \{-2, -1, 0\}$, and Set $B = \{-1, 0, 1\}$. If a is an element of set A and b is an element of Set B, for how many pairs (a, b) is the product ab a member of both Set A and Set B?

(A) 0
(B) 2
(C) 4
(D) 6
(E) 9

14. Which of the following is the complete solution set for $|2x+4| = 12$?

(F) $\{-8, 4\}$
(G) $\{-4, 8\}$
(H) $\{0, 8\}$
(J) $\{4, 8\}$
(K) $\{6, 8\}$

15. If $f(x) = \frac{(x-1)^2}{(-2-x)}$, for what value of x is $f(x)$ undefined?

(A) −2
(B) −1
(C) 0
(D) 1
(E) 2

16. For the figure below, which of the following statements is INCORRECT?

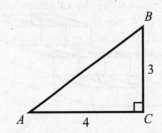

(F) $\sin(A) = \frac{3}{5}$

(G) $\cos(A) = \frac{4}{5}$

(H) $\tan(A) = \frac{3}{4}$

(J) $\cot(A) = \frac{5}{3}$

(K) $\sec(A) = \frac{5}{4}$

B. QUIZ II (21 items; 25 minutes)

1. The figure above is a plan that shows a solid set of steps to be constructed from concrete blocks of equal size. How many blocks are needed to construct the steps?

   (A) 12
   (B) 15
   (C) 18
   (D) 21
   (E) 24

2. In the figure above, what is the value of x?

   (F) 70
   (G) 60
   (H) 50
   (J) 40
   (K) 30

3. If $2^{x+1} = 4^{x-1}$, what is the value of x?

   (A) 1
   (B) 2
   (C) 3
   (D) 4
   (E) 5

4. Of the actors in a certain play, five actors are in Act I, 12 actors are in Act II, and 13 actors are in Act III. If 10 of the actors are in exactly two of the three acts and all of the other actors are in just one act, how many actors are in the play?

   (F) 17
   (G) 20
   (H) 24
   (J) 30
   (K) 38

5. In the figure above, $\overline{AB} \cong \overline{BC} \cong \overline{CA}$. What is the value of y?

   (A) 20
   (B) 60
   (C) 80
   (D) 100
   (E) 120

6. Under certain conditions, a bicycle traveling k meters per second requires $\frac{k^2}{20} + k$ meters to stop. If $k = 10$, how many <u>meters</u> does the bicycle need to stop?

   (F) 10
   (G) 12
   (H) 15
   (J) 20
   (K) 30

7. What is the slope of a line that passes through the origin and $(-3,-2)$?

(A) $\frac{3}{2}$

(B) $\frac{2}{3}$

(C) 0

(D) $-\frac{2}{3}$

(E) $-\frac{3}{2}$

8. An album contains x black-and-white photographs and y color photographs. If the album contains 24 photographs, then which of the following CANNOT be true?

(F) $x = y$

(G) $x = 2y$

(H) $x = 3y$

(J) $x = 4y$

(K) Cannot be determined from the given information

9. If $2a = 3b = 4c$, then what is the average (arithmetic mean) of a, b, and c, in terms of a?

(A) $\frac{13a}{18}$

(B) $\frac{13a}{9}$

(C) $\frac{8a}{3}$

(D) $\frac{4a}{3}$

(E) $2a$

10. If $x = 6 + y$ and $4x = 3 - 2y$, what is the value of x?

(F) 4

(G) $\frac{11}{3}$

(H) $\frac{5}{2}$

(J) $-\frac{2}{3}$

(K) $-\frac{7}{2}$

11. If $\frac{2}{3}$ is written as a decimal to 101 places, what is the sum of the first 100 digits to the right of the decimal point?

(A) 66

(B) 595

(C) 599

(D) 600

(E) 601

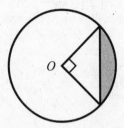

12. In the figure above, O is the center of the circle with radius 1. What is the area of the shaded region?

(F) $\frac{3\pi}{4} + \frac{1}{2}$

(G) $\frac{3\pi}{4} - \frac{1}{2}$

(H) $\frac{\pi}{4} + \frac{1}{2}$

(J) $\frac{\pi}{4} - \frac{1}{2}$

(K) $\pi - 1$

13. If $f(3) = 5$ and $f(7) = 7$, what is the slope of the graph of $f(x)$ in the coordinate plane?

(A) -2

(B) $-\frac{1}{2}$

(C) 1

(D) $\frac{1}{2}$

(E) 2

14. In a list of the first 100 positive integers, the digit 9 appears how many times?

(F) 9

(G) 10

(H) 11

(J) 19

(K) 20

15. If $\frac{x}{x+3} = \frac{3}{4}$, and $x \neq -3$, then $x = ?$

(A) 3
(B) 4
(C) 5
(D) 7
(E) 9

16. Which of the following is the complete solution set for $\sqrt{2x+3} + 2 = 5$?

(F) $\{\}$
(G) $\{-1\}$
(H) $\{3\}$
(J) $\{-1, 3\}$
(K) $\{1, 2\}$

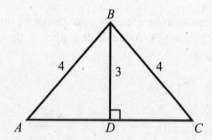

17. In the figure above, what is the length of $\overline{AC}$?

$[\sin(\angle ABD) = \frac{\sqrt{7}}{4}]$

(A) 5
(B) $2\sqrt{7}$
(C) $4\sqrt{3}$
(D) 7
(E) $3\sqrt{7}$

18. A dartboard has four concentric circles with the center as indicated in the figure above. If the diameter of each circle except for the smallest is twice that of the next smaller circle, what is the probability that a randomly thrown dart will strike the shaded portion of the figure?

(F) $\frac{3}{16}$
(G) $\frac{1}{4}$
(H) $\frac{13}{64}$
(J) $\frac{17}{64}$
(K) $\frac{1}{2}$

19. If $f(3) = 4$ and $f(-3) = 1$, what is the y-intercept of the graph of $f(x)$ in the coordinate plane?

(A) $-\frac{5}{2}$
(B) $-\frac{2}{5}$
(C) 0
(D) $\frac{2}{5}$
(E) $\frac{5}{2}$

Sales of Company *X* (in millions)

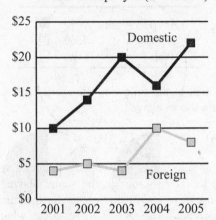

20. Which of the following pie graphs best represents the division of total sales between foreign and domestic sales for 2004?

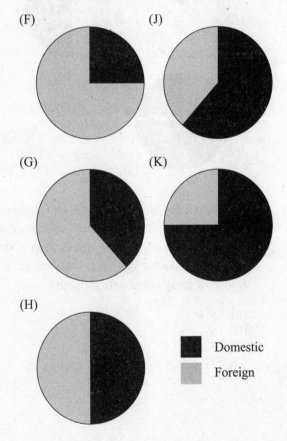

(F)

(J)

(G)

(K)

(H)

■ Domestic

▨ Foreign

21. In the figure below, the length of $\overline{AC}$ is 5 units. Which of the following is the best approximation for the number of units in the length of $\overline{BC}$? [$\tan(22°) \approx 0.4$]

(A) 2.0
(B) 3.0
(C) 7.5
(D) 12.5
(E) 16

C. QUIZ III (26 items; 25 minutes)

1. What is the average (arithmetic mean) of all integers 6 through 15 (including 6 and 15)?

    (A) 6
    (B) 9
    (C) 10.5
    (D) 11
    (E) 21

2. Which of the following numbers is the largest?

    (F) 0.08
    (G) 0.17
    (H) 0.171
    (J) 0.1077
    (K) 0.10771

3. If the rectangle above has an area of 72, then $x = ?$

    (A) 3
    (B) 4
    (C) 6
    (D) 8
    (E) 9

4. Machine X produces 15 units per minute, and Machine Y produces 12 units per minute. In one hour, Machine X will produce how many more units than Machine Y?

    (F) 90
    (G) 180
    (H) 240
    (J) 270
    (K) 360

Team Expenses		
Transportation	$240	■
Lodging	$360	▨
Meals	$120	☐

5. Which of the following pie charts represents the data shown above?

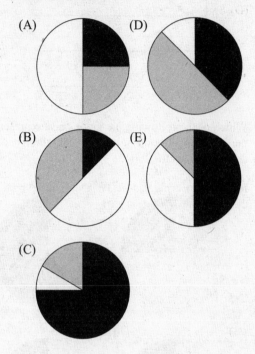

6. On the first day after being given an assignment, a student read $\frac{1}{2}$ the number of pages assigned, and on the second day, the student read 3 more pages. If the student still has 6 additional pages to read, how many pages were assigned?

    (F) 15
    (G) 18
    (H) 24
    (J) 30
    (K) 36

7. The average (arithmetic mean) of Pat's scores on three tests was 80. If the average of her scores on the first two tests was 78, what was her score on the third test?

(A) 82
(B) 84
(C) 86
(D) 88
(E) 90

8. In the figure above, $a + c - b$ is equal to which of the following?

(F) $2a - d$
(G) $2a + d$
(H) $2d - a$
(J) $2a$
(K) 180

9. If $3a + 6b = 12$, then $a + 2b = ?$

(A) 1
(B) 2
(C) 3
(D) 4
(E) 6

10. Two circles with radii r and $r + 3$ have areas that differ by 15π. What is the radius of the smaller circle?

(F) 4
(G) 3
(H) 2
(J) 1
(K) $\frac{1}{2}$

11. If x, y, and z are integers, $x > y > z > 1$, and $xyz = 144$, what is the greatest possible value of x?

(A) 8
(B) 12
(C) 16
(D) 24
(E) 36

12. For all integers, $x \, \Phi \, y = 2x + 3y$. Which of the following must be true?

    I. $3 \, \Phi \, 2 = 12$
    II. $x \, \Phi \, y = y \, \Phi \, x$
    III. $0 \, \Phi \, (1 \, \Phi \, 2) = (0 \, \Phi \, 1) \, \Phi \, 2$

(F) I only
(G) I and II only
(H) I and III only
(J) II and III only
(K) I, II, and III

13. In the figure above, what is the slope of line l?

(A) 1
(B) $\frac{1}{2}$
(C) 0
(D) $-\frac{1}{2}$
(E) -1

14. If Yuriko is now twice as old as Lisa was 10 years ago, how old is Lisa today if Yuriko is now n years old?

(F) $\frac{n}{2}+10$

(G) $\frac{n}{2}-10$

(H) $n-10$

(J) $2n+10$

(K) $2n-10$

15. In the figure above, $ABCD$ is a rectangle with sides $\overline{AB}$, $\overline{BC}$, and $\overline{CD}$ touching the circle with center O. If the radius of the circle is 2, what is the area of the shaded region?

(A) $\frac{3\pi}{2}$

(B) $\frac{3\pi}{4}$

(C) $8-2\pi$

(D) $2-\pi$

(E) $\pi-1$

16. The sum of two positive consecutive integers is n. In terms of n, what is the value of the larger of the two integers?

(F) $\frac{n-1}{2}$

(G) $\frac{n+1}{2}$

(H) $\frac{n}{2}+1$

(J) $\frac{n}{2}-1$

(K) $\frac{n}{2}$

	Old Scale	New Scale
Minimum Score	0	120
Minimum Passing Score	60	?
Maximum Score	100	180

17. The table above shows a teacher how to convert scores for a test from the Old Scale to the New Scale. What is the Minimum Passing Score on the New Scale?

(A) 108

(B) 136

(C) 156

(D) 164

(E) 208

18. If a polygon with all equal sides is inscribed in a circle, then the measure in degrees of the minor arc created by adjacent vertices of the polygon could be all of the following EXCEPT:

(F) 30

(G) 25

(H) 24

(J) 20

(K) 15

19. A jar contains 5 blue marbles, 25 green marbles, and x red marbles. If the probability of drawing a red marble at random is $\frac{1}{4}$, what is the value of x?

(A) 25

(B) 20

(C) 15

(D) 12

(E) 10

20. $\frac{1}{10^{25}}-\frac{1}{10^{26}}=?$

(F) $\frac{9}{10^{25}}$

(G) $\frac{9}{10^{26}}$

(H) $\frac{1}{10^{25}}$

(J) $-\frac{9}{10^{25}}$

(K) $-\frac{1}{10}$

21. When the 10-gallon tank of an emergency generator is filled to capacity, the generator operates without interruption for 20 hours, consuming fuel at a constant rate. Which of the graphs below represents the fuel consumption of the generator over time?

(A)

(B)

(C)

(D)

(E)

Floor Readings for the Red River

Time (p.m.)	1:00	2:00	3:00	4:00
Inches above Normal	0.5	1.5	?	13.5

22. The table above shows readings of water levels for the Red River at various times. If readings of the rise of the water level followed a geometric progression, the water level at 3:00 p.m. was how many inches above normal?

(F) 4
(G) 4.5
(H) 4.75
(J) 5
(K) 5.25

23. In the figure above, $\overline{PQ}$ is tangent to circle O at point S and $\overline{QR}$ is tangent to circle O at point T. If the radius of circle O is 2, what is the area of the shaded portion of the figure?

(A) $\frac{\pi}{3}$
(B) $\frac{2\pi}{3}$
(C) π
(D) $\frac{4\pi}{3}$
(E) 2π

Items #24–25 refer to the following table.

ANNUAL EXPENDITURES FOR THE JONES FAMILY

(percent of disposable income)

Category	2006	2007
Rent	23.0%	19.3%
Food	17.6%	18.2%
Clothing	14.2%	15.1%
Automobile	11.3%	12.3%
Utilities	10.9%	10.2%
Savings	6.2%	5.1%
Entertainment	5.2%	5.3%
Medical and Dental Care	4.0%	3.7%
Charitable Contributions	3.2%	3.9%
Household Furnishings	2.9%	3.1%
Other	1.5%	3.8%
	+	+
	100.0%	100.0%
Total Expenditures:	$34,987.00	$40,012.00

---

24. Approximately how much money did the Jones family spend on medical and dental care in 2006?

(F) $1,200
(G) $1,400
(H) $1,520
(J) $2,250
(K) $4,000

25. If the categories in the table are rank ordered from one to eleven in each year, for how many categories would the rank ordering change from 2006 to 2007?

(A) 2
(B) 3
(C) 4
(D) 5
(E) 6

26. In the figure below, the length of $\overline{AB}$ is 2 units. Which of the following is the best approximation for the number of units in the length of $\overline{BC}$? [$\cos(45°) \approx 0.7$]

(F) 0.7
(G) 1.2
(H) 1.4
(J) 2.9
(K) 3.4

CAMBRIDGE TESTPREP™

MATHEMATICS
STRATEGY SUMMARY SHEET

GENERAL STRATEGIES: When approaching a Mathematics item, there are several things to which you should pay careful attention:

1. *Figures:* Unless otherwise specifically noted, the figures included as illustrations are NOT drawn to scale. However, when all other options for answering the item fail, try the strategy of assuming the figure *is* drawn to scale. Then, use the figure to help you answer the item.

2. *Answer Choices:* Most answer choices are arranged in order of ascending or descending value and many incorrect answer choices correspond to conceptual errors.

3. *"Signal" Words:* Typically, "signal" words are capitalized (e.g., thought-reversers, such as "NOT," "CANNOT," and "EXCEPT"); however, they may sometimes be underlined or italicized (e.g., specified units). While the specific formatting of these words may vary, they can be critical to correctly understanding the item. Pay careful attention to thought-reversers, as they reverse the apparent meaning of an item.

4. *Ladder of Difficulty:* Difficult Mathematics items tend to be clustered near the end of the section. When solving items that are high on the ladder of difficulty, be wary of simplistic answers and the "Cannot be determined…" response. Remember to pace yourself—difficult, time-consuming items have the same value as the easy items.

5. *Preview Item Stems:* Read the item stem first. Only then should you read the details of the item, keeping this item stem in mind.

6. *Confirm Solutions:* Double-check the solution by confirming that it answers the particular question that is being asked. When applicable, this confirmation includes verifying that the solution is given in the units specified by the item stem.

If you are unable to either find an elegant (quick) solution or solve the item directly based on subject knowledge, the following alternative solutions strategies can be extremely helpful:

1. *"Test-the-Test" Strategy*: The correct answer to any item is always one of five given choices. Sometimes, the easiest and quickest way to solve an item is to test each of the answer choices. The "test-the-test" strategy can mean plugging answer choices back into the item (starting with the middle answer choice) to test the validity of an expression, or it can mean checking each answer choice against any stated conditions. The "test-the-test" strategy is typically useful for items with numerical solutions or variables and values that meet stated conditions.

2. *"Plug-and-Chug" Strategy*: This strategy is similar to the "test-the-test" strategy in that the item stem and answer choices (rather than direct mathematical solution strategies) are used to isolate the correct answer. The difference is that rather than testing the validity of each answer choice against the item stem conditions, the item stem and/or answer choices are evaluated by plugging in chosen numbers: "plug-and-chug." This strategy is especially helpful when solving Algebra items.

3. *"Eliminate-and-Guess" Strategy*: If unable to determine the correct answer directly by using mathematical methods or indirectly by using either the "test-the-test" or "plug-and-chug" strategy, eliminate as many

answer choices as possible and then guess from the remaining answer choices. For difficult mathematics items, eliminate answer choices that can be reached either by a single step or by copying a number from the item.

CHECKLIST OF SKILLS AND CONCEPTS:

ARITHMETIC

___ Simplifying: Fractions, Collecting Terms
___ Factoring
___ Approximation
___ The "Flying-X" Method
___ Decimal-Fraction Equivalents
___ Properties of Numbers (Odd, Even, Negative, Positive, Consecutive)
___ Sets (Union, Intersection, Elements)
___ Absolute Value
___ Percents (Change, Original Amount, Price Increase)
___ Ratios (Two-Part, Three-Part, Weighted)
___ Proportions (Direct, Indirect)

ALGEBRA

___ Evaluation of Expressions (Rational, Radical)
___ Exponents (Integer, Rational, Negative)
___ Factoring
___ Sequence
___ Solving Single Variable Equations and Inequalities
___ Absolute Value
___ Functions
___ Domain and Range
___ Solving Equations (Multi-Variable, Linear, Quadratic, Simultaneous)
___ Story Problems: Work (Joint Effort), Averages

COORDINATE GEOMETRY

___ Coordinate Plane
___ Slope of a Line
___ Slope-Intercept Form of a Linear Equation
___ Distance Formula
___ Graphing Linear Equations
___ Graphing First-Degree Inequalities
___ Graphing Quadratic Equations
___ Permutations of Equations and Graphs

GEOMETRY

___ Lines and Angles (Perpendicular, Parallel, Intersecting, Big Angle/Little Angle Theorem)
___ Triangles (Equilateral, Isosceles, Acute, Obtuse, Perimeter, Area, Altitudes, Angles, Bisectors, Pythagorean Theorem)
___ Quadrilaterals (Squares, Rectangles, Rhombuses, Parallelograms, Trapezoids, Perimeter, Area)
___ Polygons (Sum of Interior Angles)
___ Circles (Chords, Tangents, Radius, Diameter, Circumference, Area)
___ Solids (Cubes, Cylinders, Spheres, Volumes, Surface Areas)
___ Complex Figures

TRIGONOMETRY

___ Trigonometric Functions
___ Trigonometric Values
___ Trigonometric Relationships

STATISTICS AND PROBABILITY

___ Averages (Simple, Weighted), Median, and Mode
___ Probability
___ Graphs (Bar, Cumulative, Line)
___ Pie Charts
___ Tables (Matrices)
___ Scatterplots

ADDITIONAL STRATEGIES FROM IN-CLASS DISCUSSION: _____

_____

_____

_____

_____

_____

_____

_____

_____

_____

_____

_____

_____

_____

_____

_____

_____

_____

_____

_____

_____

_____

_____

_____

_____

_____

_____

_____

CALCULATOR EXERCISE

This exercise is designed to illustrate when and when not to use your calculator. Make sure that the calculator you bring to the ACT, the PLAN, or the EXPLORE is one with which you are thoroughly familiar. (The calculator requirements are the same for the ACT, the PLAN, and the EXPLORE. For more detailed information on calculator usage, including specific models that are prohibited on all three tests, go to http://www.actstudent.org/faq/answers/calculator.html.) Although no item requires the use of a calculator, a calculator may be helpful to answer some items. The calculator may be useful for any item that involves complex arithmetic computations, but it cannot take the place of understanding how to set up a mathematical item. The degree to which you can use your calculator will depend on its features. Answers are on page 594.

DIRECTIONS: Label each of the items that follow according to the following categories: (1) a calculator would be very useful (saves valuable test time), (2) a calculator might or might not be useful, or (3) a calculator would be counterproductive (wastes valuable test time).

1. What is the average of 8.5, 7.8, and 7.7?

   (A) 8.3
   (B) 8.2
   (C) 8.1
   (D) 8.0
   (E) 7.9

2. If $0 < x < 1$, which of the following is the largest?

   (F) x
   (G) $2x$
   (H) x^2
   (J) x^3
   (K) $x+1$

3. If 4.5 pounds of chocolate cost \$10, how many pounds of chocolate can be purchased for \$12?

   (A) $4\frac{3}{4}$
   (B) $5\frac{2}{5}$
   (C) $5\frac{1}{2}$
   (D) $5\frac{3}{4}$
   (E) 6

4. What is the value of $\frac{8}{9} - \frac{7}{8}$?

   (F) $\frac{1}{72}$
   (G) $\frac{15}{72}$
   (H) $\frac{1}{7}$
   (J) $\frac{1}{8}$
   (K) $\frac{15}{7}$

5. Which of the following fractions is the largest?

   (A) $\frac{111}{221}$
   (B) $\frac{75}{151}$
   (C) $\frac{333}{998}$
   (D) $\frac{113}{225}$
   (E) $\frac{101}{301}$

6. Dr. Leo's new office is 2.8 yards by 4 yards. She plans to run a decorative border around the perimeter of the office. How many yards of wallpaper border should she purchase?

   (F) 8
   (G) 13.2
   (H) 13.6
   (J) 14.2
   (K) 16.7

7. What is the value of $\frac{2}{3} - \frac{5}{8}$?

(A) 1
(B) $\frac{15}{16}$
(C) $\frac{3}{24}$
(D) $\frac{1}{24}$
(E) $\frac{1}{100}$

8. If $3x + y = 33$ and $x + y = 17$, then what is the value of x?

(F) 8
(G) 12
(H) 16
(J) 24
(K) 33

9. If the perimeter of the rectangle above is 40, what is its area?

(A) 5
(B) 15
(C) 25
(D) 45
(E) 75

10. If the price of a book increases from $10.00 to $12.50, what is the percent increase in price?

(F) 2.5
(G) 12.5
(H) 25
(J) 33
(K) 50

Reading

CAMBRIDGE TESTPREP™

READING

COURSE CONCEPT OUTLINE: WHAT YOU ABSOLUTELY MUST KNOW

I. Test Mechanics (p. 145)

II. Lesson (p. 153)

A. Preliminaries

B. Facts about Passages

1. Four Passage Topics, Unfamiliar Subjects
2. Passages Test Comprehension, Not "Speed-Reading"

C. Item-Types

1. Main Idea (Items #1–2, p. 153)
2. Explicit Detail (Items #3–5, p. 154)
3. Vocabulary (Item #6, p. 154)
4. Development (Items #7–8, p. 154)
5. Implied Idea (Items #9–11, p. 155)
6. Application (Items #12–13, p. 155)
7. Voice (Items #14–15, p. 155)

D. Strategies

1. Three Reading Comprehension Levels
   a. General Theme
   b. Specific Points
   c. Evaluation
2. Using the Three Comprehension Levels
3. Five Steps to Approaching Passages
   a. Label Passages as "Easy" or "Hard"
   b. Preview First and Last Sentences of Selection
   c. Preview Item Stems
   d. Read the Passage
   e. Answer the Items (Items #16–24, p. 156)
4. Item-Type Strategies
   a. Main Idea Clues (Items #25–27, p. 158)
   b. Explicit Detail Clues (Item #28, p. 159)
   c. Vocabulary Clues (Items #29–33, p. 159)
   d. Development Clues (Items #34–35, p. 159)
   e. Implied Idea Clues (Items #36–37, p. 159)
   f. Application Clues (Item #38, p. 160)
   g. Voice Clues (Item #39, p. 160)

TEST MECHANICS

BASICS

The Reading Test consists of four approximately 700-word reading selections, each followed by ten questions. You read a passage and answer the questions based upon what is stated or implied in the reading selection.

You'll have one passage from each of the following four categories: Prose Fiction, Humanities, Social Studies, and Natural Sciences. In most cases, the passage will be about a topic with which you are not familiar. The test-writers choose unusual topics so that the Reading Test will be one of reading skill and not of knowledge. Of course, you may find a topic that you know something about, but even so, your knowledge is probably not going to help you very much, though familiarity with a topic is a definite advantage.

The time limit for the Reading Test is 35 minutes. Given the time limit, you obviously need to work quickly. The exam, however, is not a test of "speed-reading." Instead, the exam is a test of reading <u>comprehension</u>.

ANATOMY

DIRECTIONS: The passages presented in the test are each followed by a set of items. Read the passage and choose the best answer for each item. Fill in the corresponding oval on your bubble sheet. You may refer to the passage as often as necessary to answer the passage items.

SOCIAL SCIENCE: This passage is adapted from a government publication about the history of alcohol abuse.

The movement to prohibit alcohol began in the early years of the nineteenth century with the formation of local societies in New York and Massachusetts to promote temperance in consumption of alcohol. Many
5 of the temperance societies were affiliated with Protestant evangelical denominations and met in local churches. As time passed, most temperance societies modified their goal to call for complete abstinence from all alcoholic beverages.

10 In 1919, largely in response to the lobbying efforts of the Anti-Saloon League, the Eighteenth Amendment to the Constitution was passed banning the production, transportation, and sale of all alcoholic beverages. The Amendment, also known as the
15 Prohibition Amendment, provided for concurrent enforcement by both federal and state law. By January 1920, in addition to the federal Volstead Act, the nation had laws in thirty-three states prohibiting alcohol entirely.

20 Prohibition, however, proved unworkable as bootleggers and speakeasies* quickly organized to satisfy the public's continuing thirst for alcohol. Thirteen years later, the "Noble Experiment," doomed by the impracticality of enforcement, ended with the repeal of the Prohibition Amendment.

*Bootleggers manufactured, transported, and sold illegal alcoholic beverages. Speakeasies were illegal clubs serving alcohol.

The directions make Reading items sound easy: read this and answer the questions. But there's a lot more, as you'll learn. So, the directions aren't very helpful, and you can ignore them from now on.

Most of the passages include an introductory note telling you where the passage comes from. A note may provide some useful information, so read it.

Typically, reading passages discuss an unfamiliar topic. Even if you know something about Prohibition, that information may or may not be helpful since you'll be asked about this particular passage. (Note: Given space restrictions, this passage is much shorter than those used by the ACT.)

This passage is organized chronologically. The first paragraph talks about the "early years of the nineteenth century," in other words, the early 1800s.

The second paragraph starts with 1919. Then, the passage briefly traces the events leading up to Prohibition.

The third paragraph explains why Prohibition failed: people wanted to drink, so bootleggers and illegal clubs satisfied that demand. Eventually, Prohibition was repealed.

The footnote provides two important definitions.

1. The passage is primarily concerned with the:

   A. social problems caused by alcohol abuse.
   B. founding of anti-alcohol temperance societies.
   C. origins of Prohibition and its subsequent failure.
   D. efforts to enforce Prohibition legislation.

This question asks you to identify the main idea of the passage. This is a common type of Reading question. The correct answer is (C).

2. According to the passage, in the early nineteenth century temperance societies originally:

   F. encouraged moderation in alcohol use.
   G. demanded the repeal of the Eighteenth Amendment.
   H. supported efforts to enforce the Volstead Act.
   J. refused to align with religious groups.

This question asks about something that is specifically stated in the passage. The author clearly says that the temperance societies were originally founded to promote temperance as opposed to complete prohibition, so the correct answer is (F).

3. The passage implies that Prohibition failed because:

   A. religious organizations withdrew their support for the program.
   B. the repeal of the Eighteenth Amendment was only experimental.
   C. too many states passed laws prohibiting the sale of alcohol.
   D. widespread demand for alcohol made enforcement impossible.

This question asks you to "read between the lines" of the passage. In the second paragraph, the author does not specifically say why Prohibition failed, but you can figure out from what's said there: people simply refused to quit consuming alcohol, even illegally. The correct answer is (D).

4. In line 15, "concurrent" means:

   F. unsuccessful.
   G. shared.
   H. practicable.
   J. intermittent.

This question asks you for the definition of a term in the context of the passage. The passage states that the federal government and the states were given "concurrent" authority and that the states, as well as the federal government, passed laws against alcohol. So, "concurrent" must mean something like "joint" or "shared," and the correct answer is (G).

PACING

The fact that there are four passages of approximately equal length, each with the same number of questions, and a 35-minute time limit leads naturally to the conclusion that you should spend 8.75 minutes on each passage—and that's a pretty good plan. The following tables summarize the timing for this approach:

40 questions; 35 minutes

First Passage		
Task	**Allotted Time**	**Remaining Time**
Read Passage	2.5 minutes	32.5 minutes
Answer Questions	6.25* minutes	26.25 minutes

Second Passage		
Task	**Allotted Time**	**Remaining Time**
Read Passage	2.5 minutes	23.75 minutes
Answer Questions	6.25* minutes	17.5 minutes

Third Passage		
Task	**Allotted Time**	**Remaining Time**
Read Passage	2.5 minutes	15 minutes
Answer Questions	6.25* minutes	8.75 minutes

Fourth Passage		
Task	**Allotted Time**	**Remaining Time**
Read Passage	2.5 minutes	6.25 minutes
Answer Questions	6.25* minutes	0 minutes

*Approximately 37 seconds per question

NOTE: The tables refer to "First Passage," "Second Passage," etc. These ordinal numbers, however, refer to the order in which you decide to do the passages, not to the order in which they appear in your test booklet. For reasons that we discuss in the Game Plan, below, you might choose to start with the passage that appears last. It's up to you.

GAME PLAN

1. PREVIEW THE READING TEST BEFORE STARTING TO WORK

Last-minute adjustments to the test format are theoretically (but not practically) possible, so check the subject test before you start to work, especially the number of passages, the number of questions, and the time limit.

2. DON'T READ THE DIRECTIONS

Yes, the test-writers always tell you to "read the directions carefully." But they don't tell you that you have to read them during the test. Instead, become familiar with them <u>before</u> test day. That way, you won't waste 30 seconds or more (enough time to answer a question) reading directions.

3. CHOOSE YOUR PASSAGES

Remember that you don't have to do the questions in the order in which they are presented in the booklet. For some sections, like the math section, doing problems in order (more or less) makes good sense. But in Reading, it is a sound strategy to make a choice about the order in which you're going to work through the section. You may decide to do the passages in the order presented, or you may want to change the order.

What factors should you consider? First, you may find a passage that seems familiar to you. Of course, you can't expect that you'll already know the answers to the questions, but familiarity is a definite advantage. Second, you'll feel more comfortable with some topics than with others. Like biology but hate literature? Love social science but hate art? Then do those passages that you like first.

This sets up the following game plan:

1. Choose familiar passages to do first.
2. Otherwise, choose your favorite topics to do first.
3. Repeat for your second favorite.
4. And third.
5. And fourth.

When you choose your passages, you should number them in the margin of your test booklet. Put a big "1" by the passage you'll do first, and so on.

4. READ ANY INTRODUCTORY NOTES

As already indicated on page 146 of this section, most of the passages include an introductory note telling you where the passage comes from and maybe some other information. Sometimes, this information is useful for getting a better understanding of the passage.

5. PREVIEW THE PASSAGE

Before you start reading the passages, take 15 to 30 seconds to preview key sentences. Key sentences are the first and last sentences of the passage and the first sentence of each paragraph. Why preview? First sentences are often topic sentences, so reading a series of topic sentences will tell you what the author is trying to say, and it can give you an outline of the development of the passage. Sometimes, though not always, the last sentence is a conclusion.

To see how this can work, read the following key sentences:

> *At the present time, 98 percent of world energy consumption comes from stored sources such as fossil fuels.*
>
> *Our energy consumption currently amounts to about one-ten thousandth of the energy we receive from the sun.*
>
> *It is often stated that the growth rate will decline or that energy conservation measures will preclude any long-range problem.*
>
> *The only practical means of avoiding the problem of thermal pollution is the use of solar energy.*

To see what you can learn from just a few sentences, think about these questions:

What's the passage about?
- Gas mileage.
- Space exploration.
- Solar energy.

What is a common attitude about energy conservation?
- That it doesn't work.
- That it might work.
- That it will probably work.

What's the author's view on solar energy?
- It doesn't work.
- It's unnecessary.
- It's absolutely essential.

And the answers are that the passage is about solar energy, which the author believes to be necessary, even though a lot of people think conservation could solve all our problems.

6. PREVIEW THE QUESTION STEMS

You <u>may</u> find it helpful to preview the question stems, which are presented either as questions or incomplete statements. If a stem mentions a key word or phrase, make a mental note and look for it as you read the selection. See what you would learn from the stems on the following page.

> *According to the passage, the most important disadvantage of nuclear energy is:*
>
> *According to the author, shifting climate patterns will have all of the following effects EXCEPT:*
>
> *The author's attitude toward scientists who deny that average temperatures are rising can best be described as:*
>
> *Which of the following best describes the main point of the passage?*

Previewing would tell you to look for certain information in your reading.

The first stem uses the phrase "most important disadvantage of nuclear energy." So, you know that the passage will discuss disadvantages of nuclear energy. When you find the "most important" one, mark that reference so that you can answer this question.

The second stem tells you that the author discusses "shifting climate patterns," probably in some detail since the passage mentions multiple effects. Each time you find one of the effects, mark it so that when you answer this question you can eliminate those choices that mention such effects. ("EXCEPT" means that you'll be looking for the one NOT mentioned in the passage.)

The third stem lets you know that the passage discusses average temperatures and a theory advanced by some scientists. If you find that reference in your reading, you'll have the answer to this question.

Finally, the last stem tells you to look for the main idea. That, in and of itself, is not particularly because you're always reading for the main idea—even if you don't get a question that asks about it. So, some stems are not very helpful while others are.

NOTE: Some test-takers don't like this technique. Try it, and use it if you like it. Otherwise, do not preview the question stems.

7. READ THE PASSAGE

- Read the passage quickly but carefully. You'll probably need about 2 to 3 minutes to read a passage. This is about 300 to 350 words a minute.

- Read the passage for important themes. Many of the questions will ask about important themes of the passage, such as the main point, the purpose of a particular paragraph, or the author's intention.

- Do not try to memorize details. If you need detailed information, you can always go back to the passage to find it. This is an "open-book" test.

- Pause at the end to summarize your reading. One of the most helpful reading techniques is to summarize in your own words what you have just read. What is the main point? What did the author do in the first paragraph? In the second paragraph? What did the author prove?

- Read any footnotes. Reading passages sometimes include a footnote. These notes may provide additional information, give examples, or define a key term. Be sure to pay attention to any footnote as it may contain information useful in answering a question.

8. ANSWER THE QUESTIONS

- Identify the question being asked. Test questions fall into one of seven categories such as "Main Idea," "Explicit Detail," and "Vocabulary." Specific item-types have characteristic kinds of answers. If you identify the category first, it will be easier to find the right answer. (You'll spend more time on this point in the Reading Lesson.)

- Answer the question being asked. One of the most common mistakes made by students is to read the question carelessly and then answer the "wrong" question. That is, they respond to what they think they read rather than what is actually there on the page. Since wrong answers often sound plausible, if you make this mistake, you're probably going to find a pretty good answer—to the wrong question!

- Read the answer choices carefully. You'll learn how to recognize the seven Reading item-types and what the correct answer to each should look like. As you review the choices, make sure that you read them carefully. Do this experiment. Estimate how many words are in the passage and then how many are in the answer choices. The answer choices are just about as long as the passage itself. That means reading comprehension doesn't stop at the end of the last sentence of the passage. It continues all the way through to the last word of the last answer choice to the last question.

- Pay attention to thought-reversers. Thought-reversers are words in the question stem like "NOT," "BUT," and "EXCEPT." These words turn the question upside down. What is normally the right answer is now a wrong answer, and what is normally a wrong answer is the right answer.

- Do not spend too much time on any one question. Remember that you get +1 for the hardest question and +1 for the easiest. With Reading items, the easiest ones can theoretically be the last in the group and the hardest ones can be the first. So, if you sense that you're spinning your wheels, make a guess and then move along. You should always guess, even if you are unable to eliminate any answer choices, because there is no penalty for guessing on the ACT. However, your chances improve if you are able to eliminate even one answer choice.

LESSON

The passages and items in this section accompany the Reading Lesson. They demonstrate the Reading skills and concepts that are tested by the ACT, the PLAN, and the EXPLORE. You will work through the items with your instructor in class. Answers are on page 595.

DIRECTIONS: Each passage below is followed by one or more items based on its content. Answer the items on the basis of what is stated or implied in the corresponding passage.

Items #1–15 are based on the following passage.

SOCIAL STUDIES: This passage discusses the presidential election of 1796.

To broaden their voting appeal in the Presidential election of 1796, the Federalists selected Thomas Pinckney, a leading South Carolinian, as running mate for the New Englander John Adams. But Pinckney's
5 Southern friends chose to ignore their party's intentions and regarded Pinckney as a Presidential candidate, creating a political situation that Alexander Hamilton was determined to exploit. Hamilton had long been wary of Adams' stubbornly independent brand of
10 politics and preferred to see his running mate, who was more pliant and over whom Hamilton could exert more control, in the President's chair.

The election was held under the system originally established by the Constitution. At that time, there was
15 but a single tally, with the candidate receiving the largest number of electoral votes declared President and the candidate with the second largest number declared Vice President. Hamilton anticipated that all the Federalists in the North would vote for Adams and
20 Pinckney equally in an attempt to ensure that Jefferson would not be either first or second in the voting. Pinckney would be solidly supported in the South while Adams would not. Hamilton concluded if it were possible to divert a few electoral votes from Adams to
25 Pinckney, Pinckney would receive more than Adams, yet both Federalists would outpoll Jefferson.

Various methods were used to persuade the electors to vote as Hamilton wished. In the press, anonymous articles were published attacking Adams
30 for his monarchical tendencies and Jefferson for being overly democratic, while pushing Pinckney as the only suitable candidate. In private correspondence with state party leaders, the Hamiltonians encouraged the idea that Adams' popularity was slipping, that he could not

35 win the election, and that the Federalists could defeat Jefferson only by supporting Pinckney.

Had sectional pride and loyalty not run as high in New England as in the deep South, Pinckney might well have become Washington's successor. New
40 Englanders, however, realized that equal votes for Adams and Pinckney in their states would defeat Adams; therefore, eighteen electors scratched Pinckney's name from their ballots and deliberately threw away their second votes to men who were not
45 even running. It was fortunate for Adams that they did, for the electors from South Carolina completely abandoned him, giving eight votes to Pinckney and eight to Jefferson.

In the end, Hamilton's interference in Pinckney's
50 candidacy lost him even the Vice Presidency. Without New England's support, Pinckney received only 59 electoral votes, finishing third to Adams and Jefferson. He might have been President in 1797, or as Vice President a serious contender for the Presidency in
55 1800; instead, stigmatized by a plot he had not devised, he served a brief term in the United States Senate and then dropped from sight as a national influence.

1. The main purpose of the passage is to:

   (A) propose reforms of the procedures for electing the President and Vice President.
   (B) condemn Alexander Hamilton for interfering in the election of 1796.
   (C) describe the political events that led to John Adams' victory in the 1796 Presidential election.
   (D) contrast the political philosophy of the Federalists to that of Thomas Jefferson.

2. Which of the following titles best describes the content of the passage?

(F) The Failure of Alexander Hamilton's Plan for Thomas Pinckney to Win the 1796 Presidential Election
(G) The Roots of Alexander Hamilton's Distrust of John Adams and New England's Politics
(H) Important Issues in the 1796 Presidential Campaign as Presented by the Federalist Candidates
(J) The Political Careers of Alexander Hamilton, John Adams, and Thomas Pinckney

3. According to the passage, which of the following was true of the Presidential election of 1796?

(A) Thomas Jefferson received more electoral votes than did Thomas Pinckney.
(B) John Adams received strong support from the electors of South Carolina.
(C) Alexander Hamilton received most of the electoral votes of New England.
(D) Thomas Pinckney was selected by Federalist party leaders to be the party's Presidential candidate.

4. According to the passage, Hamilton's plan included all of the following EXCEPT:

(F) articles published in newspapers to create opposition to John Adams.
(G) South Carolina's loyalty to Thomas Pinckney.
(H) private contact with state officials urging them to support Thomas Pinckney.
(J) John Adams' reputation as a stubborn and independent New Englander.

5. The passage supplies information that answers which of the following questions?

(A) How many electoral votes were cast for John Adams in the 1796 Presidential election?
(B) Under the voting system originally set up by the Constitution, how many votes did each elector cast?
(C) Who was Jefferson's running mate in the 1796 Presidential election?
(D) What became of Alexander Hamilton after his plan to have Thomas Pinckney elected President failed?

6. In line 11, the word "pliant" most nearly means:

(F) assertive.
(G) public.
(H) national.
(J) yielding.

7. Why does the author refer to the election procedure established by the original Constitution?

(A) To prove to the reader that New England as a whole had more electoral votes than the state of South Carolina
(B) To persuade the reader that Thomas Pinckney's defeat could have been avoided
(C) To alert the reader that the procedure used in 1796 was unlike that presently used
(D) To encourage the reader to study Constitutional history

8. The overall development of the passage can best be described as:

(F) refuting possible explanations for certain phenomena.
(G) documenting a thesis with specific examples.
(H) offering an explanation of a series of events.
(J) making particular proposals to solve a problem.

9. The passage implies that some electors voted for John Adams because they were:

    (A) in favor of a monarchy.
    (B) persuaded to do so by Hamilton.
    (C) afraid South Carolina would not vote for Pinckney.
    (D) anxious to have a President from their geographical region.

10. Which of the following can be inferred from the passage?

    (F) Thomas Pinckney had a personal dislike for Jefferson's politics.
    (G) The Federalists regarded themselves as more democratic than Jefferson.
    (H) The Hamiltonians contacted key Southern leaders to persuade them to vote for Adams.
    (J) Electors were likely to vote for candidates from their own geographical region.

11. It can be inferred that had South Carolina not cast any electoral votes for Jefferson, the outcome of the 1796 election would have been a:

    (A) larger margin of victory for John Adams.
    (B) victory for Thomas Jefferson.
    (C) Federalist defeat in the Senate.
    (D) victory for Thomas Pinckney.

12. The electors who scratched Pinckney's name from their ballots behaved most like which of the following people?

    (F) A newspaper publisher who adds a special section to the Sunday edition to review the week's political events
    (G) A member of the clergy who encourages members of other faiths to meet to discuss solutions to the community's problems
    (H) An artist who saves preliminary sketches of an important work even after the work is finally completed
    (J) A general who orders his retreating troops to destroy supplies they must leave behind so the enemy cannot use the supplies

13. Hamilton's strategy can best be summarized as:

    (A) divide and conquer.
    (B) retreat and regroup.
    (C) feint and counterattack.
    (D) hit and run.

14. The tone of the passage can best be described as:

    (F) witty.
    (G) comical.
    (H) scholarly.
    (J) frivolous.

15. The author's attitude toward Hamilton's plan can be described as:

    (A) angry.
    (B) approving.
    (C) analytical.
    (D) regretful.

Items #16–20 are based on the following passage.

SOCIAL STUDIES: This passage is adapted from an essay on citizenship in a social studies textbook.

The liberal view of democratic citizenship that developed in the 17th and 18th centuries was fundamentally different from that of the classical Greeks. The pursuit of private interests with as little
5 interference as possible from government was seen as the road to human happiness and progress rather than the public obligations and involvement in the collective community that were emphasized by the Greeks. Freedom was to be realized by limiting the scope of
10 governmental activity and political obligation and not through immersion in the collective life of the *polis*. The basic role of the citizen was to select governmental leaders and keep the powers and scope of public authority in check. On the liberal view, the rights of
15 citizens against the state were the focus of special emphasis.

Over time, the liberal democratic notion of citizenship developed in two directions. First, there was a movement to increase the proportion of members of
20 society who were eligible to participate as citizens— especially through extending the right of suffrage—and to ensure the basic political equality of all. Second, there was a broadening of the legitimate activities of government and a use of governmental power to redress
25 imbalances in social and economic life. Political citizenship became an instrument through which groups and classes with sufficient numbers of votes could use the state's power to enhance their social and economic well-being.

30 Within the general liberal view of democratic citizenship, tensions have developed over the degree to which government can and should be used as an instrument for promoting happiness and well-being. Political philosopher Martin Diamond has categorized
35 two views of democracy as follows. On the one hand, there is the "libertarian" perspective that stresses the private pursuit of happiness and emphasizes the necessity for restraint on government and protection of individual liberties. On the other hand, there is the
40 "majoritarian" view that emphasizes the "task of the government to uplift and aid the common man against the malefactors of great wealth." The tensions between these two views are very evident today. Taxpayer revolts and calls for smaller government and less
45 government regulation clash with demands for greater government involvement in the economic marketplace and the social sphere.

16. The author's primary purpose is to:

(F) study ancient concepts of citizenship.
(G) contrast different notions of citizenship.
(H) criticize modern libertarian democracy.
(J) describe the importance of universal suffrage.

17. It can be inferred from the passage that the Greek word "*polis*" (line 11) means:

(A) family life.
(B) military service.
(C) marriage.
(D) political community.

18. The author cites Martin Diamond in the last paragraph because the author:

(F) regards Martin Diamond as an authority on political philosophy.
(G) wishes to refute Martin Diamond's views on citizenship.
(H) needs a definition of the term "citizenship."
(J) is unfamiliar with the distinction between libertarian and majoritarian concepts of democracy.

19. According to the passage, all of the following are characteristics that would distinguish the liberal idea of government from the Greek idea of government EXCEPT:

(A) the emphasis on the rights of private citizens.
(B) the activities that government may legitimately pursue.
(C) the obligation of citizens to participate in government.
(D) the size of the geographical area controlled by a government.

20. A majoritarian would be most likely to favor legislation that would:

(F) eliminate all restrictions on individual liberty.
(G) cut spending for social welfare programs.
(H) provide greater protection for consumers.
(J) lower taxes on the wealthy and raise taxes on the average worker.

Items #21–24 are based on the following passage.

SOCIAL STUDIES: This passage is adapted from an article about John Dewey and his theories of education.

The place of public education within a democratic society has been widely discussed and debated through the years. Perhaps no one has written more widely on the subject in the United States than John Dewey,
5 sometimes called "the father of public education," whose theories of education have a large social component; that is, he places an emphasis on education as a social act and the classroom or learning environment as a replica of society.
10 Dewey defined various aspects or characteristics of education. First, it was a necessity of life inasmuch as living beings needed to maintain themselves through a process of renewal. Therefore, just as humans needed sleep, food, water, and shelter for physiological
15 renewal, they also needed education to renew their minds, assuring that their socialization kept pace with physiological growth.

A second aspect of education was its social component, which was to be accomplished by
20 providing the young with an environment that would provide a nurturing atmosphere to encourage the growth of their, as yet, undeveloped social customs.

A third aspect of public education was the provision of direction to youngsters, who might
25 otherwise be left in uncontrolled situations without the steadying and organizing influences of school. Direction was not to be of an overt nature, but rather indirect through the selection of the school situations in which the youngster participated.
30 Finally, Dewey saw public education as a catalyst for growth. Since the young came to school capable of growth, it was the role of education to provide opportunities for that growth to occur. The successful school environment is one in which a desire for
35 continued growth is created—a desire that extends throughout one's life beyond the end of formal education. In Dewey's model, the role of education in a democratic society is not seen as a preparation for some later stage in life, such as adulthood. Rather,
40 education is seen as a process of growth that never ends, with human beings continuously expanding their capacity for growth. Neither did Dewey's model see education as a means by which the past was recapitulated. Instead, education was a continuous
45 reconstruction of experiences, grounded very much in the present environment.

Since Dewey's model places a heavy emphasis on the social component, the nature of the larger society that supports the educational system is of paramount
50 importance. The ideal larger society, according to Dewey, is one in which the interests of a group are all shared by all of its members and in which interactions with other groups are free and full. According to Dewey, education in such a society should provide
55 members of the group a stake or interest in social relationships and the ability to negotiate change without compromising the order and stability of the society.

Thus, Dewey's basic concept of education in a
60 democratic society is based on the notion that education contains a large social component designed to provide direction and assure children's development through their participation in their school group.

21. Which of the following best states the main idea of this passage?

(A) The role of education is extremely complex.
(B) Dewey's notion of education contains a significant social component.
(C) Dewey's model of education is not relevant today.
(D) Direction provided in education must not be overt.

22. The phrase "a continuous reconstruction of experiences" (lines 44–45) used in reference to education means that education is:

(F) based in life experiences.
(G) a never-ending process.
(H) a meaning-based endeavor.
(J) an individual pursuit.

23. The passage implies that:

(A) true education fosters the desire for lifelong learning.
(B) a truly educated person understands physics.
(C) Dewey was a radical philosopher.
(D) education must cease at some point.

24. The tone of this passage can best be described as:

(F) humorous.
(G) serious.
(H) dramatic.
(J) informal.

Items #25–39 are based on the following passage.

SOCIAL STUDIES: This passage is adapted from an article on Aleut language and culture.

The Aleuts, residing on several islands of the Aleutian Chain, the Pribilof Islands, and the Alaskan Peninsula, have possessed a written language since 1825, when the Russian missionary Ivan Veniaminov
5 selected appropriate characters of the Cyrillic alphabet to represent Aleut speech sounds, recorded the main body of Aleut vocabulary, and formulated grammatical rules. The Czarist Russian conquest of the proud, independent sea hunters was so devastatingly thorough
10 that tribal traditions, even tribal memories, were almost obliterated. The slaughter of the majority of an adult generation was sufficient to destroy the continuity of tribal knowledge, which was dependent upon oral transmission. Consequently, the Aleuts developed a
15 fanatical devotion to their language as their only cultural heritage.

The Russian occupation placed a heavy linguistic burden on the Aleuts. Not only were they compelled to learn Russian to converse with their overseers and
20 governors, but they had to learn Old Slavonic to take an active part in church services as well as to master the skill of reading and writing their own tongue. In 1867, when the United States purchased Alaska, the Aleuts were unable to break sharply with their
25 immediate past and substitute English for any one of their three languages.

To communicants of the Russian Orthodox Church, knowledge of Slavonic remained vital, as did Russian, the language in which one conversed with the
30 clergy. The Aleuts came to regard English education as a device to wean them from their religious faith. The introduction of compulsory English schooling caused a minor renaissance of Russian culture as the Aleut parents sought to counteract the influence of the
35 schoolroom. The harsh life of the Russian colonial rule began to appear more happy and beautiful in retrospect.

Regulations forbidding instruction in any language other than English increased its unpopularity. The superficial alphabetical resemblance of Russian
40 and Aleut linked the two tongues so closely that every restriction against teaching Russian was interpreted as an attempt to eradicate the Aleut tongue. From the wording of many regulations, it appears that American administrators often had not the slightest idea that the
45 Aleuts were clandestinely reading and writing in their own tongue or that they even had a written language of their own. To too many officials, anything in Cyrillic letters was Russian and something to be stamped out. Bitterness bred by abuses and the exploitations that the
50 Aleuts suffered from predatory American traders and adventurers kept alive the Aleut resentment against the language spoken by Americans.

Gradually, despite the failure to emancipate the Aleuts from a sterile past by relating the Aleut and
55 English languages more closely, the passage of years has assuaged the bitter misunderstandings and caused an orientation away from Russian toward English as their second language, but Aleut continues to be the language that molds their thought and expression.

25. The author is primarily concerned with describing:

(A) the Aleuts' loyalty to their language and American failure to understand the language.
(B) Russian and American treatment of Alaskan inhabitants both before and after 1867.
(C) how the Czarist Russian occupation of Alaska created a written language for the Aleuts.
(D) American government attempts to persuade the Aleuts to use English as a second language.

26. The author is primarily concerned with:

(F) describing the Aleuts' loyalty to their language and American failure to understand the language.
(G) criticizing Russia and the United States for their mistreatment of the Aleuts.
(H) praising the Russians for creating a written language for the Aleuts.
(J) condemning Russia for its mistreatment of the Aleuts during the Czarist Russian occupation.

27. Which of the following titles best fits the passage?

   (A) Aleut Loyalty to Their Language: An American Misunderstanding
   (B) Failure of Russian and American Policies in Alaska
   (C) Russia's Gift to the Aleuts: A Written Language
   (D) Mistreatment of Aleuts During Russian Occupation

28. According to the passage, which of the following was the most important reason for the Aleuts' devotion to their language?

   (F) Invention of a written version of their language
   (G) Introduction of Old Slavonic for worship
   (H) Disruption of oral transmission of tribal knowledge
   (J) Institution of compulsory English education

29. In line 17, the word "linguistic" infers relation to:

   (A) orthodoxy.
   (B) commerce.
   (C) language.
   (D) laws.

30. In line 33, the word "renaissance" most nearly means:

   (F) resurgence.
   (G) rejection.
   (H) repeal.
   (J) reassessment.

31. In line 45, the word "clandestinely" most nearly means:

   (A) secretly.
   (B) reliably.
   (C) openly.
   (D) casually.

32. In line 54, the word "sterile" most nearly means:

   (F) germ-free.
   (G) unproductive.
   (H) fortunate.
   (J) ill-timed.

33. In line 56, the word "assuaged" most nearly means:

   (A) failed.
   (B) created.
   (C) intensified.
   (D) eased.

34. The passage is developed primarily by:

   (F) testing the evidence supporting a theory.
   (G) describing causes and effects of events.
   (H) weighing the pros and cons of a plan.
   (J) projecting the future consequences of a decision.

35. Why does the author mention that the Russians killed the majority of adult Aleuts?

   (A) To call attention to the immorality of foreign conquest
   (B) To urge Russia to make restitution to the children of those killed
   (C) To stir up outrage against the Russians for committing such atrocities
   (D) To explain the extreme loyalty that Aleuts feel to their language

36. Which of the following statements about the religious beliefs of the Aleuts can be inferred from the passage?

   (F) Prior to the Russian occupation they had no religious beliefs.
   (G) American traders and adventurers forced them to abandon all religious beliefs.
   (H) At no time in their history have the Aleuts had an organized religion.
   (J) The Russians forced Aleuts to become members of the Russian Orthodox Church.

37. The passage implies that:

    (A) the Cyrillic alphabet was invented for the
        Aleut language
    (B) all of the Cyrillic characters were used in
        writing the Aleut language
    (C) Russian and the Aleut language have some
        similar speech sounds
    (D) English is also written using the Cyrillic
        alphabet

38. Distributing which of the following publications
    would be most likely to encourage Aleuts to
    make more use of English?

    (F) Russian translations of English novels
    (G) English translations of Russian novels
    (H) An English-Russian bilingual text devoted to
        important aspects of Aleutian culture
    (J) An Aleut-English bilingual text devoted to
        important aspects of Aleutian culture

39. The author's attitude toward the Aleuts can best
    be described as one of:

    (A) understanding and sympathy
    (B) callousness and indifference
    (C) condemnation and reproof
    (D) ridicule and disparagement

EXTENDED LESSON

The passages and items in this section accompany the Reading Extended Lesson. You will work through the items with your instructor in class. Answers are on page 595.

DIRECTIONS: Each passage below is followed by one or more items based on its content. Answer the items on the basis of what is stated or implied in the corresponding passage.

Items #1–8 are based on the following passage.

NATURAL SCIENCES: This passage is adapted from a science magazine article about galaxies.

Galaxies come in a variety of sizes and shapes: majestic spirals, ruddy disks, elliptically shaped dwarfs and giants, and a menagerie of other, more bizarre forms. Most currently, popular theories suggest that
5 conditions prior to birth—mass of the protogalactic cloud, its size, its rotation—determine whether a galaxy will be large or small, spiral or elliptical; but about ten percent of all galaxies are members of rich clusters of thousands of galaxies. The gravitational forces of fields
10 of nearby galaxies constantly distort galaxies in the crowded central region of rich clusters. In addition, rich clusters of galaxies are pervaded by a tenuous gas with a temperature of up to 100 million degrees. Galaxies are blasted and scoured by a hot wind created by their
15 motion through the gas. In crowded conditions such as these, environment becomes a more important determinant of the size and shape of a galaxy than heredity. In fact, if our galaxy had happened to form well within the core of a cluster such as Virgo, the Sun
20 would probably never have formed, because the Sun, a second- or third-generation star located in the disk of the galaxy, was formed from leftover gas five billion years or so after the initial period of star formation. By that time, in a rich cluster, the galaxy may well have
25 already been stripped of its gas.

As a galaxy moves through the core of a rich cluster, it is not only scoured by hot gas; it encounters other galaxies as well. If the collision is one-on-one at moderate to high speeds of galaxies of approximately
30 the same size, both galaxies will emerge relatively intact, if a little distorted and ragged about the edges. If, however, a galaxy coasts by a much larger one in a slow, grazing collision, the smaller one can be completely disrupted and assimilated by the larger.
35 Under the right conditions, these cosmic cannibals can consume 50 to 100 galaxies. The accumulative

effect of these collisions is to produce a dynamic friction on the large galaxy, slowing it down. As a result, it gradually spirals in toward the center of the
40 cluster. Eventually, the gravitational forces that bind the stars to the infalling galaxy are overwhelmed by the combined gravity of the galaxies in the core of the cluster—just as the ocean is pulled away from the shore at ebb tide by the Moon, the stars are pulled away from
45 their infalling parent galaxy. If there is a large galaxy at the center of the cluster, it may ultimately capture these stars. With the passage of time, many galaxies will be torn asunder in the depths of this gravitational maelstrom and be swallowed up in the ever-expanding
50 envelope of the central cannibal galaxy.

Galactic cannibalism also explains why there are few if any bright galaxies in these clusters other than the central supergiant galaxy. That is because the bright galaxies, which are the most massive, experience the
55 greatest dynamical friction. They are the first to go down to the gravitational well and be swallowed up by the central galaxies.

Over the course of several billion years, 50 or so galaxies may be swallowed up, leaving only the central
60 supergiant and the 51st, the 52nd, etc., brightest galaxies. Given time, all the massive galaxies in the cluster will be absorbed, leaving a sparse cluster of a supergiant galaxy surrounded by clouds of small, dim galaxies.

1. In line 3, the word "menagerie" most nearly means:

   (A) odd mixture.
   (B) open environment.
   (C) uniform collection.
   (D) flat area.

2. It can be inferred from the passage that the physical features of a galaxy that does not belong to a rich cluster are determined primarily by the:

   (F) size and rotation of the protogalactic cloud.
   (G) intensity of light emanating from the galaxy.
   (H) temperature of the interstellar gas.
   (J) age of the protogalactic cloud.

3. The author implies that the currently accepted theories on galaxy formation are:

    (A) completely incorrect and misguided.
    (B) naive and out-of-date.
    (C) speculative and unsupported by observation.
    (D) substantially correct but in need of modification.

4. According to the passage, a cluster with a central, supergiant galaxy will:

    (F) contain no intermediately bright galaxies.
    (G) have 50-100 galaxies of all sizes and intensities.
    (H) consist solely of third- and fourth-generation stars.
    (J) produce only spiral and disk-shaped galaxies.

5. According to the passage, the outcome of a collision between galaxies depends on which of the following?

    (A) The relative velocities of the galaxies
    (B) The relative ages of the galaxies
    (C) The relative sizes of the galaxies
    (D) The relative velocities and sizes of the galaxies

6. According to the passage, as a galaxy falls inward toward the center of a cluster, it:

    (F) collides with the central core and emerges relatively intact.
    (G) absorbs superheated gases from the interstellar medium.
    (H) is broken apart by the gravitational forces of the core.
    (J) is transformed by collisions into a large, spiral galaxy.

7. The passage provides information that will answer which of the following questions?

    (A) What is the age of our sun?
    (B) What proportion of all galaxies are found in clusters?
    (C) Approximately how many galaxies would be found in a rich cluster?
    (D) What type of galaxy is ours?

8. The tone of the passage can best be described as:

    (F) light-hearted and amused.
    (G) objective but concerned.
    (H) detached and unconcerned.
    (J) cautious but sincere.

Items# 9–13 are based on the following passage.

NATURAL SCIENCES: This passage reviews the basic physical chemistry of atoms and radioactive decay.

An atom consists of a nucleus (containing protons and neutrons) surrounded by electrons. Each proton has a positive charge of +1, and each electron has a negative charge of –1. A neutron has no charge. The
5 number of protons in their nuclei determines the identities of the different elements. For example, hydrogen atoms have only one proton, while oxygen atoms have eight protons. The total number of protons in the nucleus is the "atomic number" of that element.
10 The total number of protons and neutrons in the nucleus is the "atomic mass" of the atom. Different atoms of the same element may contain a different number of neutrons, and so have different atomic masses. (But they will have the same number of
15 protons and the same atomic number.) Atoms of the same element with different atomic masses are called isotopes of that element.

Certain elements are radioactive—they emit various types of radiation from their atomic nuclei.
20 Two common types of radiation are alpha particles and beta particles. An alpha particle, which is the equivalent of a helium nucleus, consists of two protons and two neutrons. It is written $_2^4\text{He}$ (the superscript 4 is the mass number of the particle, and the subscript 2 is
25 its atomic number). A beta particle is an electron traveling at high speed. It is written $_{-1}^0\text{e}$. Both types of radiation are emitted at a very high speed and can easily penetrate other substances.

When atoms of a substance emit radiation, they
30 are said to undergo radioactive decay. The result is a different element with a different atomic number and a different mass number. For example, when a radium atom emits an alpha particle, it decays into an atom of radon. This reaction is shown in the following
35 equation:

$$_{88}^{226}\text{Ra} \rightarrow {}_2^4\text{He} + {}_{86}^{222}\text{Rn}$$

Note that the equation is balanced. That is, the atomic number of the original atom on the left side of the equation equals the sum of the atomic numbers of the
40 products on the right side of the equation. Similarly, the mass number of the original atom equals the sum of the mass numbers of the products. Every nuclear reaction balances in this same manner.

Some types of nuclear radiation take place very
45 slowly; other types are very rapid. The rate of radiation is measured in half-lives. A half-life is the time required for one-half the amount of a given radioactive substance to decay.

9. As radium emits alpha particles, the mass of radium will:

   (A) increase.
   (B) decrease.
   (C) stay the same.
   (D) either increase or decrease, depending on the conditions.

10. In nuclear chemistry notation, two isotopes, or forms, of cobalt are written $_{27}^{59}\text{Co}$ and $_{27}^{60}\text{Co}$. The difference between the two isotopes is:

    (F) an alpha particle.
    (G) a beta particle.
    (H) a proton.
    (J) a neutron.

11. An alpha particle has:

    (A) no electric charge.
    (B) a positive electric charge.
    (C) a negative electric charge.
    (D) a variable electric charge.

12. A beta particle has:

    (F) no electric charge.
    (G) a positive electric charge.
    (H) a negative electric charge.
    (J) a variable electric charge.

13. When an atom emits a beta particle, the atomic mass number will:

    (A) increase.
    (B) decrease.
    (C) stay the same.
    (D) either increase or decrease, depending on the conditions.

Items #14–23 are based on the following passage.

NATURAL SCIENCES: This passage discusses the development of basic inheritance theories and the role of DNA in genetic mutation processes.

In 1866, Gregor Mendel published the results of his studies on the breeding of different races of pea plants. Through his experiments, Mendel discovered a pattern of inheritance and subsequently developed the
5 concept of a "unit of inheritance."

Mendel started with a pure stock of pea plants that had recognizably different characteristics. He artificially cross-pollinated the different races of plants and noted the characteristics of the different offspring
10 over several generations. Mendel concluded that a pair of discrete "factors" governed each trait and that they segregated upon the formation of the gametes. This pair of factors is now known as the maternally and paternally derived alleles on homologous chromosomes
15 that first come together at fertilization and later segregate during meiosis.

Subsequent studies have shown that new genes could appear as mutations of existing genes and that crossing over and recombination could redistribute
20 maternal and paternal characteristics. Genes can occur in a linear sequence, and groups of genes that segregate together are called "linkage groups." The chromosome is the carrier of the linear array of genes and the physical basis of the linkage groups.

25 It was originally thought that proteins were the genetic carrier. In contrast to nucleic acids, proteins were known to mediate complex reactions and to be composed of a variety of different building blocks. There are approximately 20 different amino acids in a
30 protein, but only 4 different nucleotides in a nucleic acid molecule. It was not until 1944 that Avery *et al.* noted that deoxyribonucleic acid (DNA) was the genetic carrier, not protein. Avery and his co-workers conducted experiments on the transformation in
35 pneumococcus. Two strains of the bacteria had been isolated: one produced colonies having a smooth (S) appearance and was able to cause pneumonia in a suitable host; the other grew into rough (R) colonies because of a defect in its capsule and was non-virulent.
40 When a cell-free extract of the S bacteria was added to the medium in which the R strain was growing, a few of the R bacteria grew into smooth colonies and were virulent. They had become transformed. From the time of transformation, the progeny of that cell continued to
45 have the properties of the S strain. The transformation was a stable genetic change. Avery and his co-workers purified the contents of cells in detergent after their

disruption and found that among the contents of the cells, only the purified DNA was capable of causing
50 the transformation. As a result of these and future experiments, it was determined that in order for transformation to occur, DNA fragments entered the recipient cell intact and substituted in the bacterial chromosome for the original DNA, which was
55 eliminated. This process resulted in the creation of a genetically different microorganism.

DNA is a very long, fibrous molecule with a backbone composed of alternate sugar and phosphate groups joined by 3'-5'-phosphodiester linkages.
60 Attached to each sugar is one of four possible nitrogenous bases. There are two types of bases: the pyrimidines, cytosine (C) and thymine (T); and the purines, adenine (A) and guanine (G). The amount of purine equals the amount of pyrimidine, and, more
65 specifically, the amount of adenine equals the amount of thymine, and the amount of guanine equals the amount of cytosine.

In 1953, Watson and Crick proposed that DNA was made of two chains of nucleotides coiled around a
70 common axis, with the sugar-phosphate backbone on the outside and the bases pointing in toward the axis, and that the two chains were held together by hydrogen bonds. The hydrogen bonds occur between each base of one chain and an associated base on the other chain.
75 Based on the 20-angstrom width of the fiber, a pyrimidine from one chain is always paired with a purine from the other chain. Adenine is the only purine capable of bonding to thymine and guanine is the only purine capable of bonding to cytosine.

80 Watson and Crick proposed that the information in DNA was coded for by the linear sequence of the base pairs. They theorized that a mutation could be accounted for by a chance mistake in the formation of the sequence during duplication. Another major aspect
85 of the Watson and Crick model was the proposed complementarity between hydrogen-bonded nucleotides. For example, adenine is complementary to thymine, AGC is complementary to TCG, and one chain is complementary to the other. If the base
90 sequence of one chain is known, then the base sequence of the complementary chain can be derived. The concept of complementarity of nucleic acids in DNA and RNA chains is the basis of most research in which these classes of molecules are involved.

14. Mendel conducted his studies using the method known as:

   (F) cloning.
   (G) genetic mapping.
   (H) cross-pollination.
   (J) transformation.

15. Mendel's findings were important because they indicated that:

   I. DNA fragments can replace original DNA.
   II. specific units, handed down from one generation to the next, govern traits in organisms.
   III. proteins are composed of approximately 20 different amino acids.

   (A) I only
   (B) II only
   (C) I and III only
   (D) I, II, and III

16. Contrary to earlier beliefs, Avery *et al.* discovered that:

   (F) there are only four nucleotides in DNA.
   (G) pneumonia can be passed from host to host.
   (H) genes can mutate.
   (J) DNA, not protein, carries genetic information.

17. If you witnessed R strain pneumococcus infected with S extract and saw a few R strain pneumococcus transformed to S strain, you would expect:

   (A) the remaining R strain pneumococcus to transform later.
   (B) only the new S strain cells to survive.
   (C) offspring of those transformed cells to be S strain as well.
   (D) a few S strain pneumococcus to transform to R strain.

18. The author uses the word "non-virulent" (line 39) to mean:

   (F) harmless.
   (G) toxic.
   (H) bacterial.
   (J) sweet.

19. In contrast to the paragraphs before, the fifth paragraph is intended primarily to:

   (A) give historical genetic research information .
   (B) describe the results of Mendel's experiments.
   (C) speculate on the future of genetic research.
   (D) provide a definition for an essential element in genetic research.

20. A chain of DNA with the pattern CAG would bond with a chain with the pattern:

   (F) GAC.
   (G) TGA.
   (H) GTC.
   (J) Cannot be determined from the given information

21. Which of the following is (are) classified as a purine?

   I. cytosine
   II. guanine
   III. thymine

   (A) I only
   (B) II only
   (C) III only
   (D) I and II only

22. Watson and Crick's contribution to the study of genetics was:

   I. information about the transfer of genes across membranes.
   II. the notion that pairs of genes could work together.
   III. a suggestion about the structure of DNA.

   (F) I only
   (G) II only
   (H) III only
   (J) I, II, and III

23. The concept of complementarity in DNA is apparently important because:

(A) it contradicts the notion that proteins are the basis for genetic transformation.
(B) hydrogen bonds connect the nucleotides.
(C) if maternally and paternally derived alleles were not complementary, life could not exist.
(D) if you know one chain's sequence, you can determine that of the other.

Items #24–30 are based on to the following passage.

SOCIAL STUDIES: This passage is adapted from a policy article about attempts to change the healthcare system.

Considerable advances have been made in healthcare services since World War II. These include better access to healthcare (particularly for the poor and minorities), improvements in physical plants, and
5 increased numbers of physicians and other health personnel. All have played a part in the recent improvement in life expectancy. But there is mounting criticism of the large remaining gaps in access, unbridled cost inflation, the further fragmentation of
10 service, excessive indulgence in wasteful high-technology "gadgeteering," and breakdowns in doctor-patient relationships. In recent years, proposed panaceas and new programs, small and large, have proliferated at a feverish pace and disappointments have multiplied at
15 almost the same rate. This has led to an increased pessimism—"everything has been tried and nothing works"—that sometimes borders on cynicism or even nihilism.

It is true that the automatic "pass through" of
20 rapidly spiraling costs to government and insurance carriers produced for a time a sense of unlimited resources and allowed a mood to develop whereby every practitioner and institution could "do his own thing" without undue concern for the "Medical
25 Commons." The practice of full-cost reimbursement encouraged capital investment and now the industry is overcapitalized. Many cities have hundreds of excess hospital beds; hospitals have proliferated a superabundance of high-technology equipment; and
30 structural ostentation and luxury were the order of the day. In any given day, one-fourth of all community beds are vacant; expensive equipment is underused or, worse, used unnecessarily. Capital investment brings rapidly rising operating costs.
35 Yet, in part, this pessimism derives from expecting too much of healthcare. Care is often a painful experience accompanied by fear and unwelcome results; although there is room for improvement, it will always retain some unpleasantness
40 and frustration. Moreover, the capacities of medical science are limited. Humpty Dumpty cannot always be put back together again. Too many physicians are reluctant to admit their limitations to patients; too many patients and families are unwilling to accept such
45 realities. Nor is it true that everything has been tried and nothing works, as shown by the prepaid group practice plans at the Kaiser Foundation and Puget Sound.

However, typically such undertakings have been drowned by a veritable flood of public and private
50 moneys that have supported and encouraged the continuation of conventional practices and subsidized their shortcomings on a massive, almost unrestricted scale. Except for the most idealistic and dedicated, there were no incentives to seek change or to practice self-
55 restraint or frugality. In this atmosphere, it is not fair to condemn as failures all attempted experiments; it may be more accurate to say that many never had a fair trial.

24. In line 14, the word "feverish" most nearly means:

(F) diseased.
(G) rapid.
(H) controlled.
(J) timed.

25. According to author, the "pessimism" mentioned in line 35 is partly attributable to the fact that:

(A) there has been little real improvement in healthcare services.
(B) expectations about healthcare services are sometimes unrealistic.
(C) large segments of the population find it impossible to get access to healthcare services.
(D) advances in technology have made healthcare service unaffordable.

26. The author cites the prepaid plans (lines 46–47) as:

(F) counterexamples to the claim that nothing has worked.
(G) examples of healthcare plans that were overfunded.
(H) evidence that healthcare services are fragmented.
(J) proof of the theory that no plan has been successful.

27. It can be inferred that the sentence "Humpty Dumpty cannot always be put back together again" means that:

    (A) the cost of healthcare services will not decline.
    (B) some people should not become doctors.
    (C) medical care is not really essential to good health.
    (D) medical science cannot cure every ill.

28. With which of the following descriptions of the system for the delivery of healthcare services would the author most likely agree?

    (F) It is biased in favor of doctors and against patients.
    (G) It is highly fragmented and completely ineffective.
    (H) It has not embraced new technology rapidly enough.
    (J) It is generally effective but can be improved.

29. Which of the following best describes the logical structure of the selection?

    (A) The third paragraph is intended as a refutation of the first and second paragraphs.
    (B) The second and third paragraphs are intended as a refutation of the first paragraph.
    (C) The second and third paragraphs explain and put into perspective the points made in the first paragraph.
    (D) The first paragraph describes a problem, and the second and third paragraphs present two horns of a dilemma.

30. The author's primary concern is to:

    (F) criticize physicians and healthcare administrators for investing in technologically advanced equipment.
    (G) examine some problems affecting delivery of healthcare services and assess the severity of those problems.
    (H) defend the medical community from charges that healthcare has not improved since World War II.
    (J) analyze the reasons for the healthcare industry's inability to provide quality care to all segments of the population.

Items #31–35 are based on to the following passage.

SOCIAL STUDIES: This passage discusses the contest over the vice presidency in the 1792 election.

In 1792, there was no contest for the presidency. George Washington received the unanimous vote of the electors, Federalist and Republican alike. But the struggle over the vice presidency hinted at the
5 rekindling of old divisions and antagonisms sparked by Alexander Hamilton's system. Southern planters who in 1789 had been ready, in fact eager, to cooperate with the monied men of the North, parted with them when they realized that the policies designed to benefit
10 Northern merchants and bankers brought no profit to them as landed aristocrats. Even more, they saw themselves paying for a system that contributed to another section's prosperity. Although in 1792 they were willing to continue with Washington, they were
15 not as willing to go along with Vice President John Adams, who represented the commerce, shipbuilding, fisheries, and banking institutions of New England and the North. If the Federalists were to have the first office, then the followers of Jefferson—who had
20 already come to call themselves Republicans in contradistinction to the unpopular term anti-Federalist, insisted that they were to command the second office.

Appealing to the shopkeepers, artisans, laboring men, and farmers of the North based on their sympathy
25 with the French Revolution, and to the Southern planters with their agrarian bias, the Republicans waged a gallant but losing campaign for the second office. However, the campaign served notice to the overconfident Federalists that when the Republicans
30 became better organized nationally, they would have to be more seriously considered. This did not take long. In 1793, England went so far as to declare war with republican France over the guillotining of Louis XVI, and in 1794, John Jay's treaty terminating the United
35 States' difficulties with Britain seemed to suggest a sympathetic policy toward monarchical and conservative England, instead of republican, liberty-loving France. The treaty intensified party spirit and gave the Republicans a sense of mission that
40 legitimized their existence. The contest was now between the Republican "lovers of liberty" and the Monocrats.

31. Which of the following titles best describes the content of the passage?

(A) The Origins of Jefferson's Republican Party
(B) Jefferson's Defeat in the 1792 Election
(C) The Legacy of Hamilton's Political System
(D) Political Differences Between the Rich and the Poor

32. According to the passage, all of the following are true of the Republicans EXCEPT:

(F) they opposed the monied interests of the North.
(G) they were led by Thomas Jefferson.
(H) they disapproved of the French Revolution.
(J) they and the Federalists supported the same candidate for president in 1792.

33. It can be inferred from the passage that the term "Monocrats" (line 42) was:

(A) used by John Jay in his treaty to refer to France's King Louis XVI.
(B) invented by the Federalists to refer to the aristocratic landowners of the South.
(C) coined by the Republicans to disparage the Federalists' support of England.
(D) employed by Republicans to describe their leader, Thomas Jefferson.

34. The passage implies that Thomas Jefferson was unsuccessful in his 1792 bid for the vice presidency because the Republican Party:

(F) did not have a presidential candidate.
(G) was not as well organized as the Federalists.
(H) refused to support John Adams.
(J) appealed to workers in the North.

35. The tone of the passage can best be described as:

(A) enthusiastic and impassioned.
(B) scholarly and neutral.
(C) opinionated and dogmatic.
(D) argumentative and categorical.

Items #36–44 are based on to the following passage.

SOCIAL STUDIES: This passage is adapted from the speech "Is it a Crime for a Citizen of the United States to Vote?" by Susan B. Anthony.

Friends and fellow citizens: I stand before you tonight under indictment for the alleged crime of having voted at the last presidential election without having a lawful right to vote. It shall be my work this
5 evening to prove to you that in thus voting, I not only committed no crime, but, instead, simply exercised *my citizen's rights*, guaranteed to me and all United States citizens by the National Constitution, beyond the power of any State to deny. The preamble of the
10 Federal Constitution says: "We, the people of the United States, in order to form a more perfect union, establish justice, insure *domestic* tranquility, provide for the common defense, promote the general welfare, and secure the blessings of liberty to ourselves and our
15 posterity, do ordain and establish this Constitution for the United States of America."

It was we, the people, not we, the white male citizens; but we, the whole people, who formed the Union. And we formed it, not to give the blessings of
20 liberty, but to secure them; not to the half of ourselves and the half of our posterity but to the whole people—women as well as men. And it is a downright mockery to talk to women of their enjoyment of the blessings of liberty while they are denied the use of the only means
25 of securing them provided by this democratic-republican government—the ballot.

For any State to make sex a qualification that must ever result in the disfranchisement of one entire half of the people is a violation of the supreme law of
30 the land. By it the blessings of liberty are forever withheld from women and their female posterity. To them this government has no just powers derived from the consent of the governed. To them this government is not a democracy. It is not a republic. It is a hateful
35 oligarchy of sex. An oligarchy of learning, where the educated govern the ignorant, might be endured; but this oligarchy of sex, which makes father, brothers, husband, sons, the oligarchs or rulers over the mother and sisters, the wife and daughters of every
40 household—which ordains all men sovereigns, all women subjects, carries dissension, discord and rebellion into every home of the nation.

Webster's Dictionary defines a citizen as a person in the United States, entitled to vote and hold office.
45 The only question left to be settled now is, Are women persons? And I hardly believe any of our opponents will have the hardihood to say we are not.

Being persons, then, women are citizens; and no State has a right to make any law, or to enforce any old law,
50 that shall abridge their privileges or immunities. Hence, every discrimination against women in the constitutions and laws of the several States is today null and void.

36. The nineteenth-century feminist leader Susan B. Anthony fought long and hard to guarantee women the right to vote. In this speech, she talks as if she were a:

   (F) defendant on trial.
   (G) chairperson of a committee.
   (H) legislator arguing for a new law.
   (J) judge ruling at a trial.

37. Anthony broadens her appeal to her audience by showing how her case could affect all:

   (A) existing laws.
   (B) United States citizens.
   (C) women.
   (D) uneducated persons.

38. Anthony quotes the preamble to the Constitution (lines 10–16) in order to:

   (F) impress the audience with her intelligence.
   (G) utilize a common legalistic trick.
   (H) point out which part of the preamble needs to be changed.
   (J) add force to her argument.

39. According to Anthony, who formed the Union?

   (A) Only one-half of the people
   (B) The whole people
   (C) White male citizens only
   (D) White female citizens

40. When Anthony says that the blessings of liberty are forever withheld from women and their female posterity, she means that:

    (F) all classes of women are discriminated against.
    (G) women of the past have been victimized.
    (H) female children of the poor will be the only ones affected.
    (J) women of the present and the future will suffer.

41. Anthony argues that a government that denies women the right to vote is not a democracy because its powers do not come from:

    (A) the Constitution of the United States.
    (B) the rights of the states.
    (C) the consent of the governed.
    (D) the vote of the majority.

42. According to this speech, an "oligarchy of sex" would cause:

    (F) women to rebel against the government.
    (G) men to desert their families.
    (H) problems to develop in every home.
    (J) the educated to rule the ignorant.

43. In this speech, a citizen is defined as a person who has the right to vote and also the right to:

    (A) acquire wealth.
    (B) speak publicly.
    (C) hold office.
    (D) pay taxes.

44. Anthony argues that state laws that discriminate against women are:

    (F) being changed.
    (G) null and void.
    (H) helpful to the rich.
    (J) supported by the Constitution.

Items #45–53 are based on the following passage.

HUMANITIES: This passage is adapted from an article that discusses literary genre.

When we speak casually, we call *Nineteen Eighty-Four* a novel, but to be more exact we should call it a political fable. This requirement is not refuted by the fact that the book is preoccupied with an individual,
5   Winston Smith, who suffers from a varicose ulcer, or by the fact that it takes account of other individuals, including Julia, Mr. Charrington, Mrs. Parsons, Syme, and O'Brien. The figures claim our attention, but they exist mainly in their relation to the political system that
10 determines them. It would indeed be possible to think of them as figures in a novel, though in that case they would have to be imagined in a far more diverse set of relations. They would no longer inhabit or sustain a fable, because a fable is a narrative relieved of much
15 contingent detail so that it may stand forth in an unusual degree of clarity and simplicity. A fable is a structure of types, each of them deliberately simplified lest a sense of difference and heterogeneity reduce the force of the typical. Let us say, then, that *Nineteen Eighty-Four* is a
20 political fable, projected into a near future and incorporating historical references mainly to document a canceled past.

Since a fable is predicated upon a typology, it must be written from a certain distance. The author
25 cannot afford the sense of familiarity that is induced by detail and differentiation. A fable, in this respect, asks to be compared to a caricature, not to a photograph. It follows that in a political fable there is bound to be some tension between a political sense dealing in the
30 multiplicity of social and personal life, and a fable sense committed to simplicity of form and feature. If the political sense were to prevail, the narrative would be drawn away from fable into the novel, at some cost to its simplicity. If the sense of fable were to prevail, the
35 fabulist would station himself at such a distance from any imaginary conditions in the case that his narrative would appear unmediated, free or bereft of conditions. The risk would be considerable: a reader might feel that the fabulist has lost interest in the variety of human life
40 and fallen back upon an unconditioned sense of its types, that he has become less interested in lives than in a particular idea of life. The risk is greater still if the fabulist projects his narrative into the future: The reader cannot question by appealing to life conditions already
45 known. He is asked to believe that the future is another country and that "they just do things differently there."

In a powerful fable, the reader's feeling is likely to be mostly fear: He is afraid that the fabulist's vision of any life that could arise may be accurate. The fabulist's
50 feeling may be more various. A fable such as *Nineteen Eighty-Four* might arise from disgust, despair, or world-weariness induced by evidence that nothing, despite one's best efforts, has changed and that it is too late now to hope for the change one wants.

45. In line 15, the word "contingent" most nearly means:

(A) dependent.
(B) essential.
(C) boring.
(D) unnecessary.

46. In drawing an analogy between a fable and a caricature (lines 26–27), the author would most likely regard which of the following pairs of ideas as also analogous?

(F) The subject of a caricature and the topic of a fable
(G) The subject of a caricature and the main character in *Nineteen Eighty-Four*
(H) The subject of a fable and the artist who draws the caricature
(J) The artist who draws the caricature and a novelist

47. Which of the following would be the most appropriate title for the passage?

(A) A Critical Study of the Use of Characters in *Nineteen Eighty-Four*
(B) *Nineteen Eighty-Four*: Political Fable Rather Than Novel
(C) *Nineteen Eighty-Four*: Reflections on the Relationship of the Individual to Society
(D) The Use of Typology in the Literature of Political Fables

48. According to the passage, which of the following are characteristics of a political fable?

    (F) It is widely popular at its time of development.
    (G) The reader is unlikely to experience fear as his reaction to the political situation described.
    (H) Its time frame must treat events that occur at some point in the future.
    (J) Its characters are defined primarily by their relationship to the social order.

49. Which of the following best explains why the author mentions that Winston Smith suffers from a varicose ulcer?

    (A) To demonstrate that a political fable must emphasize type over detail
    (B) To show that Winston Smith has some characteristics that distinguish him as an individual
    (C) To argue that Winston Smith is no more important than any other character in *Nineteen Eighty-Four*
    (D) To illustrate one of the features of the political situation described in *Nineteen Eighty-Four*

50. The "tension" that the author mentions in line 29 refers to the:

    (F) necessity of striking a balance between the need to describe a political situation in simple terms and the need to make the description realistic.
    (G) reaction the reader feels because he is drawn to the characters of the fable as individuals but repulsed by the political situation.
    (H) delicate task faced by a literary critic who must interpret the text of a work while attempting to describe accurately the intentions of the author.
    (J) danger that too realistic a description of a key character will make the reader feel that the fable is actually a description of his own situation.

51. The author's attitude toward *Nineteen Eighty-Four* can best be described as:

    (A) condescending.
    (B) laudatory.
    (C) disparaging.
    (D) scholarly.

52. The author uses the phrase "another country" to describe a political fable in which:

    (F) political events described in a fable occur in a place other than the country of national origin of the author.
    (G) a lack of detail makes it difficult for a reader to see the connection between his own situation and the one described in the book.
    (H) too many minor characters create the impression of complete disorganization, leading the reader to believe he is in a foreign country.
    (J) the author has allowed his personal political convictions to infect his description of the political situation.

53. The author's primary concern is to:

    (A) define and clarify a concept.
    (B) point out a logical inconsistency.
    (C) trace the connection between a cause and an effect.
    (D) illustrate a general statement with examples.

Items #54–58 are based on the following passage.

HUMANITIES: This passage discusses the impact of Southwestern environment and culture on twentieth century artists.

Georgia O'Keeffe, whose death at age 98 closed one of the most fertile chapters of American artistic creativity, flourished as a maverick in her life and work. While other painters spent a season or two in the
5 country trying to come to terms with the scenes and settings of the Southwest, O'Keeffe stayed a lifetime. When the canvases of other artists working in the region faded from view, and then were neglected in the chronicle of American visual history, her stylized
10 images, skeletal, floral, and geological motifs made an indelible impression on countless eyes.
Between 1900 and 1945, the region now called New Mexico both fascinated and perplexed two generations of American artists—luminaries such as
15 Stuart Davis, Marsden Hartley, and John Sloan, whose reputations were built largely on depictions of gritty, modern life in Eastern urban centers. Despite successes, many of these artists wearied of the industrial world of the East. The vast expanse of the
20 American West offered a promise for inspiration. It was an ancient yet new world to their eyes—an enchanted land far removed from urban conventions.
For these artists, life and art, so separate in New York and Paris, seemed inextricably bound in
25 Southwestern cultures. Painters of every persuasion were convinced that sampling this mysterious phenomenon would strengthen and enrich their own work. Most were touched by what D.H. Lawrence called the "spirit of the place." Besides the scenic
30 possibilities bathed in clear golden light, the rich traditions of New Mexico's Native American and Latino people—their dress, crafts, adobe pueblos, plaza life, rituals, and simple dignity—became frequent subjects of the artists who traveled to Taos and Santa
35 Fe.
Some of the artists were traditionalists—local color realists; some were modernists—like O'Keeffe, avant-garde painters of the abstract. Their varied talents coupled with the attractions of the land gave
40 New Mexico's art centers a status unrivaled among other American summer colonies and contributed to their heyday in the early twentieth century.

54. This passage deals primarily with:

(F) the life of Georgia O'Keeffe.
(G) the major trends of American modern art.
(H) the mystery and spirit of the Southwest.
(J) artists in the American Southwest.

55. The author implies that the Southwest attracted artists for all of the following reasons EXCEPT:

(A) the quality of life was different from that of large urban centers.
(B) the inhabitants and culture provided interesting subject matter.
(C) New Mexico was the only state to support young, avant-garde painters.
(D) the region offered unusual geological features and landscapes.

56. The author implies that most of the artists who painted in the Southwest:

(F) originally studied in Paris.
(G) lived there only temporarily.
(H) painted only landscapes.
(J) received considerable recognition.

57. The author mentions which of the following facts about Georgia O'Keeffe?

   I. She resided permanently in the South-west.
  II. She enjoyed considerable and lasting fame.
 III. She created modern, abstract paintings.

(A) I only
(B) II only
(C) I and III only
(D) I, II, and III

58. Stuart Davis, Marsden Hartley, and John Sloan were painters who painted mainly in:

(F) Paris.
(G) New Mexico.
(H) cities in the Eastern United States.
(J) Rome.

Items #59–66 are based on the following passage.

HUMANITIES: This passage is adapted from an essay by Oliver Goldsmith that appeared in *The Citizen of the World*.

Were we to estimate the learning of the English by the number of books that are every day published among them, perhaps no country, not even China itself, could equal them in this particular. I have reckoned not
5 less than twenty-three new books published in one day, which, upon computation, makes eight thousand three hundred and ninety-five in one year. Most of these are not confined to one single science, but embrace the whole circle. History, politics, poetry, mathematics,
10 metaphysics, and the philosophy of nature are all comprised in a manual not larger than that in which our children are taught the letters. If then, we suppose the learned of England to read but an eighth part of the works which daily come from the press (and surely
15 none can pretend to learning upon less easy terms), at this rate every scholar will read a thousand books in one year. From such a calculation, you may conjecture what an amazing fund of literature a man must be possessed of, who thus reads three new books every
20 day, not one of which but contains all the good things that ever were said or written.

And yet I know not how it happens, but the English are not, in reality, so learned as would seem from this calculation. We meet but few who know all
25 arts and sciences to perfection; whether it is that the generality are incapable of such extensive knowledge, or that the authors of those books are not adequate instructors. In China, the Emperor himself takes cognizance of all the doctors in the kingdom who
30 profess authorship. In England, every man may be an author that can write; for they have by law a liberty, not only of saying what they please, but also of being as dull as they please.

Yesterday, I testified my surprise, to the man in
35 black, where writers could be found in sufficient number to throw off the books I daily saw crowding from the press. I at first imagined that their learned seminaries might take this method of instructing the world. But, to obviate this objection, my companion
40 assured me that the doctors of colleges never wrote, and that some of them had actually forgotten their reading. "But if you desire," continued he, "to see a collection of authors, I fancy I can introduce you to a club, which assembles every Saturday at seven...." I
45 accepted his invitation; we walked together, and entered the house some time before the usual hour for the company assembling.

My friend took this opportunity of letting me into the characters of the principal members of the club....
50 "The first person," said he, "of our society is Doctor Nonentity, a metaphysician. Most people think him a profound scholar, but, as he seldom speaks, I cannot be positive in that particular; he generally spreads himself before the fire, sucks his pipe, talks
55 little, drinks much, and is reckoned very good company. I'm told he writes indexes to perfection: he makes essays on the origin of evil, philosophical inquiries upon any subject, and draws up an answer to any book upon 24 hours' warning...."

59. Goldsmith's disdainful attitude toward English authors is best explicated in:

(A) lines 1–4.
(B) lines 12–17.
(C) lines 30–33.
(D) lines 42–44.

60. Goldsmith believes that:

(F) we can tell how knowledgeable English authors are by counting the number of books they publish.
(G) the number of books published in England is not up to standards set in China.
(H) the number of books published in England says nothing about English scholarship.
(J) every English scholar reads a thousand books a year.

61. Why does Goldsmith calculate the number of books published in England?

(A) To impress his readers with English erudition
(B) To make the point that anyone can be an author
(C) As defense for his argument that England is better than China
(D) As a comparison with publication quotas in other lands

62. The tone of the second paragraph may best be described as:

    (F) self-satisfied.
    (G) awestruck.
    (H) affectionate.
    (J) sardonic.

63. Goldsmith first assumes that English writers come from:

    (A) foreign lands.
    (B) seminaries.
    (C) China.
    (D) clubs.

64. The word "obviate" (line 39) means:

    (F) clarify.
    (G) obscure.
    (H) turn.
    (J) negate.

65. Goldsmith's opinion of the first member of the club is illuminated by which of the following?

    I.   His conversation with the character
    II. The given name for the character
    III. His friend's description of the character

    (A) I only
    (B) II only
    (C) I and III only
    (D) II and III only

66. One of Goldsmith's major objections to English authors is to their:

    (F) deficiency in language skills.
    (G) inclination to drink.
    (H) tendency to write about everything at once.
    (J) inability to retain information.

Items #67–71 are based on the following passage.

PROSE FICTION: This passage is adapted from Nathaniel Hawthorne's *The House of the Seven Gables*.

It still lacked a half hour of sunrise when Miss Hepzibah—we will say awoke, it being doubtful whether the poor old lady had so much as closed her eyes during the brief night of midsummer—but, at all
5 events, arose from her solitary pillow, and began the adornment of her person. She was alone in the old house—quite a house by itself, indeed—with locks, bolts, and oaken bars on all the intervening doors. Inaudible, consequently, were poor Miss Hepzibah's
10 gusty sighs, inaudible the creaking joints of her stiffened knees, as she knelt down by the bedside. And inaudible too, by mortal ear, that almost agony of prayer—now whispered, now a groan, now a struggling silence—wherewith she sought the Divine assistance
15 through the day! Evidently this is to be the day of more than ordinary trial to Miss Hepzibah, who for above a quarter of a century gone by has dwelt in strict seclusion, taking no part in the business of life, and just as little in its intercourse and pleasures.
20 Here comes Miss Hepzibah. Forth she steps into the dusky, time-darkened passage a tall figure, clad in black silk, with a long and shrunken waist, feeling her way towards the stair like a nearsighted person, which in truth she is.
25 Her scowl—as the world persisted in calling it— her scowl had done Miss Hepzibah every ill office, in establishing her character as an ill-tempered old maid; nor does it appear improbable that, by often gazing at herself in a dim looking glass, and perpetually
30 encountering her own frown within its ghostly sphere, she had been led to interpret the expression almost unjustly as the world did. But her heart never frowned.

67. According to the passage, Miss Hepzibah is all of the following EXCEPT:

(A) elderly.
(B) reclusive.
(C) religious.
(D) vain.

68. The author's portrait of Miss Hepzibah is:

(F) critical and disparaging.
(G) loving and intimate.
(H) sarcastic and mocking.
(J) interested and sympathetic.

69. It can be inferred that Miss Hepzibah views the day's coming events with:

(A) apprehension.
(B) confidence.
(C) eagerness.
(D) boredom.

70. Which of the following correctly describes the scene as set by the passage?

    I. The season is summer.
    II. The weather is threatening.
    III. The time is morning.

(F) I only
(G) III only
(H) I and II only
(J) I and III only

71. In the last paragraph, the author implies that Miss Hepzibah is:

(A) old and wicked.
(B) affable and outgoing.
(C) good-hearted but misunderstood.
(D) sincere but blasphemous.

Items #72–81 are based on the following passage.

PROSE FICTION: This passage is adapted from the short story "Mrs. Gay's Prescription" by Louisa May Alcott.

The poor little woman looked as if she needed rest but was not likely to get it; for the room was in a chaotic state, the breakfast table presented the appearance of having been devastated by a swarm of
5 locusts, the baby began to fret, little Polly set up her usual whine of "I want sumpin to do," and a pile of work loomed in the corner waiting to be done.

"I don't see how I ever shall get through it all," sighed the despondent matron as she hastily drank a
10 last cup of tea, while two great tears rolled down her cheeks, as she looked from one puny child to the other, and felt the weariness of her own tired soul and body more oppressive than ever.

"A good cry" was impending, when there came a
15 brisk ring at the door, a step in the hall, and a large, rosy woman came bustling in, saying in a cheery voice as she set a flower-pot down upon the table, "Good morning! Nice day, isn't it? Came in early on business and brought you one of my Lady Washingtons, you are
20 so fond of flowers."

"Oh, it's lovely! How kind you are. Do sit down if you can find a chair; we are all behind hand today, for I was up half the night with poor baby, and haven't energy enough to go to work yet," answered Mrs.
25 Bennet, with a sudden smile that changed her whole face, while baby stopped fretting to stare at the rosy clusters, and Polly found employment in exploring the pocket of the newcomer, as if she knew her way there.

"Let me put the pot on your stand first, girls are
30 so careless, and I'm proud of this. It will be an ornament to your parlor for a week," and opening a door Mrs. Gay carried the plant to a sunny bay window where many others were blooming beautifully.

Mrs. Bennet and the children followed to talk and
35 admire, while the servant leisurely cleared the table.

"Now give me that baby, put yourself in the easy chair, and tell me all about your worries," said Mrs. Gay, in the brisk, commanding way which few people could resist.

40 "I'm sure I don't know where to begin," sighed Mrs. Bennet, dropping into the comfortable seat while baby changed bearers with great composure.

"I met your husband and he said the doctor had ordered you and these chicks off to Florida for the
45 winter. John said he didn't know how he should manage it, but he meant to try."

"Isn't it dreadful? He can't leave his business to go with me, and we shall have to get Aunt Miranda to come and see to him and the boys while I'm gone, and
50 the boys can't bear her strict, old-fashioned ways, and I've got to go that long journey all alone and stay among strangers, and these heaps of fall work to do first, and it will cost an immense sum to send us, and I don't know what is to become of me."

55 Here Mrs. Bennet stopped for breath, and Mrs. Gay asked briskly, "What is the matter with you and the children?"

"Well, baby is having a hard time with his teeth and is croupy, Polly doesn't get over scarlet fever well,
60 and I'm used up; no strength or appetite, pain in my side and low spirits. Entire change of scene, milder climate, and less work for me, is what we want, the doctor says. John is very anxious about us, and I feel regularly discouraged."

65 "I'll spend the day and cheer you up a bit. You just rest and get ready for a new start tomorrow; it is a saving of time to stop short now and then and see where to begin next. Bring me the most pressing job of work. I can sew and see to this little rascal at the same
70 time."

72. The phrase "little woman" (line 1) refers to:

   (F) Lady Washington.
   (G) a servant.
   (H) Mrs. Bennet.
   (J) Mrs. Gay.

73. When Alcott compares the breakfast table to something "devastated by a swarm of locusts" (lines 4–5), she means:

   (A) that it is a mess left by an uncaring mob.
   (B) that children are no more meaningful than insects to Mrs. Bennet.
   (C) to illustrate the horror of Mrs. Bennet's life.
   (D) that the Bennets are pests.

74. Had Mrs. Gay not arrived when she did, the author leads us to suspect that:

   (F) Mrs. Bennet would have gone back to bed.
   (G) the children would have continued to cry.
   (H) Mrs. Bennet would have accomplished little all day.
   (J) sickness would have overtaken the entire family.

75. The phrase "rosy clusters" (lines 26–27) refers to:

   (A) Mrs. Gay's cheeks.
   (B) Mrs. Bennet's cheeks.
   (C) candies from Mrs. Gay's pockets.
   (D) flowers.

76. In lines 29–33, the author:

   (F) reveals Mrs. Bennet's only talent.
   (G) uses the sunny parlor as a symbol of hope.
   (H) contrasts Mrs. Gay's sunniness with Mrs. Bennet's dullness.
   (J) contrasts Mrs. Bennet's plants with her children.

77. When Mrs. Bennet says that she's "used up" (line 60), she means that she:

   (A) has no energy.
   (B) is abused.
   (C) is exploited.
   (D) has spent all her money.

78. The word "pressing" (line 68) means:

   (F) heavy.
   (G) ardent.
   (H) forceful.
   (J) important.

79. The disposition of Mrs. Bennet's friend is indicated by:

   I. her name.
   II. her speech.
   III. her clothing.

   (A) I only
   (B) III only
   (C) I and II only
   (D) I and III only

80. The author implies that Mrs. Bennet's real problem is:

   (F) her inability to cope.
   (G) a touch of fever.
   (H) the cold winter weather.
   (J) a lack of common sense.

81. Mrs. Gay's primary quality seems to be her:

   (A) lethargy.
   (B) anxiety.
   (C) dignity.
   (D) practical nature.

Items #82–91 are based on the following passage.

PROSE FICTION: This passage is adapted from the memoir series "Old Times on the Mississippi" by Mark Twain that appeared in *Atlantic Monthly*.

At the end of what seemed a tedious while, I had managed to pack my head full of islands, towns, bars, "points," and bends; and a curiously inanimate mass of lumber it was, too. However, inasmuch as I could shut
5 my eyes and reel off a good long string of these names without leaving out more than ten miles of river in every fifty, I began to feel that I could make her skip those little gaps. But of course my complacency could hardly get started enough to lift my nose a trifle into
10 the air, before Mr. Bixby would think of something to fetch it down again. One day he turned on me suddenly with this settler:

"What is the shape of Walnut Bend?"

He might as well have asked me my
15 grandmother's opinion of protoplasm. I reflected respectfully, and then said I didn't know it had any particular shape. My gunpowdery chief went off with a bang, of course, and then went on loading and firing until he was out of adjectives.
20 I had learned long ago that he only carried just so many rounds of ammunition, and was sure to subside into a very placable and even remorseful old smoothbore as soon as they were all gone. That word "old" is merely affectionate; he was not more than
25 thirty-four. I waited. By and by he said:

"My boy, you've got to know the *shape* of the river perfectly. It is all there is left to steer by on a very dark night. Everything else is blotted out and gone. But mind you, it hasn't the same shape in the night that it
30 has in the daytime."

"How on earth am I ever going to learn it, then?"

"How do you follow a hall at home in the dark? Because you know the shape of it. You can't see it."

"Do you mean to say that I've got to know all the
35 million trifling variations of shape in the banks of this interminable river as well as I know the shape of the front hall at home?"

"On my honor, you've got to know them *better* than any man ever did know the shapes of the halls in
40 his own house."

"I wish I was dead!"

"Now I don't want to discourage you, but..."

"Well, pile it on me; I might as well have it now as another time."
45 "You see, this has got to be learned; there isn't any getting around it. A clear starlight night throws such heavy shadows that, if you didn't know the shape

of a shore perfectly, you would claw away from every bunch of timber, because you would take the black
50 shadow of it for a solid cape; and you see you would be getting scared to death every fifteen minutes by the watch. You would be fifty yards from shore all the time when you ought to be within fifty feet of it. You can't see a snag in one of those shadows, but you know
55 exactly where it is, and the shape of the river tells you when you are coming to it. Then there's your pitch-dark night; the river is a very different shape on a pitch-dark night from what it is on a starlit night. All shores seem to be straight lines, then, and mighty dim
60 ones, too; and you'd *run* them for straight lines, only you know better. You boldly drive your boat right into what seems to be a solid straight wall (you knowing very well that in reality there is a curve there), and that wall falls back and makes way for you. Then there's
65 your gray mist. You take a night when there's one of these grisly, drizzly, gray mists, and then there isn't any particular shape to a shore. A gray mist would tangle the head of the oldest man that ever lived. Well, then different kinds of *moonlight* change the shape of
70 the river in different ways."

82. In line 12, the word "settler" is used to mean:

(F) a pioneer.
(G) a perch on the railing.
(H) a remark that decides the issue.
(J) a humbling problem.

83. When the narrator compares Bixby's question to asking his "grandmother's opinion of protoplasm" (line 15), he means that:

(A) the question is inane.
(B) the speaker is very old.
(C) he does not know the answer.
(D) his grandmother would be able to respond.

84. Comparing the chief to a gun (lines 17–19) points out the chief's:

(F) accuracy.
(G) peppery temper.
(H) love of hunting.
(J) violent past.

85. When Twain writes that Mr. Bixby "carried just so many rounds of ammunition," he means that:

(A) Bixby used a pistol to settle arguments.
(B) Bixby loaded and fired his gun at random.
(C) Bixby was an impossible employer.
(D) Bixby's hot temper would soon subside.

86. The narrator's reaction to Mr. Bixby's insistence on the need to know the river at night is:

(F) despair.
(G) elation.
(H) puzzlement.
(J) anger.

87. In the phrase "pile it on me" (line 43), "it" refers to:

(A) clothing.
(B) information.
(C) the river.
(D) the shoreline.

88. The word "cape" (line 50) means:

(F) cloak.
(G) robe.
(H) peninsula.
(J) waterway.

89. Mr. Bixby is shown to be extremely:

(A) knowledgeable.
(B) rude.
(C) condescending.
(D) fearful.

90. What is the purpose of including the lengthy explanation provided in the last paragraph of the selection?

  I. To show how well Bixby speaks
  II. To show how much a riverboat captain must know
  III. To show the many modes of the river

(F) I only
(G) II only
(H) I and III only
(J) II and III only

91. According to the passage, which of the following is true?

(A) A riverboat should always be within 50 feet of the shore.
(B) On a clear, starlit night, the shoreline is easy to see.
(C) On a pitch-dark night, the pilot cannot discern the curve of the shoreline.
(D) The river's shape gives no hint of underwater snags.

CHALLENGE ITEMS

The passages and items in this section reflect both the format and difficulty range of items on the real Reading Test, though difficult items are emphasized. Answers are on page 595.

DIRECTIONS: Each passage below is followed by items based on its content. Answer the items on the basis of what is stated or implied in each passage.

Items #1–8 are based on the following passage.

SOCIAL STUDIES: This passage discusses systems for reporting and investigating adverse drug effects.

A fundamental principle of pharmacology is that all drugs have multiple actions. Actions that are desirable in the treatment of disease are considered therapeutic, while those that are undesirable or pose
5 risks to the patient are called "effects." Adverse drug effects range from the trivial, for example, nausea or dry mouth, to the serious, such as massive gastrointestinal bleeding or thromboembolism; and some drugs can be lethal. Therefore, an effective
10 system for the detection of adverse drug effects is an important component of the healthcare system of any advanced nation. Much of the research conducted on new drugs aims at identifying the conditions of use that maximize beneficial effects and minimize the risk of
15 adverse effects. The intent of drug labeling is to reflect this body of knowledge accurately so that physicians can properly prescribe the drug or, if it is to be sold without prescription, so that consumers can properly use the drug.
20 The current system of drug investigation in the United States has proved very useful and accurate in identifying the common side effects associated with new prescription drugs. By the time a new drug is approved by the Food and Drug Administration, its
25 side effects are usually well described in the package insert for physicians. The investigational process, however, cannot be counted on to detect all adverse effects because of the relatively small number of patients involved in pre-marketing studies and the
30 relatively short duration of the studies. Animal toxicology studies are, of course, done before marketing in an attempt to identify any potential for toxicity, but negative results do not guarantee the safety of a drug in humans, as evidenced by such well
35 known examples as the birth deformities due to thalidomide.

This recognition prompted the establishment in many countries of programs to which physicians report adverse drug effects. The United States and other
40 countries also send reports to an international program operated by the World Health Organization. These programs, however, are voluntary reporting programs and are intended to serve a limited goal: alerting a government or private agency to adverse drug effects
45 detected by physicians in the course of practice. Other approaches must be used to confirm suspected drug reactions and to estimate incidence rates. These other approaches include conducting retrospective control studies, for example, the studies associating
50 endometrial cancer with estrogen use, and systematically monitoring hospitalized patients to determine the incidence of acute common side effects, as typified by the Boston Collaborative Drug Surveillance Program.
55 Thus, the overall drug surveillance system of the United States is composed of a set of information bases, special studies, and monitoring programs, each contributing in its own way to our knowledge about marketed drugs. The system is decentralized among a
60 number of governmental units and is not administered as a coordinated function. Still, it would be inappropriate at this time to attempt to unite all of the disparate elements into a comprehensive surveillance program. Instead, the challenge is to improve each
65 segment of the system and to take advantage of new computer strategies to improve coordination and communication.

1. In line 63, the word "disparate" most nearly means:

(A) useless.
(B) expensive.
(C) temporary.
(D) unconnected.

2. The author's primary concern is to discuss:

(F) methods for testing the effects of new drugs on humans.

(G) the importance of having accurate information about the effects of drugs.

(H) procedures for determining the long-term effects of new drugs.

(J) attempts to curb the abuse of prescription drugs.

3. The author implies that a drug with adverse side effects:

(A) will not be approved for use by consumers without a doctor's prescription.

(B) must wait for approval until lengthy studies prove the effects are not permanent.

(C) should be used only if its therapeutic value out-weighs its adverse effects.

(D) should be withdrawn from the marketplace pending a government investigation.

4. Which of the following can be inferred from the passage?

(F) The decentralization of the overall drug surveillance system results in it being completely ineffective in any attempts to provide information about adverse drug effects.

(G) Drugs with serious adverse side effects are never approved for distribution.

(H) Some adverse drug effects are discovered during testing because they are very rare.

(J) Some adverse drug effects cannot be detected prior to approval because they take a long time to develop.

5. The author introduces the example of thalidomide in the last sentence of the second paragraph to show that some:

(A) drugs do not have the same actions in humans that they do in animals.

(B) drug testing procedures are ignored by careless laboratory workers.

(C) drugs have no therapeutic value for humans.

(D) drugs have adverse side effects as well as beneficial actions.

6. It can be inferred that the estrogen study mentioned in the last sentence of the third paragraph:

(F) uncovered long-term side effects of a drug that had already been approved for sale by the Food and Drug Administration.

(G) discovered potential side effects of a drug that was still awaiting approval for sale by the Food and Drug Administration.

(H) revealed possible new applications of a drug that had previously been approved for a different treatment.

(J) is an example of a study that could be more efficiently conducted by a centralized authority than by volunteer reporting.

7. The author is most probably leading up to a discussion of some suggestions about how to:

(A) centralize authority for drug surveillance in the United States.

(B) centralize authority for drug surveillance among international agencies.

(C) coordinate better the sharing of information among the drug surveillance agencies.

(D) eliminate the availability and sale of certain drugs now on the market.

8. The author makes use of which of the following devices in the passage?

(F) Definition of terms
(G) Examples
(H) Analogy
(J) Definition of terms and example

Items #9–15 are based on the following passage.

NATURAL SCIENCES: This passage is adapted from a science magazine article that discusses lightning.

Lightning is an electrical discharge of immense proportions. Some 80% of lightning occurs within clouds; about 20% is cloud-to-ground lightning; and an extremely small percentage is cloud-to-sky lightning.

5 Cloud-to-ground lightning begins when complex meteorological processes cause a tremendous electrostatic charge to build up within a cloud. Typically, the bottom of the cloud is negatively charged. When the charge reaches 50 to 100 million 10 volts, air is no longer an effective insulator, and lightning occurs within the cloud itself. Ten to 30 minutes after the onset of intracloud lightning, negative charges called stepped leaders emerge from the bottom of the cloud, moving toward the earth in 50-meter 15 intervals at speeds of 100 to 200 kilometers per second and creating an ionized channel. As the leaders near the Earth, their strong electric field causes streamers of positively charged ions to develop at the tips of pointed objects that are connected directly or indirectly to the 20 ground. These positively charged streamers flow upward.

When the distance, known as the striking distance, between a stepped leader and one of the streamers reaches 30 to 100 meters, the intervening air 25 breaks down completely and the leader is joined to the Earth via the streamer. Now a pulse of current known as a return stroke ranging from thousands to hundreds of thousands of amperes moves at one tenth to one third the speed of light from the Earth through the 30 object from which the streamer emanated and up the ionized channel to the charge center within the cloud. An ionized channel remains in the air and additional negative charges called dart leaders will quickly move down this path resulting in further return strokes. This 35 multiplicity causes the flash to flicker. The entire event typically lasts about one second.

The return stroke's extremely high temperature creates the visible lightning and produces thunder by instantly turning moisture into steam. Most direct 40 damage results from the heavy return stroke current because it produces high temperatures in the channel, or from arcing at the point of ground contact. If the lightning current is carried by an enclosed conductor (e.g., within a jacketed cable, through a concrete wall, 45 or beneath a painted surface), entrapped moisture is turned into high-pressure steam that can cause a cable,

wall, or painted object to explode. Arcing frequently ignites combustibles.

Lightning causes hundreds of millions of dollars 50 in property losses annually and the majority of forest fires. Lightning is also the leading weather-related killer in the U.S., causing from 100 to 200 deaths each year.

9. In line 12, the word "intracloud" most nearly means:

    (A) between clouds.
    (B) within a cloud.
    (C) from cloud to sky.
    (D) from ground to cloud.

10. The selection defines the striking distance as the distance between:

    (F) the ground and the cloud.
    (G) a stepped leader and a dart leader.
    (H) a dart leader and a return stroke.
    (J) a streamer and a stepped leader.

11. According to the selection, the flickering appearance of a lightning strike is created by:

    (A) the stepped movement of leaders.
    (B) multiple return strokes.
    (C) water being vaporized.
    (D) arcing at ground contact.

12. What topic might the author logically address in a continuation of the passage?

    (F) Precautions to minimize lightning damage
    (G) Other weather phenomena that cause injury
    (H) Basic principles governing electricity
    (J) Identifying different types of clouds

13. According to the passage, which of the following is NOT true of stepped leaders?

(A) They develop 10 to 30 minutes after intracloud lightning.
(B) As they traverse the distance from cloud to ground, they create an ionized channel.
(C) Their powerful positive charge causes streamers to develop in grounded objects.
(D) They emerge from the bottom of the cloud and move downward in intervals of 50 meters.

14. The passage answers which of the following questions?

(F) How does lightning produce the associated thunder?
(G) How far above the ground is the bottom of the typical lightning-producing cloud?
(H) How frequently will lightning strike a given object?
(J) How long does it take a cloud to build up an electrostatic charge?

15. The author's primary concern is to:

(A) warn about the dangers posed by lightning strikes.
(B) describe the sequence of events that make up a lightning strike.
(C) discuss fundamental scientific laws pertaining to electricity.
(D) support the commonly held view that lightning strikes the ground.

Items #16–24 are based on the following passage.

SOCIAL STUDIES: This passage discusses the history of hospitals.

Public general hospitals originated in the almshouse infirmaries established as early as colonial times by local governments to care for the poor. Later, in the late eighteenth and early nineteenth centuries, the
5 infirmary separated from the almshouse and became an independent institution supported by local tax money. At the same time, private charity hospitals began to develop. Both private and public hospitals mainly provided food and shelter for the impoverished sick,
10 since there was little that medicine could actually do to cure illness, and the middle class was treated at home by private physicians.

Late in the nineteenth century, private charity hospitals began trying to attract middle-class patients.
15 Although the depression of 1890 stimulated the growth of charitable institutions and an expanding urban population became dependent on assistance, there was a decline in private contributions to these organizations that forced them to look to local government for
20 financial support. Since private institutions had also lost benefactors, they began to charge patients. In order to attract middle-class patients, private institutions provided services and amenities that distinguished between paying and nonpaying patients, making the
25 hospital a desirable place for private physicians to treat their own patients. As paying patients became more necessary to the survival of the private hospital, the public hospitals slowly became the only place for the poor to get treatment. By the end of the nineteenth
30 century, cities were reimbursing private hospitals for their care of indigent patients and the public hospitals remained dependent on the tax dollars.

The advent of private hospital health insurance, which provided middle-class patients with the
35 purchasing power to pay for private hospital services, guaranteed the private hospital a regular source of income. Private hospitals restricted themselves to revenue-generating patients, leaving the public hospitals to care for the poor. Although public hospitals
40 continued to provide services for patients with communicable diseases and outpatient and emergency services, the Blue Cross plans developed around the needs of the private hospitals and the inpatients they served. Thus, reimbursement for ambulatory care has
45 been minimal under most Blue Cross plans, and provision of outpatient care has not been a major function of the private hospital, in part because private patients can afford to pay for the services of private physicians. Additionally, since World War II, there has
50 been a tremendous influx of federal money into private medical schools and the hospitals associated with them. Further, large private medical centers with expensive research equipment and programs have attracted the best administrators, physicians, and researchers.
55 Because of the greater resources available to the private medical centers, public hospitals have increasing problems attracting highly qualified research and medical personnel. With the mainstream of health care firmly established in the private medical sector,
60 the public hospital has become a "dumping ground."

16. In line 31, the word "indigent" most nearly means:

(F) without the means to pay.
(G) having emergency medical needs.
(H) lacking health insurance.
(J) reimbursed by the government.

17. According to the passage, the very first private hospitals:

(A) developed from almshouse infirmaries.
(B) provided better care than public infirmaries.
(C) were established mainly to service the poor.
(D) were supported by government revenues.

18. It can be inferred that the author believes the differences that currently exist between public and private hospitals are primarily the result of:

    (F) political considerations.
    (G) economic factors.
    (H) ethical concerns.
    (J) legislative requirements.

19. It can be inferred that the growth of private health insurance:

    (A) relieved local governments of the need to fund public hospitals.
    (B) guaranteed that the poor would have access to medical care.
    (C) forced middle-class patients to use public hospitals.
    (D) reinforced the distinction between public and private hospitals.

20. Which of the following would be the most logical topic for the author to introduce in the next paragraph?

    (F) A plan to improve the quality of public hospitals
    (G) An analysis of the profit structure of health insurance companies
    (H) A proposal to raise taxes on the middle class
    (J) A discussion of recent developments in medical technology

21. The author's primary concern is to:

    (A) describe the financial structure of the healthcare industry.
    (B) demonstrate the importance of government support for healthcare institutions.
    (C) criticize wealthy institutions for refusing to provide services to the poor.
    (D) identify the historical causes of the division between private and public hospitals.

22. The author cites all of the following as factors contributing to the decline of public hospitals EXCEPT:

    (F) Government money was used to subsidize private medical schools and hospitals to the detriment of public hospitals.
    (G) Public hospitals are not able to compete with private institutions for top-flight managers and doctors.
    (H) Large private medical centers have better research facilities and more extensive research programs than public hospitals.
    (J) Blue Cross insurance coverage does not reimburse subscribers for medical expenses incurred in a public hospital.

23. The author's attitude toward public hospitals can best be described as:

    (A) contemptuous and prejudiced.
    (B) apprehensive and distrustful.
    (C) concerned and understanding.
    (D) enthusiastic and supportive.

24. The author implies that any outpatient care provided by a hospital is:

(F) paid for by private insurance.
(G) provided in lieu of treatment by a private physician.
(H) supplied primarily by private hospitals.
(J) a source of revenue for public hospitals.

Items #25–32 are based on the following passage.

SOCIAL STUDIES: This passage discusses a historical argument that emerged following U.S. military unification.

The National Security Act of 1947 created a national military establishment headed by a single Secretary of Defense. The legislation had been a year-and-a-half in the making—beginning when President
5 Truman first recommended that the armed services be reorganized into a single department. During that period, the President's concept of a unified armed service was torn apart and put back together several times; the final measure to emerge from Congress was
10 a compromise. Most of the opposition to the bill came from the Navy and its numerous civilian spokesmen, including Secretary of the Navy James Forrestal. In support of unification (and a separate air force that was part of the unification package) were the Army air
15 forces, the Army, and, most importantly, the President of the United States.

Passage of the bill did not end the bitter interservice disputes. Rather than unify, the act served only to federate the military services. It neither halted
20 the rapid demobilization of the armed forces that followed World War II nor brought to the new national military establishment the loyalties of officers steeped in the traditions of the separate services. At a time when the balance of power in Europe and Asia was
25 rapidly shifting, the services lacked any precise statement of United States foreign policy from the National Security Council on which to base future programs. The services bickered unceasingly over their respective roles and missions, already complicated by
30 the Soviet nuclear capability that, for the first time, made the United States subject to devastating attack. Not even the appointment of Forrestal as First Secretary of Defense allayed the suspicions of naval officers and their supporters that the role of the U.S.
35 Navy was threatened with permanent eclipse. Before the war of words died down, Forrestal himself was driven to resignation and then suicide.

By 1948, the United States military establishment was forced to make do with a budget approximately 10
40 percent of what it had been at its wartime peak. Meanwhile, the cost of weapons procurement was rising geometrically as the nation came to put more and more reliance on the atomic bomb and its delivery systems. These two factors inevitably made adversaries
45 of the Navy and the Air Force as the battle between advocates of the B-36 and the supercarrier so amply demonstrates. Given severe fiscal restraints on the one

hand, and on the other the nation's increasing reliance on strategic nuclear deterrence, the conflict between
50 these two services over roles and missions was essentially a contest over slices of an ever-diminishing pie.

Yet if in the end neither service was the obvious victor, the principle of civilian dominance over the
55 military clearly was. If there had ever been any danger that the United States military establishment might exploit, to the detriment of civilian control, the goodwill it enjoyed as a result of its victories in World War II, that danger disappeared in the interservice
60 animosities engendered by the battle over unification.

25. In line 20, the word "demobilization" most nearly means:

(A) shift to a unified military.
(B) realignment of allies.
(C) change from war to peace.
(D) adoption of new technology.

26. According to the passage, the interservice strife that followed unification occurred primarily between the:

(F) Army and Army air forces.
(G) Army and Navy.
(H) Army air forces and Navy.
(J) Air Force and Navy.

27. It can be inferred from the passage that Forrestal's appointment as Secretary of Defense was expected to:

(A) placate members of the Navy.
(B) result in decreased levels of defense spending.
(C) outrage advocates of the Army air forces.
(D) win Congressional approval of the unification plan.

28. According to the passage, President Truman supported which of the following?

(F) Elimination of the Navy
(G) A unified military service
(H) Establishment of a separate air force
(J) A unified military service and establishment of a separate air force

29. With which of the following statements about defense unification would the author most likely agree?

(A) Unification ultimately undermined United States military capability by inciting interservice rivalry.

(B) The unification legislation was necessitated by the drastic decline in appropriations for the military services.

(C) Although the unification was not entirely successful, it had the unexpected result of ensuring civilian control of the military.

(D) In spite of the attempted unification, each service was still able to pursue its own objectives without interference from the other branches.

30. According to the selection, the political situation following the passage of the National Security Act of 1947 was characterized by all of the following EXCEPT:

(F) a shifting balance of power in Europe and in Asia.

(G) fierce interservice rivalries.

(H) lack of strong leadership by the National Security Council.

(J) a lame-duck President who was unable to unify the legislature.

31. The author cites the resignation and suicide of Forrestal in order to:

(A) underscore the bitterness of the interservice rivalry surrounding the passage of the National Security Act of 1947.

(B) demonstrate that the Navy eventually emerged as the dominant branch of service after the passage of the National Security Act of 1947.

(C) suggest that the nation would be better served by a unified armed service under a single command.

(D) provide an example of a military leader who preferred to serve his country in war rather than in peace.

32. The author is primarily concerned with:

(F) discussing the influence of personalities on political events.

(G) describing the administration of a powerful leader.

(H) criticizing a piece of legislation.

(J) analyzing a political development.

Items #33–40 are based on the following passage.

SOCIAL STUDIES: This passage is adapted from an article about early American education ideology.

The founders of the American Republic viewed their revolution primarily in political rather than economic or social terms. Furthermore, they talked about education as essential to the public good—a goal
5 that took precedence over knowledge as occupational training or as a means to self-fulfillment or self-improvement. Over and over again, the Revolutionary generation, both liberal and conservative in outlook, asserted its conviction that the welfare of the Republic
10 rested upon an educated citizenry and that schools, especially free public schools, would be the best means of educating the citizenry in civic values and the obligations required of everyone in a democratic republican society. All agreed that the principal
15 ingredients of a civic education were literacy and the inculcation of patriotic and moral virtues, some others adding the study of history and the study of principles of the republican government itself.

The founders, as was the case with almost all
20 their successors, were long on exhortation and rhetoric regarding the value of civic education, but they left it to the textbook writers to distill the essence of those values for schoolchildren. Texts in American history and government appeared as early as the 1790s. The
25 textbook writers turned out to be largely of conservative persuasion, more likely Federalist in outlook than Jeffersonian, and they almost universally agreed that political virtue must rest upon moral and religious precepts. Since most textbook writers were
30 New Englanders, this meant that the texts were infused with Protestant, and above all Puritan, outlooks.

In the first half of the Republic, civic education in the schools emphasized the inculcation of civic values and made little attempt to develop participatory
35 political skills. That was a task left to incipient political parties, town meetings, churches, and the coffee or ale houses where men gathered for conversation. Additionally, as a reading of certain Federalist papers of the period would demonstrate, the press probably
40 did more to disseminate realistic as well as partisan knowledge of government than the schools. The goal of education, however, was to achieve a higher form of *unum* for the new Republic. In the middle half of the nineteenth century, the political values taught in the
45 public and private schools did not change substantially from those celebrated in the first fifty years of the Republic. In the textbooks of the day, their rosy hues if anything became golden. To the resplendent values of

liberty, equality, and a benevolent Christian morality
50 were now added the middle-class virtues—especially of New England—of hard work, honesty, integrity, the rewards of individual effort, and obedience to parents and legitimate authority. But of all the political values taught in school, patriotism was preeminent; and
55 whenever teachers explained to schoolchildren why they should love their country above all else, the idea of liberty assumed pride of place.

33. In line 5, the phrase "took precedence over" most nearly means:

(A) set an example for.
(B) formulated a policy of.
(C) enlightened someone on.
(D) had greater importance than.

34. The passage deals primarily with the:

(F) content of textbooks used in early American schools.
(G) role of education in late eighteenth- and early to mid-nineteenth-century America.
(H) influence of New England Puritanism on early American values.
(J) origin and development of the Protestant work ethic in modern America.

35. According to the passage, the founders of the Republic regarded education primarily as:

(A) a religious obligation.
(B) a private matter.
(C) an unnecessary luxury.
(D) a political necessity.

36. The author states that textbooks written in the middle part of the nineteenth century:

(F) departed radically in tone and style from earlier textbooks.
(G) mentioned for the first time the value of liberty.
(H) treated traditional civic virtues with even greater reverence.
(J) were commissioned by government agencies.

37. Which of the following would LEAST likely have been the subject of an early American textbook?

   (A) Basic rules of English grammar
   (B) The American Revolution
   (C) Patriotism and other civic virtues
   (D) Vocational education

38. The author's attitude toward the educational system discussed in the passage can best be described as:

   (F) cynical and unpatriotic.
   (G) realistic and analytical.
   (H) pragmatic and frustrated.
   (J) disenchanted and bitter.

39. The passage provides information that would be helpful in answering which of the following questions?

   (A) Why was a disproportionate share of early American textbooks written by New England authors?
   (B) Was the Federalist party primarily a liberal or conservative force in early American politics?
   (C) How many years of education did the founders believe were sufficient to instruct young citizens in civic virtue?
   (D) What were the names of some of the Puritan authors who wrote early American textbooks?

40. The author implies that an early American Puritan would likely insist that:

   (F) moral and religious values are the foundation of civic virtue.
   (G) textbooks should instruct students in political issues of vital concern to the community.
   (H) textbooks should give greater emphasis to the value of individual liberty than to the duties of patriotism.
   (J) private schools with a particular religious focus are preferable to public schools with no religious instruction.

Items #41–46 are based on the following passage.

SOCIAL STUDIES: This passage discusses the interrelationship of the United States economy and international commerce.

International commerce is woven thoroughly into the fabric of the American economy. Exports and imports amounted to more than 11 percent of the U.S. gross domestic product (GDP) in 1991, up dramatically
5 from 7.5 percent just 5 years before. More than 7 million American jobs are related to exports, and millions more depend on the overall economic activity generated by export trade. Export-related jobs pay more—almost 17 percent more than the average
10 American job.

Exports are vital to the economic health of many key sectors of the manufacturing economy. For instance, makers of computers, aerospace and heavy earthmoving equipment, and farm implements are
15 increasingly dependent on export markets. For these exports, slow growth abroad translates to declining vitality at home. The same picture is true of agriculture, where roughly one in four farm acres is now harvested for the export market. International sales of business-
20 related services—construction, finance, insurance, and engineering, among others—amount to tens of billions of dollars each year.

In the early years of the post-World War II era, the United States stood virtually alone as the industrial
25 and technological leader of the world. At that time, the U.S. produced almost half of the world's GDP, including much of the world's manufactured goods, and had roughly 80 percent of the world's hard currency reserves. Today, while the U.S. remains the
30 world's leading economy, its share of world GDP has shrunk to about 24 percent, and its share of world manufacturers is even lower. Experts agree that, relative to the size of the economy and the diversity of its industrial and technological base, the U.S. has
35 lagged far behind its export potential.

Meanwhile, the potential for growth in U.S. exports is enormous. Markets in Europe and Japan are huge and relatively stable. There is growing promise in Asia's $5.7 trillion economy and Latin America's
40 $1 trillion economy. These markets are generating a rapidly growing demand for infrastructure investment, aircraft, and high-technology capital goods—all areas in which the U.S. has real or potential strengths. In addition, new entrants into the world economy, such as
45 Central and Eastern Europe and the countries of the former Soviet Union, show real promise as potential markets for U.S. exports.

Growing world markets, however, do not automatically translate into U.S. export sales. The
50 fierce competition for international markets comes primarily from the more innovative firms in Europe and Japan. In particular, Japanese companies have set the pace with a mix of aggressive business practices and a virtually economy-wide commitment to quality,
55 rapid time to market, ongoing innovation, and customer satisfaction. American companies are beginning to try to meet the competition abroad, as well as to view their success as a benchmark for improvement, whether that best is in Chicago, Frankfurt, or Osaka.

60 The new realities of international competition yield lessons for the U.S. government as well. Persistent economic diplomacy and high-level advocacy, competitive and well-focused export financing, and improved efforts at information-
65 gathering have become necessary components of an export promotion policy. Many foreign governments have been more aggressive and more focused than the U.S. government in working with their firms to secure export sales. Senior government officials, up to and
70 including the President or Prime Minister, often will travel to support the sale of their home country's goods and services. The U.S. government needs to begin to measure its export strategy against the flexibility and effectiveness of the competition. Exports are central to
75 growth, jobs, and a rising standard of living for all Americans. Our role in building a better America at home and acting as an economic leader abroad is dependent on our ability to develop a coherent, aggressive, and effective national export strategy.

41. Which of the following U.S. economic sectors has declined most seriously since World War II?

(A) Agriculture
(B) Manufacturing
(C) High-technology products
(D) Business-related services

42. Which of the following best expresses the central point of the passage?

(F) Exports drive the U.S. economy.
(G) U.S. exports have declined since shortly after World War II.
(H) Exports are so important to the U.S. economy that steps should be taken to increase U.S. exports worldwide.
(J) The U.S. government should encourage U.S. corporations to expand into markets in Asia and Latin America.

43. Which of the following areas is NOT mentioned in the passage as a potential market for U.S. goods abroad?

(A) Asia
(B) Latin America
(C) Central Europe
(D) Northern Africa

44. The passage suggests that both U.S. corporations and the U.S. government should:

(F) discourage imports in favor of exports.
(G) focus on improving the quality of American products.
(H) try to meet the competition abroad.
(J) take steps to reduce the economy's dependence on exports.

45. With which of the following explanations for the decline in the United States' share of world GDP would the author be most likely to agree?

I. Other countries are relatively uninterested in purchasing the goods and services the U.S. has to offer.
II. Other governments have done more to encourage their countries' exports than has the U.S. government.
III. Companies in some other countries have been more enterprising in producing high-quality goods and services.

(A) II only
(B) I and II only
(C) I and III only
(D) II and III only

46. According to the passage, an increase in U.S. exports abroad would generate:

(F) more high-paying jobs for American workers.
(G) increased profits for American farmers.
(H) greater diversity in American industry.
(J) resentment among foreign competitors.

Items #47–55 are based on the following passage.

NATURAL SCIENCES: This passage details lake regions, the conditions under which the regions occur, and how various interactions between these regions create different types of lakes.

Lakes arise from sources that are almost entirely geologic in nature. Once they have formed, lakes are doomed. Because of the concave nature of the lake basin, there is a trend toward demise as the basin fills
5 in with sediment. A lake lives through youthful stages to maturity, senescence, and death when the basin is finally full. This procedure does not always follow a direct course. Periods of rejuvenation occasionally occur in some lakes. Eventually, marshes, swampy
10 meadows, and forests appear where lakes once existed. Large lakes may be far from death as a result of shoaling, but climatic changes or geologic events that result in drying out or drainage eventually lead to their ends.
15 The littoral zone of a lake is the region of the shallows. The shallows are subject to fluctuating temperatures and erosion of the shoreline through wave action and the effects of weather. The shallows are usually well lit and serve as home to rooted
20 aquatic plants. The littoral region is the region from the shoreline to the depth where the weeds disappear. Sometimes, wave action is so extreme that most aquatic vegetation is absent and only algae are present, marking the outer regions of the littoral
25 region. The littoral benthos is the bottom region of the littoral region. This region contains many species and taxonomic groups. A high diversity and high annual production set this community apart from other regions of the lake.
30 The sublittoral zone extends from the outer region of the littoral region. Sediments in the sublittoral zone are finer grained than those of the littoral zone. Although this region is dimly lit, it is usually well oxygenated. The sublittoral zone
35 community contains fewer species than does the littoral zone. This is due mainly to the reduced number of habitats.

In some lakes, the old shells of gastropods and pelecypods that inhabit the littoral zone are found
40 accumulated in the sublittoral zone. These shell zones are thought to mark the place where weather interactions and currents have carried and dropped these remains.

The profundal zone is defined as the region of a
45 lake where summer temperature stratification is apparent. Under such conditions a deep cold region is formed where currents are at a minimum and where light is greatly reduced. The temperature is mostly uniform throughout this region, and under some
50 conditions, oxygen is almost completely absent, but CO_2 and methane are prevalent. The hydrogen ion concentration is high because of the presence of carbonic acid. This stratum of water is characterized by the existence of decayed matter rather than by the
55 production of organic matter.

As solar radiation passes down from the surface of the lake, it disappears exponentially, and the heating wavelengths are usually absorbed very fast. At the end of the yearly heating period, one might
60 expect the temperature stratum to resemble the light curve; however, due to weather conditions—for example, wind—the temperature profiles of lakes are altered. The temperature difference is readily explained by the wind mixing the upper layers of
65 water and distributing downward the heat that has been absorbed by the surface layers of water.

Direct stratification occurs when dense cold water lies beneath lighter warm layers of water. Direct stratification divides a lake into three regions. The
70 upper warm region, mixed completely by wind to produce a region that is almost at a uniform temperature throughout, is called the epilimnion. At the bottom is a colder, heavier region of water, which is unaffected by wind action and therefore remains
75 stagnant. This region is called the hypolimnion. Separating these two regions is the thermocline, a region of water where temperature drops quickly with increasing depth.

Dimictic lakes are lakes that have two mixing
80 periods: vernal and autumnal. The typical dimictic lake stratifies directly during the warm months. When the cold months arrive, the surface water starts to cool, which eventually destroys the stratification and initiates complete circulation. During the fall mixing,
85 chilling of the entire water mass continues until the water mass achieves a uniform temperature of about 4 degrees Celsius.

Polymictic lakes are lakes that have many mixing periods or which have continuous circulation
90 throughout the year. Polymictic lakes are influenced more by fluctuations in temperature from day to night than by seasonal changes.

Meromictic lakes circulate at times, but incompletely. The entire water mass does not
95 participate in the mixing. A dense region of water at the bottom remains stagnant and anaerobic. The three regions of a meromictic lake have their own names. The bottom layer, which is basically stagnant and

contains a greater concentration of dissolved
100 substances, is called the monimolimnion. The upper
layer is mixed by the wind, is more dilute, and shows
seasonal changes. This region is called the
mixolimnion. Between the monimolimnion and the
mixolimnion is a region where salinity increases
105 quickly with depth. This region is called the
chemocline.

47. The author uses "doomed" in line 3 to indicate
that:

    I. he regrets the event.
    II. the lakes have a limited future.
    III. people will destroy the lakes.

(A) I only
(B) II only
(C) II and III only
(D) I, II, and III

48. Unlike the sublittoral zone, the littoral zone:

(F) has fine-grained sediment.
(G) contains many varied habitats.
(H) contains aquatic vegetation.
(J) is well oxygenated.

49. Why is aquatic vegetation absent in some lakes?

(A) Extreme wave action might uproot plants.
(B) Some lakes have no littoral or sublittoral
regions.
(C) Algae take over the littoral region.
(D) The lakes are fully mature.

50. The remains of gastropods are deposited in the
sublittoral zone by:

    I. currents.
    II. wind.
    III. animals.

(F) I only
(G) II only
(H) I and II only
(J) I and III only

51. The profundal zone is marked by:

(A) shells of organisms, low vegetation, and
high diversity.
(B) solar radiation and a vernal mixing period.
(C) increased temperatures in summer and
production of organic matter.
(D) cold temperatures, low light, and a lack of
oxygen.

52. In October, you would expect a northern
dimictic lake to:

(F) be warmer on the surface than it was in
May.
(G) cool from the surface to achieve a uniform
temperature.
(H) begin to stratify directly.
(J) slowly freeze across the surface.

53. A polymictic lake might be coldest:

(A) at night.
(B) in autumn.
(C) after sunrise.
(D) in spring.

54. The chemocline in a meromictic lake is
equivalent to:

(F) the littoral zone in a senescent lake.
(G) the profundal zone in a dimictic lake.
(H) the thermocline in a dimictic lake.
(J) the epilimnion in a polymictic lake.

55. Which of the following conclusions CANNOT
be drawn from this passage?

(A) Deep lakes are unaffected by weather.
(B) Lakes have geologic derivations.
(C) Lakes vary in temperature.
(D) All lakes will eventually die.

Items #56–62 are based on the following passage.

HUMANITIES: This passage discusses home and building construction in the Appalachian region of North America.

For nearly a century, the houses and other artificial structures of the Appalachian region have played a prominent role in its representation in books, magazines, and film. From nineteenth century
5 magazine illustrations of single-room log cabins to twentieth century television programs focusing on unpainted, one- or two-room company houses, the dominant image of the region has been the dilapidated, weather-beaten Appalachian home. While some of
10 these presentations are authentic, some are contrived, and nearly all are selective. Interpreters of Appalachian culture have tended to focus on extremes and, as a result, have misrepresented Appalachian life. A survey of the New River Gorge area in West Virginia revealed
15 a much more diverse landscape than has been described in the past. While project researchers did locate log cabins and abandoned coal towns, they also found considerable architectural variety. Contrary to past reports, the New River Gorge cultural landscape
20 reflects the history of a community that designed, built, and used its buildings according to individual tastes and principles.

The territory is dotted with homes that have had the original appearances altered to suit the occupant.
25 These individually styled facades may appear quirky to the outsider, but their meaning is revealed through an understanding of the local history. Coal companies originally constructed many of the homes for their workers. Whole towns of box houses (cheap, fast to
30 build, and temporary) were constructed at one time. While the floor plans varied, the basic construction technique did not. Vertical boards attached to sills and plates formed both the interior and exterior walls, as well as the buildings' weight-bearing supports. Today,
35 West Virginians commonly call box houses "Jinn Linns." One local resident related a story concerning the origin of the term. Jenny Lynn, a coal camp resident, decided to distinguish her home from the other identical box houses in her camp by nailing
40 narrow strips over the spaces between the vertical boards, creating the board and batten siding now characteristic of these houses. Soon, many others followed her example and eventually named the house type after her.
45 Unlike Jenny Lynn, most coal camp residents were required to maintain their box houses according to strict company standards or risk eviction. As the coal boom declined, however, companies began selling the homes to their tenants. Having obtained the freedom to
50 maintain their homes according to their own standards, residents altered facades or added rooms or porches, resulting in the variety of box houses visible in the region today. Others decided to leave the company camps altogether. Many purchased modern
55 prefabricated houses, for example, the Lustron, an all-steel factory-made home manufactured in Ohio between 1948 and 1950. The Lustron was a one-story, gable-roof ranch house with an exterior and interior skin of enameled steel panels bolted to a structural-
60 steel frame and a concrete slab foundation. Unlike the Jinn Linn, the home was durable, easy to maintain, and strong.

Innovative construction materials are also produced locally. Bluish cinder blocks and "red dog"
65 blocks, both by-products of the coal industry, have been used to construct homes, churches, gymnasiums, and barns throughout the Gorge. These and other colorful materials, including glazed tile, are often used in striking combinations, and an unusual amount of
70 care is given to decorative detail. For example, yellow and red bricks and stones are often used for window and door trims, quoins, and belt courses (projecting horizontal strips around the outside of a building).

The complex balance between formal design and
75 personal expression is a striking feature of the New River Gorge landscape. Like the quilts made in the region, much of the architecture is pieced together from locally made and recycled materials. Materials rarely used in combination in other areas are carefully pieced
80 together into a landscape filled with personal meaning.

56. The author uses the word "selective" (line 11) when describing the popular representations of Appalachian architecture to indicate that they:

   (F) present only one facet of Appalachian architecture.
   (G) focus on public buildings rather than on private homes.
   (H) show only the most attractive side of Appalachian architecture.
   (J) represent the perceptions only of the residents themselves.

57. With which of the following aspects of New River Gorge houses described in the passage would the interpreters mentioned in line 11 be most surprised?

(A) Their uniformity
(B) Their unusually large size
(C) The ease with which they were built and maintained
(D) The attention given to decorative detail in constructing them

58. Which of the following best expresses the author's main point in telling the story of Jenny Lynn (lines 37–44)?

(F) Residents of the coal camps modified their originally identical homes to suit their own preferences.
(G) The person who most influenced architecture in the New River Gorge was Jenny Lynn.
(H) Box houses are the most common type of house in the New River Gorge because they were inexpensive to construct.
(J) Coal companies had a great deal of control over the architecture of the New River Gorge.

59. Which of the following is NOT a difference between Lustron houses and Jinn Linn houses?

(A) Lustron houses were tougher than were Jinn Linn houses.
(B) Lustron houses were easier to keep up than were Jinn Linn houses.
(C) Lustron houses were made of steel while Jinn Linn houses were made of wood.
(D) Lustron houses came in several different floor plans while Jinn Linn houses always had the same plan.

60. According to the passage, Lustron houses were:

(F) less expensive than box houses.
(G) more common in Ohio than in West Virginia.
(H) ready-made in one place to be put up elsewhere.
(J) extremely popular among former coal-camp residents.

61. In what way is the architecture of the New River Gorge like the quilts made there?

   I. Both use designs or plans that originally come from outside the region.
  II. Both are made from available materials used in innovative ways.
 III. Both express the personal tastes of the makers or users.

(A) I and II only
(B) II only
(C) II and III only
(D) I, II, and III

62. Which of the following aspects of Appalachian architecture does the author appear to value most highly?

(F) Its beauty
(G) Its diversity
(H) Its practicality
(J) Its durability

TIMED-PRACTICE QUIZZES

This section contains six Reading quizzes. Complete each quiz under timed conditions. Answers are on page 595.

DIRECTIONS: Each passage below is followed by one or more items based on its content. Answer the items on the basis of what is stated or implied in the corresponding passage.

A. QUIZ I (8 items; 15 minutes)

Items #1–8 are based on the following passage.

SOCIAL STUDIES: This passage discusses the economic structure of current healthcare policy.

The healthcare economy is replete with unusual and even unique economic relationships. One of the least understood involves the peculiar roles of producer or "provider" and purchaser or "consumer" in the
5 typical doctor-patient relationship. In most sectors of the economy, the seller attempts to attract a potential buyer with various inducements of price, quality, and utility, and the buyer makes the decision. Where circumstances permit the buyer no choice because there
10 is effectively only one seller and the product is relatively essential, government usually asserts monopoly and places the industry under price and other regulations. Neither of these conditions prevails in most of the healthcare industry.
15 In the healthcare industry, the doctor-patient relationship is the mirror image of the ordinary relationship between producer and consumer. Once an individual has chosen to see a physician—and even then there may be no real choice—it is the physician
20 who usually makes all significant purchasing decisions: whether the patient should return "next Wednesday," whether x-rays are needed, whether drugs should be prescribed, etc. It is a rare and sophisticated patient who will challenge such professional decisions or raise
25 in advance questions about price, especially when the ailment is regarded as serious.

This is particularly significant in relation to hospital care. The physician must certify the need for hospitalization, determine what procedures will be
30 performed, and announce when the patient may be discharged. The patient may be consulted about some of these decisions, but in the main it is the doctor's judgments that are final. Little wonder, then, that in the eyes of the hospital, the physician is the real
35 "consumer." Consequently, the medical staff represents

the "power center" in hospital policy and decision-making, not the administration.

Although usually there are in this situation four identifiable participants—the physician, the hospital,
40 the patient, and the payer (generally an insurance carrier or government)—the physician makes the essential decisions for all of them. The hospital becomes an extension of the physician; the payer generally meets most of the bona fide bills generated
45 by the physician/hospital; and for the most part the patient plays a passive role. In routine or minor illnesses, or just plain worries, the patient's options are, of course, much greater with respect to use and price. In illnesses that are of some significance, however,
50 such choices tend to evaporate, and it is for these illnesses that the bulk of the healthcare dollar is spent. We estimate that about 75 to 80 percent of healthcare expenditures are determined by physicians, not patients. For this reason, economy measures directed at
55 patients or the public are relatively ineffective.

1. In line 1, the phrase "replete with" most nearly means:

   (A) filled with.
   (B) restricted by.
   (C) enriched by.
   (D) damaged by.

2. The author's primary purpose is to:

   (F) speculate about the relationship between a patient's ability to pay and the treatment received.
   (G) criticize doctors for exercising too much control over patients.
   (H) analyze some important economic factors in healthcare.
   (J) urge hospitals to reclaim their decision-making authority.

3. It can be inferred that doctors are able to determine hospital policies because:

(A) it is doctors who generate income for the hospital.
(B) most of a patient's bills are paid by health insurance.
(C) hospital administrators lack the expertise to question medical decisions.
(D) a doctor is ultimately responsible for a patient's health.

4. According to the author, when a doctor tells a patient to "return next Wednesday," the doctor is in effect:

(F) taking advantage of the patient's concern for his health.
(G) instructing the patient to buy more medical services.
(H) warning the patient that a hospital stay might be necessary.
(J) advising the patient to seek a second opinion.

5. The author is most probably leading up to:

(A) a proposal to control medical costs.
(B) a discussion of a new medical treatment.
(C) an analysis of the causes of inflation in the United States.
(D) a study of lawsuits against doctors for malpractice.

6. The tone of the passage can best be described as:

(F) whimsical.
(G) cautious.
(H) analytical.
(J) inquisitive.

7. With which of the following statements would the author be likely to agree?

(A) Few patients are reluctant to object to the course of treatment prescribed by a doctor or to question the cost of the services.
(B) The payer, whether an insurance carrier or the government, is less likely to acquiesce to demands for payment when the illness of the patient is regarded as serious.
(C) Today's patients are more informed as to what services and procedures they will need from their healthcare providers.
(D) The more serious the illness of a patient, the less likely it is that the patient will object to the course of treatment prescribed or to question the cost of services.

8. The author's primary concern is to:

(F) define a term.
(G) clarify a misunderstanding.
(H) refute a theory.
(J) discuss a problem.

B. QUIZ II (7 items; 15 minutes)

Items #1–7 are based on the following passage.

NATURAL SCIENCES: This passage discusses human social evolution and adaptation.

Man, so the truism goes, lives increasingly in a man-made environment. This puts a special burden on human immaturity, for it is plain that adapting to such variable conditions must depend very heavily on
5 opportunities for learning, or whatever the processes are that are operative during immaturity. It must also mean that during immaturity, man must master knowledge and skills that are neither stored in the gene pool nor learned by direct encounter, but that are
10 contained in the culture pool—knowledge about values and history, skills as varied as an obligatory natural language or an optional mathematical one, as mute as levers or as articulate as myth telling.

Yet, it would be a mistake to leap to the
15 conclusion that because human immaturity makes possible high flexibility, therefore anything is possible for the species. Human traits were selected for their survival value over a four- to five-million-year period with a great acceleration of the selection process during
20 the last half of that period. There were crucial, irreversible changes during that final man-making period: the recession of formidable dentition, a 50-percent increase in brain volume, the obstetrical paradox—bipedalism and strong pelvic girdle, larger
25 brain through a smaller birth canal—an immature brain at birth, and creation of what Washburn has called a "technical-social way of life," involving tool and symbol use.

Note, however, that hominidization consisted
30 principally of adaptations to conditions in the Pleistocene.

These preadaptations, shaped in response to earlier habitat demands, are part of man's evolutionary inheritance. This is not to say that close beneath the
35 skin of man is a naked ape, that civilization is only a veneer. The technical-social way of life is a deep feature of the species adaptation. But we would err if we assumed *a priori* that man's inheritance placed no constraint on his power to adapt. Some of the
40 preadaptations can be shown to be presently maladaptive. Man's inordinate fondness for fats and sweets no longer serves his individual survival well. Furthermore, the human obsession with sexuality is plainly not fitted for survival of the species now,
45 however well it might have served to populate the upper Pliocene and the Pleistocene. Nevertheless, note that the species responds typically to these challenges by technical innovation rather than by morphological or behavioral change. Contraception dissociates
50 sexuality from reproduction. Of course, we do not know what kinds and what range of stresses are produced by successive rounds of such technical innovation. Dissociating sexuality and reproduction, for example, surely produces changes in the structure
55 of the family, which in turn redefine the role of women, which in turn alters the authority pattern affecting the child, etc. Continuing and possibly accelerating change seems inherent in such adaptation. This, of course, places an enormous pressure on man's
60 uses of immaturity, preparing the young for unforeseeable change—the more so if there are severe restraints imposed by human preadaptations to earlier conditions of life.

1. The primary purpose of the passage is to:

   (A) refute some misconceptions about the importance of human immaturity.
   (B) introduce a new theory of the origins of the human species.
   (C) describe the evolutionary forces that formed the physical appearance of modern humans.
   (D) discuss the importance of human immaturity as an adaptive mechanism.

2. It can be inferred that the obstetrical paradox is puzzling because:

   (F) it occurred very late during the evolution of the species.
   (G) evolutionary forces seemed to work at cross purposes to each other.
   (H) technological innovations have made the process of birth easier.
   (J) an increase in brain size is not an ordinary evolutionary event.

3. Which of the following statements can be inferred from the passage?

   (A) Human beings are today less sexually active than were our ancestors during the Pleistocene era.
   (B) During the Pleistocene era, a fondness for fats and sweets was a trait that contributed to survival of humans.
   (C) Mathematics was invented by human beings during the latter half of the Pleistocene era.
   (D) The use of language and tools is a trait that is genetically transmitted from one generation to the next.

4. As used in line 32, the term "preadaptations" refers to traits that:

   (F) were useful to earlier human beings but have since lost their utility.
   (G) appeared in response to the need to learn a natural language and the use of tools.
   (H) humans currently exhibit but that developed in response to conditions of an earlier age.
   (J) are disadvantageous to creatures whose way of life is primarily technical and social.

5. The author mentions contraception to demonstrate that:

   (A) human beings may adapt to new conditions by technological invention rather than by changing their behavior.
   (B) sexual promiscuity is no longer an aid to the survival of the human species.
   (C) technological innovation is a more important adaptive mechanism than either heredity or direct encounter.
   (D) conditions during the upper Pliocene and Pleistocene eras no longer affect the course of human evolution.

6. With which of the following statements would the author LEAST likely agree?

   (F) The technical-social way of life of humans is an adaptive mechanism that arose in response to environmental pressures.
   (G) The possibility of technical innovation makes it unlikely that the physical appearance of humans will change radically in a short time.
   (H) Technological innovations can result in changes in the social structures in which humans live.
   (J) The fact that humans have a technical-social way of life makes the species immune from evolutionary pressures.

7. The author is most probably addressing which of the following audiences?

   (A) Medical students in a course on human anatomy
   (B) College students in an introductory course on archaeology
   (C) Psychologists investigating the uses of human immaturity
   (D) Biologists trying to trace the course of human evolution

C. QUIZ III (8 items; 15 minutes)

Items #1–8 are based on the following passage.

SOCIAL STUDIES: This passage is adapted from an article that discusses Japanese culture and civilization.

The uniqueness of the Japanese character is the result of two, seemingly contradictory forces: the strength of traditions, and selective receptivity to foreign achievements and inventions. As early as the
5 1860s, there were counter movements to the traditional orientation. Yukichi Fukuzawa, the most eloquent spokesman of Japan's "Enlightenment," claimed "The Confucian civilization of the East seems to me to lack two things possessed by Western civilization: science
10 in the material sphere and a sense of independence in the spiritual sphere." Fukuzawa's great influence is found in the free and individualistic philosophy of the Education Code of 1872, but he was not able to prevent the government from turning back to the canons of
15 Confucian thought in the Imperial Rescript of 1890. Another interlude of relative liberalism followed World War I, when the democratic idealism of President Woodrow Wilson had an important impact on Japanese intellectuals and, especially, students; but more
20 important was the Leninist ideology of the 1917 Bolshevik Revolution. Again, in the early 1930s, nationalism and militarism became dominant, largely because of failing economic conditions.

Following the end of World War II, substantial
25 changes were undertaken in Japan to liberate the individual from authoritarian restraints. The new democratic value system was accepted by many teachers, students, intellectuals, and old liberals, but it was not immediately embraced by the society as a
30 whole. Japanese traditions were dominated by group values, and notions of personal freedom and individual rights were unfamiliar.

Today, democratic processes are evident in the widespread participation of the Japanese people in
35 social and political life; yet, there is no universally accepted and stable value system. Values are constantly modified by strong infusions of Western ideas, both democratic and Marxist. School textbooks espouse democratic principles, emphasizing equality
40 over hierarchy and rationalism over tradition; but in practice these values are often misinterpreted and distorted, particularly by youth who translate the individualistic and humanistic goals of democracy into egoistic and materialistic ones.
45 Most Japanese people have consciously rejected Confucianism, but vestiges of the old order remain. An important feature of relationships in many institutions such as political parties, large corporations, and university faculties is the *oyabun-kobun* or parent-child
50 relation. A party leader, supervisor, or professor, in return for loyalty, protects those subordinate to him and takes general responsibility for their interests throughout their entire lives, an obligation that sometimes even extends to arranging marriages. The
55 corresponding loyalty of the individual to his patron reinforces his allegiance to the group to which they both belong. A willingness to cooperate with other members of the group and to support without qualification the interests of the group in all its external
60 relations is still a widely respected virtue. The *oyabun-kobun* creates ladders of mobility that an individual can ascend, rising as far as abilities permit, so long as he maintains successful personal ties with a superior in the vertical channel, the latter requirement usually taking
65 precedence over a need for exceptional competence. Consequently, there is little horizontal relationship between people even within the same profession.

1. As used in line 46, the word "vestiges" most nearly means:

   (A) institutions.
   (B) superiors.
   (C) traces.
   (D) subordinates.

2. Which of the following is most like the relationship of the *oyabun-kobun* described in the passage?

   (F) A political candidate and the voting public
   (G) A gifted scientist and his protégé
   (H) Two brothers who are partners in a business
   (J) A judge presiding at the trial of a criminal defendant

3. According to the passage, Japanese attitudes are NOT influenced by which of the following?

   (A) Democratic ideals
   (B) Elements of modern Western culture
   (C) Remnants of an earlier social structure
   (D) Confucianism

4. The author implies that:

   (F) decisions about promotions within the vertical channel are often based on personal feelings.
   (G) students and intellectuals do not understand the basic tenets of Western democracy.
   (H) Western values have completely overwhelmed traditional Japanese attitudes.
   (J) respect for authority was introduced into Japan following World War II.

5. In developing the passage, the author does which of the following?

   (A) Introduces an analogy
   (B) Defines a term
   (C) Presents statistics
   (D) Cites an authority

6. It can be inferred that the Imperial Rescript of 1890:

   (F) was a protest by liberals against the lack of individual liberty in Japan.
   (G) marked a return in government policies to conservative values.
   (H) implemented the ideals set forth in the Education Code of 1872.
   (J) was influenced by the Leninist ideology of the Bolshevik Revolution.

7. Which of the following is the most accurate description of the organization of the passage?

   (A) A sequence of inferences in which the conclusion of each successive step becomes a premise in the next argument
   (B) A list of generalizations, most of which are supported by only a single example
   (C) A chronological analysis of historical events leading up to a description of the current situation
   (D) A statement of a commonly accepted theory that is then subjected to a critical analysis

8. Which of the following best states the central thesis of the passage?

   (F) The value system of Japan is based upon traditional and conservative values that have, in modern times, been modified by Western and other liberal values.
   (G) Students and radicals in Japan have used Leninist ideology to distort the meaning of democratic, Western values.
   (H) The notions of personal freedom and individual liberty did not find immediate acceptance in Japan because of the predominance of traditional group values.
   (J) Modern Japanese society is characterized by hierarchical relationships in which a personal tie to a superior is often more important than merit.

D. QUIZ IV (10 items; 15 minutes)

Items #1–10 are based on the following passage.

SOCIAL STUDIES: This passage discusses the presidential election of 1796 between Thomas Jefferson and John Adams.

"Heartily tired" from the brutal, almost daily, conflicts that erupted over questions of national policy between himself and Alexander Hamilton, Thomas Jefferson resigned his position as Secretary of State in
5 1793. Although his Federalist opponents were convinced that this was merely a strategic withdrawal to allow him an opportunity to plan and promote his candidacy for the presidency should Washington step down in 1796, Jefferson insisted that this retirement
10 from public life was to be final.

But even in retirement, the world of politics pursued him. As the election grew nearer and it became apparent that Washington would not seek a third term, rumors of Jefferson's presidential ambitions grew in
15 intensity. Reacting to these continuous insinuations in a letter to James Madison, Jefferson admitted that while his enemies to impugn his political motives had originated the idea that he coveted the office of chief executive, he had been forced to examine his true
20 feelings on the subject for his own peace of mind. In so doing he concluded that his reasons for retirement—the desire for privacy, and the delight of family life— coupled with his now failing health were insuperable barriers to public service. The "little spice of ambition"
25 he had in his younger days had long since evaporated and the question of his presidency was forever closed.

Jefferson did not actively engage in the campaign on his own behalf. The Republican Party, presaging modern campaign tactics, created a grass roots
30 sentiment for their candidate by directing their efforts toward the general populace. In newspapers, Jefferson was presented as "the uniform advocate of equal rights among the citizens" while Adams was portrayed as the "champion of rank, titles, heredity, and distinctions."
35 Jefferson was not certain of the outcome of the election until the end of December. Under the original electoral system established by the Constitution, each presidential elector cast his ballot for two men without designating between them as to office. The candidate
40 who received the greater number of votes became the president; the second highest, the vice president. Based on his own calculations, Jefferson foresaw that the electoral vote would be close. He wrote to Madison that in the event of a tie, he wished for the choice to be
45 in favor of Adams. The New Englander had always

been his senior in public office, he explained, and the expression of public will being equal, he should be preferred for the higher honor. Jefferson, a shrewd politician, realized that the transition of power from the
50 nearly mythical Washington to a lesser luminary in the midst of the deep and bitter political divisions facing the nation could be perilous, and he had no desire to be caught in the storm that had been brewing for four years and was about to break. "This is certainly not a
55 moment to covet the helm," he wrote to Edward Rutledge. When the electoral vote was tallied, Adams emerged as the victor. Rejoicing at his "escape," Jefferson was completely satisfied with the decision. Despite their obvious and basic political differences,
60 Jefferson genuinely respected John Adams as a friend and compatriot. Although he believed that Adams had deviated from the course set in 1776, Jefferson never felt a diminution of confidence in Adams' integrity and was confident he would not steer the nation too far off
65 its Republican tack. Within two years, Jefferson's views would be drastically altered as measures such as the Alien and Sedition Acts of 1798 convinced him of the need to wrest control of the government from the Federalists.

1. The phrase "heartily tired" (line 1) is most probably a quotation from:

   (A) Alexander Hamilton.
   (B) Thomas Jefferson.
   (C) George Washington.
   (D) John Adams.

2. The "escape" mentioned in line 57 refers to the fact that Jefferson:

   (F) was no longer Secretary of State.
   (G) would not be burdened with the problems of the presidency.
   (H) fled the country following the election.
   (J) was hoping that the votes would be recounted.

3. According to the passage, the Republican Party appealed primarily to:

   (A) wealthy landowners.
   (B) ordinary people.
   (C) prosperous merchants.
   (D) high society.

4. The author states that all of the following were reasons Jefferson resigned as Secretary of State EXCEPT:

(F) Jefferson disliked Madison.
(G) Jefferson wanted to spend time with his family.
(H) Jefferson was weary of the demands of public service.
(J) Jefferson wished for greater privacy.

5. The author is primarily concerned with revealing the:

(A) feud between Alexander Hamilton and Thomas Jefferson.
(B) difference between the Federalists and the Republicans.
(C) strategies used by early American political parties.
(D) character and personality of Thomas Jefferson.

6. The author relies on which of the following in developing the selection?

    I. Personal correspondence
    II. Newspapers
    III. Voter registration rolls

(F) I only
(G) II only
(H) I and II only
(J) I and III only

7. One reason for Jefferson's retirement was his disagreement with:

(A) Alexander Hamilton.
(B) George Washington.
(C) James Madison.
(D) Edward Rutledge.

8. In the context of the passage, the phrase "covet the helm" (line 55) means:

(F) to aspire to be President.
(G) to desire to purchase a boat.
(H) to wish to be left in peace.
(J) to hope to become wealthy.

9. The passage suggests that two years after the 1796 election, Jefferson would:

(A) ally himself with Alexander Hamilton.
(B) ally himself with John Adams.
(C) disagree with John Adams.
(D) disagree with Edward Rutledge.

10. The newspaper depicted Jefferson and Adams as:

(F) conservative and liberal, respectively.
(G) liberal and conservative, respectively.
(H) conservatives.
(J) liberals.

E. QUIZ V (10 items; 15 minutes)

Items #1–10 are based on the following passage.

HUMANITIES: This passage discusses the voyages to North American continents by Leif Ericsson and Biarni and debates the veracity of the varied accounts.

In the summer of 999, Leif Ericsson voyaged to Norway and spent the following winter with King Olaf Tryggvason. Substantially the same account is given by both the Saga of Eric the Red and the Flat Island Book.
5 Of Leif's return voyage to Greenland the latter says nothing, but according to the former it was during this return voyage that Leif discovered America. The Flat Island Book, however, tells of another and earlier landfall by Biarni, the son of a prominent man named
10 Heriulf, and makes this Leif's inspiration for the voyage to the new land. In short, like Leif, Biarni and his companions sight three countries in succession before reaching Greenland, and to come upon each new land takes one "doegr" more than the last until Biarni
15 comes to land directly in front of his father's house in the last-mentioned country.

Most later writers have rejected this narrative, and they may be justified. Possibly, Biarni was a companion of Leif when he voyaged from Norway to
20 Greenland via America, or it may be that the entire tale is but a garbled account of that voyage and Biarni another name for Leif. It should be noted, however, that the stories of Leif's visit to King Olaf and Biarni's to that king's predecessor are in the same narrative in
25 the Flat Island Book, so there is less likelihood of duplication than if they were from different sources. Also, Biarni landed on none of the lands he passed, but Leif apparently landed on one, for he brought back specimens of wheat, vines, and timber. Nor is there any
30 good reason to believe that the first land visited by Biarni was Wineland. The first land was "level and covered with woods," and "there were small hillocks upon it." Of forests, later writers do not emphasize them particularly in connection with Wineland, though
35 they are often noted incidentally; and of hills, the Saga says of Wineland only "wherever there was hilly ground, there were vines."

Additionally, if the two narratives were from the same source, we should expect a closer resemblance of
40 Helluland. The Saga says of it: "They found there hellus" (large flat stones). According to the Biarni narrative, however, "this land was high and mountainous." The intervals of one, two, three, and four "doegr" in both narratives are suggestive, but
45 mythic formulas of this kind may be introduced into narratives without altogether destroying their historicity. It is also held against the Biarni narrative that its hero is made to come upon the coast of Greenland exactly in front of his father's home. But it
50 should be recalled that Heriulfsness lay below two high mountains that served as landmarks for navigators.

I would give up Biarni more readily were it not that the story of Leif's voyage, contained in the supposedly more reliable Saga, is almost as amazing.
55 But Leif's voyage across the entire width of the North Atlantic is said to be "probable" because it is documented in the narrative of a preferred authority, while Biarni's is "improbable" or even "impossible" because the document containing it has been
60 condemned.

1. The author's primary concern is to demonstrate that:

   (A) Leif Ericsson did not visit America.
   (B) Biarni might have visited America before Leif Ericsson.
   (C) Biarni did not visit Wineland.
   (D) Leif Ericsson visited Wineland first.

2. The passage provides information that defines which of the following terms?

   I. Doegr
   II. Hellus
   III. Heriulfsness

   (F) I only
   (G) II only
   (H) I and II only
   (J) II and III only

3. It can be inferred from the passage that scholars who doubt the authenticity of the Biarni narrative make all of the following objections EXCEPT:

(A) Biarni might have accompanied Leif Ericsson on the voyage to America, and that is why a separate, erroneous narrative was invented.
(B) the similarity of the voyages described in the Saga and in the Flat Island Book indicates that there was but one voyage, not two voyages.
(C) it seems very improbable that a ship, having sailed from America to Greenland, could have found its way to a precise point on the coast of Greenland.
(D) both the Saga of Eric the Red and the Flat Island Book make use of mythic formulas, so it is probable that the same person wrote them both.

4. The author mentions the two high mountains (lines 50–51) in order to show that it is:

(F) reasonable for Biarni to land precisely at his father's home.
(G) possible to sail from Norway to Greenland without modern navigational equipment.
(H) likely that Biarni landed on America at least 100 years before Leif Ericsson.
(J) probable that Leif Ericsson followed the same course as Biarni.

5. All of the following are mentioned as similarities between Leif Ericsson's voyage and Biarni's voyage EXCEPT:

(A) both visited Norway.
(B) on the return voyage, both visited three different lands.
(C) both returned to Greenland.
(D) both sighted Wineland.

6. It can be inferred that the author regards the historicity of the Biarni narrative as:

(F) conclusively proved.
(G) almost conclusively proved.
(H) possibly true.
(J) highly unlikely.

7. In the final paragraph, the author suggests that some authorities who regard the Saga as authentic are guilty of which of the following errors in reasoning?

(A) Oversimplification
(B) Logical contradiction
(C) False analogy
(D) Circular reasoning

8. According to the passage, Heriulf is:

(F) Leif Ericsson's son.
(G) one of Leif Ericsson's sailors.
(H) Biarni's father.
(J) King Olaf Tryggvason's son.

9. According to the author, most authorities regard the Biarni narrative as:

(A) conclusively demonstrated.
(B) probably true.
(C) probably untrue.
(D) an attempted fraud.

10. Biarni's home was in:

(F) Norway.
(G) Greenland.
(H) Wineland.
(J) Flat Island.

E. QUIZ VI (10 items; 15 minutes)

Items #1–10 are based on the following passage.

NATURAL SCIENCES: This passage reviews the basic physics of electromagnetic waves and radar specifically.

Whether used to control airplane traffic, detect speeding automobiles, or track a hurricane, radar is a very useful tool. Developed during World War II, this technology allows for remote sensing, that is, locating
5 objects that are not seen directly. The word "radar" is a contraction of "radio detection and ranging." It works in much the same way as an echo. When you shout toward a cliff or a large building, part of the sound bounces back. In radar, waves of electromagnetic
10 radiation are sent out. When they strike an object, they bounce back and are picked up by a receiver. The returning signal indicates the direction of the object; the time it takes for the signal to return indicates the distance to the object. Radar waves detect objects by
15 their varying densities. They are not deflected by atmospheric layers and therefore always travel in a straight line—in all weather, both day and night.

Radar waves are electromagnetic waves, as are light waves, electric waves, x-rays, cosmic rays, and
20 radio waves. All electromagnetic waves travel at 300,000 kilometers per second—the speed of light. Waves differ from each other in the number of times they vibrate per second; this variable is known as frequency and is usually expressed as cycles per
25 second. Waves also differ in their size, or wavelength. The speed, frequency, and wavelength of a wave are related by the wave equation in which:

$$\text{speed} = \text{frequency} \cdot \text{wavelength}$$

This shows that the product of the frequency and
30 wavelength of any given wave is always a constant— the speed of light. To find the wavelength of a wave, knowing the frequency, this formula is used:

$$\text{wavelength} = \frac{\text{speed}}{\text{frequency}}$$

For example, if a radio station broadcasts waves at
35 600,000 cycles per second (cps), the wavelength would be calculated this way:

$$\text{wavelength} = \frac{300,000 \text{ km per sec}}{600,000 \text{ cps}} = 0.5 \text{ km} = 500 \text{ m}$$

If the frequency of the wave is doubled to 1,200,000 cycles per second, its wavelength would be cut in half
40 to 250 meters. Since frequencies are so high, the unit "megahertz" is usually used; 1 megahertz = 1,000,000 cycles per second.

Wavelengths within the electromagnetic spectrum vary greatly. Radar has wavelengths that measure from
45 approximately one centimeter (0.01 meters) up to one meter. Each kind of wave has a range of wavelengths. The table compares some sample wavelengths of several kinds of electromagnetic waves.

Type of Wave (meters)	Sample Wavelength
cosmic rays	0.0000000000000001
x-rays	0.0000000001
ultraviolet rays	0.00000001
visible light	0.000001
infrared heat	0.0001
microwaves	0.001
radar	0.1
television	1.0
radio	100
long radio waves	10,000
electric power	1,000,000

1. Radio waves and radar waves have the same:

   (A) frequency.
   (B) wavelength.
   (C) cycles per second.
   (D) speed.

2. A radar signal having a frequency of 3,000 megahertz would have a wavelength of:

   (F) 0.001 km.
   (G) 0.01 km.
   (H) 10 m.
   (J) 0.1 m.

3. A radar set could not locate an airplane if it were flying:

   (A) faster than the speed of sound.
   (B) above a heavy storm.
   (C) above the atmosphere.
   (D) below the horizon.

4. It is possible to find the distance to an object from a radar set because the:

   (F) wavelength of radar is known.
   (G) frequency of radar is known.
   (H) speed of radar is 300,000 kilometers per second.
   (J) set operates at 10 megahertz.

5. The relationship between the frequency and wavelength of a wave is:

   (A) constant.
   (B) directly proportional.
   (C) exponential.
   (D) inverse.

6. An antenna picks up a signal that has a wavelength of about one meter. It is likely to be:

   (F) in the visible spectrum.
   (G) an ultraviolet ray.
   (H) a television signal.
   (J) an x-ray.

7. Radio waves will not penetrate the ionosphere, but microwaves will. Would you expect x-rays to penetrate the ionosphere?

   (A) Yes, because they have a shorter wavelength than microwaves and radio waves.
   (B) Yes, because they have a lower frequency than microwaves and radio waves.
   (C) No, because they travel more slowly than microwaves.
   (D) No, because they have fewer cycles per second than microwaves or radio waves.

8. Compared to cosmic rays, the frequency value of visible light waves is:

   (F) higher.
   (G) lower.
   (H) the same.
   (J) Cannot be determined from the given information

9. Which factor would be most important in order for radar to detect and track storms?

   (A) Radar signals travel in straight lines.
   (B) The densities of moist air masses are different from those of dry air masses.
   (C) The atmosphere does not deflect radar signals.
   (D) Radar signals travel much faster than storm tracks.

10. Like a radar reflection, an echo can be used to determine the distance of an object. This must be because:

    (F) sound is a form of radar.
    (G) sound travels at a relatively fixed rate.
    (H) sound waves have different frequencies.
    (J) sound waves are invisible.

CAMBRIDGE TESTPREP™

READING

STRATEGY SUMMARY SHEET

ITEM-TYPE STRATEGIES: Knowing the seven item-types can help you to quickly identify what an item is asking.

1. *Main Idea:* Main Idea items ask about the central theme that unifies the passage(s).

   > EXAMPLES: *Which of the following is the main point of the passage?*
   > *The primary purpose of the passage is to....*

2. *Explicit Detail:* Explicit Detail items ask about details that are specifically mentioned in the passage. This type of item differs from a Main Idea item in that explicit details are points provided by the author in developing the main idea of the passage. Explicit Detail items provide "locator words" that identify the required information in the passage.

   > EXAMPLES: *The author mentions which of the following?*
   > *According to the passage,...?*

3. *Vocabulary:* Vocabulary items test the understanding of a word or phrase in context. The nature of the Vocabulary items indicates two points. First, the correct answer choice will make sense when it is substituted for the referenced word. Second, the correct answer choice may not be the most commonly used meaning of the word; in fact, if it were, then what would be the point of including the item on the test? Thus, the general strategy for this type of item is to favor the less commonly used meaning.

   > EXAMPLES: *The word "..." in line ## means....*
   > *In line ##, what is the best definition of "   "?*

4. *Development:* Development items ask about the overall structure of the passage or about the logical role played by a specific part of the passage.

   > EXAMPLES: *The author develops the passage primarily by....*
   > *The author mentions...in order to....*

5. *Implied Idea:* Rather than ask about what is specifically stated in the passage, Implied Idea items ask about what can be logically inferred from what is stated in the passage. For example, the passage might explain that a certain organism (X) is found only in the presence of another organism (Y). An accompanying Implied Idea item might ask the following question: "If organism Y is not present, what can be inferred?" Since the passage implies that in the absence of Y, X cannot be present, the answer would be "X is not present." Since this type of item generally builds on a specific detail, "locator words" for identifying information in the passage are often provided in the item stem.

   > EXAMPLES: *The passage implies that....*
   > *The author uses the phrase "..." to mean....*

6. *Application:* Application items are similar to Implied Idea items, but they go one step further: Examinees must apply what they have learned from the passage to a new situation.

   > EXAMPLES: *With which of the following statements would the author most likely agree?*
   > *The passage is most probably taken from which of the following sources?*

7. *Voice:* Voice items ask about the author's attitude toward a specific detail or the overall tone of the passage.

> EXAMPLES: *The tone of the passage can best be described as....*
> *The author regards...as....*

GENERAL STRATEGIES: Reading strategies are not an exact science. Practice is essential to mastering the following techniques:

1. ***Read the first sentence of each passage in the Reading Test.*** The first step is to read the first sentence of each passage, and then label each passage as either "Easy" or "Hard" based on your initial understanding of the material and your level of interest. Analyze the easier passages first.

2. ***Preview the first and last sentences of each paragraph.*** There is usually an introductory paragraph for excerpted passages that identifies the author and provides a brief description of the selection. First, read this introductory material to gain clues as to the author's point of view. Then, preview the first and last sentences of each paragraph, as they often provide paragraph summaries.

3. Preview the item stems for a given passage. Code each item stem as one of the following three levels of reading comprehension:

   a. ***Level 1—General Theme (GT):*** The first level of reading, appreciation of the ***general theme***, is the most basic. Main Idea items and items about the overall development of the selection test whether you understand the passage at the most general level. The first sentence of a paragraph—often the topic sentence—may provide a summary of the content of that paragraph. Also, the last sentence of a paragraph usually provides concluding material that may also be helpful in understanding the general theme of the passage.

      > EXAMPLE: Main Idea items

   b. ***Level 2—Specific Points (SP):*** The second level of reading, understanding of ***specific points***, takes you deeper into the selection. Explicit Detail items, items about the meanings of words, and items about the logical role of details all test your ability to read carefully. Since this is an "open-book" test, you can always return to the selection. Therefore, if something is highly technical or difficult to understand, do not dwell on it for too long—come back later if necessary.

      > EXAMPLES: Explicit Detail items
      > Vocabulary items
      > Development items

   c. ***Level 3—Evaluation (E):*** The third level of reading, ***evaluation*** of the text, takes you even deeper into the selection. Implied Idea, Application, and Voice items ask not just for understanding, but require a judgment or an evaluation of what you have read. This is why these items are usually the most difficult.

      > EXAMPLES: Implied Idea items
      > Application items
      > Voice items

4. ***Read the passage.*** Ask what the author is attempting to describe, especially in the case of Evaluation items. Also, read the first sentence in each paragraph prior to reading the entire selection. This step is optional, depending on the ease of the selection, your personal preference, and the time available. Bracket difficult material, either mentally or with some sort of a mark, and then simply revisit it if necessary or if time permits. Instead of wasting time re-reading, attempt to understand the context in which the author introduces a particular concept.

5. ***Circle the answers to the items in the test booklet, and transcribe the answers to all the items for a passage to the answer sheet after finishing each passage.*** Circle the answers to the items in the test booklet. This approach helps increase accuracy and makes checking your work easier and more efficient. For each selection, transcribe the answers to the answer sheet together as a group. Only when the time limit approaches should you transcribe the answers individually.

ADDITIONAL STRATEGIES FROM IN-CLASS DISCUSSION: _____

_____

_____

_____

_____

_____

_____

_____

_____

_____

_____

_____

_____

_____

_____

_____

_____

_____

_____

_____

_____

_____

_____

Science

CAMBRIDGE TESTPREP™

SCIENCE

COURSE CONCEPT OUTLINE: WHAT YOU ABSOLUTELY MUST KNOW

I. Test Mechanics (p. 219)

II. Lesson (p. 226)

A. Preliminaries

B. Facts about Science Test

1. Three Types of Passages
   a. Data Representation
   b. Research Summary
   c. Conflicting Viewpoints
2. Science Items Test Reasoning, Not Knowledge

C. Item-Types

1. Comprehension
2. Analysis
3. Application

D. General Strategies

1. Plan Your Attack—Easiest Passages First
2. Do Not Preview Item Stems before Reading Passage
3. Underline Key Words and Phrases
4. Pay Attention to What Is There, Not What Isn't There
5. Pay Attention to Differences
6. Watch for Assumptions
7. Look for Trends
8. Transcribe Answers in Groups
9. Answer the Question That Is Being Asked
10. Work Out the Answer First
11. Make Notes to Clarify Viewpoints

E. Data Representation Review and Strategies

1. Graphs
   a. Straight Lines
   b. Parabolic Curves
   c. Graph Reading Strategies (Items #1–3, p. 226)
2. Tables
   a. Understanding Nature of Data (Items #4–5, p. 228)
   b. Recognizing Trends (Items #6–8, p. 228)
   c. Drawing Conclusions (Item #9, p. 228)
3. Typical Data Representation Items (Items #10–14, p. 230)

TEST MECHANICS

BASICS

The Science Test consists of 40 multiple-choice questions divided into seven groups. Each group of questions is based on a report of data findings, a description of an experiment, or the presentation of a debate on different scientific theories. The time limit for the Science Test is 35 minutes.

We'll call the initial presentation a "passage," whether it is a report of data (Data Representation), a description of an experiment (Research Summary), or a debate of a theory (Conflicting Viewpoints). So, just as the English and Reading Tests have passages with associated questions, the Science Test has passages (of the three types) with associated questions. We'll use this terminology even though "passage" doesn't quite fit here since the Science Test uses a lot of diagrams, pictures, tables, and graphs.

The Science Test roughly follows the content of science courses taught in grades 7 through 12. Passages use content from the following areas:

- **Biology:** botany, cellular biology, ecology, evolution, genetics, microbiology, zoology

- **Chemistry:** biochemistry, organic chemistry, nuclear chemistry, thermo-chemistry, acids and bases, kinetics and equilibria, properties of matter

- **Earth/Space Sciences:** astronomy, environmental science, geology, meteorology, oceanography

- **Physics:** mechanics, thermodynamics, fluids, solids, electromagnetism, optics

Although these are obviously "science" subjects, you don't really need to know any science—beyond some basic concepts—to do well on this part of the exam. In fact, the ACT Science Test would be more accurately labeled "Science Reasoning" Test because that phrase would emphasize that the questions test reasoning ability and not the mastery of some specific body of scientific knowledge.

ANATOMY

DIRECTIONS: The passages presented in the test are each followed by a set of items. Read the passage and choose the best answer for each item. Fill in the corresponding oval on your bubble sheet. You may refer to the passage as often as necessary to answer the passage items.

Warning: Calculator use is not permitted on this test.

A student studied the process by which malodorzane is produced by heated protocrud in a closed system and then released into the surrounding atmosphere.

Now that you've read the directions, you don't need to read them again, especially not during the test. The only thing of real significance is that you CANNOT use your calculator on this part, even though you might think it would be nice. But you should be able to remember that one point without re-reading the directions.

In this Science passage, there is a single device and a series of tables that report data from the operation of the device. You'll see examples of other types of passages later in the lesson.

Malodorzane
Detector

Check Valve

Jocularity
Meter

0   +

Outlet Pipe

Gastile
Emissions

Aerosanizen
(neutralizes
Malodorzane)

Closed
Container   Malodorzane

Probe
Thermometer

Protocrud

Electric Heating Element

Experiment 1

The concentration of malodorzane produced by the protocrud at various temperatures was measured by determining how much aerosanizen was needed to neutralize the malodorzane (Table 1).

Table 1

Temperature of Protocrud	Aerosanizen (spritz/min.)
20°C	46–198
22.5°C	199–377
25°C	378–612

Experiment 2

The student observed that the release of gastiles, whether or not the malodorzane was counteracted by aerosanizen, produced primary and secondary jocularities. The intensity of the jocularities was measured and recorded by different durations of gastiles (Table 2).

Table 2

Gastiles (seconds)	Intensity of Jocularities	
	Primary Jocularities (decibels)	Secondary Jocularities (decibels)
1.0	30 dB	—
2.0	35 dB	—
5.0	40 dB	30 dB
12.0	60 dB	40 dB
19.0	120 dB	60 dB

Note: "—" indicates that intensity was below measurable levels.

Experiment 3

The student measured and recorded the duration of the jocularities for different durations of gastiles (see Table 3).

Table 3

Gastiles (seconds)	Duration of Jocularities	
	Primary Jocularities (seconds)	Secondary Jocularities (seconds)
0.2	3	2
1.0	7	6
2.5	13	11
5.0	25	9
12.0	51	4

1. Data from the passage indicate that duration was greatest for secondary jocularities produced by gastiles of what duration?

   A. 1.0 seconds
   B. 2.5 seconds
   C. 5.0 seconds
   D. 12.0 seconds

Data for the duration of jocularities is given in Table 3, and the greatest entry, 11 seconds, corresponds to gastiles of 2.5 seconds. So, (B) is the correct answer.

2. Gastiles with a duration of 13.0 seconds would probably produce primary jocularities of a duration:

   F. between 3 and 7 seconds.
   G. between 7 and 13 seconds.
   H. between 13 and 25 seconds.
   J. greater than 51 seconds.

Again, the answer is in Table 3, but this time there is no entry for 13 seconds. The largest entry is 12.0 seconds. Therefore, the corresponding entry in the "Primary Jocularities" column, if one existed, would have to be greater than 51 seconds. So, (J) is the correct answer.

3. A primary jocularity of 90 decibels would most likely be produced by a gastile of:

   A. less than 1.0 seconds.
   B. between 1.0 and 2.0 seconds.
   C. between 12.0 and 19.0 seconds.
   D. greater than 5.0 seconds.

The relevant information is located in Table 2, but there is no entry in the table for 90 dB. However, that value is between 60 dB and 120 dB. The most likely conclusion, then, is that the corresponding entry in the first column, if one existed, would be between 12.0 and 19.0 seconds. So, (C) is the correct answer.

4. The data in Table 1 would be most useful in determining whether:

   F. the temperature of aerosanizen affects the chemical's ability to neutralize malodorzane.
   G. the volume of malodorzane varies with the chemical composition of the protocrud.
   H. the closed system produces a greater volume of malodorzane than aerosanizen.
   J. the temperature of the protocrud affects the rate of malodorzane production.

Table 1 shows the amount of aerosanizen needed to neutralize the quantity of malodorzane at various temperatures. So, the data in that table would provide information about how the temperature of the protocrud affects the rate of malodorzane production. So, (J) is the correct answer.

PACING

The table below establishes the time that you can afford to spend on various parts of the Science Test if your goal is to complete the entire test. For many people, completing the entire test may be an unrealistic goal, and it would be better to have the goal of doing just six of the seven passages. Or perhaps even only five passages. If you choose to define your goal differently than completing the entire test, then you can adjust the timing for the remaining passages so that you'll have more time (e.g., 4 minutes for 5 questions = 48 seconds per question).

You should begin work on each passage by reading the passage itself and familiarizing yourself with the main purpose of the data reports or experiments or the focus of the debate. This should be an overview of the information, not a detailed study. You are reading primarily to learn where information is located so that you can retrieve it—if a question asks about it.

Passage	Time to Spend	Remaining Time
I	5 minutes	30 minutes
II	5 minutes	25 minutes
III	5 minutes	20 minutes
IV	5 minutes	15 minutes
V	5 minutes	10 minutes
VI	5 minutes	5 minutes
VII	5 minutes	0 minutes

If you allow yourself one minute to learn about the passage, then you have 4 minutes left to answer the 5 or 6 questions, which is somewhere between 40 and 50 seconds per question. So, on the Science Test (perhaps more so than on any other test) time is of the essence.

GAME PLAN

1. ESTABLISH THE ORDER FOR DOING THE PASSAGES

You are not required to do the passages in the order in which they appear in the test booklet. You can do the first passage second, or fourth, or last; and you can do the last passage first or third. So, you have the flexibility of choosing which ones you will do before the others, and you'll want to do first those passages that seem easier. "Easier," in this context, is really a subjective matter; it means the ones with which you are most comfortable, either because of the type of presentation or the subject matter.

- First, do those passage formats that you find easiest to handle.

- Then, of the remaining passages, do the familiar ones.

- Finally, do the rest of the passages, from the simplest to the most complicated.

Put large numbers in the margins of the test booklet beside each passage to indicate where the passage comes in the order.

2. READ THE PASSAGE

For the Science Test, "reading the passage" means "reading through" the passage. You can't afford to study the passage, and don't forget that this is an "open-book" test. So, learn generally what is going on and where things are located. Then, let the questions tell you where to look more carefully.

- Read any introductory paragraph(s). Not only does this material usually explain why an experiment is being conducted or data are being collected, but it often defines a key term that is essential to understanding the connections of the various parts of the passage.

- Examine any diagrams or schematics. The focus of a passage is often a device that includes beakers, tubing, switches, pulleys, test tubes, and other paraphernalia associated with science. Try to understand what the device is designed to accomplish and how the various parts work together.

- Look at the various subparts of the passage. The subparts are things such as experiments that change initial conditions, tables of data, and graphs. Do not try to fully understand these. Just get a general notion of what they do. For example, for a graph, read the title and the labels of the x- and y-axes. For tables, read the column heads and the titles of the rows. Do not, however, read specific values on a graph or in a table. There are too many of them, and only one or two are likely to be relevant to answering one of the few questions based on that passage (compared to all the different questions that the test-writers could have chosen).

3. ANSWER THE QUESTIONS

Answer the question that is being asked. One of the most commonly made mistakes is to read the question carelessly and then answer the "wrong" question. It's just a matter of inattention, in which you respond to what you think you read rather than what is actually there on the page. Since wrong answers often correspond to wrong readings, if you make this mistake, you are probably going to find a pretty good answer—to the wrong question.

Pay attention to thought-reversers. "Thought-reversers" are words in the question stem like "NOT," "BUT," and "EXCEPT." These words turn the question upside-down. What is normally the right answer is now a wrong answer, and what is normally a wrong answer is the right answer. Circle these words and put stars beside them so that they get your attention again.

Locate the relevant information. The first and often last step in answering a question is to locate the information you need. Most question stems use a key word or phrase to tell you where to look. For example, "in Table 2" tells you that the information you need is located in Table 2; "the troposphere…" tells you that you need the graph, table, or description that supplies information about the troposphere; and "lowering the temperature" indicates that the answer is in the subpart of the passage that provides information about temperature.

4. USE THE ANSWER CHOICES

Study the answer choices for guidance. The answer choices, like a question stem, can direct you to the subpart of the passage that contains the information you need. Consider the following answer choices:

F. Sodium
G. Potassium
H. Lithium
J. Oxygen

With this array, you know to look at that table or graph or paragraph that includes that list of terms. The choices will also give you guidance as to what degree of precision is required by the question. Often, the choices are ranges of values, such as $0.015w$ to $0.018w$, rather than specific values, such as simply $0.018w$. Do not look for more precision than the choices allow.

Read the answer choices carefully. The test-writers love to put in wrong answers that look right. For example, if a particular value doubles with a decrease in temperature from 40° to 20° (it doesn't matter what scale; this is just a sketch of a question), a question might ask: "Assuming the temperature rises from 20° to 40°, what happens to the value?" The correct answer is, of course: "The value is reduced by half." But you can bet that the wrong answers will include ideas like "doubles," "increases by $\frac{1}{4}$," and "decreases by four"—or some other variation on those ideas.

5. ABOVE ALL, WHEN THE GOING GETS TOUGH, THE TOUGH GET GOING—TO THE NEXT PASSAGE

Do NOT spend too much time on any one question. Remember that you get +1 for the hardest question and +1 for the easiest question. The questions that correspond to a Science passage tend to be arranged from easiest to most difficult. (This is not an absolute rule; it is just a useful tool.) The first item may ask you to find a single number in a table. The second item may ask for a value that is the largest or smallest in a series. And the third item may require you to interpolate a value. Then, the going might get considerably more difficult. So, try the next item, and if it is completely whack, blow off the others and go to the next passage where the difficulty resets to the lowest setting.

LESSON

The passages and items in this section accompany the Science Lesson. They demonstrate the Science skills and concepts that are tested by the ACT, the PLAN, and the EXPLORE. You will work through the items with your instructor in class. Answers are on page 597.

DIRECTIONS: Each passage is followed by several items. After reading a passage, choose the best answer to each item. You may refer to the passages as often as necessary. You are NOT permitted the use of a calculator.

Passage I

The kinetic energy of an object with mass m (measured in grams) after a fall from a height h (measured in centimeters) was recorded for different heights. A graph was made representing the kinetic energy versus height.

1. If the kinetic energy is given in units of $g \cdot cm^2/s^2$ what units must the slope have?

   (A) $g \cdot cm/s$
   (B) $g \cdot cm/s^2$
   (C) $s \cdot cm/g$
   (D) $s^2/(g \cdot cm)$

2. It is discovered that if we redo the experiment with an object with twice the mass, the kinetic energy obtained for every height is doubled. The slope of the new set of experiments can be obtained by doing what to the old slope?

   (F) Multiplying by 2
   (G) Dividing by 2
   (H) Squaring
   (J) Taking the square root

3. What would be the kinetic energy in $g \cdot cm^2/s^2$ of an object of mass $\dot{m}$ if it were dropped from a height of 4.5 cm?

(A) 4.5
(B) 9.0
(C) 45
(D) 90

Passage II

A scientist investigated the variables that affect the age at which a female of the animal species *taedi periculum* first gives birth. Some of the results of this study are summarized in the table below.

Experiment	Temperature (°C)	Average food intake (grams)	Age when first gave birth (months)
1	25	15	7
2	25	30	6
3	25	45	4
4	35	15	5
5	35	30	3
6	35	45	3

4. Which of the following would be good animals to use for the experiment?

   (F) Adult females
   (G) Newborn females
   (H) Newborn males
   (J) Adult males

5. Which of the pairs of experiments listed below would be useful for studying the effect of temperature on the age of first birth?

   (A) 1 and 2
   (B) 1 and 5
   (C) 1 and 4
   (D) 2 and 6

6. If all other variables are kept constant, which of the following will result in an increase in the age at which the animals give birth?

   (F) Increase in temperature from 25° C to 35° C
   (G) Increase in food from 15 grams to 45 grams
   (H) Decrease in food from 30 grams to 15 grams
   (J) Increase in temperature from 25° C to 30° C

7. Which experiment was the control for temperature for Experiment 5?

   (A) Experiment 1
   (B) Experiment 2
   (C) Experiment 3
   (D) Experiment 6

8. If an experiment was set up with the temperature set at 30° C and the food intake at 30 grams, which of the following would be a reasonable prediction of the age in months of the animals when they first gave birth?

   (F) 7.5
   (G) 6.0
   (H) 4.5
   (J) 2.5

9. Which of the following conclusions is consistent with the data presented in the table?

   (A) The weight of the firstborn is proportional to the food intake.
   (B) The weight of the firstborn is related to the temperature.
   (C) The age of the mother at time of first offspring's birth increases with decreasing food intake.
   (D) The age of the mother at time of first offspring's birth decreases with decreasing food intake.

Passage III

The chart below shows the average blood pressure and relative total surface area associated with the different types of human blood vessels.

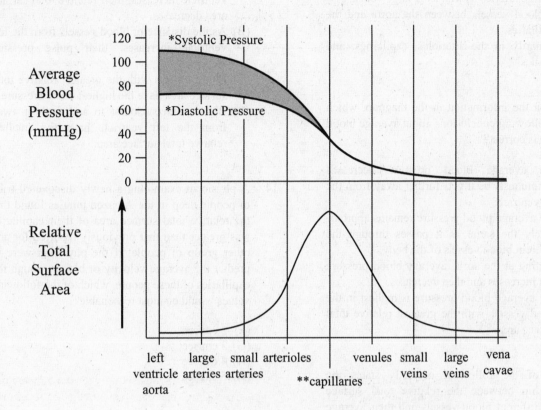

*Pulse pressure is the difference between systolic and diastolic pressure.
**Blood velocity is lowest in the capillaries (averaging 3 cm/sec).

10. According to the diagram, pulse pressure can be detected:

    (F) in large arteries only.
    (G) in large arteries as well as in large veins.
    (H) in blood vessels between the aorta and the capillaries.
    (J) primarily in the arterioles, capillaries, and venules.

11. Based on the information in the diagram, which of the following conclusions about average blood pressure is correct?

    (A) The average blood pressure decreases continuously as it gets further away from the left ventricle.
    (B) The average blood pressure remains approximately the same as it passes through the different blood vessels of the body.
    (C) Starting at the aorta, average blood pressure first increases and then decreases.
    (D) The average blood pressure is highest in the blood vessels with the greatest relative total surface area.

12. Which of the following correctly states the relationship between the relative total surface area of different blood vessels and their average blood pressure?

    (F) As relative total surface area decreases, average blood pressure increases.
    (G) As relative total surface area decreases, average blood pressure decreases.
    (H) As relative total surface area decreases, average blood pressure may increase or decrease.
    (J) Average blood pressure always changes in the opposite direction as the relative total surface area changes.

13. Which of the following conclusions can be drawn from the information provided in the diagram?

    (A) As the distance of blood vessels from the left ventricle increases, their relative total surface area decreases.
    (B) As the distance of blood vessels from the left ventricle increases, their pulse pressure increases.
    (C) Blood vessels with the greatest relative total surface area have the highest pulse pressure.
    (D) Blood vessels closest to and farthest away from the left ventricle have the smallest relative total surface area.

14. A physician examining a newly discovered tribe of people deep in the Amazon jungles found that the relative total surface area of their capillaries was greater than that previously reported for any other group of people. If the physician were to predict the average velocity of blood through the capillaries of these people, which of the following values would be most reasonable?

    (F) 2 cm/sec
    (G) 3 cm/sec
    (H) 4 cm/sec
    (J) 5 cm/sec

Passage IV

Ocean water contains "salt"—actually a mixture of ions, primarily sodium, chloride, potassium, calcium, magnesium, bicarbonate, and sulfate. The solid-line graph below indicates the percentage of these ions ("salinity") in a slab of ice that lies over seawater on a cold ocean surface. The arrow and dashed line indicate the salinity of the water beneath the ice.

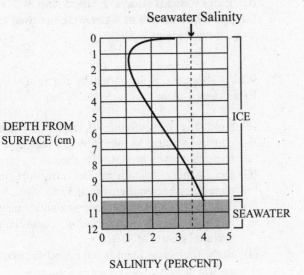

SALINITY (PERCENT)

15. According to this figure, the salt content of the ice above the ocean water:

    (A) equals 0.
    (B) is constant at all depths.
    (C) generally decreases with greater depth.
    (D) generally increases with greater depth.

16. Compared to the ocean water below it, the salinity of the ice is:

    (F) generally lower.
    (G) about the same.
    (H) generally higher.
    (J) unable to be determined.

17. The salinity of the ice at the surface of the slab is equal to the salinity of:

    (A) the ice at a depth of approximately 1.5 cm.
    (B) the ice at a depth of approximately 7.0 cm.
    (C) the ice at a depth of approximately 9.0 cm.
    (D) the water beneath the ice.

18. An experimenter wants to take a sample of ice that is one half the salinity of the seawater below. At what depth should he sample?

    (F) Between 1 and 2 cm
    (G) Between 4 and 5 cm
    (H) Either between 0 and 1 cm or between 3 and 4 cm
    (J) Between 5 and 6 cm

19. The investigator takes a 1-gram sample of ice from a depth of 10 cm, and wishes to take a sample of ice from 1.3 cm depth that will contain the same weight of total salts. How large a sample is needed?

    (A) 0.25 grams
    (B) 1.0 grams
    (C) 4.0 grams
    (D) 10 grams

Passage V

To test the hypothesis that all antibiotics are equally effective in preventing bacterial growth, the following three experiments were carried out using clear plastic plates filled with nutrient agar (a mixture of ingredients that supports the growth of bacteria).

Experiment 1: Three plates (A, B, and C) of agar were set up, each with an equal amount of bacterial culture (Bacterium X) spread over the agar surface and with a paper disk placed in the center. Plate A's disk was soaked in Antibiotic I; Plate B's disk was soaked in Antibiotic II; Plate C's disk was soaked in plain water. After incubation overnight at 37°C (body temperature), Plates A and B had a clear area, 2" in diameter surrounding the paper disk, but beyond this 2" region, the plates were cloudy. Plate C was entirely cloudy, including the area adjacent to the paper disk. When bacteria reproduce successfully, colonies form on the agar, giving it a cloudy appearance.

Experiment 2: Identical procedures were followed except that Plates A, B, and C were incubated overnight at 22°C (room temperature). After incubation, Plate A had a clear area, 2" in diameter, surrounding the paper disk. Plates B and C were entirely cloudy.

Experiment 3: Identical procedures were followed except that the concentrations of Antibiotic I (Plate A) and Antibiotic II (Plate B) were made twice as strong. After incubation overnight at 22°C, Plates A and B both had clear, 2" areas around the paper disk, while Plate C remained entirely cloudy.

20. After incubation, a clear area around a previously soaked paper disk represents a region where:

   (F) agar had washed away.
   (G) decomposition had occurred due to high incubation temperatures.
   (H) bacterial growth did not occur.
   (J) bacteria grew best.

21. Which of the following results would indicate that the antibiotics being tested have nothing to do with the control of bacterial growth?

   (A) A clear, 2" region was always observed around the disks soaked in water.
   (B) All results remained the same at the two experimental temperatures and at the two antibiotic concentration levels.
   (C) Plates A and B always remained clear.
   (D) The disks soaked in water were not used in the experiments at all.

22. Which statement is supported by the results of Experiment 1 alone?

   (F) Antibiotic I, Antibiotic II, and water are equally effective as inhibitors (preventers) of bacterial growth at 37°C.
   (G) Dry paper disks can be effective in controlling bacterial growth at 37°C.
   (H) The concentration of an antibiotic may influence its effectiveness in controlling bacterial growth at 37°C.
   (J) Both Antibiotics I and II can inhibit bacterial growth at 37°C.

23. The results of both Experiment 2 and Experiment 3 lead to which of the following conclusions?

   (A) Antibiotics I and II have similar effects on bacterial growth, regardless of concentrations.
   (B) Antibiotic II and water have similar effects on bacterial growth, regardless of concentrations.
   (C) The effectiveness of Antibiotic I at 22°C depends on its concentration.
   (D) The effectiveness of Antibiotic II at 22°C depends on its concentration.

24. Which hypothesis best explains the observation that the agar plates never appear clear beyond a 2" area surrounding the soaked paper disks?

(F) The bacteria cannot grow well within 2" of any moist paper disks.
(G) The antibiotics cannot seep through the agar beyond a distance of 2".
(H) At the experimental incubation temperatures used, the two antibiotics interfere with each other's effectiveness.
(J) The paper disks can absorb nutrients out of the agar from the distance of 2".

25. If either Antibiotic I or II could be prescribed for internal use to prevent the spread of Bacterium X infections, which recommendation, based on the experimental results, is appropriate if the cost due to the amount of antibiotic used per dose is the most critical factor (the antibiotics are equal in cost for equal concentrations)?

(A) Either Antibiotic I or II can be taken at equal cost.
(B) Antibiotic I would be less expensive.
(C) Antibiotic II would be less expensive.
(D) Neither Antibiotic I nor II would be effective in preventing the spread of Bacterium X.

Passage VI

To investigate the hypothesis that the quality of the detail of a fossil depends on the size of the particles that make up the rock surrounding the fossil, three experiments were performed using a particular type of leaf with many fine veins.

Experiment 1: A leaf was placed on a flat bed made of paste from extra-fine plaster and then completely covered with more of the same paste. A glass cover with a 5-lb weight was placed on top of the paste for one hour, until the plaster set. The plaster was then baked for 30 minutes at 25°C. When the cast was opened, the imprint of the leaf showed all of the veins, including the finest ones.

Experiment 2: A leaf was placed on a flat bed made of paste from fine-grade plaster and then completely covered with more of the same paste. A glass cover with a 5-lb weight was placed on top of the plaster for one hour, until the plaster set. The plaster was then baked for 30 minutes at 25°C. When the cast was opened, all the main veins were visible, but only isolated traces of the finer veins were found.

Experiment 3: A leaf was placed on a flat bed made of paste from coarse-grain plaster and then completely covered with more of the same paste. A glass cover with a 5-lb weight was placed on top of the plaster for one hour, until the plaster set. The plaster was then baked for 30 minutes at 25°C. When the cast was opened, only the thickest veins were visible, and some of the leaf edge was difficult to discern.

26. Should the investigator have used a different type of leaf in each experiment?

    (F) Yes: different types of structure could be studied.
    (G) Yes: in real life, many different types of fossils are found.
    (H) No: the leaf served as a controlled variable.
    (J) No: the nature of the leaf is not important.

27. When a fossil is formed, the sediment that surrounds it is normally compressed by the tons of earth deposited over it. What part of the model simulates this compressing element?

    (A) The 5-lb weight
    (B) The glass
    (C) The upper layer of paste
    (D) The baking oven

28. A fourth experiment was set up the same way as the previous three, except the paste was made by mixing equal amounts of very coarse sand with the extra-fine plaster. The investigator is likely to discover:

    (F) no change from Experiment 1 because only the plaster counts.
    (G) no change because the same kind of leaf is used.
    (H) the imprint is better than Experiment 1 because the sand provides air pockets.
    (J) the imprint is worse than Experiment 1 because the average particle size is bigger.

29. Which of the following hypotheses is supported by the results of Experiment 1 alone?

    (A) The finer the sediment the greater the detail of the resulting fossil.
    (B) Hardened sediment can preserve the imprint of a specimen.
    (C) All fossils must have been baked at high temperatures.
    (D) Only organic material can leave imprints in sediment.

30. Which of the following changes in the experiments would have permitted a test of the hypothesis that the quality of a fossil imprint depends on the pressure applied?

(F) Repeat the experiments except for using a 10-lb weight in Experiment 2, and a 20-lb weight in Experiment 3.
(G) Choose one of the plasters, and run experiments using the same plaster in all trials while varying the weights.
(H) Rerun all the experiments without the glass.
(J) Vary the depth of the leaf in each new trial, because in nature increased pressure means the fossil is at a greater depth.

Passage VII

Erosion refers to processes that wear down rocks and soil, as well as processes that transport the worn-away materials to other locations. Although these processes usually cause effects gradually (over geologic time), laboratory models can be designed to investigate which environmental factors affect erosion rate.

Three experimental sandboxes were set up that were identical in size (10 ft. • 15 ft.), had identical types of soil and rocks, and were filled to equal depths (3 ft.). The sandboxes were kept for two weeks in large environmental chambers, each maintained at a constant temperature, with a continuous wind flow of 5 mph.

Sandbox 1: One half was kept bare (just soil and rocks), while the other half had a variety of grasses and weeds planted among the soil and rocks. After two weeks, the bare half had small channels (ruts) running along its length that averaged 1 inch in width. The planted half had few channels, and those that were found averaged less than 1 inch wide.

Sandbox 2: The conditions were identical to those of Sandbox 1, with the addition that both halves were subjected to light, 15-minute showers of water every twelve hours. After two weeks, the bare half had channels averaging 4 inches wide, while the planted half had fewer channels averaging 2 inches wide.

Sandbox 3: The conditions were identical to those of Sandbox 2, but the entire box was mechanically raised to rest at an angle of 15° to simulate a steep slope. After two weeks, the bare half had channels averaging 7 inches wide, while channels in the planted half were less common and averaged 4 inches in width.

31. Results from all three sandboxes indicate that:

    (A) different types of soils and rocks are affected differently by environmental factors.
    (B) under all tested conditions, plants reduce erosion.
    (C) changing wind and temperature conditions can affect erosion patterns.
    (D) water from short periods of rain has little or no effect on erosion patterns.

32. Which of the following claims does the design and results of the experiments NOT support?

    (F) Light winds have no erosive effect.
    (G) Slopes have more erosion than level surfaces.
    (H) Water has major erosive effects.
    (J) The effects of changing temperature remain unanswered.

33. Sudden cloudbursts are known to cause more erosion than longer periods of mild rains. How could the present experiments be changed to examine this idea?

    (A) Raise the angle in Sandbox 3 to produce a steeper slope.
    (B) Add the "rain conditions" from Sandbox 2 to the conditions in Sandbox 1.
    (C) Include light, 15-minute showers every six hours instead of every twelve hours.
    (D) Every twelve hours allow the same total volume of water to fall in a 5-minute span rather than in a 15-minute span.

34. Should the investigator have used different soil types in each sandbox experiment?

    (F) Yes, because different soils may erode differently.
    (G) Yes, because a different group of plants could have been used in each sandbox as well.
    (H) No, because some soils can be washed completely away within the 2-week experiment.
    (J) No, because the soil type was a controlled variable in all three experiments.

35. Sandbox 3 specifically demonstrates the role of which particular variable in the set of experiments?

    (A) Rain
    (B) Wind
    (C) Gravity
    (D) Temperature

36. If another sandbox were set up, which of the following conditions would probably cause wider and deeper channels in the soil of the new sandbox than those in Sandbox 3?

     I. Steeper angles for the sandbox
    II. A greater volume of water during the 15-minute showers every twelve hours
   III. Removal of plants from soil

(F) I only
(G) I and II only
(H) II and III only
(J) I, II, and III

Passage VIII

Theory 1: Early in the twentieth century, many chemists believed that the stability of the molecule methane, CH_4, could be explained by the "octet" rule, which states that stability occurs when the central atom, in this case carbon, is surrounded by eight "valence," or outer, electrons. Four of these originally came from the outer electrons of the carbon itself, and four came from the four surrounding hydrogen atoms (the hydrogen atom was considered an exception to the rule since it was known to favor a closed shell of two electrons as helium has.) According to the octet rule, neither CH_3 nor CH_5 should exist as stable compounds, and this prediction has been borne out by experiment.

Theory 2: While the octet rule predicted many compounds accurately, it also had shortcomings. Ten electrons, for example, surround the compound PC_{15}. The greatest shock to the octet rule concerned noble gases such as krypton and xenon, which have eight electrons surrounding them in their atomic states, and therefore should not form compounds since no more electrons would be needed to make an octet. The discovery in 1960 that xenon could form compounds such as XeF_4 forced consideration of a new theory, which held that (a) compounds formed when electrons were completely paired, either in bonds or in non-bonded pairs; (b) the total number of shared electrons around a central atom varied, and could be as high as twelve; (c) the shapes of compounds were such as to keep the pairs of electrons as far from each other as possible.

For example, since six electrons in the atomic state surround sulfur, in the compound SF_6 it acquired six additional shared electrons from the surrounding fluorines for a total of twelve electrons. The shape of the compound is "octahedral," as shown below, since this conformation minimizes the overlap of bonding pairs of electrons.

37. According to Theory 1, the compound CH_2Cl_2:

   (A) should have eight electrons surrounding the carbon atom.
   (B) cannot exist since the original carbon atom does not have eight electrons.
   (C) should have eight electrons surrounding each hydrogen atom.
   (D) requires more electrons for stability.

38. According to Theory 1, the compound XeF_4:

   (F) exists with an octet structure around the xenon.
   (G) should not exist since more than eight electrons surround the xenon.
   (H) will have similar chemical properties to CH_4.
   (J) exists with the xenon surrounded by twelve electrons.

39. The atom boron has three outer electrons, and in bonding to boron, a fluorine atom donates one electron. The BF_3 molecule is known to exist. Which of the following is true?

    (A) BF_3 obeys Theory 1.
    (B) The existence of BF_3 contradicts Theory 2.
    (C) According to Theory 2, the structure of BF_3 is a pyramid:

    (D) According to Theory 2, the structure of BF_3 is triangular and planar:

40. A scientist seeking to explain why Theory 2 has more predictive power than Theory 1 might argue that:

    (F) eight electrons shall represent a "closed shell."
    (G) while eight electrons represent a "closed shell" for some atoms, for others the closed shell may be six, ten, or twelve.
    (H) it is incorrect to assume that a given atom always has the same number of electrons around it.
    (J) CH_4 is not as important a compound as XeF_4.

41. Theory 2 could be threatened by evidence of:

    (A) the existence of SF_4.
    (B) the existence of XeF_5.
    (C) molecules with stable octets.
    (D) the existence of SF_6.

Passage IX

Scientist 1: The atmosphere of the Earth was at one time almost totally lacking in oxygen. One piece of evidence supporting this assertion is the very fact that life got started at all. The first chemical reactions that are necessary for the origin of life, the formation of amino acids, require ultraviolet light. Most of the ultraviolet light coming from the Sun is now absorbed by oxygen in the atmosphere. If there were as much oxygen in the atmosphere then as there is now, there would have been too little ultraviolet light available to enable life to begin. Also, the oldest bacteria, the ones that have the shortest DNA, are almost all anaerobes—they either do not need oxygen or die if exposed to oxygen. Most of the oxygen that exists now entered the atmosphere later from volcanic fumes.

Scientist 2: The prevailing opinion is that the atmosphere, though thicker now than it was in the past, is not essentially different in composition. The argument that the Earth must originally have been deficient in oxygen is flawed. First of all, the presence of iron and other oxides in the rocks from this time indicates that there was oxygen available. Secondly, the requirement for a great deal of ultraviolet light holds only if there is a low concentration of the starting materials in the water. If the water in some prehistoric lake began to freeze, the starting materials would be concentrated in a small volume of unfrozen water. The high concentration of the starting materials would offset the so-called deficiency of ultraviolet light, and life could begin.

42. According to the hypothesis of Scientist 1, which of the following would have been among the last living things to evolve?

    (F) Anaerobes
    (G) Plants
    (H) Insects
    (J) Viruses

43. According to the information presented by Scientist 1, if his theory of the origin of oxygen in the atmosphere is correct, the total amount of oxygen in the air over the next million years, on the average, should:

    (A) decrease, then increase.
    (B) increase, then decrease.
    (C) increase.
    (D) decrease.

44. Underlying the argument of Scientist 2 is the assumption that the oxygen in the oxides in the rocks was:

    (F) always tied up in the rocks.
    (G) involved in biological reactions.
    (H) all gaseous during the early days of the atmosphere.
    (J) proportional to the oxygen in the atmosphere at the time.

45. Underlying Scientist 1's suggestion that the evolutionary record supports the idea of an oxygen deficiency on the early Earth is the assumption that the oldest living things:

    (A) have the shortest DNA.
    (B) have the most fragmented DNA.
    (C) have changed radically.
    (D) must have died out.

46. Which of the following is the strongest argument Scientist 1 could use to counter Scientist 2's suggested mechanism for the origin of life?

    (F) There was not enough ultraviolet light available.
    (G) Chemical reactions occurred differently then.
    (H) The temperature at the surface of the Earth at that time was always above 35°C because of geothermal heat release.
    (J) Most lakes would not have covered large enough areas to guarantee that all the essential building blocks were present.

47. To refute Scientist 1's hypothesis, Scientist 2 might best show that:

(A) the amount of oxide in rocks has changed little over the past four billion years.
(B) there are ways of making the biologically important molecules without ultraviolet light.
(C) there are complex anaerobic bacteria.
(D) the atmospheric pressure has not changed over the Earth's history.

Passage X

In the 1940s, 1950s, and 1960s, the growing field of animal behavior maintained an ongoing debate about the origin of observed behavior in many different animal species. Two extreme viewpoints were at the center of this "Nature vs. Nurture" debate.

Viewpoint 1 (Nature): Many behaviors or instincts are literally programmed by one or more genes. Genes serve as "blueprints" that enable an individual to carry out a particular stereotyped behavior (Fixed Action Pattern) as soon as the appropriate stimulus (releaser) is observed. Other individuals do not have to be observed performing the behavior. The releasing stimulus need never have been seen before. At first view of the releaser and every time thereafter, the Fixed Action Pattern will be carried out to completion in the exact same way—even if the releaser is removed before the Fixed Action Pattern is finished! Examples include: a) the pecking of baby gulls at the red spot on their mother's bill (which causes the mother gull to regurgitate food), b) song birds producing their species song without ever having heard it before, and c) a male stickle-back fish defending its territory by attacking anything red because other breeding males always have red underbellies.

Viewpoint 2 (Nurture): Many behaviors are determined by experience and/or learning during an individual's lifetime. Genes provide the limits of the "blank slate" that each individual starts out as, but then various experiences will determine the actual behavior patterns within the individual genetic range of possibilities. In other words, behavior can be modified. Examples include: a) positive ("reward") reinforcement and punishment causing a behavior to increase and decrease (respectively), and b) songbirds producing their species song only after having heard it performed by other individuals of their species.

48. The red spot on a mother gull's bill is called a(n):

   (F) Fixed Action Pattern.
   (G) instinct.
   (H) releaser.
   (J) stereotyped response.

49. To refute the strict "genetic blueprint" ideas of Viewpoint 1, a scientist could show that:

   (A) baby gulls peck at a stick with a red spot.
   (B) baby gulls will peck at mother gulls' red spot as soon as they hatch out of their eggs.
   (C) baby gulls pecking at the red spot happens exactly the same way each time.
   (D) baby gulls' accuracy in pecking at mother gulls' red spot improves with practice.

50. A food-seeking blue jay captured a distinctively colored butterfly that had a bad-tasting substance in its tissues. After spitting out the butterfly, it never again tried to capture a similarly colored butterfly. This incident seems to support:

   (F) Viewpoint 1.
   (G) Viewpoint 2.
   (H) both viewpoints.
   (J) neither viewpoint (the incident is irrelevant).

51. Which of the following supports Viewpoint 1?

   (A) A rat reaches the end of a maze by the same route, but finishes faster after each trip.
   (B) Monkey A watches other monkeys wash sweet potatoes before they eat them; then, he washes sweet potatoes before he eats them.
   (C) A male stickleback fish attacks a picture of a red mailbox held in front of his aquarium.
   (D) A bird performs its species song after hearing the song only once.

52. If baby chickens peck at grains of food on the ground when hungry, but not as much after they have recently eaten, then this:

   (F) supports Viewpoint 1.
   (G) supports Viewpoint 2.
   (H) does not refer to behavior.
   (J) is irrelevant to the Nature vs. Nurture debate.

53. It is thought that some species of birds "learn" to fly. This belief is based on observations of young birds fluttering and flapping their wings at the nest until they reach the age when flight is possible. In Species X, nestlings were kept in harmless, but tight plastic tubes in which they could not carry out such "practice movements." They were released when they reached the age of flight. Viewpoint 1 predicts that the birds will fly:

    (A) after fluttering their wings for a time.
    (B) after watching other birds flutter their wings.
    (C) after watching other birds flutter and fly.
    (D) immediately.

54. A songbird can sing its species song after it hears other birds of its own species singing. Yet, if it hears the song from another species, the bird will not sing the "foreign" song. This suggests that:

    (F) genetic "programming" and experience play a role in this species' ability to sing its song.
    (G) this species' song is a Fixed Action Pattern.
    (H) song development in this species is strictly a learned behavior with no genetic component.
    (J) genes appear to be far more important than experience in this example.

CHALLENGE ITEMS

The passages and items in this section reflect both the format and difficulty range of passages and items on the real Science Test, though difficult items are emphasized. Answers are on page 597.

DIRECTIONS: Each passage is followed by several items. After reading a passage, choose the best answer to each item. You may refer to the passages as often as necessary. You are NOT permitted the use of a calculator.

Passage I

The graph of the thin line below shows the hearing sensitivity of female moths. The auditory characteristics of certain sounds important to moth survival are also included.

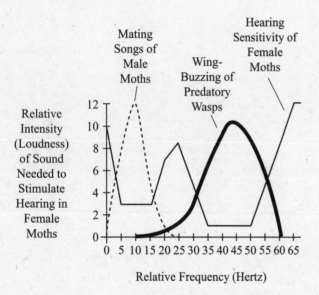

Relative Frequency (Hertz)

1. According to the graph, female moths are most sensitive to sounds between:

    (A) 0–5 Hertz.
    (B) 5–15 Hertz.
    (C) 20–25 Hertz.
    (D) 35–50 Hertz.

2. The nervous system of female moths may be set up to allow them to respond differently to sounds of different frequencies. Based on the information in the graph, which statement best describes the appropriate responses of female moths?

    (F) Approach sounds between 5–15 Hertz, withdraw from sounds between 35–50 Hertz
    (G) Approach sounds between 35–50 Hertz, withdraw from sounds between 5–15 Hertz
    (H) Approach sounds between 5–15 Hertz and 35–50 Hertz
    (J) Withdraw from sounds between 5–15 Hertz and 35–50 Hertz

3. Which of the following statements is supported by the information in the graph?

    (A) The wing-buzzing sounds of wasps occur at a narrower range of frequencies than the range of the male moth mating song.
    (B) The frequency range of the male moth mating song is narrower than the range of wasp wing-buzzing sounds.
    (C) Female moths cannot hear sounds with relative intensities less than 3.
    (D) Male moths are less sensitive to sounds than predatory wasps.

4. Which of the following statements accurately describes the relationship between the male moth mating song and female moth hearing sensitivity?

(F) The frequency range of the male song coincides with the frequency range at which females are maximally sensitive to any sound.

(G) Females need not be maximally sensitive at the frequency range of the male song because of the extremely high intensity of the song.

(H) Females cannot hear the male song if its intensity level is less than 10.

(J) The male song does not extend to an intensity level above 10.

5. If a new species of wasp were introduced into the moths' environment, which of the following wing-buzzing characteristics would make it the most successful predator of female moths?

(A) Extremely high intensity at relative frequencies between 35–50 Hertz

(B) An intensity level of 7–8 at relative frequencies between 20–25 Hertz

(C) Low intensity at relative frequencies above 60 Hertz

(D) Extremely high intensity at relative frequencies above 60 Hertz

6. A "new male" comes to town having a mating song with a frequency range between 20–25 Hertz and an intensity level of 4. What are his chances of finding a mate?

(F) Excellent

(G) Poor

(H) Good, if no wasps are present

(J) Cannot be determined from the given information

Passage II

A chemistry student wishes to study weight relationships between compounds before and after they take part in reactions. Two experiments were conducted to investigate two different reactions. The reactions are shown below, together with the amount (grams) of each substance before and after each reaction has proceeded. Equations are balanced to show the number of each type of atom before and after the reactions.

Experiment 1				
	NaBr +	AgNO$_3$ $\Rightarrow$	AgBr +	NaNO$_3$
Initial Wt.	103	170	0	0
Final Wt.	0	0	188	85

Experiment 2					
	Na$_2$CO$_3$ +	2HCl $\Rightarrow$	2NaCl +	H$_2$O (g) +	CO$_2$
Initial Wt.	106	72	0	0	(?)
Final Wt.	0	0	117	18	(?)

(The student has measured the quantities he could, but was unable to weigh the CO$_2$ because it is a gas. Since it is a gas, he assumes it has negligible weight.)

7. In Experiment 1, the data indicate that after the reaction has proceeded:

   (A) all of the Na originally present has been converted to Ag.
   (B) there are fewer molecules of NaNO$_3$ than there were molecules of AgNO$_3$ at the outset.
   (C) no NaBr remains.
   (D) no AgBr remains.

8. Which of the following is (are) conserved in the reaction in Experiment 1?

   I. mass
   II. number of atoms
   III. amount of AgNO$_3$

   (F) I only
   (G) I and II only
   (H) I and III only
   (J) I, II, and III

9. In Experiment 2, the mass of the weighed products is:

   (A) 0.
   (B) less than the mass of reactants.
   (C) equal to the mass of reactants.
   (D) greater than the mass of reactants.

10. Experiment 2 differs from Experiment 1 in that:

    (F) the number of atoms is not conserved.
    (G) the reaction does not go to completion.
    (H) there are no ionic compounds involved.
    (J) gas is evolved.

11. Assuming the student is right in neglecting the weight of one of the products in Experiment 2, he can conclude from the data that:

    (A) mass is consumed as the reaction proceeds.
    (B) mass is produced as the reaction proceeds.
    (C) energy is consumed as the reaction proceeds.
    (D) mass is conserved as the reaction proceeds.

12. The student is advised of a means to weigh the CO$_2$ gas produced in the reaction, and finds this weight to be 43 grams. The student can now state that the two experiments:

    (F) lead to similar conclusions: neither mass nor atoms are conserved.
    (G) lead to similar conclusions: both mass and atoms are conserved.
    (H) lead to different conclusions: the number of molecules is not the same for the reactants as for the products.
    (J) lead to different conclusions: gases have negligible weight.

Passage III

Jean Baptiste Lamarck hypothesized the process of biological evolution before Charles Darwin was born. Some aspects of Lamarck's ideas and Darwin's ideas are presented below.

Lamarckism: Observations of the fossil record led Lamarck to believe that several lines of descent led to nature's broad diversity of organisms. Old fossils and recent fossils showed patterns leading to the characteristics of modern species. He believed that newer forms were more complex and more "perfectly" adapted to their environment. New adaptations could arise as the environment changed. Body organs that were used to cope with the environment became stronger and larger, while those not used deteriorated. For example, giraffes stretching their necks to reach higher leaves would develop longer necks. In addition, such changes in structure could then be passed on to offspring (these acquired characteristics could be inherited).

Darwinism: Based on the fossil and geologic record, Darwin also came to believe that various modern species were related through descent from common ancestors. He also noted that the great diversity of organisms that he observed during his travels were all very well adapted to their environments. The adaptations, however, did not come about through "coping" or usage. Instead, individuals from a population can each show slight genetic or "heritable" differences (variability) in a trait. If such differences, by chance alone, give the individual some reproductive advantage (he or she can successfully produce more offspring than other members of the population), then more individuals with that trait will make up the next generation. Through this "natural selection" of individuals with characteristics that give them a slight advantage in their particular environment, species appear to become very well suited to their natural world. However, "perfection" is not a useful term since the environment is constantly changing. The adaptations that are advantageous "today" may not be advantageous "tomorrow" under different conditions.

13. A major difference between Lamarck and Darwin relates to their views on:

   (A) the diversity of organisms in the natural world.
   (B) the significance of fossils.
   (C) the importance of adaptations to the environment.
   (D) the way adaptations come about.

14. Which viewpoint supports the idea that present-day species are descended from earlier forms?

   (F) Lamarckism
   (G) Darwinism
   (H) Both viewpoints
   (J) Neither viewpoint

15. Which statement might be used by a Darwinist to explain the extinction of a species?

   (A) The environment changed, and not enough individuals had traits or adaptations well suited to the new conditions.
   (B) The environment changed, and body parts could not be manipulated enough to adapt to new conditions.
   (C) As the environment changed, the individuals present were not "perfect" enough.
   (D) As the environment changed, there was no "natural selection."

16. Darwin might dispute the Lamarckian idea of inheriting acquired characteristics by pointing out that:

   (F) giraffes with short necks may do just as well as those with long necks.
   (G) giraffes that break a leg and walk around on three legs all their lives still do not produce three-legged offspring.
   (H) giraffes had shorter necks millions of years ago.
   (J) giraffes that break a leg would not be able to reach the highest leaves.

17. Many species of moles live underground, in the dark. These species often have small, almost dysfunctional eyes. Which of the following statement(s) would a Lamarckian thinker use to explain this phenomenon?

  I. Moles without eyesight are better adapted for survival underground and therefore produce more offspring.
  II. Disuse of eyes in the dark led to their deterioration in mole species.
  III. Eye deterioration can be transferred to a mole's genes, which are then passed on to the next generation.

  (A) I only
  (B) II only
  (C) II and III only
  (D) I, II, and III

18. Which factor is vital to Darwin's ideas, but not to those of Lamarck?

  (F) The fossil record
  (G) An examination of modern species
  (H) The inheritance of adaptations
  (J) Chance

19. A few individuals in a population have an adaptation that enables them to tolerate extremely cold temperatures. In their lifetimes, the environment never reaches such extremes. If all other traits are the same among individuals, what would a Darwinist predict about the number of offspring left in the next generation by these individuals, compared to the number left by other members of the population?

  (A) These individuals will leave approximately the same number of offspring.
  (B) These individuals will leave more offspring.
  (C) These individuals will leave fewer offspring.
  (D) These individuals will probably not leave any offspring.

Passage IV

Graph I shows the relationship between the relative rates of activity of enzymes A and B and temperature. Graph II shows the relationship between the relative rates of activity of enzymes A and B and pH.

Graph I

Graph II

20. Under which conditions is enzyme A most effective?

(F) 40°C and a pH of 5
(G) 45°C and a pH of 5
(H) 45°C and a pH of 9
(J) 50°C and a pH of 9

21. The optimum environment for enzyme B is:

(A) acidic.
(B) basic.
(C) either acidic or basic.
(D) neutral.

22. At which one of the following temperatures do A and B exhibit the same relative rate of action?

(F) 6.9°C
(G) 10°C
(H) 37°C
(J) 47°C

23. At which pH do both A and B exhibit the same relative rate of action?

(A) 6.9
(B) 10
(C) 37
(D) 47

24. At what temperature does A have half the activity of B?

(F) 20°C
(G) 25°C
(H) 42°C
(J) 53°C

25. At what temperature does B have about half the activity of A?

(A) 20°C
(B) 30°C
(C) 42°C
(D) 53°C

26. Over which of the following pH ranges will both
A and B be active?

    (F) 1 to 3
    (G) 3 to 6
    (H) 6 to 8
    (J) 8 to 10

27. At what pH will both A and B be at their
maximum activity?

    (A) 2
    (B) 5
    (C) 8.5
    (D) No such pH

Passage V

A series of three experiments was designed to investigate the interrelationships between various factors known to influence gases: temperature (Kelvin), pressure (atmospheres), volume (liters), and the number of moles of gas.

Experiment 1: A gas at 200 K and a volume of 0.30 liters was found to have a pressure of 0.40 atm. After the temperature was raised to 400 K while keeping the volume the same, the pressure was found to be 0.80 atm.

Experiment 2: A gas at 200 K had a pressure of 0.50 atm. when its volume was 1 liter. Its volume was then increased to 2 liters at constant temperature. The resulting pressure was 0.25 atm.

Experiment 3: Two moles of a gas were found to occupy 44.8 liters at 1 atm. pressure and 273 K. Four moles of the same gas are added to the system with temperature and pressure held constant, resulting in a new volume of 134.4 liters.

28. Which of the following hypotheses is (are) supported by the results of Experiment 1?

    I. The pressure of the gas is proportional to its volume at constant temperature.
    II. The volume of the gas is proportional to its temperature at constant pressure.
    III. The pressure of a gas is proportional to its temperature at constant volume.

  (F) I only
  (G) I and II only
  (H) III only
  (J) II and III only

29. The results of Experiment 2 support the hypothesis that if the temperature of a gas is held constant, then the pressure:

  (A) increases as the volume increases.
  (B) decreases as the volume increases.
  (C) does not depend strongly on the volume.
  (D) Cannot be determined from the given information

30. The result of Experiment 3 supports the hypothesis that if both the pressure and the temperature of a gas are held constant, then the volume:

  (F) varies inversely with the number of moles of gas.
  (G) varies directly with the number of moles of gas.
  (H) is raised to a maximum value of 134.4 liters when additional gas is added.
  (J) does not depend on the number of moles of gas.

31. An experimenter put 0.08 moles of gas into a 4-liter flask at 273 K and 0.448 atm. pressure. She allowed 0.02 moles of the gas to escape, and she put the remaining gas into a smaller flask that caused the pressure to remain at 0.448 atm. pressure, while the temperature was kept constant as well. According to Experiment 3, the volume of the smaller flask must be:

  (A) 0.06 liter.
  (B) 0.448 liters.
  (C) 3 liters.
  (D) Cannot be determined from the given information

32. Six moles of a gas originally at 0.1 atm. pressure and 273 K occupy a volume of 13.4 liters. The temperature is then changed to 300 K and the volume changed to 10.0 liters. To predict the final pressure on the six moles of gas, a student should use the results of:

    I. Experiment 1.
    II. Experiment 2.
    III. Experiment 3.

  (F) I only
  (G) II only
  (H) I and II only
  (J) I and III only

33. The final pressure of the gas described in the previous question will be:

    (A) less than 0.1 atm. pressure.
    (B) equal to 0.1 atm. pressure.
    (C) greater than 0.1 atm pressure.
    (D) Cannot be determined from the given information

Passage VI

How did life originate on the planet Earth? Two opposing views are presented.

Scientist 1: The idea that Earth could have given rise to life independently is mistaken. Life on this planet must have come from elsewhere for several reasons. First of all, complex life appears very suddenly in the geological record. Secondly, all life on Earth has a very similar biochemistry. If life originated on Earth, one would expect regional variations in biochemistry, similar to the variations in species spread over large areas. Finally, the time when life first appeared in the geological record was also a time when large numbers of meteorites struck the Earth. The meteorites must have caused life to appear on the Earth. The simplest hypothesis is that the meteorites brought life with them.

Scientist 2: Life need not have been imported from outer space. The chemicals required for life existed on the surface of the Earth at the time life first appeared. The fact that all life has a similar biochemistry can be explained by considering that any group of chemicals that won the race to life would probably have used the "almost-living" as food. Since we can offer explanations for what happened without relying on a meteorite of unknown composition that might have fallen to Earth, we should stick to hypotheses that have fewer unknowns.

34. Which of the following is an assumption of Scientist 1?

(F) Complex life forms can develop quickly.
(G) Meteorites burn up as soon as they hit the Earth's atmosphere.
(H) There is a cause-and-effect relationship between meteors falling and the origin of life.
(J) The changes on the Earth's surface due to the presence of life attracted meteor showers.

35. Which of the following, if true, strengthens Scientist 2's argument the most?

(A) Only 5% more meteors than normal fell on the Earth during the time life began.
(B) Only 5% of the meteorites studied contained organic molecules.
(C) A simulation of early Earth chemistry showed the spontaneous formation of complex biomolecules.
(D) Meteorites containing amoebas have been found.

36. Which of the following, if true, strengthens Scientist 1's argument the most?

(F) Only 5% more meteors than normal fell on the Earth during the time life began.
(G) Only 5% of the meteorites studied contained organic molecules.
(H) A simulation of early Earth chemistry showed the spontaneous formation of complex biomolecules.
(J) Meteorites containing amoebas have been found.

37. With which explanation of the similar biochemistry of all life on Earth would Scientist 1 most likely agree?

(A) A single chemical pathway to life exists.
(B) Life arose from a single source.
(C) Life is not varied.
(D) Meteors are simple.

38. With which explanation of the similar biochemistry of all life on Earth would Scientist 2 most likely agree?

(F) A single chemical pathway to life exists.
(G) Life arose from a single source.
(H) Life is not varied.
(J) Meteors are simple.

39. Which scientist would be likely to disagree with the idea that life on different planets could have different biochemistries?

(A) Scientist 1
(B) Scientist 2
(C) Both scientists
(D) Neither scientist

40. Which of the following questions would be the most difficult for Scientist 1 to defend his theory against?

(F) Why was there more meteorite activity earlier in Earth's history?
(G) Why have other meteors not brought other life based on a different biochemistry?
(H) Why did complex life emerge suddenly?
(J) Why should meteor activity have any connection to the origin of life?

41. Could Scientist 2 believe that life exists on other planets without affecting his hypothesis?

(A) Yes, as long as he believes that life elsewhere has a different biochemistry.
(B) Yes, because wherever the chemicals required for life exist, life can begin.
(C) No, because then he has to admit that meteorites brought life from these planets.
(D) No, because then he has to admit that meteorites that came from pieces of similar planets brought life to the Earth.

Passage VII

A seismographic station can detect how far away an earthquake occurred, but it cannot determine the direction of the earthquake. Any given station can therefore report that the epicenter of an Earthquake occurred somewhere on the circumference of a circle. The map below shows the data recorded for an earthquake at three different seismic stations (A, B, and C). Intersections of the three seismic stations' curves are marked by Roman numerals.

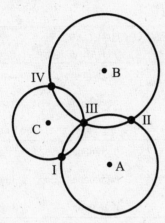

42. Which station was closest to the earthquake epicenter?

    (F) A
    (G) B
    (H) C
    (J) Cannot be determined from the given information

43. Given the information from stations A and B only, which site(s) is (are) possible for the earthquake epicenter?

    (A) I only
    (B) III only
    (C) II and III only
    (D) I and III only

44. Given the information from stations A and C only, which site(s) is (are) possible for the earthquake epicenter?

    (F) I only
    (G) III only
    (H) II and III only
    (J) I and III only

45. Given the information from all three stations, which site(s) is (are) possible for the epicenter?

    (A) I only
    (B) III only
    (C) I and III only
    (D) II and III only

46. If a fourth seismic station gave a report, at what point must its curve meet A's curve?

    (F) I
    (G) II
    (H) III
    (J) IV

47. If a fourth seismic station gave a report, at what point must its curve meet C's curve?

    (A) I
    (B) II
    (C) III
    (D) IV

48. What is the minimum number of points where two circumferences from two seismic stations, both measuring the same Earthquake, can meet?

    (F) 1
    (G) 2
    (H) 3
    (J) Infinite

Passage VIII

To investigate the factors affecting the rate at which starch is broken down to sugar by the digestive enzyme salivary amylase, two experiments were performed. In both experiments, starch (in the form of a cracker) was mixed in a beaker with the enzyme, and the samples were removed every three minutes. Dipping special sugar indicators in the sample revealed the presence of starch in a sample (indicating that the cracker had not yet been completely digested).

Experiment 1: To test the effects of different pH levels on enzyme activity rate, one cracker and a standard amount of enzyme were placed in three beakers, each containing buffers of different pH. This procedure was repeated using standard amounts of water in place of the enzyme. All tests were carried out at optimal temperature. Starch and sugar levels (starch/sugar) from selected samples are shown in Table 1.

Table 1

CONTENTS OF BEAKERS	APPROXIMATE pH LEVELS	LEVELS OF STARCH/SUGAR			
		After 3 min.	*After 9 min.*	*After 15 min.*	*After 60 min.*
cracker + enzyme + buffer	5	high/none	high/none	high/low	moderate/moderate
	7	moderate/moderate	low/high	none/high	none/high
	9	high/none	high/none	high/low	moderate/moderate
cracker + water + buffer	5	high/none	high/none	high/none	high/none
	7	high/none	high/none	high/none	high/none
	9	high/none	high/none	high/none	high/none

Experiment 2: To test the effects of temperature on enzyme activity rate, one cracker and a standard amount of enzyme were placed in 3 beakers, each kept at different temperatures. This was also repeated using standard amounts of water in place of the enzyme. All tests were carried out at optimal pH. Starch and sugar levels (starch/sugar) from selected samples are shown in Table 2.

Table 2

CONTENTS OF BEAKERS	TEMPERATURES	LEVELS OF STARCH/SUGAR			
		After 3 min.	*After 9 min.*	*After 15 min.*	*After 60 min.*
cracker + enzyme	25°C	high/none	high/none	high/low	moderate/moderate
	37°C	moderate/moderate	low/high	none/high	none/high
	45°C	high/none	high/none	high/low	moderate/moderate
cracker + water	25°C	high/none	high/none	high/none	high/none
	37°C	high/none	high/none	high/none	high/none
	45°C	high/none	high/none	high/none	high/none

49. Under what conditions does salivary amylase appear to work best?

    (A) Any pH level greater than 5 and any temperature greater than 25°C
    (B) Any pH level greater than 5 and any temperature less than 45°C
    (C) pH level of 9 and temperature equals 37°C
    (D) pH level of 7 and temperature equals 37°C

50. The ingredient used as a control for both experiments is the:

    (F) cracker.
    (G) water.
    (H) enzyme.
    (J) starch/sugar level.

51. Which of the following hypotheses is supported by the results of Experiment 1?

    (A) At the appropriate pH, water can break down starch, but at a slower rate than salivary amylase can.
    (B) At any one-time interval, no differences in the effects of the three buffers on salivary amylase activity should be detectable.
    (C) Salivary amylase can show activity at each of the three pH levels tested.
    (D) The duration of time in which starch and enzyme remain in the beakers should have no effect on the amount of sugar produced.

52. Which of the following experimental designs would test the hypothesis that enzyme concentration can affect the rate of starch digestion?

    (F) Using the same pH, temperature, and enzyme levels in all beakers, test additional samples at 90 minutes, 120 minutes, and 240 minutes.
    (G) Using different pH, temperature, and enzyme levels in all beakers, test additional samples at 90 minutes, 120 minutes, and 240 minutes.
    (H) Using the same pH and temperatures in all beakers, test additional samples with the enzyme at $\frac{1}{2} \cdot$ strength, $2 \cdot$ strength, and $4 \cdot$ strength.
    (J) Using the same pH, temperature, and enzyme levels in all beakers, test additional samples after stirring for 3 minutes, 9 minutes, 15 minutes, and 60 minutes.

53. In Experiment 2, an additional beaker was tested at 70°C (cracker + enzyme). After 60 minutes, the sample showed high levels of starch and no sugar. Which of the following best explains this result?

    (A) All the starch was destroyed at this high temperature.
    (B) The enzyme does not work at all at this high temperature.
    (C) Starch cannot be detected at this high temperature.
    (D) Iodine and sugar indicators cannot function properly at this high temperature.

54. On the basis of the results of Experiment 1, what would probably occur if Experiment 2 were carried out at a pH level of 5?

    (F) Digestion of starch to sugar would slowly begin in the beakers containing crackers plus water.
    (G) Overall, digestion of starch to sugar would probably take place less efficiently.
    (H) Overall, digestion of starch to sugar would probably take place more efficiently.
    (J) Results would not change.

Passage IX

What will the end of the universe be like? Two opposing views are presented.

Scientist 1: The universe will die out with a whimper because the energy of the big bang that created the universe will spread itself out over larger and larger regions of space. Since there is only so much energy in the universe, every cubic foot must hold, on the average, less energy as time goes on. In the end everything will get so cold that all motion will stop. That will be the true end of time.

Scientist 2: The idea that the universe will spread itself too thin and freeze is seriously flawed. Such theories do not take into account the gravitational attractions of the bits of matter in the universe for each other. Gravity can act as a cosmic glue to keep the universe from dissolving into nothingness.

55. Which of the following is a major assumption of Scientist 1?

   (A) All matter consists of atoms.
   (B) There is a limited amount of energy in the universe.
   (C) Gravity does not exist in interstellar space.
   (D) The universe is contracting.

56. Which of the following facts, if true, does not help Scientist 2's hypothesis?

   (F) It is shown that the galaxies are moving away from each other with a constant speed.
   (G) It is shown that the galaxies are moving towards each other with a constant speed.
   (H) It is shown that the galaxies are moving towards each other with a constant acceleration.
   (J) It is shown that the galaxies are not moving at all relative to each other.

57. It has been calculated that if the universe has a mass greater than or equal to m, then the universe will eventually collapse on itself. Scientist 1 would likely say that the mass of the universe:

   (A) is equal to m.
   (B) is less than or equal to m.
   (C) is greater than m.
   (D) is less than m.

58. If Scientist 2 claims that the universe is contracting, what would he expect the average temperature of the universe to be in ten billion years?

   (F) Higher than now
   (G) Lower than now
   (H) Same as now
   (J) No comparison is possible

59. What must be true about the energy content of the universe if Scientist 1 is correct?

   (A) It is increasing.
   (B) It is decreasing.
   (C) It is a constant.
   (D) It increased at the moment of the big bang, and decreased afterwards.

60. What would happen if the forces moving the galaxies farther out were exactly balanced by the forces pulling them together?

   (F) The galaxies would stop moving.
   (G) The galaxies would move in a straight line with constant speed.
   (H) The galaxies would move in a straight line with constant acceleration.
   (J) The galaxies would move back and forth in a straight line.

Passage X

A scientist investigated the number of fossils per cubic foot through several feet in a quarry. The results are presented below.

Layer	Fish	Shells	Plants	Land Reptile
1 (TOP)	0	0	3	1
2	0	1	8	2
3	1	10	4	0
4	5	18	1	0
5	7	20	0	0

61. When was the site most likely above water?

(A) During the formation of Layers 1 and 2
(B) During the formation of Layers 2 and 3
(C) During the formation of Layers 1 and 4
(D) During the formation of Layer 3

62. Was the site most recently above or below water?

(F) Above
(G) Below
(H) Borderline
(J) Cannot be determined from the given information

63. What assumption is made to relate the fossil record to the environment?

(A) No assumption
(B) That fossils do not affect the environment
(C) That the fossils are mostly from plants and animals that lived in the region
(D) That only animal fossils are important

64. No trilobite fossils were found. This proves:

(F) that no trilobites were in the region.
(G) that the layers were formed before trilobites existed.
(H) that the layers were formed after the trilobites died out.
(J) nothing about the presence of the trilobite in the region.

65. A nautilus shell was found in Layer 3. This proves that:

(A) Layer 3 formed while the nautilus still existed.
(B) Layer 3 is newer than Layer 2.
(C) Layer 3 is older than Layer 2.
(D) the nautilus once lived on land.

66. Where will the newest layer form?

(F) Under Layer 4
(G) Over Layer 1
(H) Across all the layers
(J) Layers no longer form

Passage XI

Using electrical circuits, three experiments were performed to investigate the relationship between voltage (olts), resistance (ohms) (total resistance equals sum of individual resistances), and current (amperes.) Each experiment was set up with the following circuit design:

Experiment 1: Using a 6-volt battery (far left), and two 1,000-ohm resistors (R_1 and R_2), the measured voltages between points 1 and 2 and between points 2 and 3 were 3 volts each.

Experiment 2: When the battery voltage was increased to 12 volts, and the resistors were kept the same (1,000 ohms each), the measured voltages between points 1 and 2 and between points 2 and 3 were 6 volts each.

Experiment 3: Using the original 6-volt battery, R_1 was replaced with a 2,000-ohm resistor. The voltages measured between points 1 and 2 and between points 2 and 3 were 4 volts and 2 volts, respectively.

67. Judging from the results in Experiment 1 and Experiment 2, if the battery voltage were changed to 1.5 volts, what voltage would be expected between point 1 and point 2?

    (A) 0.75 volts
    (B) 1.5 volts
    (C) 3.0 volts
    (D) 6.0 volts

68. The experimenter studies the measurement made in the previous question, as well as those made earlier in Experiments 1, 2, and 3, and hypothesizes that:

    (F) voltage measured across a resistor is inversely proportional to the value of that resistor.
    (G) voltage measured across a resistor is directly proportional to the value of that resistor.
    (H) voltage measured across a resistor is not related to the value of that resistor.
    (J) voltage measured across a resistor equals the battery voltage.

69. When the experimenter recorded the current in the circuit of Experiment 1, it measured 0.003 amperes. In Experiment 3, however, the current measured 0.002 amperes. These results show that current and total resistances are:

    (A) directly proportional.
    (B) inversely proportional.
    (C) equal.
    (D) unrelated.

70. Which of the following formulas for the current in the circuit best summarizes the above results? (The battery voltage is given by V_b and the total resistance is given by R.)

    (F) $V_b R$

    (G) $\frac{R}{V_b}$

    (H) $\frac{V_b}{R}$

    (J) $V_b + R$

71. A new circuit is set up, similar in design to those in the experiments. The battery voltage and the size of the resistors are unknown, but the current measures 0.001 amperes. If the battery voltage is doubled and one of the two resistors is replaced with one having a smaller value, which answer most accurately describes the new current?

    (A) It will be smaller than 0.001.
    (B) It will be unchanged.
    (C) It will be greater than 0.001.
    (D) Cannot be determined from the given information

72. Which of the following single changes to Experiment 2 would produce a current of 0.004 amperes?

    (F) Decrease the voltage to 8 volts.
    (G) Increase the resistance to 3,000 ohms.
    (H) Neither change will create a current of 0.004 amperes.
    (J) Either change will create a current of 0.004 amperes.

Passage XII

How old is the Earth? Two opposing views are presented.

Scientist 1: The Earth is approximately five billion years old. We know this to be true because of radioactive dating. Some chemical elements are unstable and will fall apart into smaller pieces over time. This disintegration occurs over a period of time that is very regular for the particular element. In general, we talk about the half-life of the element, which is the time necessary for one-half of the material to disintegrate. This time is constant whether we have an ounce or a ton of the material. So, by measuring the relative amounts of the material left and the disintegration products, we can form an accurate idea of how old the Earth is by determining how many half-lives have occurred.

Scientist 2: The argument that supports the hypothesis that the Earth is only five billion years old is seriously flawed. What the argument fails to take into account is that the Earth is the constant recipient of a shower of cosmic debris in the form of meteorites. These meteorites replenish the stock of radioactive material on the surface of the Earth, making it seem as though the Earth has gone through fewer half-lives than it really has. Therefore, all estimates of the age of the Earth based on radioactive dating are too low.

73. Which of the following is a major assumption of Scientist 1?

(A) The Earth has life that recycles carbon-14.
(B) The half-life of all radioactive elements is five billion years.
(C) The radioactive material was formed at the same time as the Earth.
(D) There is no longer any radioactivity on the Earth.

74. Which of the following is a major assumption of Scientist 2?

(F) The meteorites that land on the Earth are radioactive.
(G) Few meteorites have landed on the Earth.
(H) The Earth is more than five billion years old.
(J) The Earth is highly radioactive.

75. Which of the following, if true, would best refute Scientist 2's argument?

(A) Recent meteorites have been found to be radioactive.
(B) The Earth has a greater amount of radioactive material on the surface than in the mantle.
(C) The Earth's orbit intersects the orbits of a number of meteorites.
(D) Few meteorites have been found to contain radioactive material.

76. Which of the following would be most likely if Scientist 2's hypothesis were correct?

(F) The amount of radioactive material and its disintegration products on the Earth has decreased over time.
(G) The amount of radioactive material and its disintegration products has increased over time.
(H) The amount of radioactive material and its disintegration products has stayed essentially the same over time.
(J) The Earth will reach a critical mass and explode.

77. Which of the following would be most likely if Scientist 1's hypothesis were correct?

(A) The amount of radioactive material and its disintegration products has decreased over time.
(B) The amount of radioactive material and its disintegration products has increased over time.
(C) The amount of radioactive material and its disintegration products has stayed essentially the same over time.
(D) The Earth will reach a critical mass and explode.

78. Which of the following conditions, if true, would prevent an estimation of the Earth's age by Scientist 1's method?

    (F) No radioactive disintegration has occurred.
    (G) Only some of the radioactive material has disintegrated.
    (H) Eighty percent of the radioactive material has disintegrated.
    (J) All of the radioactive material has disintegrated.

TIMED-PRACTICE QUIZZES

This section contains three Science quizzes. Complete each quiz under timed conditions. Answers are on page 597.

DIRECTIONS: Each passage is followed by several items. After reading a passage, choose the best answer to each item. You may refer to the passages as often as necessary. You are NOT permitted the use of a calculator.

A. QUIZ I (10 items; 9 minutes)

Passage I

The ecological pyramid below shows the relative biomass[†] of organisms at each trophic feeding level of a marine food chain.

[†]*Biomass:* Total dry weight of organisms (useable chemical energy stored in organic matter) at each trophic level at any given time.

1. According to the diagram, the trophic level with the largest relative biomass is the:

   (A) 4° consumers.
   (B) 3° and 2° consumers.
   (C) 1° consumers.
   (D) producers.

2. From the information in the diagram, one can conclude that at any given time:

   (F) 10 seals may be found for every mackerel.
   (G) the relative dry weight of all carnivores combined is far greater than that of the herbivores alone.
   (H) only 1% of all producers live long enough to be eaten by a mackerel.
   (J) the relative dry weight of every consumer trophic level is usually less than that of the trophic level on which they feed.

3. Organisms from which trophic level are most likely to be found near the water surface where light can penetrate?

   (A) 4° consumers
   (B) 2° consumers
   (C) 3° consumers
   (D) producers

4. If there were an additional trophic level of carnivores (5° consumers), its relative biomass at any given time would be approximately:

   (F) 11 kg.
   (G) 1,000,000 kg.
   (H) 1 kg.
   (J) 111 kg.

5. The best explanation for biomass being measured as dry weight is:

(A) if water weight were included, efficiency ratios at each trophic level would be unpredictable.
(B) body fluids contribute little to the mass of marine organisms.
(C) water molecules contain little or no usable chemical energy.
(D) each trophic level contains a different amount of water.

Passage II

The table below shows various characteristics of different layers of the atmosphere.

Approximate Altitude (km)	Layers of the Atmosphere	Approximate Mean Temperature (°C)	Clouds
60,000			
6,000			
	THERMOSPHERE		
600		1200	
80		−90	
	MESOSPHERE		
50		−3	
	STRATOSPHERE		Cirrus
12		−50	
			Cirrostratus
5	TROPOSPHERE		Altostratus
0		18	Nimbostratus

6. Which statement accurately describes the relationship between the approximate altitude and the approximate mean temperature of the layers of the atmosphere?

   (F) As altitude increases, temperature increases.
   (G) As altitude increases, temperature decreases.
   (H) As altitude increases, temperature first decreases then continuously increases.
   (J) As altitude increases, temperature first decreases, then increases, then decreases, and then increases.

7. Based on the information in the table, the atmospheric layer with the narrowest range of altitude is the:

   (A) thermosphere.
   (B) troposphere.
   (C) mesosphere.
   (D) stratosphere.

8. The type of cloud(s) most likely to consist of ice crystals is (are):

   (F) nimbostratus only.
   (G) nimbostratus and altostratus.
   (H) cirrus and cirrostratus.
   (J) cirrostratus only.

9. The absorption of solar heat energy increases as the gases of the atmosphere become rarefied. The layer of the atmosphere that appears most rarefied is the:

   (A) thermosphere.
   (B) mesosphere.
   (C) stratosphere.
   (D) troposphere.

10. According to the table, which atmospheric layer shows a decrease in temperature of approximately 3°C for every 1-kilometer increase in altitude?

    (F) thermosphere
    (G) mesosphere
    (H) stratosphere
    (J) troposphere

B. QUIZ II (10 items; 9 minutes)

Passage I

The chart below shows in outline form a common means of analyzing a sample solution for various cations (positive ions). Ions above the horizontal arrows are those that are suspected to be present in the sample solution; the substances in the boxes are the reagents added as tests (0.3 M H^+ is acidic, NH_4OH is alkaline); the products shown next to the arrows pointing downward are solid precipitates resulting from the tests. Tests for specific ions need not always start from the beginning of the sequence.

1. According to the chart, which precipitate indicates if silver (Ag) is present in the sample?

   (A) AgCl
   (B) Ag
   (C) CuS
   (D) ZnS

2. If a solution containing silver (Ag) nitrate and cupric (Cu) nitrate is tested according to this scheme, an experimenter will:

   (F) first observe AgCl on treatment with Cl^-, and next observe CuS on treatment with H_2S.
   (G) first observe CuS on treatment with Cl^-, and next observe AgCl on treatment with H_2S.
   (H) first observe $CaCO_3$ on treatment with CO_3^{-2}, and next observe AgCl on treatment with Cl^-.
   (J) observe no reactions, since the scheme does not test for nitrate.

3. What is the minimum number of tests necessary to confirm the composition of an unknown solution that contains no other positive ions except Cu^{+2} or Zn^{+2}, but not both?

   (A) 1
   (B) 2
   (C) 3
   (D) 4

4. Which statement is most correct concerning the separation of Cu^{+2} from Zn^{+2} in the same solution?

   (F) Completely different test reagents are used in each of the two steps.
   (G) The same test reagents are used in each of the two steps.
   (H) The same test reagents are used, but the first step must be in an alkaline environment while the second step must be in an acidic environment.
   (J) The same test reagents are used, but the first step must be in an acidic environment while the second step must be in an alkaline environment.

5. A clear solution is found, by a method not discussed here, to contain chloride ion (Cl^-). From the information given here, what ion could not be present in the solution?

(A) Carbonate (CO^{-2})

(B) Cupric (Cu^{+2})

(C) Silver (Ag^+)

(D) Zinc (Zn^{+2})

Passage II

The chart below shows the flavor preferences of white-tailed deer when offered various fluids to drink at different ages.

6. Which category on the chart shows no preference between water and the experimental flavor?

   (F) Three months of age/sugar
   (G) Six months of age/salt
   (H) Three months of age/salt
   (J) Nine months of age/sugar

7. Which statement about white-tailed deer is supported by the information in the chart?

   (A) As age increases, the preference for all tested sugars increases.
   (B) As age increases, the preference for all tested salts increases.
   (C) As age increases, differences between sugars cannot be detected, and differences between salts cannot be detected.
   (D) As age increases, differences between sugars can be detected, and differences between salts can be detected.

8. The flavor preference that fluctuates most irregularly with age is:

   (F) moderately salty.
   (G) moderately sweet.
   (H) extremely salty.
   (J) extremely sweet.

9. Based on the trends shown in the chart, which of the following predictions is most reasonable for one-year-old white-tailed deer?

   (A) Moderately sweet and moderately salty will be most preferred.
   (B) Extremely sweet and extremely salty will be most preferred.
   (C) Moderately sweet and extremely salty will be most preferred.
   (D) Extremely sweet and moderately salty will be most preferred.

10. Which of the following conclusions about water is NOT consistent with the data in the chart?

(F) Water is never preferred over any tested flavors.

(G) Before the age of six months, white-tailed deer cannot taste the difference between water and sugar or between water and salt.

(H) At the age of three months, both salty fluids are equal to the water swallowed.

(J) As age increases, the volume of water swallowed remains the same.

C. QUIZ III (11 items; 9 minutes)

Passage I

The table below shows the first three ionization energies for the atoms hydrogen through potassium. The first ionization energy, E_1, is the energy (in kilocalories per mole of atoms) that must be added in order to remove the first electron. E_2 is the energy required to remove a second electron once the first has been removed, and E_3 is the energy needed to remove a third electron. If an atom lacks a second or third electron, no value is given in the table.

IONIZATION ENERGIES OF THE ELEMENTS (kcal/mole)				
Atomic No.	Element	E_1	E_2	E_3
1	H	313.6	-	-
2	He	566.8	1254	-
3	Li	124.3	1744	2823
4	Be	214.9	419.9	3548
5	B	191.3	580	874.5
6	C	259.6	562.2	1104
7	N	335.1	682.8	1094
8	O	314	810.6	1267
9	F	401.8	806.7	1445
10	Ne	497.2	947.2	1500
11	Na	118.5	1091	1652
12	Mg	176.3	346.6	1848
13	Al	138	434.1	655.9
14	Si	187.9	376.8	771.7
15	P	241.8	453.2	695.5
16	S	238.9	540	807
17	Cl	300	548.9	920.2
18	Ar	363.4	637	943.3
19	K	100.1	733.6	1100

1. For a given element, the ionization energies increase in the order:

   (A) E_3, E_2, E_1.
   (B) E_2, E_1, E_3.
   (C) E_1, E_2, E_3.
   (D) Order varies.

2. A student suspects that there may be an atom for which the second ionization energy is roughly twice that of the first, and the third is roughly twice that of the second. Which of the following atoms best fits this relationship?

   (F) Be
   (G) C
   (H) Ne
   (J) Ar

3. As atomic number increases, the trend in the values of E_2 is:

   (A) generally upward.
   (B) generally downward.
   (C) upward for a few values, then suddenly downward, followed by another increase, etc.
   (D) downward for a few values, then suddenly upward, followed by a decrease again, etc.

4. If the chart were continued to the element having atomic number 20, its value for E_1 would be expected to be closest to:

   (F) 20.
   (G) 90.
   (H) 140.
   (J) 730.

5. An experimenter has at her disposal a means of providing an atom with any energy up to 200 kcal/mole. From how many different atoms could she remove one electron?

   (A) 7
   (B) 8
   (C) 11
   (D) 12

Passage II

A physics student performed two sets of experiments designed to examine the factors that influence the motion of falling objects.

Experiment 1: A stone was dropped from a steep cliff while a camera, mounted on a tripod on the ground, took photographs at 1-second intervals. Back in the laboratory, the same procedure was repeated in the absence (nearly) of air inside a huge vacuum chamber.

Experiment 2: The experiments were repeated (on the cliff and inside the vacuum chamber) using a stone and a cork with identical masses dropped at the same time. At the cliff, the stone hit the ground first. In the vacuum chamber, both objects hit the ground together.

6. Assuming that air acts to resist the downward acceleration of the stone, how will the total time required to reach the ground in the vacuum chamber compare to the time required to reach the ground from the cliff?

   (F) Longer time in air than in vacuum chamber
   (G) Longer time in vacuum chamber than in air
   (H) Same time in each
   (J) Cannot be determined from the given information

7. If part of Experiment 1 were repeated on the moon, where the pull of gravity is one sixth that of the Earth, the stone's downward speed would increase as it falls (i.e., it would accelerate) but the rate of increase in speed would only be one sixth as great as on the Earth. When the photos taken at 1-second intervals on the moon are compared to the photos taken on Earth, the series of moon pictures of the stone will be:

   (A) closer together.
   (B) farther apart.
   (C) identical.
   (D) closer at some times and farther apart at others.

8. In Experiment 2, the observed results can be explained by the hypothesis that:

   (F) heavier objects fall more rapidly than lighter ones.
   (G) a cork of the same mass as a stone is smaller than the stone, and it encounters more air resistance.
   (H) a cork of the same mass as a stone is larger than the stone, and it encounters more air resistance.
   (J) the gravitational acceleration of objects toward the ground diminishes when air is not present.

9. In Experiment 1, gravity accelerates the stone as it falls from the cliff, causing it to pick up speed as it drops. Which of the following series of pictures most resembles how the stone appears as it drops?

10. The experimenter devises a means of suspending the Earth's gravity for short periods of time. Armed with this technique, he drops the stone (on Earth, in air, under conditions of normal gravity), and then suspends gravity 2 seconds after the stone has been falling and leaves it off for the next minute. Recalling that gravity causes the stone's downward speed to increase continually, choose the "photo" that best illustrates, in 1-second intervals, this experiment.

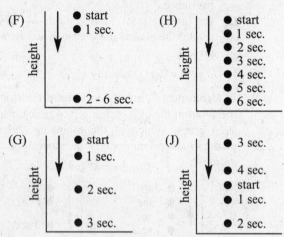

(F)
height
● start
● 1 sec.
● 2 - 6 sec.

(H)
height
● start
● 1 sec.
● 2 sec.
● 3 sec.
● 4 sec.
● 5 sec.
● 6 sec.

(G)
height
● start
● 1 sec.
● 2 sec.
● 3 sec.

(J)
height
● 3 sec.
● 4 sec.
● start
● 1 sec.
● 2 sec.

11. If Experiment 2 were repeated on the airless moon, which prediction would be correct?

(A) The cork would fall more slowly than on the Earth.
(B) The cork would fall as rapidly as the stone.
(C) Both predictions are correct.
(D) Neither prediction is correct.

CAMBRIDGE TESTPREP™

SCIENCE

STRATEGY SUMMARY SHEET

GENERAL STRATEGIES: Science items test your reasoning skills, not your scientific knowledge. So, most of the passages have all of the information that you will need to answer the items. In some cases, background information at the level of your high school general science courses is required, but do not assume data that is not given. The following are general strategies for Science:

1. Before reading any Science passage, *quickly glance over all of the passages and code them according to passage-type* in order to determine the order in which you will attack them. Identifying and coding the passages should take no more than five seconds each.

2. *Do NOT preview the item stems.* Since the Science item stems tend to be confusing without having first read the corresponding passage, previewing them will only confuse you and slow you down.

3. It is important to only *read the passage thoroughly once*, rather than to skim over it several times. The material can be difficult to understand; thus, it is important to read thoughtfully and carefully. *Be an active reader.* Use your pencil to underline key words and points of information. That way, you will be able to locate them easily when answering the items.

4. When a Science passage includes tables or graphs, make sure that you *read and understand the labels* on axes, columns, and rows. You need to know what information is being presented and what units of measure are being used.

5. Many passages will contain much more information than you need to answer a particular item. In your search for a logical conclusion, *do not be misled by data that does not relate to the item at hand*.

6. In Data Representation passages, tables and graphs present results, often of observations or experiments. Corresponding items will usually ask you to spot patterns in the data, so *look for trends*, such as upward movement, downward movement, inverse variation, etc.

7. The experiments described in Research Summary passages are based on scientific assumptions. However, if an assumption is faulty, the experiment may not prove what it claims, and conclusions drawn from it may therefore be invalid. So, for items that ask about the validity of a scientific conclusion, *consider the validity of any underlying assumptions*.

8. The arguments presented in Conflicting Viewpoints passages are also based on scientific assumptions. Again, *if the assumption is wrong, the entire argument is open to challenge*. Assumptions that are based on scientific fact add strength to an argument; faulty assumptions weaken an argument.

9. Offering the assumptions that you started with as proof of your argument is called circular reasoning, and this type of proof is not acceptable. For that reason, any conclusions discussed in Science passages or offered as answer choices must be based on additional evidence (e.g., experiments) to be valid. *Beware of any conclusions that are nothing more than a restatement of an underlying premise.*

10. All of the information that you need to answer the items is provided in the passage—do not infer any information that is not given or relate any previous experience to the passage. *Pay attention to material noted with an asterisk.*

11. *Transcribe your answers from the test booklet to the answer sheet in groups (by passage).* However, when you arrive at the last passage, transcribe each answer as it is determined.

STRATEGIES FOR EACH PASSAGE-TYPE:

- *Data Representation Passages:* When given data in the form of a graph or a chart, pay particular attention to the scale, units, legend, and other noted information.

- *Research Summary Passages:* When given multiple experiments, identify the controls and variables. Note that the controls must remain the same and that variables can only change one at a time in all experiments.

- *Conflicting Viewpoints Passages:* When given two points of view on a topic, identify the main points of difference and the logical value of each argument. After you understand the nature of the passage, attack the items.

STRATEGIES FOR EACH ITEM-TYPE:

- *Comprehension Items:* Recognize basic concepts. Read carefully. Make sure that your answers consider appropriate scales and units. Also, note the difference between absolute and percentage changes.

- *Analysis Items:* Identify relationships and trends. Pay particular attention to direct and inverse relationships.

- *Application Items:* Draw conclusions, predict outcomes, and synthesize new information. In answering Application items, beware of the following terms: "all," "none," "always," and "never." Remember that a single case of contradictory evidence is all that is necessary to disprove an absolute theory.

ADDITIONAL STRATEGIES FROM IN-CLASS DISCUSSION: _____

_____

_____

_____

_____

_____

_____

_____

_____

_____

_____

_____

Writing

CAMBRIDGE TESTPREP™

WRITING

COURSE CONCEPT OUTLINE: WHAT YOU ABSOLUTELY MUST KNOW

I. Test Mechanics (p. 283)

II. Lesson (p. 288)

    A. Preliminaries

        1. What Is Tested
        2. Directions
        3. Item Format
        4. Scoring
            a. Essay Scoring Guide
            b. Test Scores

    B. Composing the Essay

        1. Pre-Writing
        2. Beginning the Writing Process
        3. The Introduction
        4. The Body
        5. The Conclusion
        6. Revision

    C. Essay Writing Strategies

        1. Begin with the Prompt
        2. Write Only on the Assigned Topic
        3. Do Not Try to Do Too Much
        4. Outline the Essay (Item #1, p. 288)
        5. Organize Ideas into Paragraphs (Item #2, p. 289)
        6. Write Grammatically
        7. Punctuate and Spell Correctly
        8. Write Clearly, Concisely, and Legibly
        9. Proofread the Essay

III. Timed-Practice Quizzes (p. 291)

    A. Quiz I (Item #1, p. 291)

    B. Quiz II (Item #1, p. 293)

    C. Quiz III (Item #1, p. 295)

IV. Strategy Summary Sheet (p. 297)

TEST MECHANICS

BASICS

The theory underlying the Essay requirement of the test is that your response will demonstrate something about your ability to develop and express ideas in writing. It is not intended to evaluate how good a novelist you would be or how well you write when you have time to do research in the library or on the web, writing several drafts and then polishing the product before submitting it. The Essay is strictly an on-demand piece of writing that is of rough draft quality.

The Essay is not intended to test your mastery of any body of knowledge. The topic will be sufficiently vague to accommodate arguments and explanations supported by a wide range of details from your own experience, such as dance, sports, music, psychology, current events, and even, if appropriate, technology such as "twittering" and "tweeting" and video-gaming (provided you can show that these ideas are directly relevant).

The technical term for the Essay topic is "prompt," a strange term for an essay topic. The word "prompt" was chosen because it indicates that the topic is nothing more than an *excuse* for you to write something. The test could just as easily say, "During the 30 minutes provided, write an essay on anything of interest to you," but then the readers would have a couple million essays all on different topics. So, the prompt keeps everyone more or less on the same page.

Essays are scored *holistically*, which means that they are graded on the overall impression created rather than by awarding so many bonus points for a well-turned phrase and deducting penalties for mistakes in grammar. All essays are read by two graders, each of whom assigns a score of "1" to "6" (or a "0" if the essay is off-topic or otherwise not responsive to the prompt). The two scores are combined to produce an Essay subscore between "2" and "12." Then, the Essay score is combined with your English Test score to produce a Combined English/Writing scale score from "1" to "36." Your Essay score will not affect your English Test score. The Combined English/Writing score and the Writing Test score will be reported in <u>addition</u> to the English, Math, Reading, and Science scores.

ANATOMY

DIRECTIONS: This is a test of your writing skills. Before you begin planning and writing your essay, read the writing prompt carefully to understand the instructions. Your essay will be evaluated on the evidence it provides of your ability to express judgments by taking a position on the issue in the writing prompt; to maintain a focus on the topic throughout the essay; to develop a position by using logical reasoning and supporting ideas; to organize ideas in a logical way; and to use language clearly and effectively according to the conventions of standard written English.

If you finish before time is called, you may review your work. Lay your pencil down immediately when time is called.

In some schools, teachers are debating whether students should be given "must read" lists for summer break. A list would include a number of books, plays, and/or short stories, and students would be required to submit reports upon returning to school for the fall semester. Some educators think this would be a good policy because students would be exposed to additional readings in literature. They also believe that the less-structured summer break would provide students with the opportunity to enjoy reading more than they would during the school year, thereby encouraging students to read more on their own. Other educators think the requirement would not be a good idea because students would perceive the requirement as burdensome and therefore be unlikely to enjoy the reading. Additionally, these educators argue that students' summer breaks already have too many activities and too much structure. Do you think that schools should assign summer reading to their students?

The first thing to notice about the prompt is that it doesn't test any specific body of knowledge. It doesn't ask, "What were the causes of World War II?" or "What is the best recipe for chocolate cake?" Those topics might actually become a part of someone's essay (e.g., "At the start of World War II, some experts argued to wait for better intelligence on fleet movements, but there wasn't time" or "Unfortunately, the best ingredients are almost always the most expensive, and so it is sometimes necessary in baking to substitute pecans for macadamia nuts.") However, the prompt will never ask such a specific question. The second thing about the prompt is that it was constructed so that you'll be able to find everything you need for the essay answer in your own personal experience: you're a student; you read books, plays, and short stories; you have a summer break. The final thing about the prompt is that it was written to provide you encouragement. It asks you a question to get you started. All you really need to do is answer the question. (More will be discussed on this in the Writing Lesson.)

The only other part of the Essay exercise is the lined paper provided for writing your response. We don't have any insightful advice on this one—it's just lined paper, so there's nothing more to say about it. Sorry.

PACING

There is one Essay prompt with a 30-minute time limit. During the 30 minutes, you must read the prompt, formulate a position, outline your argument or analysis, write your essay, and proofread your essay. Here is a suggested breakdown for those tasks:

1 prompt; 30 minutes

Task	Time to Execute	Time Remaining
Read Prompt	1 minute	29 minutes
Formulate Position	1 minute	28 minutes
Outline Essay	2 minutes	26 minutes
Write Introduction	2 minutes	24 minutes
Write First Paragraph	7 minutes	17 minutes
Write Second Paragraph	7 minutes	10 minutes
Write Third Paragraph	7 minutes	3 minutes
Write Conclusion	2 minutes	1 minute
Proofread Essay	1 minute	0 minutes

This is a schedule for an Essay that will score at least an "8." It assumes that you'll have a short introduction, three paragraphs of development, and a brief conclusion. Obviously, if you can do more, then you should, but an "8" would be an excellent score for the vast majority of students.

GAME PLAN

Your timing in writing the essay is a critical element of your "Game Plan," but we have already covered that in the "Pacing" feature on the previous page. Your "Game Plan" for actually writing the essay includes the following points:

1. RESPOND TO THE SPECIFIC PROMPT

Don't write on a topic other than the one provided. That's an automatic score of "0" because the answer is "not responsive"—no matter how good the answer is.

2. WRITE LEGIBLY

Again, an illegible answer is an automatic "0" score. The readers can't possibly grade what they can't read. So, if your handwriting is hard to read, take a little extra time and try printing.

3. DON'T COPY THE PROMPT

Some students will begin by copying the prompt onto the lined paper. There is no reason to do this. The readers know what the topic is, and in any case, it is written right there on the page. Copying the topic makes it look as though you're trying to fill up space, and for a grader, that is like waving the red flag in front of the bull.

4. DON'T SKIP LINES

You should be able to make your answer legible without the need to skip lines. And skipping lines makes it seem as though you're padding your essay to make it look longer—another red flag.

5. USE A PENCIL

Write your essay using a pencil, not a pen, even though you may hate writing in pencil. The scanner will not pick up a response written with a pen, so note that this is another route to an automatic "0."

6. BE SPECIFIC

In the Writing Lesson, your teacher will cover a lot of important points about how to write your essay, but one of the best pieces of advice that we can offer is: BE SPECIFIC. Avoid talking in vague generalities: "Perfection in house painting is very time-consuming and requires a lot of hard work. You just can't do it in a short time; you've got to invest a lot of effort." Instead, give the reader specifics: "House painting requires attention to details. You have to prepare the surface by scraping away all old and loose paint and carefully washing it. You have to put down hundreds of strips of masking tape to protect those areas that should not receive paint, like glass panes, trim to be painted a second color, and fixtures. You have to apply a primer, then a base coat, and then the finish coat. Finally, you have to apply the second color and clean up all the mistakes. A perfect paint job would take 6 months or longer, and the cost would be prohibitive. That is why when you look closely you will always see imperfections." Specifics are the difference between a "2" or a "3" and a "4" or a "5."

LESSON

The items in this section accompany the Writing Lesson. You will work through the items with your instructor in class.

DIRECTIONS: Read the following prompt and corresponding assignment, which are written as they would appear on the ACT. Then, use the space that is provided below to create an <u>outline</u> for an essay that responds to the assignment. Include a thesis, as well as a topic sentence and a list of several examples for each part of your essay.

1. *Residents of rural areas often wonder why people would voluntarily choose to live in a large city and insist that rural life—with its open spaces, relative freedom from worries about crime, and healthful living conditions—is preferable. Conversely, residents of urban areas say that city life—with access to public transportation, cultural amenities, and many entertainment opportunities—is preferable. Which do you find more compelling, the belief that the quality of life is greater in urban areas or the belief that the quality of life is greater in rural areas?*

    In your essay, take a position on this question. You may write about either one of the two points of view given, or you may present a different point of view on this question. Use specific reasons and examples to support your position.

DIRECTIONS: Read the following prompt and corresponding assignment, which are written as they would appear on the ACT. Then, use the space that is provided below to write an <u>essay</u> that responds to the assignment. Use the essay outline from the previous item as a guide.

2. *Residents of rural areas often wonder why people would voluntarily choose to live in a large city and insist that rural life—with its open spaces, relative freedom from worries about crime, and healthful living conditions—is preferable. Conversely, residents of urban areas say that city life—with access to public transportation, cultural amenities, and many entertainment opportunities—is preferable. Which do you find more compelling, the belief that the quality of life is greater in urban areas or the belief that the quality of life is greater in rural areas?*

    In your essay, take a position on this question. You may write about either one of the two points of view given, or you may present a different point of view on this question. Use specific reasons and examples to support your position.

TIMED-PRACTICE QUIZZES

This section contains three Writing quizzes. Complete each quiz under timed conditions.

A. QUIZ I (1 item; 30 minutes)

DIRECTIONS: Plan and write an essay on the topic assigned below. DO NOT WRITE ON ANY OTHER TOPIC. AN ESSAY ON ANOTHER TOPIC IS NOT ACCEPTABLE. Think carefully about the issue presented in the following prompt and corresponding assignment below.

1.   *Some schools and districts have eliminated study hall for their students. The primary drive behind this elimination is to allow students to take additional electives and substantive subjects. Though students might have slightly more work to complete at home, they will leave school much more well-rounded with their added knowledge. Proponents of study hall argue that study hall provides an environment that is conducive to learning for students who suffer from time constraints at home. Some students may not have the luxury to complete homework assignments at home due to work or heavy extracurricular activities. In addition, proponents of study hall argue that the core classes are more important than elective courses in developing a student's future prospects; therefore, it is important to provide a quiet learning environment for students who cannot complete core class assignments at home. In your opinion, should schools and districts eliminate study hall for their students?*

In your essay, take a position on this question. You may write about either one of the two points of view given, or you may present a different point of view on this question. Use specific reasons and examples to support your position.

B. QUIZ II (1 item; 30 minutes)

DIRECTIONS: Plan and write an essay on the topic assigned below. DO NOT WRITE ON ANY OTHER TOPIC. AN ESSAY ON ANOTHER TOPIC IS NOT ACCEPTABLE. Think carefully about the issue presented in the following prompt and corresponding assignment below.

1.   *In some countries, upon graduating from or leaving high school, young people are required to perform 24 months of compulsory service. A choice is offered between military service and an alternative, community service. Some people think universal compulsory service is a good idea because young people learn valuable lessons from the experience. Other people think that such a required service engenders resentment so that no important civic lesson is learned. In your opinion, should all young people be required to participate in some form of universal compulsory service?*

In your essay, take a position on this question. You may write about either one of the two points of view given, or you may present a different point of view on this question. Use specific reasons and examples to support your position.

C. QUIZ III (1 item; 30 minutes)

DIRECTIONS: Plan and write an essay on the topic assigned below. DO NOT WRITE ON ANY OTHER TOPIC. AN ESSAY ON ANOTHER TOPIC IS NOT ACCEPTABLE. Think carefully about the issue presented in the following prompt and corresponding assignment below.

1.   *Some schools, notably military academies, have honor codes that not only prohibit cheating but require students to inform authorities of any acts of cheating by classmates of which they may be aware. Some teachers and administrators think that all schools should have honor codes because the codes teach the virtue of personal integrity and reinforce a sense of responsibility among students toward one another. Other teachers and administrators argue that honor codes are often ineffective and further that they require students to make impossible choices between loyalty to friends and the demands of the honor code. In your opinion, should schools adopt honor codes that cover all students?*

In your essay, take a position on this question. You may write about either one of the two points of view given, or you may present a different point of view on this question. Use specific reasons and examples to support your position.

CAMBRIDGE TESTPREP™

WRITING

STRATEGY SUMMARY SHEET

GENERAL STRATEGIES:

1. Begin with the prompt.

2. Write only on the assigned topic. Writing on any other topic will result in a score of "0."

3. Do not try to do too much. Try to mentally limit the scope of your topic.

4. Organize your thoughts and write an outline before beginning the essay. Do not spend more than two minutes writing the outline.

   a. Familiarize yourself with the essay prompt and assignment.

   b. Develop a point of view.

   c. Develop a thesis.

   d. Identify two to four important points.

   e. Decide on the order of presentation of the major points.

5. Organize ideas into paragraphs.

   a. Introduction

   b. Two to Four Body Paragraphs

   c. Conclusion

6. Write grammatically.

7. Write clearly, concisely, and legibly.

8. Punctuate and spell correctly.

9. Spend at least four minutes proofreading your essay.

ADDITIONAL STRATEGIES FROM IN-CLASS DISCUSSION: _____

_____

_____

_____

_____

_____

Practice Test Reinforcement

Complete four full-length ACT tests to reinforce everything you've learned in your course.

Work through the tests either all at once or by section to highlight specific skills and concepts.

Snapshot of Practice Test Reinforcement:

In this section, you will have the opportunity to apply everything that you have learned throughout the course. Each of the four practice tests has been arranged in an order and with a frequency that approximates the real ACT. Completing these practice tests will help reinforce the test content, help you become more comfortable with timing and pacing, reduce your test anxiety, and give you the chance to practice using alternative test-taking strategies. If you're working through these tests on your own, complete the first two tests without timing restrictions to practice the application of the concepts you have learned. Then, complete the second two tests with the appropriate timing to practice your pacing.

PRACTICE TEST I BUBBLE SHEET

Start with number 1 for each new section. Be sure to erase any errors or stray marks completely.

Name		Student ID Number
Date	Instructor	Course/Session Number

TEST 1—ENGLISH

1 (A) (B) (C) (D) 16 (F) (G) (H) (J) 31 (A) (B) (C) (D) 46 (F) (G) (H) (J) 61 (A) (B) (C) (D)
2 (F) (G) (H) (J) 17 (A) (B) (C) (D) 32 (F) (G) (H) (J) 47 (A) (B) (C) (D) 62 (F) (G) (H) (J)
3 (A) (B) (C) (D) 18 (F) (G) (H) (J) 33 (A) (B) (C) (D) 48 (F) (G) (H) (J) 63 (A) (B) (C) (D)
4 (F) (G) (H) (J) 19 (A) (B) (C) (D) 34 (F) (G) (H) (J) 49 (A) (B) (C) (D) 64 (F) (G) (H) (J)
5 (A) (B) (C) (D) 20 (F) (G) (H) (J) 35 (A) (B) (C) (D) 50 (F) (G) (H) (J) 65 (A) (B) (C) (D)
6 (F) (G) (H) (J) 21 (A) (B) (C) (D) 36 (F) (G) (H) (J) 51 (A) (B) (C) (D) 66 (F) (G) (H) (J)
7 (A) (B) (C) (D) 22 (F) (G) (H) (J) 37 (A) (B) (C) (D) 52 (F) (G) (H) (J) 67 (A) (B) (C) (D)
8 (F) (G) (H) (J) 23 (A) (B) (C) (D) 38 (F) (G) (H) (J) 53 (A) (B) (C) (D) 68 (F) (G) (H) (J)
9 (A) (B) (C) (D) 24 (F) (G) (H) (J) 39 (A) (B) (C) (D) 54 (F) (G) (H) (J) 69 (A) (B) (C) (D)
10 (F) (G) (H) (J) 25 (A) (B) (C) (D) 40 (F) (G) (H) (J) 55 (A) (B) (C) (D) 70 (F) (G) (H) (J)
11 (A) (B) (C) (D) 26 (F) (G) (H) (J) 41 (A) (B) (C) (D) 56 (F) (G) (H) (J) 71 (A) (B) (C) (D)
12 (F) (G) (H) (J) 27 (A) (B) (C) (D) 42 (F) (G) (H) (J) 57 (A) (B) (C) (D) 72 (F) (G) (H) (J)
13 (A) (B) (C) (D) 28 (F) (G) (H) (J) 43 (A) (B) (C) (D) 58 (F) (G) (H) (J) 73 (A) (B) (C) (D)
14 (F) (G) (H) (J) 29 (A) (B) (C) (D) 44 (F) (G) (H) (J) 59 (A) (B) (C) (D) 74 (F) (G) (H) (J)
15 (A) (B) (C) (D) 30 (F) (G) (H) (J) 45 (A) (B) (C) (D) 60 (F) (G) (H) (J) 75 (A) (B) (C) (D)

TEST 2—MATHEMATICS

1 (A) (B) (C) (D) (E) 13 (A) (B) (C) (D) (E) 25 (A) (B) (C) (D) (E) 37 (A) (B) (C) (D) (E) 49 (A) (B) (C) (D) (E)
2 (F) (G) (H) (J) (K) 14 (F) (G) (H) (J) (K) 26 (F) (G) (H) (J) (K) 38 (F) (G) (H) (J) (K) 50 (F) (G) (H) (J) (K)
3 (A) (B) (C) (D) (E) 15 (A) (B) (C) (D) (E) 27 (A) (B) (C) (D) (E) 39 (A) (B) (C) (D) (E) 51 (A) (B) (C) (D) (E)
4 (F) (G) (H) (J) (K) 16 (F) (G) (H) (J) (K) 28 (F) (G) (H) (J) (K) 40 (F) (G) (H) (J) (K) 52 (F) (G) (H) (J) (K)
5 (A) (B) (C) (D) (E) 17 (A) (B) (C) (D) (E) 29 (A) (B) (C) (D) (E) 41 (A) (B) (C) (D) (E) 53 (A) (B) (C) (D) (E)
6 (F) (G) (H) (J) (K) 18 (F) (G) (H) (J) (K) 30 (F) (G) (H) (J) (K) 42 (F) (G) (H) (J) (K) 54 (F) (G) (H) (J) (K)
7 (A) (B) (C) (D) (E) 19 (A) (B) (C) (D) (E) 31 (A) (B) (C) (D) (E) 43 (A) (B) (C) (D) (E) 55 (A) (B) (C) (D) (E)
8 (F) (G) (H) (J) (K) 20 (F) (G) (H) (J) (K) 32 (F) (G) (H) (J) (K) 44 (F) (G) (H) (J) (K) 56 (F) (G) (H) (J) (K)
9 (A) (B) (C) (D) (E) 21 (A) (B) (C) (D) (E) 33 (A) (B) (C) (D) (E) 45 (A) (B) (C) (D) (E) 57 (A) (B) (C) (D) (E)
10 (F) (G) (H) (J) (K) 22 (F) (G) (H) (J) (K) 34 (F) (G) (H) (J) (K) 46 (F) (G) (H) (J) (K) 58 (F) (G) (H) (J) (K)
11 (A) (B) (C) (D) (E) 23 (A) (B) (C) (D) (E) 35 (A) (B) (C) (D) (E) 47 (A) (B) (C) (D) (E) 59 (A) (B) (C) (D) (E)
12 (F) (G) (H) (J) (K) 24 (F) (G) (H) (J) (K) 36 (F) (G) (H) (J) (K) 48 (F) (G) (H) (J) (K) 60 (F) (G) (H) (J) (K)

TEST 3—READING

1 (A) (B) (C) (D) 9 (A) (B) (C) (D) 17 (A) (B) (C) (D) 25 (A) (B) (C) (D) 33 (A) (B) (C) (D)
2 (F) (G) (H) (J) 10 (F) (G) (H) (J) 18 (F) (G) (H) (J) 26 (F) (G) (H) (J) 34 (F) (G) (H) (J)
3 (A) (B) (C) (D) 11 (A) (B) (C) (D) 19 (A) (B) (C) (D) 27 (A) (B) (C) (D) 35 (A) (B) (C) (D)
4 (F) (G) (H) (J) 12 (F) (G) (H) (J) 20 (F) (G) (H) (J) 28 (F) (G) (H) (J) 36 (F) (G) (H) (J)
5 (A) (B) (C) (D) 13 (A) (B) (C) (D) 21 (A) (B) (C) (D) 29 (A) (B) (C) (D) 37 (A) (B) (C) (D)
6 (F) (G) (H) (J) 14 (F) (G) (H) (J) 22 (F) (G) (H) (J) 30 (F) (G) (H) (J) 38 (F) (G) (H) (J)
7 (A) (B) (C) (D) 15 (A) (B) (C) (D) 23 (A) (B) (C) (D) 31 (A) (B) (C) (D) 39 (A) (B) (C) (D)
8 (F) (G) (H) (J) 16 (F) (G) (H) (J) 24 (F) (G) (H) (J) 32 (F) (G) (H) (J) 40 (F) (G) (H) (J)

TEST 4—SCIENCE

1 (A) (B) (C) (D) 9 (A) (B) (C) (D) 17 (A) (B) (C) (D) 25 (A) (B) (C) (D) 33 (A) (B) (C) (D)
2 (F) (G) (H) (J) 10 (F) (G) (H) (J) 18 (F) (G) (H) (J) 26 (F) (G) (H) (J) 34 (F) (G) (H) (J)
3 (A) (B) (C) (D) 11 (A) (B) (C) (D) 19 (A) (B) (C) (D) 27 (A) (B) (C) (D) 35 (A) (B) (C) (D)
4 (F) (G) (H) (J) 12 (F) (G) (H) (J) 20 (F) (G) (H) (J) 28 (F) (G) (H) (J) 36 (F) (G) (H) (J)
5 (A) (B) (C) (D) 13 (A) (B) (C) (D) 21 (A) (B) (C) (D) 29 (A) (B) (C) (D) 37 (A) (B) (C) (D)
6 (F) (G) (H) (J) 14 (F) (G) (H) (J) 22 (F) (G) (H) (J) 30 (F) (G) (H) (J) 38 (F) (G) (H) (J)
7 (A) (B) (C) (D) 15 (A) (B) (C) (D) 23 (A) (B) (C) (D) 31 (A) (B) (C) (D) 39 (A) (B) (C) (D)
8 (F) (G) (H) (J) 16 (F) (G) (H) (J) 24 (F) (G) (H) (J) 32 (F) (G) (H) (J) 40 (F) (G) (H) (J)

PRACTICE TEST I ESSAY RESPONSE SHEET
(OPTIONAL)

Name

Student ID Number

Date

Instructor

Course/Session Number

S T O P

IF YOU FINISH BEFORE TIME IS CALLED, YOU MAY CHECK YOUR WORK ON THIS ESSAY ONLY.
DO NOT TURN TO ANY OTHER PORTION OF THE TEST.

PRACTICE TEST II BUBBLE SHEET

Start with number 1 for each new section. Be sure to erase any errors or stray marks completely.

Name		Student ID Number
Date	Instructor	Course/Session Number

TEST 1—ENGLISH

1 Ⓐ Ⓑ Ⓒ Ⓓ	16 Ⓕ Ⓖ Ⓗ Ⓙ	31 Ⓐ Ⓑ Ⓒ Ⓓ	46 Ⓕ Ⓖ Ⓗ Ⓙ	61 Ⓐ Ⓑ Ⓒ Ⓓ
2 Ⓕ Ⓖ Ⓗ Ⓙ	17 Ⓐ Ⓑ Ⓒ Ⓓ	32 Ⓕ Ⓖ Ⓗ Ⓙ	47 Ⓐ Ⓑ Ⓒ Ⓓ	62 Ⓕ Ⓖ Ⓗ Ⓙ
3 Ⓐ Ⓑ Ⓒ Ⓓ	18 Ⓕ Ⓖ Ⓗ Ⓙ	33 Ⓐ Ⓑ Ⓒ Ⓓ	48 Ⓕ Ⓖ Ⓗ Ⓙ	63 Ⓐ Ⓑ Ⓒ Ⓓ
4 Ⓕ Ⓖ Ⓗ Ⓙ	19 Ⓐ Ⓑ Ⓒ Ⓓ	34 Ⓕ Ⓖ Ⓗ Ⓙ	49 Ⓐ Ⓑ Ⓒ Ⓓ	64 Ⓕ Ⓖ Ⓗ Ⓙ
5 Ⓐ Ⓑ Ⓒ Ⓓ	20 Ⓕ Ⓖ Ⓗ Ⓙ	35 Ⓐ Ⓑ Ⓒ Ⓓ	50 Ⓕ Ⓖ Ⓗ Ⓙ	65 Ⓐ Ⓑ Ⓒ Ⓓ
6 Ⓕ Ⓖ Ⓗ Ⓙ	21 Ⓐ Ⓑ Ⓒ Ⓓ	36 Ⓕ Ⓖ Ⓗ Ⓙ	51 Ⓐ Ⓑ Ⓒ Ⓓ	66 Ⓕ Ⓖ Ⓗ Ⓙ
7 Ⓐ Ⓑ Ⓒ Ⓓ	22 Ⓕ Ⓖ Ⓗ Ⓙ	37 Ⓐ Ⓑ Ⓒ Ⓓ	52 Ⓕ Ⓖ Ⓗ Ⓙ	67 Ⓐ Ⓑ Ⓒ Ⓓ
8 Ⓕ Ⓖ Ⓗ Ⓙ	23 Ⓐ Ⓑ Ⓒ Ⓓ	38 Ⓕ Ⓖ Ⓗ Ⓙ	53 Ⓐ Ⓑ Ⓒ Ⓓ	68 Ⓕ Ⓖ Ⓗ Ⓙ
9 Ⓐ Ⓑ Ⓒ Ⓓ	24 Ⓕ Ⓖ Ⓗ Ⓙ	39 Ⓐ Ⓑ Ⓒ Ⓓ	54 Ⓕ Ⓖ Ⓗ Ⓙ	69 Ⓐ Ⓑ Ⓒ Ⓓ
10 Ⓕ Ⓖ Ⓗ Ⓙ	25 Ⓐ Ⓑ Ⓒ Ⓓ	40 Ⓕ Ⓖ Ⓗ Ⓙ	55 Ⓐ Ⓑ Ⓒ Ⓓ	70 Ⓕ Ⓖ Ⓗ Ⓙ
11 Ⓐ Ⓑ Ⓒ Ⓓ	26 Ⓕ Ⓖ Ⓗ Ⓙ	41 Ⓐ Ⓑ Ⓒ Ⓓ	56 Ⓕ Ⓖ Ⓗ Ⓙ	71 Ⓐ Ⓑ Ⓒ Ⓓ
12 Ⓕ Ⓖ Ⓗ Ⓙ	27 Ⓐ Ⓑ Ⓒ Ⓓ	42 Ⓕ Ⓖ Ⓗ Ⓙ	57 Ⓐ Ⓑ Ⓒ Ⓓ	72 Ⓕ Ⓖ Ⓗ Ⓙ
13 Ⓐ Ⓑ Ⓒ Ⓓ	28 Ⓕ Ⓖ Ⓗ Ⓙ	43 Ⓐ Ⓑ Ⓒ Ⓓ	58 Ⓕ Ⓖ Ⓗ Ⓙ	73 Ⓐ Ⓑ Ⓒ Ⓓ
14 Ⓕ Ⓖ Ⓗ Ⓙ	29 Ⓐ Ⓑ Ⓒ Ⓓ	44 Ⓕ Ⓖ Ⓗ Ⓙ	59 Ⓐ Ⓑ Ⓒ Ⓓ	74 Ⓕ Ⓖ Ⓗ Ⓙ
15 Ⓐ Ⓑ Ⓒ Ⓓ	30 Ⓕ Ⓖ Ⓗ Ⓙ	45 Ⓐ Ⓑ Ⓒ Ⓓ	60 Ⓕ Ⓖ Ⓗ Ⓙ	75 Ⓐ Ⓑ Ⓒ Ⓓ

TEST 2—MATHEMATICS

1 Ⓐ Ⓑ Ⓒ Ⓓ Ⓔ	13 Ⓐ Ⓑ Ⓒ Ⓓ Ⓔ	25 Ⓐ Ⓑ Ⓒ Ⓓ Ⓔ	37 Ⓐ Ⓑ Ⓒ Ⓓ Ⓔ	49 Ⓐ Ⓑ Ⓒ Ⓓ Ⓔ
2 Ⓕ Ⓖ Ⓗ Ⓙ Ⓚ	14 Ⓕ Ⓖ Ⓗ Ⓙ Ⓚ	26 Ⓕ Ⓖ Ⓗ Ⓙ Ⓚ	38 Ⓕ Ⓖ Ⓗ Ⓙ Ⓚ	50 Ⓕ Ⓖ Ⓗ Ⓙ Ⓚ
3 Ⓐ Ⓑ Ⓒ Ⓓ Ⓔ	15 Ⓐ Ⓑ Ⓒ Ⓓ Ⓔ	27 Ⓐ Ⓑ Ⓒ Ⓓ Ⓔ	39 Ⓐ Ⓑ Ⓒ Ⓓ Ⓔ	51 Ⓐ Ⓑ Ⓒ Ⓓ Ⓔ
4 Ⓕ Ⓖ Ⓗ Ⓙ Ⓚ	16 Ⓕ Ⓖ Ⓗ Ⓙ Ⓚ	28 Ⓕ Ⓖ Ⓗ Ⓙ Ⓚ	40 Ⓕ Ⓖ Ⓗ Ⓙ Ⓚ	52 Ⓕ Ⓖ Ⓗ Ⓙ Ⓚ
5 Ⓐ Ⓑ Ⓒ Ⓓ Ⓔ	17 Ⓐ Ⓑ Ⓒ Ⓓ Ⓔ	29 Ⓐ Ⓑ Ⓒ Ⓓ Ⓔ	41 Ⓐ Ⓑ Ⓒ Ⓓ Ⓔ	53 Ⓐ Ⓑ Ⓒ Ⓓ Ⓔ
6 Ⓕ Ⓖ Ⓗ Ⓙ Ⓚ	18 Ⓕ Ⓖ Ⓗ Ⓙ Ⓚ	30 Ⓕ Ⓖ Ⓗ Ⓙ Ⓚ	42 Ⓕ Ⓖ Ⓗ Ⓙ Ⓚ	54 Ⓕ Ⓖ Ⓗ Ⓙ Ⓚ
7 Ⓐ Ⓑ Ⓒ Ⓓ Ⓔ	19 Ⓐ Ⓑ Ⓒ Ⓓ Ⓔ	31 Ⓐ Ⓑ Ⓒ Ⓓ Ⓔ	43 Ⓐ Ⓑ Ⓒ Ⓓ Ⓔ	55 Ⓐ Ⓑ Ⓒ Ⓓ Ⓔ
8 Ⓕ Ⓖ Ⓗ Ⓙ Ⓚ	20 Ⓕ Ⓖ Ⓗ Ⓙ Ⓚ	32 Ⓕ Ⓖ Ⓗ Ⓙ Ⓚ	44 Ⓕ Ⓖ Ⓗ Ⓙ Ⓚ	56 Ⓕ Ⓖ Ⓗ Ⓙ Ⓚ
9 Ⓐ Ⓑ Ⓒ Ⓓ Ⓔ	21 Ⓐ Ⓑ Ⓒ Ⓓ Ⓔ	33 Ⓐ Ⓑ Ⓒ Ⓓ Ⓔ	45 Ⓐ Ⓑ Ⓒ Ⓓ Ⓔ	57 Ⓐ Ⓑ Ⓒ Ⓓ Ⓔ
10 Ⓕ Ⓖ Ⓗ Ⓙ Ⓚ	22 Ⓕ Ⓖ Ⓗ Ⓙ Ⓚ	34 Ⓕ Ⓖ Ⓗ Ⓙ Ⓚ	46 Ⓕ Ⓖ Ⓗ Ⓙ Ⓚ	58 Ⓕ Ⓖ Ⓗ Ⓙ Ⓚ
11 Ⓐ Ⓑ Ⓒ Ⓓ Ⓔ	23 Ⓐ Ⓑ Ⓒ Ⓓ Ⓔ	35 Ⓐ Ⓑ Ⓒ Ⓓ Ⓔ	47 Ⓐ Ⓑ Ⓒ Ⓓ Ⓔ	59 Ⓐ Ⓑ Ⓒ Ⓓ Ⓔ
12 Ⓕ Ⓖ Ⓗ Ⓙ Ⓚ	24 Ⓕ Ⓖ Ⓗ Ⓙ Ⓚ	36 Ⓕ Ⓖ Ⓗ Ⓙ Ⓚ	48 Ⓕ Ⓖ Ⓗ Ⓙ Ⓚ	60 Ⓕ Ⓖ Ⓗ Ⓙ Ⓚ

TEST 3—READING

1 Ⓐ Ⓑ Ⓒ Ⓓ	9 Ⓐ Ⓑ Ⓒ Ⓓ	17 Ⓐ Ⓑ Ⓒ Ⓓ	25 Ⓐ Ⓑ Ⓒ Ⓓ	33 Ⓐ Ⓑ Ⓒ Ⓓ
2 Ⓕ Ⓖ Ⓗ Ⓙ	10 Ⓕ Ⓖ Ⓗ Ⓙ	18 Ⓕ Ⓖ Ⓗ Ⓙ	26 Ⓕ Ⓖ Ⓗ Ⓙ	34 Ⓕ Ⓖ Ⓗ Ⓙ
3 Ⓐ Ⓑ Ⓒ Ⓓ	11 Ⓐ Ⓑ Ⓒ Ⓓ	19 Ⓐ Ⓑ Ⓒ Ⓓ	27 Ⓐ Ⓑ Ⓒ Ⓓ	35 Ⓐ Ⓑ Ⓒ Ⓓ
4 Ⓕ Ⓖ Ⓗ Ⓙ	12 Ⓕ Ⓖ Ⓗ Ⓙ	20 Ⓕ Ⓖ Ⓗ Ⓙ	28 Ⓕ Ⓖ Ⓗ Ⓙ	36 Ⓕ Ⓖ Ⓗ Ⓙ
5 Ⓐ Ⓑ Ⓒ Ⓓ	13 Ⓐ Ⓑ Ⓒ Ⓓ	21 Ⓐ Ⓑ Ⓒ Ⓓ	29 Ⓐ Ⓑ Ⓒ Ⓓ	37 Ⓐ Ⓑ Ⓒ Ⓓ
6 Ⓕ Ⓖ Ⓗ Ⓙ	14 Ⓕ Ⓖ Ⓗ Ⓙ	22 Ⓕ Ⓖ Ⓗ Ⓙ	30 Ⓕ Ⓖ Ⓗ Ⓙ	38 Ⓕ Ⓖ Ⓗ Ⓙ
7 Ⓐ Ⓑ Ⓒ Ⓓ	15 Ⓐ Ⓑ Ⓒ Ⓓ	23 Ⓐ Ⓑ Ⓒ Ⓓ	31 Ⓐ Ⓑ Ⓒ Ⓓ	39 Ⓐ Ⓑ Ⓒ Ⓓ
8 Ⓕ Ⓖ Ⓗ Ⓙ	16 Ⓕ Ⓖ Ⓗ Ⓙ	24 Ⓕ Ⓖ Ⓗ Ⓙ	32 Ⓕ Ⓖ Ⓗ Ⓙ	40 Ⓕ Ⓖ Ⓗ Ⓙ

TEST 4—SCIENCE

1 Ⓐ Ⓑ Ⓒ Ⓓ	9 Ⓐ Ⓑ Ⓒ Ⓓ	17 Ⓐ Ⓑ Ⓒ Ⓓ	25 Ⓐ Ⓑ Ⓒ Ⓓ	33 Ⓐ Ⓑ Ⓒ Ⓓ
2 Ⓕ Ⓖ Ⓗ Ⓙ	10 Ⓕ Ⓖ Ⓗ Ⓙ	18 Ⓕ Ⓖ Ⓗ Ⓙ	26 Ⓕ Ⓖ Ⓗ Ⓙ	34 Ⓕ Ⓖ Ⓗ Ⓙ
3 Ⓐ Ⓑ Ⓒ Ⓓ	11 Ⓐ Ⓑ Ⓒ Ⓓ	19 Ⓐ Ⓑ Ⓒ Ⓓ	27 Ⓐ Ⓑ Ⓒ Ⓓ	35 Ⓐ Ⓑ Ⓒ Ⓓ
4 Ⓕ Ⓖ Ⓗ Ⓙ	12 Ⓕ Ⓖ Ⓗ Ⓙ	20 Ⓕ Ⓖ Ⓗ Ⓙ	28 Ⓕ Ⓖ Ⓗ Ⓙ	36 Ⓕ Ⓖ Ⓗ Ⓙ
5 Ⓐ Ⓑ Ⓒ Ⓓ	13 Ⓐ Ⓑ Ⓒ Ⓓ	21 Ⓐ Ⓑ Ⓒ Ⓓ	29 Ⓐ Ⓑ Ⓒ Ⓓ	37 Ⓐ Ⓑ Ⓒ Ⓓ
6 Ⓕ Ⓖ Ⓗ Ⓙ	14 Ⓕ Ⓖ Ⓗ Ⓙ	22 Ⓕ Ⓖ Ⓗ Ⓙ	30 Ⓕ Ⓖ Ⓗ Ⓙ	38 Ⓕ Ⓖ Ⓗ Ⓙ
7 Ⓐ Ⓑ Ⓒ Ⓓ	15 Ⓐ Ⓑ Ⓒ Ⓓ	23 Ⓐ Ⓑ Ⓒ Ⓓ	31 Ⓐ Ⓑ Ⓒ Ⓓ	39 Ⓐ Ⓑ Ⓒ Ⓓ
8 Ⓕ Ⓖ Ⓗ Ⓙ	16 Ⓕ Ⓖ Ⓗ Ⓙ	24 Ⓕ Ⓖ Ⓗ Ⓙ	32 Ⓕ Ⓖ Ⓗ Ⓙ	40 Ⓕ Ⓖ Ⓗ Ⓙ

PRACTICE TEST II ESSAY RESPONSE SHEET
(OPTIONAL)

Name _____

Student ID Number _____

Date _____

Instructor _____

Course/Session Number _____

S T O P

IF YOU FINISH BEFORE TIME IS CALLED, YOU MAY CHECK YOUR WORK ON THIS ESSAY ONLY.
DO NOT TURN TO ANY OTHER PORTION OF THE TEST.

PRACTICE TEST III BUBBLE SHEET

Start with number 1 for each new section. Be sure to erase any errors or stray marks completely.

Name _____   Student ID Number _____

Date _____   Instructor _____   Course/Session Number _____

TEST 1—ENGLISH

1 Ⓐ Ⓑ Ⓒ Ⓓ	16 Ⓕ Ⓖ Ⓗ Ⓙ	31 Ⓐ Ⓑ Ⓒ Ⓓ	46 Ⓕ Ⓖ Ⓗ Ⓙ	61 Ⓐ Ⓑ Ⓒ Ⓓ
2 Ⓕ Ⓖ Ⓗ Ⓙ	17 Ⓐ Ⓑ Ⓒ Ⓓ	32 Ⓕ Ⓖ Ⓗ Ⓙ	47 Ⓐ Ⓑ Ⓒ Ⓓ	62 Ⓕ Ⓖ Ⓗ Ⓙ
3 Ⓐ Ⓑ Ⓒ Ⓓ	18 Ⓕ Ⓖ Ⓗ Ⓙ	33 Ⓐ Ⓑ Ⓒ Ⓓ	48 Ⓕ Ⓖ Ⓗ Ⓙ	63 Ⓐ Ⓑ Ⓒ Ⓓ
4 Ⓕ Ⓖ Ⓗ Ⓙ	19 Ⓐ Ⓑ Ⓒ Ⓓ	34 Ⓕ Ⓖ Ⓗ Ⓙ	49 Ⓐ Ⓑ Ⓒ Ⓓ	64 Ⓕ Ⓖ Ⓗ Ⓙ
5 Ⓐ Ⓑ Ⓒ Ⓓ	20 Ⓕ Ⓖ Ⓗ Ⓙ	35 Ⓐ Ⓑ Ⓒ Ⓓ	50 Ⓕ Ⓖ Ⓗ Ⓙ	65 Ⓐ Ⓑ Ⓒ Ⓓ
6 Ⓕ Ⓖ Ⓗ Ⓙ	21 Ⓐ Ⓑ Ⓒ Ⓓ	36 Ⓕ Ⓖ Ⓗ Ⓙ	51 Ⓐ Ⓑ Ⓒ Ⓓ	66 Ⓕ Ⓖ Ⓗ Ⓙ
7 Ⓐ Ⓑ Ⓒ Ⓓ	22 Ⓕ Ⓖ Ⓗ Ⓙ	37 Ⓐ Ⓑ Ⓒ Ⓓ	52 Ⓕ Ⓖ Ⓗ Ⓙ	67 Ⓐ Ⓑ Ⓒ Ⓓ
8 Ⓕ Ⓖ Ⓗ Ⓙ	23 Ⓐ Ⓑ Ⓒ Ⓓ	38 Ⓕ Ⓖ Ⓗ Ⓙ	53 Ⓐ Ⓑ Ⓒ Ⓓ	68 Ⓕ Ⓖ Ⓗ Ⓙ
9 Ⓐ Ⓑ Ⓒ Ⓓ	24 Ⓕ Ⓖ Ⓗ Ⓙ	39 Ⓐ Ⓑ Ⓒ Ⓓ	54 Ⓕ Ⓖ Ⓗ Ⓙ	69 Ⓐ Ⓑ Ⓒ Ⓓ
10 Ⓕ Ⓖ Ⓗ Ⓙ	25 Ⓐ Ⓑ Ⓒ Ⓓ	40 Ⓕ Ⓖ Ⓗ Ⓙ	55 Ⓐ Ⓑ Ⓒ Ⓓ	70 Ⓕ Ⓖ Ⓗ Ⓙ
11 Ⓐ Ⓑ Ⓒ Ⓓ	26 Ⓕ Ⓖ Ⓗ Ⓙ	41 Ⓐ Ⓑ Ⓒ Ⓓ	56 Ⓕ Ⓖ Ⓗ Ⓙ	71 Ⓐ Ⓑ Ⓒ Ⓓ
12 Ⓕ Ⓖ Ⓗ Ⓙ	27 Ⓐ Ⓑ Ⓒ Ⓓ	42 Ⓕ Ⓖ Ⓗ Ⓙ	57 Ⓐ Ⓑ Ⓒ Ⓓ	72 Ⓕ Ⓖ Ⓗ Ⓙ
13 Ⓐ Ⓑ Ⓒ Ⓓ	28 Ⓕ Ⓖ Ⓗ Ⓙ	43 Ⓐ Ⓑ Ⓒ Ⓓ	58 Ⓕ Ⓖ Ⓗ Ⓙ	73 Ⓐ Ⓑ Ⓒ Ⓓ
14 Ⓕ Ⓖ Ⓗ Ⓙ	29 Ⓐ Ⓑ Ⓒ Ⓓ	44 Ⓕ Ⓖ Ⓗ Ⓙ	59 Ⓐ Ⓑ Ⓒ Ⓓ	74 Ⓕ Ⓖ Ⓗ Ⓙ
15 Ⓐ Ⓑ Ⓒ Ⓓ	30 Ⓕ Ⓖ Ⓗ Ⓙ	45 Ⓐ Ⓑ Ⓒ Ⓓ	60 Ⓕ Ⓖ Ⓗ Ⓙ	75 Ⓐ Ⓑ Ⓒ Ⓓ

TEST 2—MATHEMATICS

1 Ⓐ Ⓑ Ⓒ Ⓓ Ⓔ	13 Ⓐ Ⓑ Ⓒ Ⓓ Ⓔ	25 Ⓐ Ⓑ Ⓒ Ⓓ Ⓔ	37 Ⓐ Ⓑ Ⓒ Ⓓ Ⓔ	49 Ⓐ Ⓑ Ⓒ Ⓓ Ⓔ
2 Ⓕ Ⓖ Ⓗ Ⓙ Ⓚ	14 Ⓕ Ⓖ Ⓗ Ⓙ Ⓚ	26 Ⓕ Ⓖ Ⓗ Ⓙ Ⓚ	38 Ⓕ Ⓖ Ⓗ Ⓙ Ⓚ	50 Ⓕ Ⓖ Ⓗ Ⓙ Ⓚ
3 Ⓐ Ⓑ Ⓒ Ⓓ Ⓔ	15 Ⓐ Ⓑ Ⓒ Ⓓ Ⓔ	27 Ⓐ Ⓑ Ⓒ Ⓓ Ⓔ	39 Ⓐ Ⓑ Ⓒ Ⓓ Ⓔ	51 Ⓐ Ⓑ Ⓒ Ⓓ Ⓔ
4 Ⓕ Ⓖ Ⓗ Ⓙ Ⓚ	16 Ⓕ Ⓖ Ⓗ Ⓙ Ⓚ	28 Ⓕ Ⓖ Ⓗ Ⓙ Ⓚ	40 Ⓕ Ⓖ Ⓗ Ⓙ Ⓚ	52 Ⓕ Ⓖ Ⓗ Ⓙ Ⓚ
5 Ⓐ Ⓑ Ⓒ Ⓓ Ⓔ	17 Ⓐ Ⓑ Ⓒ Ⓓ Ⓔ	29 Ⓐ Ⓑ Ⓒ Ⓓ Ⓔ	41 Ⓐ Ⓑ Ⓒ Ⓓ Ⓔ	53 Ⓐ Ⓑ Ⓒ Ⓓ Ⓔ
6 Ⓕ Ⓖ Ⓗ Ⓙ Ⓚ	18 Ⓕ Ⓖ Ⓗ Ⓙ Ⓚ	30 Ⓕ Ⓖ Ⓗ Ⓙ Ⓚ	42 Ⓕ Ⓖ Ⓗ Ⓙ Ⓚ	54 Ⓕ Ⓖ Ⓗ Ⓙ Ⓚ
7 Ⓐ Ⓑ Ⓒ Ⓓ Ⓔ	19 Ⓐ Ⓑ Ⓒ Ⓓ Ⓔ	31 Ⓐ Ⓑ Ⓒ Ⓓ Ⓔ	43 Ⓐ Ⓑ Ⓒ Ⓓ Ⓔ	55 Ⓐ Ⓑ Ⓒ Ⓓ Ⓔ
8 Ⓕ Ⓖ Ⓗ Ⓙ Ⓚ	20 Ⓕ Ⓖ Ⓗ Ⓙ Ⓚ	32 Ⓕ Ⓖ Ⓗ Ⓙ Ⓚ	44 Ⓕ Ⓖ Ⓗ Ⓙ Ⓚ	56 Ⓕ Ⓖ Ⓗ Ⓙ Ⓚ
9 Ⓐ Ⓑ Ⓒ Ⓓ Ⓔ	21 Ⓐ Ⓑ Ⓒ Ⓓ Ⓔ	33 Ⓐ Ⓑ Ⓒ Ⓓ Ⓔ	45 Ⓐ Ⓑ Ⓒ Ⓓ Ⓔ	57 Ⓐ Ⓑ Ⓒ Ⓓ Ⓔ
10 Ⓕ Ⓖ Ⓗ Ⓙ Ⓚ	22 Ⓕ Ⓖ Ⓗ Ⓙ Ⓚ	34 Ⓕ Ⓖ Ⓗ Ⓙ Ⓚ	46 Ⓕ Ⓖ Ⓗ Ⓙ Ⓚ	58 Ⓕ Ⓖ Ⓗ Ⓙ Ⓚ
11 Ⓐ Ⓑ Ⓒ Ⓓ Ⓔ	23 Ⓐ Ⓑ Ⓒ Ⓓ Ⓔ	35 Ⓐ Ⓑ Ⓒ Ⓓ Ⓔ	47 Ⓐ Ⓑ Ⓒ Ⓓ Ⓔ	59 Ⓐ Ⓑ Ⓒ Ⓓ Ⓔ
12 Ⓕ Ⓖ Ⓗ Ⓙ Ⓚ	24 Ⓕ Ⓖ Ⓗ Ⓙ Ⓚ	36 Ⓕ Ⓖ Ⓗ Ⓙ Ⓚ	48 Ⓕ Ⓖ Ⓗ Ⓙ Ⓚ	60 Ⓕ Ⓖ Ⓗ Ⓙ Ⓚ

TEST 3—READING

1 Ⓐ Ⓑ Ⓒ Ⓓ	9 Ⓐ Ⓑ Ⓒ Ⓓ	17 Ⓐ Ⓑ Ⓒ Ⓓ	25 Ⓐ Ⓑ Ⓒ Ⓓ	33 Ⓐ Ⓑ Ⓒ Ⓓ
2 Ⓕ Ⓖ Ⓗ Ⓙ	10 Ⓕ Ⓖ Ⓗ Ⓙ	18 Ⓕ Ⓖ Ⓗ Ⓙ	26 Ⓕ Ⓖ Ⓗ Ⓙ	34 Ⓕ Ⓖ Ⓗ Ⓙ
3 Ⓐ Ⓑ Ⓒ Ⓓ	11 Ⓐ Ⓑ Ⓒ Ⓓ	19 Ⓐ Ⓑ Ⓒ Ⓓ	27 Ⓐ Ⓑ Ⓒ Ⓓ	35 Ⓐ Ⓑ Ⓒ Ⓓ
4 Ⓕ Ⓖ Ⓗ Ⓙ	12 Ⓕ Ⓖ Ⓗ Ⓙ	20 Ⓕ Ⓖ Ⓗ Ⓙ	28 Ⓕ Ⓖ Ⓗ Ⓙ	36 Ⓕ Ⓖ Ⓗ Ⓙ
5 Ⓐ Ⓑ Ⓒ Ⓓ	13 Ⓐ Ⓑ Ⓒ Ⓓ	21 Ⓐ Ⓑ Ⓒ Ⓓ	29 Ⓐ Ⓑ Ⓒ Ⓓ	37 Ⓐ Ⓑ Ⓒ Ⓓ
6 Ⓕ Ⓖ Ⓗ Ⓙ	14 Ⓕ Ⓖ Ⓗ Ⓙ	22 Ⓕ Ⓖ Ⓗ Ⓙ	30 Ⓕ Ⓖ Ⓗ Ⓙ	38 Ⓕ Ⓖ Ⓗ Ⓙ
7 Ⓐ Ⓑ Ⓒ Ⓓ	15 Ⓐ Ⓑ Ⓒ Ⓓ	23 Ⓐ Ⓑ Ⓒ Ⓓ	31 Ⓐ Ⓑ Ⓒ Ⓓ	39 Ⓐ Ⓑ Ⓒ Ⓓ
8 Ⓕ Ⓖ Ⓗ Ⓙ	16 Ⓕ Ⓖ Ⓗ Ⓙ	24 Ⓕ Ⓖ Ⓗ Ⓙ	32 Ⓕ Ⓖ Ⓗ Ⓙ	40 Ⓕ Ⓖ Ⓗ Ⓙ

TEST 4—SCIENCE

1 Ⓐ Ⓑ Ⓒ Ⓓ	9 Ⓐ Ⓑ Ⓒ Ⓓ	17 Ⓐ Ⓑ Ⓒ Ⓓ	25 Ⓐ Ⓑ Ⓒ Ⓓ	33 Ⓐ Ⓑ Ⓒ Ⓓ
2 Ⓕ Ⓖ Ⓗ Ⓙ	10 Ⓕ Ⓖ Ⓗ Ⓙ	18 Ⓕ Ⓖ Ⓗ Ⓙ	26 Ⓕ Ⓖ Ⓗ Ⓙ	34 Ⓕ Ⓖ Ⓗ Ⓙ
3 Ⓐ Ⓑ Ⓒ Ⓓ	11 Ⓐ Ⓑ Ⓒ Ⓓ	19 Ⓐ Ⓑ Ⓒ Ⓓ	27 Ⓐ Ⓑ Ⓒ Ⓓ	35 Ⓐ Ⓑ Ⓒ Ⓓ
4 Ⓕ Ⓖ Ⓗ Ⓙ	12 Ⓕ Ⓖ Ⓗ Ⓙ	20 Ⓕ Ⓖ Ⓗ Ⓙ	28 Ⓕ Ⓖ Ⓗ Ⓙ	36 Ⓕ Ⓖ Ⓗ Ⓙ
5 Ⓐ Ⓑ Ⓒ Ⓓ	13 Ⓐ Ⓑ Ⓒ Ⓓ	21 Ⓐ Ⓑ Ⓒ Ⓓ	29 Ⓐ Ⓑ Ⓒ Ⓓ	37 Ⓐ Ⓑ Ⓒ Ⓓ
6 Ⓕ Ⓖ Ⓗ Ⓙ	14 Ⓕ Ⓖ Ⓗ Ⓙ	22 Ⓕ Ⓖ Ⓗ Ⓙ	30 Ⓕ Ⓖ Ⓗ Ⓙ	38 Ⓕ Ⓖ Ⓗ Ⓙ
7 Ⓐ Ⓑ Ⓒ Ⓓ	15 Ⓐ Ⓑ Ⓒ Ⓓ	23 Ⓐ Ⓑ Ⓒ Ⓓ	31 Ⓐ Ⓑ Ⓒ Ⓓ	39 Ⓐ Ⓑ Ⓒ Ⓓ
8 Ⓕ Ⓖ Ⓗ Ⓙ	16 Ⓕ Ⓖ Ⓗ Ⓙ	24 Ⓕ Ⓖ Ⓗ Ⓙ	32 Ⓕ Ⓖ Ⓗ Ⓙ	40 Ⓕ Ⓖ Ⓗ Ⓙ

PRACTICE TEST III ESSAY RESPONSE SHEET
(OPTIONAL)

Name _____

Student ID Number _____

Date _____

Instructor _____

Course/Session Number _____

S T O P

IF YOU FINISH BEFORE TIME IS CALLED, YOU MAY CHECK YOUR WORK ON THIS ESSAY ONLY.
DO NOT TURN TO ANY OTHER PORTION OF THE TEST.

PRACTICE TEST IV BUBBLE SHEET

Start with number 1 for each new section. Be sure to erase any errors or stray marks completely.

Name _____   Student ID Number _____

Date _____   Instructor _____   Course/Session Number _____

TEST 1—ENGLISH

1 Ⓐ Ⓑ Ⓒ Ⓓ	16 Ⓕ Ⓖ Ⓗ Ⓙ	31 Ⓐ Ⓑ Ⓒ Ⓓ	46 Ⓕ Ⓖ Ⓗ Ⓙ	61 Ⓐ Ⓑ Ⓒ Ⓓ
2 Ⓕ Ⓖ Ⓗ Ⓙ	17 Ⓐ Ⓑ Ⓒ Ⓓ	32 Ⓕ Ⓖ Ⓗ Ⓙ	47 Ⓐ Ⓑ Ⓒ Ⓓ	62 Ⓕ Ⓖ Ⓗ Ⓙ
3 Ⓐ Ⓑ Ⓒ Ⓓ	18 Ⓕ Ⓖ Ⓗ Ⓙ	33 Ⓐ Ⓑ Ⓒ Ⓓ	48 Ⓕ Ⓖ Ⓗ Ⓙ	63 Ⓐ Ⓑ Ⓒ Ⓓ
4 Ⓕ Ⓖ Ⓗ Ⓙ	19 Ⓐ Ⓑ Ⓒ Ⓓ	34 Ⓕ Ⓖ Ⓗ Ⓙ	49 Ⓐ Ⓑ Ⓒ Ⓓ	64 Ⓕ Ⓖ Ⓗ Ⓙ
5 Ⓐ Ⓑ Ⓒ Ⓓ	20 Ⓕ Ⓖ Ⓗ Ⓙ	35 Ⓐ Ⓑ Ⓒ Ⓓ	50 Ⓕ Ⓖ Ⓗ Ⓙ	65 Ⓐ Ⓑ Ⓒ Ⓓ
6 Ⓕ Ⓖ Ⓗ Ⓙ	21 Ⓐ Ⓑ Ⓒ Ⓓ	36 Ⓕ Ⓖ Ⓗ Ⓙ	51 Ⓐ Ⓑ Ⓒ Ⓓ	66 Ⓕ Ⓖ Ⓗ Ⓙ
7 Ⓐ Ⓑ Ⓒ Ⓓ	22 Ⓕ Ⓖ Ⓗ Ⓙ	37 Ⓐ Ⓑ Ⓒ Ⓓ	52 Ⓕ Ⓖ Ⓗ Ⓙ	67 Ⓐ Ⓑ Ⓒ Ⓓ
8 Ⓕ Ⓖ Ⓗ Ⓙ	23 Ⓐ Ⓑ Ⓒ Ⓓ	38 Ⓕ Ⓖ Ⓗ Ⓙ	53 Ⓐ Ⓑ Ⓒ Ⓓ	68 Ⓕ Ⓖ Ⓗ Ⓙ
9 Ⓐ Ⓑ Ⓒ Ⓓ	24 Ⓕ Ⓖ Ⓗ Ⓙ	39 Ⓐ Ⓑ Ⓒ Ⓓ	54 Ⓐ Ⓑ Ⓒ Ⓓ	69 Ⓐ Ⓑ Ⓒ Ⓓ
10 Ⓕ Ⓖ Ⓗ Ⓙ	25 Ⓐ Ⓑ Ⓒ Ⓓ	40 Ⓕ Ⓖ Ⓗ Ⓙ	55 Ⓐ Ⓑ Ⓒ Ⓓ	70 Ⓕ Ⓖ Ⓗ Ⓙ
11 Ⓐ Ⓑ Ⓒ Ⓓ	26 Ⓕ Ⓖ Ⓗ Ⓙ	41 Ⓐ Ⓑ Ⓒ Ⓓ	56 Ⓕ Ⓖ Ⓗ Ⓙ	71 Ⓐ Ⓑ Ⓒ Ⓓ
12 Ⓕ Ⓖ Ⓗ Ⓙ	27 Ⓐ Ⓑ Ⓒ Ⓓ	42 Ⓕ Ⓖ Ⓗ Ⓙ	57 Ⓐ Ⓑ Ⓒ Ⓓ	72 Ⓕ Ⓖ Ⓗ Ⓙ
13 Ⓐ Ⓑ Ⓒ Ⓓ	28 Ⓕ Ⓖ Ⓗ Ⓙ	43 Ⓐ Ⓑ Ⓒ Ⓓ	58 Ⓕ Ⓖ Ⓗ Ⓙ	73 Ⓐ Ⓑ Ⓒ Ⓓ
14 Ⓕ Ⓖ Ⓗ Ⓙ	29 Ⓐ Ⓑ Ⓒ Ⓓ	44 Ⓕ Ⓖ Ⓗ Ⓙ	59 Ⓐ Ⓑ Ⓒ Ⓓ	74 Ⓕ Ⓖ Ⓗ Ⓙ
15 Ⓐ Ⓑ Ⓒ Ⓓ	30 Ⓕ Ⓖ Ⓗ Ⓙ	45 Ⓐ Ⓑ Ⓒ Ⓓ	60 Ⓕ Ⓖ Ⓗ Ⓙ	75 Ⓐ Ⓑ Ⓒ Ⓓ

TEST 2—MATHEMATICS

1 Ⓐ Ⓑ Ⓒ Ⓓ Ⓔ	13 Ⓐ Ⓑ Ⓒ Ⓓ Ⓔ	25 Ⓐ Ⓑ Ⓒ Ⓓ Ⓔ	37 Ⓐ Ⓑ Ⓒ Ⓓ Ⓔ	49 Ⓐ Ⓑ Ⓒ Ⓓ Ⓔ
2 Ⓕ Ⓖ Ⓗ Ⓙ Ⓚ	14 Ⓕ Ⓖ Ⓗ Ⓙ Ⓚ	26 Ⓕ Ⓖ Ⓗ Ⓙ Ⓚ	38 Ⓕ Ⓖ Ⓗ Ⓙ Ⓚ	50 Ⓕ Ⓖ Ⓗ Ⓙ Ⓚ
3 Ⓐ Ⓑ Ⓒ Ⓓ Ⓔ	15 Ⓐ Ⓑ Ⓒ Ⓓ Ⓔ	27 Ⓐ Ⓑ Ⓒ Ⓓ Ⓔ	39 Ⓐ Ⓑ Ⓒ Ⓓ Ⓔ	51 Ⓐ Ⓑ Ⓒ Ⓓ Ⓔ
4 Ⓕ Ⓖ Ⓗ Ⓙ Ⓚ	16 Ⓕ Ⓖ Ⓗ Ⓙ Ⓚ	28 Ⓕ Ⓖ Ⓗ Ⓙ Ⓚ	40 Ⓕ Ⓖ Ⓗ Ⓙ Ⓚ	52 Ⓕ Ⓖ Ⓗ Ⓙ Ⓚ
5 Ⓐ Ⓑ Ⓒ Ⓓ Ⓔ	17 Ⓐ Ⓑ Ⓒ Ⓓ Ⓔ	29 Ⓐ Ⓑ Ⓒ Ⓓ Ⓔ	41 Ⓐ Ⓑ Ⓒ Ⓓ Ⓔ	53 Ⓐ Ⓑ Ⓒ Ⓓ Ⓔ
6 Ⓕ Ⓖ Ⓗ Ⓙ Ⓚ	18 Ⓕ Ⓖ Ⓗ Ⓙ Ⓚ	30 Ⓕ Ⓖ Ⓗ Ⓙ Ⓚ	42 Ⓕ Ⓖ Ⓗ Ⓙ Ⓚ	54 Ⓕ Ⓖ Ⓗ Ⓙ Ⓚ
7 Ⓐ Ⓑ Ⓒ Ⓓ Ⓔ	19 Ⓐ Ⓑ Ⓒ Ⓓ Ⓔ	31 Ⓐ Ⓑ Ⓒ Ⓓ Ⓔ	43 Ⓐ Ⓑ Ⓒ Ⓓ Ⓔ	55 Ⓐ Ⓑ Ⓒ Ⓓ Ⓔ
8 Ⓕ Ⓖ Ⓗ Ⓙ Ⓚ	20 Ⓕ Ⓖ Ⓗ Ⓙ Ⓚ	32 Ⓕ Ⓖ Ⓗ Ⓙ Ⓚ	44 Ⓕ Ⓖ Ⓗ Ⓙ Ⓚ	56 Ⓕ Ⓖ Ⓗ Ⓙ Ⓚ
9 Ⓐ Ⓑ Ⓒ Ⓓ Ⓔ	21 Ⓐ Ⓑ Ⓒ Ⓓ Ⓔ	33 Ⓐ Ⓑ Ⓒ Ⓓ Ⓔ	45 Ⓐ Ⓑ Ⓒ Ⓓ Ⓔ	57 Ⓐ Ⓑ Ⓒ Ⓓ Ⓔ
10 Ⓕ Ⓖ Ⓗ Ⓙ Ⓚ	22 Ⓕ Ⓖ Ⓗ Ⓙ Ⓚ	34 Ⓕ Ⓖ Ⓗ Ⓙ Ⓚ	46 Ⓕ Ⓖ Ⓗ Ⓙ Ⓚ	58 Ⓕ Ⓖ Ⓗ Ⓙ Ⓚ
11 Ⓐ Ⓑ Ⓒ Ⓓ Ⓔ	23 Ⓐ Ⓑ Ⓒ Ⓓ Ⓔ	35 Ⓐ Ⓑ Ⓒ Ⓓ Ⓔ	47 Ⓐ Ⓑ Ⓒ Ⓓ Ⓔ	59 Ⓐ Ⓑ Ⓒ Ⓓ Ⓔ
12 Ⓕ Ⓖ Ⓗ Ⓙ Ⓚ	24 Ⓕ Ⓖ Ⓗ Ⓙ Ⓚ	36 Ⓕ Ⓖ Ⓗ Ⓙ Ⓚ	48 Ⓕ Ⓖ Ⓗ Ⓙ Ⓚ	60 Ⓕ Ⓖ Ⓗ Ⓙ Ⓚ

TEST 3—READING

1 Ⓐ Ⓑ Ⓒ Ⓓ	9 Ⓐ Ⓑ Ⓒ Ⓓ	17 Ⓐ Ⓑ Ⓒ Ⓓ	25 Ⓐ Ⓑ Ⓒ Ⓓ	33 Ⓐ Ⓑ Ⓒ Ⓓ
2 Ⓕ Ⓖ Ⓗ Ⓙ	10 Ⓕ Ⓖ Ⓗ Ⓙ	18 Ⓕ Ⓖ Ⓗ Ⓙ	26 Ⓕ Ⓖ Ⓗ Ⓙ	34 Ⓕ Ⓖ Ⓗ Ⓙ
3 Ⓐ Ⓑ Ⓒ Ⓓ	11 Ⓐ Ⓑ Ⓒ Ⓓ	19 Ⓐ Ⓑ Ⓒ Ⓓ	27 Ⓐ Ⓑ Ⓒ Ⓓ	35 Ⓐ Ⓑ Ⓒ Ⓓ
4 Ⓕ Ⓖ Ⓗ Ⓙ	12 Ⓕ Ⓖ Ⓗ Ⓙ	20 Ⓕ Ⓖ Ⓗ Ⓙ	28 Ⓕ Ⓖ Ⓗ Ⓙ	36 Ⓕ Ⓖ Ⓗ Ⓙ
5 Ⓐ Ⓑ Ⓒ Ⓓ	13 Ⓐ Ⓑ Ⓒ Ⓓ	21 Ⓐ Ⓑ Ⓒ Ⓓ	29 Ⓐ Ⓑ Ⓒ Ⓓ	37 Ⓐ Ⓑ Ⓒ Ⓓ
6 Ⓕ Ⓖ Ⓗ Ⓙ	14 Ⓕ Ⓖ Ⓗ Ⓙ	22 Ⓕ Ⓖ Ⓗ Ⓙ	30 Ⓕ Ⓖ Ⓗ Ⓙ	38 Ⓕ Ⓖ Ⓗ Ⓙ
7 Ⓐ Ⓑ Ⓒ Ⓓ	15 Ⓐ Ⓑ Ⓒ Ⓓ	23 Ⓐ Ⓑ Ⓒ Ⓓ	31 Ⓐ Ⓑ Ⓒ Ⓓ	39 Ⓐ Ⓑ Ⓒ Ⓓ
8 Ⓕ Ⓖ Ⓗ Ⓙ	16 Ⓕ Ⓖ Ⓗ Ⓙ	24 Ⓕ Ⓖ Ⓗ Ⓙ	32 Ⓕ Ⓖ Ⓗ Ⓙ	40 Ⓕ Ⓖ Ⓗ Ⓙ

TEST 4—SCIENCE

1 Ⓐ Ⓑ Ⓒ Ⓓ	9 Ⓐ Ⓑ Ⓒ Ⓓ	17 Ⓐ Ⓑ Ⓒ Ⓓ	25 Ⓐ Ⓑ Ⓒ Ⓓ	33 Ⓐ Ⓑ Ⓒ Ⓓ
2 Ⓕ Ⓖ Ⓗ Ⓙ	10 Ⓕ Ⓖ Ⓗ Ⓙ	18 Ⓕ Ⓖ Ⓗ Ⓙ	26 Ⓕ Ⓖ Ⓗ Ⓙ	34 Ⓕ Ⓖ Ⓗ Ⓙ
3 Ⓐ Ⓑ Ⓒ Ⓓ	11 Ⓐ Ⓑ Ⓒ Ⓓ	19 Ⓐ Ⓑ Ⓒ Ⓓ	27 Ⓐ Ⓑ Ⓒ Ⓓ	35 Ⓐ Ⓑ Ⓒ Ⓓ
4 Ⓕ Ⓖ Ⓗ Ⓙ	12 Ⓕ Ⓖ Ⓗ Ⓙ	20 Ⓕ Ⓖ Ⓗ Ⓙ	28 Ⓕ Ⓖ Ⓗ Ⓙ	36 Ⓕ Ⓖ Ⓗ Ⓙ
5 Ⓐ Ⓑ Ⓒ Ⓓ	13 Ⓐ Ⓑ Ⓒ Ⓓ	21 Ⓐ Ⓑ Ⓒ Ⓓ	29 Ⓐ Ⓑ Ⓒ Ⓓ	37 Ⓐ Ⓑ Ⓒ Ⓓ
6 Ⓕ Ⓖ Ⓗ Ⓙ	14 Ⓕ Ⓖ Ⓗ Ⓙ	22 Ⓕ Ⓖ Ⓗ Ⓙ	30 Ⓕ Ⓖ Ⓗ Ⓙ	38 Ⓕ Ⓖ Ⓗ Ⓙ
7 Ⓐ Ⓑ Ⓒ Ⓓ	15 Ⓐ Ⓑ Ⓒ Ⓓ	23 Ⓐ Ⓑ Ⓒ Ⓓ	31 Ⓐ Ⓑ Ⓒ Ⓓ	39 Ⓐ Ⓑ Ⓒ Ⓓ
8 Ⓕ Ⓖ Ⓗ Ⓙ	16 Ⓕ Ⓖ Ⓗ Ⓙ	24 Ⓕ Ⓖ Ⓗ Ⓙ	32 Ⓕ Ⓖ Ⓗ Ⓙ	40 Ⓕ Ⓖ Ⓗ Ⓙ

PRACTICE TEST IV ESSAY RESPONSE SHEET
(OPTIONAL)

Name

Student ID Number

Date

Instructor

Course/Session Number

S T O P

IF YOU FINISH BEFORE TIME IS CALLED, YOU MAY CHECK YOUR WORK ON THIS ESSAY ONLY.
DO NOT TURN TO ANY OTHER PORTION OF THE TEST.

PRACTICE TEST PROGRESS REPORTS

The progress reports on the following pages are designed to help you monitor your progress on the multiple-choice portions of the practice tests. The reports on pages 319–320 are for your own use. The reports on pages 321–324 are to be turned in to your instructor.

Complete the assigned items by the due date given by your instructor. Practice Tests I and II should be done *without* time restrictions, and Practice Tests III and IV should be done *with* time restrictions. Correct your answers using the answers and explanations found at the back of your textbook*, and record both the number and percentage of items answered correctly on the student copies of the progress reports. Identify the date on which you completed each test. List the numbers of any items that you would like your instructor to review in class. Then, transfer this information to the corresponding instructor copies of the reports and give them to your instructor. Be sure to leave the last three columns of the instructor reports blank; these are for your instructor's use in evaluating your progress. (Note: In the first column of each report, the numbering refers to the tests and the page numbers refer to the locations of those tests in this book.)

* Consult your instructor to determine whether you will use student text answers and explanations to complete practice test progress reports.

Name: _____ Student ID: _____ Date: _____

PRACTICE TEST I STUDENT COPY

Test	Total # of Items			% of Items Correct	Date Completed	Item #s to Review
	Possible	Assigned	Correct			
1: English (p. 328)	75					
2: Mathematics (p. 340)	60					
3: Reading (p. 358)	40					
4: Science (p. 368)	40					

PRACTICE TEST II STUDENT COPY

Test	Total # of Items			% of Items Correct	Date Completed	Item #s to Review
	Possible	Assigned	Correct			
1: English (p. 384)	75					
2: Mathematics (p. 398)	60					
3: Reading (p. 414)	40					
4: Science (p. 422)	40					

PRACTICE TEST III STUDENT COPY

Test	Total # of Items			% of Items Correct	Date Completed	Item #s to Review
	Possible	Assigned	Correct			
1: English (p. 440)	75					
2: Mathematics (p. 454)	60					
3: Reading (p. 474)	40					
4: Science (p. 484)	40					

PRACTICE TEST IV STUDENT COPY

Test	Total # of Items			% of Items Correct	Date Completed	Item #s to Review
	Possible	Assigned	Correct			
1: English (p. 500)	75					
2: Mathematics (p. 514)	60					
3: Reading (p. 530)	40					
4: Science (p. 542)	40					

Name: _____ Student ID: _____ Date: _____

PRACTICE TEST I INSTRUCTOR COPY

| Test | Total # of Items | | | % of Items Correct | Date Completed | Item #s to Review | Instructor Skill Evaluation (Check One Per Section) | | |
	Possible	Assigned	Correct				Mastered	Partially Mastered	Not Mastered
1: English (p. 328)									
2: Mathematics (p. 340)									
3: Reading (p. 358)									
4: Science (p. 368)									

Name: _____ Student ID: _____ Date: _____

PRACTICE TEST II INSTRUCTOR COPY

Test	Total # of Items			% of Items Correct	Date Completed	Item #s to Review	Instructor Skill Evaluation (Check One Per Section)		
	Possible	Assigned	Correct				Mastered	Partially Mastered	Not Mastered
1: English (p. 384)									
2: Mathematics (p. 398)									
3: Reading (p. 414)									
4: Science (p. 422)									

Name: _____ Student ID: _____ Date: _____

PRACTICE TEST III INSTRUCTOR COPY

Test	Total # of Items			% of Items Correct	Date Completed	Item #s to Review	Instructor Skill Evaluation (Check One Per Section)		
	Possible	Assigned	Correct				Mastered	Partially Mastered	Not Mastered
1: English (p. 440)									
2: Mathematics (p. 454)									
3: Reading (p. 474)									
4: Science (p. 484)									

Name: _____ Student ID: _____ Date: _____

PRACTICE TEST IV INSTRUCTOR COPY

Test	Total # of Items			% of Items Correct	Date Completed	Item #s to Review	Instructor Skill Evaluation (Check One Per Section)		
	Possible	Assigned	Correct				Mastered	Partially Mastered	Not Mastered
1: English (p. 500)									
2: Mathematics (p. 514)									
3: Reading (p. 530)									
4: Science (p. 542)									

Practice Test I

DIRECTIONS

Practice Test I consists of five subject tests: English, Mathematics, Reading, Science, and Writing. Calculator use is only permitted on the Mathematics Test.

The items in each multiple-choice test are numbered and the answer choices are lettered. The provided bubble sheet (p. 304) has numbered rows that correspond to the items on the test. Each row contains lettered ovals to match the answer choices for each item on the test. Each numbered row on the bubble sheet has a corresponding item on the test.

For each item, first decide on the best answer choice. Then, locate the row number that corresponds to the item. Next, find the oval in that row that matches the letter of the chosen answer. Then, use a soft lead pencil to fill in the oval. Do not use a ballpoint pen.

Mark only one answer for each item. If you change your mind about the answer choice, thoroughly erase the first mark before marking your new answer.

Note that only responses marked on your bubble sheet will be scored. Your score on each test will be based only on the number of items that are correctly answered during the time allowed for that test. Guessing is not penalized. Therefore, it is to your best advantage to answer every item on the test, even if you must guess.

On the Writing Test, use the provided essay response sheet (p. 301) to write your response to the prompt. (Note that the Writing Test is optional.)

You may work on each test only during the time allowed for that test. If you finish a test before time is called, use the time to review your answer choices or work on items about which you are uncertain. You may not return to a test on which time has already been called and you may not preview another test. You must lay down your pencil immediately when time is called at the end of each test. You may not for any reason fill in or alter ovals for a test after time expires for that test. Violation of these rules will result in immediate disqualification from the exam.

1 1 1 1 1 1 1 1 1 1 1 1

ENGLISH TEST
45 Minutes—75 Items

DIRECTIONS: In the passages below, certain parts of the sentences have been underlined and numbered. In the right-hand column, you will find different ways of writing each underlined part; the original version is indicated by the "NO CHANGE" option. There are also items that ask about a section of the passage or the passage as a whole. These items do not refer to an underlined portion of the passage; they are identified by a number or numbers in a box.

For each item, choose the alternative that you consider to be the best. Select the answer choice that best expresses the intended idea, is most acceptable in standard written English, or is most consistent with the overall tone and style of the passage. Read the passage through once before you begin to answer the accompanying items. Finding the answers to certain items may depend on looking at material that appears several sentences beyond the item. So, be sure that you have read far enough ahead before you select your answer choice.

Answers are on page 605.

PASSAGE I

Basic Principles of Nuclear Weapons

The challenge to start to begin to make timely

1

progress toward removing the threat of nuclear war is

today the most important challenge in international

relations. Three general principles guide our defense

and negotiating policies toward such a goal, principles

based on the technical realities of nuclear war.

First, nuclear weapons are fundamentally

2

different than non-nuclear weapons. These weapons of

2

mass destruction that could do a lot of harm have a

3

1. A. NO CHANGE
B. to begin making
C. to begin the making of
D. of beginning the making of

2. F. NO CHANGE
G. different than fundamentally
H. different from fundamentally
J. fundamentally different from

3. A. NO CHANGE
B. (and they could also do a great deal of harm)
C. (owing to the fact that they could do a lot of harm)
D. OMIT the underlined portion.

GO ON TO THE NEXT PAGE.

long and deadly radioactive memory, the unknowns of
4

nuclear conflict dwarf the predictable consequences.

The number of deaths resulting from injuries and the
5

unavailability of medical care and the economic
5

damage as a result from disruption and disorganization
6

would be even more devastating than the direct loss of
7

life and property. [8]

Second, the sole purpose of nuclear weapons
9

must be to deter nuclear war, it is neither a substitute
10

for maintaining adequate conventional military forces

to meet vital national security goals but an effective
11

defense against the almost total mutual annihilation

and devastation that results from a full-scale nuclear

war. Third, arms control is an essential part of our
12

national security. Thus far, we have had no effective

controls on offensive nuclear weaponry, and it is clear

that each step forward in the arms race toward more

4. F. NO CHANGE
   G. memory. The
   H. memory the
   J. memory and the

5. A. NO CHANGE
   B. from injuries and also from the
       unavailability of medical care
   C. from the unavailability of injuries and
       medical care
   D. both from injuries and also from the
       unavailability of medical care as well

6. F. NO CHANGE
   G. as a result to
   H. resulting from
   J. with a result of

7. A. NO CHANGE
   B. is even more devastating than
   C. are even more devastating as
   D. might be more devastating even as

8. Which of the following would be an appropriate
   final sentence for this paragraph?
   F. And so I believe nuclear weapons to be a
       challenge.
   G. Nuclear war could have no winners.
   H. Nuclear conflict is very dangerous.
   J. Nuclear conflict would be rather wasteful.

9. A. NO CHANGE
   B. solely, the purpose
   C. the solely purpose
   D. the purpose solely

10. F. NO CHANGE
    G. war. They are
    H. war they are
    J. war; it is

11. A. NO CHANGE
    B. and
    C. nor
    D. including

12. F. NO CHANGE
    G. Third
    H. (Begin a new paragraph) Third
    J. (Begin a new paragraph) Third,

GO ON TO THE NEXT PAGE.

and improved weapons <u>has made less</u> our security.

13

13. **A.** NO CHANGE
    B. has lessened
    C. have lessened
    D. have made less of

Before deploying additional weapons, <u>they must</u>

14

<u>develop</u> a coherent arms control strategy.

14

14. **F.** NO CHANGE
    G. the development is necessary of
    H. it is necessary to develop
    J. it is necessarily to be developed,

> Items 15 and 16 ask about the preceding passage as a whole.

15. Which of the following best describes the overall structure of the essay?

    A. A three-part argument
    B. A two-part narrative
    C. A three-part comparison
    D. A four-part argument

16. Which of the following is the thesis of this essay?

    F. Nuclear weapons are fundamentally different from non-nuclear weapons.
    G. The sole purpose of nuclear weapons must be to deter nuclear war.
    H. There are three principles that guide our effort to remove the threat of nuclear war.
    J. Nuclear war is a frightening possibility.

PASSAGE II

Education for a New Republic

The founders of the Republic <u>viewing their</u>

17

17. **A.** NO CHANGE
    B. having viewed its
    C. viewed its
    D. viewed their

revolution primarily in political terms <u>rather as</u> in

18

18. **F.** NO CHANGE
    G. rather than
    H. but
    J. OMIT the underlined portion.

economic terms. <u>Therefore,</u> they viewed the kind of

19

education needed for the new Republic largely in

19. **A.** NO CHANGE
    B. Since
    C. However
    D. On the contrary

political terms instead of <u>as a means to</u> academic
20

excellence or individual self-fulfillment. <u>Talking about</u>
21

education as a bulwark for liberty, equality, popular

consent, and devotion to the public <u>good goals</u> that
22

<u>took precedence over</u> the uses of knowledge for self-
23

improvement or occupational preparation. Over and

over again, the Revolutionary generation, both liberal

and conservative in <u>outlook—assert their</u> faith that the
24

welfare of the Republic rested upon an educated

citizenry.

   All agreed that the principal ingredients of a

civic education <u>was</u> literacy and inculcation of patriotic
25

and moral <u>virtues some</u> others added the study of
26

history and the study of the principles of the

republican government itself. The founders, as was the

case of almost all their successors, were long on

exhortation and rhetoric regarding the value of civic

<u>education; since</u> they left it to the textbook writers to
27

distill the essence of those values for school children.

Texts in American history and government appeared as

early as the 1790s. The textbook writers <u>turned out</u>
28

<u>being</u> very largely of conservative persuasion, more
28

likely Federalist in outlook than Jeffersonian, and

20. **F.** NO CHANGE
    G. as a means or a way to
    H. to
    J. as

21. **A.** NO CHANGE
    B. Talking
    C. With the talking about
    D. They talked about

22. **F.** NO CHANGE
    G. good. Goals
    H. good, goals
    J. good; goals

23. **A.** NO CHANGE
    B. precede
    C. precede over
    D. took precedence on

24. **F.** NO CHANGE
    G. outlook, asserted its
    H. outlook; asserted its
    J. outlook asserts their

25. **A.** NO CHANGE
    B. being
    C. were
    D. were like

26. **F.** NO CHANGE
    G. virtues—some
    H. virtues, some
    J. virtues; some

27. **A.** NO CHANGE
    B. education. And
    C. education. Since
    D. education, but

28. **F.** NO CHANGE
    G. turned out to be
    H. turning out to be
    J. having turned out to be

GO ON TO THE NEXT PAGE.

universally almost agreed that political virtue must rest
²⁹

upon moral and religious precepts. Since most

textbook writers were New Englanders, this meant that

the texts had a decidedly Federalist slant.

    In the first half of the Republic, civic education

in the schools emphasized the inculcation of civic

values, put less emphasis on political knowledge, and

no attempt to develop political skills. The
³⁰

development of political skills was left to the local

parties, town meetings, churches, coffeehouses, and

ale houses where men gathered to talk. [31]

29. **A.** NO CHANGE
    B. almost, agreed universally
    C. almost universally agreed
    D. almost universally, agreed

30. **F.** NO CHANGE
    G. made no attempt to develop
    H. none at all on the development of
    J. none was put at all on developing

31. Which of the following correctly describes how
the last paragraph of the essay functions?

    A. It contradicts much of what was said before.
    B. It continues the logical development of the essay.
    C. It reiterates what was said in the first paragraph.
    D. It is a transitional paragraph to introduce a new topic.

Item 32 asks about the preceding passage as a whole.

---

32. This essay would most likely be published in a:

    F. history textbook.
    G. political science journal.
    H. journal for educators.
    J. biography of Jefferson.

GO ON TO THE NEXT PAGE.

PASSAGE III

Women and World War I

[1]

The <u>contribution of women</u> on the home front
33
during World War I was varied. It included a large

range of activities—<u>from knitting and the operation of</u>
34
drill presses—and engaged a cross section of the

female population, from housewives to society girls.

World War I <u>marked the first time</u> in the history of the
35
United States that a systematic effort was made,

through organizations like the League for Women's

Service, <u>to utilize</u> the capabilities of women in all
36
regions of the country.

[2]

While much of this volunteer work <u>falls within</u>
37
the established bounds of women's club work, many

women entered areas of industrial work <u>previously</u>
38
<u>reserved by</u> the male population. Women put on the
38
uniforms of elevator operators, streetcar conductors,

postmen, and industrial <u>workers. However, they were</u>
39
<u>employed</u> in aircraft and munitions plants as well as in
39
shipbuilding yards and steel mills.

[3]

Much of the work fell into the traditional realm

of volunteer <u>activity knitting</u> garments for the boys
40
overseas, canning for Uncle Sam, planting Victory

gardens, etc. Through these activities, every

33. A. NO CHANGE
   B. Women, their contribution
   C. The contribution of woman
   D. Woman's contribution

34. F. NO CHANGE
   G. from knitting with the operation of
   H. from knitting and operating
   J. from knitting to operating

35. A. NO CHANGE
   B. has marked the first time
   C. is the first time it is marked
   D. was marked, the first time

36. F. NO CHANGE
   G. being able to utilize
   H. utilizing
   J. and utilize

37. A. NO CHANGE
   B. fell within
   C. having fallen within
   D. fell in

38. F. NO CHANGE
   G. having previously been reserved
   H. previously reserved for
   J. reserved previous to then

39. A. NO CHANGE
   B. workers. They were employed
   C. workers, but they were employed
   D. workers. Since they were employed

40. F. NO CHANGE
   G. activity—knitting
   H. activity: knitting
   J. activity, knitting

GO ON TO THE NEXT PAGE.

homemaker could <u>demonstrate their</u> patriotism while
41

still fulfilling her role as homemaker. Women with

more time volunteered to hostess at <u>canteens: make</u>
42

bandages, and organize food and clothing drives. The

Women's Land Army, dressed in bloomer uniforms

and armed with such slogans as "The Woman with the

Hoe Must Defend the Man with the <u>Musket," was</u>
43

<u>dispatched</u> to assist farmers in processing crops.
43

[4]

Women performed ably during the war and <u>laid</u>
44

<u>the foundation</u> for more specialized jobs, increased
44

wages, better working conditions, and a more

competitive job status in the labor market.

41. **A.** NO CHANGE
    B. be demonstrating
    C. have demonstrated their
    D. demonstrate her

42. **F.** NO CHANGE
    G. canteens make
    H. canteens, make
    J. canteens; make

43. **A.** NO CHANGE
    B. Musket," which was then dispatched
    C. Musket," and it was dispatched
    D. Musket," and it got dispatched

44. **F.** NO CHANGE
    G. the foundation was laid
    H. the foundation was lain
    J. laying the foundation

Items 45 and 46 ask about the preceding passage as a whole.

---

45. Which of the following represents the most logical order for the paragraphs?

    A. 1, 4, 3, 2
    B. 1, 3, 4, 2
    C. 1, 3, 2, 4
    D. 2, 4, 3, 1

46. Is the use of the sample slogan appropriate to the essay?

    F. Yes, because it helps the reader to understand one of the points being made.
    G. Yes, because all general statements should be illustrated with an example.
    H. No, because it does not help the reader to understand the point being made.
    J. No, because it is needlessly distracting.

GO ON TO THE NEXT PAGE.

PASSAGE IV

Democracy in Japan

Following the end of World War II, substantial

changes <u>undertaken</u> in Japan to liberate the individual
₄₇

from authoritarian restraints. The new democratic

value system was <u>acceptable by</u> many teachers,
₄₈

students, intellectuals, and old <u>liberals, and</u> it was not
₄₉

immediately embraced by the society as a whole.

<u>Japanese traditions were dominated by group values,</u>
₅₀

and notions of personal freedom and individual rights

<u>being</u> unfamiliar.
₅₁

       <u>Today, the triumph of</u> democratic processes
₅₂

<u>is clear</u> evident in the widespread participation of the
₅₃

Japanese in social and political life. <u>Furthermore,</u>
₅₄

there is no universally accepted and stable value

47. A. NO CHANGE
    B. will be undertaken
    C. have been undertaken
    D. were undertaken

48. F. NO CHANGE
    G. accepted by
    H. excepted by
    J. excepted to

49. A. NO CHANGE
    B. liberals, since
    C. liberals, but
    D. liberals; consequently

50. F. NO CHANGE
    G. Dominated by group values were the
       Japanese traditions
    H. Group values were always dominating the
       Japanese traditions
    J. Dominating Japanese traditions were group
       values

51. A. NO CHANGE
    B. were
    C. was
    D. are

52. F. NO CHANGE
    G. (Do NOT begin a new paragraph) Today the
       triumph, of
    H. Today, the triumph, of
    J. (Do NOT begin a new paragraph) Today,
       owing to the fact that

53. A. NO CHANGE
    B. is
    C. is clear and also
    D. are clearly

54. F. NO CHANGE
    G. Therefore,
    H. So,
    J. Yet,

GO ON TO THE NEXT PAGE.

system, values being constantly modified by strong
55

infusions of Western ideas. School textbooks expound

democratic principles, and so emphasizing equality
56

over hierarchy and rationalism over tradition, but in

practice, these values are often sometimes distorted,
57

particularly by the youth that translated the
58

individualistic and humanistic goals of democracy into

egoistic and materialistic ones. 59

55. A. NO CHANGE
    B. system with that values are
    C. system since that values are
    D. system since values are

56. F. NO CHANGE
    G. principles, emphasizing
    H. principles and the emphasis of
    J. principles with the emphasis that

57. A. NO CHANGE
    B. had been misinterpreted and distorted often
    C. often misinterpreted and distorted
    D. are often misinterpreted and distorted

58. F. NO CHANGE
    G. that translate
    H. who translate
    J. translate

59. What type of discussion might logically follow this last paragraph?
    A. A discussion of goals of Japanese youth
    B. A discussion of democratic principles
    C. A discussion of Western education
    D. A discussion of World War II

PASSAGE V

Zoological Nature

From the beginning, humankind always has
60

shared some sort of link with the animal world. The
60

earliest and most primitive was surely that of hunter

and prey—with humans possibly playing the fatal role

of victim. Later, of course, humans reversed the roles

as they became more skillful and intelligenter.
61

60. F. NO CHANGE
    G. have always shared
    H. is always sharing
    J. has always shared

61. A. NO CHANGE
    B. so intelligent
    C. and more intelligent
    D. but intelligent

GO ON TO THE NEXT PAGE.

The later domestication of certain <u>animals and also</u> the ₆₂ discovery of agriculture, made for a more settled and stable existence and was an essential step in the not-so-orderly <u>and very chaotic</u> process of becoming civilized. ₆₃ However, the intellectual distance between regarding an animal as the source of dinner or of material comfort and <u>to consider them</u> a worthy subject for ₆₄ study is considerable.

Not until Aristotle did the animal world become a subject for serious scientific study. Although <u>he</u> ₆₅ <u>seemingly writes on</u> every <u>subject, Aristotle's work</u> in ₆₅ ₆₆ zoology—studying animals as animals—is considered his most successful. He seemed to have had a natural affinity for and curiosity about all the living creatures of the world, <u>and</u> he took special interest in marine ₆₇ life.

Aristotle's zoological writings reveal him to be a remarkably astute observer of the natural world, <u>wedding his</u> observations to what might be called ₆₈ speculative reason. He was therefore a theorist as well.

His overall theory was <u>simple. In</u> the works of ₆₉ Nature," he said, "purpose and not accident is predominant." A thing is known then when we know what it is for. He linked <u>and combined</u> theory ₇₀ and practice by saying that interpretation of an

62. **F.** NO CHANGE
   G. animals, also
   H. animals, along with
   J. animals; along with

63. **A.** NO CHANGE
   B. (and very chaotic)
   C. yet very chaotic
   D. OMIT the underlined portion.

64. **F.** NO CHANGE
   G. considering it
   H. considering them
   J. then to consider them

65. **A.** NO CHANGE
   B. he wrote (seemingly) on
   C. writing seemingly on
   D. he wrote on seemingly

66. **F.** NO CHANGE
   G. subject; Aristotles work
   H. subject Aristotles' work
   J. subject: Aristotle's work

67. **A.** NO CHANGE
   B. so
   C. but
   D. because

68. **F.** NO CHANGE
   G. who was wedded to
   H. in that he wedded
   J. with the wedding of

69. **A.** NO CHANGE
   B. simple—in
   C. simple. "In
   D. simply. "In

70. **F.** NO CHANGE
   G. combining
   H. to combine
   J. OMIT the underlined portion.

GO ON TO THE NEXT PAGE.

observed phenomenon must always be made <u>in light</u>₇₁

<u>of its purpose</u>. His zoological theory was thus a
₇₁

reflection of the essentially teleological nature of his

overall philosophy. [72]

71. **A.** NO CHANGE
    B. always keeping its purpose in mind
    C. without ever forgetting what its purpose is
    D. given an understanding of what its purpose is

72. Is the quote from Aristotle in the last paragraph appropriate?

    F. Yes, because it is important to quote the works of people you are talking about.
    G. Yes, because it is a succinct statement of Aristotle's theory.
    H. No, because the quote is irrelevant to what the author is talking about in that paragraph.
    J. No, because it is wrong to quote when you can express the idea in your own words.

Items 73–75 ask about the preceding passage as a whole.

---

73. The author probably had which of the following audiences in mind for this essay?

    A. Zoologists
    B. Students who are studying Aristotle
    C. The average person interested in science
    D. Teachers of marine biology

74. What is the actual thesis of this essay?

    F. People have always liked animals.
    G. Animals and people reversed roles.
    H. Aristotle was interested in the natural world.
    J. The animal world became a source of serious study because of Aristotle.

75. How does the first paragraph of this essay function?

    A. It poses questions to be answered.
    B. It provides general background for the rest of the passage.
    C. It introduces an argument.
    D. It provides an anecdote related to the rest of the passage.

END OF TEST 1
STOP! DO NOT TURN THE PAGE UNTIL TOLD TO DO SO.

2 2 2 2 2 2 2 2 2 2 2 2 2

MATHEMATICS TEST
60 Minutes—60 Items

DIRECTIONS: Solve each item and choose the correct answer choice. Then, fill in the corresponding oval on the bubble sheet.

Allocate time wisely. Try to solve as many items as possible, returning to skipped items if time permits.

Calculator use is permitted on this test; however, some items are best solved without the use of a calculator.

Note: Unless otherwise stated, assume all of the following.

1. Illustrative figures are NOT necessarily drawn to scale.
2. The word *average* indicates arithmetic mean.
3. The word *line* indicates a straight line.
4. Geometric figures lie in a plane.

Answers are on page 606.

---

1. If $\frac{1}{x} + \frac{1}{x} = 8$, then $x = ?$

   A. $\frac{1}{4}$
   B. $\frac{1}{2}$
   C. 1
   D. 2
   E. 4

2. If $x = 2$ and $y = -1$, then $3x - 4y = ?$

   F. -5
   G. -1
   H. 0
   J. 2
   K. 10

3. In a certain school, there are 600 boys and 400 girls. If 20 percent of the boys and 30 percent of the girls are on the honor roll, how many of the students are on the honor roll?

   A. 120
   B. 175
   C. 240
   D. 250
   E. 280

DO YOUR FIGURING HERE.

GO ON TO THE NEXT PAGE.

4. If p, q, r, s, and t are whole numbers, the expression $t[r(p+q)+s]$ must be an even number when which of the 5 numbers is even?

   F. p
   G. q
   H. r
   J. s
   K. t

5. A student conducting a lab experiment finds that the population of flies in a bottle increases by a certain multiple from week to week. If the pattern shown in the table continues, how many flies can the student expect to find in the bottle in week 5?

Results of Biology Project Conducted by Student X					
Week	1	2	3	4	5
# of flies in bottle	3	12	48	192	?

   A. 195
   B. 240
   C. 384
   D. 564
   E. 768

6. At a school assembly, 3 students are each scheduled to give a short speech. In how many different orders can the speeches be scheduled?

   F. 12
   G. 9
   H. 6
   J. 4
   K. 3

DO YOUR FIGURING HERE.

GO ON TO THE NEXT PAGE.

7. If points P and Q lie in the xy-plane and have the coordinates shown below, what is the midpoint of $\overline{PQ}$?

A. $(-2,0)$
B. $(-2,2)$
C. $(0,2)$
D. $(2,0)$
E. $(2,2)$

DO YOUR FIGURING HERE.

8. If $xy = |xy|$ and $xy \neq 0$, which of the following CANNOT be true?

F. $x > y > 0$
G. $y > x > 0$
H. $x > 0 > y$
J. $0 > x > y$
K. $0 > y > x$

9. In the scale drawing of the floor of a rectangular room *shown* below, the scale used was $1\,cm = 4\,m$. What is the actual area, in square meters, of the floor of the room?

1.2 cm

1 cm

A. 9.6
B. 13.6
C. 15
D. 19.2
E. 38.4

GO ON TO THE NEXT PAGE.

10. If $30,000 \cdot 20 = 6 \cdot 10^n$, then $n = ?$

    F. 4
    G. 5
    H. 6
    J. 7
    K. 8

11. Karen purchased 4 pounds of candy, which was a mix of chocolates and caramels. If chocolates cost \$3 per pound and caramels cost \$2 per pound, and if Karen spent a total of \$10.00, how many pounds of chocolates did she buy?

    A. 1
    B. 2
    C. 2.5
    D. 3
    E. 3.5

12. The average of Al's scores on 3 tests was 80. If the average of his scores on the first 2 tests was also 80, what was his score on the third test?

    F. 90
    G. 85
    H. 80
    J. 75
    K. 72

13. A book contains 10 photographs, some in color and some in black-and-white. Each of the following could be the ratio of color to black-and-white photographs EXCEPT:

    A. 9:1
    B. 4:1
    C. 5:2
    D. 3:2
    E. 1:1

14. If $\frac{4}{5} = \frac{x}{4}$, then $x = ?$

    F. 5
    G. $\frac{16}{5}$
    H. $\frac{5}{4}$
    J. $\frac{4}{5}$
    K. $\frac{5}{16}$

DO YOUR FIGURING HERE.

GO ON TO THE NEXT PAGE.

15. In the figure below, three equilateral triangles have a common vertex. How many degrees is $x + y + z$?

DO YOUR FIGURING HERE.

A. 60
B. 90
C. 120
D. 180
E. 240

16. Peter spent $\frac{1}{4}$ of his allowance on Monday and $\frac{1}{3}$ of the remainder on Tuesday. What part of the allowance does Peter still have?

F. $\frac{1}{12}$
G. $\frac{1}{4}$
H. $\frac{1}{2}$
J. $\frac{3}{4}$
K. $\frac{11}{12}$

17. If 100 identical bricks weigh p pounds, then how many pounds do 20 bricks weigh in terms of p?

A. $\frac{p}{20}$
B. $\frac{p}{5}$
C. $20p$
D. $\frac{5}{p}$
E. $\frac{20}{p}$

GO ON TO THE NEXT PAGE.

18. If the distances between points P, Q, and R are equal, which of the following could be true?

    I. P, Q, and R are points on a circle with center O.
    II. P and Q are points on a circle with center R.
    III. P, Q, and R are vertices of an equilateral triangle.

    F. I only
    G. I and II only
    H. I and III only
    J. II and III only
    K. I, II, and III

DO YOUR FIGURING HERE.

19. In the table below, the percent *increase* in the price of the item was greatest during which of the following periods?

Year	1980	1985	1990	1995	2000	2005
Price	$2	$4	$7	$12	$20	$30

    A. 1980–1985
    B. 1985–1990
    C. 1990–1995
    D. 1995–2000
    E. 2000–2005

20. Which of the following is a factorization of $x^2 + 4x - 12$?

    F. $(x-6)(x+2)$
    G. $(x-4)(x+3)$
    H. $(x-2)(x+6)$
    J. $(x+2)(x+6)$
    K. $(x+3)(x+4)$

21. Two cartons weigh $3x-2$ and $2x-3$. If the average weight of the cartons is 10, the heavier carton weighs how much more than the lighter carton?

    A. 2
    B. 4
    C. 5
    D. 6
    E. 10

GO ON TO THE NEXT PAGE.

22. A group of 15 students took a test that was scored from 0 to 100. If 10 students scored 75 or more on the test, what is the lowest possible value for the average score of all 15 students?

DO YOUR FIGURING HERE.

F. 25
G. 50
H. 70
J. 75
K. 90

23. For all real numbers x, 16^x is equal to which of the following expressions?

A. x^{16}
B. 2^{3x}
C. 4^{2x}
D. 8^{2x}
E. 8^{4x}

24. If the figure below is a square, what is the perimeter of the figure?

F. 28
G. 16
H. 9
J. 3
K. 2

25. If a certain rectangle has a length that is 2 times its width, what is the ratio of the area of the rectangle to the area of an isosceles right triangle with a hypotenuse equal to the width of the rectangle?

A. $\frac{1}{8}$
B. $\frac{1}{4}$
C. $\frac{1}{2}$
D. $\frac{4}{1}$
E. $\frac{8}{1}$

GO ON TO THE NEXT PAGE.

26. In the coordinate plane, what is the shortest distance between the point with (x,y) coordinates $(1,3)$ and the line with the equation $x = -2$?

    F. 1
    G. 3
    H. 4
    J. 6
    K. 9

27. If 5 pounds of coffee cost $12, how many pounds of coffee can be purchased for $30?

    A. 7.2
    B. 10
    C. 12.5
    D. 15
    E. 18

28. If the 2 triangles below are equilateral, what is the ratio of the perimeter of the smaller to that of the larger?

    3

    12

    F. $\frac{1}{36}$
    G. $\frac{1}{15}$
    H. $\frac{1}{9}$
    J. $\frac{1}{4}$
    K. $\frac{1}{3}$

29. If $f(x) = -3x^3 + 3x^2 - 4x + 8$, then $f(-2) = ?$

    A. 16
    B. 22
    C. 28
    D. 36
    E. 52

DO YOUR FIGURING HERE.

GO ON TO THE NEXT PAGE.

30. A merchant pays $120 wholesale for a dress and then adds a 30% markup. Two weeks later, the dress is put on sale at 40% off the retail price. What is the sale price of the dress?

   F. $102.40
   G. $97.30
   H. $93.60
   J. $89.40
   K. $87.00

DO YOUR FIGURING HERE.

31. If $\frac{1}{3}$ of a number is 2 more than $\frac{1}{5}$ of the number, then which of the following equations can be used to find the number x?

   A. $\frac{1}{3}x + 2 = -\frac{1}{5}x$
   B. $\frac{1}{3}x - 2 = -\frac{1}{5}x$
   C. $\frac{1}{3}x - \frac{1}{5}x = 2$
   D. $\frac{1}{3}x - \frac{1}{5}x = -2$
   E. $5(\frac{1}{3}x + 2) = 0$

32. In the figure below, the triangle is equilateral and has a perimeter of 12 centimeters. What is the perimeter, in centimeters, of the square?

   F. 9
   G. 12
   H. 16
   J. 20
   K. 24

33. If one solution of the equation $12x^2 + kx = 6$ is $\frac{2}{3}$, then $k = ?$

   A. 1
   B. $\frac{3}{2}$
   C. 2
   D. 5
   E. 9

GO ON TO THE NEXT PAGE.

34. If a 6-sided polygon has 2 sides of length $x - 2y$ each and 4 sides of length $2x + y$ each, what is its perimeter?

    F. $6x - 6y$
    G. $6x - y$
    H. $5x$
    J. $6x$
    K. $10x$

DO YOUR FIGURING HERE.

35. At the first stop on her route, a driver unloaded $\frac{2}{5}$ of the packages in her van. After she unloaded another 3 packages at her next stop, $\frac{1}{2}$ of the original number of packages in the van remained. How many packages were in the van before the first delivery?

    A. 10
    B. 18
    C. 25
    D. 30
    E. 36

36. For all x and y, $12x^3y^2 - 8x^2y^3 = $?

    F. $4x^2y^2(2xy)$
    G. $4x^2y^2(3xy)$
    H. $4x^2y^2(3x - 2y)$
    J. $2x^2y^2(4x - y)$
    K. $x^3y^3(12xy - 8xy)$

37. $\frac{1}{1 + \frac{1}{x}}$ equals which of the following expressions?

    A. $x + 1$
    B. $\frac{1}{x + 1}$
    C. $\frac{x}{x + 1}$
    D. $\frac{x + 1}{x}$
    E. $x^2 + x$

GO ON TO THE NEXT PAGE.

38. If S is 150% of T, what percent of $S+T$ is T?

    DO YOUR FIGURING HERE.

    F. $33\frac{1}{3}\%$
    G. 40%
    H. 50%
    J. 75%
    K. 80%

39. In $\triangle PQR$, the lengths of $\overline{PQ}$ and $\overline{QR}$ are equal, and the measure of $\angle Q$ is 3 times that of $\angle P$. What is the measure of $\angle R$?

    A. 24°
    B. 30°
    C. 36°
    D. 45°
    E. 60°

40. If the cost of b books is d dollars, which of the following equations can be used to find the cost, C, in dollars, of x books at the same rate?

    F. $C = xd$
    G. $C = \frac{dx}{b}$
    H. $C = \frac{bd}{x}$
    J. $C = bx$
    K. $C = \frac{bx}{d}$

41. An article is on sale for 25% off its regular price of $64. If the merchant must also collect a 5% sales tax on this reduced price, what is the total cost of the article including sales tax?

    A. $42.10
    B. $44.20
    C. $49.60
    D. $50.40
    E. $56.70

42. If $\frac{x}{z} = k$ and $\frac{y}{z} = k - 1$, then $x = $?

    F. $y - 1$
    G. $y + 1$
    H. $y + z$
    J. $z - y$
    K. $\frac{y}{z}$

GO ON TO THE NEXT PAGE.

43. If x is 25 percent of y, then y is what percent of x?

    A. 400%
    B. 300%
    C. 250%
    D. 125%
    E. 75%

44. If x is an integer that is a multiple of both 9 and 5, which of the following *must* be true?

    I. x is equal to 45.
    II. x is a multiple of 15.
    III. x is odd.

    F. I only
    G. II only
    H. III only
    J. II and III only
    K. I, II, and III

45. If each edge of a cube is 2 units long, what is the distance from any vertex to the cube's center?

    A. $\frac{\sqrt{2}}{2}$
    B. $\sqrt{3}$
    C. $2\sqrt{2}$
    D. $2\sqrt{3}$
    E. $\frac{3}{2}$

DO YOUR FIGURING HERE.

GO ON TO THE NEXT PAGE.

46. The figure below shows 2 circular cylinders, C and C'. If $r = kr'$ and $h = kh'$, what is the ratio of $\frac{\text{Volume of } C}{\text{Volume of } C'}$? ($\text{volume}_{\text{cylinder}} = \pi r^2 h$.)

F. $\frac{1}{\pi}$

G. π

H. $k\pi$

J. $\frac{1}{k^3}$

K. k^3

47. In the figure below, if the triangle has an area of 1 square unit, what is the area of the circle, in square units?

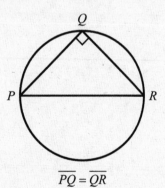

$\overline{PQ} = \overline{QR}$

A. π

B. 2π

C. $2\sqrt{3}\pi$

D. 4π

E. $4\sqrt{3}\pi$

GO ON TO THE NEXT PAGE.

48. In the figure below, the radius of the circles is 1 inch. What is the perimeter, in inches, of the shaded part of the figure?

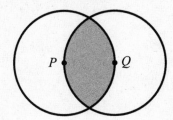

- **F.** $\frac{4\pi}{3}$
- **G.** π
- **H.** $\frac{2\pi}{3}$
- **J.** $\frac{\pi}{3}$
- **K.** $\frac{\pi}{6}$

49. A student's final grade in a certain course is the average of his scores on 10 tests graded on a scale of 0 to 100, inclusive. For the first 6 tests, the student's scores averaged 83. If x is the student's final grade for the course, then which of the following is true?

- **A.** $8.3 \le x \le 83.0$
- **B.** $49.8 \le x \le 83.0$
- **C.** $49.8 \le x \le 89.8$
- **D.** $54.7 \le x \le 89.8$
- **E.** $83.0 \le x \le 89.8$

50. What is the multiplicative inverse of the complex number $2-i$?

- **F.** $2+i$
- **G.** $i-2$
- **H.** $\frac{2+i}{3}$
- **J.** $\frac{2-i}{3}$
- **K.** $\frac{2+i}{5}$

DO YOUR FIGURING HERE.

GO ON TO THE NEXT PAGE.

DO YOUR FIGURING HERE.

51. $\log_3 \sqrt{3} = ?$

    A. -1
    B. $\frac{1}{3}$
    C. $\frac{1}{2}$
    D. $\frac{2}{3}$
    E. 2

52. If $f(x) = (x-1)^2 + 2$, then what value for x creates the minimum value for $f(x)$?

    F. -3
    G. -2
    H. 0
    J. 1
    K. 2

53. If, for all n, $2^n + 2^n + 2^n + 2^n = x(2^{n+1})$, then $x = ?$

    A. 2
    B. 4
    C. 2^n
    D. 2^{2n}
    E. 2^{n+1}

54. If $f(k) = k^2 + 2k + 1$, then what is the set of all k for which $f(k) = f(-k)$?

    F. $\{0\}$
    G. $\{1\}$
    H. $\{2\}$
    J. $\{1, 2\}$
    K. All real numbers

55. What is $\lim_{x \to 1} \frac{x^2 - 1}{x - 1}$?

    A. -1
    B. 0
    C. 1
    D. 2
    E. The limit does not exist.

GO ON TO THE NEXT PAGE.

56. If $0 \le x \le \pi$ and $\cos(x) = -1$, then $\cos(\frac{x}{2}) = $?

    F. $-\frac{\sqrt{3}}{2}$

    G. $-\frac{1}{2}$

    H. 0

    J. $\frac{1}{2}$

    K. $\frac{\sqrt{3}}{2}$

DO YOUR FIGURING HERE.

57. Which of the following defines the range of the function $f(x) = \frac{1-x}{x}$?

    A. All real numbers

    B. All real numbers except -1

    C. All real numbers except 0

    D. All real numbers except 1

    E. All real numbers greater than -1

58. Which of the following graphs represents the equations $x = 3[\sin(\theta)]$ and $y = 2[\cos(\theta)]$?

F.

J.

G.

K.

H.

GO ON TO THE NEXT PAGE.

59. For all θ such that $0° < \theta < 90°$, which of the following is equal to $\sin(\theta) \cdot \csc(\theta)$?

    A. 1
    B. $\sqrt{2}$
    C. $\tan(\theta)$
    D. $\cot(\theta)$
    E. $\sec(\theta)$

DO YOUR FIGURING HERE.

60. In $\triangle ABC$ below, the measures of $\angle ABC$, $\angle BCA$, and $\angle CAB$ are $90°$, $40°$, and $50°$, respectively. If $\overline{AB}$ is 3 units long, how many units long is $\overline{BC}$?

    F. 4
    G. 5
    H. $\sin(10°)$
    J. $3[\tan(50°)]$
    K. $3[\tan(40°)]$

END OF TEST 2
STOP! DO NOT TURN THE PAGE UNTIL TOLD TO DO SO.
DO NOT RETURN TO THE PREVIOUS TEST.

3 3 3 3 3 3 3 3 3 3 3 3

READING TEST
35 Minutes—40 Items

DIRECTIONS: The passages presented in the test are each followed by a set of items. Read the passage and choose the best answer for each item. Fill in the corresponding oval on your bubble sheet. You may refer to the passage as often as necessary to answer the passage items.

Answers are on page 607.

Passage I

SOCIAL STUDIES: This passage discusses Frederick Turner's hypothesis of the American Frontier.

In July of 1893, Frederick Jackson Turner, a historian from the University of Wisconsin, presented a paper to a group of historians convening in Chicago during the Columbian Exposition. Entitled "The
5 Significance of the American Frontier in History," Turner's paper drew little immediate reaction. Yet no theory of history has had a greater influence on the direction and methodology of inquiry and the issues of debate in American history. Later historians took issue
10 with some of Turner's interpretations; some of his own students were among those whose research proved certain of his views wrong. Yet these debates merely serve to illustrate the importance of Turner's hypothesis.

15 Turner's was an overarching hypothesis about how the settlement of the frontier had shaped the American experience and character. As with all general hypotheses in any field of study, it gave a coherent interpretation to many facts that had been largely
20 ignored by historians up to that time.

Turner used statistical evidence from the 1880 census as the basis for a startling conclusion: prior to 1880 there had been a frontier to be settled. By 1890, Turner pointed out, there was no longer any area of
25 wilderness completely untouched by settlements. The frontier had disappeared. The passing of the frontier, Turner concluded, was a historic moment.

Turner further claimed that the frontier experience had produced a distinctively American
30 character, which was not explainable simply as the predictable behavioral traits molded by English political institutions. Frontier settlers developed inquisitiveness, inventiveness, energy, and a great passion for freedom. These attributes defined a new
35 American character—one evidenced in nationalism, independence, and democracy. This new sense of national identity derived from the fact that people from every section of the country mixed at the Western frontier. Economic independence could be traced to the
40 fact that the settlers no longer depended on England for goods but had become self-sufficient. In addition, the frontier settlers, whose basic social unit was the family, enjoyed freedom from direct governmental interference. Frontier life thus reinforced the
45 fundamental ideals of populist democracy.

In addition, Turner argued that the frontier fostered democracy in the cities of the East. The availability of free land at the frontier provided a "safety-valve" against possible social unrest: those
50 discontented with social inequities and economic injustice could strike out and settle the free land available in frontier territories.

Turner's thesis was thus original in both what it said and in the methodology that Turner used in
55 formulating it. Up to the time of Turner's essay, history had been essentially the history of politics. A Midwesterner, Turner challenged this traditional approach of Eastern historians by incorporating techniques of the social sciences, showing how factors
60 of geography, economics, climate, and society influenced the development of the American West. Although now common among historians, at the time this interdisciplinary approach was novel.

GO ON TO THE NEXT PAGE.

1. Turner's essay challenged the views of:

    A. frontier writers such as Mark Twain.
    B. other American historians of his time.
    C. sociologists.
    D. European critics of America.

2. Turner's methods were original in that he:

    F. utilized research techniques from a variety of other academic fields.
    G. insulted other historians.
    H. refused to encourage further research.
    J. ignored the need for a unifying view.

3. Turner's evidence for the disappearance of the American frontier drew on:

    A. interviews with settlers.
    B. his reading of Karl Marx.
    C. diaries.
    D. the census of 1880.

4. Turner's essay affected:

    F. the reputations of American historians in Europe.
    G. future settlements in the West.
    H. the way in which population was counted.
    J. the subsequent focus of inquiry in American history.

5. One fact that would cast a doubtful light on Turner's view that the West was settled by individuals looking for escape from the pressures of Eastern city life would be if:

    A. many Western towns had few inhabitants.
    B. few people settled in mountain country.
    C. much of the land in the West and Midwest was actually bought by wealthy land speculators from the East.
    D. many people chose to settle along the banks of the Mississippi.

6. Which of the following, if true, would prove that Turner's "safety-valve" theory was false?

    F. Population movements showed that more people actually left the farms for the cities than left cities to move to the frontier.
    G. Much of the West had a desert climate.
    H. The transcontinental railroad was completed in 1869.
    J. The numbers of buffalo dropped markedly during the late nineteenth century.

7. A theory would best be defined as:

    A. a foolish notion founded on questionable data.
    B. an idle speculation that may have no basis in fact.
    C. a hypothesis that explains a large number of isolated facts.
    D. a somewhat questionable view of factual data.

8. America's frontier line moved essentially from:

    F. the South to the East.
    G. the West to the East.
    H. the East to the West.
    J. the North to the South.

9. The economic independence of Americans arose, Turner said, from the fact that:

    A. Americans rarely bought anything.
    B. many pioneers had few relatives left in Europe.
    C. Americans were buying American goods rather than English goods.
    D. few settlers ever voted in local elections.

GO ON TO THE NEXT PAGE.

10. Which of the following quotations captures the approach of historians at the time when Turner read his paper?

   F. "This history of the world is but the biography of great men."
   G. "History is past politics and politics is present history."
   H. "Those who do not heed the lessons of history are doomed to repeat them."
   J. "Anybody can make history. Only a great man can write it."

GO ON TO THE NEXT PAGE.

Passage II

HUMANITIES: In this passage, the author expresses his opinion regarding the role of philosophy.

The service of philosophy towards the human spirit is to startle it into sharp and eager observation. Every moment, and for that moment only, some form grows perfect in hand or face; some tone on the hills or
5 the sea is choicer than the rest. Not the fruit of experience, but experience itself is the end. Only a counted number of pulses are given to us of a variegated, dramatic life. How shall we pass most quickly from point to point and be present always at
10 the focus where the greatest number of vital forces unite in their purest energy?

To burn always with this hard, gemlike flame, to maintain this ecstasy, is success in life. It is only the roughness of the eye that makes any two persons,
15 things, or situations seem alike. While all melts under our feet, we may well catch at any exquisite passion, or any knowledge that seems by a lifted horizon to set the spirit free for a moment, or any stirring of the senses, strange dyes, strange colors, curious odors, or work of
20 the artist's hands or the faces of one's friends. Not to discriminate every moment some passionate attitude in those about us, and in the brilliancy of their gifts some tragic dividing of forces of their ways is, on this short day of the frost and sun, to sleep before evening. With
25 this sense of the splendor of our experience and of its awful brevity, gathering all we are into one desperate effort to see and touch, we shall hardly have time to make theories about the things we see and touch.

We are all under sentence of death but with a sort
30 of indefinite reprieve; we have an interval and then our place knows us no more. Some spend this interval in listlessness, others in high passions, the wisest—at least among the "children of this world"—in art and song. Our one chance lies in expanding this interval—
35 in getting as many pulsations as possible into the given time. Great passions may give us this quickened sense of life, ecstasy, sorrow, and love, the various forms of enthusiastic activity. Of this wisdom, the poetic passion, the desire of beauty, the love of art for art's
40 sake has most; for art comes to you professing frankly to give nothing but the highest quality to your moments as they pass, and simply for the sake of those moments.

11. Which of the following best describes the overall structure of the passage?

   A. The author raises a question and then provides an answer.
   B. The author presents a theory, which he then proves.
   C. The author studies a widely held belief and then rejects it.
   D. The author defines a term and then provides examples.

12. In the passage, the author uses the word "pulsations" (line 35) to mean:

   F. children.
   G. lives.
   H. death.
   J. experiences.

13. According to the author, the function of art is to:

   A. depict reality accurately.
   B. stimulate strong emotions.
   C. encourage social reform.
   D. express the artist's feelings.

14. With which of the following statements would the author most likely agree?

   F. A person's lifetime is merely preparation for what comes after death.
   G. Only an artist can truly enjoy life.
   H. The original experience is more important than the memory of it.
   J. A perceptive person understands that all experience is repetitious.

15. The tone of the passage can best be described as:

   A. impassioned.
   B. scholarly.
   C. informative.
   D. speculative.

GO ON TO THE NEXT PAGE.

16. In the context of this passage, the phrase "short day of the frost and sun" (lines 23–24) refers to:

    F. the transient effect of poetry.
    G. a brief moment of passion.
    H. the life of a person.
    J. stimulation of the senses.

17. The phrase "awful brevity" (line 26) means that:

    A. philosophy is not really useful.
    B. art may not satisfy everyone.
    C. life is short.
    D. passion is the greatest virtue.

18. The "children of this world" (line 33) are NOT:

    F. passionate.
    G. wise.
    H. lovers of art and song.
    J. listless.

19. According to the author, the greatest passion is the love of:

    A. beauty.
    B. one's spouse.
    C. wealth.
    D. security.

20. The phrase "then our place knows us no more" (lines 30–31) means that we:

    F. move to another town.
    G. have children.
    H. die.
    J. divorce.

GO ON TO THE NEXT PAGE.

Passage III

NATURAL SCIENCES: This passage explains how energy becomes usable through photosynthesis.

Every living cell must acquire energy in a usable form. According to the First Law of Thermodynamics, energy, which is the capacity for doing work, can be converted from one form into another without any net
5 gain or loss. An organism must have an outside source of usable energy. The Second Law of Thermodynamics states that every energy transformation reduces the free (usable) energy of the system. Living cells primarily use chemical energy derived from complex organic
10 compounds.

Photosynthesis is the process by which green plants transform sunlight into a usable energy source. Green plants utilize the energy of light to combine carbon dioxide with water to form organic material
15 (sugar) and oxygen.

$$6CO_2 + 12H_2O + \text{light} \xrightarrow{\text{Chlorophyll}} 6O_2 + C_6H_{12}O_6 + 6H_2O$$

Photosynthesis is a reduction reaction. Reduction is the addition of one or more electrons to an atom or molecule. Oxidation is the removal of electrons from
20 an atom or molecule. Reduction stores energy, while oxidation releases it. Biological systems rely on the addition or removal of an electron from hydrogen. Photosynthesis is based on two key processes. Light energy is trapped and stored, and hydrogen atoms are
25 transformed from water to carbon dioxide to form carbohydrate.

Photosynthesis takes place within the chloroplasts. The pigments within the chloroplasts are precisely arranged within the membranes of flattened
30 sacs called thylakoids. Thylakoids often lie close together in sacks called grana. The light reactions of photosynthesis take place within the thylakoid membranes, while the dark reactions take place in the colorless matrix (stroma) surrounding the thylakoids.

35 Different wavelengths of light, especially red and blue light, are trapped by various pigment molecules contained within chloroplasts. When a photon of light strikes a pigment molecule and is absorbed, the energy is transferred to an electron, which is raised to a high-
40 energy state. A specialized form of chlorophyll passes the energized electron to an acceptor molecule, X, which has a high affinity for electrons. X passes the electron to a series of acceptor molecules, each at a slightly lower energy level. After being passed from
45 molecule to molecule, the electron may return to the chlorophyll from which it started. Some of the energy

released as the electron is passed down the energy gradient is used to synthesize the compound ATP from ADP and inorganic phosphate.

50 ATP is a universal energy packet used by cells to do work. ATP is synthesized from ADP and inorganic phosphate in a process called phosphorylation. Phosphorylation is a very high energy demanding process. *Cyclic photophosphorylation* occurs when the
55 energy used for ATP synthesis comes from light-energized electrons as they are returned to the chlorophyll molecules from which they originated.

Another process that occurs in green plants is noncyclic photophosphorylation. In this reaction, some
60 electrons are passed from the chlorophyll to a different type of acceptor molecule called $NAPD_{ox}$, which retains the electron and is therefore reduced to become $NAPD_{re}$.

The ATP and $NAPD_{re}$ produced in the light
65 reaction are used to reduce carbon dioxide to carbohydrate in a series of reactions called the *Calvin cycle* (dark reaction). Basically, a five-carbon sugar, ribulose diphosphate (RuDP), is combined with CO_2. This process is called carboxyilation. The products are
70 then phosphorylated by ATP and reduced by $NAPD_{re}$ to form PGAL, a three-carbon sugar.

Under certain conditions, the very same enzyme that under more agreeable conditions would facilitate its carboxyilation oxidizes RuDP. This process, called
75 photorespiration, is seemingly a wasteful process since no ATP is created. Photorespiration predominates over photosynthesis when CO_2 levels are low and O_2 levels are high.

Some tropical angiosperm plants have a unique
80 leaf structure known as *Kranz* anatomy (C_4 plants). In Kranz plants, the bundle-sheath cells have numerous chloroplasts (other plants usually do not), and the mesophyll cells are clustered in a ring-like arrangement around the bundle sheath. These plants can carry out
85 photosynthesis under conditions of high temperature and concentrated light, when loss of water induces closure of the stomata. When the stomata close, the concentration of CO_2 in the air spaces inside the leaf falls, and the concentration of O_2 rises. Under these
90 conditions most plants (C_3) would experience a net loss of CO_2 because of photorespiration. Kranz plants (C_4) do not because of their specialized way of initially fixing CO_2. They combine CO_2 with a three-carbon compound in the mesophyll cells to form a
95 four-carbon compound that passes into the bundle-sheath cells, where the CO_2 is regenerated. Therefore, Kranz plants can maintain a CO_2 level in the bundle-

GO ON TO THE NEXT PAGE.

sheath cells that allows carboxyilation of RuDP in the Calvin cycle to predominate over its oxidation in 100 photorespiration.

21. According to this passage, "the capacity for doing work" (line 3) is the definition of:

    A. photosynthesis.
    B. energy.
    C. oxidation.
    D. thermodynamics.

22. In the equation in line 16, $C_6H_{12}O_6$ apparently names:

    F. oxygen.
    G. carbon dioxide.
    H. a sugar.
    J. photosynthesis.

23. Which of these could be considered the reverse of reduction?

    A. Oxidation
    B. Photosynthesis
    C. Transformation
    D. Phosphorylation

24. Which of the following conclusions is (are) suggested by the third paragraph?

    I. Photosynthesis involves the addition of electrons.
    II. Photosynthesis involves action on hydrogen.
    III. Photosynthesis is a form of energy release.

    F. I only
    G. II only
    H. III only
    J. I and II only

25. The fifth paragraph deals mainly with:

    A. defining terms related to plant growth.
    B. comparing one reduction reaction to another.
    C. explaining the process of photosynthesis.
    D. expressing the author's opinion.

26. Which of the following statements is NOT true about ATP?

    F. It mixes with phosphate to make ADP.
    G. It is created through phosphorylation.
    H. It serves a purpose in the Calvin cycle.
    J. It is used by cells to do work.

27. The Calvin cycle involves:

    A. the combination of carbon dioxide and a five-carbon sugar, with a three-carbon sugar as the result.
    B. the combination of oxygen and a three-carbon sugar, with a five-carbon sugar as the result.
    C. a mix of ATP and sugar to create carbon dioxide.
    D. a reduction of carbohydrate to form carbon dioxide.

28. By "more agreeable conditions" (line 73), the author probably means:

    F. conditions that produce higher levels of oxygen.
    G. conditions that produce higher levels of CO_2.
    H. conditions with higher temperatures.
    J. conditions with longer growing periods.

29. Which of the following statements names a difference between photorespiration and photosynthesis?

    I. Photorespiration involves RuDP.
    II. In photosynthesis, ATP is synthesized.
    III. Photorespiration is a reduction reaction.

    A. I only
    B. I and II only
    C. II and III only
    D. I, II, and III

GO ON TO THE NEXT PAGE.

30. Unlike the preceding paragraphs, the final paragraph discusses:

    F. plants that do not photosynthesize.
    G. living matter other than plants.
    H. plants with an unusual structure.
    J. plants that transform carbon dioxide into carbohydrate.

GO ON TO THE NEXT PAGE.

Passage IV

PROSE FICTION: In this passage, a young country man, alone in town for the first time, tries to find a relative, Major Molineux.

It was near nine o'clock of a moonlight evening, when a boat crossed the ferry with a single passenger, who had obtained his conveyance at that unusual hour by the promise of extra fare. He was a youth of barely
5 eighteen years, evidently country-bred, and now upon his first visit to town. The youth finally drew from his pocket a little province bill of five shillings, which, in depreciation in that sort of currency, satisfied the ferry-man's demand with the addition of a sex-angular piece
10 of parchment, valued at three pence. He then walked forward into the town with as light a step as if his day's journey had not already exceeded thirty miles and with as eager an eye as if he were entering London city, instead of the little metropolis of a New England
15 colony. However, before Robin had proceeded far, it occurred to him that he knew not whither to direct his steps; so he paused, and looked up and down the narrow street, scrutinizing the small and mean wooden buildings that were scattered on either side.

20 "This low hovel cannot be my kinsman's dwelling," thought he, "nor yonder old house; and truly I see none hereabouts that might be worthy of him. It would have been wise to inquire my way of the ferryman and doubtless he would have gone with me,
25 and earned a shilling from the Major for his pains. But the next man I meet will do as well."

He resumed his walk, and was glad to perceive that the street now became wide, and the houses were more respectable in their appearance. He soon
30 discerned a figure moving on moderately in advance, and he hastened his steps to overtake it. Robin laid hold of the skirt of the man's old coat, just when the light from the open door and windows of a barber's shop fell upon both their figures.

35 "Good evening to you, honored sir," said he, making a low bow, and still retaining hold of the skirt. "I pray you tell me whereabouts is the dwelling of my kinsman, Major Molineux."

The citizen answered him in a tone of excessive
40 anger and annoyance. "Let go my garment, fellow! I tell you, I know not the man you speak of. What! I have the authority, I have—hem, hem—authority; and if this be the respect you show for your betters, your feet shall be brought acquainted with the stocks by
45 daylight, tomorrow morning!"

Robin released the old man's skirt, and hastened away, pursued by an ill-mannered roar of laughter from the barber's shop. He was at first considerably surprised by the result of his question, but, being a
50 shrewd youth, he soon thought himself able to account for the mystery.

"This is some country representative," was his conclusion, "who has never seen the inside of my kins-man's door, and lacks the breeding to answer a
55 stranger civilly. Ah, Robin, Robin! Even the barber's boys laugh at you for choosing such a guide! You will be wiser in time, friend Robin."

31. In the final paragraph, the young man is talking to:

   A. the Major.
   B. the man in the coat.
   C. himself.
   D. the barbers.

32. The total cost of the young man's passage on the ferryboat was:

   F. five shillings.
   G. three pence.
   H. five shillings less three pence.
   J. five shillings plus three pence.

33. The young man believes that his relative is a:

   A. barber.
   B. wealthy person.
   C. constable.
   D. builder.

34. The incidents described in the passage take place:

   F. in the late morning.
   G. in the early afternoon.
   H. in the late afternoon.
   J. at night.

35. The passage suggests that thirty miles is:

   A. a long distance to travel in one day.
   B. easily traveled in a single day.
   C. easily traveled in an hour.
   D. a long ferryboat ride.

GO ON TO THE NEXT PAGE.

36. The young man believes that the barbers laughed at him because:

    F. his clothes clearly show that he is from the country.
    G. he asked a question of a stranger who obviously would not know the answer.
    H. he badly needs a haircut and a shave.
    J. the stranger he questioned is actually the man he is looking for.

37. The scenes in the passage are most likely set in which of the following time periods?

    A. Eighteenth century
    B. Nineteenth century
    C. Early twentieth century
    D. Present time

38. The young man approaches the stranger in the coat:

    F. respectfully.
    G. rudely.
    H. coyly.
    J. stealthily.

39. The young man is the only passenger on the ferryboat because:

    A. he paid the ferryman extra for a private charter.
    B. no one else was traveling at that hour.
    C. the Major had sent the boat especially for him.
    D. the ferryman was a good friend of the young man.

40. Just after he gets off the ferry, the young man finds himself in a:

    F. poorer neighborhood.
    G. wealthy neighborhood.
    H. forest.
    J. large city.

END OF TEST 3
STOP! DO NOT TURN THE PAGE UNTIL TOLD TO DO SO.
DO NOT RETURN TO A PREVIOUS TEST.

4 4 4 4 4 4 4 4 4 4 4 4

SCIENCE TEST
35 Minutes—40 Items

DIRECTIONS: The passages presented in the test are each followed by a set of items. Read the passage and choose the best answer for each item. Fill in the corresponding oval on your bubble sheet. You may refer to the passage as often as necessary to answer the passage items.

Warning: Calculator use is not permitted on this test.

Answers are on page 608.

Passage I

The chart below shows several physical properties of compounds called alkanes, which are long "chains" of carbons to which hydrogen atoms are attached. As an example, the compound propane, which has three carbons, has the structural formula:

$$CH_3—CH_2—CH_3$$

PHYSICAL PROPERTIES OF STRAIGHT-CHAIN ALKANES				
Name	# of Carbons	Boiling Point (°C)	Melting Point (°C)	Density
methane	1	−162	−183	0.47
ethane	2	−89	−183	0.57
propane	3	−42	−188	0.50
butane	4	0	−138	0.58
pentane	5	36	−130	0.56
hexane	6	69	−95	0.66
heptane	7	98	−91	0.68
octane	8	126	−57	0.70
nonane	9	151	−54	0.72
decane	10	174	−30	0.74

1. The general trends shown in the chart are:

   A. as the number of carbons increases, all properties increase in value (with occasional exceptions).
   B. as the number of carbons increases, boiling points and melting points decrease, while density increases.
   C. as the number of carbons increases, density decreases and other properties increase.
   D. as the number of carbons increases, all properties decrease.

2. The change in boiling point is greatest:

   F. from methane to ethane.
   G. from propane to butane.
   H. from butane to pentane.
   J. from nonane to decane.

GO ON TO THE NEXT PAGE.

3. For alkanes with more than one carbon, the change in melting point from one alkane to the next:

    A. tends to be greater from an even number of carbons to the next odd number.
    B. tends to be greater from an odd number of carbons to the next even number.
    C. is similar, whether from an even number of carbons to the next odd number, or from an odd number of carbons to the next even number.
    D. Cannot be determined from the given information.

4. Considering the alkane properties listed, if alkane X has a higher boiling point than alkane Y, then without exception, it must also have a:

    F. higher melting point.
    G. higher density.
    H. higher number of carbons.
    J. longer name.

5. The greatest percentage increase in density occurs from:

    A. ethane to propane.
    B. propane to butane.
    C. pentane to hexane.
    D. hexane to heptane.

GO ON TO THE NEXT PAGE.

Passage II

A student performs a set of physics laboratory experiments, in which objects of different masses glide "frictionlessly" along a smooth surface, collide, and then continue to glide. The momentum of each object is defined as its "mass • velocity." The momentum of a system of objects is the sum of the individual momentums.

Experiment 1: The light mass moves toward the stationary, heavy mass, and both stick together and continue to move. Table 1 shows the relevant information.

Table 1

	Object 1	Object 2
Mass	2 kg	5 kg
Initial velocity	4 m/sec	0 m/sec
Final velocity	1.14 m/sec	1.14 m/sec

Experiment 2: The student performs a similar experiment in which the objects do not stick together, but collide "elastically"—that is, rebound from each other with no loss in energy. Table 2 shows the results.

Table 2

	Object 1	Object 2
Mass	2 kg	5 kg
Initial velocity	4 m/sec	0 m/sec
Final velocity	−1.71 m/sec	2.29 m/sec

(Note that positive velocities indicate motion to the right, negative velocities indicate motion to the left.)

6. In Experiment 1, the momentum of Object 1 before the collision is:

   F. 0 kg • m/sec.
   G. 2 kg • m/sec.
   H. 4 kg • m/sec.
   J. 8 kg • m/sec.

7. After the collision in Experiment 1, the momentum of the combined masses is:

   A. much less than the initial total momentum of the two masses.
   B. about equal to the initial total momentum of the two masses.
   C. much greater than the initial total momentum of the two masses.
   D. Cannot be determined from the given information

8. After the collision in Experiment 2:

   F. both objects are moving to the right.
   G. both objects are moving to the left.
   H. Object 1 is moving to the left and Object 2 to the right.
   J. Object 1 is moving to the right and Object 2 to the left.

9. In Experiment 2, if Object 2 were replaced by another object that was far more massive than Object 1, its final velocity would be closest to:

   A. 4.0 m/sec.
   B. 2.3 m/sec.
   C. −1.7 m/sec.
   D. 0 m/sec.

10. Under the conditions described in the previous item, the final velocity of Object 1 would be closest to:

    F. −2 m/sec.
    G. −1.7 m/sec.
    H. 0 m/sec.
    J. 2 m/sec.

11. Kinetic energy is defined as $\frac{1}{2}(mv^2)$. During the collision described in Experiment 1, the kinetic energy of Object 1:

    A. increases.
    B. remains the same.
    C. decreases.
    D. Cannot be determined from the given information.

GO ON TO THE NEXT PAGE.

Passage III

The table below shows how an increase (+) or a decrease (–) in one or more plant hormones and environmental factors can affect various plant activities. The activities listed on the left occur when the combinations of conditions to the right exist at the same time. Hormones (H) are numbered; e.g., H_1, H_2, etc.

Activities	H_1	H_2	H_3	H_4	H_5	Day Length	Temperature
Plant growth	+ +		+ +				
No plant growth (1)	+ +		+ +	+ +			
No plant growth (2)	+ +		+ +		+ +		
Seed germination			+ +				
Flowering			+ +		+ +	$(+ + \, or \, - -)^\dagger$	+ +
Flower drop-off	– –	+ +					
Fruit drop-off	– –	+ +					
Leaf drop-off	– –	+ +					– –

†Different species of plants require different combinations of light and darkness to stimulate flowering.

12. Based on the information in the table, a drop in temperature will help cause:

  F. flowering.
  G. loss of leaves, fruit, and flowers.
  H. loss of leaves only.
  J. seed germination.

13. The hormones that can inhibit (prevent) plant growth are:

  A. 1 and 3.
  B. 1, 3, and 4.
  C. 1, 3, and 5.
  D. 4 and 5.

14. Which conclusion is correct about the various factors affecting plant activities?

  F. Hormone 3 influences more plant activities than any other factor.
  G. Seed germination is influenced by the fewest factors, whereas flowering is influenced by the most.
  H. For Hormone 1 to have an effect on any plant activity, it must be changing in the opposite direction of at least one other hormone.
  J. Temperature changes can affect all plant activities.

GO ON TO THE NEXT PAGE.

15. Which activity would most likely be affected by changing a houseplant's growing conditions from twelve hours of light per twelve hours of darkness to constant light?

    I.   Plant growth
   II. Loss of leaves
  III. Flowering

  A. I only
  B. II only
  C. III only
  D. I and III only

16. Which statement best describes the relationship between Hormone 1 and Hormone 2?

  F. Hormone 2 must change in the opposite direction of Hormone 1 for plant growth to occur.
  G. When Hormone 1 and Hormone 2 affect a plant activity together, no other factors influence that activity.
  H. As Hormone 1 increases, Hormone 2 always decreases; and as Hormone 1 decreases, Hormone 2 always increases.
  J. Hormone 2 only affects plant activities when Hormone 1 is also involved.

GO ON TO THE NEXT PAGE.

Passage IV

In order to examine the factors that affect the flow of substances across cell membranes, three experiments were carried out. In each experiment, semi-permeable bags (bags with small pores that allow some substances to pass through, but not others) were partially filled with a fluid, tied, and then weighed (first weighing). The bags were then submerged into a large beaker of water, and at 10-minute intervals, removed from the beaker of water and re-weighed.

Experiment 1: A bag containing a 30% red dye solution (30% red dye and 70% water) weighed 100 grams. The bag was then submerged in a beaker of pure water. After 20 minutes, the bag weighed 110 grams. The beaker water remained clear.

Experiment 2: A second bag containing 40% red dye solution (40% red dye and 60% water) weighed 100 grams before being submerged in a beaker of pure water. After only 10 minutes, the bag weighed 110 grams. The beaker water remained clear.

Experiment 3: A third bag containing only pure water and weighing 100 grams was submerged in a beaker of 50% red dye solution (50% red dye and 50% water). After 20 minutes, the bag weighed 70 grams. The bag water remained clear.

17. In Experiment 1, a gain in bag weight suggests that:

A. material passed out from bag to beaker faster than it passed in from beaker to bag.
B. material passed in from beaker to bag faster than it passed out from bag to beaker.
C. material passed in and out of the bag at approximately the same rate.
D. material did not move at all.

18. Which of the following hypotheses is supported by the results of all three experiments?

F. Red dye can leave the bag but not enter.
G. Red dye can enter the bag but not leave.
H. Red dye can enter or leave the bag.
J. Red dye cannot enter or leave the bag.

19. Which of the following represents the best approximation for the weight of the bag in Experiment 2 after 20 minutes?

A. 90 grams
B. 100 grams
C. 110 grams
D. 120 grams

20. Which of the following questions is the entire set of experiments designed to answer?

F. How does concentration of red dye affect rate and direction of water flow?
G. How does concentration of water affect rate and direction of red dye flow?
H. How does rate of red dye flow affect direction of water movement?
J. How does direction of red dye movement affect rate of water flow?

21. A control experiment was set up to confirm the investigation's conclusion. A bag containing pure water and weighing 100 grams was submerged in a beaker of pure water. What is expected to occur?

A. The bag will slowly gain weight.
B. The bag will slowly lose weight.
C. The bag will remain approximately the same weight.
D. The bag will eventually become empty, and the water level in the beaker will rise.

22. Assuming that salts cannot freely pass across a cell's membrane, what would happen to human red blood cells (approximately 1% salt and 99% water) submerged in sea water (approximately 5% salt and 95% water)?

F. The cells would shrink due to a loss of water.
G. The cells would shrink due to a loss of salt.
H. The cells would swell up due to a gain of water.
J. The cells would swell up due to a gain of salt.

GO ON TO THE NEXT PAGE.

Passage V

The chart below shows various physical characteristics of different types of soil.

PHYSICAL CHARACTERISTICS OF SOIL				
Types of Soil	Diameter of Particles (μm)	Relative Ability† to Hold Positively Charged Minerals (Ca^{+2}, K^+, Mg^{+2})	Relative Ability† to Maintain Air Spaces	Relative Ability† to Retain Water
Clay	less than 2	1	4	1
Silt	2–20	2	3	2
Sand	20–200	3	2	3
Coarse Sand	200–2,000	4	1	4

†Relative abilities are rated from 1, indicating the best (most able), to 4, indicating the worst (least able).

23. The soil type that is LEAST able to hold substances such as magnesium (Mg^{+2}) is:

    A. sand.
    B. coarse sand.
    C. silt.
    D. clay.

24. Based on the information in the chart, which of the following statements best describes the relationship between a soil's particle size and its other physical characteristics?

    F. As particle size increases, the ability to hold positively charged minerals increases.
    G. As particle size decreases, the ability to retain water decreases.
    H. As particle size decreases, the ability to maintain air spaces increases.
    J. As particle size increases, the ability to retain water decreases.

25. The size of particles in the soil type that is neither best nor worst at any of the listed abilities must be:

    A. less than 20 micrometers.
    B. more than 20 micrometers.
    C. between 2 and 200 micrometers.
    D. between 2 and 2,000 micrometers.

26. Loam is a type of soil that is mostly clay, but it also contains some sand and silt particles. Which prediction is most likely to be accurate about the ability of loam to support plant growth?

    F. Plants will grow well because loam primarily has small particles that can hold minerals and retain water, yet it also has enough large particles to provide air spaces containing oxygen.
    G. Plants will grow well because loam primarily has large particles that can provide air spaces containing oxygen, yet it also has enough small particles that can hold minerals and retain water.
    H. Plants will not grow well because although loam is excellent at maintaining air spaces for oxygen, it will not hold enough minerals or water.
    J. Plants will not grow well because although loam has enough minerals and air spaces for oxygen, it cannot retain enough water.

GO ON TO THE NEXT PAGE.

27. Based on the information provided in the chart, which of the following conclusions about soil types is NOT correct?

   A. Soils best at retaining water are also best at holding positively charged minerals.
   B. No two soil types have the exact same combination of relative abilities.
   C. Clay and coarse sand are the soil types that are most different in every physical characteristic.
   D. At each listed ability, a different type of soil is best.

GO ON TO THE NEXT PAGE.

Passage VI

Theory 1: The rate of a chemical reaction is defined as the number of moles of a specified reactant consumed in one second. Reactants must collide in order for a reaction to occur, so it might seem that rates would depend upon the concentration of reactants—the more reactants that are present, the greater the likelihood of a collision. In fact, this is the case; a concrete example makes this clear. For the reaction: $2NO + O_2 \Rightarrow 2NO_2$, the rate is proportional to the amount of NO and O_2 present. This fact is expressed as the following "rate law": rate $= k[NO]^2[O_2]^1$, where k is the rate constant, and the exponents reflect the coefficients in front of the reactants in the reaction. The relationship between numbers of reactant molecules and exponents in the rate law is a general one.

Theory 2: Theory 1 is very often true, for it expresses the reasonable insight that the greater the concentration of reactants, the greater the likelihood of a reaction. It has a great shortcoming, however, in its assumption that all reactions proceed in one fell swoop rather than in several skirmishes.

For example, let letters A, B, and C stand for molecules. In the reaction $A + 2B \Rightarrow C$, Theory 1 predicts a rate law as follows: rate $= k[A][B]^2$. However, if the reaction actually proceeds in two stages, the first one would be $A + B \Rightarrow AB$ and the second one would be $AB + B \Rightarrow C$.

Thus, Theory 2 implies that one must understand the details of the reaction, including the relative speeds of the sub-reactions, in order to predict a rate law. Theory 1 is not completely wrong, just incomplete.

28. Theory 1 relates:

F. reaction rate to the concentration of products.
G. reaction rate to the concentration of reactants.
H. the relative amounts of products to one other.
J. reaction rate to the individual rates of various stages of the reaction.

29. According to a proponent of Theory 2, Theory 1:

A. can never give a correct prediction for a rate law.
B. will give a correct result if the reactant coefficients are all equal to 1.
C. will give a correct result for a single-stage reaction.
D. is in error because it claims that collisions are required for reactions to occur.

30. According to Theory 1, the rate of the reaction $3M + 2N \Rightarrow 4P$ will be given by:

F. $k[M][N]$.
G. $k[M]^3[N]^2$.
H. $k[M]^3[N]^2[P]^4$.
J. $k([M]^3 + [N]^2)$.

31. A chemist studies the rate of the reaction $2NO_2 + F_2 \Rightarrow 2NO_2F$. According to Theory 1, the rate of the reaction is proportional to:

A. the first power of NO_2 and the first power of F_2.
B. the second power of NO_2 and the second power of NO_2F.
C. the second power of NO_2 and the second power of F_2.
D. the second power of NO_2 and the first power of F_2.

32. Supporters of Theory 2 would best be able to defend their positions if:

F. they could show that the reaction occurs in more than one stage.
G. they slowed the reaction down by cooling the reactants.
H. they sped the reaction up with additional heat.
J. they eliminated all collisions.

GO ON TO THE NEXT PAGE.

33. According to Theory 2, if in a two-stage reaction Stage 1 is much slower than Stage 2, then the overall reaction rate will be:

    A. primarily determined by the rate of Stage 1.
    B. primarily determined by the rate of Stage 2.
    C. undeterminable unless all collisions are counted.
    D. undeterminable unless the rate law is measured experimentally.

34. When discussing the rates of reactions that have more than one stage, Theory 2 would not be necessary if:

    F. all stages went quickly.
    G. all stages had different rates.
    H. the sum of the rates of each stage always equaled the rate of the reaction as a whole.
    J. the sum of the rates of each stage was never equal to the rate of the reaction as a whole.

GO ON TO THE NEXT PAGE.

Passage VII

Closely related species of butterflies are often found living in very different environments. A pair of experiments was performed in which butterfly species previously captured in either desert areas or mountain areas were tested in laboratory incubators to determine the conditions at which they could carry out important life functions such as mating, oviposition (egg-laying), and pupation (the stage in which the stationary cocoon undergoes its final development into an adult).

Experiment 1: Under conditions of 100% relative humidity (maximum moisture content of the air), 100 desert butterflies (Species D) and 100 mountain butterflies (Species M) were tested at temperature intervals of 2°C (from 0°C to 40°C) to determine if they could mate, oviposit, and pupate. Each species achieved at least 90% success at the following ranges of temperatures:

Table 1

TEMPERATURE RANGES (°C)			
	Mating	*Oviposition*	*Pupation*
Species D	10–34	14–34	4–38
Species M	6–30	10–28	4–34

Experiment 2: The experiment was repeated at 0% relative humidity (minimum moisture content of the air). The species achieved at least 90% success at the following ranges of temperatures:

Table 2

TEMPERATURE RANGES (°C)			
	Mating	*Oviposition*	*Pupation*
Species D	10–34	14–34	4–38
Species M	6–24	10–22	4–28

35. Results of Experiments 1 and 2 indicate that the life function with the narrowest range of temperature at which both species achieve 90% success is:

    A. mating.
    B. oviposition.
    C. pupation.
    D. different in Experiment 1 than it is in Experiment 2.

36. Which condition has the most detrimental effects on Species M for mating, oviposition, and pupation?

    F. Moist air at low temperatures
    G. Moist air at high temperatures
    H. Dry air at low temperatures
    J. Dry air at high temperatures

37. A third experiment was conducted at 100% relative humidity in which the temperature range for caterpillar survival (another life function) was tested in Species D and Species M. Species D achieved 90% success at 12–36 (°C), while Species M achieved 90% success at 8–30 (°C). Which temperature range is a good prediction of survival in Species D under dry conditions?

    A. 8°C–30°C
    B. 8°C–24°C
    C. 12°C–36°C
    D. 12°C–30°C

38. If an investigator wanted to set up an experiment to determine the effects of light and dark on mating ability in Species D and Species M at 100% relative humidity, which set of conditions would provide the most complete results?

    F. Test both species at 6°C in the light and 6°C in the dark.
    G. Test both species at 20°C in the light and 20°C in the dark.
    H. Test both species at 34°C in the light and 34°C in the dark.
    J. Test both species at 34°C in the light and 30°C in the dark.

GO ON TO THE NEXT PAGE.

39. Which hypothesis is NOT supported by the results of Experiment 1 and Experiment 2?

    A. For all tested life functions, dry conditions only affect Species M at the high end of its temperature ranges.

    B. For all tested life functions, dry conditions have no effects on the temperature ranges of the desert species.

    C. Species D does better than Species M at high temperatures in all tested life functions.

    D. Species M does better than Species D at low temperatures for pupation.

40. Which of the following statements best explains the broad range of temperatures for pupation observed in both butterfly species?

    F. Since the cocoon is stationary, it must be able to survive changing temperature conditions until the adult butterfly emerges.

    G. Deserts can get very hot and mountains can get very cold.

    H. Mountain butterflies would not survive long in the desert, and desert butterflies would not survive long in the mountains.

    J. The stationary cocoon must be able to survive under light and dark conditions until the adult butterfly emerges.

END OF TEST 4
STOP! DO NOT TURN THE PAGE UNTIL TOLD TO DO SO.
DO NOT RETURN TO A PREVIOUS TEST.

5 5 5 5 5 5 5 5 5 5 5 5

WRITING TEST (OPTIONAL)
30 Minutes—1 Essay Prompt

DIRECTIONS: This is a test of your writing skills. Before you begin planning and writing your essay, read the writing prompt carefully to understand the instructions. Your essay will be evaluated on the evidence it provides of your ability to express judgments by taking a position on the issue in the writing prompt; to maintain a focus on the topic throughout the essay; to develop a position by using logical reasoning and supporting ideas; to organize ideas in a logical way; and to use language clearly and effectively according to the conventions of standard written English.

If you finish before time is called, you may review your work. Lay your pencil down immediately when time is called.

Writing Test Prompt

Some educators and parents advocate changing from the traditional nine-month school year to a twelve-month program. They point out that the nine-month school year was first adopted when students were needed to work on family farms during the summer months, a need that no longer exists. They also state that year-round school would improve academic achievement because it would eliminate the need to review each previous year's work at the beginning of a new school year and allow teachers to cover material in greater detail. Other teachers and parents are opposed to such a change. They point out that summer is the traditional time for family vacations and that in addition to giving students a needed break from academic work, the summer vacation is the time for part-time jobs, summer camp, and special trips, all of which are also learning experiences. Do you think that schools should change from a nine-month school year to a twelve-month school year?

In your essay, take a position on this issue. You may address either of the two points described above, or you may offer an entirely different perspective on the issue. Be sure to use specific reasons and examples to support your analysis.

END OF TEST 5
STOP! DO NOT RETURN TO ANY OTHER TEST.

Practice Test II

DIRECTIONS

Practice Test II consists of five subject tests: English, Mathematics, Reading, Science, and Writing. Calculator use is only permitted on the Mathematics Test.

The items in each multiple-choice test are numbered and the answer choices are lettered. The provided bubble sheet (p. 305) has numbered rows that correspond to the items on the test. Each row contains lettered ovals to match the answer choices for each item on the test. Each numbered row on the bubble sheet has a corresponding item on the test.

For each item, first decide on the best answer choice. Then, locate the row number that corresponds to the item. Next, find the oval in that row that matches the letter of the chosen answer. Then, use a soft lead pencil to fill in the oval. Do not use a ballpoint pen.

Mark only one answer for each item. If you change your mind about the answer choice, thoroughly erase the first mark before marking your new answer.

Note that only responses marked on your bubble sheet will be scored. Your score on each test will be based only on the number of items that are correctly answered during the time allowed for that test. Guessing is not penalized. Therefore, it is to your best advantage to answer every item on the test, even if you must guess.

On the Writing Test, use the provided essay response sheet (p. 306) to write your response to the prompt. (Note that the Writing Test is optional.)

You may work on each test only during the time allowed for that test. If you finish a test before time is called, use the time to review your answer choices or work on items about which you are uncertain. You may not return to a test on which time has already been called and you may not preview another test. You must lay down your pencil immediately when time is called at the end of each test. You may not for any reason fill in or alter ovals for a test after time expires for that test. Violation of these rules will result in immediate disqualification from the exam.

1 1 1 1 1 1 1 1 1 1 1 1

ENGLISH TEST
45 Minutes—75 Items

DIRECTIONS: In the passages below, certain parts of the sentences have been underlined and numbered. In the right-hand column, you will find different ways of writing each underlined part; the original version is indicated by the "NO CHANGE" option. There are also items that ask about a section of the passage or the passage as a whole. These items do not refer to an underlined portion of the passage; they are identified by a number or numbers in a box.

For each item, choose the alternative that you consider to be the best. Select the answer choice that best expresses the intended idea, is most acceptable in standard written English, or is most consistent with the overall tone and style of the passage. Read the passage through once before you begin to answer the accompanying items. Finding the answers to certain items may depend on looking at material that appears several sentences beyond the item. So, be sure that you have read far enough ahead before you select your answer choice.

Answers are on page 609.

PASSAGE I

The Philosophy of Botany

[1]

Botany is surely <u>the more gentler of</u> sciences.
 ₁

The careful observation of a flower is a calm,

<u>ostentatious</u> action—the peaceful contemplation of a
₂

beautiful object. Reduced to its <u>essentials, it</u> requires
 ₃

no laboratory <u>but the natural world,</u> a few tools and
 ₄

the naked eye. Botany in its most scientific or purest

1. **A.** NO CHANGE
    B. the most gentle of
    C. the gentler of
    D. the gentlest in the

2. **F.** NO CHANGE
    G. unobtrusive
    H. violent
    J. chaotic

3. **A.** NO CHANGE
    B. essentials; it
    C. essentials; botany
    D. essentials, botany

4. **F.** NO CHANGE
    G. but you do need the natural world
    H. and the natural world is needed
    J. but the natural world is necessary

GO ON TO THE NEXT PAGE.

form consists about seeking to know more about the
5
plant simply for the sake of that knowledge. Plants

have not always been regarded as worthy of knowing
6
or studying in and of themselves, not on their merits

as sources of food or drugs but as life-forms. In fact,

the history of botany can be viewed in terms of

repeated rediscoveries of this one theme—that plants

are worthy of study in and of themselves, quite apart
7
from any use they might have for mankind.

[2]

8 The practical motives behind plant study should

not be disparaging—the bulk of our medical history,
9
for instance, is made up of accounts of herbal

remedies. Nonetheless, the study of the medicinal
10
properties of plants contained a self-limiting

mechanism: if a plant seemed to have no utilitarian

value, it was disregarded, and no further study of it is
11
made. The Renaissance attitude towards nature
11
changed this overly practical bent and initiated the

scientific study of plants.

5. **A.** NO CHANGE
　　B. consists of
　　C. consists in
　　D. consist of

6. **F.** NO CHANGE
　　G. for knowledge
　　H. of knowledge
　　J. to know

7. **A.** NO CHANGE
　　B. by themselves
　　C. themselves
　　D. by and for themselves

8. Beginning Paragraph 2 with which of the following might make the transition from Paragraph 1 to Paragraph 2 clearer?
　　F. However,
　　G. Since
　　H. Heretofore
　　J. Hence

9. **A.** NO CHANGE
　　B. disparaged—the bulk
　　C. disparaging, the bulk
　　D. disparaged; the bulk

10. **F.** NO CHANGE
　　G. Consequently
　　H. Thus
　　J. Moreover

11. **A.** NO CHANGE
　　B. had been made
　　C. were made
　　D. was made

GO ON TO THE NEXT PAGE.

[3]

Botany, as a pure science, has certain characteristics and makes certain assumptions that prove thought provoking and interesting. One of its unspoken or basic assumptions is an implicit respect
<u>12</u>
and regard for all living things. The botanist who

studies a plant's structure or tries <u>to have understood</u>
<u>13</u>
<u>their</u> functions confronts nature on its own terms.
13
Investigations of how a plant thrives or reproduces, or studies of the purposefulness of a flower's coloration and structure, are almost implicitly egalitarian and tautological. The botanist studies the flower because <u>they exist, but</u> because it exists, it is worthy of study.
14

12. F. NO CHANGE
G. because
H. and thus
J. yet

13. A. NO CHANGE
B. to understand its
C. understanding their
D. having understood its

14. F. NO CHANGE
G. it exists, but
H. it exists and
J. it exists, and

Item 15 asks about the preceding passage as a whole.

15. The last sentence of the essay is actually a restatement of which of the following ideas?

A. The study of the medicinal properties of plants has a self-limiting mechanism.
B. The botanist who tries to understand a plant's function confronts nature on its own terms.
C. Botany is a gentle science.
D. The study of plants and flowers is egalitarian and tautological.

GO ON TO THE NEXT PAGE.

PASSAGE II

Poverty in America

The main characteristic of poverty is, <u>of course,</u>
₁₆
lack of money. A family is defined as poor when its

annual income <u>falls below a certain dollar amount,</u>
₁₇
calculated by the U.S. Federal Government to be the

minimum a family of <u>their</u> size would need to
₁₈
maintain a minimally decent standard of living. In

certain areas of rural America, <u>consequently,</u> poverty is
₁₉
the rule rather than the exception. As many as 50

percent of the families may earn <u>less than</u> the poverty
₂₀
level, and some may manage to subsist somehow on

amounts even less than half the official poverty level

income. ☐21

<u>Although</u> lack of money is the defining
₂₂
characteristic of poverty, poverty is more than simply

lack of money. Poverty is an entire complex of

symptoms. Low levels of formal schooling among

16. The use of the phrase "of course" is:
- **F.** appropriate because someone who is poor obviously lacks money.
- **G.** appropriate because it is not obvious that someone who is poor lacks money.
- **H.** questionable since someone might be poor in spirit.
- **J.** appropriate because it disrupts the flow of the sentence.

17. **A.** NO CHANGE
- **B.** falls and is under a certain dollar amount,
- **C.** is under a certain specified dollar amount,
- **D.** OMIT the underlined portion.

18. **F.** NO CHANGE
- **G.** there
- **H.** its
- **J.** it's

19. **A.** NO CHANGE
- **B.** and therefore, as a result of this,
- **C.** moreover, due to this fact,
- **D.** OMIT the underlined portion.

20. **F.** NO CHANGE
- **G.** lower than
- **H.** less as
- **J.** lower as

21. The first paragraph provides which of the following?
- **A.** A definition
- **B.** An argument
- **C.** A comparison
- **D.** A narrative

22. **F.** NO CHANGE
- **G.** (Do NOT begin a new paragraph) Although
- **H.** Since
- **J.** (Do NOT begin a new paragraph) Since

GO ON TO THE NEXT PAGE.

adults parallel low-income levels. Additionally, in
23
families below the poverty level, the number of

children and aged who depend on those who work is in

general higher than the national average for all

families. As a consequence, fewer workers support a
24
greater number of non-workers than in other, more

prosperous families.

Often, the schooling provided in low-income

areas are as inadequate like incomes. In particular,
25
rural children get poorer schooling than city children,

and many rural poor are severely handicapped by it.
26
The general rural average is only 8.8 years of school

completed. Moreover, low educational levels seem to

just keep repeating and repeating themselves. If the
27
head of a rural poor family have little schooling, the
28
children are often handicapped in their efforts to get an

education. It is especially difficult for people who are

handicapped educationally to acquire new skills, get

new jobs, or otherwise adjust to an increasingly

23. **A.** NO CHANGE
    B. go along with
    C. are a lot like
    D. very often go together with

24. **F.** NO CHANGE
    G. However,
    H. Surprisingly,
    J. Fortunately,

25. **A.** NO CHANGE
    B. is—like family income, inadequate
    C. is so inadequate as family income
    D. is, like family income, inadequate

26. **F.** NO CHANGE
    G. education
    H. their education
    J. their lack of education

27. **A.** NO CHANGE
    B. be self-perpetuating of themselves
    C. be self-perpetuating
    D. cause the same thing to happen all over
       again

28. **F.** NO CHANGE
    G. have had
    H. has had
    J. was to have

GO ON TO THE NEXT PAGE.

urbanized society. This is as true on the farm <u>rather</u>₂₉

<u>than</u>₂₉ in urban industry, since modern farming <u>of the</u>₃₀

<u>present day</u>₃₀ requires skills that <u>poor educated</u>₃₁ people

lack. Lacking in education, the rural poor either take

low-paying jobs on the farm or elsewhere in rural areas

or swell the ranks of the unemployed or under-

employed.

29. A. NO CHANGE
   B. rather as
   C. as they are
   D. as it is

30. F. NO CHANGE
   G. of the present
   H. presently
   J. OMIT the underlined portion.

31. A. NO CHANGE
   B. poorly educated
   C. educated poor
   D. poor education

Item 32 asks about the preceding passage as a whole.

---

32. The author does NOT use which of the following in the development of the essay?

   F. Definitions
   G. Explanation
   H. Statistics
   J. Personal experience

PASSAGE III

School Dropouts

One out of every four children who entered the

fifth grade in the fall of 1966 <u>fail to graduate</u>₃₃ with his

33. A. NO CHANGE
   B. failed to graduate
   C. failed graduation
   D. fails to graduate

GO ON TO THE NEXT PAGE.

or her class. The total number that should of graduated
34
was 4.1 million, but approximately 900,000 fell by
the wayside.

Those who do not make it are called school dropouts. (Official statistics define a dropout as a person
who has not yet attained the age of 16 and leaves
school before graduation for any reason except
transfer.) School officials who work with dropouts
who leave school say a student will usually starting
35   36
thinking about dropping out about two years before
36

he or she ceases to attend school: roughly at age 14.
37
Absenteeism, class cutting, lack of motivation, and

lack of interest in school is often early signs of the
38
potential dropout. Also, many students drop out
39
mentally very early in their school career, despite their
physical presence until graduation.

The dropout is most often a boy who mostly,
40
frequently leaves school at the age of 16 while in the
40

tenth grade. He is most likely than those who stay in
41
school to score low on an intelligence test and is likely

34. F. NO CHANGE
     G. that should of been
     H. who should of
     J. who should have

35. A. NO CHANGE
     B. who have left school
     C. who are leaving school
     D. OMIT the underlined portion.

36. F. NO CHANGE
     G. usually will be starting thinking
     H. starts usually thinking
     J. usually starts to think

37. A. NO CHANGE
     B. school but roughly
     C. school and roughly
     D. school, roughly

38. F. NO CHANGE
     G. is oftentimes
     H. are often
     J. were often

39. A. NO CHANGE
     B. dropout also
     C. dropout many
     D. dropout but also

40. F. NO CHANGE
     G. frequently and often
     H. frequently
     J. sometimes often

41. A. NO CHANGE
     B. more likely than those
     C. most likely as one
     D. more likely than one

GO ON TO THE NEXT PAGE.

to be failing in school at the time <u>of him dropping out</u>.
₄₂

Yet most dropouts <u>are really not less bright</u> than
₄₃
students who remain in school until graduation. The

dropout typically comes from the lower-income class

and most often leaves school for financial reasons. His

absences from school <u>increasing noticeably</u> during the
₄₄

eighth grade and he participates little <u>or none</u> in extra-
₄₅
curricular activities. The reasons a student drops out of

school <u>goes deeper as</u> a mere desire to be rid of school.
₄₆
Dropping out is a symptom; the roots of the problem

are usually below the surface. 47

42. **F.** NO CHANGE
    G. he drops out
    H. of his having dropped out
    J. he dropped out

43. **A.** NO CHANGE
    B. really they are no less bright than are the students who remain
    C. are, than the students who remain, really no less bright
    D. than the students who remain are really no less bright

44. **F.** NO CHANGE
    G. increase so that
    H. increase noticeably
    J. increased to the point where it was noticed

45. **A.** NO CHANGE
    B. and not at all
    C. or not much
    D. or not at all

46. **F.** NO CHANGE
    G. go more deeply than
    H. go deeper as
    J. go deeper than

47. A logical continuation of the essay would be a discussion of:

    A. the financial reasons a student might leave school.
    B. a student's lack of motivation.
    C. possible extracurricular activities.
    D. why students might drop out of school.

> Item 48 asks about the preceding passage as a whole.

48. Is the use of the official definition of dropout in the second paragraph appropriate?

    F. Yes, because without a definition, the article would not be understandable.
    G. Yes, because the nature of a "dropout" is one of the central themes of the passage.
    H. No, because the definition has nothing to do with what the author is discussing in the second paragraph.
    J. No, because the author then redefines the word.

GO ON TO THE NEXT PAGE.

PASSAGE IV

Wind Machines

The idea of generating electricity with wind power is not new. But the kind of attention that idea is getting today, in terms of research and <u>development, are</u> both new and encouraging to planners looking for
49

renewable energy sources <u>satisfying</u> growing national
50
demands. An effort is being made in the United States to use one of humankind's oldest energy sources to solve one of <u>its</u> most modern <u>problems, to find</u>
51   52
reliable and cost-effective ways to harness the wind to produce electricity.

Wind machines are not the simple devices <u>that</u>
53
<u>they may be appearing to be,</u> and the lessons they
53
teach seldom come easy. <u>On the other hand,</u> the
54
potential reward to a nation that needs more energy from a renewable source is beyond calculation. Rewards for using wind power <u>have been gathered</u> by
55
civilizations and cultures since early in recorded history.

No record survives of the earliest wind machine. It <u>may have been built</u> in China more than three
56
thousand years ago. It may have been built on the windy plains of Afghanistan. History hints at some

49. A. NO CHANGE
 B. development, is
 C. developing, is
 D. development are

50. F. NO CHANGE
 G. that would have satisfied
 H. to satisfy
 J. with the satisfaction of

51. A. NO CHANGE
 B. their
 C. it's
 D. your

52. F. NO CHANGE
 G. problems: to find
 H. problems, finding
 J. problems. To find

53. A. NO CHANGE
 B. they may be
 C. it may seem to be
 D. they may appear to be

54. F. NO CHANGE
 G. Therefore,
 H. As a consequence
 J. This means that

55. A. NO CHANGE
 B. has been gathering
 C. is gathering
 D. will have been gathered

56. F. NO CHANGE
 G. may have been
 H. was being built
 J. has been building

GO ON TO THE NEXT PAGE.

sort of wind power used in the Pharaoh's Egypt for the
57

 drawing of water for agriculture, long before the birth
 57

of Christ. Hammurabi may have taken time out

from developing a legal code about 2,000 BC to

sponsor development of some sort of wind machine.

The earliest confirmed wind machines are in that

same region. Persian writers described gardens

irrigated through the means of wind-driven water
58

lifts several centuries before the birth of Christ.
59

Ultimately, we can only guess at the origin of the
60

windmill.
60

Persian machines were horizontal devices,
61

carousel-like contraptions that revolved around a

center pole and caught the wind with bundles of reeds.

57. **A.** NO CHANGE
    B. to draw water
    C. in order that water be drawn
    D. in order to draw water

58. **F.** NO CHANGE
    G. irrigated by means of
    H. which were then irrigated by means of
    J. irrigated by

59. **A.** NO CHANGE
    B. lifts several,
    C. lifts but several
    D. lifts and several

60. **F.** NO CHANGE
    G. the origin of the windmill can only be guessed at
    H. the origin of the windmill can only be guessed at by us
    J. the origin of the windmill could only be guessed at

61. **A.** NO CHANGE
    B. (Do NOT begin a new paragraph) Persian machines were horizontal devices,
    C. Since Persian machines were
    D. It was discovered that Persian machines were horizontal devices,

GO ON TO THE NEXT PAGE.

The carousel is perhaps the <u>more simple design for capturing</u> the wind; it cares nothing for the direction of the breeze, but revolves no matter where on the compass the wind may originate. From the Middle East, wind-machine technology may have been carried to Europe by returning Crusaders. Accurate records do not exist, but soon after the Crusades, windmills appeared in northern Europe and soon were found on the British Isles.

For a while, windmills flourished in Europe, but with the advent of steam power, they <u>come close to</u> extinction for the wind is <u>real iffy</u>. It can fail to blow just when it is needed the most, or it can <u>rage into a gale</u> when it is not needed at all.

62. **F.** NO CHANGE
   G. most simplest design for capturing
   H. simpler design to capture
   J. simplest design for capturing

63. **A.** NO CHANGE
   B. came close to
   C. are coming closer to
   D. come close upon

64. **F.** NO CHANGE
   G. likely to blow sometimes and not to others
   H. here today and gone tomorrow isn't
   J. capricious

65. The author's use of the phrase "rage into a gale" is:
   A. appropriate because it creates a vivid image.
   B. appropriate because it minimizes the importance of weather.
   C. inappropriate because images are out of place in scientific writing.
   D. inappropriate because wind is sometimes calm.

GO ON TO THE NEXT PAGE.

PASSAGE V

The Development of Television Programming

Television and its programs do not just happen.

It is planned products of a huge, wealthy, and highly
66

competitive commercial enterprise. The television

industry, which includes stations, networks, production

companies, actors, and writers, are responsible for
67

selecting, creating, and distributing programs. The

three most popular programs are the episodic series, the
68

made-for-television movie, and the mini-series.

In the 1970s, the episodic series, both dramatic

and comic, was the most popular of these. With the
69   70

advent of cable and pay television and of video disks
70

and tapes, the television movie is rapidly gaining in
71

popularity. The past ten years have seen several
72

changes in television drama. The action-adventure

police drama has lost and the situation comedy has
73

grew in popularity. Topics previously considered
73

taboo emerged. Unmarried couples living together,
74

divorces, and single parents. Even topics that are

---

66. **F.** NO CHANGE
    G. They are
    H. They would be
    J. It was

67. **A.** NO CHANGE
    B. writers, is
    C. writers are
    D. writers—is

68. **F.** NO CHANGE
    G. episodic series the
    H. episodic, series the
    J. episodic series the,

69. **A.** NO CHANGE
    B. was the more
    C. were the most
    D. were the more

70. **F.** NO CHANGE
    G. Including the advent
    H. Notwithstanding the advent
    J. With the beginning of the advent

71. **A.** NO CHANGE
    B. has rapidly gained in
    C. is rapidly gaining
    D. will rapidly gain in

72. **F.** NO CHANGE
    G. see
    H. will see
    J. would be seeing

73. **A.** NO CHANGE
    B. has grown
    C. grew
    D. grow

74. **F.** NO CHANGE
    G. emerged, unmarried
    H. emerged unmarried
    J. emerged: unmarried

GO ON TO THE NEXT PAGE.

<u>politically controversy</u> can now be the focus of
₇₅

programs.

75. **A.** NO CHANGE
    B. politically controversial
    C. politics controversy
    D. political controversy

END OF TEST 1
STOP! DO NOT TURN THE PAGE UNTIL TOLD TO DO SO.

2 2 2 2 2 2 2 2 2 2 2 2

MATHEMATICS TEST
60 Minutes—60 Items

DIRECTIONS: Solve each item and choose the correct answer choice. Then, fill in the corresponding oval on the bubble sheet.

Allocate time wisely. Try to solve as many items as possible, returning to skipped items if time permits.

Calculator use is permitted on this test; however, some items are best solved without the use of a calculator.

Note: Unless otherwise stated, assume all of the following.

1. Illustrative figures are NOT necessarily drawn to scale.
2. The word *average* indicates arithmetic mean.
3. The word *line* indicates a straight line.
4. Geometric figures lie in a plane.

Answers are on page 610.

---

1. $121,212 + (2 \cdot 10^4) = ?$

   A. 312,212
   B. 141,212
   C. 123,212
   D. 121,412
   E. 121,232

2. If $6x + 3 = 21$, then $2x + 1 = ?$

   F. 1
   G. 2
   H. 3
   J. 6
   K. 7

3. At a recreation center, it costs \$3 per hour to rent a ping pong table and \$12 per hour to rent a lane for bowling. For the cost of renting a bowling lane for 2 hours, it is possible to rent a ping pong table for how many hours?

   A. 4
   B. 6
   C. 8
   D. 18
   E. 36

DO YOUR FIGURING HERE.

GO ON TO THE NEXT PAGE.

4. If j, k, l, and m are natural numbers and $j < k < l < m$, which of the following could be true?

    F. $k = k + l$
    G. $j = l + m$
    H. $j + k = l + m$
    J. $j + k + m = l$
    K. $j + m = k + l$

5. Which of the following is greater than $\frac{1}{2}$?

    A. $\frac{6}{11}$
    B. $\frac{9}{19}$
    C. $\frac{7}{15}$
    D. $\frac{4}{9}$
    E. $\frac{3}{7}$

6. Out of a group of 360 students, exactly 18 are on the track team. What percent of the students are on the track team?

    F. 5%
    G. 10%
    H. 12%
    J. 20%
    K. 25%

7. In the figure below, 3 lines intersect as shown. Which of the following *must* be true?

    I. $a = x$
    II. $y + z = b + c$
    III. $x + a = y + b$

    A. I only
    B. II only
    C. I and II only
    D. I and III only
    E. I, II, and III only

DO YOUR FIGURING HERE.

GO ON TO THE NEXT PAGE.

8. In the figure below, $x = ?$

DO YOUR FIGURING HERE.

F. 15
G. 30
H. 45
J. 60
K. 90

9. Which of the following is the prime factorization of 60?

A. (2)(3)(10)
B. (3)(4)(5)
C. (2)(2)(3)(5)
D. (2)(2)(3)(6)
E. (3)(3)(3)(5)

10. The average height of 4 buildings is 20 meters. If 3 of the buildings are each 16 meters tall, what is the height, in meters, of the fourth building?

F. 32
G. 28
H. 24
J. 22
K. 18

11. In the figure below, what is the value of x?

A. 15
B. 20
C. 30
D. 45
E. 60

GO ON TO THE NEXT PAGE.

12. In the figure below, what is the length of $\overline{PQ}$?

   F. 0.09
   G. 0.11
   H. 0.12
   J. 0.13
   K. 0.16

13. What is the perimeter of the rectangle below?

$2a-1$

$3a-2$

   A. $10a-6$
   B. $10a-3$
   C. $6a-3$
   D. $5a-6$
   E. $5a-3$

14. If the average of x, x, x, 56, and 58 is 51, then $x = ?$

   F. 43
   G. 47
   H. 49
   J. 51
   K. 53

15. For how many integers x is $-2 \le 2x \le 2$?

   A. 1
   B. 2
   C. 3
   D. 4
   E. 5

DO YOUR FIGURING HERE.

GO ON TO THE NEXT PAGE.

16. For all real numbers x, 8^x equals which of the following?

    F. $8x$
    G. x^8
    H. 2^{2x}
    J. $x^{\frac{2}{3}}$
    K. 2^{3x}

DO YOUR FIGURING HERE.

17. What is the sum of the areas of 2 squares with sides of 2 and 3 unit lengths, respectively?

    A. 1
    B. 5
    C. 13
    D. 25
    E. 36

18. If the rectangular solid shown below has a volume of 54 cubic inches, what is the value of x, in inches?

    F. 2
    G. 3
    H. 6
    J. 9
    K. 12

19. If x is 80 percent of y, then y is what percent of x?

    A. $133\frac{1}{3}\%$
    B. 125%
    C. 120%
    D. 90%
    E. 80%

GO ON TO THE NEXT PAGE.

20. From which of the following statements can it be deduced that $m > n$?

   F. $m + 1 = n$
   G. $2m = n$
   H. $m + n > 0$
   J. $m - n > 0$
   K. $mn > 0$

21. If $f(x) = x^2 + x$, then what is the value of $f(f(2))$?

   A. 42
   B. 38
   C. 32
   D. 18
   E. 4

22. The circle below with center O has a radius with a length of 2. If the total area of the shaded regions is 3π, then $x = ?$

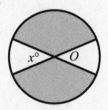

   F. 270
   G. 180
   H. 120
   J. 90
   K. 45

23. If a bar of metal alloy consists of 100 grams of tin and 150 grams of lead, what percent of the entire bar, by weight, is tin?

   A. 10%
   B. 15%
   C. $33\frac{1}{3}\%$
   D. 40%
   E. $66\frac{2}{3}\%$

DO YOUR FIGURING HERE.

GO ON TO THE NEXT PAGE.

24. If $\frac{1}{x}+\frac{1}{y}=\frac{1}{z}$, then $z = ?$

   DO YOUR FIGURING HERE.

   F. $\frac{1}{xy}$
   G. xy
   H. $\frac{x+y}{xy}$
   J. $\frac{xy}{x+y}$
   K. $\frac{2xy}{x+y}$

25. $|-5|+|-12|-|-2|+(-6) = ?$

   A. 2
   B. 3
   C. 6
   D. 9
   E. 14

26. If the average of $2x$, $2x+1$, and $2x+2$ is $x-1$, which of the following equations could be used to find x?

   F. $6x+3 = x-1$
   G. $6x+3 = 3(x-1)$
   H. $3(6x+3) = x-1$
   J. $(6x+3)+(x-1) = 3$
   K. $(6x+3)(x-1) = 3$

27. Members of a civic organization purchase boxes of candy for \$1 each and sell them for \$2 each. If no other expenses are incurred, how many boxes of candy must they sell to earn a net profit of \$500?

   A. 250
   B. 500
   C. 1,000
   D. 1,500
   E. 2,000

28. $(-2)^2 - (-2)^3 = ?$

   F. 16
   G. 12
   H. 2
   J. -2
   K. -8

GO ON TO THE NEXT PAGE.

29. The sum, the product, and the average of 3 different integers are equal. If 2 of the integers are x and $-x$, the third integer is:

    A. $\frac{x}{2}$
    B. $2x$
    C. -1
    D. 0
    E. 1

DO YOUR FIGURING HERE.

30. In a school with a total enrollment of 360, 90 students are seniors. What percent of all students enrolled in the school are seniors?

    F. 25%
    G. $33\frac{1}{3}$%
    H. 50%
    J. $66\frac{2}{3}$%
    K. 75%

31. The perimeter of the square below is:

    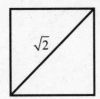

    A. 1
    B. $\sqrt{2}$
    C. 4
    D. $4\sqrt{2}$
    E. 8

32. If 2 straight lines intersect as shown, what is the value of x?

    F. 15
    G. 30
    H. 45
    J. 60
    K. 75

GO ON TO THE NEXT PAGE.

33. The figure below is a scale drawing of the floor of a dining hall. If 1 centimeter on the drawing represents 5 meters, what is the area, in square meters, of the floor?

0.8 cm

8 cm

4 cm

    A. 144
    B. 156
    C. 784
    D. 796
    E. 844

34. A triangle has one side with a length of 4 and another side with a length of 11. What are the *greatest* and *least* possible integer values for the length of the remaining side?

    F. 7 and 4
    G. 11 and 4
    H. 14 and 8
    J. 15 and 7
    K. 16 and 7

35. Which of the following is the solution set for the equation $-x^2 = 3 - 4x$?

    A. $\{-3, -1\}$
    B. $\{-3, 1\}$
    C. $\{1, 3\}$
    D. $\{1, 4\}$
    E. $\{3, 5\}$

GO ON TO THE NEXT PAGE.

DO YOUR FIGURING HERE.

36. A school club spends $\frac{2}{5}$ of its budget for one project and $\frac{1}{3}$ of what remains for another project. If the club's entire budget is $300, how much of the budget is left after the 2 projects?

   F. $60
   G. $90
   H. $120
   J. $180
   K. $240

37. If the cost of n nails is c cents, which of the following equations could be used to determine d, the cost in dollars, of x nails?

   A. $d = 100cnx$
   B. $d = 100\frac{cx}{n}$
   C. $d = \frac{100nx}{c}$
   D. $d = \frac{nx}{100c}$
   E. $d = \frac{cx}{100n}$

38. If $a^2b^3c < 0$, which of the following inequalities *must* be true?

   F. $b^3 < 0$
   G. $b^2 < 0$
   H. $b < 0$
   J. $c < 0$
   K. $bc < 0$

39. If the figure below is an equilateral triangle, what is its perimeter?

$2x+1$ $y+2$
$2x+y$

   A. 1
   B. 3
   C. 9
   D. 12
   E. 15

GO ON TO THE NEXT PAGE.

40. In the coordinate plane, what is the distance between the point with (x,y) coordinates $(2,1)$ and the point with (x,y) coordinates $(5,5)$?

    F. $\sqrt{3}$
    G. $2\sqrt{3}$
    H. $3\sqrt{2}$
    J. 5
    K. 6

41. $\sqrt{45} - \sqrt{20} + \sqrt{5} = ?$

    A. 0
    B. $2 - \sqrt{5}$
    C. $2 + \sqrt{5}$
    D. $2\sqrt{5}$
    E. 10

42. What is the least positive integer x for which $12 - x$ and $15 - x$ will yield non-zero results with opposite signs?

    F. 3
    G. 4
    H. 11
    J. 12
    K. 13

43. The solution set to the pair of equations $mx + ny = 15$ and $nx + my = 13$ is $x = 3$ and $y = 1$. What are the values of m and n?

    A. $m = 5; n = 3$
    B. $m = 4; n = 3$
    C. $m = 3; n = 4$
    D. $m = 3; n = 5$
    E. $m = 2; n = 6$

DO YOUR FIGURING HERE.

GO ON TO THE NEXT PAGE.

44. In the figure below, line segments intersecting each other at 90° join equally spaced points. If the total length of all line segments in the figure is 24, what is the area of the shaded part?

DO YOUR FIGURING HERE.

F. 1
G. 4
H. 8
J. 12
K. 16

45. All of the following are true for all real numbers EXCEPT:

A. $|a| = |-a|$
B. $|a-b| = |b-a|$
C. $|a-b| = -|b-a|$
D. $|a+b| \le |a| + |b|$
E. $|a-b| \le |a| + |b|$

46. $\text{Arccos}[\cos(\frac{\pi}{2})] = ?$

F. 0
G. $\frac{\pi}{4}$
H. $\frac{\pi}{2}$
J. π
K. $\frac{3\pi}{2}$

47. $\triangle ABC$ has coordinates $A\ (-1,-2)$, $B\ (0,4)$, and $C\ (3,-1)$. Which of the following provides the coordinates of $\triangle A'B'C'$, respectively, the image of $\triangle ABC$ after a reflection in the line $y = -x$?

A. $(2,1), (-4,0), (1,-3)$
B. $(1,2), (0,-4), (-3,1)$
C. $(2,1), (4,0), (1,-3)$
D. $(3,2), (5,1), (2,-2)$
E. $(4,0), (3,-1), (-1,-2)$

GO ON TO THE NEXT PAGE.

48. If $\sin(x) = \cos(x)$, then x terminates only in the:

DO YOUR FIGURING HERE.

    F. first quadrant
    G. second quadrant
    H. first or third quadrants
    J. second or third quadrants
    K. second or fourth quadrants

49. If the line $x = k$ is tangent to the circle $(x-2)^2 + (y+1)^2 = 4$, then which of the following is the point of tangency?

    A. $(-6,-1)$ or $(2,-1)$
    B. $(-2,-1)$ or $(6,-1)$
    C. $(0,-1)$ or $(4,-1)$
    D. $(0,1)$ or $(4,1)$
    E. $(2,1)$ or $(6,1)$

50. What is the last term in the expansion $(2x + 3y)^4$?

    F. y^4

    G. $9y^4$

    H. $27y^4$

    J. $81y^4$

    K. $(xy)^4$

51. Which of the following could be a graph of the equation $y = ax^2 + bx + c$, where $b^2 - 4ac = 0$?

A.

D.

B.

E.

C.

GO ON TO THE NEXT PAGE.

52. For any acute angle θ, which of the following is equal to $\frac{\sin(\theta)}{\cos(\theta)}$?

    F. 0.5
    G. 1
    H. $\tan(\theta)$
    J. $\cot(\theta)$
    K. $\sec(\theta)$

53. An angle that measures $\frac{3}{2}\pi$ radians measures how many degrees?

    A. 60
    B. 90
    C. 120
    D. 180
    E. 270

54. What is the solution set for $|2x-1| = 3$?

    F. All real numbers
    G. The empty set
    H. $\{-1\}$
    J. $\{2\}$
    K. $\{-1,2\}$

55. The end points of a line have coordinates of (2,5) and (2,−4). What are the coordinates of the midpoint of the line?

    A. (0,1)
    B. $(2,\frac{1}{2})$
    C. (2,1)
    D. (2,9)
    E. (4,9)

56. What is the slope of the line with the equation $2x+3y-2=0$?

    F. $-\frac{3}{2}$
    G. $-\frac{2}{3}$
    H. $\frac{2}{3}$
    J. 4
    K. 6

DO YOUR FIGURING HERE.

GO ON TO THE NEXT PAGE.

57. $\frac{1}{\sqrt{3}-1} = ?$

    A. $\frac{\sqrt{3}-1}{4}$

    B. $\frac{\sqrt{3}-1}{3}$

    C. $\frac{\sqrt{3}-1}{2}$

    D. $\frac{\sqrt{3}+1}{2}$

    E. $\sqrt{3}+1$

58. $(-2)^2 - 2^{-2} = ?$

    F. -5

    G. -3

    H. 3

    J. $3\frac{3}{4}$

    K. $4\frac{1}{4}$

59. $\frac{-3+\sqrt{5}}{2}$ is 1 root of the equation $x^2 + 3x + 1 = 0$.

What is the other root?

    A. $\frac{3+\sqrt{5}}{2}$

    B. $\frac{3-\sqrt{5}}{2}$

    C. $\frac{-3-\sqrt{5}}{2}$

    D. $3+\frac{\sqrt{5}}{2}$

    E. $3-\frac{\sqrt{5}}{2}$

GO ON TO THE NEXT PAGE.

60. The figure below represents which of the following equations?

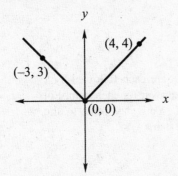

F. $y = x$

G. $y = -x$

H. $y = |x|$

J. $y = 2x$

K. $y = x^2$

DO YOUR FIGURING HERE.

END OF TEST 2
STOP! DO NOT TURN THE PAGE UNTIL TOLD TO DO SO.
DO NOT RETURN TO THE PREVIOUS TEST.

3 3 3 3 3 3 3 3 3 3 3 3

READING TEST
35 Minutes—40 Items

DIRECTIONS: The passages presented in the test are each followed by a set of items. Read the passage and choose the best answer for each item. Fill in the corresponding oval on your bubble sheet. You may refer to the passage as often as necessary to answer the passage items.

Answers are on page 611.

Passage I

PROSE FICTION: In this passage, the narrator shares his exasperation with and sympathy for an employee.

Turkey was a short, pursy Englishman, of about my own age—that is, somewhere not far from sixty. In the morning, one might say, his face was of a fine florid hue, but after twelve o'clock, meridian—his
5 dinner hour—it blazed like a grate full of Christmas coals; and continued blazing—but, as it were, with a gradual wane—till six o'clock p.m., or thereabouts; after which, I saw no more of the proprietor of the face, which, gaining its meridian with the Sun, seemed
10 to set with, to rise, culminate, and decline the following day, with the like regularity and undiminished glory. There are many singular coincidences I have known in the course of my life, not the least among which was the fact that, exactly when
15 Turkey displayed his fullest beams from his red and radiant countenance, just then, too, at that critical moment, began the daily period when I considered his business capacities as seriously disturbed for the remainder of the twenty-four hours.

20 Not that he was absolutely idle, or averse to business then; far from it. The difficulty was he was apt to be altogether too energetic. There was a strange, inflamed, flurried, flighty recklessness of activity about him. He would be incautious in dipping his pen into his
25 inkstand. All his blots upon my documents were dropped there after twelve o'clock, meridian. Indeed, not only would he be reckless, and sadly given to making blots in the afternoon, but, some days, he went further, and was rather noisy. At such times, too, his
30 face flamed with augmented blazonry, as if cannel coal had been heaped upon anthracite. He made an unpleasant racket with his chair; spilled his sand box;

in mending his pens, impatiently split them all to pieces, and threw them on the floor in a sudden
35 passion; stood up, and leaned over his table, boxing the papers about in a most indecorous manner, very sad to behold in an elderly man like him.

Nevertheless, as he was in many ways a most valuable person to me, and all the time before twelve
40 o'clock, meridian, was the quickest, steadiest creature, too, accomplishing a great deal of work in a style not easily to be matched—for these reasons, I was willing to overlook his eccentricities, though, indeed, occasionally, I remonstrated with him. I did this very
45 gently, however, because, though the civilest, nay, the blandest and most reverential of men in the morning, in the afternoon he was disposed, upon provocation, to be slightly rash with his tongue—in fact, insolent. Now, valuing his morning services as I did, and resolved not
50 to lose them—yet, at the same time, made uncomfortable by his inflamed ways after twelve o'clock—and being a man of peace, unwilling by my admonitions to call forth unseemly retorts from him, I took upon me, one Saturday noon (he was always
55 worse on Saturdays) to hint to him, very kindly, that perhaps, now that he was growing old, it might be well to abridge his labors; in short, he need not come to my chambers after twelve o'clock, but, dinner over, had best go home to his lodgings, and rest himself till
60 teatime. But no; he insisted upon his afternoon devotions. His countenance became intolerably fervid, as he oratorically assured me—gesticulating with a long ruler at the other end of the room—that if his services in the morning were useful, how
65 indispensable, then, in the afternoon?

"With submission, sir," said Turkey, on this occasion, "I consider myself your right-hand man. In the morning I but marshal and deploy my columns; but

GO ON TO THE NEXT PAGE.

in the afternoon I put myself at their head, and
70 gallantly charge the foe, thus"—and he made a violent
thrust with the ruler.

"But the blots, Turkey," intimated I.

"True; but, with submission sir, behold these
hairs! I am getting old. Surely, sir, a blot or two of a
75 warm afternoon is not to be severely urged against gray
hairs. Old age—even if it blot the page—is honorable.
With submission, sir, we *both* are getting old."

This appeal to my fellow-feeling was hardly to be
resisted. At all events, I saw that go he would not. So, I
80 made up my mind to let him stay, resolving,
nevertheless, to see to it that, during the afternoon, he
had to do with my less important papers.

1. The narrator is Turkey's:

   A. older brother.
   B. physician.
   C. employer.
   D. co-worker.

2. The passage suggests that Turkey is a:

   F. copyist.
   G. painter.
   H. fencing instructor.
   J. sales clerk.

3. A logical explanation for Turkey's behavior is
   that he:

   A. becomes fatigued.
   B. is growing old.
   C. drinks alcohol.
   D. dislikes the narrator.

4. The "fellow-feeling" mentioned in the final
   paragraph is based on the fact that:

   F. Turkey is the narrator's right-hand man.
   G. Turkey and the narrator are the same age.
   H. the narrator also makes ink blots.
   J. the ink blots are not very serious.

5. The narrator's final resolution of the problem is
   to:

   A. find a replacement for Turkey.
   B. give Turkey Saturdays off.
   C. give Turkey afternoons off.
   D. give Turkey less important work after noon.

6. According to the narrator, Turkey's face is
   reddest:

   F. in early morning.
   G. at noon.
   H. in midafternoon.
   J. in early evening.

7. It can be inferred that when cannel coal is heaped
   on anthracite, a fire:

   A. burns more intensely.
   B. burns less intensely.
   C. goes out altogether.
   D. begins to sputter and spit.

8. The narrator's attitude toward Turkey's afternoon
   behavior is one of:

   F. amusement.
   G. discomfort.
   H. indifference.
   J. outrage.

9. The narrator finds Turkey's work in the mornings
   to be:

   A. entirely satisfactory.
   B. frequently unsatisfactory.
   C. almost always unsatisfactory.
   D. inconsistent.

10. Which of the following does NOT characterize
    Turkey's behavior in the afternoon?

    F. Frenzied activity
    G. Excessive carelessness
    H. Idleness
    J. Verbal insolence

GO ON TO THE NEXT PAGE.

Passage II

SOCIAL STUDIES: This passage discusses punishment for individuals who have violated the law.

Justice in society must include both a fair trial to the accused and the selection of an appropriate punishment for those proved guilty. Because justice is regarded as one form of equality, we find in its earlier
5 expressions the idea of a punishment equal to the crime. Recorded in the Old Testament is the expression "an eye for an eye, and a tooth for a tooth." That is, the individual who has done wrong has committed an offense against society. To atone for this offense,
10 society must get even. Only inflicting an equal injury upon him can do this. This conception of retributive justice is reflected in many parts of the legal codes and procedures of modern times. It is illustrated when we demand the death penalty for a person who has
15 committed murder.

The German idealist, Hegel, supported this philosophy of punishment. He believed that society owed it to the criminal to administer a punishment equal to the crime committed. The criminal has by his
20 own actions denied his true self, and it is necessary to do something to restore the self that has been denied. To the murderer, nothing less than giving up his own life will pay his debt. The exaction of the death penalty is a right the state owes the criminal, and it should not
25 deny him his due.

Modern jurists have tried to replace retributive justice with the notion of corrective justice. The aim of the latter is not to abandon the concept of equality but to find a more adequate way to express it. It tries to
30 preserve the ideal of equal opportunity for each individual to realize the best that is in him. The criminal is regarded as being socially ill and in need of treatment that will enable him to become a normal member of society. Before treatment can be adminis-
35 tered, the causes that led to antisocial behavior must be found. If the causes can be removed, provisions must be made to have this done.

Only those criminals who are incurable should be permanently separated from the rest of society. This
40 does not mean that criminals will escape punishment or be quickly returned to take up careers of crime. It means that justice is to heal the individual, not simply to get even with him. If severe punishment is the only adequate means for accomplishing this, it should be
45 administered. However, the individual should be given every opportunity to assume a normal place in society. His conviction of crime must not deprive him of the

opportunity to make his way in the society of which he is a part.

11. The best title for this selection is:

   A. Fitting Punishment to the Crime.
   B. Approaches to Just Punishment.
   C. Improvement in Legal Justice.
   D. Attaining Justice in the Courts.

12. Hegel would view the death sentence for murder as:

   F. inadequate justice.
   G. the best way for society to get revenge.
   H. the most efficient method of removing a known danger.
   J. an inalienable right of the murderer.

13. The passage implies that the basic difference between retributive justice and corrective justice is:

   A. the type of crime that was committed.
   B. the severity of the punishment.
   C. the reason for the sentence.
   D. the outcome of the trial.

14. The punishment that would be most inconsistent with the views of corrective justice is:

   F. forced brain surgery.
   G. solitary confinement.
   H. life imprisonment.
   J. the electric chair.

15. The Biblical expression "an eye for an eye, and a tooth for a tooth" was presented in order to:

   A. justify the need for punishment as a part of law.
   B. give moral backing to retributive justice.
   C. show that humanity has long been interested in justice as a form of equality.
   D. indicate the lack of social development during Biblical times.

GO ON TO THE NEXT PAGE.

16. The concept of retributive justice still reflected in many modern legal codes is:

    F. giving the accused a fair trial.
    G. rehabilitating the criminal.
    H. separating incurable criminals from the rest of society.
    J. inflicting equal injury on the criminal.

17. A major goal of modern jurists is to:

    A. ensure that criminals do not escape punishment.
    B. preserve the notion of equality.
    C. restore states' rights.
    D. select an appropriate punishment for a crime.

18. Under the notion of corrective justice, assuming "a normal place in society" (line 46) most likely means:

    F. acting in one's best interests.
    G. denying one's true self.
    H. curing antisocial behavior.
    J. accepting punishment.

19. The author's tone in the passage is best described as:

    A. argumentative.
    B. sympathetic.
    C. explanatory.
    D. conciliatory.

20. According to the author, criminals cannot be treated until:

    F. they have been punished properly for their crime.
    G. they have received a fair trial.
    H. a legal code for treatment has been established.
    J. the causes of antisocial behavior have been found.

GO ON TO THE NEXT PAGE.

Passage III

HUMANITIES: This passage describes events leading to and the effects of World War I.

The event that touched off World War I occurred in Sarajevo, the capital of the Austro-Hungarian province of Bosnia, on June 28, 1914. There the Archduke Francis Ferdinand, the Hapsburg heir to the
5 throne of the Austro-Hungarian Empire, was shot and killed by a young Serbian nationalist seeking revenge against the Austrians for their annexation of Bosnia. Austria issued an ultimatum to Serbia. The Serbians acquiesced, in an attempt to stave off war. Austria,
10 however, was intent on exacting retribution and in July of that year declared war on Serbia.

For almost a century, since the Congress of Vienna in 1815, European diplomats had prevented any real threat to the delicate balance of power
15 achieved by the Congress. This time, though, they seemed powerless to stop the movement toward war. The assassination provoked a fateful series of failed diplomatic attempts that led suspicious Russia to mobilize its armed forces as Serbia's ally. Austria
20 sought and received the mobilization aid of its ally Germany. The other members of the Triple Entente, France and Great Britain, soon joined their ally Russia against Austria. In 1917, the United States was drawn into the battle as an ally of France and Great Britain.

25 World War I was unlike any other war fought before or since. The profound shock it generated dramatically affected the progression of life in Europe and America and changed the course of world politics. Moreover, the war shocked millions of people through-
30 out Europe into confronting the terrible losses and the grim and brutal realities of modern war. The few wars that had been fought since 1815 were distant colonial wars. Europeans had always been victorious, and the battles seemed nothing more than skirmishes that
35 offered chances to experience adventure and to demonstrate bravery and heroism. The trenches and battle-fields of Europe introduced millions of young men and women to a world of pain and death that they had never imagined.

40 The war altered the collective social sensibility of the people of Europe. It destroyed the spirit of optimism that had prevailed in the nineteenth century. Civilized, polite behavior now seemed archaic and utterly hypocritical. Moreover, the impression that
45 there appeared to be no sane way to end the carnage only added to the sense of futility. The war changed relationships between members of the same social class. Before the war, the upper classes of Europe felt a common bond that united them across national borders.
50 After the war, national boundaries defined social consciousness in a way that destroyed the solidarity of class.

World War I produced several dramatic changes in the political landscape of Europe. The breakup of
55 the Austro-Hungarian, Russian, and German empires led to the reemergence of the state of Poland and the formation of other independent nation states in Europe. The war acted as a catalyst for European revolutionar-ies. The Russian Revolution of 1917 set the stage for
60 the Bolshevik seizure of power, the exercise of total power by the Communist party; and the rise of Stalin as the absolute dictator of the Russian state (renamed the Union of Soviet Socialist Republics). World War I bore bitter fruit in Central and Southern Europe as
65 well. The rise of Nazism in Germany and fascism in Italy led many historians to conclude that World War II, which was begun by Nazi Germany in 1939, was in actuality the continuation of the Great War that destroyed the social fabric of Europe in 1914.

21. The precipitating cause of World War I was:

    A. an assassination.
    B. a coronation.
    C. a rebellion.
    D. a plebiscite.

22. The event occurred in the city of:

    F. Sarajevo in Bosnia.
    G. Vienna in Austria.
    H. Trieste in Italy.
    J. Budapest in Hungary.

23. Before World War I, a balance of power had existed for:

    A. nearly 15 years.
    B. almost a quarter century.
    C. almost 100 years.
    D. nearly 10 years.

GO ON TO THE NEXT PAGE.

24. The chief reason European countries other than Austria and Serbia were drawn into the conflict was that they:

    F. were members of the two alliance systems to which the combatants belonged.
    G. feared the Hapsburgs.
    H. wanted to ensure freedom of the seas.
    J. wanted the land of neighboring countries.

25. Mobilization for war resulted swiftly when:

    A. the United States declared war.
    B. attempts at diplomacy failed.
    C. Russia refused to help Serbia.
    D. Italy joined the conflict.

26. The way in which class relationships changed as a result of the outbreak of World War I suggests that:

    F. nationalism might have weakened had the war never occurred.
    G. the middle classes had no real love of country.
    H. the upper classes had eagerly anticipated war.
    J. everyone sanctioned the war.

27. The forces of militant nationalism that were unleashed during World War I culminated in the breakup of the Russian Empire and the German Empire. The political regimes that came to power in Germany and the Soviet Union before World War II were:

    A. democracies that isolated themselves from world politics.
    B. ruthless dictatorships dedicated to world conquest.
    C. weak states allied with the United States.
    D. members of a Europe-wide common market.

28. The sense of futility felt throughout Europe during and after World War I would be evident in a study of:

    F. American investment policies.
    G. statistics concerning foreign language study in America.
    H. European literature of the 1920s, 1930s, and 1940s.
    J. the number of transatlantic voyages between 1920 and 1930.

29. World War I and its aftermath suggest the idea that:

    A. nationalism has little to do with world conflict.
    B. war feeds on nationalist sympathies.
    C. the cause of peace is best aided by reinvigorating the spirit of nationalism.
    D. diplomacy never works.

30. Archduke Francis Ferdinand, as the heir to the Austro-Hungarian Empire, was a member of the:

    F. Hohenzollern family.
    G. Hanover family.
    H. Hapsburg family.
    J. Stuart family.

GO ON TO THE NEXT PAGE.

Passage IV

NATURAL SCIENCES: This selection discusses the information gathered about the planet Uranus by the Voyager 2 spacecraft.

When the Voyager 2 spacecraft flew past Uranus and its moons in 1986, it gathered startling new information about these extraordinary celestial objects. Uranus had long been known to be different from all
5 the other planets in one important respect: It lies tipped over on its side and instead of spinning like a top, it rolls like a ball along the path of its orbit. Its geographic poles, instead of being on the top and bottom of the planet as Earth's are, are located on
10 either side, one facing the Sun and one facing away— as if they were the ends of a gigantic axle. Voyager found another oddity: Uranus' magnetic poles, instead of lying close to the geographic poles as Earth's do, are located not far from the planet's equator, 60° away
15 from the geographic poles. Still another discovery is that the clouds in the Uranian atmosphere move in the same direction as the planet rotates; that is, from top to bottom and back to top, rather than horizontally, as Earth's clouds move.

20 The Uranian moons proved to have equally striking features. Miranda, the moon nearest the planet, bears tremendous markings where terrains of completely different types appear to have been wedged together. On Ariel, the next moon out, the landscape
25 has been stretched apart, creating huge faults where the ground has broken apart and sunk inward. However, there is no evidence of any geological activity. Umbriel, the third moon, seems to be "painted" with some dark substance. On one side of Umbriel is a
30 large, round bright marking called the "donut." It is presumably some type of impact crater. Each of Uranus' other seven moons is equally odd and unique in its own way. Furthermore, between the orbit of Miranda and Uranus' surface are up to one hundred
35 charcoal-colored rings, ringlets, and bands of dust, and between some of these rings are still more tiny moonlets.

The moons and rings of Uranus are odd in still another way. Like the clouds in the planet's atmos-
40 phere, they circle Uranus in the same direction as the planet rotates. That is, they orbit over the top and bottom of the planet rather than around the sides, as Earth's moon does.

31. Because of the odd way in which Uranus rotates, one geographic pole:

   A. alternates between daylight and darkness.
   B. receives only indirect sunlight.
   C. varies between heat from the Sun and cold.
   D. is always in darkness.

32. The warmest spot on Uranus would most likely be located at:

   F. one of the magnetic poles.
   G. the equator.
   H. one of the geographic poles.
   J. a spot midway between a geographic pole and the equator.

33. On Uranus, a surface location that receives sunlight:

   A. will alternate between daylight and darkness.
   B. will always be in daylight.
   C. will occasionally be in darkness.
   D. must be near one of the magnetic poles.

34. The Uranian equator extends:

   F. around the planet horizontally, as Earth's does.
   G. around the planet through the geographic poles.
   H. around the planet from top to bottom.
   J. around the planet through the magnetic poles.

35. An observer at the Uranian equator would most likely experience:

   A. a regular succession of days and nights.
   B. constant, indirect sunlight.
   C. a regular succession of warmth and cold.
   D. only darkness.

GO ON TO THE NEXT PAGE.

36. Auroras are sky phenomena that generally appear near a planet's magnetic poles. On Earth, auroras can be seen at extreme north or south latitudes. On Uranus, auroras would most likely:

F. be visible near the planet's geographic poles.
G. never be visible.
H. be visible not far from the planet's equator.
J. be visible from everywhere on the planet's surface.

37. On Earth, atmospheric circulation patterns are largely controlled by the varying amounts of sunlight received at different latitudes. On Uranus:

A. atmospheric circulation functions in an identical way.
B. there is no atmospheric circulation.
C. the atmosphere circulates from one geographic pole to the other.
D. some other factor besides sunlight controls atmospheric circulation.

38. It has been suggested that the moon Miranda was shattered into pieces by a collision with some other object. Gravity then caused the pieces to reassemble; however, great "seam" marks most likely remained because:

F. the gravitational forces involved were weak.
G. the lack of atmosphere meant that no erosion ever took place.
H. the second object remained nearby, exerting gravitational pull.
J. the force of the collision was so great.

39. The great faults observed on the moon Ariel could have been caused by:

A. moonquakes.
B. continental drift.
C. the gravitational pull of other nearby moons.
D. volcanic activity.

40. Uranus has how many moons?

F. 3
G. 7
H. 10
J. 12

END OF TEST 3
STOP! DO NOT TURN THE PAGE UNTIL TOLD TO DO SO.
DO NOT RETURN TO A PREVIOUS TEST.

4 4 4 4 4 4 4 4 4 4 4 4

SCIENCE TEST

35 Minutes—40 Items

DIRECTIONS: The passages presented in the test are each followed by a set of items. Read the passage and choose the best answer for each item. Fill in the corresponding oval on your bubble sheet. You may refer to the passage as often as necessary to answer the passage items.

Warning: Calculator use is not permitted on this test.

Answers are on page 612.

Passage I

The table below shows selected elements from the periodic table, together with atomic radii in angstrom units (Å) and electronegativities (second number). When two atoms form a covalent bond, the approximate bond length may be calculated by adding together the two atomic radii.

H 0.37 Å 2.20						
Li 1.35 Å 0.98	Be 0.90 Å 1.57	B 0.80 Å 2.04	C 0.77 Å 2.55	N 0.70 Å 3.04	O 0.66 Å 3.44	F 0.64 Å 3.98
Na 1.54 Å 0.93	Mg 1.30 Å 1.31	Al 1.25 Å 1.61	Si 1.17 Å 1.90	P 1.10 Å 2.19	S 1.04 Å 2.58	Cl 0.99 Å 3.16
K 1.96 Å 0.82						Br 1.14 Å 2.96
Rb 2.11 Å 0.82						I 1.33 Å 2.66

The electronegativity has important chemical significance. If two atoms form a bond, the difference in the two electronegativities indicates the degree to which the bond is covalent (indicated by a small difference) or ionic (indicated by a large difference).

1. What occurs when moving down the table's columns?

   A. Radii decrease; electronegativities decrease.
   B. Radii increase; electronegativities increase.
   C. Radii decrease; electronegativities increase.
   D. Radii increase; electronegativities decrease.

2. The greatest electronegativity in the table is:

   F. fluorine (F).
   G. chlorine (Cl).
   H. rubidium (Rb).
   J. hydrogen (H).

3. The bond length in the P-Cl bond is:

   A. 0.11 angstroms.
   B. 0.97 angstroms.
   C. 2.09 angstroms.
   D. 5.35 angstroms.

4. The bond between which of the following is likely to have the most covalent character?

   F. Sodium (Na) and iodine (I)
   G. Magnesium (Mg) and oxygen (O)
   H. Sulfur (S) and oxygen (O)
   J. Carbon (C) and nitrogen (N)

5. The table indicates that bonds of greatest ionic character generally occur:

   A. between elements by each other in a row.
   B. between elements that are near each other in a column but far apart along a row.
   C. between elements that are far apart along a column but close in a row.
   D. between elements far apart along a column and far apart in a row.

GO ON TO THE NEXT PAGE.

6. The element cesium (Cs) lies directly below rubidium (Rb) in the Periodic Table. The electronegativity difference in CsF is likely to be:

   F. less than 3.16.
   G. equal to 3.16.
   H. greater than 3.16.
   J. Cannot be determined from the given information

GO ON TO THE NEXT PAGE.

Passage II

A set of experiments was carried out to investigate the relative sizes of the planets of our solar system and the relative distances from the Sun. Table 1 was given to all students performing the experiments.

Experiment 1: Using a compass, ruler, and paper (11 in. x 14 in.), students were asked to compare the sizes of the planets. Calling the size of Earth 1.00 (Earth diameter = 5 in.), a circle was made by inserting the point of the compass in the center of the paper. The circle had a radius of 2.5 in. to produce a circle with a diameter of 5 in. representing the Earth. All other planets were drawn to scale based on the size of their diameters relative to one Earth diameter (Table 1).

Table 1

Planet	Approximate Diameter (in Earth diameters)	Approximate Distance from the Sun (A.U.)
Mercury	0.38	0.40
Venus	0.95	0.70
Earth	1.00	1.00
Mars	0.54	1.50
Jupiter	11.20	5.20
Saturn	9.50	9.50
Uranus	3.70	19.20
Neptune	3.50	30.00
Pluto	0.47	40.00

Experiment 2: Using the equipment from Experiment 1, students were also asked to compare planetary distances from the Sun. The Earth is 93 million miles from the Sun. This distance is called 1.00 Astronomical Unit (1 A.U. = 0.5 inches), and it was used as a reference distance when the other planets were drawn at their proper distances (Table 1) from the Sun (a planet twice as far as the Earth is from the Sun would be drawn 2 A.U., or 1.0 inches, from the Sun).

7. In Experiment 1, the two planets represented by circles most similar in size on the paper are:

   A. Earth and Venus.
   B. Mars and Pluto.
   C. Uranus and Neptune.
   D. Mercury and Pluto.

8. In Experiment 2, if the paper were held the "long way" and the left-hand paper edge represented the Sun, which planet(s) would not fit on the paper?

   F. Uranus, Neptune, and Pluto
   G. Neptune and Pluto
   H. Pluto only
   J. All planets would fit on the paper.

9. Which of the following statements is supported by the data in Table 1?

   A. The larger the planet, the greater is its distance from the Sun.
   B. The smaller the planet, the greater is its distance from the Sun.
   C. Only planets larger than the Earth are farther away from the Sun.
   D. There is no consistent pattern between a planet's size and its distance from the Sun.

10. A planet's "year" is how long it takes to orbit the Sun and it is related to the distance of that planet from the Sun. If asteroids are found 2.8 A.U. from the Sun, an "asteroid year" should be:

    F. longer than a "Mars year" but shorter than a "Jupiter year."
    G. longer than an "Earth year" but shorter than a "Mars year."
    H. longer than an "Earth year" but shorter than a "Neptune year."
    J. longer than a "Neptune year" but shorter than a "Uranus year."

11. In Experiment 1, how large would a circle representing the Sun be if its diameter is approximately 110 times greater than that of the Earth?

    A. It would have a radius of approximately 550 inches.
    B. It would have a diameter of approximately 550 inches.
    C. It would have a radius of approximately 55 inches.
    D. It would have a diameter of approximately 55 inches.

GO ON TO THE NEXT PAGE.

12. A third experiment was conducted in which the mass of each planet was described relative to the mass of the Earth (Jupiter had the greatest mass, Saturn had the next largest mass, Mercury and Pluto had the smallest masses). If the planets were placed in an order based on how they compared to Earth for the variables measured in all three experiments, which two orders would be expected to be most similar?

F. Diameter and distance from the Sun
G. Mass and distance from the Sun
H. Diameter and mass
J. All three orders would be similar.

Passage III

It is known that during photosynthesis, leaf pigments absorb light energy that eventually results in the production of glucose and other carbohydrates to be used by the green plant. Oxygen gas (O_2) is also produced during the process. Various factors affecting the rate of photosynthesis were investigated by counting the number of oxygen bubbles produced under the conditions described in the following three experiments.

Experiment 1: A sample of leaf extract (a mixture of pigments previously separated from other leaf components) from the pond plant *Elodea* was placed in a beaker containing water and a standard concentration of carbon dioxide (CO_2) (both are necessary ingredients for photosynthesis). Light of varying intensity was used to illuminate the beaker, and the number of oxygen bubbles emitted by the plant each minute was recorded. The results are illustrated in Figure 1.

Figure 1

Experiment 2: An identical experiment was conducted in which the concentration of leaf extract was reduced four-fold (the mixture was one-fourth as concentrated as in Experiment 1). The results are shown in Figure 2.

Figure 2

Experiment 3: Visible light consists of many different colors, or light wavelengths. Only those wavelengths that are absorbed by leaf pigments can provide the energy to maintain photosynthesis in the leaf. Different light wavelengths were used separately to illuminate two samples of leaf extract, each containing a different *Elodea* leaf pigment. Oxygen (O_2) bubbles were counted again as a measure of the rate of photosynthesis. Figure 3 summarizes the results.

Figure 3

GO ON TO THE NEXT PAGE.

13. When running Experiment 1, which of the following changes in CO_2 should be made in order to determine its effect on the rate of photosynthesis?

    A. Repeat the experiment using the same concentration of CO_2 in the beaker of water, but with different species of green plants.
    B. Repeat the experiment using first no CO_2 and then varying concentrations of carbon dioxide in the beaker of water.
    C. Repeat the experiment using different levels of water in the beaker containing a standard concentration of CO_2.
    D. Repeat the experiment using additional light intensities.

14. The results in Experiments 1 and 2 demonstrate that in order to maintain a continued increase in the photosynthesis rate:

    F. adequate amounts of light are needed.
    G. adequate amounts of carbon dioxide are needed.
    H. adequate amounts of oxygen are needed.
    J. adequate amounts of leaf pigments are needed.

15. Based on the information in Figure 3, which of the following statements is correct?

    A. Pigment A primarily absorbs light at 450 and 650 nanometers, while Pigment B absorbs light at 500–575 nanometers.
    B. Pigment B primarily absorbs light at 450 and 650 nanometers, while Pigment A primarily absorbs light at 500–575 nanometers.
    C. Pigment A can influence the rate of photosynthesis, while Pigment B cannot.
    D. Pigment B can influence the rate of photosynthesis, while Pigment A cannot.

16. If the concentration of *Elodea* leaf extract was increased in Experiment 2, which of the following results could be expected?

    F. A decrease in the number of oxygen bubbles
    G. An increase in the number of oxygen bubbles
    H. No change in the number of oxygen bubbles
    J. A gradual dimming of light intensity

17. In Experiments 1 and 2, approximately how many oxygen bubbles/minute were produced at a light intensity level of 4?

    A. 20–30
    B. 30–40
    C. 40–50
    D. Between 0 and 10

18. According to the information in Figure 3, if an additional experiment were conducted, which condition would be LEAST effective in maintaining photosynthetic rate in *Elodea*?

    F. Using blue light only
    G. Using red light only
    H. Using yellow light only
    J. Using orange light only

GO ON TO THE NEXT PAGE.

Passage IV

The accompanying figure shows how the world records for various footraces have improved during a portion of this century. Speeds are given in both meters/minute and minutes/mile.

Modified from H.W. Ryder, H.J. Carr, and P. Herget, "Future performance in footracing," *Sci. Amer.* 234 (6): 109–114, 1976.

19. In what race and in what year was the greatest speed in meters/minute achieved?

    A. The 440-yard dash in 1900
    B. The 100-yard dash in 1930
    C. The 100-yard dash in 1962
    D. The 1-mile run in 1947

20. The trend in the graphs of meters/minute for the various distances shows:

    F. roughly a linear increase.
    G. roughly a linear decrease.
    H. a linear increase for short distances and a linear decrease for long distances.
    J. no systematic pattern.

21. For 1960, the ratio of minutes/mile values for the 1-mile run to that for the 440-yard dash is roughly:

    A. 3/4
    B. 4/5
    C. 5/4
    D. 4/3

22. The increase in speed, in meters/minute, for the 2-mile run from 1925 to 1967 is roughly:

    F. 0.3
    G. 10
    H. 30
    J. 100

23. If the trends shown can be expected to hold for later years, then the value of minutes per mile for the 880-yard run in 1980 is expected to be:

    A. 3.5
    B. 3.8
    C. 420
    D. 460

GO ON TO THE NEXT PAGE.

Passage V

Two experiments were performed in which constant amounts of heat were added continuously to samples over a defined period of time. The temperatures of the samples were monitored while the heat was added. The results from the two experiments are shown below.

24. The results of Experiment 1 may be interpreted to show that:

  F. it takes longer to heat a hot sample than a cold one.
  G. the temperature of the sample rises proportionately with time as heat is applied.
  H. temperature is not related to heat.
  J. temperature and time measure the same thing.

25. Experiment 2 differs from Experiment 1 in that:

  A. only the starting temperature is different in the two experiments.
  B. the graph in Experiment 2 is not a straight line; there must have been experimental error.
  C. Experiment 2 has a lower starting temperature and a time period when the temperature does not rise.
  D. in Experiment 2, the heat went off for a while in the middle of the experiment.

26. The experimenter wants to explain the flat part of the graph from Experiment 2. It could represent:

  F. a period when the clock was turned off.
  G. a period when the heat was turned off.
  H. a period when heat was added but some process that did not occur in the first experiment (such as absorption of heat), caused the temperature to remain constant.
  J. a period when less heat was added.

27. The "phase" of the sample changes (an example of a phase change is the melting of a solid, or the boiling of a liquid) in conjunction with the flat part of the graph in Experiment 2. From the temperature data given, the phase change might be:

  A. the boiling of water.
  B. the melting of ice.
  C. the melting of iron.
  D. the boiling of iron.

28. The results of these experiments demonstrate that:

  F. heat and temperature are basically the same.
  G. heat and temperature are not the same.
  H. a pause in heating can lead to a pause in temperature change.
  J. constant heating leads to constant change.

GO ON TO THE NEXT PAGE.

29. If the experimenter extends Experiment 2 to higher temperatures, using water as a sample, which graph best illustrates the expected results?

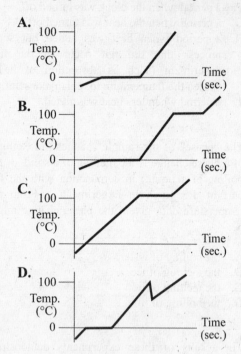

Passage VI

The following chart shows the generalized sequence of early developmental stages (terms in boxes) observed in most vertebrates.

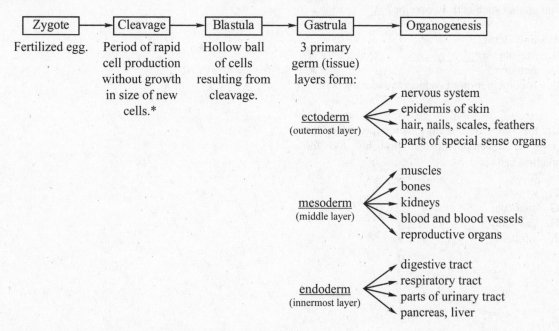

*New cells form as the zygote and its subsequent daughter cells divide and re-divide.

30. According to the chart, the stage of development when the three primary tissue layers form is:

   F. cleavage.
   G. blastula.
   H. gastrula.
   J. organogenesis.

31. Differentiation refers to a period of cell maturation during which time cells become specialized in structure and function. At which stage of development would most differentiation be expected to occur?

   A. Cleavage
   B. Blastula
   C. Gastrula
   D. Organogenesis

32. Based on the information in the diagram, which conclusion is NOT correct?

   F. Vertebrates develop three primary germ layers.
   G. Most bones develop from the innermost primary germ layer.
   H. Diverse structures such as scales, feathers, and hair always develop from the same primary germ layer.
   J. Before an organism can form different primary tissue layers, it must go through a stage in which it is in the form of a hollow ball of cells.

GO ON TO THE NEXT PAGE.

33. If a species of monkey were found to have extraordinary vision due to special receptor cells that were highly sensitive to different colors of light, from which primary germ layer(s) would you predict such cells to develop?

A. Endoderm
B. Mesoderm
C. Ectoderm
D. A combination of endoderm and mesoderm

34. On the basis of the information provided, the stage of development that probably has the smallest cells is:

F. zygote.
G. cleavage.
H. gastrula.
J. adult.

GO ON TO THE NEXT PAGE.

Passage VII

The following are two theories regarding the proportions of chemicals that will react to form products.

Theory 1: Although a chemical reaction is more than simple mixing, the two are similar in that any amounts of reactants may be brought together to form chemical products that contain the same elements as the reactants. For example, in the chemical reaction "hydrogen + oxygen $\Rightarrow$ water," we may use 1 mole of hydrogen and 1 mole of oxygen, or 2 to 1, or 1 to 2, etc. The reaction will adjust to the proportions given.

Theory 2: Only certain proportions of reactants will combine chemically. For example, when hydrogen and oxygen are reacted, the amounts that will combine will be *exactly* 2 grams of hydrogen for every 32 grams of oxygen. We can show, using molecular weights, that these weights of reactants (which correspond to 2 moles of hydrogen and 1 mole of oxygen), imply the following reaction:

$$2H_2 + O_2 \Rightarrow 2H_2O$$

From this statement about the proportions of hydrogens and oxygens that react with each other, we can conclude that two hydrogen molecules must react with a single oxygen molecule to form two molecules of water.

35. Theory 1 does NOT predict which of the following?

  A. 2 moles of zinc may react completely with 2 moles of sulfur.
  B. 2 moles of zinc may react completely with 3 moles of sulfur.
  C. 7 moles of zinc may react completely with 4 moles of sulfur.
  D. If 3 moles of zinc were mixed with 4 moles of sulfur, 1 mole of sulfur would be left unreacted.

36. According to Theory 1, how many moles of water would be produced by the reaction of 2 moles of hydrogen and 1 mole of oxygen?

  F. 1
  G. 2
  H. 4
  J. Cannot be determined from the given information

37. An experimenter finds that when 170 grams of $AgNO_3$ is reacted with 58.5 grams of NaCl to form products, none of the original reactants remain in appreciable amounts. When the original amount of $AgNO_3$ is increased to 175 grams, then all of the NaCl is used up, but 5 grams of $AgNO_3$ remains. This result is:

  A. consistent with Theory 1.
  B. consistent with Theory 2.
  C. consistent with both Theory 1 and Theory 2.
  D. not consistent with either theory.

38. According to Theory 2, how might the remaining 5 grams of $AgNO_3$ be used up?

  F. Add more of the reactant NaCl.
  G. Remove some of the reactant NaCl.
  H. Add even more of the reactant $AgNO_3$.
  J. There is no mechanism for using the 5 grams of $AgNO_3$.

39. An experimenter wishes to determine which theory better fits her data for an experiment in which iron (Fe) is chemically combined with oxygen (O). She finds that 2 moles of Fe will react completely with 2 moles of O; she also finds that 2 moles of Fe will react completely with 3 moles of O. At this point she is confident that Theory 1, which is in opposition to the idea of "definite proportions," is correct. What further experiment might she do to test the success of Theory 1 over Theory 2?

  A. Add 1 mole of Fe to 1 mole of O.
  B. Add 2 moles of Fe to 4 moles of O.
  C. Add 3 moles of Fe to 4.5 moles of O.
  D. Add 4 moles of Fe to 4 moles of O.

GO ON TO THE NEXT PAGE.

40. According to Theory 1, the product of the reaction of hydrogen and oxygen:

    F. is H_2O.
    G. could be anything.
    H. must contain hydrogen and oxygen, but lacks a specific formula.
    J. has a definite proportion of hydrogen to oxygen.

END OF TEST 4
STOP! DO NOT TURN THE PAGE UNTIL YOU ARE TOLD TO DO SO.
DO NOT RETURN TO A PREVIOUS TEST.

5 5 5 5 5 5 5 5 5 5 5 5

WRITING TEST (OPTIONAL)
30 Minutes—1 Essay Prompt

DIRECTIONS: This is a test of your writing skills. Before you begin planning and writing your essay, read the writing prompt carefully to understand the instructions. Your essay will be evaluated on the evidence it provides of your ability to express judgments by taking a position on the issue in the writing prompt; to maintain a focus on the topic throughout the essay; to develop a position by using logical reasoning and supporting ideas; to organize ideas in a logical way; and to use language clearly and effectively according to the conventions of standard written English.

If you finish before time is called, you may review your work. Lay your pencil down immediately when time is called.

Writing Test Prompt

The founders of this country viewed public education as a way to instill civic virtues such as patriotism, honesty, hard work, and personal responsibility. Some people think that schools today do not place enough emphasis on these virtues and say that schools should require a course in civics as part of each year of the high school curriculum. Only by producing a population, they say, that knows the value of these virtues will it be possible to maintain a secure and prosperous nation. Other people think that the purpose of public schools is purely educational and that the schools should not attempt to teach civic virtues. They note that while people tend to agree that patriotism, honesty, hard work, and responsibility are virtuous, people disagree on what these ideas mean in specific circumstances. They point out, for example, that many people think it is unpatriotic to protest when the country is at war while others think that it is patriotic to oppose an unjust or unwise war. Consequently, this group says that teaching about these virtues should be left to family, religion, and other civic organizations. Do you think that schools should teach civic virtues such as patriotism, honesty, hard work, and personal responsibility?

In your essay, take a position on this issue. You may address either of the two points described above, or you may offer an entirely different perspective on the issue. Be sure to use specific reasons and examples to support your analysis.

END OF TEST 5
STOP! DO NOT RETURN TO ANY OTHER TEST.

Practice Test III

DIRECTIONS

Practice Test III consists of five subject tests: English, Mathematics, Reading, Science, and Writing. Calculator use is only permitted on the Mathematics Test.

The items in each multiple-choice test are numbered and the answer choices are lettered. The provided bubble sheet (p. 312) has numbered rows that correspond to the items on the test. Each row contains lettered ovals to match the answer choices for each item on the test. Each numbered row on the bubble sheet has a corresponding item on the test.

For each item, first decide on the best answer choice. Then, locate the row number that corresponds to the item. Next, find the oval in that row that matches the letter of the chosen answer. Then, use a soft lead pencil to fill in the oval. Do not use a ballpoint pen.

Mark only one answer for each item. If you change your mind about the answer choice, thoroughly erase the first mark before marking your new answer.

Note that only responses marked on your bubble sheet will be scored. Your score on each test will be based only on the number of items that are correctly answered during the time allowed for that test. Guessing is not penalized. Therefore, it is to your best advantage to answer every item on the test, even if you must guess.

On the Writing Test, use the provided essay response sheet (p. 309) to write your response to the prompt. (Note that the Writing Test is optional.)

You may work on each test only during the time allowed for that test. If you finish a test before time is called, use the time to review your answer choices or work on items about which you are uncertain. You may not return to a test on which time has already been called and you may not preview another test. You must lay down your pencil immediately when time is called at the end of each test. You may not for any reason fill in or alter ovals for a test after time expires for that test. Violation of these rules will result in immediate disqualification from the exam.

1 1 1 1 1 1 1 1 1 1 1 1 1

ENGLISH TEST
45 Minutes—75 Items

DIRECTIONS: In the passages below, certain parts of the sentences have been underlined and numbered. In the right-hand column, you will find different ways of writing each underlined part; the original version is indicated by the "NO CHANGE" option. There are also items that ask about a section of the passage or the passage as a whole. These items do not refer to an underlined portion of the passage; they are identified by a number or numbers in a box.

For each item, choose the alternative that you consider to be the best. Select the answer choice that best expresses the intended idea, is most acceptable in standard written English, or is most consistent with the overall tone and style of the passage. Read the passage through once before you begin to answer the accompanying items. Finding the answers to certain items may depend on looking at material that appears several sentences beyond the item. So, be sure that you have read far enough ahead before you select your answer choice.

Answers are on page 613, and explanations begin on page 616.

PASSAGE I

Trade in the Northwest Territory

[1]

In 1849, San Francisco became the first official port of entry on the Pacific Coast. In 1851, <u>on account of</u> the rapid growth of lumbering activity and a
₁
corresponding expansion of population in the Northwest Territory, the government established the Puget Sound District of the Bureau of Customs. <u>Nonetheless,</u> smuggling grew rapidly, fostered by the
₂
tempting proximity of British havens and the natural cover afforded by vast forested areas and by the coves and inlets of <u>countless heavy</u> timbered islands.
₃

1. **A.** NO CHANGE
   B. since
   C. because of
   D. for

2. **F.** NO CHANGE
   G. Therefore,
   H. Consequently,
   J. On the contrary,

3. **A.** NO CHANGE
   B. countless, heavy
   C. countless, heavily
   D. countlessly heavy

GO ON TO THE NEXT PAGE.

[2]

Such fears were <u>well foundationed</u>. In 1851, U.S.
4

customs officers <u>seize</u> the Hudson Bay
5

Company's steamer *Beaver* <u>for a technical violation of</u>
6

<u>the revenue laws</u>. This incident signaled an end to the
6

era of unrestricted trade in the Pacific Northwest and

drove some traders on both sides of the international

border into illicit commercial arrangements. British

wool, blankets, and liquor <u>were the principle articles</u>
7

of this trade. <u>In fact,</u> so much British wool was
8

smuggled into the San Juan Islands <u>selling</u> as domestic
9

wool by American <u>sheepmen one</u> naive textbook writer
10

credited San Juan sheep with a world's record annual

production of 150 pounds of wool per animal.

[3]

<u>Although</u> American settlers in the Northwest
11

4. F. NO CHANGE
G. well founded
H. founded well
J. well found

5. A. NO CHANGE
B. seized
C. were seizing
D. have seized

6. F. NO CHANGE
G. on account of violating the revenue laws
H. for technically being in violation of the revenue laws
J. in that they were in technical violation of the revenue laws

7. A. NO CHANGE
B. were the principal articles
C. was the principle article
D. was the principal article

8. F. NO CHANGE
G. Furthermore,
H. Moreover,
J. On the contrary,

9. A. NO CHANGE
B. and sold
C. and would be sold
D. to sell

10. F. NO CHANGE
G. sheepmen, one
H. sheepmen that one
J. sheepmen, and a

11. A. NO CHANGE
B. Since
C. Therefore
D. Thus

GO ON TO THE NEXT PAGE.

Territory <u>welcomed</u> the assertion of national control to
₁₂

the forty-ninth parallel, they were less amenable to

restrictions on the trade with Vancouver Island. They

wanted the duty-free rum and woolens offered by the

British <u>but were fearing</u> that the imposition and
₁₃

enforcement of permanent tariffs on goods from British

North America <u>might be resulting in the losing</u> of
₁₄

British markets for American products.

12. **F.** NO CHANGE
    G. welcoming
    H. would welcome
    J. were welcomed by

13. **A.** NO CHANGE
    B. and were fearing
    C. and was fearful
    D. but feared

14. **F.** NO CHANGE
    G. might result in the losing
    H. might result in the loss
    J. results in the loss

Items 15 and 16 ask about the preceding passage as a whole.

---

15. Which of the following represents the most logical order of the three paragraphs?

    A. 1, 2, 3
    B. 1, 3, 2
    C. 2, 3, 1
    D. 3, 1, 2

16. Which of the following does NOT represent a technique used in the development of the essay?

    F. Narrative
    G. Example
    H. Statistics
    J. Quotations

PASSAGE II

Mapping the Cosmos

One of the beauties of astronomy <u>is that one does</u>
₁₇

<u>not have to be an expert to enjoy it</u>. Anyone can step
₁₇

outside on a clear, moonless night, gaze at thousands

17. **A.** NO CHANGE
    B. is the not having to be an expert to enjoy it
    C. is that the enjoying of it does not have to be done by an expert
    D. is that one doesn't necessarily have to be an expert in order to derive some enjoyment from it

GO ON TO THE NEXT PAGE.

of stars shining across the vast interstellar spaces, and
                                                    __18__

then one can become intoxicated by a heady mix of
_____
     18

grandeur and existential chill. The same questions

come to mind time and again, how far away are the
                             _____
                               19

stars? How many are there? Are they strewn endlessly

through space, or are we a part of an island universe of

suns ending abruptly somewhere out there in the black
     _____
       20

ocean of space?

    It has been the sometimes heroic and often

frustrating task of astronomers since the dawn of

science to chart our position in the cosmic ocean. In
        _____
          21

the twentieth century, significant progress had been
                                            _____
                                              22

made in constructing an accurate map of the cosmos.
____
 22

We know, for example, that our solar system is part of

a much larger system of hundreds of billions of stars.

As such, this system is the Milky Way Galaxy, a huge
_____
    23

disk of stars and gas. We also know that ours is not

the only galaxy in the universe. As far as the largest

telescopes in the world can see, there are galaxies in

every direction. The nearest galaxies to our own are the
                ____
                 24

18. F. NO CHANGE
   G. spaces—and became
   H. spaces, and become
   J. spaces and becomes

19. A. NO CHANGE
   B. again and how
   C. again how
   D. again. How

20. F. NO CHANGE
   G. that ends
   H. that end
   J. ended

21. A. NO CHANGE
   B. charting
   C. having charted
   D. who charted

22. F. NO CHANGE
   G. was made
   H. is made
   J. will be made

23. A. NO CHANGE
   B. Obviously, this
   C. Doubtless, this
   D. This

24. F. NO CHANGE
   G. These
   H. (Begin a new paragraph here rather than after "skies") The
   J. (Begin a new paragraph here rather than after "skies") As the

GO ON TO THE NEXT PAGE.

Magellanic Clouds; the "crown jewels" of the southern
₂₅
skies.

Since they are so near, they offer a laboratory in
which astronomers can study the evolution of stars and
galaxies. The nearest large galaxy to the Milky Way is
the Andromeda Galaxy, which is about two million
light years away. It is a giant spiral galaxy, much like
₂₆
our own in size, shape, and number and type of stars.

This nearby sister galaxy provides to us an opportunity
₂₇
to get a bird's eye view of a galaxy much like our

own—in effect, to see ourselves as others do.
₂₈

25. **A.** NO CHANGE
    B. Clouds, the crown jewels
    C. Clouds which is the "crown jewels"
    D. Clouds, the "crown jewels"

26. **F.** NO CHANGE
    G. much as
    H. like much
    J. much the same like

27. **A.** NO CHANGE
    B. provides us
    C. provide us
    D. providing to us

28. **F.** NO CHANGE
    G. to see ourselves the way other people tend to see us
    H. so that we would be seeing ourselves the way other people would be seeing us
    J. so that in this way we would see ourselves as others do

Item 29 asks about the preceding passage as a whole.

29. Which of the following is NOT one of the reasons the author poses a series of questions in the first paragraph?

    A. To give the reader a sense of the "grandeur and existential chill"
    B. To stimulate the reader's interest in astronomy
    C. To give specific examples of questions about the cosmos that are still unanswered
    D. To alert the reader that answers to these questions will follow later in the passage

GO ON TO THE NEXT PAGE.

PASSAGE III

A Brief History of the Mercury Space Program

The first astronauts entered the Mercury program in April 1959. They were volunteer, military pilots, graduated of test pilot schools. Each were required having a bachelor's degree in engineering (or its equivalent) and at least 1,500 hours of jet time. Of the first group of sixty candidates called to Washington to hear about the program, more than 80 percent volunteered. Only seven got chosen. (Officials

assumed that no more than seven men would have the opportunity to fly.) ☐33 These men were true

pioneers, they volunteered at a time when the plans for space travel were only on paper and no one knew what the chance of success was.

Scientists were able to learn from each failure.

30. F. NO CHANGE
    G. pilots graduates
    H. pilots; graduates
    J. pilots, graduates

31. A. NO CHANGE
    B. was required to have
    C. required having
    D. had been required to have

32. F. NO CHANGE
    G. were
    H. had been
    J. has been

33. Is the second use of parentheses in the first paragraph appropriate?
    A. Yes, because the information explains something the author said but is not vital to the understanding of the passage.
    B. Yes, because the information contained in the parentheses is irrelevant to the passage.
    C. No, because the material is vital to the understanding of the author's main argument.
    D. No, because an entire sentence should never be placed in parentheses.

34. F. NO CHANGE
    G. pioneers but
    H. pioneers yet
    J. pioneers. They

35. Which of the following phrases would best replace the word "scientists" to provide a transition from the first to the second paragraph?
    A. It was lucky that the men volunteered because scientists
    B. There were failures as well as successes in the Mercury program, but scientists
    C. Since the chances for success were unknown, scientists
    D. Since the volunteers were also engineers, scientists

GO ON TO THE NEXT PAGE.

Fortunately they had these failures early in the program. The astronauts and the animal passengers as well were

flown without mishap when their time came for them.

[3]

The most spectacular failure in the Mercury [38]

program came to be known as the "tower flight."

The escape tower, the parachutes, and the peroxide fuel

were all deployed on the launching pad in front of the

domestic and international press. A relatively simple

ground-circuit defect in the Redstone launch vehicle

caused the main rocket engine to ignite and then

shutting down immediately after liftoff from the

launching pad. The "flight" lasted only a second and

covered a distance of inside only two inches. [41]

One of the requirements of the Mercury program

36. **F.** NO CHANGE
    G. Fortunately, they had these failures occurring
    H. These failures occurred fortunately
    J. Fortunately, these failures occurred

37. **A.** NO CHANGE
    B. the time for them finally came
    C. their time finally came for them
    D. their time came

38. Is the use of the word "spectacular" in the first sentence of the third paragraph appropriate?
    F. Yes, because the author is using the word in an ironic sense.
    G. Yes, because the author obviously disapproves of the Mercury program.
    H. No, because the reader might be misled about goals of the Mercury program.
    J. No, because the failure cited was caused by a simple defect.

39. **A.** NO CHANGE
    B. relative and simple
    C. relative simple
    D. simple relatively

40. **F.** NO CHANGE
    G. and then will shut
    H. and then they shut
    J. and then to shut

41. The author put the word "flight" in quotation marks because:
    A. the article is quoting from another source.
    B. there was no real flight at all.
    C. the word is a technical term used by astronauts.
    D. the word is often repeated in the passage.

42. **F.** NO CHANGE
    G. (Do NOT begin a new paragraph) One of the requirements
    H. (Do NOT begin a new paragraph) One requirement
    J. (Do NOT begin a new paragraph) A requirement

GO ON TO THE NEXT PAGE.

was that an animal <u>had to precede man into space</u>. The
                                    43
flight of Ham, the chimpanzee, was a major milestone

in the program. Again, there were some problems.

The pickup of the spacecraft was delayed, and <u>water</u>
                                                 44
<u>had leaked into</u> the capsule. Ham, however, was
      44

eventually rescued <u>unharmed</u>.
                       45

     Sending a man into zero gravity was among the

greatest medical experiments of all time. Fortunately,

all astronauts found the weightlessness to be no

problem. All <u>returning</u> to Earth with no medical
                46
difficulties whatsoever. In this area, the only question

left unanswered by the Mercury program was how long

man <u>will tolerate</u> weightlessness. It <u>seemed like,</u>
        47   48
however, that longer flights would require only that

astronauts <u>to have</u> suitable methods of exercise and
              49
nutrition. [50]

43. **A.** NO CHANGE
   B. had to be the one to precede man in space
   C. was going to have to go into space before
      man
   D. needed to be the one to go into space before
      man did

44. **F.** NO CHANGE
   G. water leaked into
   H. water leaks in
   J. leaking water into

45. **A.** NO CHANGE
   B. (Place before the word "was")
   C. (Place before the word "eventually")
   D. (Place before the word "rescued")

46. **F.** NO CHANGE
   G. return
   H. returned
   J. will return

47. **A.** NO CHANGE
   B. will be able to tolerate
   C. was able to tolerate
   D. could tolerate

48. **F.** NO CHANGE
   G. seemed,
   H. seemed as,
   J. seemed to be,

49. **A.** NO CHANGE
   B. have
   C. had had
   D. are sure to have

50. Which of the following might be an appropriate
    concluding sentence for the essay?

   F. Although the Mercury program had some
      failures, it was on the whole a successful part
      of the space program.
   G. Although the Mercury program had some
      successes, it was on the whole a failure.
   H. Many people have objected that it is immoral
      to use animals in testing programs.
   J. Science fiction writers have often written
      about space travel.

GO ON TO THE NEXT PAGE.

PASSAGE IV

Advances in Modern Medicine

It was not until the nineteenth century that

medicine was able, in any broad and real way, to help
                                              51

the suffering individual. During this century, technical

advances aided the diagnostician and also the surgeon,
                                        52

and the beginnings of an understanding of the

fundamental mechanisms of disease had been
                                        53

emerging. All aspects of medicine—from the research
53

laboratory to the operating table—was enjoying the
                                       54

benefits of the rigorous application of the scientific

method.

By the end of the nineteenth century, a person's

chances were fairly good that a doctor could not only

give a name to his medical complaint yet probably had
                                         55

an elementary understanding of what it was and how it

progressed. With somewhat more luck, the doctor

could select the proper treatment and he could also
                                         56

mitigate the symptoms if not cure the disease
56

altogether.

This transition to modern medicine depended on

three important advances. First, it required an

understanding of the true nature and origin of disease.

Second, it required that an organized body of standard

medical practice be available to guide physicians in
                    57

51. A. NO CHANGE
     B. way of help
     C. way to help
     D. way, of helping

52. F. NO CHANGE
     G. as well as
     H. with
     J. as opposed to

53. A. NO CHANGE
     B. was emerging
     C. were emerging
     D. emerged

54. F. NO CHANGE
     G. were enjoying
     H. is enjoying
     J. enjoys

55. A. NO CHANGE
     B. but probably had
     C. consequently probably has
     D. but, probably would have

56. F. NO CHANGE
     G. but could mitigate
     H. and mitigate
     J. and can mitigate

57. A. NO CHANGE
     B. was available to
     C. is available for
     D. be available as

GO ON TO THE NEXT PAGE.

diagnosis and treatment of disease. Last, <u>it presupposes</u>
58

a degree of medical technology never before available.

<u>Among the more dramatic</u> nineteenth century
59

medical advances were those in the field of human

physiology. ⬚60 In 1822, an obscure American army

camp surgeon practicing medicine <u>near where the</u>
61

<u>Canadian frontier is</u> was transformed almost overnight
61

into a specialist on the mechanism of human digestion.

The physician, William Beaumont, was called to treat

a young trapper, accidentally shot in the stomach.

<u>Beaumont's operating skill</u> saved the boy's life but the
62

patient was left with an abnormal opening leading to

the stomach. To Beaumont's credit, he recognized this

unique opportunity to study the human digestive

<u>process, but</u> for the next ten years he conducted
63

hundreds of experiments with the reluctant cooperation

of his not-so-willing patient.

From his experiments, Beaumont was able to

describe the physiology of digestion, demonstrating

---

58. **F.** NO CHANGE
G. it is presupposed
H. it presupposed
J. they presuppose

59. **A.** NO CHANGE
B. (Do NOT begin a new paragraph) Among the more dramatic
C. Since
D. (Do NOT begin a new paragraph) Since

60. Which of the following correctly describes the function of the first sentence of this paragraph?
F. It introduces a topic that has nothing to do with the material discussed in the first three paragraphs.
G. It introduces material that will contradict what was discussed in the first three paragraphs.
H. It provides a transition that sets up a contrast to the material that came before.
J. It provides a transition that moves from a general discussion to a more specific, but related topic.

61. **A.** NO CHANGE
B. near where the Canadian frontier is,
C. near where the Canadian frontier was
D. near the Canadian frontier

62. **F.** NO CHANGE
G. (Begin a new paragraph) Beaumont's operating skill
H. The skill of Beaumont at operating
J. (Begin a new paragraph) The skill of Beaumont at operating

63. **A.** NO CHANGE
B. process, and
C. process,
D. process. But

GO ON TO THE NEXT PAGE.

the characteristics of gastric motility <u>and describe</u> the
₆₄ properties of gastric juice. He determined that the
stomach contained hydrochloric acid and that it broke
down food by a chemical process and not by
maceration or putrefaction. Beaumont's pioneering
work made him a famous man. The young trapper did
not fare as well; he was forced to tour medical schools
as "the man with the window in his stomach."

64. **F.** NO CHANGE
    G. to describe
    H. that describe
    J. and describing

GO ON TO THE NEXT PAGE.

PASSAGE V

All About Babies

Newborn babies are not the passive creatures most
people assume him to be. Recent research shows that the
                    65

newborn comes well-endowed of charm and full potentia
                           66
for social graces. His eyes are equipped with surprisingly
good vision. Shortly after birth, he begins to watch his
mother's face, which he soon comes to recognize. He
also learns to know her voice and will turn toward her
when he hears it. This is about the time when affection
               67
begins. The infant's cry alerts the mother and causes a

biological including an emotional reaction. The infant's
          68
ability to cling and cuddle communicates a pleasurable

warmth to the mother, and the infant's odor is
pleasant and uniquely its own. The newborn also
smiles. The human infant, unfortunately, is in
                        69   70
possession of a collection of attributes that are
70   71
guaranteeing its attractiveness.
71

        Although there is some argument about whether

the child sparks the development of love or whether or
                                     72
not a special physiological state of the mother prompts
72

her to interact with the new infant. But most
                            73
researchers agree that the newborn does mold or trigger
adult behavior. The neonate organizes the mother's

65. A. NO CHANGE
     B. he was
     C. them to be
     D. it is

66. F. NO CHANGE
     G. for
     H. with
     J. by

67. A. NO CHANGE
     B. it, this
     C. it this
     D. it

68. F. NO CHANGE
     G. and
     H. with
     J. but

69. A. NO CHANGE
     B. on the other hand
     C. nevertheless
     D. in fact

70. F. NO CHANGE
     G. possessed
     H. possesses
     J. are in possession of

71. A. NO CHANGE
     B. guaranteed
     C. guarantees
     D. guarantee

72. F. NO CHANGE
     G. or whether
     H. and whether if
     J. or whether if

73. A. NO CHANGE
     B. infant: but most
     C. infant. Most
     D. infant, most

GO ON TO THE NEXT PAGE.

behavior by crying and by eye-to-eye contact. The

newborn is not a passive creature at all.

Items 74 and 75 ask about the preceding passage as a whole.

74. Which of the following best describes the function of the last sentence of the essay?

    F. It introduces a new topic for the reader to investigate.

    G. It contradicts everything that was said before.

    H. It reiterates the main theme of the passage.

    J. It establishes the author as an authority.

75. Which of the following best describes the overall development of the essay?

    A. A comparison and contrast using anecdotes

    B. A narrative using examples

    C. A description using statistics

    D. An argument using examples

END OF TEST 1

STOP! DO NOT TURN THE PAGE UNTIL TOLD TO DO SO.

MATHEMATICS TEST
60 Minutes—60 Items

DIRECTIONS: Solve each item and choose the correct answer choice. Then, fill in the corresponding oval on the bubble sheet.

Allocate time wisely. Try to solve as many items as possible, returning to skipped items if time permits.

Calculator use is permitted on this test; however, some items are best solved without the use of a calculator.

Note: Unless otherwise stated, assume all of the following.

1. Illustrative figures are NOT necessarily drawn to scale.
2. The word *average* indicates arithmetic mean.
3. The word *line* indicates a straight line.
4. Geometric figures lie in a plane.

Answers are on page 614, and explanations begin on page 623.

---

1. A barrel contained 5.75 liters of water and 4.5 liters evaporated. How many liters of water remain in the barrel?

   A. 0.75
   B. 1.25
   C. 1.75
   D. 2.25
   E. 13.25

2. Which of the following expressions correctly describes the mathematical relationship below?

   3 less than the product of 4 times x

   F. $4x - 3$
   G. $3x - 4$
   H. $4(x - 3)$
   J. $3(4x)$
   K. $\frac{4x}{3}$

3. If $\frac{3}{4}$ of x is 36, then $\frac{1}{3}$ of $x = ?$

   A. 9
   B. 12
   C. 16
   D. 24
   E. 42

DO YOUR FIGURING HERE.

GO ON TO THE NEXT PAGE.

4. In the figure below, what is the value of $x + y$?

    DO YOUR FIGURING HERE.

    F. 45
    G. 60
    H. 75
    J. 90
    K. 120

5. If n is a multiple of 3, which of the following expressions is also a multiple of 3?

    A. $2 + n$
    B. $2 - n$
    C. $2n - 1$
    D. $2n + 1$
    E. $2n + 3$

6. Which of the following is NOT equal to the ratio of 2 whole numbers?

    F. $\left(\frac{1}{5}\right)^2$
    G. 5%
    H. $\frac{1}{5}$
    J. 0.25
    K. $\frac{\sqrt{5}}{1}$

7. If the area of a square is 16 square inches, what is the perimeter, in inches?

    A. 2
    B. 4
    C. 8
    D. 16
    E. 32

8. If $12 + x = 36 - y$, then $x + y = $?

    F. −48
    G. −24
    H. 3
    J. 24
    K. 48

GO ON TO THE NEXT PAGE.

9. What is the greatest factor of the expression $3x^2y^3z + 6x^3yz^3 + 2xy^2z^2$?

   A. $3x^2y^2z^2$
   B. $2x^2y^2z^2$
   C. $x^3y^3z^3$
   D. xyz
   E. xz

DO YOUR FIGURING HERE.

10. Depending on the value of k, the expression $3k + 4k + 5k + 6k + 7k$ may or may not be divisible by 7. Which of the terms, when eliminated from the expression, guarantees that the resulting expression is divisible by 7 for every positive integer k?

    F. $3k$
    G. $4k$
    H. $5k$
    J. $6k$
    K. $7k$

11. If $\frac{1}{3} < x < \frac{3}{8}$, which of the following is a possible value of x?

    A. $\frac{3}{16}$
    B. $\frac{17}{48}$
    C. $\frac{9}{24}$
    D. $\frac{5}{12}$
    E. $\frac{1}{2}$

12. If $x^2 - y^2 = 3$ and $x - y = 3$, then $x + y = ?$

    F. 0
    G. 1
    H. 2
    J. 3
    K. 9

GO ON TO THE NEXT PAGE.

13. If *n* is a positive integer, which of the following *must* be an even integer?

    A. $n+1$
    B. $3n+1$
    C. $3n+2$
    D. n^2+1
    E. n^2+n

14. If the area of a square inscribed in a circle is 16 square centimeters, what is the area of the circle, in square centimeters?

    F. 2π
    G. 4π
    H. 8π
    J. 16π
    K. 32π

15. Ellen bought a CD player on sale for 25 percent off the usual price of $120. If the store also collected an 8-percent sales tax on the sale price of the CD player, how much did Ellen pay for the CD player, including sales tax?

    A. $106.30
    B. $101.40
    C. $97.20
    D. $95.10
    E. $88.44

16. A certain mixture of gravel and sand consists of 2.5 kilograms of gravel and 12.5 kilograms of sand. What percent of the mixture, by weight, is gravel?

    F. 10%
    G. $16\frac{2}{3}\%$
    H. 20%
    J. 25%
    K. $33\frac{1}{3}\%$

DO YOUR FIGURING HERE.

GO ON TO THE NEXT PAGE.

17. The figure below is the top-view of a folding room divider, hinged at P and Q. If sections PR and QS are moved as shown until R and S meet, what will be the enclosed area, in square feet? (Ignore the thickness of the hinges and the screen's sections.)

   A. 6
   B. 12
   C. 6π
   D. 24
   E. 12π

18. Motorcycle A averages 40 kilometers per liter of gasoline while Motorcycle B averages 50 kilometers per liter. If the cost of gasoline is $2 per liter, what will be the difference in the cost of operating the 2 motorcycles for 300 kilometers?

   F. $3
   G. $6
   H. $12
   J. $15
   K. $20

19. If $f(x) = x^2 - 2x + 1$, then what is $f(f(3))$?

   A. 3
   B. 9
   C. 14
   D. 27
   E. 39

20. For a positive integer k, which of the following equals $6k + 3$?

   F. $\frac{1}{2}(k+1)$
   G. $\frac{1}{k} + 4$
   H. $2k + 1$
   J. $3(k + 1)$
   K. $3(2k + 1)$

DO YOUR FIGURING HERE.

GO ON TO THE NEXT PAGE.

21. Mailing a letter costs x cents for the first ounce and y cents for every additional ounce or fraction of an ounce. What is the cost, in cents, to mail a letter weighing a whole number of ounces, w?

    A. $w(x+y)$
    B. $x(w-y)$
    C. $x(x-1)+y(w-1)$
    D. $x+wy$
    E. $x+y(w-1)$

22. $|-3| \cdot |2| \cdot \left|-\frac{1}{2}\right| + (-4) = ?$

    F. -1
    G. 0
    H. 1
    J. $\frac{3}{2}$
    K. 4

23. In the figure below, the area of the square $OPQR$ is 2 square inches, what is the area of the circle with center O (in square inches)?

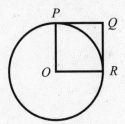

    A. $\frac{\pi}{4}$
    B. $\pi\sqrt{2}$
    C. 2π
    D. $2\sqrt{2}\pi$
    E. 4π

GO ON TO THE NEXT PAGE.

24. Which of the following *must* be an odd number?

    I. The product of a prime number and a prime number

    II. The sum of a prime number and a prime number

    III. The product of an odd number and another odd number

    F. I only
    G. III only
    H. I and II only
    J. II and III only
    K. I, II, and III

DO YOUR FIGURING HERE.

25. What is the area of the shaded portion of the figure below, expressed in terms of a and b?

    A. $a(b-a)$
    B. $a(a-b)$
    C. $b(a-b)$
    D. $b(b-a)$
    E. ab

26. $\sqrt{(43-7)(29+7)} = ?$

    F. $3\sqrt{3}$
    G. 6
    H. 36
    J. 42
    K. 1,296

GO ON TO THE NEXT PAGE.

27. A concrete mixture contains 4 cubic yards (yd.^{3}) of cement for every 20 yd.^{3} of grit. If a mason orders 50 yd.^{3} of cement, how much grit (in yd.^{3}) should he order if he is to use all of the cement?

    A. 250
    B. 200
    C. 100
    D. 80
    E. 10

DO YOUR FIGURING HERE.

28. In the figure below, $\overline{QT} = \overline{QR}$. If $x° = 120°$, then $y = ?$

    F. 30
    G. 60
    H. 75
    J. 90
    K. 120

29. If $\frac{x}{y} = -1$, then $x + y = ?$

    A. 2
    B. 1
    C. 0
    D. −1
    E. −2

GO ON TO THE NEXT PAGE.

30. According to the table below, which fabric costs the LEAST per yard?

Fabric	Cost
F	3 yards for $8
G	2 yards for $6
H	4 yards for $9
J	5 yards for $7
K	6 yards for $4

F. F
G. G
H. H
J. J
K. K

31. In $\triangle PQR$ below, if $\overline{PQ} \parallel \overline{ST}$, then $y = ?$

A. 20
B. 40
C. 45
D. 50
E. 55

32. $\dfrac{10^3(10^5 + 10^5)}{10^4} = ?$

F. 10^4

G. 10^6

H. $2(10^2)$

J. $2(10^4)$

K. $2(10^9)$

GO ON TO THE NEXT PAGE.

33. What is the solution set for the following equation: $x^2 - 5x + 4 = 0$?

    A. $\{-4, -1\}$
    B. $\{-3, -1\}$
    C. $\{-1, 3\}$
    D. $\{1, 4\}$
    E. $\{2, 3\}$

DO YOUR FIGURING HERE.

34. The average of seven different positive integers is 12. What is the greatest that any one integer could be?

    F. 19
    G. 31
    H. 47
    J. 54
    K. 63

35. If $x = b + 4$ and $y = b - 3$, then in terms of x and y, $b = ?$

    A. $x + y - 1$
    B. $x + y + 1$
    C. $x - y - 1$
    D. $\frac{x + y + 1}{2}$
    E. $\frac{x + y - 1}{2}$

36. If $5x = 3y = z$, and x, y, and z are positive integers, all of the following must be an integer EXCEPT:

    F. $\frac{z}{xy}$
    G. $\frac{z}{5}$
    H. $\frac{z}{3}$
    J. $\frac{z}{15}$
    K. $\frac{x}{3}$

37. What is the width of a rectangle with an area of $48x^2$ and a length of $24x$?

    A. 2
    B. $2x$
    C. $24x$
    D. $2x^2$
    E. $3x^2$

GO ON TO THE NEXT PAGE.

38. If $x = \frac{1}{y+1}$ and $y \neq -1$, then $y = ?$

DO YOUR FIGURING HERE.

  F. $x+1$
  G. x
  H. $\frac{x+1}{x}$
  J. $\frac{x-1}{x}$
  K. $\frac{1-x}{x}$

39. In the figure below, if the area of the triangle is 54, then $x = ?$

  A. $3\sqrt{3}$
  B. $2\sqrt{3}$
  C. 3
  D. 2
  E. $\sqrt{2}$

40. A drawer contains 4 green socks, 6 blue socks, and 10 white socks. If socks are pulled out of the drawer at random and not replaced, what is the minimum number of socks that must be pulled out of the drawer to *guarantee* that 2 of every color have been pulled out of the drawer?

  F. 6
  G. 7
  H. 11
  J. 12
  K. 18

GO ON TO THE NEXT PAGE.

41. In the figure below, the circle with center O has a radius that is 4 units long. If the area of the shaded region is 14π square-units, what is the value of x?

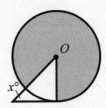

A. 90
B. 75
C. 60
D. 55
E. 45

42. In the figure below, a circle is inscribed in a square that is in turn inscribed in a larger circle. What is the ratio of the area of the larger circle to that of the smaller circle?

F. 8:1
G. 4:1
H. $2\sqrt{2}$:1
J. 2:1
K. $\sqrt{2}$:1

43. $2^0 + 2^3 - 2^{-2} = ?$

A. 4
B. $6\frac{1}{4}$
C. 7
D. $8\frac{3}{4}$
E. $9\frac{3}{4}$

GO ON TO THE NEXT PAGE.

44. The graph of $y = x^2 - 3$ is a parabola with the axis of symmetry given by the equation $x = 0$. Which of the following are the (x,y) coordinates of the point on the parabola that is symmetric, with respect to the axis of symmetry, to the point with coordinates $(-1,-2)$?

    F. $(-2,-1)$
    G. $(-1,2)$
    H. $(0,-3)$
    J. $(1,-2)$
    K. $(1,2)$

45. If 2 lines with equations $y = m_1 x + b_1$ and $y = m_2 x + b_2$ are perpendicular, which of the following *must* be true?

    A. $m_1 = m_2$
    B. $m_1 m_2 = 1$
    C. $m_1 m_2 = -1$
    D. $b_1 = b_2$
    E. $b_1 b_2 = -1$

46. The figure below has lengths as marked, in units. What is the area, in square units, of the figure?

    F. 36
    G. 48
    H. 56
    J. 64
    K. 80

DO YOUR FIGURING HERE.

GO ON TO THE NEXT PAGE.

DO YOUR FIGURING HERE.

47. For all $x > 0$ and $y > 0$, the radical expression
$\dfrac{\sqrt{x}}{2\sqrt{x} - \sqrt{y}}$ is equivalent to:

   A. $\dfrac{2\sqrt{x} - \sqrt{y}}{2}$

   B. $\dfrac{2\sqrt{x} + \sqrt{y}}{4xy}$

   C. $\dfrac{2x + \sqrt{xy}}{2x - y}$

   D. $\dfrac{2x + \sqrt{xy}}{4x - y}$

   E. $\dfrac{4x + \sqrt{xy}}{4x - y}$

48. In the figure below, if $l_1 \parallel l_2$, then $x = ?$

   F. 20
   G. 30
   H. 45
   J. 65
   K. 130

49. The graph of $y = 2[\cos(2x)] + 2$ intersects the y-axis where $y = ?$

   A. 0
   B. 2
   C. 3
   D. 4
   E. 5

GO ON TO THE NEXT PAGE.

50. In the figure below, *PQRS* is a square, and each of the 4 circles has a radius of *r*. What fractional part of the area of the square is shaded?

F. $\dfrac{\pi - 4}{2}$

G. $\dfrac{4 - \pi}{4}$

H. $\dfrac{\pi}{4}$

J. $\dfrac{4}{\pi}$

K. π

51. If $0° < \theta < 90°$, $\dfrac{\sin^2(\theta) + \cos^2(\theta)}{\sin(\theta)}$ is equivalent to:

A. $\sin(\theta)$

B. $\cos(\theta)$

C. $\csc(\theta)$

D. $\tan(\theta)$

E. $\cot(\theta)$

52. In the figure below, ABC is a right triangle. If $\sin(35°) \approx 0.57$ and $\tan(55°) \approx 1.4$, which of the following is the best approximation of the length of $\overline{AC}$?

DO YOUR FIGURING HERE.

F. 3.42
G. 4.28
H. 8.57
J. 10.50
K. 12.25

53. What are the values for which $\frac{x(x+3)}{(x-1)(x+2)}$ is undefined?

A. −3 only
B. −2 only
C. 1 only
D. −2 and 1 only
E. −3, −2, and 1

54. What is the maximum value of $3y$ for x and y satisfying the system of inequalities below?

$$x \geq 0$$
$$y \geq 0$$
$$x + y \leq 6$$

F. −3
G. 0
H. 6
J. 12
K. 18

GO ON TO THE NEXT PAGE.

55. Which of the following graphs in the standard (x,y) coordinate plane correctly shows the points on the graph of $y = \left| x^2 - 3 \right|$ for $x = -1, 0,$ and 1?

DO YOUR FIGURING HERE.

A.

B.

C.

D.

E.

GO ON TO THE NEXT PAGE.

56. The figure below is a graph of which of the following equations?

DO YOUR FIGURING HERE.

F. $y = -3x + 5$
G. $y = -2x + 2$
H. $y = -\frac{3}{2}x - 2$
J. $y = \frac{2}{3}x + 3$
K. $y = x + 2$

57. The roots of equation $ax^2 + bx + c = 0$ are $\frac{-3+\sqrt{5}}{2}$ and $\frac{-3-\sqrt{5}}{2}$. Which of the following could be the equation?

A. $x^2 + 3x + 1 = 0$
B. $x^2 - 3x + 1 = 0$
C. $x^2 + 3x - 1 = 0$
D. $x^2 - 3x - 1 = 0$
E. $-x^2 + 3x + 1 = 0$

58. The relation defined by the set of ordered pairs $\{(0,3), (2,1), (3,0), (-1,2), (0,5),$ and $(-2,5)\}$ is NOT a function. Deleting which of the ordered pairs will make the resulting set a function?

F. $(0,3)$
G. $(2,1)$
H. $(3,0)$
J. $(-1,2)$
K. $(-2,5)$

GO ON TO THE NEXT PAGE.

59. Trapezoid *ABCD* has lengths, in units, and angle measures as marked in the figure below. What is the area of the trapezoid *ABCD*?

DO YOUR FIGURING HERE.

A. $18+8\sqrt{2}$
B. $18+8\sqrt{3}$
C. $36+8\sqrt{2}$
D. $36+8\sqrt{3}$
E. 42

60. What is $\tan(\theta)$ if $\sin(\theta) = \frac{3}{5}$ and $\cot(\theta) = \frac{4}{3}$?

F. $\frac{9}{20}$
G. $\frac{3}{4}$
H. $\frac{7}{8}$
J. $\frac{5}{3}$
K. $\frac{20}{9}$

END OF TEST 2
STOP! DO NOT TURN PAGE UNTIL TOLD TO DO SO.
DO NOT RETURN TO THE PREVIOUS TEST.

3 3 3 3 3 3 3 3 3 3 3 3

READING TEST
35 Minutes—40 Items

DIRECTIONS: The passages presented in the test are each followed by a set of items. Read the passage and choose the best answer for each item. Fill in the corresponding oval on your bubble sheet. You may refer to the passage as often as necessary to answer the passage items.

Answers are on page 615, and explanations begin on page 631.

Passage I

HUMANITIES: This passage explores the contributions of Josquin des Prez to Western music.

Until Josquin des Prez (1440–1521), Western music was liturgical, designed as an accompaniment to worship. Like the intricately carved gargoyles perched atop medieval cathedrals beyond sight of any human,
5 music was composed to please God before anybody else; its dominant theme was reverence. Emotion was there, but it was the grief of Mary standing at the foot of the Cross, the joy of the faithful hailing Christ's resurrection. Even the secular music of the Middle
10 Ages was tied to predetermined patterns that sometimes seemed to stand in the way of individual expression.

While keeping one foot firmly planted in the divine world, Josquin stepped with the other into the
15 human world. He scored magnificent masses, but also newly expressive motets such as the lament of David over his son Absalom or the "Deploration d'Ockeghem," a dirge on the death of Ockeghem, the greatest master before Josquin, a motet written all in
20 black notes, and one of the most profoundly moving scores of the Renaissance. Josquin was the first composer to set psalms to music. But alongside *Benedicite omnia opera Domini Domino* ("Bless the Lord, all ye works of the Lord") he put *El Grillo* ("The cricket is a
25 good singer who manages long poems") and *Allegez moy* ("Solace me, sweet pleasant brunette"). Martin Luther praised Josquin, for his music blends respect for tradition with a rebel's willingness to risk the horizon. What Galileo was to science, Josquin was to music.
30 While preserving their allegiance to God, both asserted a new importance for man.

Why then should Josquin languish in relative obscurity? The answer has to do with the separation of concept from performance in music. In fine art,
35 concept and performance are one; both the art lover and the art historian have thousands of years of paintings, drawings, and sculptures to study and enjoy. Similarly with literature: Poetry, fiction, drama, and criticism survive on the printed page or in manuscript
40 for judgment and admiration by succeeding generations. But musical notation on a page is not art, no matter how lofty or excellent the composer's conception; it is, crudely put, a set of directions for producing art.

45 Being highly symbolic, musical notation requires training before it can even be read, let alone performed. Moreover, because the musical conventions of other days are not ours, translation of a Renaissance score into modern notation brings difficulties of its own. For
50 example, the Renaissance notation of Josquin's day did not designate the tempo at which the music should be played or sung. It did not indicate all flats or sharps; these were sounded in accordance with musician rules, which were capable of transforming major to minor,
55 minor to major, diatonic to chromatic sound, and thus affect melody, harmony, and musical expression. A Renaissance composition might include several parts— but it did not indicate which were to be sung or played, or whether instruments were to be used at all.

60 Thus, Renaissance notation permits several interpretations and an imaginative musician may give an interpretation that is a revelation. But no matter how imaginative, few modern musicians can offer any interpretation of Renaissance music. The public for it is
65 small, limiting the number of musicians who can afford to learn, rehearse, and perform it. Most of those who attempt it at all are students organized in *collegia*

GO ON TO THE NEXT PAGE.

musica whose memberships have a distressing habit of changing every semester, thus preventing directors 70 from maintaining the year-in, year-out continuity required to achieve excellence of performance. Finally, the instruments used in Renaissance times— krummhorns, recorders, rausch-pfeifen, shawms, sackbuts, organettos—must be specially procured.

1. The primary purpose of the passage is to:

   A. introduce the reader to Josquin and account for his relative obscurity.
   B. describe the main features of medieval music and show how Josquin changed them.
   C. place Josquin's music in an historical context and show its influence on later composers.
   D. enumerate the features of Josquin's music and supply critical commentary.

2. The passage contains information that would help answer all of the following items EXCEPT:

   F. What are the titles of some of Josquin's secular compositions?
   G. What are the names of some Renaissance musical instruments?
   H. Who was the greatest composer before Josquin?
   J. What are the names of some of Josquin's most famous students?

3. It can be inferred from the passage that modern musical notation has which of the following characteristics?

   I. The tempo at which a composition is to be played is indicated in the notation.
   II. Whether a note is sharp or a flat is indicated in the notation.
   III. The notation indicates which parts of the music are to be played by which instruments.

   A. I only
   B. II only
   C. I and III only
   D. I, II, and III

4. The author would most likely agree with which of the following statements?

   F. Music is a better art form than painting or sculpture.
   G. Music can be said to exist only when it is being performed.
   H. Josquin was the greatest composer of the Middle Ages.
   J. Renaissance music is superior to music produced in modern times.

5. The passage leads most logically to a proposal to:

   A. establish more *collegia musica*.
   B. study Josquin's compositional techniques in greater detail.
   C. include Renaissance music in college studies.
   D. provide funds for musicians to study and play Josquin.

6. The author cites all of the following as reasons for Josquin's relative obscurity EXCEPT:

   F. the difficulty one encounters in attempting to read his musical notation.
   G. the inability of modern musicians to play instruments of the Renaissance.
   H. the difficulty of procuring unusual instruments needed to play the music.
   J. the lack of public interest in Renaissance music.

7. The author's attitude toward Galileo can best be described as:

   A. admiring.
   B. critical.
   C. accepting.
   D. analytical.

8. Which of the following statements about liturgical music is consistent with the selection?

   F. It is lacking in any emotion.
   G. It is written to entertain people.
   H. It is intended to be reverential.
   J. It treats primarily nonreligious themes.

GO ON TO THE NEXT PAGE.

9. Which of the following is NOT an example of fine art as that term is used in the passage?

    A. A ballet
    B. A novel
    C. A poem
    D. A mural

10. Josquin des Prez is important in the history of music because he:

    F. wrote motets using only black notes.
    G. wrote only nonliturgical music.
    H. wrote both liturgical and nonliturgical music.
    J. invented new musical instruments for his music.

GO ON TO THE NEXT PAGE.

Passage II

PROSE FICTION: In this passage, the character Miss Mix experiences an exciting robbery and learns a great deal about her employer, Mr. Rawjester.

My pupil was a bright little girl, who spoke French with a perfect accent. She said to me: "Miss Mix, did you ever have the *grande passion*? Did you ever feel a fluttering here?" and she placed her hand
5 upon her small chest. "There is to be company here tomorrow," she added, rattling on with childish naiveté, "and papa's sweetheart—Blanche Marabout— is to be here. You know they say she is to be my mamma."

10 What thrill was this shot through me? But I rose calmly, and administering a slight correction to the child, left the apartment.

Blunderbore House, for the next week, was the scene of gaiety and merriment. That portion of the
15 mansion closed with a grating was walled up, and the midnight shrieks no longer troubled me.

But I felt more keenly the degradation of my situation. I was obliged to help Lady Blanche at her toilette and help her to look beautiful. For what? To
20 captivate him? Oh-no, no—but why this sudden thrill and faintness? Did he really love her? I had seen him pinch and swear at her. But I reflected that he had thrown a candlestick at my head, and my foolish heart was reassured.

25 It was a night of festivity, when a sudden message obliged Mr. Rawjester to leave his guests for a few hours. "Make yourselves merry, idiots," he said, under his breath, as he passed me. The door closed and he was gone.

30 A half-hour passed. In the midst of the dancing a shriek was heard, and out of the swaying crowd of fainting women and excited men, a wild figure strode into the room. One glance showed it to be a highwayman, heavily armed, holding a pistol in each
35 hand.

"Let no one pass out of this room!" he said, in a voice of thunder. "The house is surrounded and you cannot escape. The first one who crosses yonder threshold will be shot like a dog. Gentlemen, I'll
40 trouble you to approach in single file, and hand me your purses and watches."

Finding resistance useless, the order was ungraciously obeyed.

"Now, ladies, please to pass up your jewelry and
45 trinkets."

This order was still more ungraciously complied with. As Blanche handed to the bandit captain her bracelet, she endeavored to conceal a diamond necklace, the gift of Mr. Rawjester, in her bosom. But,
50 with a demoniac grin, the powerful brute tore it from its concealment.

It was now my turn. With a beating heart, I made my way to the robber chieftain and sank at his feet. "Oh, sir, I am nothing but a poor governess, pray let
55 me go."

"Oh, ho! A governess? Give me your last month's wages, then. Give me what you have stolen from your master!" and he laughed fiendishly.

I gazed at him quietly, and said, in a low voice, "I
60 have stolen nothing from you, Mr. Rawjester!"

"Ah, discovered! Hush! Listen, girl!" he hissed in a fiercer whisper, "utter a syllable to frustrate my plans and you die—aid me, and—" but he was gone.

In a few moments the party, with the exception of
65 myself, were gagged and locked in the cellar. The next moment, torches were applied to the rich hangings, and the house was in flames. I felt a strong hand seize me, and bear me out in the open air and place me upon the hillside, where I could overlook the burning mansion.
70 It was Mr. Rawjester.

"Burn!" he said, as he shook his fist at the flames. Then sinking on his knees before me, he said hurriedly:

"Mary Jane, I love you; the obstacles to our union are or will be soon removed. In yonder mansion were
75 confined my three crazy wives. One of them, as you know, attempted to kill me! Ha! This is vengeance! But will you be mine?"

I fell, without a word, upon his neck.

11. The name of the narrator is:

   A. Blanche Blunderbore.
   B. Blanche Mix.
   C. Mary Jane Mix.
   D. Mary Jane Rawjester.

GO ON TO THE NEXT PAGE.

12. Mr. Rawjester leaves the party in order to:

    F. obtain more refreshments for his guests.
    G. attend to an urgent business matter.
    H. disguise himself and return to the party as a robber.
    J. check on the whereabouts of his daughter.

13. The degradation the narrator describes in the fourth paragraph (lines 17–19) comes from:

    A. having to help the fiancée of the man she loves.
    B. having to tutor a small child who speaks French.
    C. her inability to earn more money.
    D. her inability to sleep through the night without being disturbed.

14. What is the narrator's position at Blunderbore house?

    F. The master's wife
    G. The master's mistress
    H. The child's governess
    J. Blanche Marabout's sister

15. Mr. Rawjester's attitude towards his guests is one of:

    A. warmth.
    B. revulsion.
    C. indifference.
    D. admiration.

16. The child believes that:

    F. Blanche Marabout is her natural mother.
    G. Blanche Marabout is to marry her father.
    H. the narrator is her natural mother.
    J. her father dislikes the narrator.

17. It can be inferred that the narrator:

    A. denounces Mr. Rawjester to his guests.
    B. cooperates with Mr. Rawjester.
    C. defends herself against Mr. Rawjester's attack.
    D. gives the highwayman her month's wages.

18. The purpose of the visit of the highwayman is to:

    F. obtain valuable jewelry.
    G. kidnap the narrator.
    H. kill the child.
    J. deflect suspicion from Mr. Rawjester.

19. Blanche was unable to hide the diamond necklace because:

    A. the highwayman had given it to her and knew she had it.
    B. the narrator told the highwayman where it was hidden.
    C. some of the other guests insisted that she give it up.
    D. the child whispered its location to the highwayman.

20. The exchange between the narrator and the highwayman that takes place in the house was heard:

    F. only by those two persons.
    G. by the child.
    H. by Blanche.
    J. by every guest in the room.

GO ON TO THE NEXT PAGE.

Passage III

SOCIAL STUDIES: This passage discusses legislation for the regulation of corporate takeovers.

American financial markets are regulated by the federal government through the Securities and Exchange Commission and by various state agencies. In recent years, there has been considerable discussion
5 of the need for more regulation because of the increased number of corporate takeovers. Many observers of the economic scene argue that much of this activity has had harmful effects not only on stockholders but also on the economy as a whole.

10 Many corporate takeovers are hostile; that is, an outside group or company tries to seize control of an existing company whose management opposes the takeover. Most hostile takeovers begin with a tender offer in which the outside raiders offer to buy a
15 sufficient amount of the company's outstanding stock at a stated price—usually well above the current market price. Another takeover strategy is to orchestrate a proxy battle in which a vote of shareholders of record on a specific date is taken to
20 approve or reject a new slate of directors put forth by the raiders. The raiders generally argue that the new directors will make the company more profitable and thereby enhance the value of the stock for the existing stockholders.

25 Regardless of the takeover strategy employed, most raiders must purchase a significant portion of the company's stock at a price above its current market value. Outsiders usually finance such large purchases of stock through the sale of bonds that pay a very high
30 rate of interest. The raiders argue that the debt to be incurred can easily be paid off by selling parts of the targeted company or by drawing on the additional profits that the new management insists it can make.

In 1986 and 1987, charges emerged that
35 individuals within Wall Street firms specializing in raising capital for corporate takeovers were, in fact, selling inside information about future takeover attempts. Some of the individuals involved have already been sentenced to jail terms. In addition, such
40 scandals have added to pressure on Congress and the Securities and Exchange Commission to provide more effective regulation of the financial aspects of attempted corporate takeovers.

Critics of hostile corporate takeovers believe that
45 the managers of the company to be taken over usually engage in short-term activities that have very negative long-term effects. In order to avoid hostile takeovers, managers of companies generally take measures to make the takeovers less desirable. For instance, they
50 may insert a *golden parachute clause* in employment contracts. This clause requires a company to pay very large bonuses to any management members who are fired after a takeover. Another tactic, the *poison pill,* restructures the financial base of the corporation so that
55 an attempted takeover would make the company less profitable. Yet another anti-raid tactic is to pay *greenmail* to the raiders; that is, the target of the takeover pays the raiders, who have acquired a significant percentage of the stock at a premium, to sell
60 those shares back to the targeted company at a much higher price. This prevents the takeover, but it usually adds a substantial sum to the company's debt.

Supporters of corporate raiders counter-argue that, in fact, it is the threat of a takeover that makes
65 managers more efficient. For instance, it may cause managers to sell parts of the corporation that they are not managing well in order to raise the money to fend off the takeover. In addition, those who believe that takeovers are good argue that the existing shareholders
70 always do better in a hostile takeover since they invariably get a higher price for each share of stock than the current market value.

21. Which statement expresses the main idea of this passage?

A. The government is regulating the financial aspects of corporate takeovers adequately.
B. There has been recent debate over the need for additional government regulation of corporate takeovers.
C. Hostile corporate takeovers are beneficial to the targeted corporation.
D. Trading insider secrets has become a common problem in hostile corporate takeovers.

GO ON TO THE NEXT PAGE.

22. A corporation's board of directors votes to approve a new company policy. According to the plan, each member of the board and of upper management would receive severance of two to five years' pay if the new owner fired the member after a corporate takeover. This action would be considered:

    F. a poison pill.
    G. a golden parachute.
    H. greenmail.
    J. a hostile takeover.

23. What is the most important difference between a hostile and a non-hostile takeover?

    A. In a hostile takeover, stockholders must pay greenmail to the existing directors.
    B. In a non-hostile takeover, raiders sell bonds with high interest rates.
    C. In a hostile takeover, the existing management is opposed to the takeover.
    D. In a non-hostile takeover, existing management uses golden parachutes.

24. According to the passage, which of the following parties in a hostile takeover will likely incur new debt?

    F. The raiders, because they need money to buy large blocks of stock
    G. The Securities and Exchange Commission, because it must oversee the transactions more closely
    H. The stockholders, because they must furnish additional funds works
    J. The critics of hostile takeovers, because they make less money in the stock market

25. According to the passage, a poison pill strategy involves:

    A. paying the raiders high prices to buy back the company's stock from them.
    B. paying high bonuses to the members of the old management who are fired by the new management.
    C. more regulation by the Securities and Exchange Commission.
    D. restructuring the financial base of the company so that it will be less profitable or valuable to the raiders.

26. According to the passage, supporters of corporate takeovers believe that:

    F. the shareholders always lose money because a takeover profits only the raiders.
    G. fear of being targeted for a takeover makes managers more efficient.
    H. insider trading should be made legal.
    J. a proxy fight is the best way to win control.

27. According to the passage, in a proxy fight:

    A. the raiders sell bonds to buy the targeted company's stock.
    B. the raiders offer to buy stock at a higher-than-market price.
    C. insider information is traded illegally.
    D. a stockholders' meeting is called to vote for approval or rejection of a new board of directors put forth by the raiders.

28. The management of a business recently targeted for takeover decides to sell two of its unprofitable subsidiaries to raise cash and cut expenses. Supporters of corporate takeovers would say that this action:

    F. is an example of how the greenmail strategy works.
    G. is an example of how a golden parachute strategy works.
    H. is an example of how the fear of a takeover makes managers more efficient.
    J. is an example of how the poison pill strategy works.

GO ON TO THE NEXT PAGE.

29. The Securities and Exchange Commission is a:

   A. state regulatory agency that polices financial markets.
   B. federal regulatory agency that polices financial markets.
   C. source of funding for hostile takeovers.
   D. board of business executives who promote fair business practices.

30. Some individuals working on Wall Street have been sentenced to jail terms for:

   F. attempting to greenmail other companies.
   G. forcing companies to swallow a poison pill.
   H. selling inside information about takeover attempts.
   J. agreeing to pay greenmail to corporate raiders.

GO ON TO THE NEXT PAGE.

Passage IV

NATURAL SCIENCES: This passage discusses supernova explosions and their effects.

About twice every century, the light reaches us from one of the massive stars in our galaxy that blew apart millions of years ago in a supernova explosion that sends massive quantities of radiation and matter
5 into space and generates shock waves that sweep through the arms of the galaxy. The shock waves heat the interstellar gas, evaporate small clouds, and compress larger ones to the point at which they collapse under their own gravity to form new stars. The
10 general picture that has been developed for the supernova explosion and its aftermath goes something like this. Throughout its evolution, a star is much like a leaky balloon; it keeps its equilibrium figure through a balance of internal pressure against the tendency to
15 collapse under its own weight. The pressure is generated by nuclear reactions in the core of the star that must continually supply energy to balance the energy that leaks out in the form of radiation. Eventually, the nuclear fuel is exhausted, and the
20 pressure drops in the core. With nothing to hold it up, the matter in the center of the star collapses inward, creating higher and higher densities and temperatures, until the nuclei and electrons are fused into a super-dense lump of matter known as a neutron star.

25 As the overlying layers rain down on the surface of the neutron star, the temperature rises until, with a blinding flash of radiation, the collapse is reversed. A thermonuclear shock wave runs through the now expanding stellar envelope, fusing lighter elements into
30 heavier ones and producing a brilliant visual outburst that can be as intense as the light of 10 billion suns. The shell of matter thrown off by the explosion plows through the surrounding gas, producing an expanding bubble of hot gas, with gas temperatures in the millions
35 of degrees. This gas will emit most of its energy at x-ray wavelengths, so it is not surprising that x-ray observatories have provided some of the most useful insights into the nature of the supernova phenomenon. More than twenty supernova remnants have now been
40 detected in x-ray studies.

Recent discoveries of meteorites with anomalous concentrations of certain isotopes indicate that a supernova might have precipitated the birth of our solar system more than four and a half billion years
45 ago. Although the cloud that collapsed to form the Sun and the planets was composed primarily of hydrogen and helium, it also contained carbon, nitrogen, and oxygen, elements essential for life as we know it. Elements heavier than helium are manufactured deep

50 in the interior of stars and would, for the most part, remain there if it were not for the cataclysmic supernova explosions that blow giant stars apart. Additionally, supernovas produce clouds of high-energy particles called cosmic rays. These high-energy
55 particles continually bombard the Earth and are responsible for many of the genetic mutations that are the driving force of the evolution of species.

31. According to the passage, we can expect to observe a supernova in our galaxy about:

   A. twice each year.
   B. 100 times each century.
   C. once every 50 years.
   D. once every other century.

32. According to the passage, all of the following are true of supernovas EXCEPT:

   F. they are extremely bright.
   G. they are an explosion of some sort.
   H. they are emitters of large quantities of x-rays.
   J. they are caused by the collision of large galaxies.

33. The author employs which of the following to develop the first paragraph?

   A. Analogy
   B. Deduction
   C. Generalization
   D. Example

34. It can be inferred from the passage that the "meteorites" mentioned by the author (line 41):

   F. contain dangerous concentrations of radioactive materials.
   G. give off large quantities of x-rays.
   H. include material not created in the normal development of our solar system.
   J. are larger than the meteors normally found in a solar system like ours.

GO ON TO THE NEXT PAGE.

35. The author implies that:

A. it is sometimes easier to detect supernovas by observation of the x-ray spectrum than by observation of visible wavelengths of light.

B. life on Earth is endangered by its constant exposure to radiation forces that are released by a supernova.

C. recently discovered meteorites indicate that the Earth and other planets of our solar system survived the explosion of a supernova several billion years ago.

D. lighter elements are formed from heavier elements during a supernova as the heavier elements are torn apart.

36. According to the passage, what is the first event in the sequence that leads to the occurrence of a supernova?

F. An ordinary star begins to emit tremendous quantities of x-rays.

G. A superheated cloud of gas envelops a neutron star.

H. An imbalance between light and heavy elements causes an ordinary star to collapse.

J. An ordinary star exhausts its supply of nuclear fuel and begins to collapse.

37. According to the passage, a neutron star is:

A. a gaseous cloud containing heavy elements.

B. an intermediate stage between an ordinary star and a supernova.

C. the residue that is left by a supernova.

D. the core of an ordinary star that houses the thermonuclear reactions.

38. The author is primarily concerned with:

F. speculating about the origins of our solar system.

G. presenting evidence proving the existence of supernovas.

H. discussing the nuclear reaction that occurs in the core of a star.

J. describing a theory about the causes of supernovas.

39. How long ago was our galaxy formed?

A. 100 million years
B. 1 billion years
C. 2 billion years
D. Over 4.5 billion years

40. What is the connection between supernovas and the evolution of species on Earth?

F. There is no connection.

G. Cosmic radiation from supernovas retards evolution.

H. Cosmic radiation from supernovas drives evolution.

J. Evolution makes possible future supernovas.

END OF TEST 3
STOP! DO NOT TURN THE PAGE UNTIL TOLD TO DO SO.
DO NOT RETURN TO A PREVIOUS TEST.

4 4 4 4 4 4 4 4 4 4 4 4

SCIENCE TEST
35 Minutes—40 Items

DIRECTIONS: The passages presented in the test are each followed by a set of items. Read the passage and choose the best answer for each item. Fill in the corresponding oval on your bubble sheet. You may refer to the passage as often as necessary to answer the passage items.

Warning: Calculator use is not permitted on this test.

Answers are on page 616, and explanations begin on page 634.

Passage I

Before making their historic first powered flight, the Wright Brothers made extensive lift tests in 1901 using a glider. Their data differed from that obtained twelve years earlier by the German, Otto Lilienthal.

Results of both tests (Wright: thin line; Lilienthal: thick line) are shown below. "Lift" is the force that pulls the wing away from the Earth, in a direction perpendicular to the flight path, and the "angle of incidence" is the angle that the flight path makes with the horizon.

Modified from Culick, F.E.C, "The Wright 'Flyer' was the outcome of an intensive program of research." *Sci. Amer. 241* (1): 86–100, 1979.

1. The two curves differ chiefly in that:

   A. the Wright's data were more accurate.
   B. lift was generally greater in the Wright's experiments.
   C. lift was generally greater in Lilienthal's experiments.
   D. the peak value for lift was greater in Lilienthal's experiments.

2. In the Wright's experiments, the greatest lift occurred at an angle of incidence of about:

   F. 5.5 degrees.
   G. 0 degrees.
   H. 16 degrees.
   J. 46 degrees.

3. At an angle of incidence of 50 degrees, by how much would you expect the two experiments to show a difference in lift?

   A. 0–1 pounds/sq. ft.
   B. 1–2 pounds/sq. ft.
   C. 2–3 pounds/sq. ft.
   D. 3–4 pounds/sq. ft.

GO ON TO THE NEXT PAGE.

4. The two sets of experiments differed most in lift at which of the following angles?

    F. 10 degrees
    G. 15 degrees
    H. 30 degrees
    J. 40 degrees

5. The widest range of angles, in degrees, over which the Lilienthal values for lift continuously exceeded the Wright's values was:

    A. 10.
    B. 19.
    C. 25.
    D. 43.

GO ON TO THE NEXT PAGE.

Passage II

Two experiments were performed to determine the effects of temperature on the rate of cellular respiration* in germinating peas.

*Summary Equation: $C_6H_{12}O_6$ + $6O_2$ ⇒ $6CO_2$ + $6H_2O$
(glucose) (oxygen)   (carbon dioxide) (water)

Experiment 1: A simple respirometer was used, primarily consisting of a large test tube partially filled with germinating peas. The peas were covered with a layer of cotton and a small amount of potassium hydroxide (KOH), a substance that can absorb and remove carbon dioxide from the tube. The remainder of the tube, with its starting volume of air sealed inside (200 ml.), was closed to the outside with a rubber stopper. Attached was a meter designed to detect and measure any changes in gas volume in the tube during the experiment. The experiment was conducted at room temperature (22°C), and the respirator was monitored for 15 minutes. At the end of 15 minutes, the volume of gas inside the tube had *decreased* to 120 ml.

Experiment 2: An identical experiment was conducted at 30°C. At this temperature, the volume of gas inside the tube after 15 minutes had decreased from 200 ml (starting volume) to 60 ml.

6. Separate control experiments were performed alongside Experiments 1 and 2. The control contained plastic beads (the same size as peas) instead of germinating peas. All other conditions were identical. Any decrease in gas volume inside the control tube would suggest that:

   F. plastic beads utilize oxygen at approximately the same rate as germinating peas.
   G. plastic beads produce carbon dioxide at about the same rate as germinating peas.
   H. plastic beads carry out all aspects of cellular respiration at approximately the same rate as germinating peas.
   J. factors having nothing to do with cellular respiration must be responsible.

7. In both experiments, the decrease in volume in the tube was mainly due to a change in the volume of what specific gas?

   A. Oxygen
   B. Carbon dioxide
   C. Potassium hydroxide
   D. All of the above

8. If potassium hydroxide (KOH) were not included in the tubes, what would happen to the volume of gas during each experiment?

   F. Final volumes would be higher than starting volumes.
   G. Final volumes would decrease faster than what was observed in Experiments 1 and 2.
   H. Final volumes would approximately be the same as starting volumes.
   J. Results would not be different from what was observed in Experiments 1 and 2.

9. Experiment 2 showed a greater decrease in gas volume in the tube because:

   A. at higher temperatures, peas use oxygen slower.
   B. at higher temperatures, peas produce carbon dioxide faster.
   C. at higher temperatures, peas use oxygen faster.
   D. at lower temperatures, peas use oxygen slower than they produce carbon dioxide.

GO ON TO THE NEXT PAGE.

10. An additional set of experiments with germinating peas is conducted in the dark at 22°C and 30°C. All other conditions are identical to those in Experiments 1 and 2. After 15 minutes, if the final gas volume inside the tube at 22°C is 120 ml, and the final gas volume inside the tube at 30°C is 60 ml, which hypothesis best explains the results?

   F. Darkness affects cellular respiration in germinating peas the same way that a rise in temperature affects cellular respiration in germinating peas.
   G. Light/dark conditions have little or no effect on cellular respiration in germinating peas.
   H. Cellular respiration in germinating peas occurs faster in the light than in the dark.
   J. Cellular respiration in germinating peas occurs faster in the dark than in the light.

11. The summary equation in the passage shows that during cellular respiration, germinating peas must consume glucose. In Experiments 1 and 2, glucose molecules:

   A. were in the peas.
   B. were not available.
   C. were consumed at equal rates.
   D. were available but not consumed at all.

GO ON TO THE NEXT PAGE.

Passage III

Two different views of the Earth's past are presented below.

Scientist 1: The history of our planet has been marked by sudden spectacular events that have no counterpart in the natural processes observed today (Catastrophism). Today's valleys formed during periods of downward slippage by fragments of the Earth's crust. Mountains rose due to gigantic upheavals of land during the Earth's beginnings. The three major types of rock formed when one worldwide ocean precipitated out great masses of different materials during three sudden and separate events. Substances such as granite were precipitated first (today's igneous rocks), while materials in the flat upper layers precipitated last (today's sedimentary rocks). This was followed by the disappearance of much of this great ocean's water (perhaps by evaporation during years of intensive heat). Distinct assemblages of animal and plant fossils, found in successive rock layers of a region, can be explained by local catastrophic events, such as massive fires or floods. Old forms were wiped out, and eventually new forms replaced them as foreign species immigrated from other geographic areas.

Scientist 2: Processes now in operation are adequate to account for changes in the Earth's past (Principle of Uniform Change). Although today's processes seem to have negligible effects on the landscape, great changes can result from ongoing processes, if given long enough periods of time. Valleys form as flowing water cuts through the sides and bottom of the land and rock they pass across. Rocks and mountains can be formed, destroyed and reformed by processes still going on today such as volcanic activity, heat and pressure under the Earth's surfaces, erosion, weathering, and even shifts and movements that can lift massive areas below the land and ocean surfaces to high elevations. Different fossil types in successive layers of rocks represent the changes in form that can take place among related organisms as a result of evolutionary processes over vast periods of time.

12. One major difference between the views of Scientist 1 and Scientist 2 relates to:

   F. where fossils are found.
   G. when the processes that shape the Earth take place.
   H. the size of mountain ranges.
   J. whether water played a role in forming any of the Earth's characteristics.

13. Which of the following provides the strongest evidence against Scientist 1's point about mountain formation?

   A. The beginnings of the Earth are not well documented.
   B. Floods and fires have never been massive enough to eliminate fossils from all mountain areas.
   C. Volcanic activity, weathering, and erosion are believed to be less common today than in years past.
   D. Fossils of recent sea creatures can be found in rocks on mountain peaks.

14. Based on the differences between Scientist 1 and Scientist 2 stated above, which description is most accurate concerning their views about the time span needed for the Earth's geologic characteristics to form?

   F. Scientist 1 makes references to time span and suggests a longer Earth history than Scientist 2.
   G. Scientist 2 makes no references to time span, but implies a shorter Earth history than Scientist 1.
   H. Scientist 2 makes references to time span and suggests a longer Earth history than does Scientist 1.
   J. Neither scientist refers to time span or implies any difference in length of Earth history.

GO ON TO THE NEXT PAGE.

15. According to Scientist 1, which of the major types of rocks should be found at the lowest levels?

    A. Igneous (granite)
    B. Metamorphic (marble)
    C. Sedimentary (limestone)
    D. Cannot be determined from the given information

16. According to the views of Scientist 1, the number of major rock types will most likely:

    F. remain unchanged.
    G. decrease.
    H. increase.
    J. Cannot be determined from the given information

17. To refute Scientist 2's point of view about strictly uniform processes of change, Scientist 1 could argue that:

    A. the streams of today are not measurably effective in cutting through the sides and bottoms of rock they pass across.
    B. fossils are not found everywhere today.
    C. at some early point in time, the actual formation of the Earth had to involve very different processes from those now in evidence.
    D. no mountain ranges have formed in our lifetime.

18. Which argument does NOT support the views of Scientist 2?

    F. There are many regions of lava where no volcanoes are present today.
    G. There are three major types of rock that exist today.
    H. Many rivers today are flowing far below their former channels.
    J. Distinctive fossils in upper layers of rock show similarities to those in lower layers, yet they are never found in any other geographic areas.

GO ON TO THE NEXT PAGE.

Passage IV

Cold-blooded animals (poikilotherms) cannot regulate their body temperatures internally. Their body temperature varies as the environmental temperature varies. Consequently, the rates of many bodily processes also vary as outside temperatures change (as environmental temperatures increase, body temperature as well as the rates of bodily processes also may increase). Warm-blooded animals (homeotherms), on the other hand, can maintain their body temperatures internally. Therefore, the rates of their bodily processes can remain relatively stable when environmental temperatures change.

Experiments were set up to determine how the bodily process heart rate may be affected by different temperatures in two species of live laboratory animals.

Experiment 1: Ten individuals from Species A and ten individuals from Species B were kept in 20 separate containers at room temperature (22°C) for 30 minutes. Their heart rates (heart beats/minute) were recorded every 10 minutes. Average heart rates for the entire experiment were then calculated for each species. Results were as follows: Species A had an average heart rate of 150 beats/minute, while Species B averaged 100 beats/minute.

Experiment 2: Identical procedures were used to repeat the original experiment except that the containers holding the individuals of each species were placed in an incubator set at 35°C. At the end of 30 minutes, the average heart rate for both species was 148 beats/minute.

19. How many values were used to calculate the average heart beats for each species in each of these experiments?

   A. 1
   B. 10
   C. 20
   D. 30

20. Which of the following hypotheses is supported by the results of both experiments?

   F. Species A is most likely poikilothermic.
   G. Species B is most likely poikilothermic.
   H. Both species are most likely poikilothermic.
   J. Neither species is poikilothermic.

21. Which of the following statements best explains why ten individuals of each species were used in the experiments?

   A. In case a few died, there would still be others available for testing.
   B. If only one individual was used, it would be lonely.
   C. An average value for ten individuals reduces the chance of getting an extreme value for any one individual.
   D. If only one individual was chosen from each species, it would be difficult to show differences.

22. If a third experiment were conducted at 6°C, which set of results for average heart rates (in beats/minute) is closest to what might be expected?

   F. Species A = 146; Species B = 146
   G. Species A = 50; Species B = 146
   H. Species A = 50; Species B = 50
   J. Species A = 146; Species B = 50

23. Which statement is accurate concerning Species A and Species B?

   A. At 22°C, Species A has a higher average heart rate than Species B.
   B. Species A has a larger average size than Species B.
   C. As environmental temperature increases, average heart rate increases more for Species A than Species B.
   D. As environmental temperature decreases, average heart rate increases more for Species A than Species B.

GO ON TO THE NEXT PAGE.

24. If the average body temperature for ten individuals of each species were recorded during Experiments 1 and 2, which results would be expected?

   F. Species A: Temperature stays the same in both experiments. Species B: Temperature increases in Experiment 2.
   G. Species A: Temperature increases in Experiment 2. Species B: Temperature stays the same in both experiments.
   H. Both Species: Temperature increases in Experiment 2.
   J. Both Species: Temperature stays the same in both experiments.

GO ON TO THE NEXT PAGE.

Passage V

The chart below shows a set of "energy levels" that an electron in molecule X can occupy. The value of the energy in each level is shown to the right.

Energy Levels
E_5 ------ 2.07
E_4 ------ 1.75
E_3 ------ 1.52
E_2 ------ 1.20
E_1 ------ 0.60

An electron can move from one level to the next (transition) in two ways:

(a) the molecule can absorb a particle of light, called a "photon," of just the right energy to lift the electron to a higher level. For example, an electron in level 4 can be raised to level 5 if the molecule absorbs a photon whose energy is 0.32.

(b) the molecule can emit, or give off, a photon of just the right energy necessary to lower an electron to another level. For example, an electron in level 4 can move to level 3 if the molecule emits a photon whose energy is 0.23.

25. A sample containing many X molecules absorbs light, each photon of which carries 0.60 units of energy. As the light is absorbed:

   A. an electron moves from level 1 to level 2.
   B. an electron moves from level 2 to level 4.
   C. an electron moves from level 2 to level 1.
   D. an electron moves from level 4 to level 2.

26. A sample of molecule X emits light, each photon of which carries 0.32 units of energy. Which of the following statements best explains this observation?

   F. An electron moved from level 3 to level 2.
   G. An electron moved from level 2 to level 3.
   H. An electron moved from level 5 to level 4.
   J. An electron moved from level 3 to level 2 or from level 5 to level 4.

27. A sample of molecule X emits light whose photons each carry 0.92 units of energy. As the light is emitted:

   A. an electron moves from level 5 to level 2.
   B. an electron moves from level 1 to level 5.
   C. an electron moves from level 1 to level 3.
   D. an electron moves from level 3 to level 1.

28. Suppose that in a sample of molecule X, all of the electrons are in level 1. Based on the information in the chart, photons of how many different energies could be absorbed by the sample?

   F. 1
   G. 2
   H. 3
   J. 4

29. Assume that each of the molecules in a sample of molecule X has only 1 electron, whose level is not known. Light is passed through the sample, and photons, each of energy 0.23, are absorbed. A very short time later, photons of the same energy are emitted. It is likely that:

   A. electrons are being promoted from level 1 to level 2.
   B. electrons are moving from level 4 to level 3, and then back again to level 4.
   C. electrons are moving from level 3 to level 4, then back again to level 3.
   D. electrons are moving from level 5 to level 4.

30. If photons whose individual energies are each 2.07 encounter a sample of molecule X, then:

   F. electrons will be promoted from level 1 to level 5.
   G. electrons will be promoted from all levels to level 5.
   H. electrons will drop from level 5 to level 1.
   J. no electron transitions will occur.

GO ON TO THE NEXT PAGE.

Passage VI

A student performs a set of three experiments in which a light beam passes through water and air. The "refraction angles" are the angles that the light beam makes with a vertical line. In the water, this angle is called θ_1. When the beam leaves the water and passes into air, a second angle, θ_2, can be measured. Figure 1 illustrates θ_1 and θ_2.

Figure 1

Experiment 1: The entry angle, θ_1, and the exit angle, θ_2, are both equal to zero.

Experiment 2: The angles observed are shown in Figure 2.

Experiment 3: The angles observed are shown in Figure 3.

Figure 3

31. Which of the following diagrams could represent the observations of Experiment 1?

32. The student attempts to draw a conclusion from Experiments 1 and 2 that may apply to all other measurements as well. Which of the following is justified by the data?

    F. Refraction angles in water are greater than those in air.
    G. Refraction angles in water are less than those in air.
    H. Refraction angles are equal in air and in water.
    J. Refraction angles in water are equal to or less than those in air.

33. In Experiment 3, the beam travels through the water and:

    A. is reflected back down from the surface of the water.
    B. enters the air.
    C. is absorbed completely.
    D. is reflected back on itself.

GO ON TO THE NEXT PAGE.

34. An observer in the air attempts to see the beam of light in Experiments 2 and 3. She will:

   F. be able to observe the light in each experiment, provided she is in the right place.
   G. be unable to observe the light in either experiment, regardless of position.
   H. be able to observe the light in Experiment 2 but not Experiment 3.
   J. be able to observe the light in Experiment 3 but not Experiment 2.

35. A student attempts to summarize the results of all three experiments. Which of the following is most consistent with the observations?

   A. The angle of refraction in water is less than that in air.
   B. The angle of refraction in air is less than that in water.
   C. The angle of refraction in water is less than or equal to that in air, but at high angles in the water, the light is reflected back into the water.
   D. The angle of refraction in water is less than or equal to that in air.

GO ON TO THE NEXT PAGE.

Passage VII

The table below presents the results of a study in which butterflies of different size and color were captured in flight for marking with a chemical, and then recaptured in flight a few weeks later.

SIZE	WHITE		TAN		DARK BROWN	
	# marked	Recaptured	# marked	Recaptured	# marked	Recaptured
Small (less than 20 mm)	35	30	40	10	20	10
Medium (20–40 mm)	30	15	40	20	20	10
Large (greater than 40 mm)	50	25	60	30	30	10

36. For all sizes of butterflies, the color that seems most difficult to capture for marking is:

   F. white.
   G. tan.
   H. dark brown.
   J. Both tan and dark brown are almost equally difficult

37. The specific type of butterfly that is easiest to recapture after being marked is:

   A. between 10–20 mm and tan.
   B. greater than 40 mm and tan.
   C. greater than 40 mm and dark brown.
   D. less than 20 mm and white.

38. Based on the information in the table, which statement best represents the relationship between a butterfly's size and its tendency to be captured for marking?

   F. The larger the butterfly, the harder it is to be captured for marking.
   G. The larger the butterfly, the easier it is to be captured for marking.
   H. Medium-sized butterflies are consistently the easiest to capture for marking.
   J. The smaller the butterfly, the easier it is to be captured for marking.

39. The chemical used to mark all the butterflies was found to be poisonous to one specific type because it was being absorbed through the wings. Based on the data in the table, which type of butterfly appears most likely to have suffered from the effects of the marking chemical?

   A. Greater than 40 mm and white
   B. Less than 20 mm and tan
   C. Greater than 40 mm and dark brown
   D. Less than 20 mm and white

40. Which conclusion is correct concerning the information in the table?

   F. For tan butterflies, the proportion of individuals that are recaptured always stays the same.
   G. For medium-sized butterflies, the proportion of individuals that are recaptured always stays the same.
   H. For small-sized butterflies, the proportion of individuals recaptured always stays the same.
   J. For all sizes of butterflies, the darker the color the easier it is to recapture an individual.

END OF TEST 4
STOP! DO NOT TURN THE PAGE UNTIL TOLD TO DO SO.
DO NOT RETURN TO A PREVIOUS TEST.

5 5 5 5 5 5 5 5 5 5 5 5

WRITING TEST (OPTIONAL)
30 Minutes—1 Essay Prompt

DIRECTIONS: This is a test of your writing skills. Before you begin planning and writing your essay, read the writing prompt carefully to understand the instructions. Your essay will be evaluated on the evidence it provides of your ability to express judgments by taking a position on the issue in the writing prompt; to maintain a focus on the topic throughout the essay; to develop a position by using logical reasoning and supporting ideas; to organize ideas in a logical way; and to use language clearly and effectively according to the conventions of standard written English.

If you finish before time is called, you may review your work. Lay your pencil down immediately when time is called.

Sample essays begin on page 636.

Writing Test Prompt

Doctors and government leaders have become increasingly concerned about what is called the "obesity epidemic" in America. Many people are overweight, and researchers now believe that childhood eating habits have a major effect on whether an adult will be overweight. Some people now argue that schools should eliminate all "junk food" from the cafeteria offerings, remove all vending machines that sell soda pop and sugary snacks, and prohibit students from bringing into the school cafeteria from outside foods that are considered unhealthy. Other people oppose this idea. They say that the choice of what to eat should be left to individuals and families. Those parents who do not want their children eating "junk food" can take steps to regulate their diet; other parents can determine how often their children may eat such food and how much of it. Do you think that schools should take steps to ensure that only healthful foods are served and consumed on school premises?

In your essay, take a position on this issue. You may address either of the two points described above, or you may offer an entirely different perspective on the issue. Be sure to use specific reasons and examples to support your analysis.

END OF TEST 5
STOP! DO NOT RETURN TO ANY OTHER TEST.

Practice Test IV

DIRECTIONS

Practice Test IV consists of five subject tests: English, Mathematics, Reading, Science, and Writing. Calculator use is only permitted on the Mathematics Test.

The items in each multiple-choice test are numbered and the answer choices are lettered. The provided bubble sheet (p. 313) has numbered rows that correspond to the items on the test. Each row contains lettered ovals to match the answer choices for each item on the test. Each numbered row on the bubble sheet has a corresponding item on the test.

For each item, first decide on the best answer choice. Then, locate the row number that corresponds to the item. Next, find the oval in that row that matches the letter of the chosen answer. Then, use a soft lead pencil to fill in the oval. Do not use a ballpoint pen.

Mark only one answer for each item. If you change your mind about the answer choice, thoroughly erase the first mark before marking your new answer.

Note that only responses marked on your bubble sheet will be scored. Your score on each test will be based only on the number of items that are correctly answered during the time allowed for that test. Guessing is not penalized. Therefore, it is to your best advantage to answer every item on the test, even if you must guess.

On the Writing Test, use the provided essay response sheet (p. 314) to write your response to the prompt. (Note that the Writing Test is optional.)

You may work on each test only during the time allowed for that test. If you finish a test before time is called, use the time to review your answer choices or work on items about which you are uncertain. You may not return to a test on which time has already been called and you may not preview another test. You must lay down your pencil immediately when time is called at the end of each test. You may not for any reason fill in or alter ovals for a test after time expires for that test. Violation of these rules will result in immediate disqualification from the exam.

1 1 1 1 1 1 1 1 1 1 1 1 1

ENGLISH TEST
45 Minutes—75 Items

DIRECTIONS: In the passages below, certain parts of the sentences have been underlined and numbered. In the right-hand column, you will find different ways of writing each underlined part; the original version is indicated by the "NO CHANGE" option. There are also items that ask about a section of the passage or the passage as a whole. These items do not refer to an underlined portion of the passage; they are identified by a number or numbers in a box.

For each item, choose the alternative that you consider to be the best. Select the answer choice that best expresses the intended idea, is most acceptable in standard written English, or is most consistent with the overall tone and style of the passage. Read the passage through once before you begin to answer the accompanying items. Finding the answers to certain items may depend on looking at material that appears several sentences beyond the item. So, be sure that you have read far enough ahead before you select your answer choice.

Answers are on page 639, and explanations begin on page 642.

PASSAGE I

An American Christmas

As befits a nation made up of immigrants from all over the Christian world, Americans have no distinctive Christmas symbols, but we have taken the symbols of all the nations and made them our own. The Christmas tree, the holly and the ivy, the mistletoe, the exchange of gifts, the myth of Santa Claus, the carols of all nations, the plum pudding, and the wassail bowl are all elements in the American Christmas of the early twenty-first century as we know it today. Though we have no Christmas symbols of our own, the American Christmas still has a distinctive aura by virtue of two character elements.

1. **A.** NO CHANGE
   B. symbols but
   C. symbols; but
   D. symbols: but

2. **F.** NO CHANGE
   G. as it is known today
   H. known as it is today
   J. OMIT the underlined portion.

3. **A.** NO CHANGE
   B. characters
   C. characterized
   D. characteristic

GO ON TO THE NEXT PAGE.

The first of these is when, as might be expected
                    4
in a nation as dedicated to the carrying on of business

as the American nation, the dominant role of the

Christmas festivities has become to serve as a
                      5
stimulus to retail business. The themes of Christmas

advertising begin to appear as early as September, and

the open season on Christmas shopping begins in

November. 50 years ago, Thanksgiving Day was
          6

regarded like it was the opening day of the season for
          7
Christmas shopping; today, the season opens

immediately after Halloween. Thus, virtually a whole

month has been added to the Christmas season—for
                                            8
shopping purposes.

Second, the Christmas season of festivities has

insensibly combined with the New Years celebration
                                9
into one lengthened period of Saturnalia. This starts

with office parties a few days before Christmas
                                       10
continues on Christmas Eve, now the occasion in
10
America of one of two large-scale revels that mark the

season, and continues in spirited euphoria until New

Year's Eve, the second of the large-scale revels. New

Year's Day is spent resting, possibly regretting

4. F. NO CHANGE
    G. is that
    H. is which
    J. is where

5. A. NO CHANGE
    B. have become
    C. having become
    D. becomes

6. F. NO CHANGE
    G. 50 year ago
    H. Fifty years ago
    J. One time ago

7. A. NO CHANGE
    B. like as
    C. as
    D. like

8. F. NO CHANGE
    G. season. For
    H. season, for
    J. season: for

9. A. NO CHANGE
    B. New Year's
    C. New Years'
    D. New Year

10. F. NO CHANGE
    G. Christmas, continues
    H. as Christmas continues
    J. Christmas as continues

GO ON TO THE NEXT PAGE.

somebody's excesses, and watching a football "bowl"
11   12
game.

11. **A.** NO CHANGE
    B. everyone's
    C. someone's
    D. one's

12. Is the use of quotation marks appropriate?

    F. No, because the essay has no dialogue.
    G. No, because commas would be more appropriate.
    H. Yes, because quotation marks are used to set off words used out of context.
    J. Yes, because quotation marks are used around titles of books, plays, and poems.

PASSAGE II

The Myth of a Criminal Physique

[1]

Can you spot a criminal by his physical characteristics? [13] When the science of criminology was founded in the nineteenth century, an imaginative Italian observer decided that criminals are

13. Is the use of a question appropriate to begin Paragraph 1?

    A. No, because questions are not used in formal writing.
    B. No, because the question is not answered.
    C. Yes, because it varies sentence structure and interests the reader.
    D. Yes, because an essay should always begin with a question.

born that way and are distinctly by certain physical
                        14
marks. They are, he claimed, "a special species, a subspecies having distinct physical and mental characteristics. In general, all criminals have long, large, protruding ears; abundant hair; a thin beard; prominent front sinuses; a protruding chin; and large cheekbones." Rapists, he argued, have "brilliant eyes, delicate faces" and murderers may be distinguished by "cold, glassy eyes; nose always large and frequently

14. **F.** NO CHANGE
    G. distinguish
    H. distinguished
    J. distinguishing

GO ON TO THE NEXT PAGE.

aquiline; jaws strong; cheekbones large; hair curly,

dark, and abundant." $\boxed{15}$

15. Is the use of quotation marks in this paragraph appropriate?
    A. No, because it contains no dialogue.
    B. No, because too much physical detail is confusing.
    C. Yes, because it discusses a theory of criminology.
    D. Yes, because quotation marks are used around direct quotations.

[2]

But the myth does not die underline{easily}. During the
                                 16
1930s, a German criminologist, Gustav Aschaffenburg,

declared that stout, squat people with large abdomens

are more underline{like} to be occasional offenders, while slender
        17
builds and slight muscular development are common

among habitual offenders. In the 1940s, according to

writer Jessica Mitford, a group of Harvard sociologists

underline{who study sociology,} decided that criminals are most
                     18
likely to be "mesomorphs," muscular types with large

trunks who walk assertively, talk noisily, and behave

aggressively. Watch out for underline{those kind of}
                                      19
characteristics.

16. F. NO CHANGE
    G. easy
    H. easiest
    J. easier

17. A. NO CHANGE
    B. likely
    C. likely apt
    D. possible

18. F. NO CHANGE
    G. whom study sociological changes,
    H. who studied sociology,
    J. OMIT the underlined portion.

19. A. NO CHANGE
    B. those sort of
    C. them kind of
    D. those

[3]

underline{Around about} the turn of the century, a British
          20
physician made a detailed study of the faces of three

thousand convicts and underline{compared} them with a like
                             21
number of English college students, measuring the

underline{noses ears eyebrows and chins} of both groups. He
                          22
could find no correlation among physical types and

criminal behavior.

20. F. NO CHANGE
    G. At about
    H. Around
    J. OMIT the underlined portion.

21. A. NO CHANGE
    B. compare
    C. compares
    D. comparing

22. F. NO CHANGE
    G. noses ears and eyebrows and chins
    H. noses; ears; eyebrows and chins
    J. noses, ears, eyebrows, and chins

GO ON TO THE NEXT PAGE.

Items 23 and 24 ask about the preceding passage as a whole.

23. This essay was probably excerpted from:

   A. a general sociology textbook.
   B. a technical monograph on criminology.
   C. a news magazine.
   D. a biography of Gustav Aschaffenburg.

24. Choose the order of paragraph numbers that will make the essay's structure most logical.

   F. NO CHANGE
   G. 3, 2, 1
   H. 1, 3, 2
   J. 2, 3, 1

PASSAGE III

Scientific Advances Pose Global Risks

[1]

The history of modern pollution problems show that most have resulted from negligence and ignorance. We have an appalling tendency to interfere with nature before all of the possible consequences of our actions have been studied into completeness. We produce and distribute radioactive substances, synthetic chemicals, and many other potent compounds before fully comprehending their effects on living organisms.

Synthetic means manmade. Many of today's fashions are made with synthetic fibers. Our education is dangerously incomplete.

25. A. NO CHANGE
   B. shown
   C. shows
   D. showed

26. F. NO CHANGE
   G. a lot
   H. for completeness
   J. in depth

27. A. NO CHANGE
   B. effectiveness
   C. affect
   D. affects

28. F. NO CHANGE
   G. Synthetic fibers are manmade.
   H. Many of today's fashions are made with synthetic fibers.
   J. OMIT the underlined portion.

GO ON TO THE NEXT PAGE.

[2]

It will be argued that the purpose of science is to move into unknown territory; to explore, and to discover. It can be said that similar risks have been taken before and that these risks are necessary to technological progress. [30]

29. **A.** NO CHANGE
B. territory:
C. territory,
D. territory

30. The writer could most effectively bolster the essay at this point by:
F. including an example of one of the risks argued by some to be necessary for technological progress.
G. adding rhetorical emphasis with the sentence "The risks are necessary."
H. briefly describing an unknown territory.
J. defining the word "science."

[3]

These arguments overlook an important element. In the past, risks taken in the name of scientific progress were restricted to a small place and brief period of time. The effects of the processes we now strive to master are not either localized nor brief. Air pollution covers vast urban areas. Ocean pollutants have been discovered in nearly every part of the world. Synthetic chemicals spread over huge stretches of forest and farmland may remain in the soil for decades and years to come. Radioactive pollutants will be found in the biosphere for generations. The size and persistent of these problems have grown with the expanding power of modern science.

31. **A.** NO CHANGE
B. a important
C. importance
D. important

32. **F.** NO CHANGE
G. either
H. not neither
J. neither

33. **A.** NO CHANGE
B. for decades
C. for years to come in decades
D. for decades and years

34. **F.** NO CHANGE
G. persistence
H. persevering
J. persisting

[4]

One might also argue that the hazards of modern

GO ON TO THE NEXT PAGE.

pollutants are small <u>comparison for</u> the dangers
                            35
associated with other human activity. No estimate of

the actual harm done by smog, fallout, or chemical

residues can obscure the reality that the risks are being

taken before being fully understood.

[5]

The importance of these issues lies in the failure

of science to predict and <u>control. Human</u> intervention
                                        36
into natural processes. The true measure of the danger

is represented by the hazards we will encounter if we

enter the new age of technology without first

evaluating our responsibility to the environment.

35. **A.** NO CHANGE
    B. consideration for
    C. comparing with
    D. compared to

36. **F.** NO CHANGE
    G. control human
    H. control; human
    J. control and human

Items 37 and 38 ask about the preceding passage
as a whole.

37. Choose the order of paragraph numbers that will
    make the essay's structure most logical.

    A. NO CHANGE
    B. 2, 4, 3, 1, 5
    C. 1, 3, 2, 4, 5
    D. 5, 1, 2, 3, 4

38. This essay was probably intended for readers
    who:

    F. lack an understanding of the history of
    technology.
    G. are authorities on pollution and its causes.
    H. are interested in becoming more aware of
    our environmental problems and the possible
    solutions to these problems.
    J. have worked with radioactive substances.

GO ON TO THE NEXT PAGE.

PASSAGE IV

The Changing Scientific Workplace

[1]

Many researchers can be of greatest service to a company by staying around in the laboratory. A

39. A. NO CHANGE
B. remaining
C. remaining around
D. staying up

single outstanding discovery may of had a far greater impact on the company's five-year profit picture than

40. F. NO CHANGE
G. maybe
H. might of had
J. may have

the activities of even the most able administrator. It is simply good sense—and good economics—to allow qualified researchers to continue their work. Granting these researchers maximum freedom to explore their scientific ideas is also eminently good sense.

41. A. NO CHANGE
B. most ablest
C. more ablest
D. most abled

[2]

In recent years however this theory has fallen

42. F. NO CHANGE
G. years, however
H. years, however,
J. years however,

into wide disrepair. Companies find that many researchers continue to be highly productive throughout their careers. There is every reason to allow these researchers to continue their pioneering work.

43. A. NO CHANGE
B. argument
C. ill repute
D. disrepute

[3]

Some years ago, the theory was rampant that after the age of about 40, the average researcher began losing their creative spark. The chance of one making a major discovery was believed to drop off sharply. Hence, there really wasn't much point to

44. F. NO CHANGE
G. its
H. his or her
J. theirs

GO ON TO THE NEXT PAGE.

encouraging a person of 45 or 50 to do research. [45]

[4]

Companies are also convinced that the traditional guideposts in establishing salaries are not completely valid. In former years of long ago, the size of a man's paycheck was determined primarily by the size of his annual budget. On this basis, the researcher—however brilliant—who had perhaps one assistant and never spent much money made an extremely poor showing. Companies now realize that the two very important criteria that must also be considerable are a man's actual contributions to the company and his creative potential.

[5]

In today's era of scientific manpower shortages, companies have more reason than ever to encourage scientists to do the work for which they are most qualified. They also have greater reason than ever to provide within the laboratory the environment in which the creative processes of research can be carried out most effectively.

45. If, at this point in the essay, the writer wanted to increase the information about creative contributions from researchers, which of the following additions would be most relevant to the passage as a whole?
A. A bibliography of books about retirement
B. A description of a few of the contributions older researchers have made to science
C. A list of today's most prominent researchers
D. A brief description of a model retirement benefits plan

46. F. NO CHANGE
G. a long time ago
H. long ago
J. OMIT the underlined portion.

47. A. NO CHANGE
B. be considered
C. most considerable
D. considerable of

48. F. NO CHANGE
G. about which
H. of which
J. into which

GO ON TO THE NEXT PAGE.

Items 49 and 50 ask about the preceding passage as a whole.

49. Choose the order of paragraph numbers that will make the essay's structure most logical.

   A. NO CHANGE
   B. 1, 2, 4, 3, 5
   C. 1, 2, 3, 5, 4
   D. 3, 2, 1, 4, 5

50. Is the author's use of dashes appropriate in the essay?

   F. No, because dashes are never used in formal writing.
   G. No, because commas would have been as effective for emphasis.
   H. Yes, because dashes give emphasis to the sudden break in thought or interruption in the sentence in which they were used.
   J. Yes, because using dashes adds excitement to the essay.

PASSAGE V

An Argument in Favor of Scientific Contributions

[1]

What are those of us <u>whom</u> have chosen careers
       51

in science and engineering able to do about meeting

our current <u>problems?</u>
    52

[2]

Second, we can identify the many areas in which

science and technology, more considerately used, can

be of <u>greatest</u> service in the future than in the past to
   53

improve the quality of life. While we can make many

speeches and pass many laws, the quality of our

51. **A.** NO CHANGE
    B. who
    C. whose
    D. what

52. **F.** NO CHANGE
    G. problems.
    H. problems!
    J. problems;

53. **A.** NO CHANGE
    B. great
    C. more great
    D. greater

GO ON TO THE NEXT PAGE.

environment will be improved only <u>threw</u> better
54

knowledge and better application of that knowledge.

[3]

Third, we can recognize that much of the

dissatisfaction we suffer today results from our very

successes of former years <u>in the past</u>. We have been so
55

eminently successful in attaining material goals that

we are deeply dissatisfied <u>of the fact that</u> we cannot
56

attain other goals more rapidly. We have achieved a

better life for most people, but we are unhappy that we

have not spread it to all people. We have illuminated

many sources of environmental deterioration, <u>because</u>
57

<u>of</u> we are unhappy that we have not conquered all of
57

them. It is our <u>raising</u> expectations rather than our
58

failures that now cause our distress.

[4]

First, we can help destroy the false impression

that science and engineering have caused the current

54. **F.** NO CHANGE
     G. through
     H. though
     J. from

55. **A.** NO CHANGE
     B. of the past
     C. being in the past
     D. OMIT the underlined portion.

56. **F.** NO CHANGE
     G. in the fact that
     H. about
     J. that

57. **A.** NO CHANGE
     B. despite
     C. but
     D. also

58. **F.** NO CHANGE
     G. arising
     H. rising
     J. raised

GO ON TO THE NEXT PAGE.

world troubles. Quite the contrary, science and
                      59
engineering have made vast contributions to better

living for more people. 60

[5]

Although many of our current problems must

be cured more by social, political, and economic

instruments rather than by science and technology,

science and technology must still be the tools to make

further advances in such things as clean air, clean
        61

water, better transportation, better housing, better

medical care, more adequate welfare programs, purer

food, conservation of resources, and many other areas.

59.
A. NO CHANGE
B. Contrary to,
C. Contrasted with,
D. OMIT the underlined portion.

60. Suppose, at this point, that the writer wanted to add more information about the benefits of science and engineering. Which of the following additions would be most relevant?
F. A list of the colleges with the best science and engineering degree programs
G. Specific examples of contributions from the areas of science and engineering that have improved the standard of living
H. A brief explanation of the current world troubles
J. The names of several famous scientists and engineers

61.
A. NO CHANGE
B. advances, in
C. advances. In
D. advances—in

Items 62 and 63 ask about the preceding passage as a whole.

62. This essay was probably written for readers who:
F. are college graduates.
G. are interested in an environmental services career.
H. are in a career or contemplating a career in science or engineering.
J. are frustrated with the current world problems.

63. Choose the order of paragraph numbers that will make the essay's structure most logical.
A. NO CHANGE
B. 1, 4, 2, 3, 5
C. 5, 4, 2, 3, 1
D. 4, 2, 3, 1, 5

GO ON TO THE NEXT PAGE.

PASSAGE VI

Youth Market of Europe

With increasing prosperity, West European <u>youth am</u> having a fling that is creating distinctive consumer and cultural patterns.
₆₄

The result has been the increasing emergence in Europe of that phenomenon well known in America as the "youth market." This <u>here</u> is a market in which
₆₅
enterprising businesses cater to the demands of teen-agers and older youths in all their rock mania and pop art forms. The evolving European youth market has both <u>similarities</u> and differences from the American youth
₆₆
market.

The <u>markets</u> basis is essentially the same—more
₆₇
spending power and freedom to use it in the hands of teenagers and older youths. Young consumers also make up an <u>increasing high</u> proportion of the
₆₈
population.

Youthful tastes in the United States and Europe include a similar range of products—records and record players, tapes and CDs, VCRs and DVD players, leather jackets, "trendy" clothing, cosmetics, and soft <u>drinks, generally</u> it now is difficult to tell in
₆₉

which direction <u>transatlantic</u> teenage influences are
₇₀
flowing.

As in the United States, where "teen" and "teenager" have become merchandising terms,

64. **F.** NO CHANGE
    G. youths is
    H. youth be
    J. youth is

65. **A.** NO CHANGE
    B. here idea
    C. here thing
    D. OMIT the underlined portion.

66. **F.** NO CHANGE
    G. similarity
    H. similarities to
    J. similar

67. **A.** NO CHANGE
    B. markets'
    C. market's
    D. market

68. **F.** NO CHANGE
    G. increasingly high
    H. increasing higher
    J. high increasing

69. **A.** NO CHANGE
    B. drinks. Generally,
    C. drinks, in general
    D. drinks generally

70. **F.** NO CHANGE
    G. Trans-Atlantic
    H. trans-Atlantic
    J. Trans-atlantic

GO ON TO THE NEXT PAGE.

Europeans also have <u>adapted</u> similar terminology. In
71
Flemish and Dutch, it is "tiener" for "teenagers." The
French have simply adopted the English word
"teenager." In West Germany, the key word in
advertising addressed to teenagers is "freizeit,"
meaning "holidays" or "time off."

The most obvious difference <u>among</u> the youth
72
market in Europe and that in the United States is in
size. In terms of volume and variety of sales, the
market in Europe is only a shadow of its American
counterpart, but it is a growing shadow.

71. **A.** NO CHANGE
    B. picked up
    C. added
    D. adopted

72. **F.** NO CHANGE
    G. betwixt
    H. amongst
    J. between

Items 73–75 ask about the preceding passage as a whole.

---

73. Is the author's use of quotation marks appropriate in this essay?

    A. No, because quotation marks are used to set off a direct quote.
    B. No, because the essay has no dialogue.
    C. Yes, because quotation marks are used to set off words used in a special sense.
    D. Yes, because quotation marks indicate a conversation.

74. This essay was probably written for readers who:

    F. are interested in new trends in the consumer patterns of the world's youth.
    G. are parents of teenagers.
    H. are teenagers.
    J. are interested in the different cultural patterns of West Germany.

75. Is the use of the dash appropriate in this essay?

    A. Yes, because the dash is used to set off interruptions, additions, and illustrations.
    B. No, because the dash is never used in formal writing.
    C. Yes, because the dash adds flair to the essay.
    D. Yes, because the dash is more effective than brackets or parentheses.

END OF TEST 1
STOP! DO NOT TURN THE PAGE UNTIL TOLD TO DO SO.

2 2 2 2 2 2 2 2 2 2 2 2

MATHEMATICS TEST
60 Minutes—60 Items

DIRECTIONS: Solve each item and choose the correct answer choice. Then, fill in the corresponding oval on the bubble sheet.

Allocate time wisely. Try to solve as many items as possible, returning to skipped items if time permits.

Calculator use is permitted on this test; however, some items are best solved without the use of a calculator.

Note: Unless otherwise stated, assume all of the following.

1. Illustrative figures are NOT necessarily drawn to scale.
2. The word *average* indicates arithmetic mean.
3. The word *line* indicates a straight line.
4. Geometric figures lie in a plane.

Answers are on page 640, and explanations begin on page 646.

---

1. What is the additive inverse of $-\frac{2}{3}$?

   DO YOUR FIGURING HERE.

   A. $-\frac{3}{2}$
   B. 0
   C. $\frac{2}{3}$
   D. 1
   E. $\frac{3}{2}$

2. In the figure below, if $\angle AOC$ is a central angle and equals 70°, what is the measure of $\angle ABC$?

   F. 22°
   G. 35°
   H. 50°
   J. 70°
   K. 140°

GO ON TO THE NEXT PAGE.

3. Which of the following is an element of the solution set of the equation $x^2 + 6x + 8 = 0$?

   A. -8
   B. -2
   C. 4
   D. 6
   E. 8

DO YOUR FIGURING HERE.

4. In the figure below $l_1 \parallel l_2$. If $\angle x = 70°$ and $\angle y = 105°$, what is the measure of $\angle r$?

   F. $35°$
   G. $45°$
   H. $85°$
   J. $145°$
   K. $175°$

5. $A = \dfrac{2gr}{g+r}$. What is the value of g when $r = 1$ and $A = 4$?

   A. -2
   B. $\frac{4}{7}$
   C. $\frac{8}{5}$
   D. 2
   E. 4

GO ON TO THE NEXT PAGE.

6. The figure below represents which of the following equations?

DO YOUR FIGURING HERE.

F. $y = x$
G. $y = -x$
H. $y = |x|$
J. $|y| = x$
K. $y = x^2$

7. Which of the following is an illustration of the distributive property?

A. $(12 \cdot 25)(4) = 12(25 \cdot 4)$
B. $7n + 2 - 3n = 7n - 3n + 2$
C. $(17)(b^2)(5) = (17)(5)(b)^2$
D. $ab + ac = ba + ca$
E. $x(x + 2) = x^2 + 2x$

8. Joshua buys a television that costs $600. If the sales tax is 7%, what is the total cost of the purchase?

F. $4.20
G. $42.00
H. $420.00
J. $604.20
K. $642.00

9. What is the value of $-x^2 - 2x^3$ when $x = -1$?

A. -3
B. -1
C. 0
D. 1
E. 3

GO ON TO THE NEXT PAGE.

10. What is the average of $n+3$, $2n-1$, and $3n+4$?

    F. $\frac{5n+6}{3}$
    G. $2n+2$
    H. $3n+3$
    J. $\frac{6n+7}{3}$
    K. $6n+6$

11. If $x=9$, what is the value of $x^0 + x^{\frac{1}{2}} + x^{-2}$?

    A. $3\frac{1}{81}$
    B. $4\frac{1}{81}$
    C. $5\frac{7}{18}$
    D. $76\frac{1}{2}$
    E. $77\frac{1}{2}$

12. $4\sqrt{3} + 3\sqrt{27} = ?$

    F. $7\sqrt{30}$
    G. $10\sqrt{3}$
    H. $13\sqrt{3}$
    J. 63
    K. 108

13. Jessica Dawn received marks of 87, 93, and 86 on 3 successive tests. What grade must she receive on a fourth test in order to have an average grade of 90?

    A. 90
    B. 91
    C. 92
    D. 93
    E. 94

14. In terms of x, what is the total number of cents in $4x$ dimes?

    F. $0.04x$
    G. $0.4x$
    H. $4x$
    J. $40x$
    K. $400x$

DO YOUR FIGURING HERE.

GO ON TO THE NEXT PAGE.

15. Which of the following is shown by the graph below?

A. $-5 \le x < 3$
B. $-5 < x$ or $x < 3$
C. $-5 \le x$ or $x > 3$
D. $-5 \le x \le 3$
E. $-5 \ge x$ or $x > 3$

16. $2\frac{2}{5} - 1\frac{7}{8} = ?$

F. $\frac{11}{40}$

G. $\frac{19}{40}$

H. $\frac{21}{40}$

J. $\frac{7}{13}$

K. $1\frac{5}{40}$

17. In a circle with a radius of 6, what is the measure (in degrees) of an arc whose length is 2π?

A. $20°$
B. $30°$
C. $60°$
D. $90°$
E. $120°$

18. If $\frac{2x}{3\sqrt{2}} = \frac{3\sqrt{2}}{x}$, what is the positive value of x?

F. 9
G. 3
H. $2\sqrt{3}$
J. $\sqrt{6}$
K. $\sqrt{3}$

19. If $f(x) = 2x - x^2$ and $g(x) = x - 4$, what is the value of $g(f(2))$?

A. -8
B. -4
C. -2
D. 0
E. 3

GO ON TO THE NEXT PAGE.

20. What is the solution set of the equation $|5-2x|=7$?

    F. $\{6,-1\}$
    G. $\{6\}$
    H. $\{-1\}$
    J. $\{1\}$
    K. The empty set

21. Which of the following is equivalent to $\frac{3-\frac{3}{x}}{x-1}$?

    A. $\frac{1}{x-1}$
    B. $\frac{1}{3}$
    C. $x+1$
    D. 3
    E. $\frac{3}{x}$

22. What is the slope of the line that passes through the points $(-3,5)$ and $(4,7)$?

    F. $\sqrt{53}$
    G. $\frac{7}{2}$
    H. 2
    J. $\frac{1}{2}$
    K. $\frac{2}{7}$

23. In the figure below, diameter $\overline{AB}$ is perpendicular to chord $\overline{CD}$ at point E. If chord $\overline{CD}=8$ inches and $\overline{OE}=3$ inches, what is the length of the radius of the circle, in inches?

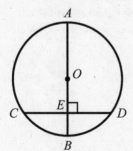

    A. $\sqrt{3}$
    B. $\sqrt{5}$
    C. $\sqrt{7}$
    D. $\sqrt{15}$
    E. 5

DO YOUR FIGURING HERE.

GO ON TO THE NEXT PAGE.

DO YOUR FIGURING HERE.

24. The diagonals of parallelogram $ABCD$ intersect at point E. If $\overline{DB} = 4x + 2$ and $\overline{DE} = x + 4$, what is the value of x?

    F. 3
    G. 2
    H. 1
    J. $\frac{2}{3}$
    K. 0

25. If the measure of the central angle of a sector of a circle is $120°$, what is the area, in square units, of the sector if the radius is 6 units long?

    A. 4π
    B. 6π
    C. 8π
    D. 10π
    E. 12π

26. If the statement "if two triangles are red, then they are equal in area" is true, then which of the following *must* be true?

    F. If the two triangles are not equal in area, then they are not red.
    G. If the two triangles are equal in area, then they are red.
    H. If the two triangles are equal in area, then they are not red.
    J. If the two triangles are not red, then they are not equal in area.
    K. If the two triangles are red, then they are not equal in area.

27. If $\frac{a}{b} = \frac{r}{t}$, then which of the following is NOT necessarily true?

    A. $\frac{a}{r} = \frac{b}{t}$
    B. $\frac{a}{t} = \frac{b}{r}$
    C. $\frac{a+b}{b} = \frac{r+t}{t}$
    D. $\frac{b}{a} = \frac{t}{r}$
    E. $at = br$

GO ON TO THE NEXT PAGE.

28. If $-2x + 5 = 2 - (5 - 2x)$, then $x = ?$

DO YOUR FIGURING HERE.

    F. 6
    G. 5
    H. 4
    J. 3
    K. 2

29. $\dfrac{[1 + \sin(x)][1 - \sin(x)]}{[1 + \cos(x)][1 - \cos(x)]}$ is equivalent to which of the following?

    A. $\cos(x)$
    B. $\tan(x)$
    C. $\tan^2(x)$
    D. $\cos^2(x)$
    E. $\cot^2(x)$

30. In the figure below, $\triangle ACB$ is a right triangle. $\overline{CE}$ is the median to hypotenuse $\overline{AB}$, and $\overline{AB} = 14$ centimeters. What is the length, in centimeters, of $\overline{CE}$?

    F. 5
    G. 6
    H. 7
    J. 8
    K. Cannot be determined from the given information

31. If y varies directly as x, and $y = 10$ when $x = \frac{1}{5}$, what is the value of y when $x = \frac{1}{2}$?

    A. 1
    B. 4
    C. 7
    D. 16
    E. 25

GO ON TO THE NEXT PAGE.

32. $\frac{(-1)(2)(-3)(4)(-5)}{(5)(-4)(3)(-2)(1)} = ?$

DO YOUR FIGURING HERE.

    F. −2
    G. −1
    H. 1
    J. 2
    K. 3

33. In the diagram below, chords $\overline{AB}$ and $\overline{CD}$ of circle O intersect at point E. If $\overline{AE} = 6$ units long, $\overline{EB} = 4$ units long, $\overline{CE} = x$, and $\overline{ED} = 6x$, then how many units long is x?

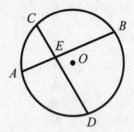

    A. 1
    B. $1\frac{3}{7}$
    C. 2
    D. 4
    E. 6

34. The measure of the vertex angle of an isosceles triangle is 50°. What is the measure, in degrees, of each base angle?

    F. 40°
    G. 50°
    H. 65°
    J. 75°
    K. 130°

GO ON TO THE NEXT PAGE.

35. Using the table below, what is the median of the following data?

Score	Frequency
20	4
30	4
50	7

A. 20
B. 30
C. 40
D. 50
E. 60

DO YOUR FIGURING HERE.

36. Which of the following number lines represents the solution set of $x^2 - 2x - 3 > 0$?

F.

G.

H.

J.

K.

37. The expression $\sin(x) + \dfrac{\cos^2(x)}{\sin(x)}$ is equal to which of the following?

A. 1
B. $\sin(x)$
C. $\cos(x)$
D. $\dfrac{1}{\sin(x)}$
E. $\dfrac{1}{\cos(x)}$

GO ON TO THE NEXT PAGE.

38. The value of $(2.5 \cdot 10^5)^2$ is equal to which of the following?

    F. $6.25 \cdot 10^7$

    G. $6.25 \cdot 10^{10}$

    H. $2.5 \cdot 10^7$

    J. $2.7 \cdot 10^{10}$

    K. $5 \cdot 10^7$

39. If $A * B$ is defined as $\frac{AB - B}{-B}$, what is the value of $-2 * 2$?

    A. -3
    B. -1
    C. 0
    D. 1
    E. 3

40. If 1 of the roots of the equation $x^2 + kx - 12 = 0$ is 4, what is the value of k?

    F. -1
    G. 0
    H. 1
    J. 3
    K. 7

41. In the figure below, D is a point on $\overline{AB}$ and E is a point on $\overline{BC}$ such that $\overline{DE} \parallel \overline{AC}$. If $\overline{DB} = 4$ units long, $\overline{AB} = 10$ units long, and $\overline{BC} = 20$ units long, how many units long is $\overline{EC}$?

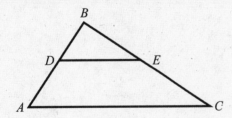

    A. 4
    B. 6
    C. 8
    D. 10
    E. 12

DO YOUR FIGURING HERE.

GO ON TO THE NEXT PAGE.

42. $(x+2)(x-4)-(x+4)(x-2) = ?$

   F. 0
   G. $2x^2 + 4x - 16$
   H. $-4x$
   J. $4x$
   K. $-4x - 16$

43. If the sum of the measures of the interior angles of a polygon equals the sum of the measures of the exterior angles, how many sides does the polygon have?

   A. 3
   B. 4
   C. 5
   D. 6
   E. 7

44. If the perimeter of an equilateral triangle is 12 inches, what is its area, in square inches?

   F. $2\sqrt{3}$
   G. $4\sqrt{3}$
   H. 8
   J. $6\sqrt{3}$
   K. $36\sqrt{3}$

45. If the ratio of 2 complementary angles is 8:1, what is the measure, in degrees, of the smaller angle?

   A. 10
   B. 20
   C. 30
   D. 40
   E. 80

DO YOUR FIGURING HERE.

GO ON TO THE NEXT PAGE.

46. Given a square, a rectangle, a trapezoid, and a circle, if one figure is selected at random, what is the probability that the figure has four right angles?

   F. 1
   G. $\frac{3}{4}$
   H. $\frac{1}{2}$
   J. $\frac{1}{4}$
   K. 0

DO YOUR FIGURING HERE.

47. A man travels 320 miles in 8 hours. If he continues at the same rate, how many miles will he travel in the next 2 hours?

   A. 6
   B. 40
   C. 80
   D. 120
   E. 240

48. $\frac{\sin(x)}{\cos(x)} + \frac{\cos(x)}{\sin(x)} = ?$

   F. 1
   G. $\sin(x)$
   H. $\frac{1}{\sin(x)\cos(x)}$
   J. $\tan(x)$
   K. $\frac{\sin(x) + \cos(x)}{\sin(x)\cos(x)}$

49. The average temperatures for 5 days were 82°, 86°, 91°, 79°, and 91°. What is the mode of these temperatures?

   A. 79°
   B. 82°
   C. 85.8°
   D. 86°
   E. 91°

GO ON TO THE NEXT PAGE.

50. A booklet contains 30 pages. If 9 pages in the booklet have drawings, what percentage of the pages in the booklet has drawings?

    F. 30%
    G. 9%
    H. 3%
    J. 1%
    K. $\frac{3}{10}$%

51. Which of the following represents $-7t + 6t^2 - 3$ when it is completely factored?

    A. $(3t - 1)(2t + 3)$
    B. $(3t + 1)(2t - 3)$
    C. $(6t - 1)(t + 3)$
    D. $(6t + 1)(t - 3)$
    E. $(2t - 1)(3t + 3)$

52. What is the solution set of $2^{x^2 + 2x} = 2^{-1}$?

    F. $\{1\}$
    G. $\{-1\}$
    H. $\{1, -1\}$
    J. $\{2\}$
    K. The empty set

53. Jessica is 3 years younger than Joshua. If x represents Joshua's age now, what was Jessica's age four years ago in terms of x?

    A. $x - 1$
    B. $x - 3$
    C. $x - 4$
    D. $x - 6$
    E. $x - 7$

DO YOUR FIGURING HERE.

GO ON TO THE NEXT PAGE.

54. In a drama club, x students contributed y dollars each to buy an $18 gift for their advisor. If three more students had contributed, each student could have contributed one dollar less to buy the same gift. Which of the following sets of equations expresses this relationship?

    F. $xy = 18$ and $(x+3)(y-1) = 18$
    G. $xy = 18$ and $(x-3)(y+1) = 18$
    H. $xy = 18$ and $(x+3)(y+1) = 18$
    J. $xy = 18$ and $(x-3)(y-1) = 18$
    K. $xy = 18$ and $(x+1)(y-3) = 18$

55. $\frac{1}{2}\sqrt{112} - \sqrt{28} + 2\sqrt{63} = ?$

    A. $6\sqrt{7}$
    B. $7\sqrt{7}$
    C. $8\sqrt{7}$
    D. $9\sqrt{7}$
    E. $10\sqrt{7}$

56. What is the value of x for the following set of simultaneous equations?

    $$\frac{1}{x} + \frac{1}{y} = \frac{1}{4}$$
    $$\frac{1}{x} - \frac{1}{y} = \frac{3}{4}$$

    F. 4
    G. 2
    H. $\frac{1}{2}$
    J. $\frac{1}{4}$
    K. -4

57. Which set could represent the lengths of the sides of a triangle?

    A. $\{1, 3, 6\}$
    B. $\{2, 4, 7\}$
    C. $\{2, 10, 12\}$
    D. $\{4, 6, 8\}$
    E. $\{4, 4, 10\}$

DO YOUR FIGURING HERE.

GO ON TO THE NEXT PAGE.

58. What is the solution set, in terms of a and b, for the following system of equations?

$$ax + y = b$$
$$2ax + y = 2b$$

F. $\{-\frac{b}{a}, 1\}$

G. $\{-a, b\}$

H. $\{\frac{b}{a}, 0\}$

J. $\{\frac{b}{a}, \frac{a}{b}\}$

K. $\{\frac{2a}{b}, \frac{2b}{a}\}$

DO YOUR FIGURING HERE.

59. In the figure below, $\sin(\theta) = \frac{r}{4}$. What is the value of $\cos(\theta)$?

A. $\frac{\sqrt{16 - r^2}}{4}$

B. $\frac{4 - r}{4}$

C. $\frac{16 - r^2}{2}$

D. $\frac{4 - r}{2}$

E. $\frac{16 - r^2}{r}$

60. If 3 copier machines can copy 300 sheets in 3 hours, assuming the same rate, how long, in hours, will it take 6 such copiers to copy 600 sheets?

F. 2

G. 3

H. 4

J. 6

K. 9

END OF TEST 2
STOP! DO NOT TURN THE PAGE UNTIL TOLD TO DO SO.
DO NOT RETURN TO THE PREVIOUS TEST.

3 3 3 3 3 3 3 3 3 3 3 3

READING TEST

35 Minutes—40 Items

DIRECTIONS: The passages presented in the test are each followed by a set of items. Read the passage and choose the best answer for each item. Fill in the corresponding oval on your bubble sheet. You may refer to the passage as often as necessary to answer the passage items.

Answers are on page 641, and explanations begin on page 653.

Passage I

NATURAL SCIENCES: This passage discusses the production of electromagnetic radiation.

Whenever a changing electric field is produced, electromagnetic radiation is also produced. If you run a comb through your hair, you disturb electrons (negatively charged subatomic particles) in both hair
5 and comb, producing static electricity. Every electron is surrounded by an electric field. Any sudden change in the electron's motion gives rise to *electromagnetic radiation*. If you were to run a comb through your hair while standing near an AM radio, you would produce
10 radio static. These previous examples illustrate an important principle: Whenever you change the motion of an electron, you generate electromagnetic waves.

If you apply this principle to a heated object, you must first determine what is meant by heat. When an
15 object is hot, its atoms are vibrating rapidly. The hotter an object becomes, the faster the atoms vibrate. The vibrating atoms collide with the electrons in the material. Each time the motion of an electron is disturbed, it emits a photon. Therefore, you should
20 expect a heated object to emit electromagnetic radiation. This type of radiation, called *black body radiation,* is very common and is responsible for the light emitted from an incandescent light bulb.

A *spectrum* is an array of electromagnetic
25 radiation in order of wavelength. The spectrum of visible light, such as what you see when you look at a rainbow, is most familiar, but the visible spectrum is just a small segment of the much larger electromagnetic spectrum.

30 The average wavelength of visible light is about 0.0005 mm. Because this unit is so small (50 light waves could be lined up end to end across the thickness of ordinary plastic wrap), wavelengths are measured in *Angstroms*. One Angstrom (Å) is 10^{-10} m.
35 The wavelength of visible light ranges from 4,000 Å to 7,000 Å. Light near the short wavelength end of the visible spectrum (4,000 Å) looks violet, and light near the long wavelength end (7,000 Å) looks red (Figure 1). Beyond the red end of the visible spectrum lies
40 infrared radiation, where wavelengths range from 7,000 Å to 1 mm. At wavelengths shorter than violet, there is ultraviolet radiation. These wavelengths range from 4,000 Å down to about 100 Å. At wavelengths shorter than these are x-rays and gamma rays. Long
45 wavelength radiation (7,000 Å to 1 mm) can be observed in "heat lamps," where our skin senses infrared wavelengths as heat. These lower-energy infrared photons can warm you, but because of their low energy, they cannot give you a tan. In contrast are
50 the short wavelengths, which contain a high amount of energy. These wavelengths can be dangerous. Small doses can give you a suntan, larger doses produce sunburns, and extreme doses might produce skin cancers.

55 When a filament is heated, two types of collisions take place among the electrons. Gentle collisions produce low-energy photons with long wavelengths, and violent collisions produce high-energy photons with short wavelengths. A graph of the energy emitted
60 at different wavelengths produces a curve like that in Figure 2. The curve indicates that gentle collisions and violent collisions occur infrequently. Most collisions lie somewhere in between, producing photons of intermediate wavelengths.

65 The *wavelength of maximum* (λ_{max}) is the wavelength at which an object emits the maximum amount of energy. The wavelength of maximum depends on the object's temperature. As an object is heated, the

GO ON TO THE NEXT PAGE.

average collision becomes more violent, producing
70 high-energy, shorter-wavelength photons. The hotter
the object is, the shorter the λ_{max} is (Figure 2). Physics
shows that λ_{max} in Angstroms equals 30 million
divided by the temperature in degrees Kelvin.

$$\lambda_{max} = \frac{30 \cdot 10^6}{T}$$

75   This is a very important point in astronomy, since
with this equation it is possible to determine the
temperature of a star from its light. It is also possible to
estimate the temperature of a star from the color of
light it emits. For a hot star λ_{max} lies in the ultraviolet
80 spectrum and most of the radiation cannot be seen, but
in the visible range the star emits more blue than red.
Thus, a hot star looks blue. In contrast, a cooler star
radiates its maximum energy in the infrared. In the
visible range of the spectrum it radiates more red than
85 blue and therefore looks red.

The total amount of radiation emitted at all
wavelengths depends on the number of collisions per
second. If an object's temperature is high, there are
many collisions and it emits more light than a cooler
90 object of the same size. Energy is measured in units
called *ergs*. The total radiation given off by 1 cm^2 of
the object in ergs per second equals a constant number,
represented by s ($5.67 \cdot 10^{-5}$ ergs/cm^2 sec degree^4)
times the temperature raised to the fourth power.

95      $$E = sT^4 \, (\text{ergs/sec/cm}^2)$$

It can be seen from this equation that doubling an
object's temperature would cause the object to radiate
2^4, or 16, times more energy.

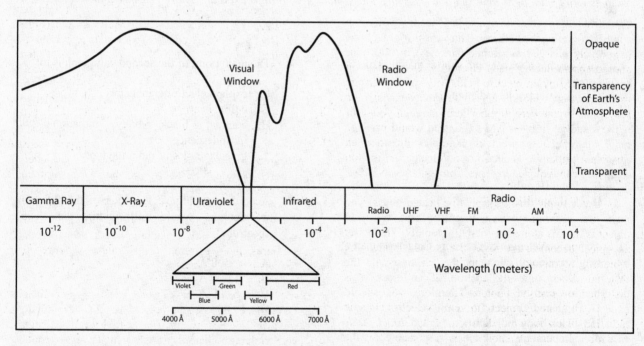

Figure 1: The electromagnetic spectrum includes all wavelengths of electromagnetic radiation. Earth's atmosphere is relatively opaque at most wavelengths. Visual and radio windows allow light and some radio waves to reach Earth's surface.

GO ON TO THE NEXT PAGE.

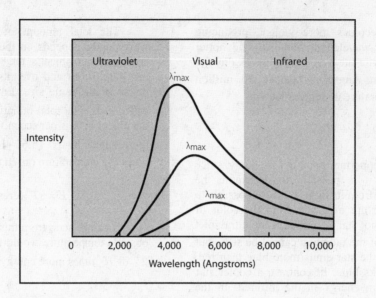

Figure 2: The intensity of radiation emitted by a heated body depends on wavelength. λ_{max} designates the wavelength of maximum intensity. Hotter objects radiate more energy and have shorter λ_{max} than cooler objects. A hot object radiates more blue light than red and therefore looks blue. A cool object radiates more red than blue and therefore looks red.

1. An x-ray has a wavelength shorter than that of:

    I. ultraviolet radiation.
    II. infrared radiation.
    III. 500 Å.

    A. I only
    B. III only
    C. I and III only
    D. I, II, and III

2. A short wavelength can be more dangerous than a long wavelength due to its:

    F. low energy.
    G. high energy.
    H. black body radiation.
    J. temperature.

3. At $\lambda_{max} = \frac{30 \cdot 10^6}{T}$ an object:

    A. turns blue.
    B. produces gentle collisions of electrons.
    C. releases radio static.
    D. emits a maximum amount of energy.

4. The main point of the second paragraph is to:

    F. explain electromagnetism.
    G. define heat.
    H. contrast black body radiation with incandescence.
    J. give examples of radiation types.

5. According to Figure 1, which of the following wavelengths would fall within the visible spectrum?

    A. 500 Å
    B. 1,000 Å
    C. 5,000 Å
    D. 10,000 Å

6. In the equation shown in line 95, what is T?

    F. Time
    G. Wavelength
    H. Number of photons emitted
    J. Temperature

GO ON TO THE NEXT PAGE.

7. An astronomer views two stars of different temperatures. Which is hotter?

    A. The one that is larger
    B. The one that is smaller
    C. The one that is redder
    D. The one that is bluer

8. Lines 87–88 refer to "collisions per second," meaning collisions of:

    I. photons.
    II. electrons.
    III. photons with electrons.

    F. I only
    G. II only
    H. III only
    J. I, II, and III

9. According to Figure 2, which of the following statements is true?

    A. λ_{max} of a hot object varies with size.
    B. Temperature is unrelated to wavelength.
    C. A cool object radiates red.
    D. Ultraviolet light has a longer wavelength than infrared light.

10. Heating an object from an initial temperature of 2,000 K to a final temperature of 4,000 K would:

    F. multiply its radiated energy by 16.
    G. decrease its radiated energy by half.
    H. have no effect on the energy released.
    J. cause it to radiate more red light.

GO ON TO THE NEXT PAGE.

Passage II

PROSE FICTION: This passage is adapted from the short story "Paul's Case" by Willa Cather.

It was Paul's afternoon to appear before the faculty of Pittsburgh High School to account for his various misdemeanors. He had been suspended a week ago, and his father had called at the Principal's office
5 and confessed his perplexity about his son. Paul entered the faculty room suave and smiling. His clothes were a trifle outgrown, and the tan velvet on the collar of his open overcoat was frayed and worn; but for all that there was something of the dandy in him, and he
10 wore an opal pin in his neatly knotted black four-in-hand, and a red carnation in his buttonhole. This latter adornment the faculty somehow felt was not properly significant of the contrite spirit befitting a boy under the ban of suspension.

15 Paul was tall for his age and very thin, with high, cramped shoulders and a narrow chest. His eyes were remarkable for a certain hysterical brilliancy, and he continually used them in a conscious, theatrical sort of way, peculiarly offensive in a boy. The pupils were
20 abnormally large, as though he was addicted to belladonna, but there was a glassy glitter about them, which that drug does not produce.

When questioned by the Principal as to why he was there Paul stated, politely enough, that he wanted
25 to come back to school. This was a lie, but Paul was quite accustomed to lying; he found it, indeed, indispensable for overcoming friction. His teachers were asked to state their respective charges against him, which they did with such a rancor and
30 aggrievement as evinced that this was not a usual case. Disorder and impertinence were among the offenses named, yet each of his instructors felt that it was scarcely possible to put into words the real cause of the trouble, which lay in a sort of hysterically defiant
35 manner of the boy's, in the contempt which they all knew he felt for them, and which he seemingly made not the least effort to conceal. Once, when he had been making a synopsis of a paragraph at the blackboard, his English teacher had stepped to his side and attempted
40 to guide his hand. Paul had started back with a shudder and thrust his hands violently behind him. The astonished woman could scarcely have been more hurt and embarrassed had he struck at her. The insult was so involuntary and definitely personal as to be
45 unforgettable. In one way or another he had made all his teachers, men and women alike, conscious of the same feeling of physical aversion. In one class he habitually sat with his hand shading his eyes; in another he always looked out of the window during the
50 recitation; in another he made a running commentary on the lecture, with humorous intention.

His teachers felt this afternoon that his whole attitude was symbolized by his shrug and his flippant red carnation flower, and they fell upon him without
55 mercy, his English teacher leading the pack. He stood through it smiling, his pale lips parted over his white teeth. (His lips were continuously twitching, and he had a habit of raising his eyebrows that was contemptuous and irritating to the last degree.) Older
60 boys than Paul had broken down and shed tears under that baptism of fire, but his set smile did not once desert him, and his only sign of discomfort was the nervous trembling of the fingers that toyed with the buttons of his overcoat, and an occasional jerking of
65 the other hand that held his hat. Paul was always smiling, always glancing about him, seeming to feel that people might be watching him and trying to detect something. This conscious expression, since it was as far as possible from boyish mirthfulness, was usually
70 attributed to insolence or "smartness."

11. This short story is subtitled "A Study in Temperament," which suggests that Cather wants to examine:

   A. a certain type of character.
   B. reactions under pressure.
   C. how people change over time.
   D. people and their settings.

12. The introductory phrases "something of the dandy" (line 9), "hysterical brilliancy" (line 17), and "peculiarly offensive" (line 19):

   I. describe Paul's reaction to his peers.
   II. show the narrator's distaste for Paul.
   III. reveal Paul as an unpleasant character.

   F. I only
   G. III only
   H. I and II only
   J. II and III only

GO ON TO THE NEXT PAGE.

13. Cather makes it clear in the first paragraph that the faculty of the high school:

   A. is perplexed by Paul's actions.
   B. finds Paul's demeanor inappropriate.
   C. cannot understand Paul's words.
   D. wants only the best for Paul.

14. The words "hysterical" and "hysterically," as used in lines 17 and 34, respectively, seem to imply:

   F. delirium.
   G. raving.
   H. uncontrolled behavior.
   J. frothing.

15. Cather implies that the most serious flaw Paul has is his:

   A. inability to complete his work.
   B. flippant sense of humor.
   C. drug use.
   D. failure to hide his contempt for others.

16. To keep the reader from sympathizing with the faculty, Cather compares them metaphorically to:

   F. rabbits.
   G. wolves.
   H. dictators.
   J. comedians.

17. Cather uses the phrase "baptism of fire" (line 61) to denote the:

   A. challenge faced by students in a faculty inquisition.
   B. youthfulness of Paul and his fellow students.
   C. obstacles adolescents confront while growing up.
   D. fury with which Paul faced the faculty.

18. "Smartness" (line 70) is used to mean:

   F. wit.
   G. intelligence.
   H. impudence.
   J. reasonableness.

19. Which adjective does NOT describe Paul as he is presented in this story?

   A. Defiant
   B. Proud
   C. Flippant
   D. Candid

20. By the end of the selection, we find that the faculty:

   F. resent and loathe Paul.
   G. admire and trust Paul.
   H. struggle to understand Paul.
   J. are physically revolted by Paul.

GO ON TO THE NEXT PAGE.

Passage III

HUMANITIES: This passage is adapted from Thomas Bulfinch's *Mythology*.

Minerva was the goddess of wisdom, but on one occasion she did a very foolish thing; she entered into competition with Juno and Venus for the prize of beauty. It happened thus: At the nuptials of Peleus and
5 Thetis all the gods were invited with the exception of Eris, or Discord. Enraged at her exclusion, the goddess threw a golden apple among the guests, with the inscription, "For the fairest." Thereupon Juno, Venus, and Minerva each claimed the apple. Jupiter, not
10 willing to decide in so delicate a matter, sent the goddesses to Mount Ida, where the beautiful shepherd Paris was tending his flocks, and to him was committed the decision. The goddesses accordingly appeared before him. Juno promised him power and riches,
15 Minerva glory and renown in war, and Venus the fairest of women for his wife, each attempting to bias his decision in her own favour. Paris decided in favour of Venus and gave her the golden apple, thus making the two other goddesses his enemies. Under the
20 protection of Venus, Paris sailed to Greece, and was hospitably received by Menelaus, king of Sparta. Now Helen, the wife of Menelaus, was the very woman whom Venus had destined for Paris, the fairest of her sex. She had been sought as a bride by numerous
25 suitors, and before her decision was made known, they all, at the suggestion of Ulysses, one of their number, took an oath that they would defend her from all injury and avenge her cause if necessary. She chose Menelaus, and was living with him happily when Paris
30 became their guest. Paris, aided by Venus, persuaded her to elope with him, and carried her to Troy, whence arose the famous Trojan War, the theme of the greatest poems of antiquity, those of Homer and Virgil.

Menelaus called upon his brother chieftains of
35 Greece to fulfill their pledge, and join him in his efforts to recover his wife. They generally came forward, but Ulysses, who had married Penelope, and was very happy in his wife and child, had no disposition to embark in such a troublesome affair. He therefore hung
40 back and Palamedes was sent to urge him. When Palamedes arrived at Ithaca, Ulysses pretended to be mad. He yoked an ass and an ox together to the plough and began to sow salt. Palamedes, to try him, placed the infant Telemachus before the plough, whereupon
45 the father turned the plough aside, showing plainly that he was no madman, and after that could no longer refuse to fulfill his promise. Being now himself gained for the undertaking, he lent his aid to bring in other reluctant chiefs, especially Achilles. This hero was the
50 son of that Thetis at whose marriage the apple of

Discord had been thrown among the goddesses. Thetis was herself one of the immortals, a sea-nymph, and knowing that her son was fated to perish before Troy if he went on the expedition, she endeavored to prevent
55 his going. She sent him away to the court of King Lycomedes, and induced him to conceal himself in the disguise of a maiden among the daughters of the king. Ulysses, hearing he was there, went disguised as a merchant to the palace and offered for sale female
60 ornaments, among which he had placed some arms. While the king's daughters were engrossed with the other contents of the merchant's pack, Achilles handled the weapons and thereby betrayed himself to the keen eye of Ulysses, who found no great difficulty
65 in persuading him to disregard his mother's prudent counsels and join his countrymen in the war.

21. By describing Jupiter as "not willing to decide in so delicate a matter" (lines 9–10), the author implies that:

   A. Jupiter is usually heavy-handed.
   B. any decision is bound to offend someone.
   C. Jupiter is overly sensitive.
   D. the problems are so obscure that no one can judge them.

22. The word "disposition" (line 38) is used to mean:

   F. inclination.
   G. nature.
   H. integrity.
   J. value.

23. All of the following assertions are examples of the author's inserting himself into the narrative EXCEPT:

   A. Minerva did a foolish thing.
   B. The poems of Homer and Virgil were great.
   C. Helen was the fairest of her sex.
   D. The greatest poems of antiquity were about the Trojan War.

GO ON TO THE NEXT PAGE.

24. The sowing of salt (line 43) is intended to show:

   F. Ulysses' attempt to be found insane.
   G. the difficulty of cultivating in rocky soil.
   H. how the tears of the gods created the sea.
   J. Ulysses' talent as a soldier rather than a farmer.

25. When Palamedes tries Ulysses (lines 43–47), he:

   A. finds him guilty.
   B. judges him.
   C. tests him.
   D. attempts to help him.

26. The author reveals that Thetis is a sea-nymph in order to explain:

   F. why she married Peleus.
   G. why she dislikes the idea of war.
   H. the effect of the apple of Discord.
   J. her ability to predict the future.

27. Among the chieftains of Greece apparently are:

   A. Juno, Venus, and Minerva.
   B. Paris and Lycomedes.
   C. Ulysses, Achilles, and Menelaus.
   D. Eris and Thetis.

28. Why does Ulysses display arms among the ornaments?

   F. To trick Achilles into revealing himself
   G. As a declaration of war
   H. To mislead the daughters of the king
   J. To complete his disguise as a merchant

29. This passage foreshadows which of the following events?

   I. The death of Achilles
   II. The advent of war
   III. The downfall of Paris

   A. I only
   B. II only
   C. I and II only
   D. II and III only

30. A reasonable title for this narrative might be:

   F. "Achilles and Ulysses"
   G. "The Apple of Discord Leads to War"
   H. "Beauty and the Beast"
   J. "The Pettiness of the Gods"

GO ON TO THE NEXT PAGE.

Passage IV

SOCIAL STUDIES: This passage discusses the history of African Americans in Congress.

Only with the enforcement of the Reconstruction Act of 1867 and the ratification of the Fifteenth Amendment to the Constitution—nearly 70 years after the ratification of the U.S. Constitution—did African
5 Americans first win seats in Congress. Hiram Revels of Mississippi became the first African American to serve in Congress when he took his seat in the Senate on February 25, 1870. Joseph Rainey of South Carolina became the first African American member of the
10 House of Representatives later in 1870. In the next 80 years, nearly seventy African Americans served in Congress.

African Americans throughout the South became politically active soon after emancipation and the close
15 of the Civil War. State conventions and local political societies such as the Union League provided an opportunity for freed African Americans to articulate their vision of full participation in the political and economic life of the former slave states. Out of this
20 broad-based political mobilization emerged a generation of African American leaders who nearly unanimously adhered to the Republican Party because it had championed the rights of African Americans. African Americans elected to Congress during Reconstruction
25 found the national legislature an effective forum for the advocacy of political equality. Following the end of federal Reconstruction in 1877, African Americans continued to win election to Congress and they carried on the struggle for civil rights and economic
30 opportunity. The African American congressional representatives of the late nineteenth century were the most prominent indication of the persistence of political organization on a local level in the South.

During the 1890s and early 1900s, no African
35 American won election to Congress, in part because of restrictive state election codes in some southern states. During World War I and in the following decade, however, African American migration to northern cities established the foundation for political
40 organization in urban centers. Oscar DePriest's election in 1928 as a representative from Chicago began a slow but steady succession of political victories in the North. Over the next three decades African Americans won congressional seats in New
45 York City, Detroit, and Philadelphia. In the wake of the civil rights movement and the enforcement of the Voting Rights Act of 1965, African Americans regained seats in the South. Since the 1930s, nearly all African American representatives have been
50 Democrats.

Since the nineteenth century, African American members of Congress have served as advocates for all African Americans as well as representatives for their constituencies. During Reconstruction and the late
55 nineteenth century, African American representatives called on their colleagues to protect the voting rights of African Americans. These members of Congress, many of them former slaves, also called for expanded educational opportunities and land grants for freed
60 African Americans. In the mid-twentieth century, African American representatives turned to the needs of urban communities and urged federal programs for improved housing and job training. As the most prominent African American office-holders of the
65 time, these representatives served as defenders of the civil rights movement and proponents of legislation to end segregation. In 1971, the establishment of the Congressional Black Caucus offered a formal means of representing the combined interests of African
70 Americans. The caucus has demonstrated a special concern for the protection of civil rights; the guarantee of equal opportunity in education, employment, and housing; and a broad array of foreign and domestic policy issues.

75 African Americans in Congress have been further united by their shared experience in the African American community. Many of the early Black representatives were born in slavery. The political and economic opportunities of Reconstruction offered these
80 representatives the hope that African Americans might achieve genuine equality in American society, while the opposition of some white Southerners reminded them of the need for federal protection of the liberties won in the aftermath of the Civil War.

85 Since the victories of the civil rights movement in the 1960s, African American men and women have won election to Congress from increasingly diverse regions of the country. Whether from largely urban districts, suburban areas, or more recently from rural
90 Mississippi, these members of Congress have maintained their common concern with economic issues that affect African Americans and with the protection of civil rights.

The collected biographies of African Americans
95 who served in the House and Senate provide an important perspective on the history of the Congress and the role of African Americans in American politics. Their stories offer eloquent testimony to the long struggle to extend the ideals of the founders to
100 encompass all citizens of the United States.

GO ON TO THE NEXT PAGE.

31. According to the passage, the first African American to serve in the House of Representatives was:

   A. Hiram Revels.
   B. Joseph Rainey.
   C. from Chicago.
   D. a former slave.

32. The passage suggests that, in contrast to African Americans elected to Congress during and shortly after Reconstruction, African Americans selected to Congress today are more likely to:

   F. come from urban areas in the North.
   G. be members of the Republican Party.
   H. work for full political equality for all African Americans.
   J. come from districts in which the majority is African American.

33. One difference between African American congressional representatives in the nineteenth century and those in the mid-twentieth century was:

   A. the political party to which they were likely to belong.
   B. their commitment to education for African Americans.
   C. the strength of their ties to the African American community as a whole.
   D. the extent to which they represented all African Americans and not just their constituents.

34. When the African American representatives "turned to" (line 60) certain issues in the mid-twentieth century, they:

   F. became antagonistic toward those issues.
   G. reversed their positions on those issues.
   H. devoted themselves to those issues.
   J. referred to those issues.

35. According to the passage, one reason African Americans began to be elected to Congress from cities in the northern United States after the 1930s was that:

   A. more African Americans lived in northern cities at that time than had been the case previously.
   B. African Americans in northern cities had better political organizations than did African Americans in the rural South.
   C. African American politicians in the North were more likely to be members of the Democratic Party than were those in the South.
   D. African American politicians in the North were more likely to focus on voting rights for African Americans than were those in the South.

36. Which one of the following is NOT mentioned in the passage as a common concern of African American congressional representatives?

   F. Enforcing voting rights for African Americans
   G. Increasing educational opportunities for African Americans
   H. Ensuring opportunities for employment for African Americans
   J. Protecting people of African descent in other countries

37. One reason cited in the passage for the election of African Americans to Congress from both southern states after Reconstruction and northern states after World War I is the:

   A. success of the civil rights movement.
   B. passage and enforcement of the Fifteenth Amendment.
   C. strength of local African American political organizations.
   D. predominance of African Americans in certain districts.

GO ON TO THE NEXT PAGE.

38. According to the passage, the Congressional Black Caucus:

    F. focused its attention almost exclusively on domestic issues.

    G. was the first organization founded exclusively for African American congressional representatives.

    H. was intended to replace local African American political organizations with one large national organization.

    J. provided a forum in which African American representatives could deal with issues of concern to all African Americans.

39. The last paragraph suggests that this passage might serve as:

    A. a call to political involvement on the part of African Americans.

    B. an introduction to biographies of African American members of Congress.

    C. the conclusion of a history of African Americans in the United States.

    D. part of a longer work on the history of the United States Congress.

40. The author expresses admiration toward the African American congressional representatives discussed in the passage for their:

    F. political acumen.

    G. attempts to ensure the rights of all Americans.

    H. single-minded devotion to the struggle for civil rights.

    J. focus on providing economic opportunity for African Americans.

END OF TEST 3
STOP! DO NOT TURN THE PAGE UNTIL TOLD TO DO SO.
DO NOT RETURN TO A PREVIOUS TEST.

4 4 4 4 4 4 4 4 4 4 4 4

SCIENCE TEST
35 Minutes—40 Items

DIRECTIONS: The passages presented in the test are each followed by a set of items. Read the passage and choose the best answer for each item. Fill in the corresponding oval on your bubble sheet. You may refer to the passage as often as necessary to answer the passage items.

Warning: Calculator use is not permitted on this test.

Answers are on page 642, and explanations begin on page 656.

Passage I

The solubility of materials in liquids depends not only on the nature of the solute and the solvent, but also on temperature. A graph showing the solubilities of several substances in water is presented below.

Solubility Curves

Note: NH_3 is a gas.

1. Which of the following has the most temperature sensitive solubility throughout the range shown?

    A. $NaNO_3$
    B. KNO_3
    C. NaCl
    D. NH_3

2. The solubility of sodium (Na) salts is:

    F. high because sodium is an alkali metal.
    G. low because sodium combines with anions to make salts.
    H. dependent on what salt it forms.
    J. always greater than 20 grams per 100 grams of water.

3. A 250 ml alcoholic solution of KNO_3 at 50°C contains how many grams KNO_3 at saturation?

    A. 80
    B. 200
    C. 30
    D. Cannot be determined from the given information

GO ON TO THE NEXT PAGE.

4. A solution containing equal amounts of $NaNO_3$ and KNO_3 is allowed to cool until a white powder begins to appear at the bottom of the flask. That powder is:

   F. KNO_3.
   G. $NaNO_3$.
   H. a mixture of both.
   J. Cannot be determined from the given information

5. The solubility curve of NH_3 suggests an explanation of why:

   A. divers get the bends (nitrogen bubbles in the blood) if they rise too quickly.
   B. soda goes flat.
   C. warm lemonade is sweeter than cold lemonade.
   D. hot air balloons rise.

GO ON TO THE NEXT PAGE.

Passage II

Part of our understanding of Earth comes from a consideration of its physical properties. A table of selected properties is presented below.

Property	Value
Mass	$6 \cdot 10^{24}$ kg
Diameter	$6 \cdot 10^{6}$ m
Orbital Radius	$1.5 \cdot 10^{11}$ m
Period of Revolution	365.3 days
Period of Rotation	24 hours

Below is a table comparing the other planets of the solar system to Earth.

	Earth	Jupiter	Mars	Mercury	Neptune	Pluto	Saturn	Uranus	Venus
Diameter	1	10	0.55	0.38	4.3	?	9.4	4.1	0.98
Mass	1	320	0.10	0.58	17	?	95	14	0.83
Surface Gravity	1	2.7	0.40	0.40	1.2	?	1.2	1.1	0.90
Volume	1	1,320	0.15	0.58	42	0.729	760	50	0.90
Average Distance to Sun	1	5.3	1.5	0.40	30	40	10	19	0.70
Period of Revolution	1	12	2	0.25	165	248	30	84	0.60
Period of Rotation	1	0.40	1	60	0.50	0	0.40	0.50	240

The following are a few basic equations:

(1) density $= \frac{\text{mass}}{\text{volume}}$

(2) distance $=$ rate $\cdot$ time

(3) volume$_{\text{sphere}} = \frac{4}{3}\pi r^3$ ($r =$ radius$_{\text{sphere}}$)

6. Based on the table above, what is the approximate ratio of the period of revolution in days to the period of rotation in days for Mercury?

   F. 240
   G. $\frac{3}{2}$
   H. $\frac{2}{3}$
   J. $\frac{1}{240}$

7. Which planet is as dense as the planet Earth?

   A. Mercury
   B. Venus
   C. Mars
   D. None

8. Which planet orbits the sun at the slowest rate?

   F. Mercury
   G. Jupiter
   H. Neptune
   J. Pluto

9. Analysis of the tables above shows that surface gravity most likely depends on:

   A. mass alone.
   B. distance and mass.
   C. density alone.
   D. density of the planet and proximity to the sun.

GO ON TO THE NEXT PAGE.

10. Assuming that both Earth and Pluto are spherical, the diameter of Pluto is:

    F. 0.729 • the radius of the Earth.

    G. 0.9 • the radius of the Earth.

    H. 1.8 • the radius of the Earth.

    J. 2.7 • the radius of the Earth.

11. How many meters separate the orbits of the farthest apart planetary neighbors?

    A. 40 • orbital radius of the Earth

    B. 11 • orbital radius of the Earth

    C. 10 • orbital radius of the Earth

    D. 9 • orbital radius of the Earth

GO ON TO THE NEXT PAGE.

Passage III

Four groups of 1,000 men each were placed on strict diets that contained different intakes of cholesterol. The men stayed on the diet for 40 years, and their history of illness over that time is recorded below.

Illness	Death rate, standardized/1,000			
	No cholesterol	Men taking in a daily average of		
		0–5 grams	6–20 grams	20+ grams
Cancer				
Colon	0.01	0.03	0.04	0.02
Prostate	2.02	0.06	1.03	4.01
Lung	0.03	0.06	0.40	0.20
Coronary				
Thrombosis	5.02	1.01	4.00	10.05
Arrest	6.00	0.98	5.09	11.00
Cardiovascular	5.96	0.65	4.97	9.08
Cerebral Clot	4.01	0.02	0.50	4.01
Depression	5.01	0.30	0.30	0.30

12. Which of the following statements is best supported by the data?

   F. A man ingesting no cholesterol is approximately twice as likely to die of prostate cancer as a man ingesting 10 grams per day.

   G. Any ingestion of cholesterol decreases the risk of dying from all three forms of cancer listed here.

   H. Ingestion of cholesterol seems unrelated to the probability of coronary disease.

   J. Cerebral clots are the most prevalent form of death among the group consuming the most cholesterol.

13. What might one conclude about the relationship between cholesterol ingestion and depression based on the information above?

   A. Cholesterol causes depression.

   B. Ingestion of cholesterol has no effect on the occurrence of depression.

   C. Small amounts of cholesterol are most effective in combating depression.

   D. Large and small amounts of cholesterol are equally effective in reducing the depression death rate.

GO ON TO THE NEXT PAGE.

14. For which of the following diseases does the highest cholesterol diet increase the probability of death most, compared relatively to the non-cholesterol diets?

    F. Cerebral clots
    G. Coronary arrest
    H. Cardiovascular disease
    J. Coronary thrombosis

15. For which of the following groups of diseases does a daily intake of 0–5 grams of cholesterol reduce the probability of death?

    A. Cerebral clot, coronary thrombosis, and lung cancer
    B. Cerebral clot, depression, and colon cancer
    C. Depression, coronary arrest, and prostate cancer
    D. Depression, coronary thrombosis, and colon cancer

16. What might be involved in determining a standardized death rate for men?

    F. Ignoring deaths that do not conform to the average results
    G. Adjusting death rates according to discrepancies in age
    H. Assuming that the natural death rate is 0 deaths per 1,000 men
    J. Comparing data with a similar experiment involving women

GO ON TO THE NEXT PAGE.

Passage IV

The resistance (R) of a material is directly proportional to the resistivity (r) of the material, resistivity is measured in ohm-meters. The voltage (V, measured in volts) in a circuit is directly proportional to both the resistance (R, measured in ohms) and the current (I, measured in amperes). Resistors in series act as one resistor according to the formula:

$$R_s = R_1 + R_2 + R_3 + \ldots$$

and resistors in parallel act as one resistor according to the formula:

$$\frac{1}{R_p} = \frac{1}{R_1} + \frac{1}{R_2} + \frac{1}{R_3} + \ldots$$

The resistivities of several materials are listed below.

Substance	Resistivity, r (ohm-meters)
Aluminum	$2.63 \cdot 10^{-8}$
Copper	$1.72 \cdot 10^{-8}$
Germanium	$6.00 \cdot 10^{-1}$
Silicon	$2.30 \cdot 10^{3}$
Silver	$1.47 \cdot 10^{-8}$
Sulfur	$1.00 \cdot 10^{15}$

17. According to the information provided, the best formula for the voltage in a circuit, where voltage is V, current is I, and resistance is R is:

   A. $V = \frac{I}{R}$.
   B. $V = I + R$.
   C. $V = IR$.
   D. $V = I - R$.

18. According to the information provided, how would the voltage in a circuit with a silver resistor compare to the voltage in a circuit with a germanium resistor of the same size? (Current is the same in both circuits.)

   F. The voltage in the silver circuit would be greater.
   G. The voltage in the germanium circuit would be greater.
   H. The voltage would be the same in both circuits.
   J. Cannot be determined from the given information

19. Two resistors with $R = 2$ are placed in series. How does the voltage in the circuit compare with the voltage in a circuit with only one resistor, $R = 2$? (Assume current remains constant.)

   A. The voltage is doubled.
   B. The voltage is halved.
   C. The voltage is the same.
   D. The voltage is zero.

20. A resistor with $R = 4$ is put in parallel with an identical resistor, $R = 4$. What is R_p?

   F. 0
   G. $\frac{1}{2}$
   H. 1
   J. 2

21. Power is defined as $P = I^2 R$. If R is a constant, then power would increase —— with an increase in the current. (Fill in the blank space with the best answer choice.)

   A. logarithmically
   B. directly
   C. exponentially
   D. inversely

GO ON TO THE NEXT PAGE.

22. In order to keep the current in a circuit constant, if one increases the voltage, one must:

    F. lengthen the circuit.
    G. shorten the circuit.
    H. decrease the resistance.
    J. increase the resistance.

GO ON TO THE NEXT PAGE.

Passage V

In order to discover the steps by which a chemical reaction occurs, the dependence of the initial rate of reaction on the concentration of the reactants is determined. Three experiments exploring the mechanism of a reaction are presented below.

Experiment 1: Compound *A* is injected into a rapidly stirred solution of *B* in hexamethyl phosphoramide. As *A* and *B* react, they form a compound that has a characteristic absorption at 520 nanometers. The concentration of product, and therefore the rate of reaction, can be calculated by measuring the strength of the absorption. Results are presented below:

Trial	Concentration A	Concentration B	Rate
1	4	4	60
2	2	2	30
3	4	2	30
4	4	8	120

Experiment 2: Compound *A* is injected into a rapidly mixed solution of *B* in carbon tetrachloride. The product of the reaction is identical to the product in Experiment 1. The course of the reaction is followed by spectrophotometric methods as in Experiment 1.

Trial	Concentration A	Concentration B	Rate
1	3	3	27
2	6	6	108
3	6	3	54
4	12	6	216

Experiment 3: Compound *A* is injected in a swirling solution of *B* in a 1:1-by-volume mixture of carbon tetrachloride and hexamethyl phosphoramide. The formation of product, as before, is followed by spectrophotometry.

Trial	Concentration A	Concentration B	Rate
1	9	9	54
2	9	4.5	27
3	4	4.5	18
4	4	9	36

23. Which of the following statements best describes the effect of Concentration *A* on the rate of reaction in Experiment 1?

   A. Rate increases with increasing *A*.
   B. Rate increases by the square of *A*'s concentration.
   C. Rate increases by the square root of *A*'s concentration.
   D. Rate is independent of *A*'s concentration.

24. Which of the following statements best describes the effect of Concentration *A* on the rate of reaction in Experiment 2?

   F. Rate increases with increasing *A*.
   G. Rate increases by the square of *A*'s concentration.
   H. Rate increases by the square root of *A*'s concentration.
   J. Rate is independent of *A*'s concentration.

25. Which of the following statements best describes the effect of Concentration *A* on the rate in Experiment 3?

   A. Rate increases with increasing *A*.
   B. Rate increases by the square of *A*'s concentration.
   C. Rate increases by the square root of *A*'s concentration.
   D. Rate is independent of *A*'s concentration.

26. What is the likeliest explanation for the results obtained in Experiment 3?

   F. A mechanism intermediates between the ones found in Experiments 1 and 2.
   G. Some of the molecules react by Experiment 1's mechanism, others by Experiment 2's mechanism.
   H. A different mechanism is responsible.
   J. There is an averaging of the mechanisms.

GO ON TO THE NEXT PAGE.

27. What is the best conclusion that can be drawn from this set of experiments?

    A. Rate is increased by changing solvents.
    B. Reactions may depend on solvent effects as well as on the nature of the reactants.
    C. Mechanisms can always be changed by use of an appropriate solvent.
    D. Reactions depend on solvent effects as well as on the nature of the reactants.

GO ON TO THE NEXT PAGE.

Passage VI

Acceleration is defined as the change in the velocity of an object divided by the length of time during which that change took place. Contrary to popular belief, Galileo did not base his conclusion of the acceleration of gravity on experiments done with cannonballs dropped from the Leaning Tower of Pisa. Instead, he used the motion of objects moving down an inclined plane to develop his theory. In the following sets of experiments, a student studies the motion of bodies on an inclined plane.

For all of the following experiments, time is measured in seconds, distance in meters, and velocity in meters per second. The distance (*d*) an object travels at a constant acceleration (*a*) in time (*t*), assuming it starts from rest, is given by the equation: $d = \frac{1}{2}at^2$.

Experiment 1: A student set up a smooth wooden board at an angle of 30° from horizontal. The board had a length of 10 meters. Using a stroboscope, the student was able to determine the position of a 100-gram steel ball that was rolled down the incline. Velocity was determined by means of a radar gun. The results are presented below:

Time	Distance (m)	Velocity (m/sec)
0	0	0
0.5	0.44	1.75
1.0	1.75	3.5
1.5	3.94	5.25
2.0	7.00	7.00

Experiment 2: The same 10-meter wooden board was used in Experiment 2. The angle used was again 30°. The object used this time was a 100-gram sled made of the same material as the ball in Experiment 1. The stroboscope and the radar gun were used to determine its position and velocity as it slid down the inclined plane. The results are presented below:

Time	Distance (m)	Velocity (m/sec)
0	0	0
0.5	1.13	2.45
1.0	2.45	4.90
1.5	5.51	7.35
2.0	9.80	9.80

Experiment 3: The same board at the same angle was used in the third experiment as in the previous two. In this experiment, a 100-gram box made of the same material as the ball and the sled was used. The same recording devices were used, and the results are presented below:

Time	Distance (m)	Velocity (m/sec)
0	0	0
1.0	0.33	0.66
2.0	1.31	1.32
3.0	2.97	1.98
4.0	5.28	2.64
5.0	8.25	3.30

Experiment 4: The board in the previous experiments was carefully oiled. Once again, the board was placed at an angle of 30° from horizontal. Each of the objects was then allowed to move down the inclined plane, and the time required to reach the bottom of the plane is recorded below:

Object	Time
sled	2.02
ball	2.39
box	4.08

GO ON TO THE NEXT PAGE.

28. Which object in the first three experiments has the greatest acceleration?

   F. Ball
   G. Sled
   H. Box
   J. Ball and sled are equal.

29. The acceleration of the ball relative to that of the sled is due to the ball's:

   A. rolling.
   B. friction.
   C. rolling and friction.
   D. being the same mass as the sled, and therefore having the same acceleration.

30. The acceleration of the ball relative to that of the box is due to:

   F. the ball's rolling only.
   G. the ball's friction only.
   H. the ball's rolling and the box's friction.
   J. the ball's having the same mass as the box, and therefore having the same acceleration.

31. Based on these four experiments, the ratio of the acceleration of the ball to the acceleration of the sled is:

   A. 1.
   B. $\frac{5}{7}$.
   C. dependent on the amount of friction.
   D. dependent on time.

32. Based on these four experiments, the ratio of the acceleration of the ball to the acceleration of the box is:

   F. 1.
   G. $\frac{5}{7}$.
   H. dependent on the amount of friction.
   J. dependent on time.

GO ON TO THE NEXT PAGE.

Passage VII

What was the fate of Neanderthal man? Two differing views are presented below.

Scientist 1: Neanderthals were very similar to modern humans in appearance. It is true that Neanderthals were somewhat more muscular than modern humans and that the way the muscles seem to have been arranged on the skeleton was, in a few minor ways, different. This we are able to deduce from the places on the surviving bones that mark where the ligaments were once attached. For example, the neck and wrists of Neanderthals were far thicker than is natural to modern humans. Some of the facial structure was also different, especially the protrusion of the brow. But differences between the appearance of Neanderthals and modern humans have been exaggerated since they are based on the skeleton of one individual who was later discovered to have been suffering from severe arthritis. It is not unlikely that, because of the low population density and the nomadic lifestyle that spread the few individuals over ever-larger areas, Neanderthal and early modern humans interbred and eventually merged into one species. The notion that some sort of "war" broke out between these different species (or, more likely, subspecies) of humans is an attempt to look out of early human eyes with a modern perspective.

Scientist 2: Whenever two species compete for the same niche there is a conflict. In this conflict the loser either moves to a different niche or dies out. It is unusual for two species to interbreed. The difference between early modern humans and Neanderthals physically may not appear great to an anatomist, but to the average man on the street, or prehistoric man in the forest, the differences are not subtle. And it was these individuals, not the anatomists, who had to decide whether or not to mate. Even if early modern humans and Neanderthals did mate, the result—us—would look more like a mix of the two rather than like modern humans. Early modern humans and Neanderthals, because they were so close to each other physically, must have been deadly enemies. The population was thinly dispersed at that time because the resources available would not support a greater population density. There literally was not room enough on the planet for the two species. They could not combine because they were so different in appearance, so only one answer remained. We survived because we killed our cousin.

33. Underlying the hypothesis of Scientist 1 is the assumption that:

   A. early modern humans and Neanderthals did not compete for the same kinds of food.
   B. early modern humans and Neanderthals were genetically close.
   C. early modern humans and Neanderthals did not necessarily live in the same area.
   D. early modern humans and Neanderthals often fought.

34. Underlying the hypotheses of both scientists is the assumption that:

   F. early modern humans and Neanderthals understood the consequences of their actions.
   G. early modern humans and Neanderthals both lived in exactly the same type of environment.
   H. early modern humans and Neanderthals both lived in the same geographical regions.
   J. early modern humans were more intelligent than Neanderthals.

35. If an isolated community of Neanderthals was discovered, whose hypothesis would be more damaged?

   A. Scientist 1's because his theory does not allow for such a community to survive
   B. Scientist 2's because the descendants of early modern humans inhabit all the Earth and therefore there should be no community of Neanderthals
   C. Both hypotheses are disproved.
   D. Neither hypothesis is affected.

GO ON TO THE NEXT PAGE.

36. Which of the following, if true, would most support the hypothesis of Scientist 2?

    F. The camps of early modern humans are often close to the camps of Neanderthals.

    G. The camps of early modern humans are never close to Neanderthal camps.

    H. Bones of Neanderthals and early modern humans are often found near each other.

    J. Chipped Neanderthal bones are found with early modern human weapons.

37. The fact that lions and tigers fight when brought together even though they can be interbred supports which hypothesis to the greater extent?

    A. Scientist 1's hypothesis, because it proves two species can interbreed

    B. Scientist 1's hypothesis, because two species still exist that share the same niche

    C. Scientist 2's hypothesis, because it suggests that two species that can interbreed may not do so under natural conditions

    D. Scientist 2's hypothesis, because lions and tigers fight when brought together

38. According to the hypothesis of Scientist 2, what should be the result of interbreeding lions and tigers?

    F. The offspring should be infertile.

    G. The offspring will resemble one parent only.

    H. The offspring will possess a mixture of traits.

    J. Scientist 2's hypothesis makes no conjectures on the point because lions and tigers would not interbreed.

39. What other assumption do both Scientist 1 and Scientist 2 make about Neanderthals and early modern humans?

    A. That early modern humans were directly involved in the disappearance of Neanderthals

    B. That early modern humans were the more intelligent of the two

    C. That Neanderthals differed little from early modern humans

    D. That early modern humans only inhabited regions that were hospitable for Neanderthals

40. If a burial site containing over one hundred early modern humans and Neanderthal remains was discovered, and if two Neanderthal skeletons were found with early modern human spearpoints in them, which hypothesis would be the most strengthened?

    F. Scientist 1's hypothesis, because spearpoints need not have been what killed the two Neanderthals

    G. Scientist 2's hypothesis, because two Neanderthals were killed by early modern humans and no early modern humans were killed by Neanderthals

    H. Scientist 2's hypothesis, because the spearpoints prove that the early modern humans had more developed weapons

    J. Scientist 1's hypothesis, because only a couple of the individuals buried together died violently

END OF TEST 4
STOP! DO NOT TURN THE PAGE UNTIL TOLD TO DO SO.
DO NOT RETURN TO A PREVIOUS TEST.

5 5 5 5 5 5 5 5 5 5 5 5

WRITING TEST (OPTIONAL)
30 Minutes—1 Essay Prompt

DIRECTIONS: This is a test of your writing skills. Before you begin planning and writing your essay, read the writing prompt carefully to understand the instructions. Your essay will be evaluated on the evidence it provides of your ability to express judgments by taking a position on the issue in the writing prompt; to maintain a focus on the topic throughout the essay; to develop a position by using logical reasoning and supporting ideas; to organize ideas in a logical way; and to use language clearly and effectively according to the conventions of standard written English.

If you finish before time is called, you may review your work. Lay your pencil down immediately when time is called.

Sample essays begin on page 660.

Writing Test Prompt

Some people believe that schools do not emphasize enough the concept of public service. They point out that volunteer service is a tradition in America and mention organizations such as the Girl and Boy Scouts, volunteer fire departments and rescue squads, and Big Brother and Sister. They believe that high schools should encourage volunteerism by offering students academic credit for such activities. They state that allowing academic credit would release students from studies to do volunteer work and further that such service would strengthen the sense of community. Other people say that volunteer service should be voluntary and that release time from school is a form of compensation for students. Students who receive such compensation would not really be doing volunteer work. Opponents of release time point out that students have opportunities to volunteer after school, on weekends, and during the summer months.

In your essay, take a position on this issue. You may address either of the two points described above, or you may offer an entirely different perspective on the issue. Be sure to use specific reasons and examples to support your analysis.

END OF TEST 5
STOP! DO NOT RETURN TO ANY OTHER TEST.

Post-Assessment

Highlights:

See how far you have come and measure your improvement with this second, official test.

Practice working through the test quickly without losing accuracy.

Put into action all of the content knowledge you have learned.

Analyze your assessment scores and course performance to anticipate your adjusted plan of action.

Snapshot of Post-Assessment:

It's time to measure your progress. You will put into action everything that you've learned during this second "dress rehearsal." After taking this final exam, you will be able to compare your pre- and post-assessment scores and see how much you have improved. You will have a chance to identify any remaining areas of weakness so that you know where to focus your studies as you continue to improve your skills.

POST-ASSESSMENT ADMINISTRATION

At the end of the course, you will take a post-assessment. This post-assessment consists of an official, retired ACT, PLAN, or EXPLORE. When you take the post-assessment, you should bring the following items to the classroom, in addition to anything else your teacher instructs you to bring:

1. Sharpened, soft-lead No. 2 pencils

2. A calculator that is approved for use on the test. This includes any four-function, scientific, or graphing calculator, except for those with the following features:

    - Built-in computer algebra systems

    - Pocket organizers or PDAs

    - Handheld or laptop computers

    - Electronic writing pad or pen-input devices

    - Calculators built into any electronic communication device, such as a cell phone

    - Models with a QWERTY (typewriter) keypad (Calculators with letters on the keys are permitted as long as the keys are not arranged in a QWERTY keypad.)

    You may use the following types of calculators if you make appropriate modifications:

    - Models with paper tape: the paper must be removed.

    - Models that make noise: the sound feature must be turned off.

    - Models that have an infrared data port: the port must be covered with duct tape, electrician's tape, or another heavy, opaque material.

    - Models that have a power cord: the power cord must be removed.

    (For more detailed information on calculator usage, go to www.actstudent.org/faq/answers/calculator.html.)

3. A watch (to pace yourself as you work through each test section)

As you take the test, remember the following points about marking the bubble sheet:

- The bubble for each answer choice must be completely darkened. If the letter within the bubble can be read through the pencil mark, then it is not dark enough. Mechanical pencils, even with No. 2 pencil lead, often fail to leave a dark mark.

- Stay within the lines.

- When erasing pencil marks, be sure to erase the marks completely. Do not leave any stray marks!

- Circle the answer choices in the test booklet. Towards the end of the section, or after each completed group of items, transfer the selected answers as a group to the answer form. Not only does this minimize erasing on the answer form, but it also saves time and minimizes transcription errors.

- When changing an answer, over-darken the final answer choice after completely erasing the original mark. This extra density tends to offset the residue left over from the original answer choice.

If your program has ordered post-assessment student summary reports, you will receive one of these reports with your post-assessment results. This report will help you determine the areas in which you need continued study. You can then utilize your study time to prepare in those areas so that when you take the real test, you are ready to do your best. Refer to the *How to Use the Pre-Assessment Report* section found in volume 1 of your student text (p. 35) to learn more about how to read and use the student summary report.

ESSAY RESPONSE SHEET
(OPTIONAL)

Name _____

Student ID Number _____

Date _____

Instructor _____

Course/Session Number _____

_____

S T O P

IF YOU FINISH BEFORE TIME IS CALLED, YOU MAY CHECK YOUR WORK ON THIS ESSAY ONLY.
DO NOT TURN TO ANY OTHER PORTION OF THE TEST.

ACT • PLAN • EXPLORE BUBBLE SHEET

Start with number 1 for each new section. If a section has fewer items than answer spaces, leave the extra answer spaces blank. Be sure to erase any errors or stray marks completely.

Name _____ Student ID Number _____

Date _____ Instructor _____ Course/Session Number _____

TEST 1—ENGLISH

1 Ⓐ Ⓑ Ⓒ Ⓓ	16 Ⓕ Ⓖ Ⓗ Ⓙ	31 Ⓐ Ⓑ Ⓒ Ⓓ	46 Ⓕ Ⓖ Ⓗ Ⓙ	61 Ⓐ Ⓑ Ⓒ Ⓓ
2 Ⓕ Ⓖ Ⓗ Ⓙ	17 Ⓐ Ⓑ Ⓒ Ⓓ	32 Ⓕ Ⓖ Ⓗ Ⓙ	47 Ⓐ Ⓑ Ⓒ Ⓓ	62 Ⓕ Ⓖ Ⓗ Ⓙ
3 Ⓐ Ⓑ Ⓒ Ⓓ	18 Ⓕ Ⓖ Ⓗ Ⓙ	33 Ⓐ Ⓑ Ⓒ Ⓓ	48 Ⓕ Ⓖ Ⓗ Ⓙ	63 Ⓐ Ⓑ Ⓒ Ⓓ
4 Ⓕ Ⓖ Ⓗ Ⓙ	19 Ⓐ Ⓑ Ⓒ Ⓓ	34 Ⓕ Ⓖ Ⓗ Ⓙ	49 Ⓐ Ⓑ Ⓒ Ⓓ	64 Ⓕ Ⓖ Ⓗ Ⓙ
5 Ⓐ Ⓑ Ⓒ Ⓓ	20 Ⓕ Ⓖ Ⓗ Ⓙ	35 Ⓐ Ⓑ Ⓒ Ⓓ	50 Ⓕ Ⓖ Ⓗ Ⓙ	65 Ⓐ Ⓑ Ⓒ Ⓓ
6 Ⓕ Ⓖ Ⓗ Ⓙ	21 Ⓐ Ⓑ Ⓒ Ⓓ	36 Ⓕ Ⓖ Ⓗ Ⓙ	51 Ⓐ Ⓑ Ⓒ Ⓓ	66 Ⓕ Ⓖ Ⓗ Ⓙ
7 Ⓐ Ⓑ Ⓒ Ⓓ	22 Ⓕ Ⓖ Ⓗ Ⓙ	37 Ⓐ Ⓑ Ⓒ Ⓓ	52 Ⓕ Ⓖ Ⓗ Ⓙ	67 Ⓐ Ⓑ Ⓒ Ⓓ
8 Ⓕ Ⓖ Ⓗ Ⓙ	23 Ⓐ Ⓑ Ⓒ Ⓓ	38 Ⓕ Ⓖ Ⓗ Ⓙ	53 Ⓐ Ⓑ Ⓒ Ⓓ	68 Ⓕ Ⓖ Ⓗ Ⓙ
9 Ⓐ Ⓑ Ⓒ Ⓓ	24 Ⓕ Ⓖ Ⓗ Ⓙ	39 Ⓐ Ⓑ Ⓒ Ⓓ	54 Ⓕ Ⓖ Ⓗ Ⓙ	69 Ⓐ Ⓑ Ⓒ Ⓓ
10 Ⓕ Ⓖ Ⓗ Ⓙ	25 Ⓐ Ⓑ Ⓒ Ⓓ	40 Ⓕ Ⓖ Ⓗ Ⓙ	55 Ⓐ Ⓑ Ⓒ Ⓓ	70 Ⓕ Ⓖ Ⓗ Ⓙ
11 Ⓐ Ⓑ Ⓒ Ⓓ	26 Ⓕ Ⓖ Ⓗ Ⓙ	41 Ⓐ Ⓑ Ⓒ Ⓓ	56 Ⓕ Ⓖ Ⓗ Ⓙ	71 Ⓐ Ⓑ Ⓒ Ⓓ
12 Ⓕ Ⓖ Ⓗ Ⓙ	27 Ⓐ Ⓑ Ⓒ Ⓓ	42 Ⓕ Ⓖ Ⓗ Ⓙ	57 Ⓐ Ⓑ Ⓒ Ⓓ	72 Ⓕ Ⓖ Ⓗ Ⓙ
13 Ⓐ Ⓑ Ⓒ Ⓓ	28 Ⓕ Ⓖ Ⓗ Ⓙ	43 Ⓐ Ⓑ Ⓒ Ⓓ	58 Ⓕ Ⓖ Ⓗ Ⓙ	73 Ⓐ Ⓑ Ⓒ Ⓓ
14 Ⓕ Ⓖ Ⓗ Ⓙ	29 Ⓐ Ⓑ Ⓒ Ⓓ	44 Ⓕ Ⓖ Ⓗ Ⓙ	59 Ⓐ Ⓑ Ⓒ Ⓓ	74 Ⓕ Ⓖ Ⓗ Ⓙ
15 Ⓐ Ⓑ Ⓒ Ⓓ	30 Ⓕ Ⓖ Ⓗ Ⓙ	45 Ⓐ Ⓑ Ⓒ Ⓓ	60 Ⓕ Ⓖ Ⓗ Ⓙ	75 Ⓐ Ⓑ Ⓒ Ⓓ

TEST 2—MATHEMATICS

1 Ⓐ Ⓑ Ⓒ Ⓓ Ⓔ	13 Ⓐ Ⓑ Ⓒ Ⓓ Ⓔ	25 Ⓐ Ⓑ Ⓒ Ⓓ Ⓔ	37 Ⓐ Ⓑ Ⓒ Ⓓ Ⓔ	49 Ⓐ Ⓑ Ⓒ Ⓓ Ⓔ
2 Ⓕ Ⓖ Ⓗ Ⓙ Ⓚ	14 Ⓕ Ⓖ Ⓗ Ⓙ Ⓚ	26 Ⓕ Ⓖ Ⓗ Ⓙ Ⓚ	38 Ⓕ Ⓖ Ⓗ Ⓙ Ⓚ	50 Ⓕ Ⓖ Ⓗ Ⓙ Ⓚ
3 Ⓐ Ⓑ Ⓒ Ⓓ Ⓔ	15 Ⓐ Ⓑ Ⓒ Ⓓ Ⓔ	27 Ⓐ Ⓑ Ⓒ Ⓓ Ⓔ	39 Ⓐ Ⓑ Ⓒ Ⓓ Ⓔ	51 Ⓐ Ⓑ Ⓒ Ⓓ Ⓔ
4 Ⓕ Ⓖ Ⓗ Ⓙ Ⓚ	16 Ⓕ Ⓖ Ⓗ Ⓙ Ⓚ	28 Ⓕ Ⓖ Ⓗ Ⓙ Ⓚ	40 Ⓕ Ⓖ Ⓗ Ⓙ Ⓚ	52 Ⓕ Ⓖ Ⓗ Ⓙ Ⓚ
5 Ⓐ Ⓑ Ⓒ Ⓓ Ⓔ	17 Ⓐ Ⓑ Ⓒ Ⓓ Ⓔ	29 Ⓐ Ⓑ Ⓒ Ⓓ Ⓔ	41 Ⓐ Ⓑ Ⓒ Ⓓ Ⓔ	53 Ⓐ Ⓑ Ⓒ Ⓓ Ⓔ
6 Ⓕ Ⓖ Ⓗ Ⓙ Ⓚ	18 Ⓕ Ⓖ Ⓗ Ⓙ Ⓚ	30 Ⓕ Ⓖ Ⓗ Ⓙ Ⓚ	42 Ⓕ Ⓖ Ⓗ Ⓙ Ⓚ	54 Ⓕ Ⓖ Ⓗ Ⓙ Ⓚ
7 Ⓐ Ⓑ Ⓒ Ⓓ Ⓔ	19 Ⓐ Ⓑ Ⓒ Ⓓ Ⓔ	31 Ⓐ Ⓑ Ⓒ Ⓓ Ⓔ	43 Ⓐ Ⓑ Ⓒ Ⓓ Ⓔ	55 Ⓐ Ⓑ Ⓒ Ⓓ Ⓔ
8 Ⓕ Ⓖ Ⓗ Ⓙ Ⓚ	20 Ⓕ Ⓖ Ⓗ Ⓙ Ⓚ	32 Ⓕ Ⓖ Ⓗ Ⓙ Ⓚ	44 Ⓕ Ⓖ Ⓗ Ⓙ Ⓚ	56 Ⓕ Ⓖ Ⓗ Ⓙ Ⓚ
9 Ⓐ Ⓑ Ⓒ Ⓓ Ⓔ	21 Ⓐ Ⓑ Ⓒ Ⓓ Ⓔ	33 Ⓐ Ⓑ Ⓒ Ⓓ Ⓔ	45 Ⓐ Ⓑ Ⓒ Ⓓ Ⓔ	57 Ⓐ Ⓑ Ⓒ Ⓓ Ⓔ
10 Ⓕ Ⓖ Ⓗ Ⓙ Ⓚ	22 Ⓕ Ⓖ Ⓗ Ⓙ Ⓚ	34 Ⓕ Ⓖ Ⓗ Ⓙ Ⓚ	46 Ⓕ Ⓖ Ⓗ Ⓙ Ⓚ	58 Ⓕ Ⓖ Ⓗ Ⓙ Ⓚ
11 Ⓐ Ⓑ Ⓒ Ⓓ Ⓔ	23 Ⓐ Ⓑ Ⓒ Ⓓ Ⓔ	35 Ⓐ Ⓑ Ⓒ Ⓓ Ⓔ	47 Ⓐ Ⓑ Ⓒ Ⓓ Ⓔ	59 Ⓐ Ⓑ Ⓒ Ⓓ Ⓔ
12 Ⓕ Ⓖ Ⓗ Ⓙ Ⓚ	24 Ⓕ Ⓖ Ⓗ Ⓙ Ⓚ	36 Ⓕ Ⓖ Ⓗ Ⓙ Ⓚ	48 Ⓕ Ⓖ Ⓗ Ⓙ Ⓚ	60 Ⓕ Ⓖ Ⓗ Ⓙ Ⓚ

TEST 3—READING

1 Ⓐ Ⓑ Ⓒ Ⓓ	9 Ⓐ Ⓑ Ⓒ Ⓓ	17 Ⓐ Ⓑ Ⓒ Ⓓ	25 Ⓐ Ⓑ Ⓒ Ⓓ	33 Ⓐ Ⓑ Ⓒ Ⓓ
2 Ⓕ Ⓖ Ⓗ Ⓙ	10 Ⓕ Ⓖ Ⓗ Ⓙ	18 Ⓕ Ⓖ Ⓗ Ⓙ	26 Ⓕ Ⓖ Ⓗ Ⓙ	34 Ⓕ Ⓖ Ⓗ Ⓙ
3 Ⓐ Ⓑ Ⓒ Ⓓ	11 Ⓐ Ⓑ Ⓒ Ⓓ	19 Ⓐ Ⓑ Ⓒ Ⓓ	27 Ⓐ Ⓑ Ⓒ Ⓓ	35 Ⓐ Ⓑ Ⓒ Ⓓ
4 Ⓕ Ⓖ Ⓗ Ⓙ	12 Ⓕ Ⓖ Ⓗ Ⓙ	20 Ⓕ Ⓖ Ⓗ Ⓙ	28 Ⓕ Ⓖ Ⓗ Ⓙ	36 Ⓕ Ⓖ Ⓗ Ⓙ
5 Ⓐ Ⓑ Ⓒ Ⓓ	13 Ⓐ Ⓑ Ⓒ Ⓓ	21 Ⓐ Ⓑ Ⓒ Ⓓ	29 Ⓐ Ⓑ Ⓒ Ⓓ	37 Ⓐ Ⓑ Ⓒ Ⓓ
6 Ⓕ Ⓖ Ⓗ Ⓙ	14 Ⓕ Ⓖ Ⓗ Ⓙ	22 Ⓕ Ⓖ Ⓗ Ⓙ	30 Ⓕ Ⓖ Ⓗ Ⓙ	38 Ⓕ Ⓖ Ⓗ Ⓙ
7 Ⓐ Ⓑ Ⓒ Ⓓ	15 Ⓐ Ⓑ Ⓒ Ⓓ	23 Ⓐ Ⓑ Ⓒ Ⓓ	31 Ⓐ Ⓑ Ⓒ Ⓓ	39 Ⓐ Ⓑ Ⓒ Ⓓ
8 Ⓕ Ⓖ Ⓗ Ⓙ	16 Ⓕ Ⓖ Ⓗ Ⓙ	24 Ⓕ Ⓖ Ⓗ Ⓙ	32 Ⓕ Ⓖ Ⓗ Ⓙ	40 Ⓕ Ⓖ Ⓗ Ⓙ

TEST 4—SCIENCE

1 Ⓐ Ⓑ Ⓒ Ⓓ	9 Ⓐ Ⓑ Ⓒ Ⓓ	17 Ⓐ Ⓑ Ⓒ Ⓓ	25 Ⓐ Ⓑ Ⓒ Ⓓ	33 Ⓐ Ⓑ Ⓒ Ⓓ
2 Ⓕ Ⓖ Ⓗ Ⓙ	10 Ⓕ Ⓖ Ⓗ Ⓙ	18 Ⓕ Ⓖ Ⓗ Ⓙ	26 Ⓕ Ⓖ Ⓗ Ⓙ	34 Ⓕ Ⓖ Ⓗ Ⓙ
3 Ⓐ Ⓑ Ⓒ Ⓓ	11 Ⓐ Ⓑ Ⓒ Ⓓ	19 Ⓐ Ⓑ Ⓒ Ⓓ	27 Ⓐ Ⓑ Ⓒ Ⓓ	35 Ⓐ Ⓑ Ⓒ Ⓓ
4 Ⓕ Ⓖ Ⓗ Ⓙ	12 Ⓕ Ⓖ Ⓗ Ⓙ	20 Ⓕ Ⓖ Ⓗ Ⓙ	28 Ⓕ Ⓖ Ⓗ Ⓙ	36 Ⓕ Ⓖ Ⓗ Ⓙ
5 Ⓐ Ⓑ Ⓒ Ⓓ	13 Ⓐ Ⓑ Ⓒ Ⓓ	21 Ⓐ Ⓑ Ⓒ Ⓓ	29 Ⓐ Ⓑ Ⓒ Ⓓ	37 Ⓐ Ⓑ Ⓒ Ⓓ
6 Ⓕ Ⓖ Ⓗ Ⓙ	14 Ⓕ Ⓖ Ⓗ Ⓙ	22 Ⓕ Ⓖ Ⓗ Ⓙ	30 Ⓕ Ⓖ Ⓗ Ⓙ	38 Ⓕ Ⓖ Ⓗ Ⓙ
7 Ⓐ Ⓑ Ⓒ Ⓓ	15 Ⓐ Ⓑ Ⓒ Ⓓ	23 Ⓐ Ⓑ Ⓒ Ⓓ	31 Ⓐ Ⓑ Ⓒ Ⓓ	39 Ⓐ Ⓑ Ⓒ Ⓓ
8 Ⓕ Ⓖ Ⓗ Ⓙ	16 Ⓕ Ⓖ Ⓗ Ⓙ	24 Ⓕ Ⓖ Ⓗ Ⓙ	32 Ⓕ Ⓖ Ⓗ Ⓙ	40 Ⓕ Ⓖ Ⓗ Ⓙ

HOW TO USE THE POST-ASSESSMENT REPORT

In the transition from Post-Assessment to Personal Action Plan, you and your teacher will use the results of your post-assessment to recognize your individual strengths and weaknesses. Additionally, be sure at this point in the course that you have not only reviewed the *Setting a Test Score Target*, *Overcoming Test Anxiety*, and *Overall Time Management* sections in the Pre-Assessment/Course Planning part of your book but have also followed through on your schedule for the course.

You will receive the results of your official post-assessment in the form of a student summary report. This report provides details about your performance and helps you determine where to focus your efforts until the real test. (You should receive your student summary report for the post-assessment approximately 10 days after taking the test.) When you receive your post-assessment results, you can more strategically target those skills, concepts, and strategies that will help you to improve in your areas of weakness. Just as you did with the pre-assessment, review the details of the student summary report on pages 35–37 in volume 1 so that you are familiar with its contents.

Once you have received your post-assessment student summary report, you can make connections between the report and the specific skills, concepts, and strategies that you need to study. Just as with the pre-assessment, you will be given a checklist for your post-assessment. Referring to your student summary report, put an "X" beside those items that you answered incorrectly and a "?" by those that you do not fully understand. The descriptions on the checklist tell you where you can look in the item index (pp. 665–687) to find the appropriate items in your book. Then, once you have your checklist of items to study, make a "to do" list using the following pages.

TOPIC	START DATE	DATE TO BE COMPLETED	DATE COMPLETED

Personal Action Plan

Highlights:

With the post-assessment data, create a focused action plan with the help of your instructor so you know what to review.

Don't waste time on areas you've already mastered; target any remaining areas of weakness.

Learn valuable information on preparing your college applications and writing college admissions essays.

Snapshot of Personal Action Plan:

Based on the results of the post-assessment, you will collaborate with your instructor to develop a personalized action plan. You may be asked to return to items you've already reviewed but have not yet mastered. If there are any items you have not yet completed, this is the time to return to those areas. You may need to review specific test-taking strategies; to focus on pacing, timing, and guessing; or to focus on other weaknesses. In addition to developing a plan to deliver your best test performance, you will also begin to learn the nuts and bolts of the college application process.

PLANNING FOR FURTHER STUDY

Up until this point, you have spent a great deal of time preparing for the real test both in class and on your own. After receiving the results of your post-assessment and finishing the Cambridge ACT • PLAN • EXPLORE review course, you will most likely have some spare time before test day. So, spend this time wisely to make the best effort in preparation for the exam.

Planning a study schedule between the post-assessment and the real test is critical in order to reinforce and maintain the skills, concepts, and strategies that you have learned throughout the course. Depending on whether several weeks or several days remain before the exam date, you will want to plan your study differently. If there are several weeks remaining before the day of the test, you should plan to review more material than if there are only a few days remaining. If only a few days remain, a quick summary review is a better choice.

Many topics that are related to planning a study schedule have already been covered in the *Pre-Assessment/Course Planning* part of this book. It is important for you to review the material in that step when designing your study plan. In particular, you should balance a plan that will leave you confident of your preparation but also calm and rested for the day of the exam.

The largest problem that most students face on the exam is not a lack of subject knowledge but poor management of time. If you have not yet done so, take Practice Tests III and IV included in this book. These practice tests not only serve to reinforce skills and strategies, but they also emphasize the importance of time management since they are to be administered *with* time restrictions. These time restrictions are put in place to simulate the experience of the real test. Therefore, when taking these practice tests, hold rigorously to the allotted times. It is always worthwhile to return to a practice test to address skipped or unfinished items, but you should do so only at the conclusion of the allotted time.

Besides helping your pacing and preparedness, the practice tests are also an excellent guide to targeting your study plan. Look out for things that you know you could improve upon if you had the opportunity to peek at your notes. These areas are likely targets for review as you approach the day of the exam. Listing a few concrete topics for review sets a firm starting ground for your study plan.

Remember that the most significant aspect of an effective study plan is that it is a written plan. A written study plan is more concrete than one that you simply draw on from memory. So, when creating your plan, write out a day-by-day schedule for reviewing all of the materials that are necessary to succeed on the real test. This written format will provide a clear and dependable guide for study. The schedule should be prioritized according to the time that you will devote to each of the different core subjects based on the amount of time that you have remaining before the day of the exam. Plan to review all of the materials equally several weeks before test day. Then, when the test date approaches, start focusing on the core subjects that are giving you the most difficulty. Divide your time proportionally among these subjects based on your assessment of their difficulty. In the final days before the test, you will not be able to learn a great deal of new material. Therefore, unless there is a long span of time between the end of your review course and the date of the exam, you should focus on practicing the skills, concepts, and strategies that you have already learned.

As you examine the schedule that you set for yourself at the beginning of the course, consider how you can plan your study time from this point forward, specifically focusing on areas that you may have missed. You should devote your remaining study time to any particular areas of weakness that you recognized in your post-assessment results (see *How to Use the Post-Assessment Report*, pp. 564–568). For example, if you are satisfied with your English Test scores but have not attained your goals for the Mathematics Test, you might consider designing a study plan that emphasizes mathematics. On the other hand, if you are more comfortable with mathematics, you may want to review diagramming sentences, grammar and mechanics, and reading. While you may consider returning to vocabulary that you have already learned, it is probably too late to begin memorizing new word lists. Rather, a focus on concepts is a better use of your time.

Once you have determined your rubric for study, stick to it without fail. Such discipline will surely reward you on the day of the test. However, do not study too much. An hour or two of studying each day will be more productive than a severe study schedule that leaves you physically and mentally exhausted when the time comes to take the real test. Think of this process as training for a sport. While it is necessary to practice every day, it is counterproductive to overexert yourself and to practice too much.

Make copies of the following empty calendars, and use them to develop a plan of action, determining what topics you will study each day and allotting time to study those sections of the book and complete the relevant exercises. Remember that it is not necessary for you to do everything all at once. Instead, picking a few things to focus on each week will help you to better manage your time between now and the real test. After you have designed a basic study plan, ask your teacher for insight. He or she can help you set goals for each core subject and may be able to suggest further strategies or a subtle re-allotment of your time.

Sunday	*Monday*	*Tuesday*	*Wednesday*	*Thursday*	*Friday*	*Saturday*

Sunday	*Monday*	*Tuesday*	*Wednesday*	*Thursday*	*Friday*	*Saturday*

Sunday	Monday	Tuesday	Wednesday	Thursday	Friday	Saturday

Sunday	Monday	Tuesday	Wednesday	Thursday	Friday	Saturday

Sunday	Monday	Tuesday	Wednesday	Thursday	Friday	Saturday

APPLICATION PREPARATION

WINNING STRATEGIES

The title of this section echoes our analysis of the admissions process in the *Setting a Test Score Target* section (Volume 1, p. 3). To maximize your chances of success, you must create an application that satisfies the needs of the school to which you are applying. This does not mean that you enhance your application with fabricated details, but it does mean that you organize and present your experiences in a way that depicts you in the most favorable light.

HIGHLIGHT YOUR UNIQUE QUALITIES WITHIN THE APPLICATION

You must create an application that satisfies the needs of the school to which you are applying in order to maximize your chances of admissions success. Many times, this means that you should have a certain GPA and ACT score, while at the same time exhibiting unique characteristics that differentiate you from other students. You should never create a deceptive, fictitious, or over-embellished application, but you should strive to present yourself as well as possible.

Most of the application questions that you will be asked require only short answers. For example: "Did you work while you were in school?" "What clubs did you join?" "What honors or awards did you receive?" When answering such questions, you do not have much room to maneuver, but you should try to communicate as much information as possible in your short answers. Compare the following pairs of descriptions:

Member of Orchestra	*Second Violinist of the Orchestra*
Played Intra-Mural Volleyball	*Co-captain of the Volleyball Team*
Member of the AD's CSL	*One of three members on the Associate Dean's Committee on Student Life*
Worked at Billy's Burger Barn	*Assistant Manager at Billy's Burger Barn (25 hours per week)*

In addition to the short-answer questions, some college applications invite or even require you to answer in writing one or more college admissions essay questions. The admissions essay—also called an application essay, personal statement, personal essay, essay question, or admissions question—is a written composition from a student, generally submitted to a college at the same time as the application documents. Some college admissions essay questions ask for only a limited degree of additional information. For example: "In a paragraph, explain to us one reason why you want to attend this college." Other essay questions are open-ended and require providing more information: "Tell us additional information about yourself that you think would assist us in the selection process." Still others are more thought provoking and require a reasoned and clearly articulated answer to the specific question: "Describe a character in fiction, a historical figure, or a creative work (as in art, music, science, etc.) that has had an influence on you, and explain that influence." The point of the admissions essay questions is for you to give the admissions decision-makers helpful information that might not be available from your test scores, GPA, and short-answer questions.

You should consider the admissions essay to be a highly significant part of your application for two reasons. First, answers to the essay questions will be your argument to the admissions personnel for your acceptance. The answers will give them additional reasons why they should accept you. Second, the admissions essay is one aspect of the application over which you can exercise real control. Your work experience has been accumulated over the years, your GPA is already settled, and your ACT has been scored. Those aspects of the application cannot easily be manipulated. The writing of the admissions essay, however, is completely under your present control.

What information should be included in an open-ended admissions essay (one that asks generally for more information about yourself)? You should devise arguments that interpret your academic, employment, and personal histories in such a way as to indicate that you have the ability to complete college and that you are committed to studying and later to pursuing a career in your chosen area of study. Clearly, you should stress your strengths. Your essay answer must not be a simple restatement of facts that are already in the application. Imagine, for example, a submitted essay that reads as follows:

I went to high school where I got a 3.5 GPA. I was a member of the Associate Dean's Committee on Student Life, and I worked as the assistant manager on the night shift at Billy's Burger Barn. Then, I took the ACT and got a 25. I know that I will make a really good B.A. candidate and will enjoy my job.

This essay is not very interesting. Furthermore, all of that information is redundant because it is already included in the answers to the standard questions on the application.

Instead, describe the facts of your life in such a way that they will be interpreted as good reasons for accepting you. Let's start with your GPA. If your GPA is lower than you would like, try to highlight certain academic facts that would suggest that your abilities exceed and are therefore not reflective of your overall GPA. Did you have a particularly challenging academic schedule that included honors or advanced placement classes? Did you have one especially bad semester (during which you took physics, calculus, and Latin) that pulled your average down? Did you participate in any unusual courses that required special activities, such as field research or independent study? Also, try to emphasize any non-academic facts that would legitimately be considered "important distractions" from your studies. Was there a death in the family or some other difficult set of circumstances that interfered with your studies? How many hours did you work in an average week? What extracurricular or family commitments took time away from your studies?

These points are significant and may have an impact on the admissions committee. For example:

The committee will see that my final GPA is 3.5. I should point out that the average would have been higher had I not needed to work 20 hours each week to save for my college education. Additionally, my grades in the first semester of my junior year were disappointing because my grandmother, who lived with my family and with whom I was very close, died. Finally, in order to fulfill the requirements for the honors program, I wrote a 20-page honors thesis on the Dutch fishing industry of the 18th century. I have included a copy of the introduction to my thesis with this application.

You should take the same approach to your work experience. For example:

During my junior and senior years in high school, I worked an average of 20 hours per week at Billy's Burger Barn as the manager on the night shift. I would report to work at midnight and get off at four a.m. As night manager, I supervised eight other employees and was responsible for making emergency repairs on kitchen equipment. For example, once I was able to keep the deep fryer in operation by using a length of telephone cable to repair a faulty thermostat. The night manager was also responsible for maintaining order. It's no easy job to convince intoxicated students who become too rowdy to leave without calling the police. Also, we were robbed at gunpoint not once but twice.

Of course, if you have considerable work experience (e.g., if you graduated from high school several years ago rather than just recently), you will want to describe that experience in more detail.

Can you say anything about your ACT score? Probably not much—the ACT score is fairly simple and not usually open to interpretation. However, there are certain exceptions that may be taken into consideration, such as a history of poor scores on standardized exams. For example:

I believe that my ACT score of 21 understates my real ability, for I have never had much success on aptitude tests. Yet, I finished high school with a 3.6 GPA.

The committee will see that I have two ACT scores, 22 and 25. During the first test, I had the flu and a fever and simply could not concentrate.

A history of poor test performance and illness are the two most common types of excuses for a disappointing test score.

Finally, you must also persuade the admissions committee that you are serious about obtaining your college degree. You must be able to give an example of something in your background that explains why you want to go to college. Also, it will help your case if you can suggest what you might do with a college degree. For example:

As a prospective environmental science major, I interned with the Student Environmental Association. Working with private company executives who had themselves satisfied E.P.A. emissions standards, we convinced the University to stop polluting the Ten-Mile Run Creek. From this experience, I learned how business helps to protect our environment. I plan to make environmental resources my area of study, and I hope to work for the government or a private agency to protect the environment.

A word of warning is in order regarding your career objectives: they must be believable. It will not be sufficient to write, "I plan to solve the environmental problems of American industry." Such a statement is much too abstract. College admissions officers are also not interested in a general discourse on the advantages of democracy or the hardship of poverty. If you write, "I want to eliminate damage to the planet and to help private industries help themselves environmentally," then there had better be something in your experience that makes this statement believable.

Finally, with regard to motivation, do not imagine that there is a preferred political position that you should adopt. College admissions officers span the political spectrum.

Thus far, we have discussed the issues of ability and motivation. You may also wish to include information in a general essay answer that demonstrates to the school how you would help create a diverse student body with interesting talents, abilities, and perspectives. This additional information can be something dramatic:

One morning, a patron choked on a burger and lost consciousness. I used the Heimlich maneuver to dislodge the food and performed CPR until a team of paramedics arrived. The patron recovered fully, in large part, according to her doctors, because of my first aid.

Or, the information may not be dramatic:

My parents are Armenian immigrants, so I am fluent in Armenian as well as English. I would enjoy meeting others who share an interest in the politics, legal developments, and culture of that part of the world.

However, do not overestimate the value of this kind of information. It is, so to speak, the icing on the cake. These details about your life make you a more interesting individual and might tip the scale in your favor when all other things are equal. Keep in mind, though, that it will not get you accepted into a school for which you would not otherwise be competitive in terms of ACT and GPA.

Now, we turn our attention to matters of style. Your arguments for acceptance need to be presented in an organized fashion. There is no single preferred format, but you might start with the following outline:

    I. I have the ability to succeed in college.
        A. My high school studies are good.
            1. I had one bad semester due to an illness in the family.
            2. I was in the accelerated program.
            3. I wrote a comprehensive term paper.
        B. My work experience is good.
            1. I worked during three years of high school.
            2. I was promoted to shift leader at my job.
    II. I have the desire to earn a college degree.

      A. During my internship, I worked with Ph.D. recipients on the pollution problem.

      B. I want to become a specialist in environmental chemistry.

  III. I have unique characteristics.

The prose that you use should display your own natural style of writing. Do not write something that appears contrived. Admissions officers do not want to read essays that are written as manuscripts, with footnoted "documentary evidence." You should create your outline using as many arguments as possible. Then, you must begin to edit. For most people, the final document should not be more than a page to a page and a half in length—typed, of course! During the editing process, you should strive for an economy of language so that you can convey as much information as possible. Additionally, you will be forced to make considered judgments about the relative importance of various points. You will be forced to delete those ideas that are not really very compelling. In order to compose a really good essay, it may be necessary to reduce five or six pages to a single page, and the process may require more than 20 drafts. Make sure that you have at least one other person look at your essay—a teacher, counselor, or parent would be a good resource.

Because a number of colleges elevate the importance of the college admissions essay, more thorough recommendations are presented in the section of this book entitled *Six Ways to Jumpstart Your College Admissions Essays* (p. 579).

SOLICIT EFFECTIVE LETTERS OF RECOMMENDATION

Perhaps the best advice that we can give you about so-called "letters of recommendation" is that you should think of them as evaluations rather than recommendations. Indeed, many admissions officers refer to letter-writers as evaluators. These letters can be very important factors in an application, so who should actually write them?

First of all, some schools require a letter from the dean of students (or some similar functionary) at your high school. Essentially, this requirement serves as an inquiry into your behavior. However, colleges do not really expect that this person will have much to say about your application since in many cases students do not become acquainted with their deans. This letter is merely intended to evoke any information about disciplinary problems that might not otherwise surface. So, the best response from a dean, and the one that most people tend to receive, is just a statement to the effect that there is nothing much to say regarding your behavior. In addition to the dean's letter, most schools require, or at least permit, you to submit two or three letters of evaluation from other sources. Who should write these letters? Remember that a letter of evaluation does not necessarily have to come from a well-known person. How effective is the following letter?

Francis Scott
Chairperson of the Board

    To the Admissions Committee:

    I am recommending Susan Roberts for college. Her mother is a member of our board
    of directors. Susan's mother earned her doctorate at the University of Chicago and
    she regularly makes significant contributions to our corporate meetings. Susan,
    following in her mother's footsteps, will make a fine college candidate.

    Sincerely,
    Francis Scott

The letterhead holds great promise, but the body of the letter is worthless. It is obvious that Francis Scott does not really have any basis for his conclusion that Susan Roberts "will make a fine college candidate."

Find people who know you very well to write the very best letters of recommendation (e.g., a teacher with whom you took several courses, your intern supervisor, or an associate with whom you have worked closely). A good evaluation will incorporate personal knowledge into the letter and will make references to specific events and activities. For example:

Mary P. Weiss
White, Waste, and Blanche

To the Admissions Committee:

White, Waste, and Blanche is a consulting firm that advises corporations on environmental concerns. Susan Roberts has worked for us as an intern for the past two summers. Her work is outstanding, and she is an intelligent and genial person.

Last summer, as my assistant, Susan wrote a 5-page report that outlined a way of altering a client's exhaust stack to reduce sulfur emissions. The report was organized so that it was easy to follow and written in a style that was clear and easy to understand. Additionally, Susan assisted with a live presentation during a meeting with the client's board of directors and engineers. She was confident and handled some very difficult questions in an easy manner.

Finally, Susan made an important contribution to our company softball team. The team finished in last place, but Susan played in every game. Her batting average wasn't anything to brag about, but her enthusiasm more than made up for it.

Sincerely,
Mary Weiss

This letter demonstrates that the writer knows the applicant very well. The writer is able to address several aspects of the applicant's character, personality, and work ethic from a position of familiarity. A letter like this one makes for a very meaningful contribution to any college application, so you should strive to receive this type of recommendation as part of your application portfolio.

SIX WAYS TO JUMPSTART YOUR COLLEGE ADMISSIONS ESSAYS

An admissions director sits behind a well-lit desk in a paper-strewn office. Her window overlooks a large, rolling college campus. At mid-morning, students freckle the walkways, ambling to and from the surrounding lecture halls. Of current concern for this college admissions director are not the students already enrolled but the hundreds or even thousands of students who are seeking admission for the fall semester. Near the edge of her desk rises an already teetering stack of college applications, representing the academic hopes and dreams of soon-to-be high school graduates. Students from a wide range of high schools—big, small, public, private, home-based, rural, suburban, urban—have submitted their vital statistics: test score(s); high school transcripts with summaries of classes; GPAs; class rank; extracurricular activities; and references from teachers, coaches, club advisors, and counselors. These application papers assist her in differentiating one level of student from another (e.g., students with "As" and "Bs" versus students with "Bs" and "Cs"). She pulls out two applications with very similar test scores and GPAs and considers which of these two students will receive the coveted stamp of "admitted" on his or her file. Following this task, she will move on to the even more challenging task of mining through applications to find the small percentage of students who are "diamonds in the rough"; these students did not fully flourish in high school for various reasons, but they have the potential to succeed in a college environment.

As a high school student, your goals and aspirations are tightly interwoven with your ability to obtain admission to the college of your choice. Thus, as a student applying to various colleges, it is important for you to understand the selection or admissions process that these institutions of higher education use to narrow the pool of applicants. You should, with great curiosity, ask a number of probing questions about the process: What criteria do colleges use to admit students? How does the college admissions director decide between the merits of students who hold similar test scores and grades? How does a college discover those rare, under-qualified students who have not fully demonstrated their potential in high school through grades or test scores?

Of course, college admissions directors assess potential students using tools such as GPA, test score(s), teacher references, and extracurricular participation records. But colleges also use an evaluation instrument known as the admissions essay as a significant component in determining which students will or will not receive acceptance letters.

The admissions essay—also referred to as an application essay, a personal statement, or a personal essay—is a written composition from a student, generally submitted to a college at the same time as the application documents. The written essay—typically from 100 to 500 words in length—may answer a directed content question (e.g., an opinion on some current event), or it may respond to a simple "tell us about yourself" question.

The essay prompts listed below reflect actual examples of those delivered alongside recent college admissions applications.

- *Write an essay in which you tell us about someone who has made an impact on your life, and explain how and why this person is important to you.*

- *Choose an issue of importance to you—the issue could be personal, school related, local, political, or international in scope—and write an essay in which you explain the significance of that issue to yourself, your family, your community, or your generation.*

- *Evaluate a significant experience or achievement, risk you have taken, or ethical dilemma you have faced and its impact on you.*

- *Discuss some issue of personal, local, national, or international concern and its importance to you.*

- *Describe a character of fiction, a historical figure, or a creative work (as in art, music, science, etc.) that has had an influence on you, and explain that influence.*

- *Make a rational argument for a position that you do not personally support.*

- *Share an experience through which you have gained respect for intellectual, social, or cultural differences. Comment on how your personal experiences and achievements would contribute to the diversity of our college.*

- *As you prepare to pursue a career in music, theatre, or dance, describe your thoughts on the relationship between the arts and today's society. How relevant has your art been to your community and to you?*

- *What outrages you?*

- *If you were given a grant to research a scientific or medical issue that you deem important to the world, what would it be, why would you choose it, and what kind of research do you think would have the greatest chance of being productive?*

- *What have you read recently that you found enlightening?*

- *Consider the books, essays, poems, or journal articles that you have read over the last year or two, either for school or leisure. Discuss the way in which one of these writings has changed your understanding of the world, of other people, or of yourself.*

The admissions essay provides you with an opportunity to "sell" yourself and hopefully elevate your status from a potential student to a future student in the eyes of a college. In submitting this essay, it is important to view the process as a chance to catapult yourself beyond the other candidates. Confidently articulate why a particular college needs you as a student by emphasizing your unique goals, values, aptitudes, and abilities.

What follows are six strategies to help you jumpstart the writing of a college admissions essay. While these strategies can tell you neither exactly what types of questions will be asked (since some colleges ask questions that are quite broad while others ask questions that are very targeted and specific) nor what assessment criteria specific colleges use for evaluating the admissions essay (since each institution tightly guards this type of assessment information), they should provide valuable insights to consider as you begin the essay writing process.

PRESENT YOURSELF AS UNIQUE, EXCEPTIONAL, OR TALENTED

Because college admissions directors read thousands of essays, you must write in a way that distinguishes you from the crowd of applying students. A large number of college applicants submit adequate to excellent GPAs along with solid test scores. Many have been involved in extracurricular activities, such as athletics, honors clubs, music, or drama. Others have participated in a wide range of leadership or volunteer roles. Given this large pool of truly qualified students, you must leave an impression that makes you positively memorable as a candidate for admission by seizing the opportunity to compose a well-crafted essay that highlights your best characteristics and your achievements.

In preparation for writing the essay, think clearly and creatively about what makes you unique, exceptional, or talented as a potential college student. What unique experiences have you had? Do you have abilities or aptitudes that set you apart from other students? In what special events or activities have you participated? What unique cultural experiences have you encountered? Is there anything special about how or where you grew up? Have you met famous or unique people who have influenced you? Are you exceptionally talented in a particular area, such as music, art, or drama? What motivates you to succeed beyond other students? Do you have atypical work or employment experiences? How have you overcome an individual setback, struggle, or limitation? Have you participated in significant and/or memorable athletic events? Can you identify a unique hobby in which you participate? Have you volunteered or served in your community and made a significant contribution? Do you have a one-of-a-kind talent? Have you received any special awards or commendations? Have you distinguished yourself as a leader in clubs or organizations?

On the following page are examples of opening essay sentences that include the positive characteristics upon which a student might desire to focus in an essay. Consider how these statements might serve as springboards for powerful admissions essays.

- *Because my grandmother moved into my family's home when I was just ten days old, I have vicariously experienced a distinct and dissimilar culture from my own. I flood my days with friends and activities found in the high-tech, suburban, media-driven, adolescent-controlled culture of Tri-City High School. During the evening hours, however, I wander in a completely different culture immersed in the foods, songs, stories, and language of the "Old World" where my grandmother lived for more than fifty years.*

- *I personally do not know of any other high school student at South High School who has willingly dined on goat intestines, but while traveling over the summer with an international student exchange program, I embraced the opportunity to feast on this unique delicacy.*

- *Senator-elect Jamison shook my hand vigorously and commented to all those within earshot that he was sure my efforts had played a significant role in contributing to his recent election.*

- *Not every seventeen-year-old might jump at the opportunity to witness a three-hour long cardiac surgery from the operating room window of a teaching hospital. But I certainly did! Dr. Rose provided me with just such a privilege in celebration of my fourth year of serving as a volunteer hospital aid at New City Hospital.*

- *Performing with a choir at the governor's mansion may seem like less than a life-changing experience. But after speaking personally with the governor following the performance and asking her one simple question, my perspective regarding the world of women in politics radically changed.*

- *Losing every single game as a senior football player at Old Lake High School may not have taught me much about celebrating victories, but I did learn valuable lessons about perseverance, dedication, and humility.*

- *I never thought I'd write a computer program that other people would regularly use. But after a friend introduced me to the world of open-source coding, I fervently dove into writing new code and improving existing code on a variety of programs that some major companies utilize every day.*

- *Working weekends at Billy B's Barbeque during high school not only allowed me to earn money for college, but it also brought me face to face with a host of truly fascinating "regulars" whose life stories I will never forget.*

- *For years, because of my love for reading, each and every librarian at the Key City public library knew me by name. But now, because of my love for writing, everyone who reads the Key City Times newspaper also knows me by name.*

- *I was shocked and honored when my name was called as the regional swimmer of the year, especially considering that my pediatrician had warned me that childhood asthma would forever hinder my ability to compete in athletics.*

Remember that the main goal in writing an admissions essay is to distinguish yourself from the other applicants. Note how this next example of a 400-word college essay shines light on a unique relationship that led to exceptional experiences.

<u>*What has influenced your desire to study history at New College University?*</u>

At first blush, I look like a typical all-American girl. But I truly live a double identity. From the very day that my grandmother moved into my family's home when I was just ten days old, I have vicariously experienced a distinct and dissimilar culture from my own. I flood my days with friends and activities found in the high-tech, suburban, media-driven, adolescent-controlled culture of Tri-City High School. During the evening hours, however, I wander in a completely different culture immersed in the foods, songs, stories, and language of the "Old World" where my grandmother lived for more than fifty years.

Seeded by the nightly songs and stories of my grandmother, I had for years envisioned scenes of the Italian countryside with narrow streets and quiet villas. In an almost mystical manner, I could smell chickens roasting on open-air fireplaces, feel the breezes off the sea of the Sicilian coast, see the workers harvesting grapes in the hillside vineyards, and hear the after-dinner songs rising from family gatherings. But as a junior at Tri-

City High School, those far-away images became reality after I traveled to Italy to spend the summer of my junior year in Sicily as a participant in an International Student Exchange Unlimited program. I was amazed at how my grandmother's stories took tangible shape and substance over twelve memorable and life-transforming weeks.

I knew I would learn valuable lessons traveling the Italian countryside, visiting historical sites, and meeting a rich variety of local characters, but I did not anticipate that this adventure would change my perspective on the world and redirect my future. In my final weeks of the student exchange program, I joined a group digging for archaeological relics just outside the town of Salina. Through listening to the archaeology lectures from local university professors, I discovered that civilizations had for thousands of years settled and resettled the Sicilian shores and hillsides. As I participated in the archaeological dig, I touched shards of pottery left by some of the very earliest inhabitants of the island and helped uncover the burial grounds of ancient people. I read research and became acquainted with civilizations that I never knew had even existed.

This experience, spawned by my grandmother's influence in my life, launched in me a desire to study ancient civilizations and cultures. So, now I'm applying to New College University in order to study history and archaeology. I'm convinced that as a student at New College University I will continue to live a double identity, wonderfully captured between the pull of contemporary and ancient cultures.

TELL AN ENGAGING STORY

"The universe is made of stories, not atoms." Muriel Rukeyser

To effectively communicate how you are a unique candidate, tell an engaging story—or stories if word limits permit—of experiences that highlight those personal characteristics that distinguish you from other students.

Think about the last journalistic photograph in a newspaper, magazine, or website that captured your attention. The best photographs tell a story. As you look at a great journalistic picture, you gain an emerging sense of the event, the context, the emotion, the tension, the thrill, or the struggle embedded in the image. In the same manner, the best admissions essays also portray a story that imprints a lasting mark on the reader. When the essay prompts allow, you should consider organizing your essay around meaningful and moving stories that communicate how your hopes and dreams draw you to this particular college and a specific area of study.

Bear in mind this word of warning. As you write your essay, reemphasizing your GPA, ACT score, or class rank in a bland format does little to draw attention to yourself. Remember that the pages of your college application and high school transcript already list these figures. Yes, these numbers do provide important information to the college. (That, in fact, is why the college requires you to provide them in the first place.) However, these numbers are not central to the purpose of an admissions essay. The core function of this essay is to determine whether you can clearly and concisely articulate, in written fashion, who you are and why you make a great candidate for entrance into a particular college. If your scores are exceptional and you can communicate them in a creative manner, include them in the essay.

Review the following examples of essay paragraphs, and note how telling significant information in a story or narrative form creates a more engaging and readable essay paragraph.

- Essay Paragraph 1

   Poor Example:
   As a student at Newbury High School, I was involved in four years of Student Council, Art Club, and the Yearbook. My GPA was a 3.9. I graduated in the top 5% of students in my class. I enjoy photography. I want to be an Art teacher.

Better Example:

The janitor laughed loudly as he saw my sweeping red hair catapult over the empty wastebaskets strewn in the hall after school. Again, I was literally running (down the school corridor) from my responsibilities as the Student Council representative for the Senior Class to join in assisting the Yearbook production team in hitting another important deadline. As one of two student photographers for Newbury High School, I had worked late into the night selecting the last three pictures to appear on the Yearbook cover and was now excited to hear the reaction of Mrs. Jensen, the Yearbook advisor, and the rest of the production team. During lunch, I had shown the photographs to other members of the Art Club, and they all gave them two huge "thumbs up." I was really hoping to please Mrs. Jensen with these pictures, since over my four years of high school, she had mentored and encouraged me, pushing me to achieve to the highest degree not only with my academics—I have a 3.9 GPA and will graduate in the top 5% of my class—but also with my many extracurricular activities. Because of Mrs. Jensen's example, I too want to be an Art teacher who pushes students to take new challenges and to succeed in both academic and extracurricular endeavors.

- Essay Paragraph 2

Poor Example:

I was selected as the #1 golfer in our state my senior year in high school. In my junior year, I was ranked in the top ten. I think my test scores and my GPA are high enough for you to consider me for a scholarship. I also play in the Jazz Band.

Better Example:

Innovation. For me, there is a deep sense of satisfaction in finding a unique or creative solution to a problem. In last spring's state high school golf tournament, I was leading the field by a single stroke walking toward the final green. An errant tee shot on my part had landed my ball behind a stand of bushes, and my coaches had groaned when they saw the precarious position of my lie. Thinking quickly—and innovatively—I grabbed my two iron and shot the ball not over the bushes as all would have expected, but under a gap below the bushes, rolling the ball cleanly toward the middle of the green. I sunk a remaining seven-foot putt and won not only the state high school golf tournament but also the #1 ranking that accompanied the win. Throughout my four years of high school varsity golf, I over and over again discovered innovative ways to succeed. It is this deep desire to innovate, to create new avenues to answers, and to find solutions to challenges that drives my love for problem-solving in the areas of mathematics and science. As a member of the Blackstone High School Jazz Band, innovation, too, is what drives my love for creative musical expression. And this love for innovation is what drives me to apply to the honors program at Lake City University, which is known nationally for its unique approach to educating students.

Telling an engaging story about some life experience is a powerful tool in distinguishing yourself from other students. Note that not every essay prompt can be addressed through the use of a story. Some call for a more logical or deductive approach. Nevertheless, when the opportunity to tell a story presents itself within the context of a specific essay prompt, you should seize upon that opportunity to tell why you are a great potential student.

NARROW YOUR ESSAY TO A SPECIFIC THEME

A college admissions essay is typically limited to a certain number of words. As you can imagine, an admissions director does not have the time to read a multiple page treatise covering your entire life story from birth to high school graduation. As you organize your essay, focus your essay on one or two major ideas or themes that express your experiences, abilities, goals, attitudes, ideas, talents, or thoughts. Do not ramble aimlessly or muse recklessly without any focus or overarching structure. Instead, narrow the thrust of your essay to a specific and manageable theme.

Read the following winning essay submitted for a college scholarship contest. Note how the student tells how just one experience in her life—being cast in a play—caused her perspectives on life to mature and grow. Consider how she narrows her theme.

My heart was pounding out of my chest in an unfamiliar rhythm. I longed for water but knew there was not time. In the crowded area, pushed up against others, I could feel their breathing, as rapid and tense as my own. The anticipation was killing me as I swallowed hard and closed my eyes. Overcome with emotion, I cracked my knuckles three times—a habit I perform during extreme nervousness. My mind was flooded with last minute worries, and I tried with difficulty to push them away. I sensed a comforting hand on my shoulder and felt a rush of momentary calmness. "Everything is going to be O.K.," someone said reassuringly.

As the show was about to begin, my anticipation was replaced by excitement. As I looked out tentatively at the audience, I felt strangely secure rather than vulnerable on the stage. Suddenly, as if by magic, my worries were gone. I was no longer Malinda Spry, a seventeen-year-old-girl concerned about monologues, dance routines, and solos; I was someone else. I was Eve, and as the heart-wrenching words to "Children of Eve" escaped my mouth, the scene of expulsion from the beautiful Garden of Eden became my reality.

When I was cast in "Children of Eve," a musical chronicling the events of the New Testament, I was overwhelmed with giving voice to Eve. I was extremely grateful to be given this unique opportunity to represent such a complex character. As the woman held accountable for the presence of sin in the world, Eve is viewed as the villain in the creation story. However, before long, I saw the other side of Eve, the intelligent, curious, gifted side; the one responsible for humanity's successes in the world rather than its defeat. Although Eve carried the burden of original sin, she was amazingly strong and blessed with an innate desire to learn. I knew that it was my responsibility to portray the story of creation through her eyes. My portrayal of Eve included her passionate response to life in and out of paradise. Inspired, I recognized a parallel between Eve and myself.

I was exhilarated to bring Eve to life. She was never content with paradise, perfection, or the Garden, as Adam was. Instead, Eve asked the difficult questions and refused to accept life the way it was presented to her. She ardently claimed that it was God's will for humanity to be expelled from Eden in order to discover free will. Although Eve defied God, she found that He never abandoned her, a fact that strengthened my own faith in life.

During the closing moments of the performance, Eve implores God and the rest of creation—her children—for forgiveness. "We were just humans, to error prone," she says, looking around. The song brought tears to my eyes as I realized Eve's influence in all of creation and her profound lesson of forgiveness, not of betrayal, of love, not of hate. As I glanced around the audience, whose faces were filled with sympathy, I knew that they too understood the creation story from Eve's perspective—as it was meant to be told.

START WITH AN ENGAGING HOOK AND END WITH A POWERFUL PUNCH

An effective essay begins with an enticing start. In your essay, write an introduction that hooks the admissions director, compelling him or her to finish reading your composition. Craft your first two or three lines in such a way that they creatively engage the reader. These first sentences are so important that you may need to work and rework them until you find a great combination of words, setting a compelling hook and subsequent direction for your essay.

Here are some tips for creating engaging hooks (not all of them will be used at once, of course):

- Use active verbs (avoid passive verbs).

- Give a sense of feeling or emotion.

- Use a moving literary, historical, or provocative quotation.

- Provide a surprise, logical twist, or emotional shock.

- Use hyperbole.

- Present a definition.

- Interject a puzzle or riddle.

- Introduce an anecdote.

- Draw an example from a current event.

- Create suspense or drama.

- Convey humor (ONLY if you can do it naturally and tastefully).

- Avoid dull facts and figures.

- Ask a question that cannot be answered.

Remember that your introductory sentences must flow naturally into the entire theme of your essay. The introduction directs the reader toward your remaining thoughts or arguments.

As you develop a powerful hook, do not forget that your essay must answer the question that is asked. Make sure your introductory sentences help you to focus clearly and intentionally on the answer to the essay prompt. No matter how powerful your essay is, if you fail to directly address the prompt that is presented, you fail the essay.

Here are three examples of essay introductions that hook the reader into an engaging story.

Example 1:
My feet clamped to the floor, immovable, after Mr. Smith called my name as Washington High School's "Student of the Year" at the annual award ceremony. As my shock faded and I coerced my limbs to stand and walk to the stage, I thought of all the people who had helped me achieve this award. There was Mr. Paulsen, my varsity basketball coach, Mrs. Simpson, my orchestra director, and Mr. Smith, the Honor Society advisor who had nominated me for the award.

Example 2:
"Diplomacy is the art of saying 'Nice doggie' until you can find a rock," quipped Will Rogers, the U.S. humorist and showman. The danger in practicing this particular philosophy of political diplomacy is that on occasion the dog wakes from its passivity, growls ferociously, and bites aggressively, all before the rock is found and exploited as a defense. Current research in the field of political science provides effective alternatives to this overused passive/aggressive approach to diplomacy that Will Rogers humorously presented.

Example 3:
Why do I always smell barbequed pork ribs, deep-fried hushpuppies, and large mugs of black coffee in my mind when I think of my love for history? Working weekends at Billy B's Barbeque during high school not only allowed me to save money for college, but it also brought me face to face with a host of truly fascinating "regulars" whose life stories I will never forget. In Mr. Brown's World History class I had studied the causes and results of the Korean War. But it was not until I met Mr. Jacob Abbot—"Jake" to his friends—that I came face to face with the real history of that military conflict.

Here is an example of an entire essay that was submitted for a scholarship contest. Observe how this student creatively hooks the reader into the history of her deep desire to become a broadcast journalist.

"Where are my spoons," my mother would ask, commenting on the ever-dwindling supply as she washed dishes. By the time I was seven, my mother discovered that her missing spoons served as microphones, enabling me to host a "live" news show with my younger siblings. With the assistance of my "guests," we performed daily newscasts from our kitchen and living room. As the clock approached our bedtime, I would usher a "breaking news" segment.

Eventually, I learned that the profession of journalism involves more than "breaking news" or playing dress-up for a make-believe camera. As I became a devout viewer of Ted Koppel and "60 Minutes," several things became apparent. Journalism required remaining abreast of both historical and contemporary events, as well as a firm belief that public issues be viewed through the lens of people's everyday experiences.

As a junior in high school, I applied to and was accepted as a student intern at the local television station. This allowed me to move even further from the world of playing broadcast journalism to truly living and breathing it. The weekend news crew took me under their wings and allowed me to try almost every facet of creating the evening news.

While many years have passed since my broadcast days from my living room, I cannot disassociate myself from that little girl and her microphone. Indeed, that girl's dream has not dimmed, nor has the insatiable desire to transform it into reality. As an aspiring broadcast journalist, I hope to ultimately inform and advance larger discourses that affect the social, political, and economic welfare of our society. If admitted to Lincoln University, I want to hone my skills in order to one day tell stories of people at their best and their worst, narratives that speak of our curiosities, our hopes, and our struggles.

You must write your introduction to capture the imagination of the reader. Remember, however, that you must also construct a meaningful ending or conclusion. In the conclusion, attempt to answer the "why," "what next," or "so what" questions of your essay in a meaningful final sentence. Although the conclusion is a summary, do not merely summarize or reword your arguments or thoughts. Give the reader an understanding of the final step or next steps following your essay. Having told a moving story or made a powerful argument, now tell the reader what you want them to remember or do with your essay.

Consider these examples of conclusions:

- *If admitted to Lincoln University, I want to hone my skills in order to one day tell stories of people at their best and their worst, narratives that speak of our curiosities, our hopes, and our struggles.*

- *Now, having held a newborn baby in my hands, I strongly desire to invest my life in preparing to become a caring and skilled pediatrician.*

- *How did meeting Senator Smithson influence my desire to study at Big Valley College? Inspiration, inspiration, inspiration! I, and other women, can indeed succeed in the world of politics.*

- *Yes, my body was still shaking with frustration, anger, and even outrage from the experience. Those memories, to this day, still motivate me to pursue study in the field of clinical psychology.*

ORGANIZE THE ESSAY TIGHTLY AND ARRANGE IT MEANINGFULLY

Because most essay prompts allow for 500 words or fewer, the organization of your essay answer must be concise and clear. Your introduction should flow smoothly into your first paragraph. Each paragraph must meaningfully follow the previous one. Between the paragraphs should exist a natural parallelism in the alignment of thoughts, arguments, or ideas.

Prepare for writing your essay by developing a formal outline of your presentation. The elements of the outline must thoughtfully connect. Here are some ways that an essay might be organized.

- Comparison and Contrast
- Point and Counterpoint
- Before and After
- Chronological Sequence

- Cause and Effect

- Logical Progression

- Increasingly Effective Arguments

- Differing Scenes or Locations

- Conflict and Resolution

Read the following example paragraph written in a "before and after" format. Notice how the paragraph is tightly wound around a single theme but moves smoothly from the "before" to the "after."

> *I failed English class—twice! After the second failure, I sobbed intensely even as my guidance counselor comforted me by explaining this was quite forgivable given that I knew absolutely no English when I had arrived in the United States just two years before. Even in the midst of great compassion, I fretted over my inability to understand a noun from a pronoun, a verb from an adverb, or an infinitive from a gerund. My high school life, so I thought, was doomed, like a never-ending hell, to repeating freshman English over and over and over again. But then Mrs. Butler arrived. Like some rare powered superhero, this gifted teacher had the strength to bend my mind to understand not only the basics of the English language but also the complexities of story, poetry, and verse. With her help, I passed not only freshman English, sophomore Composition, and junior Literature, but I also passed the English Advanced Placement exam with high scores. So now, even as I apply to become an English major at Jefferson State College, I'm determined to return to the high school classroom, and like Mrs. Butler, rescue those who desire not to fail anymore.*

USE PROPER ENGLISH

This might sound like overly simplistic advice, but college admissions directors use the essay to determine whether you can write on a college-appropriate level. To impress a college, you must write in a style that follows all the rules of formal English.

As you edit your essay, check for (among other things):

- Proper grammar

- Correct punctuation

- Appropriate word usage

- Normal capitalization

- Proper spelling

- Appropriate abbreviations

- Correct notation of sources (if used)

- Normal pagination and spacing

Find someone to help proofread your essay before you submit it to the college. Consult an English instructor at your high school for direct help in proofreading your essay or for references to someone else who might be available to help.

BONUS TIPS

Here are some additional tips to consider as you compose college admissions essays.

- Do not over embellish, lie about, or fabricate your experiences.

- Research and double-check any facts, dates, or numbers that you use.

- Do not overuse words from a thesaurus that you do not normally use.

- Never plagiarize an essay or portions of an essay.

- Do not tell someone else's story or experience as your own.

- Be yourself; find your own voice; be natural.

- Write about something you are passionate about.

- Do not drop names (especially if you do not have a real relationship with the person).

- Avoid clichés and slang.

- Do not try to be overly cute or trite.

- Use specific details, not just generalizations.

- Start the writing process early.

- Write, rewrite, and rewrite again.

- Ask a teacher or advisor to read your essay and provide feedback.

- Do not beg. ("I really, really, really want to attend your college.")

- Avoid odd fonts or unusual paper that might distract from the content of your essay).

- Proofread, proofread, and proofread!

CONCLUSION

"A finished person is a boring person." Anna Quindlen

For the vast majority of college admissions essays there exist no right or perfect answers. Instead, the college provides you blank space to fill with a well-composed and creative statement reflecting your uniqueness as a person. The questions asked will vary. But always remember that the answers you provide should point to yourself as a future college student who has untapped potential, talent, and ability. Good luck!

Answer Keys:

Test Mechanics, Concepts, and Strategies

ENGLISH ANSWER KEY

LESSON (p. 15)

1. A	20. J	39. B	58. G	77. C	96. H	115. –	134. B
2. G	21. C	40. F	59. C	78. K	97. D	116. D	135. F
3. B	22. F	41. B	60. H	79. B	98. K	117. J	136. B
4. H	23. E	42. G	61. B	80. H	99. D	118. D	137. F
5. D	24. H	43. A	62. K	81. B	100. G	119. G	138. D
6. G	25. E	44. K	63. B	82. K	101. A	120. B	139. H
7. C	26. J	45. D	64. K	83. E	102. F	121. F	140. A
8. H	27. A	46. H	65. A	84. K	103. B	122. B	141. F
9. B	28. G	47. C	66. C	85. A	104. J	123. J	142. B
10. F	29. A	48. H	67. B	86. K	105. C	124. A	143. J
11. A	30. J	49. D	68. H	87. B	106. G	125. F	144. D
12. K	31. B	50. H	69. E	88. H	107. B	126. B	145. H
13. E	32. J	51. A	70. J	89. A	108. J	127. G	
14. F	33. A	52. F	71. B	90. H	109. B	128. C	
15. D	34. J	53. D	72. G	91. B	110. J	129. G	
16. G	35. D	54. F	73. D	92. H	111. A	130. E	
17. D	36. G	55. A	74. H	93. E	112. H	131. J	
18. H	37. D	56. G	75. A	94. K	113. A	132. B	
19. C	38. J	57. C	76. H	95. B	114. K	133. J	

CHALLENGE ITEMS (p. 35)

1. A	7. A	13. A	19. D	25. A	31. B	37. C	43. C
2. J	8. F	14. J	20. G	26. H	32. H	38. G	44. H
3. B	9. D	15. A	21. D	27. A	33. A	39. A	45. A
4. H	10. H	16. G	22. G	28. F	34. G	40. F	46. F
5. A	11. A	17. B	23. B	29. B	35. D	41. A	47. B
6. F	12. F	18. G	24. J	30. H	36. G	42. H	48. H

TIMED-PRACTICE QUIZZES (p. 43)

QUIZ I

1. B	5. C	9. A	13. B	17. B	21. C	25. B	29. C
2. F	6. F	10. J	14. H	18. H	22. F	26. H	30. G
3. B	7. D	11. C	15. A	19. C	23. A	27. D	31. B
4. F	8. J	12. J	16. J	20. J	24. G	28. G	32. H

QUIZ II

1. D	5. C	9. A	13. B	17. D	21. A	25. D	29. B
2. F	6. F	10. F	14. G	18. F	22. J	26. H	
3. D	7. B	11. B	15. D	19. C	23. B	27. D	
4. J	8. G	12. F	16. F	20. G	24. H	28. F	

ANSWER KEYS

QUIZ III

1. B	5. C	9. D	13. A	17. C	21. A	25. A	29. A
2. H	6. F	10. J	14. F	18. J	22. G	26. H	30. G
3. B	7. C	11. C	15. C	19. C	23. A	27. C	31. B
4. F	8. H	12. G	16. J	20. F	24. G	28. J	

MATHEMATICS ANSWER KEY

LESSON (p. 77)

1. C	32. F	63. C	94. K	125. B	156. F	187. C	218. J
2. H	33. C	64. K	95. D	126. H	157. D	188. H	219. E
3. D	34. G	65. B	96. J	127. A	158. K	189. C	220. F
4. J	35. C	66. K	97. D	128. K	159. C	190. H	221. D
5. C	36. J	67. C	98. H	129. B	160. J	191. A	222. H
6. F	37. A	68. H	99. B	130. F	161. D	192. G	223. D
7. E	38. K	69. A	100. K	131. D	162. G	193. C	224. F
8. G	39. A	70. F	101. C	132. G	163. C	194. H	225. E
9. C	40. J	71. C	102. H	133. C	164. H	195. A	226. F
10. J	41. D	72. K	103. D	134. G	165. C	196. H	227. D
11. B	42. H	73. B	104. K	135. D	166. K	197. E	228. K
12. J	43. D	74. J	105. C	136. K	167. B	198. J	229. A
13. D	44. G	75. B	106. F	137. C	168. J	199. E	230. G
14. J	45. D	76. G	107. A	138. K	169. B	200. H	231. C
15. E	46. K	77. D	108. K	139. C	170. H	201. E	232. H
16. J	47. E	78. F	109. D	140. K	171. E	202. K	233. E
17. C	48. J	79. C	110. F	141. B	172. K	203. A	234. G
18. K	49. C	80. J	111. C	142. G	173. B	204. K	235. E
19. C	50. J	81. D	112. F	143. B	174. K	205. C	236. J
20. G	51. B	82. J	113. A	144. F	175. A	206. H	237. B
21. D	52. K	83. E	114. K	145. B	176. F	207. D	238. G
22. H	53. D	84. J	115. A	146. K	177. A	208. H	239. A
23. B	54. H	85. C	116. F	147. A	178. H	209. D	240. G
24. H	55. C	86. H	117. B	148. K	179. D	210. H	241. B
25. D	56. F	87. D	118. J	149. D	180. H	211. D	242. G
26. K	57. A	88. K	119. C	150. H	181. D	212. J	243. D
27. E	58. J	89. B	120. J	151. C	182. K	213. B	244. J
28. H	59. D	90. J	121. D	152. G	183. C	214. G	
29. D	60. H	91. D	122. H	153. C	184. J	215. C	
30. H	61. A	92. F	123. B	154. G	185. E	216. H	
31. C	62. K	93. D	124. H	155. C	186. K	217. E	

CHALLENGE ITEMS (p. 116)

1. B	6. J	11. A	16. K	21. B	26. F	31. D
2. H	7. B	12. J	17. B	22. G	27. E	32. H
3. C	8. J	13. C	18. G	23. A	28. H	33. E
4. K	9. C	14. K	19. C	24. G	29. C	34. K
5. D	10. J	15. B	20. H	25. B	30. J	

TIMED-PRACTICE QUIZZES (p. 123)

QUIZ I

1. A	3. D	5. D	7. E	9. B	11. D	13. D	15. A
2. K	4. H	6. J	8. J	10. H	12. J	14. F	16. J

QUIZ II

1. C	4. G	7. B	10. H	13. D	16. H	19. E
2. F	5. C	8. J	11. D	14. K	17. B	20. J
3. C	6. H	9. A	12. J	15. E	18. H	21. D

QUIZ III

1. C	5. D	9. D	13. A	17. C	21. C	25. E
2. H	6. G	10. J	14. F	18. G	22. G	26. H
3. E	7. B	11. D	15. C	19. E	23. D
4. G	8. F	12. F	16. G	20. G	24. G

CALCULATOR EXERCISE (p. 138)

1. 1	3. 2	5. 1	7. 3	9. 3
2. 2	4. 3	6. 2	8. 3	10. 3

READING ANSWER KEY

LESSON (p. 153)

1. C	6. J	11. A	16. G	21. B	26. F	31. A	36. J
2. F	7. C	12. J	17. D	22. G	27. A	32. G	37. C
3. A	8. H	13. A	18. F	23. A	28. H	33. D	38. J
4. J	9. D	14. H	19. D	24. G	29. C	34. G	39. A
5. B	10. J	15. C	20. H	25. A	30. F	35. D	

EXTENDED LESSON (p. 161)

1. A	13. C	25. B	37. B	49. B	61. B	73. A	85. D
2. F	14. H	26. F	38. J	50. F	62. J	74. H	86. F
3. D	15. B	27. D	39. B	51. D	63. B	75. D	87. B
4. F	16. J	28. J	40. J	52. G	64. J	76. G	88. H
5. D	17. C	29. C	41. C	53. A	65. D	77. A	89. A
6. H	18. F	30. G	42. H	54. J	66. H	78. J	90. J
7. B	19. D	31. A	43. C	55. C	67. D	79. C	91. C
8. G	20. H	32. H	44. G	56. G	68. J	80. F	
9. B	21. B	33. C	45. D	57. D	69. A	81. D	
10. J	22. H	34. G	46. F	58. H	70. J	82. J	
11. B	23. D	35. B	47. B	59. C	71. C	83. C	
12. H	24. G	36. F	48. J	60. H	72. H	84. G	

CHALLENGE ITEMS (p. 182)

1. D	9. B	17. C	25. C	33. D	41. B	49. A	57. D
2. G	10. J	18. G	26. J	34. F	42. H	50. H	58. F
3. C	11. B	19. D	27. A	35. D	43. D	51. D	59. D
4. J	12. F	20. F	28. J	36. H	44. H	52. G	60. H
5. A	13. C	21. D	29. C	37. D	45. D	53. A	61. C
6. F	14. F	22. J	30. J	38. G	46. F	54. H	62. G
7. C	15. B	23. C	31. A	39. B	47. B	55. A	
8. J	16. F	24. G	32. J	40. F	48. G	56. F	

TIMED-PRACTICE QUIZZES (p. 199)

QUIZ I

1. A	3. A	5. A	7. D
2. H	4. G	6. H	8. J

QUIZ II

1. D	3. B	5. A	7. C
2. G	4. H	6. J	

QUIZ III

1. C	3. D	5. B	7. C
2. G	4. F	6. G	8. F

QUIZ IV

1. B	3. B	5. D	7. A	9. C
2. G	4. F	6. H	8. F	10. G

QUIZ V

1. B	3. D	5. D	7. D	9. C
2. J	4. F	6. H	8. H	10. G

QUIZ VI

1. D	3. D	5. D	7. A	9. B
2. J	4. H	6. H	8. G	10. G

SCIENCE ANSWER KEY

LESSON (p. 226)

1. B	10. H	19. C	28. J	37. A	46. H
2. F	11. A	20. H	29. B	38. G	47. B
3. C	12. H	21. A	30. G	39. D	48. H
4. G	13. D	22. J	31. B	40. G	49. D
5. C	14. F	23. D	32. F	41. B	50. G
6. H	15. D	24. G	33. D	42. H	51. C
7. D	16. F	25. A	34. J	43. C	52. F
8. H	17. B	26. H	35. C	44. J	53. D
9. C	18. H	27. A	36. J	45. A	54. F

CHALLENGE ITEMS (p. 244)

1. D	14. H	27. D	40. G	53. B	66. G
2. F	15. A	28. H	41. B	54. G	67. A
3. B	16. G	29. B	42. H	55. B	68. G
4. G	17. C	30. G	43. C	56. F	69. B
5. C	18. J	31. C	44. J	57. D	70. H
6. G	19. A	32. H	45. B	58. F	71. C
7. C	20. G	33. C	46. H	59. C	72. J
8. G	21. B	34. H	47. C	60. G	73. C
9. B	22. H	35. C	48. F	61. A	74. F
10. J	23. A	36. J	49. D	62. F	75. D
11. A	24. G	37. B	50. G	63. C	76. G
12. G	25. C	38. G	51. C	64. J	77. C
13. D	26. H	39. D	52. H	65. A	78. J

TIMED-PRACTICE QUIZZES (p. 264)

QUIZ I

1. D	3. D	5. C	7. B	9. A
2. J	4. H	6. J	8. H	10. G

QUIZ II

1. A	3. A	5. C	7. D	9. C
2. F	4. J	6. H	8. F	10. G

QUIZ III

1. C	3. C	5. A	7. A	9. B	11. C
2. G	4. H	6. F	8. H	10. G	

WRITING ANSWER KEY

LESSON (p. 288)

1. Sample Outline

    I. Introduction
        A. Thesis: Rural life offers the best quality of life.

    II. Urban life is stressful.
        A. "Street people" (who may need intervention)
        B. Traffic (delays during travel from one place to another)
        C. Lack of community

    III. In rural areas, each person can have more of an impact within the community.
        A. Shared problems and solutions within a small community lead to personal responsibility.
        B. Because the community is small, there is more chance of recognition.

    IV. Less demands on personal time
        A. Less commuting
        B. Less traffic
        C. Fewer lines

    V. Conclusion
        A. Restatement of Thesis: Rural life provides the best quality of life because it is less stressful; it provides a good sense of community; and it allows for better usage of time.

2. Sample Essays

Below Average Response

Residents of rural areas insist that their life is better. People living in urban city areas prefer the lively life that they lead. Each has a viewpoint, but I feel that the city life is much better. Urban areas have good streets and roads and many things to do.

A city is closer together than rural areas. Everything can be reached pretty quickly by car, bus, or even bicycle. The streets are maintained by the city in winter and summer. My Aunt in the mountains is snowed in each winter for days at a time. Sometimes traffic is a problem in urban areas, but that's the price you pay.

The urban areas have so many activities to do. Lots of movies, concerts, and sports events are always going on. Because the urban areas have more people and money, more famous artists visit and perform there.

Some really important things in cities include good hospitals and healthcare. With lots of people there is a need for specialist doctors and great hospitals, even for children. I feel that I can find people in the city that share my interests whatever I decide on.

In conclusion, urban areas are the best places to live. Americans, and people around the world are moving from rural areas more each day to get to the excitement and opportunity of urban areas.

Above Average Response

The question of the quality of the rural life versus the life of a city dweller is an interesting one that faces each adult making a decision about their life activities. Plainly, United States citizens "voted with their feet" and have flocked to the cities in the 20th century. But recently there has been some movement back to rural areas and the "simple life" that they represent. I feel that a more rural area offers the best quality of life in the beginning of the 21st century. This opinion is based on the issues of emotional health, community involvement and opportunity, and best usage of my time.

Life in urban areas can be very stressful and difficult. Noise and traffic go on 24 hours a day. "Street people" who may need intervention may be outside your door in a downtown area. Traffic may make your voyage to work or entertainment difficult and lengthy. In rural areas the noise level is lessened, the roads less crowded, and more humane contact is likely.

In a more rural area, each person can have more of an impact within the community. The problems and challenges may be shared community wide and not just in your own neighborhood as in a large city. You can more easily be known and make a difference in a rural area. A contrary view contends that newcomers are sometimes not part of the "community family" in a small town. Gaining acceptance can be harder than in cities used to an influx of new people.

A rural area places less demands on my personal time: less traffic, less commuting, and fewer lines of people waiting to get services. I could get home faster from work and pursue my own interests.

In conclusion, I prefer rural areas. Keeping in communication and accessing healthcare used to be a problem there. But the Internet and satellite dishes helped alleviate the first concern. Regional health centers and rapid transportation have helped make "big city" healthcare available to rural areas.

TIMED-PRACTICE QUIZZES (p. 291)

QUIZ I

Below Average Response

The study hall time I have each day is very important to me. Some schools have cut it out to add another subject to school. We only have so much time in the evening, and without study hall, students might never get their homework done. Study hall really helps students who need to work harder and students with part-time jobs, lots of chores, or athletics.

Students that have to put in a lot of extra work in subjects, really welcome study hall. They may have a poor environment for class work at home. Sometime help is available in study hall for problem subjects. Study hall has reference books not always available in the home. If you have study hall, you at least don't get more homework at that time. Some students just rest in study hall, and don't work on school. That is their choice if they want to waste time.

If you have a part-time job you really need study hall to do at least some of your homework. This also applies to athletes. They have hours of practice each evening and may be too tired afterwards to study well. Study hall provides a good break in the hard day at school, and lets students keep up better in the classroom subjects.

Above Average Response

Study hall is beneficial to many students and should therefore not be eliminated from school. It provides the extra time needed to complete homework, review for a test, or even prepare ahead for future assignments. Since students are given the opportunity to take elective classes throughout the school day, study hall should be integrated into their schedule so that they may better manage their studies. Study hall especially helps students in the areas of time management, outside activities, and improved performance in subject areas.

Students under the strains of time management may require study hall to just keep up with their studies. Extracurricular activities, athletics, and after-school jobs can be very time-consuming and tend to distract students from their studies. In order to accommodate these activities, many students deprive themselves of sleep due to late hours of study at home. To a student who works after school to earn some extra spending money, or to help support his or her family, study hall may be the only chance to complete course work.

By allowing for some free time, study hall enables a student to broaden his or her skills and grow as a well-rounded person. Extracurricular activities and after-school jobs provide the necessary outlet for students to relax and socialize with their peers. Many students are even able to apply to their studies new skills learned in other environments.

Study hall is an elective that actually supports the required curriculum. Although many electives may be fun and interesting, students who take study hall can actually devote more time to math, science, and English. Study hall also provides a supportive educational environment that may not be available in every home due to the living arrangements.

In summary, study hall has many more benefits compared to those of having just another subject class. Students under oppressive time pressures can catch up with studies, expand their horizons with reading, and keep up in the face of outside activity demands with the help of study hall.

QUIZ II

Below Average Response

Its my opinion that high school graduates and young people leaving high school should not have to have universal compulsory service because it disrupts plans and interferes with freedoms. I'm not talking about the draft when there is a big war or something, because it is necessary. But having service when there isn't a war or anything is disruptive and inteferes with freedoms.

One of our basic rights is freedom. The government isn't supposed to tell us where or when we can go that we want. But universal compulsory service will tell everyone when they graduate or leave high school when and where they have to go for two years. That's not freedom.

Also, people graduate and leave high school with important plans. Some young people want to go on to college. Some young people are going to get jobs and make decent livings. Some young people will go in the military because that's what they plan to do. When the government tells people it can't do these things, they intefere with the important plans of people as individual persons.

During World War II there was a draft and everyone had to go in the military. But remember that the U.S. was facing terrible enemies, even though Germany and Japan are our allies now. To keep them from taking over the world and the U.S. we had to have a military. That is not now the case. The military is volunteering.

Universal compulsory service would interfere with plans and violate freedom. For these reasons, it should not be done.

Above Average Response

At first universal compulsory service might seem to be a good requirement because it is successful in other countries. But the real question for us is whether it would be a good idea here in America. I don't think so. America is unique in many very important ways. First, our way of life makes the idea of universal compulsory service unnecessary. Second, there are already many opportunities for volunteer work for those who want such an experience. Third, our fundamental notion of freedom means that service (such as the draft) can be required only in times of national emergency.

First, requiring universal compulsory service is not needed. When young people graduate or leave high school, they usually find jobs. Even those who go on to college will eventually get jobs when they graduate again. People that work, and that means young people too, pay taxes, and taxes are used to pay for government programs like roads, water and sewage, and aid to people in need. So, in a sense, everyone who is no longer in school and is working is already performing a compulsory service by paying taxes. There is no need to make those individuals do the actual work themselves.

Secondly, I believe that there's already a lot of opportunities for young people to volunteer for service. There is the Peace Corps for young people that might want to volunteer to help people in other countries. There is Habitat for Humanity for young people that like to work with their hands. There is the National Guard for young people who want military training. There is Big Brother/Sister for young people who want to work with children. Because there's already so many opportunities to volunteer for service, there's no need to make service compulsory. Anyone who wants the experience of service can already get it voluntarily.

Last, but certainly not least, America is built on freedom. Although this country is not perfect (slavery was an evil), most people believe that is wrong to force other people to do something they do not want to do. We do not tell people what Church to go to, when to get up or when to go to bed, and where they have to live and work, or who they should marry. The very notion of compulsory universal service is based on compulsion. And requiring people to do work they don't want to do contradicts our very notion of freedom.

There are some times when compulsory service is needed, as in time of war. And hopefully, during such times, young people will gladly serve their country. But drafting young people into the military should be the exception and not the rule. In fact, the whole purpose of having a military is to defend our basic freedoms. It seems upside-down to sacrifice those freedoms in order to protect them.

In conclusion, I am strongly opposed to compulsory universal service. We don't need it in the first place because we pay taxes. Other kinds of service are already available for those who want to serve. And, most important, compulsory service is contradictory with our notion of freedom.

QUIZ III

Below Average Response

I must agree with the teachers and administrators who say that honor code is a good idea. Honor code stands for honor and tells students what they are supposed to do. Students who know what they are supposed to do will behave different from students who don't know what they are supposed to do. If you don't know that there is cheating going on, then you can learn about them and report them.

Honor code can also make a regular school more like a military academy. When a regular school has the honor code, then it will have students that behave like military students. Everyone will trust everyone because they will know that no one is trying to get ahead with an unfair advantage such as cheating.

All students do not support the honor code. And I'm not just talking about the cheaters. Some students wont like the idea of having to report their friends who are cheating. That's tough. When someone is cheating, they are going against honor codes so they should be reported.

For the reasons that honor codes make schools more military and tell students not to cheat they would be a good idea. Thus, I am in favor of those teachers and administrators who like them.

Above Average Response

The idea of an honor code is not new. West Point (the Military Academy) is famous for its honor code. It requires cadets to refrain from cheating and says that they must tell their superiors when they know about any cheating. Would this model be a good idea for other schools? I doubt it. In the first place, the honor codes at military academies don't always work. Secondly, requiring students to "inform" on other students would break down the morale of the school. Lastly, even though an honor code might be appropriate in a military setting, it is not necessary in a regular school environment.

First, even though the leaders of military academies might think that an honor code is a good idea, the codes don't always work as they are supposed to work. Over the years, there have been scandals at the military academies. Sometimes these involve cheating, but sometimes they involve other kinds of unacceptable behavior such as sexual harassment. (Although sexual harassment is not the same thing as cheating, the idea of a "code" could apply here too.) These scandals don't occur all the time, but one thing is clear. When they do, they often involve many students. An entire class of math students might get caught cheating on the final exam. In other words, a lot of people are cheating. And with so many students cheating, a lot more must have known it and not said anything. That means that even in military schools honor codes don't work perfectly.

In the second place, an honor code would require students to "tell" on their classmates, and no one likes a tattletell. A student who "informs" will be ostrichsized by his/her classmates, even those who aren't cheating. Sometimes it may not be possible to know for sure when someone is cheating. Maybe you suspect someone of cheating but don't have any real proof. For example, you think they copied a paper from the web, but you google it and can't find it. Should you go to a teacher or the principle? What if you're wrong? But if you don't, then you're violating the honor code. An honor code would create a lot of problems like these.

Finally, there is a big difference between military school and regular school. A military school is built on discipline because that's they way the military operates. They are training soldiers, or pilots, or officers. In *these jobs, people are expected to behave more honorably. In civilian life, people are not supposed to cheat, but they don't have to tell on other people who do. They have the option of just not being friends with them.*

It seems that sometimes when there is a problem a drastic solution is needed. So if there is cheating, we need an honor code. We already have rules against cheating. If we obey those rules, we don't have a problem. If some people violate those rules, then the authorities should enforce them. In this way, the existing rules can do everything that we need to do.

Answers and Explanations:

Practice Test Reinforcement

PRACTICE TEST I ANSWER KEY

TEST 1: ENGLISH (p. 328)

ANSWER KEY DIRECTIONS: For the *correct* answer, check the corresponding unshaded box. Then, total the number of checkmarks for each of the content areas, and add these totals in order to determine the raw score for that test.

ENGLISH TEST—ANSWER KEY

UM RH		UM RH		UM RH		UM RH		UM RH
1. B	16. H	31. B	46. F	61. C
2. J	17. D	32. H	47. D	62. H
3. D	18. G	33. A	48. G	63. D
4. G	19. A	34. J	49. C	64. G
5. A	20. F	35. A	50. F	65. D
6. H	21. D	36. F	51. B	66. F
7. A	22. H	37. B	52. F	67. A
8. G	23. A	38. H	53. B	68. F
9. A	24. G	39. B	54. J	69. C
10. G	25. C	40. H	55. D	70. J
11. C	26. J	41. D	56. G	71. A
12. J	27. D	42. H	57. D	72. G
13. B	28. G	43. A	58. H	73. B
14. H	29. C	44. F	59. A	74. J
15. A	30. G	45. C	60. J	75. B

Usage and Mechanics (UM): _____ /44   Rhetorical Skills (RH): _____ /31   Raw Score (UM + RH): _____ /75

TEST 2: MATHEMATICS (p. 340)

MATHEMATICS TEST—ANSWER KEY

#	Ans		#	Ans		#	Ans		#	Ans
1.	A		16.	H		31.	C		46.	K
2.	K		17.	B		32.	H		47.	A
3.	C		18.	K		33.	A		48.	F
4.	K		19.	A		34.	K		49.	C
5.	E		20.	H		35.	D		50.	K
6.	H		21.	D		36.	H		51.	C
7.	D		22.	G		37.	C		52.	J
8.	H		23.	C		38.	G		53.	A
9.	D		24.	F		39.	C		54.	F
10.	G		25.	E		40.	G		55.	D
11.	B		26.	G		41.	D		56.	H
12.	H		27.	C		42.	H		57.	B
13.	C		28.	J		43.	A		58.	K
14.	G		29.	E		44.	G		59.	A
15.	D		30.	H		45.	B		60.	J

Each answer is classified by column: EA, AG, GT.

Pre-Algebra/Elementary Algebra (EA): _____ /30

Int. Algebra/Coordinate Geometry (AG): _____ /13

Plane Geometry/Trigonometry (GT): _____ /17

Raw Score (EA + AG + GT): _____ /60

TEST 3: READING (p. 358)

READING TEST—ANSWER KEY

	SS	AL
1. B		■
2. F		■
3. D		■
4. J		■
5. C		■
6. F		■
7. C		■
8. H		■
9. C		■
10. G		■
11. A	■	
12. J	■	
13. B	■	
14. H	■	
15. A	■	

	SS	AL
16. H	■	
17. C	■	
18. J	■	
19. A	■	
20. H	■	
21. B		■
22. H		■
23. A		■
24. J		■
25. C		■
26. F		■
27. A		■
28. G		■
29. B		■
30. H		■

	SS	AL
31. C	■	
32. J	■	
33. B	■	
34. J	■	
35. A	■	
36. G	■	
37. A	■	
38. F	■	
39. B	■	
40. F	■	

Social Studies/Sciences (SS): _____ /20

Arts/Literature (AL): _____ /20

Raw Score (SS + AL): _____ /40

TEST 4: SCIENCE (p. 368)

SCIENCE TEST—ANSWER KEY

	B	C	P	ES
1. A				
2. F				
3. B				
4. H				
5. C				
6. J				
7. B				
8. H				
9. D				
10. F				
11. C				
12. H				
13. D				
14. G				
15. C				

	B	C	P	ES
16. J				
17. B				
18. J				
19. D				
20. F				
21. C				
22. F				
23. B				
24. J				
25. C				
26. F				
27. D				

	B	C	P	ES
28. G				
29. C				
30. G				
31. D				
32. F				
33. A				
34. H				
35. B				
36. J				
37. C				
38. G				
39. D				
40. F				

Biology (B): _____ /17

Chemistry (C): _____ /12

Physics (P): _____ /6

Earth/Space Sciences (ES): _____ / 5

Raw Score (B + C + P + ES): _____ /40

PRACTICE TEST II ANSWER KEY

TEST 1: ENGLISH (p. 384)

ANSWER KEY DIRECTIONS: For the *correct* answer, check the corresponding unshaded box. Then, total the number of checkmarks for each of the content areas, and add these totals in order to determine the raw score for that test.

ENGLISH TEST—ANSWER KEY

	UM RH		UM RH		UM RH		UM RH		UM RH
1. B		16. F		31. B		46. J		61. A	
2. G		17. A		32. J		47. D		62. J	
3. D		18. H		33. B		48. G		63. B	
4. F		19. D		34. J		49. B		64. J	
5. B		20. F		35. D		50. H		65. A	
6. F		21. A		36. J		51. A		66. G	
7. A		22. F		37. D		52. H		67. B	
8. F		23. A		38. H		53. D		68. F	
9. D		24. F		39. A		54. F		69. A	
10. F		25. D		40. H		55. A		70. F	
11. D		26. J		41. B		56. F		71. B	
12. J		27. C		42. G		57. B		72. F	
13. B		28. H		43. A		58. J		73. B	
14. J		29. D		44. H		59. A		74. J	
15. D		30. J		45. D		60. F		75. B	

Usage and Mechanics (UM): _____ /45   Rhetorical Skills (RH): _____ /30   Raw Score (UM + RH): _____ /75

TEST 2: MATHEMATICS (p. 398)

MATHEMATICS TEST—ANSWER KEY

#	Ans	EA	AG	GT
1.	B			
2.	K			
3.	C			
4.	K			
5.	A			
6.	F			
7.	C			
8.	G			
9.	C			
10.	F			
11.	E			
12.	K			
13.	A			
14.	G			
15.	C			
16.	K			
17.	C			
18.	G			
19.	B			
20.	J			
21.	A			
22.	K			
23.	D			
24.	J			
25.	D			
26.	G			
27.	B			
28.	G			
29.	D			
30.	F			
31.	C			
32.	G			
33.	C			
34.	H			
35.	C			
36.	H			
37.	E			
38.	K			
39.	C			
40.	J			
41.	D			
42.	K			
43.	B			
44.	G			
45.	C			
46.	H			
47.	A			
48.	H			
49.	C			
50.	J			
51.	A			
52.	H			
53.	E			
54.	K			
55.	B			
56.	G			
57.	D			
58.	J			
59.	C			
60.	H			

Pre-Algebra/Elementary Algebra (EA): _____ /27   Plane Geometry/Trigonometry (GT): _____ /17

Int. Algebra/Coordinate Geometry (AG): _____ /16   Raw Score (EA + AG + GT): _____ /60

TEST 3: READING (p. 414)

READING TEST—ANSWER KEY

	SS	AL
1. C	▓	
2. F	▓	
3. C	▓	
4. G	▓	
5. D	▓	
6. G	▓	
7. A	▓	
8. G	▓	
9. A	▓	
10. H	▓	
11. B	▓	
12. J	▓	
13. C	▓	
14. J	▓	
15. C	▓	

	SS	AL
16. J	▓	
17. B	▓	
18. F	▓	
19. C	▓	
20. J	▓	
21. A		▓
22. F		▓
23. C		▓
24. F		▓
25. B		▓
26. J		▓
27. B		▓
28. H		▓
29. B		▓
30. H		▓

	SS	AL
31. D		▓
32. H		▓
33. B		▓
34. H		▓
35. B		▓
36. H		▓
37. D		▓
38. G		▓
39. C		▓
40. H		▓

Social Studies/Sciences (SS): _____ /20

Arts/Literature (AL): _____ /20

Raw Score (SS + AL): _____ /40

TEST 4: SCIENCE (p. 422)

SCIENCE TEST—ANSWER KEY

	B	C	P	ES
1. D				
2. F				
3. C				
4. J				
5. D				
6. H				

	B	C	P	ES
7. A				
8. G				
9. D				
10. F				
11. B				
12. H				

	B	C	P	ES
13. B				
14. J				
15. A				
16. G				
17. C				
18. J				

	B	C	P	ES
19. C				
20. F				
21. D				
22. H				
23. A				

	B	C	P	ES
24. G				
25. C				
26. H				
27. B				
28. G				
29. B				

	B	C	P	ES
30. H				
31. D				
32. G				
33. C				
34. G				

	B	C	P	ES
35. D				
36. J				
37. B				
38. F				
39. B				
40. H				

Biology (B): _____ /11

Chemistry (C): _____ /12

Physics (P): _____ /11

Earth/Space Sciences (ES): _____ / 6

Raw Score (B + C + P + ES): _____ /40

PRACTICE TEST III ANSWER KEYS

TEST 1: ENGLISH (p. 440)

ANSWER KEY DIRECTIONS: For the *correct* answer, check the corresponding unshaded box. Then, total the number of checkmarks for each of the content areas, and add these totals in order to determine the raw score for that test.

ENGLISH TEST—ANSWER KEY

	UM RH			UM RH			UM RH			UM RH			UM RH
1. C			16. J			31. B			46. H			61. D	
2. F			17. A			32. G			47. D			62. F	
3. C			18. H			33. A			48. G			63. B	
4. G			19. D			34. J			49. B			64. J	
5. B			20. G			35. B			50. F			65. C	
6. F			21. A			36. J			51. A			66. H	
7. B			22. G			37. D			52. G			67. A	
8. F			23. D			38. F			53. D			68. G	
9. B			24. H			39. A			54. G			69. D	
10. H			25. D			40. J			55. B			70. H	
11. A			26. F			41. B			56. H			71. C	
12. F			27. B			42. F			57. A			72. G	
13. D			28. F			43. A			58. H			73. D	
14. H			29. D			44. G			59. A			74. H	
15. B			30. J			45. A			60. J			75. D	

Usage and Mechanics (UM): _____ /46   Rhetorical Skills (RH): _____ /29   Raw Score (UM + RH): _____ /75

TEST 2: MATHEMATICS (p. 454)

MATHEMATICS TEST—ANSWER KEY

	EA	AG	GT
1. B			
2. F			
3. C			
4. J			
5. E			

	EA	AG	GT
6. K			
7. D			
8. J			
9. D			
10. G			

	EA	AG	GT
11. B			
12. G			
13. E			
14. H			
15. C			

	EA	AG	GT
16. G			
17. D			
18. F			
19. B			
20. K			

	EA	AG	GT
21. E			
22. F			
23. C			
24. G			
25. A			

	EA	AG	GT
26. H			
27. A			
28. G			
29. C			
30. K			

	EA	AG	GT
31. A			
32. J			
33. D			
34. K			
35. E			

	EA	AG	GT
36. F			
37. B			
38. K			
39. B			
40. K			

	EA	AG	GT
41. E			
42. J			
43. D			
44. J			
45. C			

	EA	AG	GT
46. K			
47. D			
48. H			
49. D			
50. G			

	EA	AG	GT
51. C			
52. G			
53. D			
54. K			
55. D			

	EA	AG	GT
56. G			
57. A			
58. F			
59. D			
60. G			

Pre-Algebra/Elementary Algebra (EA): _____ /26
Int. Algebra/Coordinate Geometry (AG): _____ /16
Plane Geometry/Trigonometry (GT): _____ /18
Raw Score (EA + AG + GT): _____ /60

TEST 3: READING (p. 474)

READING TEST—ANSWER KEY

		SS	AL
1.	A	▓	
2.	J	▓	
3.	D	▓	
4.	G	▓	
5.	D	▓	
6.	G	▓	
7.	A	▓	
8.	H	▓	
9.	A	▓	
10.	H	▓	
11.	C	▓	
12.	H	▓	
13.	A	▓	
14.	H	▓	
15.	B	▓	

		SS	AL
16.	G	▓	
17.	B	▓	
18.	J	▓	
19.	A	▓	
20.	F	▓	
21.	B		▓
22.	G		▓
23.	C		▓
24.	F		▓
25.	D		▓
26.	G		▓
27.	D		▓
28.	H		▓
29.	B		▓
30.	H		▓

		SS	AL
31.	C		▓
32.	J		▓
33.	A		▓
34.	H		▓
35.	A		▓
36.	J		▓
37.	B		▓
38.	J		▓
39.	D		▓
40.	H		▓

Social Studies/Sciences (SS): _____ /20

Arts/Literature (AL): _____ /20

Raw Score (SS + AL): _____ /40

TEST 4: SCIENCE (p. 484)

SCIENCE TEST—ANSWER KEY

	B	C	P	ES
1. C				
2. H				
3. A				
4. H				
5. C				

	B	C	P	ES
6. J				
7. A				
8. H				
9. C				
10. G				
11. A				

	B	C	P	ES
12. G				
13. D				
14. H				
15. A				
16. F				
17. C				
18. G				

	B	C	P	ES
19. D				
20. G				
21. C				
22. J				
23. A				
24. F				

	B	C	P	ES
25. A				
26. J				
27. D				
28. J				
29. C				
30. J				

	B	C	P	ES
31. C				
32. J				
33. A				
34. H				
35. C				

	B	C	P	ES
36. H				
37. D				
38. G				
39. B				
40. G				

Biology (B):	/17	Earth/Space Sciences (ES):	/ 7
Chemistry (C):	/ 6	Raw Score (B + C + P + ES):	/40
Physics (P):	/10		

PRACTICE TEST III EXPLANATIONS

TEST 1: ENGLISH (p. 440)

1. **(C)** *English/Usage and Mechanics/Grammar and Usage/Diction.* The original sentence is not idiomatic. "On account of" should not be used as a substitute for "because of." (C) makes the needed correction. (B) is wrong because "since" is a conjunction that introduces a dependent clause, but the material that follows is not a clause—it contains no verb. As for (D), although "for" can be a preposition, its meaning is not appropriate in this context.

2. **(F)** *English/Rhetorical Skills/No Change.* The original sentence is correct. "Nonetheless" means "in spite of this." (G) and (H) are wrong because the author means to say that smuggling grew in spite of government efforts, not because of government efforts. As for (J), although "on the contrary" does signal an opposition, it does not have the "in spite of" meaning needed here.

3. **(C)** *English/Usage and Mechanics/Grammar and Usage/Adjectives versus Adverbs* and *Punctuation/Commas.* The original sentence contains two errors. First, an adverb is needed to modify the adjective "timbered"—"heavy" should be "heavily." Second, since "countless" is intended to modify "islands" and not "heavily timbered," a comma must be placed after "countless." (C) makes both of these corrections.

4. **(G)** *English/Usage and Mechanics/Grammar and Usage/Diction.* The original sentence and (H) and (J) are not idiomatic. The correct idiom is "well founded."

5. **(B)** *English/Usage and Mechanics/Grammar and Usage/Sequence and Verb Tense.* The tense of the verb in the original sentence is not consistent with the other verbs in the paragraph. The author is describing past events, so the past tense "seized" should be used. Although (C) and (D) can be used to refer to past actions, they have meanings that are inappropriate in this context. First, "were seizing" (the progressive form of the past tense) implies an action that continued for some time in the past (e.g., during this period, customs officials were seizing tons of wool each month). Second, "have seized" (the present perfect) implies an action that began in the past but continues into the present (e.g., the British have repeatedly seized our ships).

6. **(F)** *English/Rhetorical Skills/No Change.* The original sentence is correct. By comparison, (G) and (J) are awkward and needlessly wordy. In (H), "technically" modifies "being," whereas "technical" modifies "violation."

7. **(B)** *English/Usage and Mechanics/Grammar and Usage/Diction.* The original sentence contains an error of diction. "Principle" means "rule"; "principal" means "main or important." (C) fails to correct this problem. (D) makes the needed correction, but the verb "was" does not agree with the subject of the sentence. The subject of the sentence is a compound subject—a series of elements joined by "and"—and requires the use of a plural verb.

8. **(F)** *English/Rhetorical Skills/No Change.* "In fact" signals an idea that will provide an illustration of or give special emphasis to a point that came just before. This is exactly what the author does. As for (G) and (H), these words are used to alert the reader that what follows is a continuation of an idea and that the following idea has the same status as the first idea. Thus, (G) and (H) are not suited to this sentence. Finally, as for (J), "on the contrary" signals a contrast of ideas, but the author does not intend to present contrasting ideas.

9. **(B)** *English/Usage and Mechanics/Grammar and Usage/Verb Tense.* The only role for "selling" in the original sentence would be that of an adjective, but there is nothing for "selling" to modify. (B) corrects this problem by converting "selling" to a conjugated form. The sentence reads: "was smuggled… and sold." (C) is wrong because "would be sold" is not parallel to "smuggled." (D) is wrong for the same reason. There is no logical role for the infinitive "to sell."

10. **(H)** *English/Usage and Mechanics/Grammar and Usage/Diction.* The idiom "so much…that" is not completed in the original sentence. (H) completes the idiom: "so much was smuggled and sold… that one…." (G) and (J) fail to complete the expression.

11. **(A)** *English/Rhetorical Skills/No Change.* The original sentence is correct. "Although" sets up the contrast between the ideas of the settlers welcoming national control and their not liking the restrictions.

12. **(F)** *English/Usage and Mechanics/No Change.* The original sentence is correct. The simple past tense is consistent with the other verbs in the passage. (G) is wrong because it eliminates the only conjugated verb in the clause introduced by "although." (H) is wrong because the tense is inconsistent with the other tenses in the paragraph. (J) destroys the logic of the sentence.

13. **(D)** *English/Usage and Mechanics/Grammar and Usage/Diction.* The original sentence is not idiomatic—the correct idiom is "were fearful," not "were fearing." (D) avoids the problem by using "feared," and the past tense is parallel to the other verb in the sentence, "wanted." (B) fails to correct the problem of the original sentence. (C) uses the correct idiom, but the verb "was" does not agree with the subject of the sentence, "they."

14. **(H)** *English/Usage and Mechanics/Grammar and Usage/Sequence and Verb Tense* and *Diction.* The original sentence contains two errors. First, the underlined verb is in the present tense and is therefore inconsistent with the use of the past tense in the rest of the paragraph. Second, "in the losing of" is not idiomatic; the phrase "in the loss of" is better used. (H) makes both the needed corrections. (G) makes one correction but not the other. (J) uses the indicative "results," but it lacks the element of contingency: "they feared that this results." A verb is needed that suggests something might or might not occur: "they feared that this would result or might result."

15. **(B)** *English/Rhetorical Skills/Organization/Passage-Level Structure.* The passage should be arranged in chronological order. [1] should come first because it describes the first event (the opening of the customs office). [3] should be second because it describes the events that come next in time (Americans were leery of the new office). [2] should be last because it is the final development (the fears turned out to be true).

16. **(J)** *English/Rhetorical Skills/Organization/Passage-Level Structure.* The author describes events, so "narrative" is a part of the passage. The author also gives a specific example of a ship—the *Beaver*—that was seized. The author gives statistics about wool. However, the author does not quote from another source.

17. **(A)** *English/Rhetorical Skills/No Change.* The original sentence is the best choice. The other choices are awkward and needlessly wordy.

18. **(H)** *English/Usage and Mechanics/Sentence Structure/Faulty Parallelism.* The original sentence suffers from a lack of parallelism. All three verbs ("step," "gaze," and "become") are governed by the first instance of "can," so the additional "can" in the original sentence creates a series in which the elements do not have the same form. (H) brings the third verb into line with the other two. (G) fails to provide the needed parallelism, and (J) is wrong because "becomes" does not agree in number with the subject, "anyone."

19. **(D)** *English/Usage and Mechanics/Sentence Structure/Comma Splices.* The original sentence is incorrectly punctuated. The comma creates a run-on sentence. (D) solves this problem by starting a new sentence, while (B) and (C) do not.

20. **(G)** *English/Usage and Mechanics/Sentence Structure/Misplaced Modifiers.* The original sentence is ambiguous. "Ending" seems to be an adjective modifying "suns," but the author intends for "ending" to modify "island universe." (G) corrects this problem by creating a relative clause that modifies "island universe." (H) also creates a new clause, but "ends" does not agree with the antecedent of "that," which is "universe." Finally, (J) suffers from the same defect as the original because "ended" seems to modify "suns."

21. **(A)** *English/Usage and Mechanics/No Change.* The original sentence is correct as written. (B) is not idiomatic. Correct English requires the use of the infinitive "to chart" in this situation, not the gerund "charting." (C) is wrong because there is nothing for a participle like "having charted" to modify. (D) destroys the logic of the sentence.

22. **(G)** *English/Usage and Mechanics/Grammar and Usage/Verb Tense.* The verb tense of the original sentence is wrong. The past perfect "had been made" implies that the progress was made at a time in the past, *before* the twentieth century. However, since the author intends to say that the progress was made "in the twentieth century," the simple past "was made" is required. So, (G) is the correct answer choice. (H) is wrong because the present tense "is made" lacks the implication of a past action. (J), which uses the future tense, indicates that the progress has not yet been made.

23. **(D)** *English/Rhetorical Skills/Strategy/Effective Transitional Sentence.* In the original sentence, "as such" signals that the second idea is what it is by virtue of the first idea. However, the Milky Way is not called the Milky Way because our solar system is a part of it. (B) and (C) also disrupt the logical connection between the two ideas.

24. **(H)** *English/Rhetorical Skills/Organization/Paragraph-Level Structure.* The material in this sentence belongs with that of the next paragraph. Thus, a new paragraph should be started here, and no new paragraph should be started at the end of the sentence. (H) and (J) make the required change. However, (J) is wrong because "as" is used to introduce a dependent clause, resulting in a dependent clause with no supporting independent clause.

25. **(D)** *English/Usage and Mechanics/Punctuation/Commas.* The original sentence is incorrect because a comma and not a semicolon must be used to separate an appositive phrase from the main part of the sentence. The semicolon is too powerful and makes a fragment out of everything that follows it. (B) is wrong because it is necessary to place the phrase "crown jewels" in quotation marks. (C) is wrong because the verb "is" does not agree with "Magellanic Clouds."

26. **(F)** *English/Usage and Mechanics/No Change.* The original sentence is correct as written. The other choices simply are not idiomatic.

27. **(B)** *English/Rhetorical Skills/Style/Conciseness.* "To" is superfluous and makes the phrasing stilted. Eliminate it. (B) and (C) both make the needed correction, but (C) is wrong because "provide" does not agree with the subject of the sentence, "galaxy."

28. **(F)** *English/Rhetorical Skills/No Change.* The original sentence is the best rendering. Study the other choices—they are all stilted or needlessly wordy.

29. **(D)** *English/Rhetorical Skills/Organization/Paragraph-Level Structure.* The author poses the questions because they are questions about the stars that are still unanswered. He will not provide answers.

30. **(J)** *English/Usage and Mechanics/Grammar and Usage/Diction.* At first, it appears that "graduated" is intended to be a verb in a phrase such as "graduated from test pilot schools." Unfortunately, the structure of the sentence does not permit that reading. (J) clarifies the issue by making "graduated" a noun, and "graduates" can function as an appositive for "pilots." (G) and (H) are wrong because the appositive must be set off by a comma and nothing else.

31. **(B)** *English/Usage and Mechanics/Grammar and Usage/Subject-Verb Agreement* and *Diction.* The original sentence has two errors. First, "were" fails to agree in number with its subject, "each." Second, the use of the gerund "having" is not idiomatic. (B) corrects both errors. (C) fails to correct the second error. (D) corrects both errors, but the past perfect "had been required" is inconsistent with the other verbs in the paragraph.

32. **(G)** *English/Rhetorical Skills/Style/Idiomatic Expression.* The original sentence contains low-level usage. Do not use "got" to suggest the passive voice. Use some form of the verb "to be." (G) makes the needed correction. (H) is a form of the passive voice, but the use of the past perfect is not consistent with the other verbs in the paragraph. (J) is wrong for two reasons. First, the present perfect "has been" is not consistent with the other verbs in the paragraph. Second, "has" is a singular verb, but the subject "seven" is plural.

33. **(A)** *English/Rhetorical Skills/Strategy/Appropriate Supporting Material.* The information contained in the parentheses explains why only seven astronauts were chosen. However, it is not vital to the development of the passage. By placing the remark in parentheses, the author signals to the reader that the information is not vital.

34. **(J)** *English/Usage and Mechanics/Sentence Structure/Comma Splices.* The original sentence contains a comma splice. (J) corrects the problem of the run-on sentence by starting a new sentence. Neither (G) nor (H) addresses the problem.

35. **(B)** *English/Rhetorical Skills/Strategy/Effective Transitional Sentence.* The second paragraph introduces the topic of failures. (B) provides a good transition by signaling to the reader that this will be the topic of the paragraph.

36. **(J)** *English/Usage and Mechanics/Grammar and Usage/Pronoun Usage.* The original sentence uses the ubiquitous "they." "They" has no referent. (H) and (J) correct the error; however, the usage of "fortunately" is not correct in (H).

37. **(D)** *English/Rhetorical Skills/Style/Conciseness.* The original sentence is needlessly wordy as indicated by comparison with (D).

38. **(F)** *English/Rhetorical Skills/Strategy/Appropriate Supporting Material.* By using the word "spectacular," the author is suggesting that the incident was sensational, but it did not actually have particularly significant consequences. The irony is intended due to the incongruity between the anticipated and actual results of the incident.

39. **(A)** *English/Usage and Mechanics/No Change.* The original sentence is correct. An adverb, such as "relatively," is needed to modify an adjective, such as "simple."

40. **(J)** *English/Usage and Mechanics/Sentence Structure/Faulty Parallelism.* The underlined verb is not parallel to the other verb: "to ignite" and "shutting down." (J) corrects the problem: "to ignite and then to shut down." Neither (G) nor (H) solves the problem. (H) suffers from the further defect that "they" does not have a referent.

41. **(B)** *English/Usage and Mechanics/Punctuation/Quotation Marks.* This is another example of irony. The rocket was never really launched. The quotation marks signal that the author is using the word "flight" in a non-standard way.

42. **(F)** *English/Rhetorical Skills/No Change.* The original sentence is correct as written. A new paragraph should be started here because the author is taking up a new topic, switching from a discussion of failures in the problem to a discussion of animals in flight. Therefore, (G), (H), and (J) are wrong.

43. **(A)** *English/Rhetorical Skills/No Change.* The original sentence is the most concise. The other choices are stilted and wordy.

44. **(G)** *English/Usage and Mechanics/Grammar and Usage/Sequence and Verb Tense.* The verb tense of the original sentence is wrong. "Delay" and "leak" belong to the same time frame, so both should be in the same tense.

45. **(A)** *English/Usage and Mechanics/No Change.* The original sentence is correct. None of the other suggested positions for "unharmed" are idiomatic.

46. **(H)** *English/Usage and Mechanics/Sentence Structure/Fragments.* "Returning" is not a conjugated verb and thus it cannot be the main verb. All three choices supply conjugated verbs, but (H) is the only tense that is consistent with the other verbs in the paragraph.

47. **(D)** *English/Usage and Mechanics/Grammar and Usage/Sequence and Verb Tense.* The question mentioned was, at the time, still unanswered. Thus, the choice of verb should reflect that: "could tolerate."

48. **(G)** *English/Usage and Mechanics/Grammar and Usage/Diction.* "Like" in the original sentence is both superfluous and not idiomatic. (G) corrects the error by eliminating the extra word. (H) and (J) are not idiomatic.

49. **(B)** *English/Usage and Mechanics/Grammar and Usage/Verb Tense.* The original sentence contains an error of grammar: "longer flights would require that astronauts to have." The infinitive cannot be the verb for the subject "astronauts." Instead, a conjugated verb is needed. Each of the alternatives supplies a conjugated verb form, but only (B) is consistent with the rest of the sentence. (C) is wrong because the past perfect "had had" suggests a sequence of events that is not supported by the meaning of the sentence. (D) is wrong because the sentence now reads: "would require that the astronauts are sure to have."

50. **(F)** *English/Rhetorical Skills/Strategy/Effective Concluding Sentence.* The author emphasizes the successes of the program and downplays its failures. (F) best summarizes this development.

51. **(A)** *English/Usage and Mechanics/No Change.* The original sentence is correct. (B) makes two mistakes. First, it leaves out an essential comma. The end of the aside beginning with "in" must be marked. Second, "of" introduces a prepositional phrase that has nothing to modify. (C) is wrong because it fails to mark the close of the aside. (D) is wrong because "of helping" is not idiomatic.

52. **(G)** *English/Rhetorical Skills/Style/Conciseness.* The original sentence is needlessly wordy. "And" and "also" mean the same thing, so they should not both be used. (G) solves this problem by substituting "as well as," a phrase which also means "and." (H) is wrong because "with" does not have an appropriate meaning in this context. (J) is wrong because "as opposed to" signals a contrast between two ideas that is not suggested by the content of the sentence.

53. **(D)** *English/Usage and Mechanics/Grammar and Usage/Sequence and Verb Tense.* The verb tense of the original sentence is inconsistent with that of the other verb in the sentence: "aided" and "had been emerging." The simple past verb form should be used: "aided" and "emerged." Only (D) makes the needed correction.

54. **(G)** *English/Usage and Mechanics/Grammar and Usage/Subject-Verb Agreement.* The original sentence is incorrect because "was enjoying" does not agree with the subject of the sentence, "aspects." (G) makes the needed correction. (H) and (J) are wrong because they are singular.

55. **(B)** *English/Usage and Mechanics/Grammar and Usage/Diction.* The original sentence is not idiomatic. The correct idiom is "not only this but that." (B) supplies the correct idiom. (C) is wrong because "not only this consequently that" is not idiomatic. As for (D), although it supplies the correct idiom, it also contains two errors. First, the comma following "but" illogically disrupts the idiom. Second, the verb "would have" is inconsistent with the other verb in the sentence.

56. **(H)** *English/Usage and Mechanics/Sentence Structure/Run-On Sentences.* The original sentence is a run-on sentence since the clause that follows "treatment" is an independent clause. Because separating the clauses with a comma is not provided as an option, the underlined part should be rewritten to share the subject that is presented earlier in the sentence. (H) makes this change, eliminating the run-on sentence and expressing the thought more concisely. (G) is wrong because "but" illogically signals a contrast where none is intended. (J) destroys the parallelism of the sentence: "…the doctor could select…and can mitigate…."

57. **(A)** *English/Usage and Mechanics/No Change.* The original sentence is correct. (B) and (C) use inappropriate verb forms: "require that something was available" and "require that something is available." The technical explanation for this is that it is one of the last vestiges in English of the subjunctive. (D) is wrong because "as" does not have the same meaning as "to."

58. **(H)** *English/Usage and Mechanics/Grammar and Usage/Sequence and Verb Tense.* In the original sentence, the present tense "presupposes" conflicts with the other past tense verbs in the paragraph. Although (G) also makes the correction, the passive voice is needlessly indirect. (H) makes the needed correction and is more concise.

59. **(A)** *English/Rhetorical Skills/No Change.* The original sentence is correct. A new paragraph is required here because the author is taking up a new topic (a discussion of a particular doctor). Therefore, (B) and (D) are wrong. As for (C), "since" is a subordinate conjunction and is used to introduce a dependent clause. The resulting construction would be a dependent clause with no supporting independent clause.

60. **(J)** *English/Rhetorical Skills/Organization/Sentence-Level Structure.* The first three paragraphs are a general discussion of medical advances in the nineteenth century. The last two paragraphs are a discussion of a particular advance. The first sentence of the fourth paragraph sets the stage for this transition.

61. **(D)** *English/Rhetorical Skills/Style/Conciseness.* The original sentence, (B), and (C) are all needlessly wordy. (D) clearly conveys the idea.

62. **(F)** *English/Rhetorical Skills/No Change.* The original sentence is correct. A new paragraph should not be started here because the following material continues the discussion about Dr. Beaumont. Thus, (G) and (J) are wrong. (H) is awkward. Compare the wording of (H) with the more direct wording of the original sentence.

63. **(B)** *English/Usage and Mechanics/Sentence Structure/Problems of Coordination and Subordination.* The original sentence is grammatically correct; however, "but" signals an inappropriate contrast. The second clause explains the outcome of the first clause. (B) solves this problem. (C) is wrong because the resulting construction would be a comma splice. (D) is grammatically correct; however, "but" is out of place.

64. **(J)** *English/Usage and Mechanics/Sentence Structure/Faulty Parallelism.* The original sentence suffers from faulty parallelism. The verb "describe" has the same function in the sentence as the verb "demonstrate," so they

—621—

need parallel forms. Only (J) makes the needed correction. The verb forms of (G) and (H) do not create the needed parallelism.

65. **(C)** *English/Usage and Mechanics/Grammar and Usage/Pronoun Usage.* The original sentence contains an error of pronoun usage. "Him" refers to "babies." (C) makes the needed correction by using the plural "them." (B) and (D) are wrong because, among other things, they use singular pronouns.

66. **(H)** *English/Usage and Mechanics/Grammar and Usage/Diction.* The original sentence is not idiomatic. The correct idiom is "endowed with." As for (J), although "endowed by" is idiomatic, it is not appropriate here. It would be used in a different way: "…endowed by their Creator with certain inalienable rights."

67. **(A)** *English/Usage and Mechanics/No Change.* The original sentence is correct. The other choices, however, are not acceptable. (B) and (C) both create run-on sentences. (D) destroys the logical structure of the sentence. Two occurrences of "it" are required: one to be the object of "hears" and the other to function as the subject of the second clause.

68. **(G)** *English/Usage and Mechanics/Sentence Structure/Problems of Coordination and Subordination.* The sentence intends to state that an infant's cry causes two parallel reactions, one biological and the other emotional. As written, "including" illogically implies that an emotional reaction is a kind of biological reaction. Only a word like "and" will do the trick.

69. **(D)** *English/Rhetorical Skills/Strategy/Effective Transitional Sentence.* The word "unfortunately" has a meaning that is not appropriate here. The author intends the last sentence of the paragraph to be a conclusion that is proved by the remainder of the paragraph: the infant does this and that, so he is in possession of certain attributes. The use of "in fact" conveys this idea and adds a special emphasis.

70. **(H)** *English/Rhetorical Skills/Style/Conciseness.* The original sentence is needlessly indirect and wordy. (H) is more direct and concise. (G) also is concise, but it uses a verb tense that is inconsistent with the other verbs in the paragraph. (J) is too wordy. Furthermore, the verb "are" does not agree with the singular subject of the sentence.

71. **(C)** *English/Usage and Mechanics/Grammar and Usage/Verb Tense.* In English, sometimes the present progressive is used to give special emphasis to an idea: (e.g., But Mom, I am doing my homework!). But nothing suggests that the author would want special emphasis here. (C) corrects the problem by using the simple present tense, which is the same tense used for the other verbs. (B) is wrong because the past tense is out of place. (D) is wrong because the subject of "guarantee" is "that," which in turn refers to the singular "collection."

72. **(G)** *English/Usage and Mechanics/Grammar and Usage/Diction.* Although "whether or not" is a typical English idiom, its use here is not idiomatic. The first "whether" in the sentence has set up the comparison: "whether" this or "whether" that. (G) makes the needed correction. (H) and (J) are wrong because "whether if" is not idiomatic.

73. **(D)** *English/Usage and Mechanics/Sentence Structure/Fragments.* "Although" introduces a long and complex dependent clause that ends with the period. The original sentence is wrong because the dependent clause is not attached to an independent clause. (D) makes the needed correction.

74. **(H)** *English/Rhetorical Skills/Organization/Sentence-Level Structure.* The final sentence serves to summarize in an emphatic way the point the author has been laboring to prove: the newborn infant is not a passive creature.

75. **(D)** *English/Rhetorical Skills/Organization/Passage-Level Structure.* The passage is an argument. The author is trying to persuade the reader that the newborn infant is not a passive creature. The author uses examples of behavior to prove this point.

TEST 2: MATHEMATICS (p. 454)

1. **(B)** *Mathematics/Arithmetic/Simple Manipulations.* Perform the indicated operation: $5.75 - 4.5 = 1.25$.

2. **(F)** *Mathematics/Algebra/Manipulating Algebraic Expressions/Basic Algebraic Manipulations.* The product of 4 times x is written as $4x$. 3 less than that would be $4x - 3$.

3. **(C)** *Mathematics/Algebra/Manipulating Algebraic Expressions/Evaluating Expressions.* This question really just tests fractions. If $\frac{3}{4}$ of x equals 36, then: $\frac{3}{4}x = 36 \Rightarrow x = 36 \cdot \frac{4}{3} = 48$ and $\frac{1}{3}$ of 48 is 16.

4. **(J)** *Mathematics/Geometry/Lines and Angles.* The measure of the unlabeled angle in the top triangle is 90°. The angle vertically opposite it in the bottom triangle is also equal to 90°. Therefore: $x + y + 90° = 180°$ and $x + y = 90°$.

5. **(E)** *Mathematics/Arithmetic/Common Arithmetic Items/Properties of Numbers.* There are two ways to attack this question. One is to reason as follows:

   A. $2 + n$ cannot be a multiple of 3. Since n is a multiple of 3, when $2 + n$ is divided by 3 there will be a remainder of 2.
   B. $2 - n$ cannot be a multiple of 3 for the same reason that $2 + n$ cannot be a multiple of 3.
   C. $2n - 1$ cannot be a multiple of 3. Since n is a multiple of 3, $2n$ will also be a multiple of 3, and $2n - 1$ cannot be a multiple of 3.
   D. $2n + 1$ cannot be a multiple for the same reason that $2n - 1$ cannot be a multiple of 3.
   E. $2n + 3$ is a multiple of 3. $2n$ is a multiple of 3; 3 is a multiple of 3; thus, $2n + 3$ is a multiple of 3.

   Alternatively, substitute an assumed value into the choices. Let $n = 3$:

   A. $2 + n = 2 + 3 = 5$ (Not a multiple of 3)
   B. $2 - n = 2 - 3 = -1$ (Not a multiple of 3)
   C. $2n - 1 = 2(3) - 1 = 6 - 1 = 5$ (Not a multiple of 3)
   D. $2n + 1 = 2(3) + 1 = 6 + 1 = 7$ (Not a multiple of 3)
   E. $2n + 3 = 2(3) + 3 = 6 + 3 = 9$ (A multiple of 3)

6. **(K)** *Mathematics/Arithmetic/Common Arithmetic Items/Ratios.* A ratio is just another way of writing a fraction. Simply inspect each of the answers. As for (F), $\left(\frac{1}{5}\right)^2$ is equal to $\frac{1}{25}$, and both 1 and 25 are whole numbers. As for (H), $\frac{1}{5}$ is the ratio of 1 to 5, so (H) is not the correct choice. As for (J), 0.25 is equal to $\frac{1}{4}$, the ratio of two whole numbers. Answer choice (G) is not the correct because 5 percent can be written as $\frac{5}{100}$, or $\frac{1}{20}$, which is the ratio of two whole numbers. Finally, $\sqrt{5}$ is not a whole number, so the expression in (K) is not the ratio of two whole numbers.

7. **(D)** *Mathematics/Geometry/Rectangles and Squares.* If the area of a square is known, the perimeter can be found, and vice versa. $\text{Area}_{\text{square}} = \text{side} \cdot \text{side} = 16 \Rightarrow s^2 = 16 \Rightarrow s = \pm 4$. Distances are always positive. Therefore, the perimeter is equal to $4s$, or $4 \cdot 4 = 16$.

8. **(J)** *Mathematics/Algebra/Solving Algebraic Equations with Two Variables.* This problem presents one equation with two variables. It is not possible to solve for x or y individually, but that is not necessary. Just rewrite the equation in the form of $x + y$: $12 + x = 36 - y \Rightarrow x + y = 36 - 12 = 24$.

9. **(D)** *Mathematics/Algebra/Manipulating Algebraic Expressions/Factoring Expressions.* The coefficients are 3, 6, and 2, and 1 is the only common factor of those numbers. The smallest term containing the variable x is simply

x. Thus, the greatest factor of those terms is just *x*. The same is true for the terms containing *y* and *z* and the greatest common factor is *xyz*.

10. **(G)** *Mathematics/Arithmetic/Common Arithmetic Items/Properties of Numbers.* This item can be analyzed as follows: the sum of $3k$, $4k$, $5k$, $6k$, and $7k$ is $25k$, which is divisible by 7 if the value of k is divisible by 7. If, however, the coefficient of k were divisible by 7, then that number would be divisible by 7 regardless of the value of k. Dropping the term $4k$ from the group, the sum of the remaining terms is $21k$. Since 21 is divisible by 7, $21k$ will be divisible by 7 regardless of the value of k.

11. **(B)** *Mathematics/Arithmetic/Complicated Manipulations/Decimal-Fraction Equivalents.* Do not try to convert each of these fractions to decimals to find the value that lies between $\frac{1}{3}$ and $\frac{3}{8}$. Instead, find an escape route. Use a benchmark, approximate, or use whatever else is available. First, eliminate (E): $\frac{1}{2}$ is more than $\frac{3}{8}$. Next, eliminate (A): $\frac{3}{15}$ is equal to $\frac{1}{3}$, so $\frac{3}{16}$ is smaller than $\frac{1}{3}$. (B) is close to and slightly less than $\frac{18}{48}$, which is $\frac{3}{8}$. Therefore, (B) is the correct choice. As for (C), $\frac{9}{24}$ is equal to $\frac{3}{8}$, not less than $\frac{3}{8}$. Finally, as for (D), $\frac{5}{12}$ is equal to $\frac{10}{24}$, and $\frac{3}{8}$ is equal to $\frac{9}{24}$.

12. **(G)** *Mathematics/Algebra/Manipulating Algebraic Expressions/Factoring Expressions.* Simply factor the expression: $x^2 - y^2 = (x+y) \cdot (x-y)$. Since $(x-y) = 3$, then $(x+y)(3) = 3 \Rightarrow x+y = 1$.

13. **(E)** *Mathematics/Arithmetic/Common Arithmetic Items/Properties of Numbers.* As for (A), whether $n+1$ is odd or even will depend on whether n is odd or even. The same is true for (B) and (C) since whether $3n$ is odd or even will depend on whether n is odd or even. As for (D), n^2 will be odd or even depending on whether n is odd or even. However, (E) is even regardless of whether n is odd or even. $n^2 + n$ can be factored as $n(n+1)$. Since either n or $n+1$ is even, the product must be even.

14. **(H)** *Mathematics/Geometry/Complex Figures* and *Rectangles and Squares* and *Circles.* Since the square has an area of 16, it has a side of 4 and a diagonal of $4\sqrt{2}$. The diagonal of the square is also the diameter of the circle. Therefore, the circle has a diameter of $4\sqrt{2}$ and a radius of $2\sqrt{2}$. Finally, a circle with a radius of length $2\sqrt{2}$ has an area of $\pi r^2 = \pi(2\sqrt{2})^2 = 8\pi$.

15. **(C)** *Mathematics/Arithmetic/Common Arithmetic Items/Percents.* First, calculate the sale price of the CD player that Ellen bought: $\$120 - (25\% \text{ of } \$120) = \$120 - (0.25 \cdot \$120) = \$120 - \$30 = \$90$. Next, calculate the sales tax: $\text{tax} = 8\% \text{ of } \$90 = 0.08 \cdot \$90 = \$7.20$. Therefore, the total price was $\$90 + \$7.20 = \$97.20$.

16. **(G)** *Mathematics/Arithmetic/Solving Complicated Arithmetic Application Items* and *Common Arithmetic Items/Percents.* Use the "is-over-of" equation. The "of," which is the denominator of the fraction, is the mixture. How much of the mixture is there? $2.5 + 12.5 = 15$. The word "is," which is the numerator of the fraction, is the 2.5 kilograms of gravel. Thus: $\frac{\text{is}}{\text{of}} = \frac{\text{gravel}}{\text{mixture}} = \frac{2.5}{15} = \frac{1}{6}$. Remember that $\frac{1}{6} = .01666 = 16\frac{2}{3}\%$.

17. **(D)** *Mathematics/Geometry/Triangles/Working with Triangles.* The triangle has sides of 6, 8, and 10 (multiples of 3, 4, and 5). Therefore, the triangle is a right triangle. The sides of 6 and 8 form the right angle, so they can be used as altitude and base for finding the area: $\text{area}_{\text{triangle}} = \frac{1}{2} \cdot \text{altitude} \cdot \text{base} = \frac{1}{2} \cdot 6 \cdot 8 = 24$.

18. **(F)** *Mathematics/Arithmetic/Common Arithmetic Items/Proportions and Direct-Inverse Variation.* Proportions make this calculation easy. First, complete the calculation for Motorcycle A: $\frac{\text{Fuel Used } X}{\text{Fuel Used } Y} = \frac{\text{Miles Driven } X}{\text{Miles Driven } Y} \Rightarrow \frac{1}{x} = \frac{40}{300} \Rightarrow 40x = 300 \Rightarrow x = 7.5$. Thus, Motorcycle A uses 7.5 liters of fuel for the 300-mile trip. Now, do the same for

Motorcycle B: $\frac{1}{x} = \frac{50}{300} \Rightarrow 50x = 300 \Rightarrow x = 6$. Therefore, Motorcycle B uses 6 liters of fuel for the trip. Since Motorcycle A uses $7.5 - 6 = 1.5$ liters more than Motorcycle B, the fuel for Motorcycle A costs $1.5 \cdot \$2 = \$3$ more.

19. **(B)** *Mathematics/Algebra/Expressing and Evaluating Algebraic Functions/Function Notation.* First, substitute 3 for x: $f(3) = 3^2 - 2(3) + 1 = 9 - 6 + 1 = 4$. Now, substitute 4 for x: $f(4) = 4^2 - 2(4) + 1 = 16 - 8 + 1 = 9$. Therefore, $f(f(3)) = 9$.

20. **(K)** *Mathematics/Algebra/Manipulating Algebraic Expressions/Factoring Expressions.* Factor $6k + 3$: $6k + 3 = 3(2k + 1)$. Substituting 1 for k in the answer choices also works. The correct answer choice, (K), yields the value 9: $6k + 3 = 6(1) + 3 = 6 + 3 = 9$.

21. **(E)** *Mathematics/Algebra/Manipulating Algebraic Expressions/Creating Algebraic Expressions.* Devise the formula as follows. The formula will be x, the cost for the first ounce, plus some expression to represent the additional postage for each additional ounce over the first ounce. The postage for the additional weight is y cents per ounce, and the additional weight is w minus the first ounce, or $w - 1$. Therefore, the additional postage is $y(w - 1)$, and the total postage is $x + y(w - 1)$.

Alternatively, assume some numbers. For ease of calculations, assume that the first ounce costs 1 cent and every additional ounce is free. If $x = 1$ and $y = 0$, then a letter, of say, 10 ounces ($w = 10$) will cost 1 cent. Substitute 1 for x, zero for y, and 10 for w into the choices. The correct formula will generate the value 1. (A), (B), and (C) are eliminated. One more set of assumptions will give the correct answer.

22. **(F)** *Mathematics/Arithmetic/Common Arithmetic Items/Absolute Value.* $|-3| = 3$ and $\left|-\frac{1}{2}\right| = \frac{1}{2}$. Therefore: $|-3| \cdot |2| \cdot \left|-\frac{1}{2}\right| + (-4) = 3 \cdot 2 \cdot \frac{1}{2} - 4 = 3 - 4 = -1$.

23. **(C)** *Mathematics/Geometry/Complex Figures* and *Rectangles and Squares* and *Circles.* The side of the square is also the radius of the circle. Since the square has an area of 2, its side is: $s \cdot s = 2 \Rightarrow s^2 = 2 \Rightarrow s = \sqrt{2}$. $\sqrt{2}$ is the radius of the circle. Therefore, the area of the circle is $\pi r^2 = \pi(\sqrt{2})^2 = 2\pi$.

24. **(G)** *Mathematics/Arithmetic/Common Arithmetic Items/Properties of Numbers.* Test each statement. As for statement (I), 2 is the first prime number, and the product of 2 and any other number must be even. Thus, (I) is not part of the correct answer. As for (II), the sum of two prime numbers might be odd, (e.g., $2 + 3 = 5$), but the sum of two prime numbers might also be even, (e.g., $3 + 5 = 8$). As for (III), however, the product of two odd numbers is necessarily odd.

25. **(A)** *Mathematics/Coordinate Geometry/The Coordinate System.* The coordinates establish that this figure is a rectangle. The width of the rectangle is a, and the length is $b - a$. Therefore, the area is $a(b - a)$.

Alternatively, "test-the-test," assuming that $a = 2$ and $b = 4$. The rectangle has a width of 2, a length of $4 - 2 = 2$, and an area of $2 \cdot 2 = 4$. Substitute 2 for a and 4 for b into the answer choices and the correct formula will yield 4.

26. **(H)** *Mathematics/Arithmetic/Simple Manipulations.* $\sqrt{(43 - 7)(29 + 7)} = \sqrt{(36)(36)} = 36$.

27. **(A)** *Mathematics/Arithmetic/Common Arithmetic Items/Proportions and Direct-Inverse Variation.* Set up a direct proportion: $\frac{\text{Cement } X}{\text{Cement } Y} = \frac{\text{Grit } X}{\text{Grit } Y} \Rightarrow \frac{4}{50} = \frac{20}{x} \Rightarrow 4x = (20)(50) \Rightarrow x = \frac{(20)(50)}{4} = 250$.

28. **(G)** *Mathematics/Geometry/Lines and Angles.* Label the other two angles in the triangle:

$x + z = 180 \Rightarrow 120 + z = 180 \Rightarrow z = 60$; $z + w + y = 180$. Since $\overline{QT} = \overline{QR}$, $y = w$. $60 + y + y = 180 \Rightarrow 2y = 120 \Rightarrow y = 60$.

29. **(C)** *Mathematics/Algebra/Solving Algebraic Equations with Two Variables.* There is only one equation but two variables, so x and y cannot be solved for individually. Instead, look for a way to rewrite the first equation to give the information needed: $\frac{x}{y} = -1 \Rightarrow x = -y \Rightarrow x + y = 0$.

30. **(K)** *Mathematics/Statistics and Probability/Data Representation/Tables (Matrices)* and *Arithmetic/Common Arithmetic Items/Decimal-Fraction Equivalents.* Do not do lengthy calculations. Set up the cost of each fabric as a fraction and compare the fraction directly, using a benchmark:

F. $\frac{8}{3}$

G. $\frac{6}{2} = 3$

H. $\frac{9}{4}$

J. $\frac{7}{5}$

K. $\frac{4}{6}$

(K), $\frac{4}{6}$, is less than 1. The other fractions are greater than 1, so (K) is the smallest.

31. **(A)** *Mathematics/Geometry/Lines and Angles.* Since $\overline{PQ} \parallel \overline{ST}$, the "big angle/little angle" theorem establishes that $x = y$. Solve for x since this equals y: $75 + 65 + x + x = 180 \Rightarrow 2x + 140 = 180 \Rightarrow 2x = 40 \Rightarrow x = 20$. Therefore, $y = 20$.

32. **(J)** *Mathematics/Arithmetic/Complicated Manipulations/Simplifying.* $\frac{10^3(10^5 + 10^5)}{10^4} = \frac{10(10^4 + 10^4)}{10} = 2(10^4)$.

33. **(D)** *Mathematics/Algebra/Solving Quadratic Equations.* Factor and solve for x: $x^2 - 5x + 4 = 0 \Rightarrow (x - 4)(x - 1) = 0$. So, either $x - 4 = 0$ and $x = 4$, or $x - 1 = 0$ and $x = 1$.

Alternatively, substitute the values in the choices back into the equation to find the set that works.

34. **(K)** *Mathematics/Statistics and Probability/Averages.* Use the method for finding the missing elements of an average. The smallest possible sum for 6 different positive integers is $1 + 2 + 3 + 4 + 5 + 6 = 21$. The sum of all 7 integers is $7 \cdot 12 = 84$. Therefore, the largest that the seventh number could be (with the average of the seven numbers still 12) is $84 - 21 = 63$.

35. **(E)** *Mathematics/Algebra/Solving Simultaneous Equations.* To find b in terms of x and y, set b equal to x and equal to y:

46. **(K)** *Mathematics/Geometry/Complex Figures* and *Triangles/Working with Triangles* and *Rectangles and Squares.* Draw some additional lines to carve the figure up into some more familiar shapes, and use the Pythagorean theorem to determine the length of the shared third side of the two small triangles: $a^2 + 8^2 = 10^2 \Rightarrow a^2 + 64 = 100 \Rightarrow a^2 = 36 \Rightarrow a = 6$.

The area of the large rectangle is $16 \cdot 2 = 32$. Using 6 and 8 as the altitude and base of each triangle, respectively, determine the area of each triangle: $\frac{1}{2} \cdot 6 \cdot 8 = 24$. Therefore, the area of the composite figure is: $32 + 24(2) = 32 + 48 = 80$.

47. **(D)** *Mathematics/Algebra/Manipulating Algebraic Expressions/Evaluating Expressions.* Rationalize the denominator: $\frac{\sqrt{x}}{2\sqrt{x} - \sqrt{y}} \cdot \frac{2\sqrt{x} + \sqrt{y}}{2\sqrt{x} + \sqrt{y}} = \frac{2x + \sqrt{xy}}{4x + 2\sqrt{xy} - 2\sqrt{xy} - y} = \frac{2x + \sqrt{xy}}{4x - y}$.

Alternatively, assume some values for x and y. Since the problem involves square roots, pick a couple of perfect squares, e.g., $x = 9$ and $y = 4$. The expression in the question stem becomes: $\frac{\sqrt{9}}{2\sqrt{9} - \sqrt{4}} = \frac{3}{2(3) - 2} = \frac{3}{4}$. Now, substitute 9 for x and 4 for y into the answer choices. The correct choice will generate the value $\frac{3}{4}$:

A. $\frac{2\sqrt{x} - \sqrt{y}}{2} = \frac{2\sqrt{9} - \sqrt{4}}{2} = \frac{2(3) - 2}{2} = \frac{4}{2} = 2$ ✗

B. $\frac{2\sqrt{x} + \sqrt{y}}{4xy} = \frac{2\sqrt{9} + \sqrt{4}}{4(9)(4)} = \frac{2(3) + 2}{144} = \frac{8}{144}$ ✗

C. $\frac{2\sqrt{x} + \sqrt{xy}}{2x - y} = \frac{2\sqrt{9} + \sqrt{(9)(4)}}{2(9) - 4} = \frac{6 + 6}{14} = \frac{12}{14}$ ✗

D. $\frac{2x + \sqrt{xy}}{4x - y} = \frac{2(9) + \sqrt{(9)(4)}}{4(9) - 4} = \frac{18 + 6}{32} = \frac{24}{32} = \frac{3}{4}$ ✓

E. $\frac{4x + \sqrt{xy}}{4x - y} = \frac{4(9) + \sqrt{(9)(4)}}{4(9) - 4} = \frac{36 + 6}{36 - 4} = \frac{42}{32}$ ✗

48. **(H)** *Mathematics/Geometry/Lines and Angles.* This question requires the deduction of further conclusions based on the given information. Since opposite angles are equal, the figure becomes:

The center triangle has angles 30, 105, and x. Solve for x: $30 + 105 + x = 180 \Rightarrow x = 45$.

49. **(D)** *Mathematics/Trigonometry/Determining Trigonometric Values.* The graph intersects the y-axis where $x = 0$: $y = 2[\cos(2 \bullet 0)] + 2 = 2[\cos(0)] + 2$. Since $\cos(0) = 1$: $y = 2(1) + 2 = 4$.

50. **(G)** *Mathematics/Geometry/Complex Figures* and *Rectangles and Squares* and *Circles.* This is a typical "shaded area" question. The shaded area will be the whole square minus the four circles: $\text{area}_{\text{shaded}} = \square - (4 \bullet \bigcirc)$. The entire solution statement is: $\frac{\text{area}_{\text{shaded}}}{\text{area}_{\text{square}}}$. On the assumption that each circle has a radius of r, the side of the square must be $4r$, and the area of the square is $4r \bullet 4r = 16r^2$. This is the denominator of the solution statement, and it is also an element in the calculation of the shaded area. To complete the calculation of the shaded area, reason that each circle with radius r has an area of πr^2. Therefore, $\text{area}_{\text{shaded}} = 16r^2 - 4\pi r^2$. Fill in the solution statement: $\frac{16r^2 - 4\pi r^2}{16r^2} = \frac{4r^2(4 - \pi)}{16r^2} = \frac{4 - \pi}{4}$.

A little common sense goes a long way when applied to the answer choices. Since π is less than 4, (F) is a negative number and is therefore impossible. Both (J) and (K) are greater than 1, asserting that the shaded area is larger than the square, an equally absurd conclusion. Now, there are only two answer choices remaining: (G) asserts that the shaded area is a little less than one-quarter of the square, and (H) asserts that the shaded area is about three-quarters of the square. After careful inspection of the figure, it is safe to assume that (G) is correct.

51. **(C)** *Mathematics/Trigonometry/Trigonometric Relationships.* One of the Pythagorean identities is: $\sin^2(\theta) + \cos^2(\theta) = 1$. Therefore, the expression given in the question stem is equivalent to $\frac{1}{\sin(\theta)}$. The reciprocal identity for the sine function is the cosecant function.

52. **(G)** *Mathematics/Trigonometry/Definitions of the Six Trigonometric Functions.* $\tan(\theta) = \frac{\text{side opposite } \theta}{\text{side adjacent to } \theta}$. Therefore, $\tan(55°) = \frac{6}{AC}$: $1.4 \approx \frac{6}{AC} \Rightarrow \overline{AC} \approx \frac{6}{1.4} \approx 4.28$.

53. **(D)** *Mathematics/Algebra/Manipulating Algebraic Expressions/Evaluating Expressions.* When $x = 1$, $x - 1 = 0$, so the entire expression is undefined. Similarly, when $x = -2$, $x + 2 = 0$, and the expression is undefined. When $x = -3$, $x + 3 = 0$, so the value of the expression is 0.

54. **(K)** *Mathematics/Algebra/Solving Simultaneous Equations.* Since the sum of x and y is less than or equal to 6, y will have its maximum value when x has its minimum value. The minimum value of x is 0; the maximum value of y is 6. $3(6) = 18$.

Alternatively, test the answer choices. Since the question asks for the maximum value of y, start with the largest choice: 18. If $3y = 18$, then $y = 6$. $x + y \le 6 \Rightarrow x + 6 \le 6 \Rightarrow x \le 0$. Since x can be 0, $y = 6$ satisfies the system of inequalities. 18 is the largest answer choice, and therefore it must be the largest value possible for $3y$.

55. **(D)** *Mathematics/Coordinate Geometry/The Coordinate System.* Find the corresponding values for y:

$$y = \left|(-1)^2 - 3\right| = |1 - 3| = |-2| = 2$$
$$y = \left|(0)^2 - 3\right| = |-3| = 3$$
$$y = \left|(1)^2 - 3\right| = |1 - 3| = |-2| = 2$$

(D) is the correct plotting of the points $(-1, 2)$, $(0, 3)$, and $(1, 2)$.

56. **(G)** *Mathematics/Coordinate Geometry/Graphs of Linear Equations.* Calculate the slope: $m = \frac{(-2) + (-4)}{(2) - (-1)} = \frac{-6}{3} = -2$. Since the answer choices are equations of a line in slope-intercept form, each with a different slope, (G) is the correct answer.

57. **(A)** *Mathematics/Algebra/Solving Quadratic Equations.* There are at least three different ways of attacking this problem, but one method is clearly superior. Use the roots to create the equation. If $x = a$ or $x = b$, then $x - a = 0$ or $x - b = 0$. The factors of the equation are $(x - a)$ and $(x - b)$, and the equation is: $(x - a)(x - b) = x^2 - ax - bx + ab = 0$. Given the roots of this equation, that will take a little time.

Similarly, substitute the solutions into each of the equations to find the equation that will accept both solutions. This, too, is a lot of work.

The best approach is to see that the roots are expressed in a form that is suggestive of the quadratic formula. Thus, $-b = -3$, so $b = 3$. Eliminate (B) and (D). Next, $2a = 2$, so $a = 1$; eliminate (E). Finally, $b^2 - 4ac = 5$. Since $b = 3$ and $a = 1$: $b^2 - 4ac = 5 \Rightarrow (3)^2 - 4(1)(c) = 5 \Rightarrow 9 - 4c = 5 \Rightarrow 4c = 4 \Rightarrow c = 1$. Thus, the equation is $x^2 + 3x + 1 = 0$.

58. **(F)** *Mathematics/Algebra/Expressing and Evaluating Algebraic Functions/Concepts of Domain and Range.* A function is a relationship such that each element of the domain is paired with one and only one element in the range. In the relationship given in the question stem, one element of the domain, 0, is paired with two different elements in the range: 3 and 5. Therefore, the relationship given in the question stem is not a function. By dropping the first set of pairs, this duplication is eliminated and the set becomes a function.

59. **(D)** *Mathematics/Geometry/Complex Figures* and *30°-60°-90° Triangles* and *Rectangles and Squares.* Consider the trapezoid as a composite figure. Draw a line from point B perpendicular to $\overline{CD}$. The trapezoid is a combination of a right triangle and a rectangle. Since the triangle has degree measures of 30, 60, and 90, the side opposite the 30° angle has a length half that of the hypotenuse, or a length of 4. Thus, the rectangle has sides of 4 and 9 and an area of 36. Then, the side of the triangle opposite the 60° angle has a length equal to $4\sqrt{3}$. The area of the triangle is: $\frac{1}{2}(a)(b) = \frac{1}{2}(4)(4\sqrt{3})$. The area of the triangle is $8\sqrt{3}$. So, the area of the trapezoid is $36 + 8\sqrt{3}$.

60. **(G)** *Mathematics/Trigonometry/Trigonometric Relationships.* There are several routes by which to reach the right conclusion. The shortest is to reason that the cotangent and tangent are reciprocal functions, so if $\cot(\theta) = \frac{4}{3}$, then $\tan(\theta) = \frac{3}{4}$.

TEST 3: READING (p. 474)

1. **(A)** *Reading/Humanities/Main Idea.* The passage actually makes two points: who Josquin is, and why we have never heard of him. (A) mentions both of these points.

2. **(J)** *Reading/Humanities/Explicit Detail.* (F) is answered in the second paragraph ("Solace me"). (G) is answered in the final paragraph (sackbut). (H) is answered in the second paragraph (Ockeghem). (J) must be the correct answer since the author never makes reference to any students.

3. **(D)** *Reading/Humanities/Implied Idea.* In the fourth paragraph, the author lists certain difficulties in reading a Renaissance score: no tempo specified, missing flats and sharps, and no instrument/voice indication. Since these are regarded as deficiencies of Renaissance scoring, it is inferable that modern music notation contains all of these.

4. **(G)** *Reading/Humanities/Implied Idea.* In the third paragraph, the author discusses the distinction between concept and performance. The author states that music does not exist as printed notes. The notation is just a set of instructions for producing music. Therefore, the author would agree with (G).

5. **(D)** *Reading/Humanities/Application.* There is merit to each of the choices, but the best answer is the one that is most closely connected to the passage. The author discusses the lack of funding as one important reason for

Josquin's obscurity, an obscurity that the author deplores. The argument might be used to support a proposal for funds to promote Josquin's music, (D).

6. **(G)** *Reading/Humanities/Explicit Detail.* (H) and (J) are mentioned in the final paragraph. (F) is mentioned in the third paragraph. (G) is never mentioned. The author states that musicians who read modern notation have difficulty reading Renaissance notation—not that these musicians lack talent.

7. **(A)** *Reading/Humanities/Implied Idea.* The author compares Josquin to Galileo in order to praise Josquin. This suggests that the author has a very high opinion of Galileo.

8. **(H)** *Reading/Humanities/Implied Idea.* The first paragraph states that the dominant theme of liturgical music is reverence.

9. **(A)** *Reading/Humanities/Implied Idea.* In the third paragraph, the author says that in fine art such as painting and poetry, concept and performance are one. For example, the painting is what it is—a physical object. However, in music, the concept exists only during a performance. Ballet is like music in this respect.

10. **(H)** *Reading/Humanities/Implied Idea.* In the first paragraph, the author states that up to the time of Josquin des Prez, Western music was liturgical. In the second paragraph, the author says that Josquin des Prez wrote both religious and nonreligious music.

11. **(C)** *Reading/Prose Fiction/Explicit Detail.* At the beginning of the story, the child addresses the narrator as Miss Mix. At the end of the story, Mr. Rawjester calls her Mary Jane.

12. **(H)** *Reading/Prose Fiction/Implied Idea.* As the narrator surmises, the highwayman is in reality Mr. Rawjester. He assumes the role of a robber in order to make sure that he is not suspected of setting the fire.

13. **(A)** *Reading/Prose Fiction/Implied Idea.* The narrator is employed as a governess by Mr. Rawjester. Apparently, she is required to help Blanche make herself up. This is degrading since the narrator herself has feelings for the master of the house.

14. **(H)** *Reading/Prose Fiction/Explicit Detail.* This can be deduced from the conversation between the narrator and the child. It becomes clear when the narrator identifies herself to the highwayman as a governess.

15. **(B)** *Reading/Prose Fiction/Implied Idea.* As he leaves the party, he calls his guests "idiots" under his breath.

16. **(G)** *Reading/Prose Fiction/Explicit Detail.* At the beginning of the story, the child tells the narrator that her father's sweetheart is about to become her mother.

17. **(B)** *Reading/Prose Fiction/Implied Idea.* Since the narrator survives the encounter with the highwayman, she must have chosen to cooperate with him.

18. **(J)** *Reading/Prose Fiction/Explicit Detail.* As already noted, the highwayman is a trick designed to allow Mr. Rawjester to dispose of his three crazy wives while avoiding suspicion.

19. **(A)** *Reading/Prose Fiction/Explicit Detail.* Since the highwayman is Mr. Rawjester, he knows about the necklace.

20. **(F)** *Reading/Prose Fiction/Implied Idea.* Notice that the conversation takes place in a low voice and a whisper.

21. **(B)** *Reading/Social Studies/Main Idea.* This is the only statement general enough to cover the specific information in the piece. (A) is contradicted by the text. (C) and (D) are specific details and, therefore, too narrow in scope to be the main idea of the passage.

22. **(G)** *Reading/Social Studies/Application.* Since the policy approved by the board involves the payment of large bonuses to any management member who is fired after a takeover, the policy is, by definition, a golden parachute.

23. **(C)** *Reading/Social Studies/Implied Idea.* According to the second paragraph, the defining characteristic of a hostile takeover is the existing management's opposition.

24. **(F)** *Reading/Social Studies/Explicit Detail.* This statement is supported by the beginning of the third paragraph, which tells of the methods used by raiders to raise the cash they need to buy a targeted company's stock.

25. **(D)** *Reading/Social Studies/Explicit Detail.* The fifth paragraph defines the three anti-takeover strategies. (A) defines the greenmail strategy. (B) defines the golden parachute theory. (C) is not supported by anything in the passage.

26. **(G)** *Reading/Social Studies/Explicit Detail.* This argument is made at the beginning of the last paragraph. The topics of statements (F), (H), and (J) are all mentioned in the passage, but the passage does not support any of these statements.

27. **(D)** *Reading/Social Studies/Explicit Detail.* The meaning of a proxy fight is presented in the second paragraph. The other choices are all true but do not involve a proxy battle.

28. **(H)** *Reading/Social Studies/Application.* This point is explicitly made at the beginning of the last paragraph. All the other choices are properly defined in the second-to-last paragraph.

29. **(B)** *Reading/Social Studies/Explicit Detail.* The role of the Securities and Exchange Commission is defined in the first sentence of the selection.

30. **(H)** *Reading/Social Studies/Explicit Detail.* In the fourth paragraph, the passage states that some people have been convicted of selling inside information about takeovers.

31. **(C)** *Reading/Natural Sciences/Explicit Detail.* In the first sentence of the passage, the author says a supernova occurs about twice every century, or about once every fifty years.

32. **(J)** *Reading/Natural Sciences/Explicit Detail.* (F) is stated in the second paragraph. (G) is stated in the first paragraph. (H) is stated in the second paragraph. Although the word "galaxy" is used in the selection, the author does not say that colliding galaxies cause supernovas. (J) is the one detail not mentioned in the selection.

33. **(A)** *Reading/Natural Sciences/Development.* In the first paragraph, the author compares a star to a leaky balloon. That is an analogy.

34. **(H)** *Reading/Natural Sciences/Implied Idea.* The key word for this question is "anomalous." The author states that the unexpected makeup of the meteorites is evidence that a supernova helped form our solar system. However, this evidence supports the conclusion only if the strange content is foreign to our solar system. Only (H) explains the connection between the theory of the origin of our solar system and the strange makeup of the meteors.

35. **(A)** *Reading/Natural Sciences/Implied Idea.* In the last two sentences of the second paragraph, the author states that supernovas emit most of their energy as x-rays and notes that x-ray observations provide the most useful insights into the nature of supernovas. He adds that remnants of supernovas have been found using x-ray studies. These remarks suggest that it is easier to find a supernova using equipment that detects x-rays than it is using equipment for viewing visible light.

36. **(J)** *Reading/Natural Sciences/Explicit Detail.* In the first paragraph, the author describes the start of the sequence of events that leads to a supernova. It begins when a star runs out of fuel and collapses.

37. **(B)** *Reading/Natural Sciences/Explicit Detail.* In the first paragraph, the author describes the collapse of an ordinary star. The result is a neutron star. In the second paragraph, the author describes what follows—a supernova. Thus, the neutron star is an intermediate stage between the ordinary star and its final phase, a supernova.

38. **(J)** *Reading/Natural Sciences/Main Idea.* (F), (G), and (H) are incorrect—each makes the mistake of elevating a part of the passage to the status of main idea. (J) is the best description of the passage. The author describes the sequence of events that leads to a supernova and then describes what events follow the supernova.

39. **(D)** *Reading/Natural Sciences/Explicit Detail.* The last paragraph dates the formation of our galaxy at over 4.5 billion years ago.

40. **(H)** *Reading/Natural Sciences/Implied Idea.* The last paragraph notes that the cosmic radiation generated by supernovas is responsible for many of the genetic mutations that propel evolution.

TEST 4: SCIENCE (p. 484)

1. **(C)** *Science/Data Representation/Analysis.* Generally, the Wright data show lower lift at a given angle than the Lilienthal data.

2. **(H)** *Science/Data Representation/Comprehension.* The highest point on the graph is at 16 degrees (approximately 5.5 pounds/sq. ft.).

3. **(A)** *Science/Data Representation/Comprehension.* By extending both lines to the 50° mark, the difference between them is clearly observed to be less than 1 pound/sq. ft.

4. **(H)** *Science/Data Representation/Comprehension.* Count the crossing points of the two curves.

5. **(C)** *Science/Data Representation/Comprehension.* The widest region is between 18° and 43°.

6. **(J)** *Science/Research Summary/Analysis.* Since plastic beads are not alive, they cannot possibly carry out cellular respiration. This control is designed to detect any atmospheric changes (in the laboratory) that may cause a change in gas volume inside the tubes.

7. **(A)** *Science/Research Summary/Comprehension.* Oxygen in the air of the tube is consumed by the peas during cellular respiration (see summary equation).

8. **(H)** *Science/Research Summary/Analysis.* Without KOH to remove the carbon dioxide produced during cellular respiration, the same number of gas molecules ($6CO_2$) would always be added to the tube as gas molecules were being consumed in the tube ($6O_2$).

9. **(C)** *Science/Research Summary/Analysis.* Experiment 2 was conducted at a higher temperature than Experiment 1. The greater decrease in gas in the same time period (15 minutes) demonstrates a faster consumption of oxygen.

10. **(G)** *Science/Research Summary/Analysis.* If results are identical in light and dark (Experiments 1 and 2), then light/dark conditions are irrelevant to cellular respiration rates in the experiment; only temperature conditions are important.

11. **(A)** *Science/Research Summary/Comprehension.* Glucose must be consumed in order for cellular respiration to occur. Since cellular respiration did not occur at equal rates in Experiments 1 and 2, (A) is the only possible answer. Peas are seeds containing a supply of glucose.

12. **(G)** *Science/Conflicting Viewpoints/Analysis.* Scientist 1 believes that processes associated with sudden events in the past shaped the Earth, whereas Scientist 2 believes that the processes are continuing in the present.

13. **(D)** *Science/Conflicting Viewpoints/Analysis.* Mountains could not have formed only when land masses were raised at the beginnings of the Earth if recent fossils of sea creatures are found at mountain tops. This evidence suggests that the rocks were underwater relatively recently.

14. **(H)** *Science/Conflicting Viewpoints/Analysis.* Scientist 1 never refers to time or how old the Earth may be. Scientist 2 refers to "long" or "vast" periods of time.

15. **(A)** *Science/Conflicting Viewpoints/Comprehension.* If the worldwide ocean precipitated granite first, it must be the lowest layer, with other precipitated materials covering it later.

16. **(F)** *Science/Conflicting Viewpoints/Comprehension.* If the major rock types (three) formed when the worldwide ocean precipitated different materials on three occasions, no further types can be expected since this ocean no longer exists (possibly due to evaporation).

17. **(C)** *Science/Conflicting Viewpoints/Analysis.* Processes cannot be uniform from the beginning. Processes that formed the Earth at its origin must have differed from those that maintain and mold the Earth as an existing planet.

18. **(G)** *Science/Conflicting Viewpoints/Analysis.* Scientist 1 refers to three rock types forming during three separate precipitations. Regions of lava (with no present volcanoes), rivers presently continuing to cut their channels, and "related" fossils that could not have immigrated from other geographic areas are factors that support the views of Scientist 2.

19. **(D)** *Science/Research Summary/Comprehension.* Ten individuals had their heart rates recorded every 10 minutes during a 30-minute experiment (three times). Therefore, 30 values were used to calculate the average heart rate for each of the experiments.

20. **(G)** *Science/Research Summary/Analysis.* Since Species B had an increase in heart rate when environmental temperature increased, it is the likely species to be poikilothermic (Species A's heart rate stayed about the same).

21. **(C)** *Science/Research Summary/Analysis.* Just by chance alone, any one individual might have an extremely high or extremely low heart rate. The larger the sample of individuals tested, the lower the chances of getting extreme average values.

22. **(J)** *Science/Research Summary/Analysis.* Since Species B (poikilothermic) had an increase in average heart rate when environmental temperature increased, a decrease in average heart rate is likely when temperatures drop. Species A should have approximately the same average heart rate at all three temperatures.

23. **(A)** *Science/Research Summary/Analysis.* At 22°C, Species A had an average heart rate of 150 beats/minute, while Species B averaged 100 beats/minute.

24. **(F)** *Science/Research Summary/Analysis.* The poikilothermic Species B should have an increase in body temperature in Experiment 2 (35°C conditions in the incubator compared to 22°C in Experiment 1). The homeothermic Species A should have no significant change in body temperature during the experiments.

25. **(A)** *Science/Data Representation/Comprehension.* Each photon can promote an electron from level 1 to level 2 since the difference in energies is 0.60. (Note that the actual value of level 1 alone, which happens to be 0.60 also, does not determine the answer. Differences in energy are what matter.)

26. **(J)** *Science/Data Representation/Comprehension.* There is no way to distinguish between the two emissions since each releases a photon of equal energy.

27. **(D)** *Science/Data Representation/Comprehension.* Only the level 3 to level 1 emission has an energy difference of 0.92.

28. **(J)** *Science/Data Representation/Comprehension.* Each electron can go from level 1 to any of 4 other levels, with each of the four transitions requiring a photon of a different energy.

29. **(C)** *Science/Data Representation/Analysis.* Since absorption of photons occurs first, then emission, electrons must be promoted (gaining the necessary energy from the absorbed photons), then emitted. Transitions between levels 3 and 4 have the necessary energies, namely 0.23.

30. **(J)** *Science/Data Representation/Comprehension.* Although 2.07 is the absolute energy of level 5, there is no difference of energy levels anywhere on the diagram that equals 2.07; hence, the photons will not be absorbed.

31. **(C)** *Science/Research Summary/Comprehension.* Note how θ_1 and θ_2 are defined on the original drawing, then imagine how the diagram will change as the angles become smaller. (B) would be correct if the angles were defined as those between the ray and the horizontal, not vertical, axis.

32. **(J)** *Science/Research Summary/Analysis.* Only the last choice fits both experiments.

33. **(A)** *Science/Research Summary/Comprehension.* This question simply requires interpretation of the meaning of the diagram.

34. **(H)** *Science/Research Summary/Comprehension.* The beam of light only passes into the air for observation in Experiment 2.

35. **(C)** *Science/Research Summary/Analysis.* This response covers all elements of the three diagrams.

36. **(H)** *Science/Data Representation/Comprehension.* The number of butterflies captured for marking is found under the heading: "# marked". Reading across the table for each size group, the "dark brown" category always has the fewest butterflies marked.

37. **(D)** *Science/Data Representation/Comprehension.* By comparing the number of butterflies recaptured to the number marked, students can derive a proportion that represents how easy it is to recapture each type of butterfly. The proportion for small, white butterflies (30/35) is much higher than that for any of the other choices.

38. **(G)** *Science/Data Representation/Analysis.* An examination of the table shows that for all colors, as size increases the number of butterflies marked gets larger.

39. **(B)** *Science/Data Representation/Application.* A poisonous chemical will have adverse effects on the butterfly after marking (perhaps by killing or by preventing flight). The group with the lowest number (and proportion) of individuals recaptured in flight ($10/40 = 1/4$ recaptured) is the group consisting of small, tan butterflies.

40. **(G)** *Science/Data Representation/Analysis.* For medium-sized butterflies, the proportion of individuals recaptured in each color is as follows: white ($15/30 = 1/2$), tan ($20/40 = 1/2$), and dark brown ($10/20 = 1/2$).

TEST 5: WRITING (p. 496)

Below Average Response

Some people will argue that a total ban on unhealthy food will interfere with the freedom of students to choose what they eat. Freedom to eat what one chooses is not like freedom of speech of freedom from policy brutality. In the big picture, being told that one cannot buy "Twinkle Cakes" from the machine in the cafeteria is not like being told that one can't criticize the government. Banning foods from school doesn't mean that these foods are banned altogether. One can still buy them and eat them before and after school and on weekends. All that the ban means is that you can't eat them in school when you are under the school's authority.

By banning unhealthy food from schools, students would be getting only healthy food. This means that for at least one meal (lunch), they wouldn't be eating junk. That would mean that they would be eating food that contains important nutrients and doesn't have all of the calories and additives that are usually found in regular junk food. This alone would probably have an important impact on the health of the country. Students would learn about good nutrition. Many students now may not understand that they need certain vitamins and minerals and these usually come from eating foods like broccoli and fresh fruit. You just don't find a lot of vitamins in "Twinkle Cakes." Junk food often contains additives and preservatives that are not good for us. Someone who eats too much junk food gets too much of these bad elements. This would be especially important for younger children because their nutritional needs are more significant than older children. They would begin to learn at an earlier age the important difference between healthy food and junk food. And these lessons would stay with them.

Having schools set a good example might help adults as well. When parents see that their children are eating right, they could also become interested in having better diets. If everyone were eating better, then there would be less incentive to eat things that are bad, and everyone would benefit.

Banning unhealthy foods in school is not the first step to a dictatorship. Schools prohibit a lot of behavior (think of obscene T-shirts) that is allowed outside of school. So a new policy really would hurt anyone. Plus, the new policy would have some definite benefits, so it should be accepted.

Position on issue:

The writer never clearly explains the position. The writer begins the essay with "some people will argue that a total ban on unhealthy food will interfere with the freedom of students to choose what they eat," which leaves the writer's actual position ambiguous.

Topic development and essay organization:

This is obviously the same essay as the second but with some minor changes. Much of the organizational scheme has been removed. There is no use of the words "three benefits" or any other words that would signal when the writer is passing from one point to another. The point is to see how very important the organizational scheme is in an essay. The two essays make essentially the same points, but the second one is much more effective.

Language usage, sentence structure, and punctuation:

The essay should have a more formal tone.

Summary and conclusions:

This first essay would probably receive a "3" rather than a "4," although the elimination of the organization is artificial, so we can't say for certain. This much, however, does seem clear. The second would be more likely to receive the "4" than would the first.

Above Average Response

I think that it would be a good for schools to ban all food that is not healthy for students. Although some people will argue that a total ban on unhealthy food will interfere with the freedom of students to choose what they eat, there are two points to remember. One, freedom to eat what one chooses is not like freedom of speech of freedom from policy brutality. In the big picture, being told that one cannot buy "Twinkle Cakes" from the machine in the cafeteria is not like being told that one can't criticize the government. Two, banning foods from school doesn't mean that these foods are banned altogether. One can still buy them and eat them before and after school and on weekends. All that the ban means is that you can't eat them in school when you are under the school's authority.

Banning unhealthy food from schools would have three benefits. First, during the school day, students would be getting only healthy food. This means that for at least one meal (lunch), they wouldn't be eating junk. That would mean that they would be eating food that contains important nutrients and doesn't have all of the calories and additives that are usually found in regular junk food. This alone would probably have an important impact on the health of the country. Second, students would learn about good nutrition. Many students now may not understand that they need certain vitamins and minerals and these usually come from eating foods like broccoli and fresh fruit. You just don't find a lot of vitamins in "Twinkle Cakes." Also, junk food often contains additives and preservatives that are not good for us. Someone who eats too much junk food gets too much of these bad elements. This would be especially important for younger children because their nutritional needs are more significant than older children. They would begin to learn at an earlier age the important difference between healthy food and junk food. And these lessons would stay with them.

Third, having schools set a good example might help adults as well. When parents see that their children are eating right, they could also become interested in having better diets. If everyone were eating better, then there would be less incentive to eat things that are bad, and everyone would benefit.

Banning unhealthy foods in school is not the first step to a dictatorship. Schools prohibit a lot of behavior (think of obscene T-shirts) that is allowed outside of school. So a new policy really would not hurt anyone. Plus, the new policy would have some definite benefits, so it should be accepted.

Position on issue:

In this essay, the writer takes a clear position and begins by handling a possible objection to that position.

Topic development and essay organization:

The writer develops three benefits that would flow from a school policy banning certain foods. The three benefits are each discussed in separate paragraphs, and the writer nicely signals for the reader what each paragraph is about. The one criticism that might be made about the essay is that it doesn't seem to develop the points in sufficient detail. Yes, the writer mentions examples such as "Twinkle Cakes" (presumably a humorous reference to "Twinkies" and a nice touch), broccoli, and fresh fruit, but the writer never connects these to the issue of obesity. To be sure, it would be legitimate to let the essay range over a lot of nutritional issues, but then the writer really should explain to the reader that these additional points are further thoughts about the issue, e.g., "In addition to having an impact on the obesity epidemic, a policy of 'Healthy Foods Only' would improve nutrition in other ways."

Language usage, sentence structure, and punctuation:

In general, the writer uses correct grammar and ties ideas together logically.

Summary and conclusions:

As written, the essay makes some good points but they seem to be wide of the mark. A tighter focus would earn a higher mark. As it stands, this essay would probably get a "4." It's hard to imagine that anyone would think of it as a "3," and perhaps a handful of readers might think of it as a "5."

PRACTICE TEST IV ANSWER KEYS

TEST 1: ENGLISH (p. 500)

ANSWER KEY DIRECTIONS: For the *correct* answer, check the corresponding unshaded box. Then, total the number of checkmarks for each of the content areas, and add these totals in order to determine the raw score for that test.

ENGLISH TEST—ANSWER KEY

UM RH		UM RH		UM RH		UM RH		UM RH
1. C		16. F		31. A		46. J		61. A
2. J		17. B		32. J		47. B		62. H
3. D		18. J		33. B		48. F		63. B
4. G		19. D		34. G		49. D		64. J
5. A		20. H		35. D		50. H		65. D
6. H		21. A		36. G		51. B		66. H
7. C		22. J		37. A		52. F		67. C
8. F		23. A		38. H		53. D		68. G
9. B		24. H		39. B		54. G		69. B
10. G		25. C		40. J		55. D		70. F
11. D		26. J		41. A		56. J		71. D
12. H		27. A		42. H		57. C		72. J
13. C		28. J		43. D		58. H		73. C
14. H		29. C		44. H		59. A		74. F
15. D		30. F		45. B		60. G		75. A

Usage and Mechanics (UM): _____ /55   Rhetorical Skills (RH): _____ /20   Raw Score (UM + RH): _____ /75

TEST 2: MATHEMATICS (p. 514)

MATHEMATICS TEST—ANSWER KEY

#	Ans	EA AG GT		#	Ans	EA AG GT		#	Ans	EA AG GT		#	Ans	EA AG GT
1.	C			16.	H			31.	E			46.	H	
2.	G			17.	C			32.	G			47.	C	
3.	B			18.	G			33.	C			48.	H	
4.	F			19.	B			34.	H			49.	E	
5.	A			20.	F			35.	B			50.	F	
6.	H			21.	E			36.	F			51.	B	
7.	E			22.	K			37.	D			52.	G	
8.	K			23.	E			38.	G			53.	E	
9.	D			24.	F			39.	E			54.	F	
10.	G			25.	E			40.	F			55.	A	
11.	B			26.	F			41.	E			56.	G	
12.	H			27.	B			42.	H			57.	D	
13.	E			28.	K			43.	B			58.	H	
14.	J			29.	E			44.	G			59.	A	
15.	E			30.	H			45.	A			60.	G	

Pre-Algebra/Elementary Algebra (EA): _____ /26   Plane Geometry/Trigonometry (GT): _____ /19

Int. Algebra/Coordinate Geometry (AG): _____ /15   Raw Score (EA + AG + GT): _____ /60

TEST 3: READING (p. 530)

READING TEST—ANSWER KEY

		SS	AL
1.	D		▒
2.	G		▒
3.	D		▒
4.	G		▒
5.	C		▒
6.	J		▒
7.	D		▒
8.	G		▒
9.	C		▒
10.	F		▒
11.	A	▒	
12.	J	▒	
13.	B	▒	
14.	H	▒	
15.	D	▒	

		SS	AL
16.	G	▒	
17.	A	▒	
18.	H	▒	
19.	D	▒	
20.	F	▒	
21.	B	▒	
22.	F	▒	
23.	C	▒	
24.	F	▒	
25.	C	▒	
26.	J	▒	
27.	C	▒	
28.	F	▒	
29.	C	▒	
30.	G	▒	

		SS	AL
31.	B		▒
32.	F		▒
33.	A		▒
34.	H		▒
35.	A		▒
36.	J		▒
37.	C		▒
38.	J		▒
39.	B		▒
40.	G		▒

Social Studies/Sciences (SS): _____ /20

Arts/Literature (AL): _____ /20

Raw Score (SS + AL): _____ /40

TEST 4: SCIENCE (p. 542)

SCIENCE TEST—ANSWER KEY

	B	C	P	ES
1. B				
2. H				
3. D				
4. J				
5. B				

	B	C	P	ES
6. G				
7. A				
8. J				
9. B				
10. H				
11. B				

	B	C	P	ES
12. F				
13. D				
14. J				
15. C				
16. G				

	B	C	P	ES
17. C				
18. G				
19. A				
20. J				
21. C				
22. J				

	B	C	P	ES
23. D				
24. F				
25. C				
26. H				
27. B				

	B	C	P	ES
28. G				
29. A				
30. H				
31. B				
32. H				

	B	C	P	ES
33. B				
34. H				
35. D				
36. J				
37. C				
38. H				
39. A				
40. G				

Biology (B): _____ /13   Earth/Space Sciences (ES): _____ / 6

Chemistry (C): _____ /10   Raw Score (B + C + P + ES): _____ /40

Physics (P): _____ /11

PRACTICE TEST IV EXPLANATIONS

TEST 1: ENGLISH (p. 500)

1. **(C)** *English/Usage and Mechanics/Punctuation/Semicolons.* A semicolon is used between clauses joined by a coordinating conjunction when one or more of the clauses contain commas.

2. **(J)** *English/Rhetorical Skills/Style/Conciseness.* This is redundant and not necessary to the sentence.

3. **(D)** *English/Usage and Mechanics/Grammar and Usage/Adjectives versus Adverbs.* The correct adjective is "characteristic," which means distinctive.

4. **(G)** *English/Usage and Mechanics/Grammar and Usage/Diction.* "When" is not used with "is." Replace "when" with "is that."

5. **(A)** *English/Usage and Mechanics/No Change.* The original sentence is correct. "Has become" is correct in both number and tense.

6. **(H)** *English/Rhetorical Skills/Style/Idiomatic Expression.* Numbers are generally written out, especially at the beginning of a sentence.

7. **(C)** *English/Usage and Mechanics/Grammar and Usage/Diction.* "As" is the standard usage for comparison.

8. **(F)** *English/Usage and Mechanics/Punctuation/Dashes.* The dash is used for separation and emphasis.

9. **(B)** *English/Usage and Mechanics/Punctuation/Apostrophes.* The apostrophe is used to show possession.

10. **(G)** *English/Usage and Mechanics/Punctuation/Commas.* The comma is needed for separation and clarity.

11. **(D)** *English/Usage and Mechanics/Grammar and Usage/Pronoun Usage.* "One's" is the correct possessive pronoun.

12. **(H)** *English/Usage and Mechanics/Punctuation/Quotation Marks.* Quotation marks indicate that "bowl" is used in an unusual way.

13. **(C)** *English/Rhetorical Skills/Strategy/Effective Opening Sentence.* The question gives the reader the main focus of the passage and piques his or her interest.

14. **(H)** *English/Usage and Mechanics/Grammar and Usage/Adjectives versus Adverbs.* The correct adjective is "distinguished," which means separated from others by extraordinary qualities.

15. **(D)** *English/Usage and Mechanics/Punctuation/Quotation Marks.* The quoted material is the words of the imaginative Italian observer mentioned in the second sentence.

16. **(F)** *English/Usage and Mechanics/No Change.* "Easily" is the correct adverb modifying the verb "die."

17. **(B)** *English/Usage and Mechanics/Grammar and Usage/Diction.* "Likely" should be used to indicate probability. "Like" is incorrect as it is used in the original.

18. **(J)** *English/Rhetorical Skills/Style/Conciseness.* This is redundant and not necessary since sociologists, by definition, study sociology.

19. **(D)** *English/Usage and Mechanics/Grammar and Usage/Diction.* "Those kind of" is a nonstandard expression. "Those" is plural and "kind" is singular.

20. **(H)** *English/Usage and Mechanics/Grammar and Usage/Diction.* The correct adverb is "around."

21. **(A)** *English/Usage and Mechanics/No Change.* The original sentence is correct. The verb "compared" continues the past tense used throughout the sentence.

22. **(J)** *English/Usage and Mechanics/Punctuation/Commas.* Commas are used to separate items in a list.

23. **(A)** *English/Rhetorical Skills/Strategy/Audience.* Criminology is a topic in the study of sociology, but the passage is not technical in nature; thus, (B) is wrong. (C) is too general, while (D) is too specific.

24. **(H)** *English/Rhetorical Skills/Organization/Passage-Level Structure.* [1] refers to the nineteenth century, [3] to the turn of the century, and [2] to the twentieth century.

25. **(C)** *English/Usage and Mechanics/Grammar and Usage/Subject-Verb Agreement.* "Shows" is necessary for agreement with the singular subject "history."

26. **(J)** *English/Usage and Mechanics/Grammar and Usage/Diction.* "In depth" is the correct prepositional phrase.

27. **(A)** *English/Usage and Mechanics/No Change.* The original sentence is correct. "Effects" is the noun that means "results."

28. **(J)** *English/Rhetorical Skills/Strategy/Appropriate Supporting Material.* This information has no relevance to the paragraph, so it should be omitted.

29. **(C)** *English/Usage and Mechanics/Punctuation/Commas.* A comma is used to separate words, phrases, or clauses in a series.

30. **(F)** *English/Rhetorical Skills/Strategy/Appropriate Supporting Material.* An example of the risks being discussed would make the discussion more concrete to the reader.

31. **(A)** *English/Usage and Mechanics/No Change.* The original sentence is correct. "An" is used before a word beginning with a vowel.

32. **(J)** *English/Usage and Mechanics/Grammar and Usage/Diction.* "Neither" agrees with "nor" in the sentence.

33. **(B)** *English/Rhetorical Skills/Style/Conciseness.* "And years to come" is redundant and not necessary to the sentence.

34. **(G)** *English/Usage and Mechanics/Grammar and Usage/Nouns and Noun Clauses.* "Persistence" is the correct noun.

35. **(D)** *English/Usage and Mechanics/Grammar and Usage/Diction.* "Compared" is the correct verb and "to" is the correct preposition.

36. **(G)** *English/Usage and Mechanics/Punctuation/Punctuating for Clarity.* No punctuation is necessary.

37. **(A)** *English/Rhetorical Skills/Organization/Passage-Level Structure.* The original order is correct. [1] introduces the topic of the entire essay: modern pollution problems—therefore, only (A) and (C) need to be considered. [2] begins with "these arguments," which refers to arguments previously mentioned. Only (A) has [2] arranged before [3], so (A) is the correct choice.

38. **(H)** *English/Rhetorical Skills/Strategy/Audience.* The passage discusses pollution problems, not a history of technology; thus, (F) is wrong. Because the information presented is general, not technical in nature, (G) is also wrong. (J) is too narrow; the passage covers radioactive substances and more.

39. **(B)** *English/Usage and Mechanics/Grammar and Usage/Diction.* "Remaining" is the correct gerund. The addition of "around" or "up" is unnecessary.

40. **(J)** *English/Usage and Mechanics/Grammar and Usage/Diction.* Use of "of had" in place of "have had" is nonstandard. "Maybe" is an adverb, not a verb.

41. **(A)** *English/Usage and Mechanics/No Change.* The original sentence is correct. "Most" is used correctly to modify the adjective "able."

42. **(H)** *English/Usage and Mechanics/Punctuation/Commas.* Commas are used to set off adverbs that compare or contrast some preceding idea.

43. **(D)** *English/Usage and Mechanics/Grammar and Usage/Diction.* "Disrepute" is the correct noun. It means having a bad reputation.

44. **(H)** *English/Usage and Mechanics/Grammar and Usage/Pronoun Usage.* The singular pronoun "his or her" is needed for agreement with the singular noun "researcher."

45. **(B)** *English/Rhetorical Skills/Strategy/Appropriate Supporting Material.* The paragraph discusses a theory about the usefulness of the researcher after age 40. Thus, discussing contributions of older researchers would now be appropriate. (A) and (D) are irrelevant; (C) is too general. The correct answer is (B).

46. **(J)** *English/Rhetorical Skills/Style/Conciseness.* "Of long ago" is redundant and not necessary to the sentence.

47. **(B)** *English/Usage and Mechanics/Grammar and Usage/Diction.* "Be considered" is the correct verb phrase.

48. **(F)** *English/Usage and Mechanics/No Change.* "In" is the correct preposition.

49. **(D)** *English/Rhetorical Skills/Organization/Passage-Level Structure.* The most logical order is to contrast views of creativity in the past [3] with those of the present [2] and [1], and then of salary guideposts in the past [4] to those of today [5].

50. **(H)** *English/Usage and Mechanics/Punctuation/Dashes.* The correct answer is (H). "However brilliant" should be emphasized.

51. **(B)** *English/Usage and Mechanics/Grammar and Usage/Pronoun Usage.* "Who" is correct as the subject of the verb phrase "have chosen."

52. **(F)** *English/Usage and Mechanics/Punctuation/End-Stop Punctuation.* Question marks are used after direct questions.

53. **(D)** *English/Usage and Mechanics/Grammar and Usage/Faulty or Illogical Comparisons.* "Greater" is the correct comparative adjective. "Greatest" is in the superlative and is not required in this sentence.

54. **(G)** *English/Usage and Mechanics/Grammar and Usage/Diction.* "Through," meaning "by means of," is the correct preposition. "Threw" is the past tense of the verb "throw."

55. **(D)** *English/Rhetorical Skills/Style/Conciseness.* "In the past" is redundant.

56. **(J)** *English/Usage and Mechanics/Grammar and Usage/Diction.* The conjunction "that" is the only word needed to introduce the clause that follows.

57. **(C)** *English/Usage and Mechanics/Sentence Structure/Problems of Coordination and Subordination.* "But" establishes the contrast between the two clauses and parallels the construction of the previous sentence.

58. **(H)** *English/Usage and Mechanics/Grammar and Usage/Diction.* "Rising," which means "moving upward," is correct. "Raising" means "causing to move upward."

59. **(A)** *English/Rhetorical Skills/No Change.* The original sentence is correct. "Quite the contrary" is the only phrase that makes sense in the sentence.

60. **(G)** *English/Rhetorical Skills/Strategy/Appropriate Supporting Material.* The paragraph discusses the contributions that science and engineering have made. Therefore, specific examples are appropriate.

61. **(A)** *English/Usage and Mechanics/No Change.* The original sentence is correct. No punctuation is required here.

62. **(H)** *English/Rhetorical Skills/Strategy/Audience.* The passage is concerned with solving problems in the fields of science and engineering. It begins by addressing those who have chosen these fields.

63. **(B)** *English/Rhetorical Skills/Organization/Passage-Level Structure.* [1] introduces the main concern of this section. [4], [2], and [3] begin with "first," "second," and "third," respectively. [5] summarizes the author's point of view and is the conclusion.

64. **(J)** *English/Usage and Mechanics/Grammar and Usage/Subject-Verb Agreement.* The singular subject "youth" requires the singular verb "is."

65. **(D)** *English/Usage and Mechanics/Grammar and Usage/Pronoun Usage.* "This here" is nonstandard usage for the pronoun "this."

66. **(H)** *English/Usage and Mechanics/Grammar and Usage/Diction.* "Similarities" is not completed by "from." It requires the preposition "to" ("similarities to" the American market).

67. **(C)** *English/Usage and Mechanics/Punctuation/Apostrophes.* "Market's" is the correct possessive. The apostrophe followed by an "s" is used to show singular possession.

68. **(G)** *English/Usage and Mechanics/Grammar and Usage/Adjectives versus Adverbs.* The adverb "increasingly" correctly modifies the adjective "high."

69. **(B)** *English/Usage and Mechanics/Punctuation/End-Stop Punctuation.* The use of the comma creates a run-on sentence. The two sentences must be separated by a period, and then "generally" must be capitalized and also followed by a comma.

70. **(F)** *English/Usage and Mechanics/No Change.* "Transatlantic" is one word and an adjective, not a noun. No capitalization or hyphenation is necessary.

71. **(D)** *English/Usage and Mechanics/Grammar and Usage/Diction.* "Adopted," meaning "to have taken up and practice as one's own," is the correct verb. "Adapted" means "to have adjusted."

72. **(J)** *English/Usage and Mechanics/Grammar and Usage/Diction.* "Between" is used for two persons or things and "among" and "amongst" are used for more than two persons or things.

73. **(C)** *English/Usage and Mechanics/Punctuation/Quotation Marks.* The correct answer is (C). Words in quotation marks have meanings that are specific to the context of this essay.

74. **(F)** *English/Rhetorical Skills/Strategy/Audience.* The passage deals with the youth markets of Western Europe and America; therefore, its readers would probably be people who are interested in the consumer patterns of youth worldwide.

75. **(A)** *English/Usage and Mechanics/Punctuation/Dashes.* The original sentence is correct. The dash sets off an illustration.

TEST 2: MATHEMATICS (p. 514)

1. **(C)** *Mathematics/Arithmetic/Simple Manipulations.* Two numbers that add up to zero are additive inverses. $(a)+(-a)=0$. The additive inverse is the opposite of the original value. $\frac{2}{3}$ is the additive inverse of $-\frac{2}{3}$.

2. **(G)** *Mathematics/Geometry/Lines and Angles* and *Circles.* $\angle AOC$ is a central angle and equals 70°. A central angle is equal to its intercepted arc. $\overarc{AC}=70°$. An inscribed angle is equal to one-half the measure of its intercepted arc. The measure of $\angle ABC = \frac{1}{2}m \cdot (\overarc{AC}) \Rightarrow \angle ABC = 35°$.

3. **(B)** *Mathematics/Algebra/Solving Quadratic Equations.* $x^2 + 6x + 8 = 0 \Rightarrow (x+4)(x+2) = 0 \Rightarrow x+4 = 0$ or $x + 2 = 0$. Therefore, $x = -4$ or -2.

4. **(F)** *Mathematics/Geometry/Lines and Angles.*

The measure of $\angle b$ is 70°, and because it is an alternate interior angle with $\angle x$. The measure of $\angle a$ is 75° because it is the supplement of $\angle y$. The three angles form a triangle: $\angle r + \angle a + \angle b = 180°$. Thus, $\angle r + 75° + 70° = 180° \Rightarrow \angle r = 35°$.

5. **(A)** *Mathematics/Algebra/Manipulating Algebraic Expressions/Evaluating Expressions.* $A = \frac{2gr}{g+r} \Rightarrow 4 = \frac{2g(1)}{g+(1)} \Rightarrow 4 = \frac{2g}{g+1}$. Cross-multiply: $4(g+1) = 2g \Rightarrow 4g+4 = 2g \Rightarrow 2g = -4 \Rightarrow g = -2$.

6. **(H)** *Mathematics/Coordinate Geometry/Graphs of Linear Equations.* V-shaped graphs usually indicate absolute value functions. Substitute the given coordinates (2,2), (0,0), and (−3,3) into the answer choices: only $y = |x|$ satisfies all the ordered pairs.

7. **(E)** *Mathematics/Algebra/Manipulating Algebraic Expressions/Basic Algebraic Manipulations.* The distributive property indicates multiplication over addition $[a(b+c) = ab+ac]$ and multiplication over subtraction $[a(b-c) = ab-ac]$. Thus, $x(x+2) = x^2 + 2x$.

8. **(K)** *Mathematics/Arithmetic/Common Arithmetic Items/Percents.* The sales tax is 7% of $600: $\frac{7}{100} \cdot 600 = \frac{7(600)}{100} = \$42$. Thus, the total cost is $\$600 + \$42 = \$642$.

9. **(D)** *Mathematics/Algebra/Expressing and Evaluating Algebraic Functions/Function Notation.* Substitute the value −1 for x: $-x^2 - 2x^3 \Rightarrow -(-1)^2 - 2(-1)^3 = -(1) - 2(-1) = -1 + 2 = 1$.

10. **(G)** *Mathematics/Statistics and Probability/Averages.* The average is the sum of the numbers divided by the quantity of numbers:

$$\text{average} = \frac{(n+3) + (2n-1) + (3n+4)}{3} = \frac{6n+6}{3} = 2n+2$$

11. **(B)** *Mathematics/Algebra/Manipulating Algebraic Expressions/Evaluating Expressions.* Substitute 9 for x: $x^0 + x^{\frac{1}{2}} + x^{-2} = 9^0 + 9^{\frac{1}{2}} + 9^{-2} = 1 + \sqrt{9} + \frac{1}{9^2} = 1 + 3 + \frac{1}{81} = 4\frac{1}{81}$.

12. **(H)** *Mathematics/Arithmetic/Simple Manipulations.* In order to add radicals, the number in the square root must be the same: $4\sqrt{3} + 3\sqrt{27} = 4\sqrt{3} + 3(3\sqrt{3}) = 4\sqrt{3} + 9\sqrt{3} = 13\sqrt{3}$.

13. **(E)** *Mathematics/Statistics and Probability/Averages.* The average is the sum of the test scores divided by the quantity of tests:

$$\text{average} = 90 = \frac{87 + 93 + 86 + x}{4} \Rightarrow 4(90) = 87 + 93 + 86 + x \Rightarrow 360 = 266 + x \Rightarrow x = 94$$

14. **(J)** *Mathematics/Algebra/Manipulating Algebraic Expressions/Creating Algebraic Expressions.* Each dime is 10 cents. Three dimes would be $3(10) = 30$ cents. $4x$ dimes would be $4x(10) = 40x$ cents.

15. **(E)** *Mathematics/Arithmetic/Simple Manipulations.* The shaded circle at -5 indicates either $\geq$ or $\leq$, and the unshaded circle at 3 indicates either $>$ or $<$, without the equal sign. The arrow pointing to the left, $<$, indicates "less than," and the arrow pointing to the right, $>$, indicates "greater than." The graph indicates $x \leq -5$ or $x > 3$. The answers are connected by "or." Therefore, the answer is $x \leq -5$ or $x > 3$.

16. **(H)** *Mathematics/Arithmetic/Simple Manipulations.* $2\frac{2}{5} - 1\frac{7}{8} = \frac{12}{5} - \frac{15}{8}$. The lowest common denominator is 40. Thus, $\frac{12}{5} - \frac{15}{8} = \frac{96}{40} - \frac{75}{40} = \frac{21}{40}$.

17. **(C)** *Mathematics/Geometry/Circles.* Circumference $= 2\pi r = 2\pi(6) = 12\pi$. 2π is $\frac{2\pi}{12\pi} = \frac{1}{6}$ of the circumference. In turn, the central angle is $\frac{1}{6}(360°) = 60°$ or $\frac{\text{arc length}}{\text{circumference}} = \frac{x°}{360°} \Rightarrow \frac{2\pi}{12\pi} = \frac{x}{360} \Rightarrow \frac{1}{6} = \frac{x}{360} \Rightarrow 6x = 360 \Rightarrow x = 60$.

18. **(G)** *Mathematics/Algebra/Solving Algebraic Equations or Inequalities with One Variable/Equations Involving Rational Expressions* and *Equations Involving Radical Expressions.* $\frac{2x}{3\sqrt{2}} = \frac{3\sqrt{2}}{x} \Rightarrow 2x(x) = (3\sqrt{2})(3\sqrt{2}) \Rightarrow 2x^2 = 9(2) = 18 \Rightarrow x^2 = 9 \Rightarrow x = \pm 3$. The positive value of x is 3.

19. **(B)** *Mathematics/Algebra/Expressing and Evaluating Algebraic Functions/Function Notation.* $f(x) = 2x - x^2 \Rightarrow f(2) = 2(2) - (2)^2 = 4 - 4 = 0$. $g(x) = x - 4 \Rightarrow g(0) = 0 - 4 = -4$. Therefore, $g(f(2)) = g(0) = -4$.

20. **(F)** *Mathematics/Algebra/Solving Algebraic Equations or Inequalities with One Variable/Equations Involving Absolute Value.* Since 7 is set equal to the absolute value of the equation involving x ($7 = |5 - 2x|$), then $5 - 2x = \pm 7$. Solve for the possible values of x: $5 - 2x = -7 \Rightarrow -2x = -12 \Rightarrow x = 6$ and $5 - 2x = -7 \Rightarrow -2x = 2 \Rightarrow x = -1$. Therefore, the possible solution set is $\{6, -1\}$, (F).

21. **(E)** *Mathematics/Algebra/Manipulating Algebraic Expressions/Evaluating Expressions.* Multiply the top and bottom of the fraction by the lowest common denominator, which is x:

$$\frac{x(3 - \frac{3}{x})}{x(x-1)} = \frac{x(3) - x(\frac{3}{x})}{x(x-1)} = \frac{3x - 3}{x(x-1)} = \frac{3(x-1)}{x(x-1)} = \frac{3}{x}$$

22. **(K)** *Mathematics/Coordinate Geometry/Slope of a Line.* Slope $= m = \frac{y_2 - y_1}{x_2 - x_1} = \frac{7 - 5}{4 - (-3)} = \frac{2}{7}$.

23. **(E)** *Mathematics/Geometry/Circles* and *Triangles/Pythagorean Theorem.*

A diameter drawn perpendicular to the chord bisects the chord. Therefore, $\overline{AB}$ bisects $\overline{CD}$. A constructed radius $\overline{OC}$ forms right ΔOEC with $\overline{OC}$ as the hypotenuse. Since $\overline{OE} = 3$ inches and $\overline{CE} = 4$ inches, use the Pythagorean theorem:

$$(\text{Hypotenuse})^2 = (\text{Leg}_1)^2 + (\text{Leg}_2)^2 \Rightarrow (\overline{OC})^2 = (\overline{OE})^2 + (\overline{CE})^2 \Rightarrow x^2 = 3^2 + 4^2 \Rightarrow x^2 = 25 \Rightarrow x = 5$$

24. **(F)** *Mathematics/Geometry.*

The diagonals of a parallelogram bisect each other. $\overline{DB} = 2(\overline{DE}) \Rightarrow 4x + 2 = 2(x + 4) \Rightarrow 4x + 2 = 2x + 8 \Rightarrow 2x = 6 \Rightarrow x = 3$.

25. **(E)** *Mathematics/Geometry/Lines and Angles* and *Circles.*

$\frac{\text{area of sector}}{\text{area of circle}} = \frac{\text{central angle}}{360°} \Rightarrow \frac{x}{\pi r^2} = \frac{120°}{360°} \Rightarrow \frac{x}{36\pi} = \frac{1}{3} \Rightarrow 3x = 36\pi \Rightarrow x = 12\pi$.

26. **(F)** *Mathematics/Geometry/Triangles.* If a statement is true, its contrapositive must be true. If the original statement is $p \Rightarrow q$, the contrapositive is "not $q \Rightarrow$ not p."

27. **(B)** *Mathematics/Algebra/Manipulating Algebraic Expressions/Basic Algebraic Manipulations.* Compare all the answer choices to the original using cross-multiplication. The original is: $\frac{a}{b} = \frac{r}{t} \Rightarrow at = br$.

    A. $\frac{a}{r} = \frac{b}{t} \Rightarrow at = br$ ✓

    B. $\frac{a}{t} = \frac{b}{r} \Rightarrow ar = bt$ ✗

    C. $\frac{a+b}{b} = \frac{r+t}{t}$

        $t(a+b) = b(r+t)$

        $at + bt = br + bt$

        $at = br$ ✓

    D. $\frac{b}{a} = \frac{t}{r} \Rightarrow at = br$ ✓

    E. $at = br$ ✓

28. **(K)** *Mathematics/Algebra/Solving Algebraic Equations or Inequalities with One Variable/Simple Equations.* $-2x + 5 = 2 - (5 - 2x) = 2 - 5 + 2x = -3 + 2x \Rightarrow 5 = -3 + 4x \Rightarrow 8 = 4x \Rightarrow x = 2$.

29. **(E)** *Mathematics/Trigonometry/Trigonometric Relationships.* $\frac{[1 + \sin(x)][1 - \sin(x)]}{[1 + \cos(x)][1 - \cos(x)]} = \frac{1 - \sin(x) + \sin(x) - \sin^2(x)}{1 - \cos(x) + \cos(x) - \cos^2(x)} = \frac{1 - \sin^2(x)}{1 - \cos^2(x)}$. Since $\sin^2(x) + \cos^2(x) = 1$, $\sin^2(x) = 1 - \cos^2(x)$ and $\cos^2(x) = 1 - \sin^2(x)$. Therefore, by substitution: $\frac{1 - \sin^2(x)}{1 - \cos^2(x)} = \frac{\cos^2(x)}{\sin^2(x)} = \cot^2(x)$.

30. **(H)** *Mathematics/Geometry/Triangles/Working with Triangles.* The median to the hypotenuse of a right triangle is equal in length to half the hypotenuse: $\overline{BE} = \overline{AE} = \overline{CE}$.

31. **(E)** *Mathematics/Arithmetic/Common Arithmetic Items/Proportions and Direct-Inverse Variation.* y varies directly as x: $\frac{y_1}{x_1} = \frac{y_2}{x_2}$. Therefore, $\frac{10}{\frac{1}{5}} = \frac{y}{\frac{1}{2}} \Rightarrow 10(5) = y(2) \Rightarrow 50 = 2y \Rightarrow y = 25$.

32. **(G)** *Mathematics/Arithmetic/Complicated Manipulations/Simplifying.* $\frac{(-1)(2)(-3)(4)(-5)}{(5)(-4)(3)(-2)(1)} = \frac{-120}{120} = -1$.

33. **(C)** *Mathematics/Geometry/Circles.* The product of the segments of one chord is equal to the product of the segments of the other.

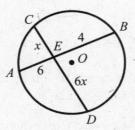

$\overline{CE} \cdot \overline{ED} = \overline{AE} \cdot \overline{EB} \Rightarrow x(6x) = 6(4) \Rightarrow 6x^2 = 24 \Rightarrow x^2 = 4 \Rightarrow x = \pm 2$. Lengths are positive, so $x = 2$.

34. **(H)** *Mathematics/Geometry/Triangles/Working with Triangles* and *Lines and Angles.* An isosceles triangle has two equal sides and two equal base angles: $50 + x + x = 180 \Rightarrow 50 + 2x = 180 \Rightarrow 2x = 130 \Rightarrow x = 65$.

35. **(B)** *Mathematics/Statistics and Probability/Median.* The median is the "middle" data element when the data are arranged in numerical order: 20, 20, 20, 20, 30, 30, 30, 30, 50, 50, 50, 50, 50, 50, 50. The "middle" data element is 30.

36. **(F)** *Mathematics/Algebra/Solving Quadratic Equations.* $x^2 - 2x - 3 > 0 \Rightarrow (x-3)(x+1) > 0$. This is true for two situations: $(+) \cdot (+)$ and $(-) \cdot (-)$. $|x-3|$ is positive for $x > 3$ and negative for $x < 3$. $x+1$ is positive for $x > -1$ and negative for $x < -1$. Therefore, the two situations for which $(x-3) \cdot (x+1) > 0$ are $(x > 3)(x > -1)$ and $(x < 3)(x < -1)$. To keep both parentheses true in each situation, x must be larger than 3 or less than -1. This is two intervals: numbers less than -1 and numbers greater than $+3$, (F).

37. **(D)** *Mathematics/Trigonometry/Trigonometric Relationships.* To evaluate $\frac{\sin(x)}{1}$, a common denominator is required in order to add the fractions. The lowest common denominator is $\sin x$: $\frac{\sin(x)}{1} \cdot \frac{\sin(x)}{\sin(x)} + \frac{\cos^2(x)}{\sin(x)} = \frac{\sin^2(x)}{\sin(x)} + \frac{\cos^2(x)}{\sin(x)} = \frac{\sin^2(x) + \cos^2(x)}{\sin(x)}$. Since $\sin^2(x) + \cos^2(x) = 1$, the expression reduces to $\frac{1}{\sin(x)}$.

38. **(G)** *Mathematics/Arithmetic/Simple Manipulations.* $(2.5 \cdot 10^5)^2 = (2.5 \cdot 10^5)(2.5 \cdot 10^5) = 6.25 \cdot 10^{10}$.

39. **(E)** *Mathematics/Algebra/Expressing and Evaluating Algebraic Functions/Function Notation.* $A * B = \frac{AB - B}{-B} \Rightarrow -2 * 2 = \frac{(-2)(2) - 2}{-2} = \frac{-4 - 2}{-2} = \frac{-6}{-2} = 3$.

40. **(F)** *Mathematics/Algebra/Solving Quadratic Equations.* Substitute the root into the equation for the value of x: $0 = x^2 + kx - 12 = (4)^2 + k(4) - 12 = 16 + 4k - 12 = 4k + 4 \Rightarrow 4k = -4 \Rightarrow k = -1$.

41. **(E)** *Mathematics/Geometry/Triangles/Working with Triangles.* $\triangle ABC$ and $\triangle DBE$ are similar; create a proportion between the sides of the two triangles. If $\overline{AB} = 10$ and $\overline{DB} = 4$, $\overline{DA} = 6$; if $\overline{BC} = 20$ and $\overline{EC} = x$, $\overline{BE} = 20 - x$.

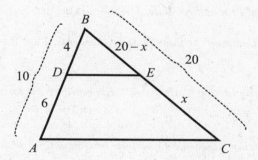

Therefore, $\frac{4}{10} = \frac{20 - x}{20} \Rightarrow 80 = 200 - 10x \Rightarrow 10x = 120 \Rightarrow x = 12$.

42. **(H)** *Mathematics/Algebra/Manipulating Algebraic Expressions/Basic Algebraic Manipulations.* Evaluate the expression using the FOIL (First, Outer, Inner, Last) method: $(x+2)(x-4) - (x+4)(x-2) = x^2 - 4x + 2x - 8 - (x^2 - 2x + 4x - 8) = x^2 - 2x - 8 - x^2 + 2x - 4x + 8 = (x^2 - x^2) + (-2x + 2x - 4x) + (-8 + 8) = -4x$.

43. **(B)** *Mathematics/Geometry/Lines and Angles.* The sum of the measures of the exterior angles of a polygon is $360°$ for all polygons. The sum of the measures of the interior angles of a polygon can be expressed as $180°(n-2)$, where n is the number of sides. Therefore, $180(n-2) = 360 \Rightarrow n-2 = 2 \Rightarrow n = 4$.

44. **(G)** *Mathematics/Geometry/Triangles/Working with Triangles.* If the perimeter is 12, then each side of the triangle is: $\frac{12}{3} = 4$. $\text{Area}_{\text{triangle}} = \frac{1}{2}(\text{base})(\text{height})$, so draw a figure:

Use the Pythagorean theorem to solve for h: $2^2 + h^2 = 4^2 \Rightarrow h^2 = 16 - 4 = 12 \Rightarrow h = \sqrt{12} = 2\sqrt{3}$. $\text{Area}_{\text{triangle}} = \frac{1}{2}(\text{base})(\text{height}) = \frac{1}{2}(4)(2\sqrt{3}) = 4\sqrt{3}$.

45. **(A)** *Mathematics/Geometry/Lines and Angles.* Let $8x$ equal one angle and x equal the other angle. Since complementary angles add to $90°$, $8x + x = 90 \Rightarrow 9x = 90 \Rightarrow x = 10$.

46. **(H)** *Mathematics/Statistics and Probability/Probability.* A square has four right angles; a rectangle has four right angles; a trapezoid does not have four right angles; a circle has no angles. Thus, the probability of four right angles is $\frac{\#\,\text{of successes}}{\#\,\text{of possibilities}} = \frac{2}{4} = \frac{1}{2}$.

47. **(C)** *Mathematics/Arithmetic/Common Arithmetic Items/Proportions and Direct-Inverse Variation.* Distance = rate $\cdot$ time $\Rightarrow$ rate $= \frac{\text{distance}}{\text{time}} \Rightarrow \frac{320\text{ miles}}{8\text{ hours}} = 40$ miles per hour. Therefore, the distance traveled in two hours is 40 miles per hour $\cdot$ 2 hours = 80 miles.

48. **(H)** *Mathematics/Trigonometry/Trigonometric Relationships.* Use the common denominator, $\sin(x) \cdot \cos(x)$, to simplify the expression: $\frac{\sin(x)}{\cos(x)} \cdot \frac{\sin(x)}{\sin(x)} + \frac{\cos(x)}{\sin(x)} \cdot \frac{\cos(x)}{\cos(x)} = \frac{\sin^2(x)}{\sin(x)\cos(x)} + \frac{\cos^2(x)}{\sin(x)\cos(x)} = \frac{\sin^2(x) + \cos^2(x)}{\sin(x)\cos(x)} = \frac{1}{\sin(x)\cos(x)}$.

49. **(E)** *Mathematics/Statistics and Probability/Mode.* The mode is the data element with the greatest frequency: $91°$.

50. **(F)** *Mathematics/Arithmetic/Common Arithmetic Items/Percents.* Find the percentage: $\frac{\text{part}}{\text{whole}} \cdot 100 = \frac{9}{30} \cdot 100 = 30\%$.

51. **(B)** *Mathematics/Algebra/Manipulating Algebraic Expressions/Factoring Expressions.* Rearrange the expression and then factor: $-7t + 6t^2 - 3 = 6t^2 - 7t - 3 = (3t + 1)(2t - 3)$.

52. **(G)** *Mathematics/Algebra/Solving Algebraic Equations or Inequalities with One Variable/Equations Involving Integer and Rational Exponents.* If $2^{x^2 + 2x} = 2^{-1}$, then $x^2 + 2x = -1$. Therefore, $x^2 + 2x + 1 = (x + 1)(x + 1) = 0$. This equation holds true only if $x = -1$.

53. **(E)** *Mathematics/Algebra/Manipulating Algebraic Expressions/Evaluating Expressions.* If Joshua is x years old now and Jessica is 3 years younger, then Jessica is now $x - 3$ years old. Four years ago she was $(x - 3) - 4 = x - 7$ years old.

54. **(F)** *Mathematics/Algebra/Manipulating Algebraic Expressions/Creating Algebraic Expressions.* The amount collected is equal to the number of students multiplied by the amount that each student contributed. Therefore, $(x)(y) = 18$ and $(x + 3)(y - 1) = 18$.

55. **(A)** *Mathematics/Arithmetic/Complicated Manipulations/Simplifying.* $\frac{1}{2}\sqrt{112} = \frac{1}{2}(\sqrt{16})(\sqrt{7}) = \frac{1}{2}(4)(\sqrt{7}) = 2\sqrt{7}$. $\sqrt{28} = \sqrt{4}\sqrt{7} = 2\sqrt{7}$. $2\sqrt{63} = 2(\sqrt{9})(\sqrt{7}) = 2(3)(\sqrt{7}) = 6\sqrt{7}$. Thus, $2\sqrt{7} - 2\sqrt{7} + 6\sqrt{7} = 6\sqrt{7}$.

56. **(G)** *Mathematics/Algebra/Solving Simultaneous Equations.* Add the two equations:

$$\begin{array}{r} \frac{1}{x} + \frac{1}{y} = \frac{1}{4} \\ + \quad \frac{1}{x} - \frac{1}{y} = \frac{3}{4} \\ \hline \frac{2}{x} = 1 \Rightarrow x = 2 \end{array}$$

57. **(D)** *Mathematics/Geometry/Triangles/Working with Triangles.* The sum of the lengths of any two sides of a triangle must exceed the length of the third side. Check each of the answer choices:

$$
\begin{array}{lll}
\text{A.} & 1+3 > 6 & \textbf{✗} \\
\text{B.} & 2+4 > 7 & \textbf{✗} \\
\text{C.} & 2+10 > 12 & \textbf{✗} \\
\text{D.} & 4+6 > 8 & \\
 & 4+8 > 6 & \\
 & 6+8 > 4 & \textbf{✓} \\
\text{E.} & 4+4 > 10 & \textbf{✗}
\end{array}
$$

58. **(H)** *Mathematics/Algebra/Solving Simultaneous Equations.* To eliminate the variable y, multiply the first equation by -1 and add the equations:

$$
\begin{array}{l}
-1(ax + y = b) \\
+\ 2ax + y = 2b \\
\hline
ax = b \Rightarrow x = \frac{b}{a}
\end{array}
$$

Substitute the value of x into the first equation and solve for y: $ax + y = b \Rightarrow a(\frac{b}{a}) + y = b \Rightarrow b + y = b \Rightarrow y = 0$. The solution set is $\left\{ \frac{b}{a}, 0 \right\}$.

59. **(A)** *Mathematics/Trigonometry/Determining Trigonometric Values* and *Geometry/Triangles/Pythagorean Theorem.* From the given information, draw a figure:

The third side of the triangle, x, is found using the Pythagorean theorem: $x^2 + r^2 = 4^2 = 16 \Rightarrow x^2 = 16 - r^2 \Rightarrow x = \sqrt{16 - r^2}$. Since $\cos(\theta) = \frac{\text{side adjacent to } \theta}{\text{hypotenuse}}$, $\cos(\theta) = \frac{\sqrt{16 - r^2}}{4}$.

60. **(G)** *Mathematics/Arithmetic/Common Arithmetic Items/Proportions and Direct-Inverse Variation.* The number of sheets is directly proportional to the number of machines, as well as directly proportional to the amount of time. Thus, $\left(\frac{\text{sheets}}{\text{\# of machines} \cdot \text{time}} \right)_1 = \left(\frac{\text{sheets}}{\text{\# of machines} \cdot \text{time}} \right)_2 \Rightarrow \frac{300}{3(3)} = \frac{600}{6(t)} \Rightarrow \frac{300}{9} = \frac{600}{6t} \Rightarrow \frac{100}{3} = \frac{100}{t} \Rightarrow 100t = 300 \Rightarrow t = 3$.

TEST 3: READING (p. 530)

1. **(D)** *Reading/Natural Sciences/Explicit Detail.* In the fourth paragraph, lines 43–44 state that x-rays are found at wavelengths shorter than 100 Å, the lower end of ultraviolet radiation, (I). Lines 39–41 state that infrared radiation, (II), has wavelengths longer than 7,000 Å. Since (I), (II), and (III) are true, the answer is (D).

2. **(G)** *Reading/Natural Sciences/Explicit Detail.* As stated in lines 49–51, short wavelengths contain a high amount of energy, which makes them more dangerous than long wavelengths.

3. **(D)** *Reading/Natural Sciences/Explicit Detail.* This definition appears in lines 65–67.

4. **(G)** *Reading/Natural Sciences/Main Idea.* The first line of the paragraph states this main idea.

5. **(C)** *Reading/Natural Sciences/Explicit Detail.* The figure shows that the visible spectrum ranges from 4,000 Å to 7,000 Å.

6. **(J)** *Reading/Natural Sciences/Explicit Detail.* Line 94 states that T refers to temperature: "…the temperature raised to the fourth power."

7. **(D)** *Reading/Natural Sciences/Explicit Detail.* Lines 75–85 refer to the temperature of stars. Line 81 states that "a hot star looks blue."

8. **(G)** *Reading/Natural Sciences/Explicit Detail.* Returning to lines 55–59 provides the answer to this question.

9. **(C)** *Reading/Natural Sciences/Explicit Detail.* (A) is never discussed. (B) is certainly not true, as the caption of the figure proves, and (D) is directly contradicted by the graph. Only (C) is true.

10. **(F)** *Reading/Natural Sciences/Application.* As stated in lines 96–98: "doubling an object's temperature would radiate 16 times more energy."

11. **(A)** *Reading/Prose Fiction/Main Idea.* Only the first choice explains the subtitle. The other choices may be included under the idea "A Study in Temperament," but they are not the main idea.

12. **(J)** *Reading/Prose Fiction/Implied Idea.* Paul is shown in a very unsympathetic light; one of the interesting things about this passage is the lack of sentiment in the description. Paul is plainly unpleasant, and even the narrator dislikes him.

13. **(B)** *Reading/Prose Fiction/Explicit Detail.* The first paragraph focuses on the faculty's feeling that Paul's dress and behavior are not properly contrite.

14. **(H)** *Reading/Prose Fiction/Vocabulary.* Paul seems to be unable to control his odd mannerisms, but he is not actually frenzied, as (F), (G), or (J) would suggest.

15. **(D)** *Reading/Prose Fiction/Implied Idea.* It is the inability to hide his contempt for others that has landed Paul in trouble, as evidenced in lines 40–51.

16. **(G)** *Reading/Prose Fiction/Explicit Detail.* The faculty "fell upon him without mercy, his English teacher leading the pack" (lines 54–55). The comparison is to a pack of wolves.

17. **(A)** *Reading/Prose Fiction/Implied Idea.* "Older boys than Paul had broken down and shed tears under that baptism of fire" (lines 59–61). Paul has just undergone an inquisition by the faculty and has borne up without crying, unlike many other students.

18. **(H)** *Reading/Prose Fiction/Vocabulary.* All of these choices could mean "smartness," but only "impudence" makes sense in context.

19. **(D)** *Reading/Prose Fiction/Implied Idea.* There is evidence for every other choice in the descriptions of Paul's actions. The point is made in lines 25–27 that Paul often lies; he cannot be called "candid."

20. **(F)** *Reading/Prose Fiction/Implied Idea.* Paul is physically revolted by the faculty, not vice versa, (J). The faculty's attack on Paul indicates their hatred for him.

21. **(B)** *Reading/Humanities/Implied Idea.* Jupiter is being asked to decide which of three goddesses is the fairest—it is a no-win decision since it is bound to anger two of the three.

22. **(F)** *Reading/Humanities/Vocabulary.* Ulysses has no inclination to embark on the adventure since he is happy at home with his family.

23. **(C)** *Reading/Humanities/Voice.* Venus, one of the characters in the narrative, selected Helen as "the fairest of her sex." The other assertions are all opinions of the author.

24. **(F)** *Reading/Humanities/Implied Idea.* "Ulysses pretended to be mad" (lines 41–42), and one of the methods he chose was to hitch a mismatched team and sow something that could not grow.

25. **(C)** *Reading/Humanities/Implied Idea.* Palamedes does not buy Ulysses' mad act; he thinks up a way to test him. Since Ulysses is unwilling to run over his own son, he is obviously not as mad as he pretends to be.

26. **(J)** *Reading/Humanities/Implied Idea.* Rather than say that Thetis, being a sea-nymph, can read the future, the author merely mentions her immortal status and expects the reader to understand that this means that she knows "her son was fated to perish."

27. **(C)** *Reading/Humanities/Explicit Detail.* The names in (A) are those of goddesses; Paris, (B), is a "beautiful shepherd." In (D), Eris is the goddess of Discord and Thetis is a sea-nymph.

28. **(F)** *Reading/Humanities/Implied Idea.* Readers are expected to understand Ulysses' clever ploy without its being spelled out. Achilles is disguised as a woman, but he is inappropriately interested in manly objects.

29. **(C)** *Reading/Humanities/Development.* Thetis' foreknowledge predicts Achilles' death, and the preparations for war on the part of the chieftains foreshadow the Trojan conflict.

30. **(G)** *Reading/Humanities/Main Idea.* This is an accurate summary of the main themes in the passage.

31. **(B)** *Reading/Social Studies/Explicit Detail.* Lines 5–8 say that Hiram Revels was the first African American in Congress, but he was elected to the Senate, not the House of Representatives. Therefore, (A) is incorrect. However, lines 8–10 state that Rainey was the first African American elected to the House. (D) may be true but is not mentioned in the passage.

32. **(F)** *Reading/Social Studies/Implied Idea.* The second paragraph says that the first African American representatives were from the South; the third paragraph describes the shift to northern cities.

33. **(A)** *Reading/Social Studies/Explicit Detail.* Compare lines 19–23 and 48–50.

34. **(H)** *Reading/Social Studies/Implied Idea.* The context makes it clear that "turned to" means "concentrated on" or "devoted themselves to."

35. **(A)** *Reading/Social Studies/Explicit Detail.* Lines 37–40 indicate that many African Americans moved to northern cities during World War I and in the following decade.

36. **(J)** *Reading/Social Studies/Explicit Detail.* Voting rights are mentioned or implied in lines 29, 56, and 71; educational opportunities in lines 59 and 72; and employment in lines 63 and 72.

37. **(C)** *Reading/Social Studies/Explicit Detail.* Political organizations in southern states in the nineteenth century are mentioned in lines 15–19 and 30–33; political organizations in northern states in the twentieth century are cited in lines 37–40.

38. **(J)** *Reading/Social Studies/Explicit Detail.* This answer is a paraphrase of lines 67–70.

39. **(B)** *Reading/Social Studies/Main Idea.* The last paragraph specifically mentions "collected biographies of African Americans who served in the House and Senate" and "their stories."

40. **(G)** *Reading/Social Studies/Implied Idea.* In an otherwise factual account, the author expresses admiration only in the last paragraph, where the representatives' "long struggle to extend the ideals of the founders to encompass all citizens of the United States" is cited.

TEST 4: SCIENCE (p. 542)

1. **(B)** *Science/Data Representation/Comprehension.* The sharpest sloping curve is for potassium nitrate (KNO_3).

2. **(H)** *Science/Data Representation/Analysis.* The sodium salts, $NaCl$ and $NaNO_3$, have different solubilities, indicating that solubility depends on more than the nature of sodium. Thus, (F) and (G) must be incorrect. (J) is incorrect because it is not known whether the solubility curves for all sodium compounds have been given. (H) is correct because it takes into account the differences in solubilities of different sodium salts.

3. **(D)** *Science/Data Representation/Comprehension.* The table gives data only for aqueous solutions, not alcoholic.

4. **(J)** *Science/Data Representation/Comprehension.* Since the solubility curves cross at 71°F, the temperature needs to be known.

5. **(B)** *Science/Data Representation/Application.* Soda goes flat as gas (carbon dioxide) leaves the liquid. The warmer the soda, the faster it goes flat. (A) shows the effect of pressure, not temperature, on solubility. (C) shows the solubility of a solid (sugar), which has nothing to do with the solubility characteristics of a gas. (D) deals with relative densities of gases and not with solubilities.

6. **(G)** *Science/Data Representation/Comprehension.* Mercury's period of revolution equals $0.25 \cdot$ period of Earth's revolution $= 0.25 \cdot 365.3$ days ≈ 90 days. Mercury's period of rotation equals $60 \cdot$ period of Earth's rotation $= 60 \cdot 1$ day $= 60$ days. The ratio of revolution to rotation $= \frac{90}{60} = \frac{3}{2}$.

7. **(A)** *Science/Data Representation/Comprehension.* Mercury's density equals that of the Earth. Density is mass divided by volume. $\text{Density}_{Mercury} = \frac{\text{mass}_{Mercury}}{\text{volume}_{Mercury}} = \frac{0.58 \cdot \text{mass}_{Earth}}{0.58 \cdot \text{volume}_{Earth}} = \frac{\text{mass}_{Earth}}{\text{volume}_{Earth}} = \text{density}_{Earth}$.

8. **(J)** *Science/Data Representation/Comprehension.* Rate is distance divided by time. Divide the average distance to the sun by the period of revolution to get the relative rate. The smallest relative rate is the slowest. In this specific case, the planet with the greatest relative period of revolution orbits the sun at the slowest rate.

9. **(B)** *Science/Data Representation/Analysis.* Gravity depends on both the distance between the centers of objects (and thereby the volume—assuming the planets are roughly spherical in shape) and on the mass of the objects. Compare Mars and Mercury to see the effect of volume (by considering their diameters). Mars is more massive, but the smaller size of Mercury gives it an equivalent surface gravity. Density, a ratio of mass and volume, is not enough because gravity depends on the amount of mass and the amount of distance, not their ratio.

10. **(H)** *Science/Data Representation/Comprehension.* $\frac{\text{Volume}_{Pluto}}{\text{Volume}_{Earth}} = 0.729 \Rightarrow \frac{\frac{4}{3}\pi r^3_{Pluto}}{\frac{4}{3}\pi r^3_{Earth}} = 0.729 \Rightarrow \frac{r^3_{Pluto}}{r^3_{Earth}} = 0.729 \Rightarrow$ $\frac{r_{Pluto}}{r_{Earth}} = \sqrt[3]{0.729} = 0.9$. $\text{Diameter}_{Pluto} = 2 \cdot (0.9 \cdot \text{radius}_{Earth}) = 1.8 \cdot \text{radius}_{Earth}$.

11. **(B)** *Science/Data Representation/Comprehension.* The neighbors that are farthest from each other are Uranus and Neptune. Relative distances to the sun are as follows:

$$\frac{\text{Mercury}}{0.4} < \frac{\text{Venus}}{0.7} < \frac{\text{Earth}}{1} < \frac{\text{Mars}}{1.5} < \frac{\text{Jupiter}}{5.3} < \frac{\text{Saturn}}{10} < \frac{\text{Uranus}}{19} < \frac{\text{Neptune}}{30} < \frac{\text{Pluto}}{40}$$

The largest difference is $(30-19)=11$.

12. **(F)** *Science/Data Representation/Analysis.* The death rate for the 6–20 gram/day cholesterol eater from prostate cancer is 1.03, while that for a non-cholesterol eater is 2.02. Thus, (F) is correct. (G) contradicts the data for colon cancer; (H) ignores the direct relationship between coronary deaths and cholesterol intake; and cardiac arrest is a more common form of death than cerebral clots for the 20+ eaters.

13. **(D)** *Science/Data Representation/Analysis.* The death rate for all three groups of cholesterol-eaters from depression is 0.30. This number is lower than for non-cholesterol-eaters, so (A) and (B) are both wrong. According to the data, large amounts of cholesterol are just as effective in combating depression as small amounts, so (C) is incorrect.

14. **(J)** *Science/Data Representation/Comprehension.* Although the 20+ diet increases coronary arrest to the highest absolute death rate, the percentage increase is less than 100% (from 6.00 to 11.00). The percentage increase for coronary thrombosis is greater than 100% (from 5.02 to 10.05).

15. **(C)** *Science/Data Representation/Comprehension.* (C) is the only group in which low intake of cholesterol decreases the death rate from all three diseases. Intake of 0 to 5 grams raises the probability of death for lung and colon cancer only. This question is probably best answered by recognizing that fact and eliminating those choices that include either lung or colon cancer.

16. **(G)** *Science/Data Representation/Application.* Standardizing the death rate involves correcting for variables inherent in the subject groups but not involved in the experiment. Age, weight, genetic histories, and accidental deaths are just some of the variables that the scientist must consider. However, (F) does not correct for intrinsic variables; rather, it ignores results that might not conform to a "neat" result. This does not standardize the death rate so much as "fudge" it. (H) involves an arbitrary assumption that is in fact incorrect. Assuming a zero death rate in the male population distorts the result of this experiment and does not correct for variations within the subject groups. (J) is incorrect because this experiment does not consider women at all. It might be valid to compare results with a different experiment involving women, but the actual death rates for men and women for different diseases are not necessarily similar (e.g., the gender-related differences for breast cancer).

17. **(C)** *Science/Data Representation/Analysis.* Since voltage is directly related to current, voltage increases by the same factor as current if other variables are held constant. The same applies for resistance; therefore, the only correct formula is (C).

18. **(G)** *Science/Data Representation/Analysis.* $V = IR$, so the circuit with the greater resistance would have the greater voltage. Since resistance is directly proportional to resistivity, the germanium circuit would have the greater resistance and voltage.

19. **(A)** *Science/Data Representation/Application.* The total resistance R_s of the series resistors is $R_1 + R_2 = 2 + 2 = 4$. This resistance is double that of the circuit where $R = 2$. If R doubles, then the voltage doubles as long as the current remains the same.

20. **(J)** *Science/Data Representation/Application.* According to the formula for resistors in parallel: $\frac{1}{R_p} = \frac{1}{4} + \frac{1}{4} = \frac{2}{4} = \frac{1}{2} \Rightarrow R_p = 2$.

21. **(C)** *Science/Data Representation/Application.* If R is constant, then P increases with I^2; this is the definition of exponential growth.

22. **(J)** *Science/Data Representation/Analysis.* $V = IR \Rightarrow I = \frac{V}{R}$. To keep I constant if V increases, R must be increased.

23. **(D)** *Science/Research Summary/Analysis.* Compare Trials 2 and 3 to see what changing the concentration of only one component has on rate. In this case, there is no change in rate with change in concentration of A, so rate is independent of concentration.

24. **(F)** *Science/Research Summary/Analysis.* Compare Trials 2 and 4 or Trials 1 and 3 to see what changing the concentration of only one component has on rate. In this case, rate increases with increasing A.

25. **(C)** *Science/Research Summary/Analysis.* Compare Trials 1 and 4 or Trials 2 and 3 to see what changing the concentration of only one component has on rate. In this case, rate increases by the square of the starting A concentration.

26. **(H)** *Science/Research Summary/Analysis.* Averaging or intermediate mechanisms do not work because one mechanism has no dependence on A with regard to rate. (G) is unlikely because a well-mixed solution should be homogeneous and have no pockets for mechanisms 1 and 2.

27. **(B)** *Science/Research Summary/Analysis.* This is a subtle question. (C) and (D) are incorrect because they over-generalize from a single case. It cannot be said that mechanisms can always be changed, (C), or that in every case the mechanism depends on solvent effects, (D). (A) is a special case of (D), where the claim is made that all reactions are solvent dependent. (B) alone allows for the possibility that solvents need not have an effect (note the word "may").

28. **(G)** *Science/Research Summary/Comprehension.* Acceleration $= \dfrac{D_v}{D_t} = \dfrac{\text{change in velocity}}{\text{change in time}}$.

Experiment 1 (steel ball): The acceleration is constant at 3.50 m/sec^2. This can be demonstrated by choosing a time interval and dividing the corresponding velocity change during the time interval by the length of the time interval. For example, between 1 and 2 seconds, the velocity changes from 3.5 m/sec to 7 m/sec; therefore, acceleration equals $\frac{\Delta v}{\Delta t} = \frac{7-3.5}{2-1} = \frac{3.5}{1} = 3.5$ m/sec^2.

For a time interval from 0.5 seconds to 1 second, the corresponding velocity would change from 1.75 m/sec to 3.5 m/sec; thus, the acceleration equals $\frac{\Delta v}{\Delta t} = \frac{3.5-1.75}{1-0.5} = \frac{1.75}{0.5} = 3.5$ m/sec^2.

Experiment 2 (sled): The acceleration is a constant 4.9 m/sec^2. For example, the change in velocity corresponding to the time interval from 0.5 seconds to 1 second is 4.90 m/sec $-$ 2.45 m/sec $=$ 2.45 m/sec. The acceleration $= \frac{\Delta v}{\Delta t} = \frac{4.90-2.45}{1-0.5} = \frac{2.45}{0.5} = 4.9$ m/sec^2

Experiment 3 (box): The acceleration is constant at 0.66 m/sec^2.

29. **(A)** *Science/Research Summary/Analysis.* When friction is reduced in Experiment 4, the sled and the ball still travel at about the same accelerations as in the previous experiments. This can be demonstrated by using the equation $d = 0.5at^2$, which relates the distance that an object travels starting from rest to the time (traveling at constant acceleration) it takes to travel the indicated distance. Since the board is 10 meters in length, the distance that each travels is 10 meters.

For the sled:
$$d = \tfrac{1}{2}at^2$$
$$10 = \tfrac{1}{2}a(2.02)^2 \approx \tfrac{1}{2}(a)(4)$$
$$a = 5 \text{ m/sec}^2$$

For the ball:
$$d = \tfrac{1}{2}at^2$$

$$10 = \tfrac{1}{2}a(2.39)^2 \approx \tfrac{1}{2}(a)(5.7)$$
$$a = 3.50 \ \text{m/sec}^2$$

The ball and sled travel at about the same accelerations before and after oiling, so the differences in their relative accelerations must be due to something other than friction. The difference is the rolling of the ball.

30. **(H)** *Science/Research Summary/Analysis.* Experiment 4 shows that friction affects the relative acceleration between the box and either the sled or ball. Calculate the acceleration for the box: $d = \tfrac{1}{2}at^2 \Rightarrow 10 = \tfrac{1}{2}a(4.08)^2 \approx \tfrac{1}{2}a(16) \Rightarrow a = 1.25 \ \text{m/sec}^2$.

Because the oiling in Experiment 4 caused a change in the box's acceleration, friction is a factor. Rolling must also be a factor as per the answer explanation to item #29.

31. **(B)** *Science/Research Summary/Comprehension.* The acceleration of the ball is constant at 3.50 m/sec² (either Experiment 1 or 4). The acceleration of the sled is constant at 4.90 m/sec² (Experiment 2 or 4). Ratio = $\frac{3.50}{4.90} = \frac{5}{7}$.

32. **(H)** *Science/Research Summary/Comprehension.* Although the acceleration of the ball is relatively insensitive to the amount of friction, the acceleration of the box is very sensitive to friction. Therefore, in a ratio, the effect of changing the amount of friction will change the numerator (ball acceleration) only slightly, whereas the denominator (box acceleration) will change significantly depending on friction. (J) is not correct because the acceleration remains constant within each experiment.

33. **(B)** *Science/Conflicting Viewpoints/Analysis.* Two genetically distant species cannot breed.

34. **(H)** *Science/Conflicting Viewpoints/Analysis.* For early modern humans to completely replace Neanderthals, there could not have been a region containing Neanderthals that did not also contain early modern humans.

35. **(D)** *Science/Conflicting Viewpoints/Analysis.* Neither hypothesis necessarily rules out isolated communities. Both are concerned about areas where contact occurred.

36. **(J)** *Science/Conflicting Viewpoints/Analysis.* This information suggests that early modern humans killed Neanderthals, which supports Scientist 2.

37. **(C)** *Science/Conflicting Viewpoints/Analysis.* This fact shows that even if two species can breed, they may not do so voluntarily. Scientist 2 can therefore use this case as an example of the fact that two genetically compatible but dissimilar-looking animals choose not to interbreed. (D) is not readily relevant because lions and tigers are brought together artificially. No one disputed the notion that animals can interbreed, so (A) does not enter the argument. (B) is incorrect because lions and tigers do not share the same niche (tigers are solitary forest hunters while lions are group-hunting plains dwellers), and their ranges rarely overlap.

38. **(H)** *Science/Conflicting Viewpoints/Comprehension.* The mixing of traits is part of Scientist 2's objections to Scientist 1's hypothesis.

39. **(A)** *Science/Conflicting Viewpoints/Analysis.* Both hypotheses attribute the disappearance of Neanderthals to early modern humans.

40. **(G)** *Science/Conflicting Viewpoints/Analysis.* (F) is a perfectly logical argument but it does not strengthen the position of Scientist 1. (J) does not strengthen the position of Scientist 1 since there is no way to prove from the given information whether others also died violently (clubs may have been used, or spearpoints that were used may have been valuable and were taken by the victors). Even if (J) is acceptable, it does not strengthen the position of Scientist 1. It only casts doubt on the position of Scientist 2. (H) is true in general. The only possible answer that strengthens a scientist's argument is (G).

TEST 5: WRITING (p. 556)

Below Average Response

It is my opinion that they should let students ought of school to do some volunteering. In America, volunteering is a good idea, and everyone should be ready, willing, and able to help other people. But you can't always help someone else if you're too busy helping yourself. One way of avoiding this problem is to give students time to help other people. Once students learn that they will be allowed to volunteer instead of going to class, they will volunteer more. And more volunteers will help people more.

Position on issue:

The position is stated in the first sentence; however, the several grammar errors within the sentence hinder it from being a strong opening sentence.

Topic development and essay organization:

This essay lacks any form of development. The paragraph needs to be split into several organized paragraphs that discuss each point the writer will make. The writer fails to explain the reasoning behind the points that are listed in the paragraph. Although the writer presents an argument in a logical manner, it is not explained enough to present a strong essay.

Language usage, sentence structure, and punctuation:

This essay contains several grammar mistakes and does not flow well.

Summary and conclusions:

It's probably necessary after all of the examples to look at an essay that would likely receive a low score, a "1." There are many ways of talking about the deficiencies of this response: it lacks development, it doesn't engage the topic, the writer doesn't use examples, and it has no organization. But ultimately these can all be traced back to a fundamental weakness: the writer really never gets started.

Above Average Response

Volunteerism is an important American tradition, and schools should do more to encourage it. In today's world, most students are very busy. They attend classes for most of the day, and then may participate in one or two after school activities. Many students also manage to hold down part-time jobs such as working at a fast-food restaurant. Because they are so busy, most of them don't have time to volunteer to help others. Schools could encourage volunteering by giving students release time from school to participate in such activities.

In the first place, volunteerism is important. During emergencies, the Boy Scouts stuffing sandbags on the levee as the river rises are volunteers hoping to help their neighbors save their homes and businesses. The rescue workers the television shows walking through the woods all night with flashlights searching for a lost child are volunteers. The people who pass out cold drinks to marathon runners are volunteers. Without these volunteers, these efforts could not take place. While students may not be eligible to fight fires, they can do many other jobs, and the way to get involved is to join an organization that helps out.

Unfortunately, many students find it difficult to find time to join. To really be of service in an emergency, you need to have some sort of training, and that means going to meetings and learning what role to play in a rescue or disaster. Less dramatic, you can join a group that does things like visit sick people or clean up roads. You need to be an active member of the club or organization that is doing the public service. But if your day is booked solid with classes, there may just not be time left over to do meaningful volunteer work. If schools gave one or two hours a week off, say Friday after lunch, then many other students could volunteer.

Some people might say that release time is not really volunteering because you get something for your effort. But having free time that has to be used for volunteering isn't good for anything else. If you are working to clean up a public park, then you can't be making money at your job. So you really are giving up something by volunteering.

There are many other reasons why release time would work. But the most important one is that it gives students time to do some volunteer work.

Position on issue:

The position is nicely stated in the first paragraph.

Topic development and essay organization:

The main weakness of the essay is that, in spite of the appropriate use of paragraphs and signals, it doesn't really engage the topic in an original and passionate way. To take just one point as an example, the writer, in a good authorial way, uses a paragraph to raise and dispose of a possible objection to the position. The writer argues that release time is not compensation because it cannot, under the terms of the program, be used except for volunteer work. The difficulty here is that this point doesn't come to grips with the objection raised in the prompt that being given the free time to do volunteer work doesn't require the sacrifice that one ordinarily expects with volunteerism. This idea is complex and needs to be explored in greater detail.

The same criticism could be applied to the other points made by the essay. The third paragraph, to be very critical, is really just a restatement of the problem posed by the prompt: students may not have a lot of time to volunteer. That point is probably not going to be disputed. No one has unlimited time. What the reader would probably expect to see is instead some discussion of the moral issue of giving up something for someone else's benefit, not just a statement that to volunteer requires sacrifice.

Language usage, sentence structure, and punctuation:

In general, the language is appropriate and the grammar adequate. There are, however, some errors throughout the essay.

Summary and conclusions:

This essay is a fairly consistent, if somewhat predictable, response to the prompt. It's not inspired, but it is not grossly deficient. For that reason, it is likely to receive a "4."

This criticism should not be given too much weight because, after all, the essay is pretty good—a "4" is above average, and there are only two marks higher. But the criticism is intended to suggest a way that this essay, and essays of this sort, could be improved in general.

ERROR CORRECTION AND SUGGESTION FORM

Name/Location:_____ Day Phone:_____ E-mail Address:_____

Review Course(s): ☐ ACT ☐ SAT ☑ Skills ☐ GRE ☐ GMAT ☐ LSAT ☐ MCAT
☐ TOEFL ☐ GED ☐ Praxis ☐ PSAE ☐ ITBS ☐ WorkKeys ☐ Basic Math

Part of Materials: ☐ Student Text, Specify Section:_____ Page:_____ Item:_____

☐ Teacher's Guide, Specify Section:_____ Page:_____ Item:_____

☐ Test Explanations, Specify Year/Form Code:_____ Page:_____ Item:_____

Error/Suggestion:_____

_____

_____

Review Course(s): ☐ ACT ☐ SAT ☐ Skills ☐ GRE ☐ GMAT ☐ LSAT ☐ MCAT
☐ TOEFL ☐ GED ☐ Praxis ☐ PSAE ☐ ITBS ☐ WorkKeys ☐ Basic Math

Part of Materials: ☐ Student Text, Specify Section:_____ Page:_____ Item:_____

☐ Teacher's Guide, Specify Section:_____ Page:_____ Item:_____

☐ Test Explanations, Specify Year/Form Code:_____ Page:_____ Item:_____

Error/Suggestion:_____

_____

_____

Review Course(s): ☐ ACT ☐ SAT ☐ Skills ☐ GRE ☐ GMAT ☐ LSAT ☐ MCAT
☐ TOEFL ☐ GED ☐ Praxis ☐ PSAE ☐ ITBS ☐ WorkKeys ☐ Basic Math

Part of Materials: ☐ Student Text, Specify Section:_____ Page:_____ Item:_____

☐ Teacher's Guide, Specify Section:_____ Page:_____ Item:_____

☐ Test Explanations, Specify Year/Form Code:_____ Page:_____ Item:_____

Error/Suggestion:_____

_____

_____

Review Course(s): ☐ ACT ☐ SAT ☐ Skills ☐ GRE ☐ GMAT ☐ LSAT ☐ MCAT
☐ TOEFL ☐ GED ☐ Praxis ☐ PSAE ☐ ITBS ☐ WorkKeys ☐ Basic Math

Part of Materials: ☐ Student Text, Specify Section:_____ Page:_____ Item:_____

☐ Teacher's Guide, Specify Section:_____ Page:_____ Item:_____

☐ Test Explanations, Specify Year/Form Code:_____ Page:_____ Item:_____

Error/Suggestion:_____

_____

_____

Fax form to 1-847-299-2933. For curricular assistance, call 1-800-444-4373 or e-mail testprep@CambridgeEd.com. Visit our Web site at www.CambridgeEd.com.

ITEM INDEX

In the following index, all of the numeric references are designed as follows: Item #/Page # on which that item appears. Page numbers for the Lesson, Challenge, Timed-Practice Quizzes, and Calculator Exercise items refer to the Test Mechanics, Concepts, and Strategies portion of the *Cambridge ACT • PLAN • EXPLORE Victory Student Text, Volume 2, 9th Edition*, and page numbers for the Practice Test items refer to the Practice Test Reinforcement portion of the *Cambridge ACT • PLAN • EXPLORE Victory Student Text, Volume 2, 9th Edition*. The parenthetical information beside each item category refers to the subject-area in which that item category appears.

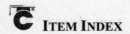

Basic Algebraic Manipulations (Mathematics)

Lesson: 86–87/88
Practice Test I: 10/343; 37/349
Practice Test II: 24/404; 38/407
Practice Test III: 2/454; 38/464
Practice Test IV: 7/516; 27/520; 42/525

Circles (Mathematics)

Lesson: 8–9/78; 27/81; 199/106; 204–205/107; 208/108
Challenge Items: 8/117
Quiz II: 12/127
Quiz III: 10/131; 15/132; 23/133
Practice Test I: 18/345; 47/352; 48/353
Practice Test II: 22/403
Practice Test III: 14/457; 23/459; 41–42/465; 50/468
Practice Test IV: 2/514; 17/518; 23/519; 25/520; 33/522

Clarity of Meaning (English)

Lesson: 134/31
Quiz I: 29/47

Colons (English)

Lesson: 106–107/26
Challenge Items: 18/38
Quiz III: 7/53
Practice Test I: 40/333

Comma Splices (English)

Lesson: 59–60/20
Practice Test III: 19/443; 34/445

Commas (English)

Lesson: 81–82/23; 87–88/24; 90–92/24; 95–100/25; 136/33
Challenge Items: 17–18/38; 42/41
Quiz II: 3/48; 5/48; 19/51
Quiz III: 8/53
Practice Test I: 22/331; 24/331; 42/334; 62/337
Practice Test II: 37/390
Practice Test III: 3/440; 25/444
Practice Test IV: 10/501; 22/503; 29/505; 42/507

Common Arithmetic Items (Mathematics)

Lesson: 17–20/80; 23/80; 25/81; 28–29/81; 45–47/83; 48–55/84; 56–64/85; 65–71/86; 72–79/87
Challenge Items: 3/116; 5/116; 9–10/117; 12–13/118; 20/119; 24–25/120; 27–28/120
Quiz I: 5–6/124; 13/125
Quiz II: 14/127
Quiz III: 2/130; 4/130; 11/131; 16–17/132; 24/134
Calculator Exercise: 2–3/138; 10/139
Practice Test I: 3/340; 4/341; 13/343; 17/344; 19/345; 27/347; 30/348; 38/350; 40–41/350; 44/351; 50/353

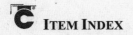

Data Representation (Science)

Lesson: 1–2/226; 3/227; 4–9/228; 10–14/230; 15–19/231
Challenge Items: 1–3/244; 4–6/245; 20–25/249; 26–27/250; 42–48/255; 61–66/259
Quiz I: 1–4/264; 5/265; 6–10/266
Quiz II: 1–4/267; 5/268; 6–9/269; 10/270
Quiz III: 1–2/271; 3–5/272
Practice Test I: 1–2/368; 3–5/369; 12–14/371; 15–16/372; 23–26/374; 27/375
Practice Test II: 1–5/422; 6/423; 19–23/428; 30–32/431; 33–34/432
Practice Test III: 1–4/484; 5/485; 25–30/492; 36–40/495
Practice Test IV: 1–3/542; 4–5/543; 6–9/544; 10–11/545; 12–13/546; 14–16/547; 17–21/548; 22/549

Decimal-Fraction Equivalents (Mathematics)

Lesson: 41–42/83
Quiz II: 11/127
Calculator Exercise: 5/138
Practice Test II: 5/399
Practice Test III: 11/456; 30/462

Definitions of the Six Trigonometric Functions (Mathematics)

Lesson: 11/79; 217–218/110
Challenge Items: 30/121; 32/121; 34/122
Quiz I: 11/124; 16/125
Quiz II: 17/128; 21/129
Quiz III: 26/134
Practice Test I: 59/356
Practice Test III: 52/469

Determining Trigonometric Values (Mathematics)

Challenge Items: 33/121
Practice Test I: 56/355
Practice Test II: 48/410
Practice Test III: 49/467
Practice Test IV: 59/529

Development (Reading)

Lesson: 7–8/154; 18/156; 34–35/159
Extended Lesson: 19/165; 26/167; 29/168; 49/173; 53/173; 90/181
Challenge Items: 5/183; 31/190
Quiz II: 5/202
Quiz III: 5/204; 7/204
Practice Test I: 11/361
Practice Test III: 33/482
Practice Test IV: 29/537

Diction (English)

Lesson: 51–56/20
Challenge Items: 35/40; 37/41; 44/42
Quiz I: 11/44; 26/47
Quiz II: 11/49; 25/51; 27/52
Quiz III: 2/53; 22/55; 26/56

Distance Formula (Mathematics)

Double Negatives (English)

Effective Concluding Sentence (English)

Effective Opening Sentence (English)

Effective Transitional Sentence (English)

End-Stop Punctuation (English)

Equations Involving Absolute Value (Mathematics)

Equations Involving Integer and Rational Exponents (Mathematics)

Equations Involving Radical Expressions (Mathematics)

Lesson: 109–112/91
Quiz II: 16/128
Practice Test IV: 18/518

Equations Involving Rational Expressions (Mathematics)

Lesson: 3/77; 105–106/90; 107/91
Quiz II: 15/128
Practice Test I: 1/340
Practice Test IV: 18/518

Evaluating Expressions (Mathematics)

Lesson: 88–89/88; 90–91/89
Challenge Items: 26/120; 28/120
Quiz II: 8/127
Quiz III: 9/131
Practice Test I: 31/348; 33/348
Practice Test II: 20/403; 50/410
Practice Test III: 3/454; 47/467; 53/469
Practice Test IV: 5/515; 11/517; 21/519; 53/527

Evaluating Sequences Involving Exponential Growth (Mathematics)

Lesson: 2/77; 99–102/90
Quiz I: 12/125
Quiz III: 22/133

Explicit Detail (Reading)

Lesson: 3–5/154; 19/156; 28/159
Extended Lesson: 4–6/162; 9/163; 11–12/163; 14–16/165; 21–22/165; 23/166; 25/167; 32/169; 37/170; 39/170; 40–44/171; 48/173; 50/173; 52/173; 57–58/174; 59/175; 63/176; 65/176; 67/177; 70/177; 79/179; 91/181
Challenge Items: 10–11/184; 13–14/185; 17/186; 22/187; 26/189; 28/189; 30/190; 35–36/191; 39/192; 41/193; 43–46/194; 48–51/196; 59–61/198
Quiz I: 4/200
Quiz II: 3/202
Quiz IV: 3/205; 4/206; 6–7/206
Quiz V: 2/207; 5/208; 8–10/208
Quiz VI: 1/209; 3/209; 4–6/210; 8/210
Practice Test I: 1–4/359; 8–9/359; 13/361; 18/362; 21–24/364; 26/364; 29/364; 32/366; 36/367
Practice Test II: 5–6/415; 10/415; 12/416; 16/417; 20/417; 21–23/418; 24–25/419; 27/419; 30/419; 31/420; 34/420; 40/421
Practice Test III: 2/475; 6/475; 11/477; 14/478; 16/478; 18–19/478; 24–27/480; 29–30/481; 31–32/482; 36–37/483; 39/483
Practice Test IV: 1–3/533; 5–9/533; 13/535; 16/535; 27/537; 31/539; 33/539; 35–37/539; 38/540

Expressing and Evaluating Algebraic Functions (Mathematics)

Lesson: 4–5/77; 122–125/92; 126–134/93
Quiz I: 15/125
Quiz II: 6/126
Quiz III: 12/131
Practice Test I: 2/340; 29/347; 52/354; 54/354; 57/355

Humanities (Reading)

Idiomatic Expression (English)

Implied Idea (Reading)

Incomplete Split Constructions (English)

Inequalities Involving Absolute Value (Mathematics)

Inequalities Involving Rational Expressions (Mathematics)

Lines and Angles (Mathematics)

Practice Test III: 4/455; 28/461; 31/462; 41/465; 48/467
Practice Test IV: 2/514; 4/515; 25/520; 34/522; 43/525; 45/525

Main Idea (English)

Lesson: 118/28; 127/31
Quiz III: 13/54
Practice Test I: 16/330; 74/338
Practice Test II: 15/386

Main Idea (Reading)

Lesson: 1/153; 2/154; 16/156; 21/157; 25–26/158; 27/159
Extended Lesson: 7/162; 30/168; 31/169; 47/172; 54/174; 66/176
Challenge Items: 2/183; 15/185; 21/187; 32/190; 34/191; 42/194; 58/198
Quiz I: 2/199; 8/200
Quiz II: 1/201
Quiz III: 8/204
Quiz IV: 5/206
Quiz V: 1/207
Practice Test I: 25/364; 30/365
Practice Test II: 11/416
Practice Test III: 1/475; 21/479; 38/483
Practice Test IV: 4/533; 11/534; 30/537; 39/540

Manipulating Algebraic Expressions (Mathematics)

Lesson: 86–89/88; 90–98/89; 146–153/95; 154–157/95
Challenge Items: 14/118; 23/119; 26/120; 28/120
Quiz II: 8/127
Quiz III: 9/131; 14/132
Practice Test I: 10/343; 20/345; 23/346; 31/348; 33/348; 36–37/349; 53/354; 55/354
Practice Test II: 2/398; 16/402; 20/403; 24/404; 37–38/407; 50/410
Practice Test III: 2–3/454; 9/456; 12/456; 20/458; 21/459; 38/464; 47/467; 53/469
Practice Test IV: 5/515; 7/516; 11/517; 14/517; 21/519; 27/520; 42/525; 51/527; 53/527; 54/528

Manipulating Expressions Involving Exponents (Mathematics)

Lesson: 92–93/89
Practice Test I: 23/346; 53/354
Practice Test II: 16/402

Median (Mathematics)

Lesson: 229/111
Practice Test IV: 35/523

Misplaced Modifiers (English)

Lesson: 76–77/22; 78/23; 145/34
Practice Test I: 65/337
Practice Test II: 20/387

Mode (Mathematics)

Lesson: 230/111
Practice Test IV: 49/526

Proportions and Direct-Inverse Variation (Mathematics)

Lesson: 20/80; 73–79/87
Challenge Items: 9–10/117; 20/119
Quiz I: 5/124
Quiz III: 4/130; 17/132
Calculator Exercise: 3/138
Practice Test I: 17/344; 27/347; 40/350
Practice Test II: 3/398
Practice Test III: 18/458; 27/461
Practice Test IV: 31/521; 47/526; 60/529

Prose Fiction (Reading)

Extended Lesson: 67–71/177; 72–74/178; 75–81/179; 82–84/180; 85–91/181
Practice Test I: 31–35/366; 36–40/367
Practice Test II: 1–10/415
Practice Test III: 11/477; 12–20/478
Practice Test IV: 11–12/534; 13–20/535

Punctuating for Clarity (English)

Lesson: 115/27; 138/33
Practice Test IV: 36/506

Punctuation (English)

Lesson: 81–82/23; 87–88/24; 90–92/24; 95–100/25; 103–110/26; 112/27; 114–115/27; 136/33; 138/33
Challenge Items: 17–18/38; 23/38; 42/41
Quiz I: 28/47
Quiz II: 3/48; 5/48; 19/51
Quiz III: 7–8/53
Practice Test I: 22/331; 24/331; 40/333; 42/334; 62/337; 69/337
Practice Test II: 9/385; 37/390
Practice Test III: 3/440; 25/444; 41/446
Practice Test IV: 1/500; 8–10/501; 12/502; 15/503; 22/503; 29/505; 36/506; 42/507; 50/509; 52/509; 67/512; 69/512; 73/513; 75/513

Pythagorean Theorem (Mathematics)

Lesson: 9/78; 190/104; 214/109
Challenge Items: 29/120
Quiz II: 17/128
Practice Test I: 45/351; 47/352
Practice Test IV: 23/519; 59/529

Qualitative Behavior of Graphs of Functions (Mathematics)

Lesson: 181–182/102
Quiz III: 21/133

Quotation Marks (English)

Practice Test I: 69/337
Practice Test III: 41/446
Practice Test IV: 12/502; 15/503; 73/513

Ratios (Mathematics)

Lesson: 17–18/80; 23/80; 71/86; 72/87
Challenge Items: 25/120
Quiz I: 6/124
Practice Test I: 13/343
Practice Test III: 6/455

Rectangles and Squares (Mathematics)

Lesson: 196/105; 197–198/106; 204/107; 206/107; 207/107; 208/108; 215/109
Challenge Items: 1–2/116; 15/118; 18/119
Quiz III: 3/130; 15/132
Calculator Exercise: 6/138; 9/139
Practice Test I: 9/342; 24–25/346; 32/348
Practice Test II: 13/401; 17/402; 31/405; 33/406; 44/409
Practice Test III: 7/455; 14/457; 23/459; 37/463; 46/466; 50/468; 59/472

Research Summary (Science)

Lesson: 20–23/232; 24–25/233; 26–29/234; 30/235; 31–35/236; 36/237
Challenge Items: 7–12/246; 28–32/251; 33/252; 49–54/257; 67–70/260; 71–72/261
Quiz III: 6–9/273; 10–11/274
Practice Test I: 6–11/370; 17–22/373; 35–39/378; 40/379
Practice Test II: 7–11/424; 12/425; 13–18/427; 24–28/429; 29/430
Practice Test III: 6–9/486; 10–11/487; 19–23/490; 24/491; 31–33/493; 34–35/494
Practice Test IV: 23/536; 24–30/537; 31–32/539

Rhetorical Skills (English)

Lesson: 116–118/28; 119–121/29; 122–125/30; 126–134/31; 135/32; 143–144/34
Challenge Items: 2–3/35; 6–9/36; 11/36; 13–16/37; 19/38; 21–22/38; 24/38; 28/39; 30/40; 33–34/40; 36/41; 38/41; 41/41; 43/41; 48/42
Quiz I: 2–3/43; 7/44; 10/44; 13/44; 14–17/45; 18/46; 27/47; 29/47; 31–32/47
Quiz II: 2/48; 6–8/48; 10/49; 15/49; 16–17/50; 21/51; 24/51; 28–29/52
Quiz III: 3–4/53; 9/53; 13–15/54; 16/55; 20/55; 23/55; 29–31/56
Practice Test I: 1/328; 3/328; 5/329; 8/329; 12/329; 13/330; 15–16/330; 19/330; 31–32/332; 33/333; 35/333; 43/334; 45–46/334; 50/335; 52–54/335; 55/336; 57/336; 59/336; 63/337; 68/337; 70/337; 71–75/338
Practice Test II: 4/384; 7–8/385; 10/385; 15/386; 16–17/387; 19/387; 21–22/387; 23–24/388; 27/388; 30/389; 32/389; 35/390; 40/390; 43/391; 47–48/391; 53–54/392; 57–61/393; 64–65/394; 70/395
Practice Test III: 2/440; 6/441; 8/441; 11/441; 15–17/442; 23–24/443; 27–29/444; 32–33/445; 35/445; 37–38/446; 42/446; 43/447; 50/447; 52/448; 59–62/449; 69–70/451; 74–75/452
Practice Test IV: 2/500; 6/501; 13/502; 18/503; 23–24/504; 28/505; 30/505; 33/505; 37–38/506; 45–46/508; 49/509; 55/510; 59–60/511; 62–63/511; 74/513

Run-On Sentences (English)

Lesson: 57–58/20
Quiz I: 12/44
Quiz II: 26/52
Quiz III: 27/56
Practice Test I: 4/329; 10/329; 26/331
Practice Test III: 56/448